THE BOOK OF
BIRTHDAYS

by

Russell Grant

A Dell Trade Paperback

A DELL TRADE PAPERBACK

Published by
Dell Publishing
a division of
Random House, Inc.
1540 Broadway
New York, New York 10036

DTP and the colophon are trademarks of Random House, Inc.

ISBN: 0-440-50889-4

Reprinted by arrangement with Boxtree, an imprint of Macmillan Publishers Ltd

Printed in the United States of America

Published simultaneously in Canada

October 1999

10 9 8 7 6 5 4 3 2 1

CONTENTS

INTRODUCTION

Many Happy Returns to you all! (Or should I say Many Happy Solar Returns! 'Solar' because the Sun returns to the same place as it was on the day you were born. Hence the saying!)

I'm delighted to welcome you to my *Book of Birthdays*, a venture which has been tremendously exciting and rewarding to develop, and which is borne from many years studying astrology, the great systems of the universe and the fascinating people of every race and nation who dwell within our world. As a Sun and Moon Aquarian, I am a natural observer of individual people and their characters.

My life as an astrologer has brought me into contact with incalculable numbers of people over the last thirty years, through viewers' direct and personal response to my appearances on television, my columns in national and regional newspapers, and as a result of my many astrological books. I have also had the opportunity to meet people from all over the world who have sought my help. They range from members of our own Royal Family, to business magnates in the City here and Wall Street in America, politicians, television pundits, actors, actresses, editors of our own national newspapers and magazines, to people from all sorts of less high-profile professions and jobs. Rich or poor, we are all concerned about our destiny and certainly want to make the best of it. I count many clients among my dearest friends.

But, of course, apart from astrology, I am also deeply involved in other allied disciplines. Chinese astrology and other Oriental belief systems have taken my interest for many years and become an integral part of my professional and personal pursuit of knowledge. Other studies include my own work on systems of numerology, palmistry, some forms of magic and many areas of ancient Celtic wisdom. Perhaps one of my most personally rewarding studies, and indeed discoveries, has been the Astro-Tarot pack, created by me and taken up by followers all over the world. This acted as the tool through which I could channel my psychic energy and fulfilled my ambition to combine my expertise of the tarot with my knowledge of astrology, making the Astro-Tarot a school for learning both disciplines.

Astrologers and followers of these other studies have always accepted that we are all influenced by the geographical place, date and timing of our birth. Birth rituals to record this are performed in ancient religions and cultures all over the world. And we accept that certain characteristics are associated with each birth sign motivated by a particular planet in a sensitive area of our own unique natal chart. But in my own studies I have long held the opinion that your character is not only affected by your sun sign but by the exact date you were born, and the intricate astrological influences that are cast from it. Even Carl Jung, the great psychologist, stressed that each and every one of us is born with a huge collective of characteristics in a kind of universal archetype, influenced by the time we are born within the natural cycle of the year. The rhythms of the year are determined by the seasons – the changes between spring, summer, autumn and winter – along with the lengthening and shortening of days and nights. It corresponds that those born in the heat of the summer differ to those born in the cold light of a short winter's day (and of course this still applies if you are born in the southern hemisphere where the seasons are reversed).

With this awareness of the undeniable pull of nature combined with the basic principles of psychology and astrology it seems clear to me that destiny is influenced by the individual date of birth, irrespective of the year, allowing us to make personal choices in our own exclusive way. Dr Marc Edmunds Jones, in his stimulating and penetrating book *The Sabian Symbols in Astrology*, draws similar conclusions by emphasising not the actual date of birth but the symbolic meaning attached to each of the 360 degrees of the zodiac wheel.

What has also cemented this conviction for me is the knowledge gained from my perhaps less well-known psychic and Spiritualist experiences. For many years I have practised as a medium and have had the privilege to work with my dear friend, one of the wisest psychics of all, Doris Stokes, now passed on to a greater world. I have many clients with this work. Some come to me for healing, others simply to consult through my clairvoyant ability. As President Emeritus of the prestigious body, The British Astrological-Psychic Society, I am able to keep in touch with current thinking about the New Age. Using this psychic ability I have been able to synthesise knowledge and experience, honing them to an outline of the characteristics of individual dates – hence the '**psycheology**' of every birthday in the year.

You'll find that each psycheology gives an insightful outline of the characteristics you might find for every birthday boy or girl as well as snippets of information about events that occurred on your date of birth, a thought for the day, the element (fire, earth, air or water) attributed to your sun sign and the names of celebrities born on the same day. It also includes sections loosely gathered under the headings 'Mind' and 'Body'. These can cover a whole range of physical and emotional attributes and are written to appeal to each birthdate's individual character and interests.

Remember that each psycheology, as with all astrological readings, acts rather like a signpost – the road doesn't have to be taken. This is a book which is invaluable as a guide, not as an ordinance on how you *must* lead your life. Glean from it what you can in the journey to discover more about the inherent nature and destiny of yourself, your friends and loved ones, and the choices that are open to fulfil your self-potential.

The word psycheology may be new in our language at least – but it describes something in us all that is as old as time.

The Book of Birthdays begins with a general outline of the characteristics of each sun sign archetype. Every sign is subdivided into three equal segments called **decanates** or decans. A decanate is a different vibration of the three signs and their ruling planets associated with the element (fire, earth, air or water) from which they form a part. The first decanate always starts with the nature of the sign in question followed in correct order with the next two from the family of the same element.

I have rounded off the decanate dates to come up with the most accurate and acceptable periods possible. This is because the start and finish of both star signs and decanates will, of course, alter yearly.

We then follow with **psycheologies** for every birthday of the year. Several of the psycheologies utilise the principles of my Astro-Tarot for added insight into the character and personality of a particular birthday. On occasion, numerology has also been used. If you would like to know more about my Astro-Tarot and personal systems of numerology, please send an S.A.E. to me c/o:

PO Box 5757, Royal Lytham St Annes, Lancashire FY8 2TE, Great Britain.

ARIES

RULER: Mars, the God of War, planet of virility, vitality and sexuality. It is this red star which imbues Aries with the assertion and aggression characteristic of this first sign of the zodiac.

LOVES: Being first, competition and being the winner at all costs. Honesty in people pleases them and they adore sex.

LOATHES: Losing, being a team player, apologising and admitting they are wrong. Deceitful people and folk who sit on the fence.

NEEDS TO CULTIVATE: Humility, co-operation and restraint for 'out of the frying pan into the fire' is something every Aries learns the minute they take the initiative and get their fingers burnt for the first time.

NEEDS TO TONE DOWN: Selfishness and turn up selflessness and put others first once in a while. Using patience to control their angry temper will earn them a little respect and make them more approachable.

ARIES–MARS DECANATE ....March 20/21 until March 30

This decanate is Aries and Mars ruled, so if their birthday is celebrated between the Equinox and the end of March, a fiery side to their character is emphasised. But beware, for they could easily rage out of control like a forest fire that zips through the land consuming everything in its path. If they contain the eternal conflagration which burns within them like a fire in a furnace they can create something wonderful from the liquid of their talents or give hand-warming comfort as would a fire in a hearth. Aries, the archetype of this decanate, is the pioneer whose resolve and true grit was how the West was won. Here lies the true Olympian spirit.

LEO–SUN DECANATE ....March 31 until April 9

Aries and Leo together is an eternal dynamic force which can dazzle the world with creative genius but can also make Aries fall in love with their own golden successes. A Narcissus complex coils around their ego waiting to spring forth and turn back the love heaped on by an adoring audience. If Aries covets the adulation from an awestruck world, they must not let the glory go to their heads – an Aries part of the anatomy. Instead, they must be all heart – the Leo area of the body – and then they will conquer all as only love can.

SAGITTARIUS–JUPITER DECANATE ....April 10 until April 20/21

They leap around like a candle in the wind, restless and desperate to move on from wherever they are physically or cerebrally, always searching, always wanting to better themselves. But perhaps they have what they want sitting right in front of them, if only they'd look and didn't drift. So they should pause a while and see how far they have come – it's so much further than they thought. Their fire is the fire which moulded ancient amulets from civilisations many Moons before – which goes to show that what they create can last forever and be an inspiration to others.

TAURUS

April 21 – May 21

RULER: Venus, not the sweet'n'treat Venus that rules Libra but the buxom, voluptuous wench of sensuously tactile Taurus. Here she reveals her possessive envious nature – *Take me I'm yours,* she yelps *and you're mine…*she adds, reclining whilst peeling another grape.

LOVES: La dolce vita – why make do with half when you can have the whole? Total loyalty and natural beauty please them too.

LOATHES: Infidelity and those folk who take a lot and give nothing in return. Also parsimonious people who are neither grateful nor generous.

NEEDS TO CULTIVATE: A less tangible and material approach to life. A more sharing attitude where everything is not always mine or yours.

NEEDS TO TONE DOWN: Their infuriating inflexibility which borders on a fixed fanaticism based on nothing more than a stubborn bee buzzing in their biased bonnet.

TAURUS–VENUS DECANATE ....April 20/21 until April 30

Now here's a fine kettle of fish, or should that be a happy herd of cows? Whichever way you look at it the combination of Taurus with Taurus and Venus with Venus is as comfortable as fresh bacon and eggs at a farmhouse bed and breakfast in the bosom of the country. These are meadow-sweet bovine beasts who only want the best that life can offer, it's a first class trip matey or *I'm not going at all.* Luxury with knobs on for these grazers, but they can often lack the motivation to obtain the wherewithal to afford the good things they desire and that is when this placid bull can turn to raging avarice making Silas Marner look like Sweet Charity. You can see them on the platform of life clutching their meal ticket ready to catch the first gravy train that pulls in complete with five star restaurant car and plush velvet reservation.

VIRGO–MERCURY DECANATE ....May 1 until May 10

If the previous decanate is creamiest cheese on offer then meet chalk, the dustiest old stick going! This decanate thinks but finds it hard to feel, and putting theory into practice is where this hard-to-please Taurean falls down. But what they lack in emotion they can make up for in sheer hard, practical business sense as this Venus/Mercury link is good for dealing with and working for others as much as for themselves. Once they have irrigated their arid emotions then out will flood a gifted, demonstrative people-person ready to wash away the dry, wry sarcasm that can spoil such a nice guy or gal.

CAPRICORN–SATURN DECANATE ....May 11 until May 21/22

The Bull and the Goat can have a good thing going just so long as they remember that sex isn't everything and use their fertile libido to be passionate about life in general. This prosaic bunch will miss by a mile if it's all about lust rather than love for the difference might be sublime but it would be ridiculous to ignore that there is a difference. So when you meet these folk and they undress you with their eyes don't misconstrue their look as love as they have the same lascivious leer when it comes to cash. But once their loins have been girded then they can strike it rich through the sheer blood and guts of their unwavering willpower and unequivocal effort.

GEMINI

RULER: Mercury, but this is the sprite, the Jack o' Lantern or Will o' the Wisp archetype, not the seeker of knowledge and learning which Virgo claims. Peter Pan is an apt description, for this planet never grows up and at the very least despises the onset of old age.

LOVES: Being as free as air with no constraints or anyone to clamp down on how they think, what they do or when they do it. People who stimulate their mind and make no demands on their emotions.

LOATHES: Being in one place, knowing it could be for the rest of their lives – or for a minute more than they want. The ignorant who make no effort to improve their mind or Philistines or idiots. Thugs who use fists rather than reason to win their arguments.

NEEDS TO CULTIVATE: A more consistent approach to all things for so often this Jack of all trades is a master of none because boredom sets in half-way through the task in hand. They must learn to express their feelings warmly, tenderly and honestly.

NEEDS TO TONE DOWN: Their superficial attitude and glib remarks which portray them as intellectual snobs but which when tested proves their knowledge is skin deep. Must try to stop lying to get out of doing something or to avoid taking the wrap.

GEMINI–MERCURY DECANATE ....May 21/22 until May 31

Meet the brainchild – here is the most brilliant specimen of boffinry that you are ever likely to meet, as their grey matter is coloured by the vibrancy of invention and initiative that only Aquarius can match. But this boffin can turn buffoon if they do not utilise and recognise what a superb cerebrum they have at their disposal. Settling down with 2 point something children or securely based in a semi on the outskirts of town will fascinate for a while, but once the routine starts to pall then this double Mercury can fall into those bad Gemini ways of cheating and lying and become attracted by low-life activities to escape the trap *they* walked into.

LIBRA–VENUS DECANATE ....June 1 until June 10

The softness of Venus tenderises the coolness of Mercury and like a woman with her toy-boy, teaches the whys, ways, wherefores and wonders of the world. This decanate has seen life and what it hasn't seen it will go out and experience. The intellect of air is given the appreciation of beauty by Libra and the gift of eloquence by Gemini, turning this child into a protégé of Terpsichore or prodigy of the classical arts. But this is also a wandering mind whose love alights on anything that is vivacious and fascinating, so although the waft of sweet-scented pollen attracts their voracious appetite in the first flush of spring, once the season is over it is on to the next new blossom which takes their fancy.

AQUARIUS–URANUS DECANATE ....June 11 until June 21/22

Cast your mind back to *Thunderbirds (Are Go!)* and take a peek at Brains for you'll recognise him here. So far ahead of their time, these mental cases are Bernstein, Epstein and Einstein combined! Their minds buzz with ideas and dazzle with a genius that is beyond compare, and their unique thoughts are out of this world. But if they think like a calculator and react like a computer then the same could be said of their emotions and there's the rub, for jumping on the super technological highway might slake their intellectual thirst, but it won't assuage their more primitive urges which will remain dormant, causing a gridlock of sexual desires unless they feel, touch and see life using *all* their senses.

AIR ────────────────

CANCER

June 22 – July 23

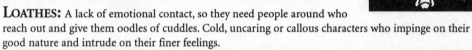

RULER: The Moon's waxing and waning creates the ebb and flow of Cancer's fluctuating emotions. This silvery lady has no light of her own but beams out the reflected glory of the golden Sun, so how *you* feel reflects on your Cancerian's mood and vice versa.

LOVES: Belonging to a family group and being with people they know and are familiar with, for old habits die hard and the sense of cosy and comfortable security they derive from 'feeling at home' is mother's milk to them.

LOATHES: A lack of emotional contact, so they need people around who reach out and give them oodles of cuddles. Cold, uncaring or callous characters who impinge on their good nature and intrude on their finer feelings.

NEEDS TO CULTIVATE: A less sensitive soul and spirit as they can take offence where none was ever intended, so they must grow a much thicker skin and learn to let some things wash over them like water off a duck's back.

NEEDS TO TONE DOWN: Claustrophobic clinginess and a tendency to hold on to a situation after it's gone. Take the best of the past, lose bad attachments, drop any emotional baggage and move on.

CANCER–MOON DECANATE ....June 21/22 until July 1

This moonchild is out of this world, for their heart beats to a very sensitive rhythm which you may find unworldly and even mystical. Their instincts are all-powerful with an intuition so advanced they are psychic. But their spirituality can make them hypersensitive to such a degree they worry over nothing, allow doubt to emerge out of thin air and behave neurotically, reading hidden meanings into ordinary things. With their sixth sense antennae they have the capacity to home in on problems miles away. Their control centre alerts them to retreat back into their carapace and in true crab-like fashion they walk sideways around the precipice and survive until the next red alert.

SCORPIO–PLUTO DECANATE ....July 2 until July 11

The intensity generated by the Moon/Pluto decanate arouses the most profound feelings. They range from dark, brooding suspicions to jealousy that is greener than any emerald, to unforgiveness which transgresses all reasonable behaviour. These Cancerians see anything unfamiliar as the potential for a personal assault, and even just an inkling that an attack is imminent mobilises their defences and sends them scurrying to the battlements of their castle of life built on the shifting sands of their emotions. If controlled their feelings radiate enormous compassion and protection and they can be your shoulder to lean on in your hour of need. Just make sure you're around in theirs.

PISCES–NEPTUNE DECANATE ....July 12 until July 23/24

Welcome to the weird and wonderful watery world where the Moon meets Neptune and nothing is real. That's their problem – what is real? Even if they can touch or see something they read a supernatural meaning into the most down to earth things. For them keeping their feet on the ground is as fruitless as Canute commanding the tide to go back. Their head is caught in the foaming surf of the wild ocean and they ride the waves better than they could ever walk the earth. This dolphin of the zodiac is happiest when swimming with the aesthetic, elevated and cultured people of the earth, to dance with gay abandon to the music of foreign shores and to extend their extraordinary gifts to create something which is beautiful and banish that which is ugly and grotesque from their world.

WATER

LEO

RULER: The Sun to whom our world looks to for he is the centre of the universe. This star proffers vitality and is the power from which new life is created.

LOVES: Loves to be in love! For Leo is the sign who loves with all of their heart and flirts with all of their might. They fiercely defend their honour and court glory with a sovereign pride as befits this regal sign.

LOATHES: Mealy-mouthed people who whinge and complain. People who are greedy and don't pull their weight or give their fair share – the ungenerous will find no friend here.

NEEDS TO CULTIVATE: Much more tolerance and forgiveness, for their inflexible nature makes them store up such fixed ideas about people or situations they refuse to budge on their first impressions, even when they are wrong. Humility.

NEEDS TO TONE DOWN: That ego! Thinking they are God's gift and their Hollywood theatrics Dahling, for a true star doesn't need to draw attention off stage. Vanity.

LEO–SUN DECANATE ....July 23/24 until August 2

So much sun can frazzle and dazzle so easily, yet if it is tempered and nurtured it is life-giving vitality, but too much and there is a drought. This double dose of Sun can be tropical and carnival or searing and humid and depends upon the state of their heart. Love makes their world go round and if they are embroiled with amour then it's Club Tropicana all day and all night but if they are crushed, unrequited or blown out then it's the Copacabana in winter – bedraggled feathers and not a spotlight in sight. But the creative brilliance locked in these little sunbeams can fire the furnace of white-heat which only very few can withstand, but those who reach their true potential will discover the alchemist's dream for they have the Midas touch. Just call them Goldfinger.

SAGITTARIUS–JUPITER DECANATE ....August 3 until August 13

Joy oh joy! The inner warm that is mustered by the alignment of Sun and Jupiter is like listening to the choir of King's College, Cambridge, at Christmas, cracking open Maine lobsters and dipping them into glistening clarified butter from Vermont or stealing away at the crack of dawn or first twinkle of twilight to a place with a memory that's gone or the hope of many to come. These folk can provide the fulfilment of all you pray for and disable the lack of hope in others. In them lies the new dawn of optimism and the infectious enthusiasm that picks folk up when they fall down. Their fault lies in giving too much and expecting everyone else to do the same. They have to learn it doesn't work like that.

ARIES–MARS DECANATE ....August 14 until August 23/24

Magnificent in defeat. Don't you believe it, for with this fiery combo sparks fly if they don't win. They might appear magnanimous but their competitive spirit only wants to be in the premier league. Like a child who sulks because they can't have their own way this Sun/Mars connection will never be content with a silver medal when the gold one shines so brightly. They must learn to count their blessings and then the vital Sun and virile Mars will create a winner where success is a frequent visitor. It's hard for them to resist when the prospect of adoration reaches their voracious ego, and here lies their Achilles' heel, a glorious Narcissus complex. Who loves ya baby? You do!

FIRE

VIRGO

RULER: Mercury, but not the Mercury that governs Gemini. Here lies the teacher in *Educating Rita* – Michael Caine is the Virgo Mercury, the server of knowledge and Julie Walters is the Gemini Mercury, who savours knowledge.

LOVES: Small things – everything to be as perfect as possible for they are the paragons of the zodiac. A neat and orderly life with everything in its place.

LOATHES: Not knowing – not knowing information, not knowing where something is and not knowing what their next move will be. People who are ignorant who make no effort to improve their mind.

NEEDS TO CULTIVATE: A less critical outlook especially when it comes to themselves, not to push their capabilities beyond their capacity. More warmth, expressive emotion and a philosophical approach if things don't go according to their masterplan.

NEEDS TO TONE DOWN: Their analytical approach to life and realise if something isn't broken then it doesn't need fixing. The urge to interfere, stick their nose in and give advice when it's not wanted.

VIRGO–MERCURY DECANATE ....August 23/24 until September 2

So much Virgo and Mercury can drive a person crazy – whether it's self-inflicted or gets on other people's nerves. They have a ready wit which manifests in a cleverness that is bright, informative and mentally on the ball, but this can often lead to acerbic, sarcastic comments which label them the Acid Queen – or King. Unless they let their hearts get one over their heads once in a while then living or working with them can be like a vacation down on Cold Comfort Farm. Though they have a mind that ticks along like clockwork their feelings are a flop, but with a little conscious effort and a more demonstrative outlook they can pull the emotional rabbit out the hat.

CAPRICORN–SATURN DECANATE ....September 3 until September 12

This Virgo has so much gravitas. Virgo is a sanguine earth sign, much more ethereal and airy than either Taurus or Capricorn, so Capricorn/Saturn – and they don't come much earthier than that – consolidates this decanate, bonding these folk with their home element, giving them the roots they need to settle down and imbuing them with the ability to see something through to a conclusion. This endows these folk with authority, determination, dedication and true grit. They also possess a red-raw sexuality – for, in case you hadn't noticed, Virgo's nocturnal activities can be pretty racy. They like to try things out and are turned on by the touch of hot flesh and pulsating bodies so put them together and *voilà*. It leads to an adept exploration of the physical body as well as of the mind.

TAURUS–VENUS DECANATE ....September 13 until September 23/24

Meet the culture vulture, for the love of the arts manifested by Venus and the adoration of the mind meted out by Mercury is an exquisite match that makes this person tasteful, elegant and refined. This is the kind of guy or gal you can invite into your home knowing they will be an intellectual and charming nexus for all those they interact with. Their detached heart is warmed by the cosmic Gulf Stream that washes out from dulcet Venus, for in this decanate Virgo attains the perfection that is denied by almost any other combination. Beauty with brains.

EARTH

LIBRA

RULER: Candy-floss Venus, so different from the Mother Earth lass that rules Taurus. This Venus trips the light fantastic looking for love and compliments. She is easily flattered but gay and good to have around and can be an acquired taste.

LOVES: Beauty and all things that are lovely. Adores people who are fun, good-natured, courteous and who appreciates them and tells 'em so!

LOATHES: Bad manners, bad language and anything beastly. Ugliness in all its forms.

NEEDS TO CULTIVATE: A more definite outlook which doesn't include wondering what people think of them. To choose for themselves and not do something just to please others.

NEEDS TO TONE DOWN: Being so sweet it turns to cloying saccharine and going completely over the top to win friends and favours. They should learn that what you see is what you get and if you don't like it, tough!

LIBRA–VENUS DECANATE ....September 23/24 until October 3

The synergy between Venus and Libra here can at times be all too much, over the top and wearying and wearing for other people. They want so much attention it's like having to constantly please a little girl or boy. This is the most indecisive of all the Libran decanates, constantly searching for the best balance but they search for so long they lose the initiative and allow vacillation and vanity to take over. But artistically and musically they can reign supreme for they possess pulchritudinous potential that if developed can make them a shining star in their own particular firmament. Relationships too can suffer if they enter a marriage or commitment thinking they have the perfect partner, so they must approach life with a warts-and-all concept if they don't want to be continually disappointed.

AQUARIUS–URANUS DECANATE ....October 4 until October 13

Now here's someone who is different but charming. Gone is the ever so sweet honey-dripping Libran lips replaced by Aquarian avant-garde tinged with elegance. They have an aura of charisma which is hard to resist for they vibrate to a rhythm of life so very different to the norm, and that is what makes them so attractive. These bonny babes are unusual in that they want you for yourself and not what you can give them. But this very airy decanate does not want to be pinned down and operates best when given the freedom to see what lies beyond their realm. So you must either go with them and discover life together or live a lonely life knowing you were close to stardust but let it slip through your fingers.

GEMINI–MERCURY DECANATE ....October 14 until October 23/24

Should the other man's grass be greener then this bohemian bunch will want to know its texture, make-up and consistency. Like Maria in *The Sound of Music* they won't conform and will do something at least once in their lives that will more than raise an eyebrow or two – possibly in the cause of love. But if their hearts are ribboned by a romantic halo then their minds have the ring of confidence, as they are determined to find out about life and that is what drives them on. Only the most caring, considerate and intellectually on par partner can satisfy them. If not they are off changing their usual uniform for an Indiana Jones trilby and leather jerkin for this Venus/Mercury soul often wants to play games for the wrong reasons – just for fun.

AIR

SCORPIO

October 24 –November 22

RULER: Scorpio's traditional ruler is Mars which gives rise to their sexy tag but it is the planet Pluto who is afforded their modern rulership – the planet of orgasm.

LOVES: Anything that pleases their senses down to hidden depths. This sign is not into anything transient or temporary but a permanent experience which truly, madly, deeply moves them like nothing else on earth.

LOATHES: Superficial people who don't 'feel' something from the bottom of their heart … or even lower. Indiscreet, unfaithful or treacherous types, it is they who will beg the legendary Scorpio sting.

NEEDS TO CULTIVATE: Forgiveness. More than anything they find it hard to forgive and, like Cancer, forget. But if they could it would then prevent vengeance, jealousy and hate from gaining a foothold.

NEEDS TO TONE DOWN: Secretive behaviour and abuse of any power they have. Being as enigmatic as the Mona Lisa is one thing but to play psychological mind games is self-destructive.

SCORPIO–PLUTO DECANATE ....October 23/24 until November 2

I'm put in mind of Jules Verne's *20,000 Leagues Under The Sea* for this is the essence of this Scorpio decanate – but even this isn't deep enough. Their emotions are a complex maze of feelings, senses and desires which require so much understanding and patience by others, and much, much more. To plumb the depths of this Scorpio ocean you need enough oxygen to last for an eternity and still you will never really understand or know this mysterious man or woman. Besides, every so often you need to come up for air as being with them can cut you off from the outside world and suffocate you. Fate has a greater hold over the children of this decanate more than any other and gaining control over their life's destiny is their life's work – but such a target can only be likened to the 12 labours of Hercules.

PISCES–NEPTUNE DECANATE ....November 3 until November 12

Here strokes a much softer touch, for the ever-moving waves of Pisces ruffles the dark, stagnant pond of Scorpio and refreshes it with a sensitive aeration of emotion that allows the folk they love and know to dip in and understand them. Gone is the enigmatic man, replaced by a compassionate soul who cares, the dove of peace which wants so much to find a solution to terror and not play on it with a psychological free-for-all. Here you find someone who is spiritually mature, someone who cares, who cares what *you* think, feel or believe and isn't motivated by power, money or control. But within every Scorpio's heart lies envy and jealousy and this combination can be as lethal or manipulative as the Borgias with a deft touch for emotional blackmail if ever crossed. You have been warned.

CANCER–MOON DECANATE ....November 13 until November 22/23

Searching for a mother figure or a strong woman can produce problems for their partner in life, unless they fit the bill. Their desire for familiar things is mega important to their insecure psyche for whatever happens they always return to their roots. The emotions emanated by this decanate are as vast as the seven seas, for their feelings and moods are governed by the ebb and flow of life and they are acutely aware of every nuance and motion that affects their own life. With their psychic telepathy there is little you can keep from their all-seeing third eye. They command great loyalty in others – or create sworn secret enemies, for they are hard to resist or must be resisted at all costs.

WATER

SAGITTARIUS
November 23 – December 21

RULER: Jupiter in his most noble Olympian guise. This is Zeus to the Greeks, who ruled from his mountain top and frequently made sexual sorties to mortals or sent thunderbolts crashing down in displeasure. This could be you!

LOVES: Doing nothing by halves but indulging in Bacchanalian frolics, and, if there's time, the odd orgy or two! People who are as enthusiastic, positive and optimistic about life as they are.

LOATHES: Depressives, doubting Thomases and Job's Comforters. Any person who is a pessimist.

NEEDS TO CULTIVATE: Moderation in all things and an elegant sufficiency. They have an innate desire to take on more than they can handle.

NEEDS TO TONE DOWN: Exaggeration, for all that bluff and bluster has to deliver in the end. Great expectations which often come to nought as they forget that they are only human.

SAGITTARIUS–JUPITER DECANATE ....November 22/23 until December 2

The fizz and bubble can get right up your nose but, like champagne, you know you're dealing with someone of quality and style and while there's no doubt they have plenty of both, you can have too much of a good thing. So one glass at time or you'll be bowled over by the rat-a-tat-tat of ideas and plans that flow from their lips. That's the problem, they have so many things they want to do but they should concentrate on one thing at a time. But this philosophical decanate with its gigantic philanthropic heart is the pick-me-up you need when you are down, for they will make sure you oounce right back from any adversity or setback.

ARIES–MARS DECANATE ....December 3 until December 12

There is something incredibly sexy about this decanate. It kinda grabs you right here and there's no way you can say 'no' to them, for whatever they want, they want it now and you have no choice but to give it! Even their friendly persuasion is backed up by so much oomph you just love 'em! But will they leave you when your relationship cools or becomes too familiar? There is a chance, for though they are initially hot to trot, once the novelty wears off or you give in too easily and the hunt is over, so their interest diminishes. These lusty people need constant challenge and cannot live without exercising their zest for life, so always try to keep something in reserve and then they'll be doing the panting and you'll be pulling the strings.

LEO–SUN DECANATE ....December 13 until December 21/22

Take the first three letters of Sagittarius and put an 'e' after it, and there you have it – sage. This divine mixture of Jupiter and Sun is creatively in control. The fixity of Leo tempering the 'in your face' side of Sagittarius results in a soul who is a cut above the rest. In some cases they may know it, demanding luxury, first-class treatment and possessing an arrogance and pomposity that is positively infuriating, but one day someone will come along and burst their bubble. When that happens they start to grow in all directions, spiritually as well as emotionally, and that's when they are at their best. Not motivated by money, but realising that the fidelity of a friend, the thanks of a stranger and the bountiful blessings of Providence are far greater riches than Mammon could ever offer.

FIRE

December 22 – January 20 CAPRICORN

RULER: Saturn, the ringed planet, and there's the rub. Capricorns can be hemmed in by circumstances or their own selves. Every so often they should remember: *rules are made to be broken.*

LOVES: The security of knowing that something will happen at a certain time of day. Success and achievement.

LOATHES: People who waste anything. People who are late, people who expect an easy ride and people who are stupid, incompetent or who don't care and ruin the efforts of those who do. Failure and rejection.

NEEDS TO CULTIVATE: The acceptance that not everything is perfect or can be done perfectly. Homing in on what is good and not concentrating on what is bad. A more optimistic outlook and positive thinking.

NEEDS TO TONE DOWN: A defeatist nature and throwing cold water on other people's plans and ideas. Being so self-critical that it hurts no one but harms their own morale or self-confidence. Being too matter of fact and hard on themselves.

CAPRICORN–SATURN DECANATE ....December 21/22 until December 31

Think of Eeyore in *Winnie the Pooh* and you have the character of this decanate in one: they don't miss a chance to be morose, maudlin and hard done by. There is a basic insecurity that stems from feeling unloved, but they believe it is their duty to carry on despite it all. They despise failure and so adopt a guilty conscience or feel ashamed that they have been part of something which was their responsibility to make a success. Add to this rejection, an inferiority or persecution complex and you might want to give up on them. But don't. For beneath this negative exterior is someone with a giddy sense of humour and endless ambition, and when inspired there ain't a mountain they can't climb. Stick with 'em. They will never let you down.

TAURUS–VENUS DECANATE ....January 1 until January 10

Here's a real softie but first you must get through the crusty skin and discover the tender heart that beats inside. Here lies rich earth which in everyday terms translates into money or sex or both! They believe that you transcend the spiritual to get to the material. OK, so it's cock-eyed, but with the right person by their side they are willing to be taught, even if it takes time. But what this combo lacks in finesse it makes up for in ambition, as here is the fair and just achiever, not someone who does something simply for financial reward, but for personal satisfaction too. These earthlings might not play hard but they sure do work hard, and love hard too!

VIRGO–MERCURY DECANATE ....January 11 until January 20/21

Only the intellectually primed Capricorn can reach the goal set by the tie which draws together Mercury and Saturn. For though compassion and sympathy is conspicuous by its absence, they are clever and astute in what they do do. But that often isn't enough for their partner so they can end up lonely unless they learn to love a little more and be less formal in their feelings. When their emotions melt then their life falls into place. They want perfection at a price, but once they realise it's impossible, things will start to happen. The business acumen registered here is second to none – Paul Getty here they come! They also have the capacity to be cunning, crafty and conniving – a latter day tricky Dicky Nixon – but realise that by using their brain for self-improvement they'll get what they want without the anguish or tears.

— EARTH

AQUARIUS January 21 – February 19

RULER: Uranus. Some Aquarians march to the off-beat tune conducted by this radical star, but there are others who are more self-disciplined and are happier dancing to the more conservative Saturn tune.

LOVES: Doing anything that annoys others – they are almost perverse in their desire to shock people, and especially the Establishment.

LOATHES: Strait-laced people and conforming to authority of any kind. They will use everything within their anarchic personality to upset the status quo.

NEEDS TO CULTIVATE: Patience and tolerance more than anything else, for they can't abide anything from queues to fools.

NEEDS TO TONE DOWN: Defiance and wilful behaviour which make them many enemies. If they don't like what society convenes as upright or proper then they should seek to reform it reasonably rather than attack it irrationally.

AQUARIUS–URANUS DECANATE ....January 20/21 until January 30

Meet Mr Spaceman (or woman) for this is a decanate of equality who in true *Star Trek* fashion goes where no one else will. They are possessed by the spirit of adventure and a desire to discover the unknown. They have foresight and vision and incredible intuition, with a piercing perception about people and life. When the song 'Aquarius' was written for the musical *Hair* it was to become their anthem. But though they possess altruism and can be humanitarian to a Mother Theresa degree their feelings and emotions are much more exclusive and have to be earned by loved ones around them. They tend to hurt the ones they love whilst giving their all to complete strangers – you either love 'em or hate 'em, there is no middle road.

GEMINI–MERCURY DECANATE ....January 31 until February 9

The lateral thinkers of the zodiac, they are out on their own intellectually and it takes some time for people to get a handle on them. They are ingenious and gifted in their own particular walk of life and are able to diversify more than most Aquarians, as mutable Gemini allows them to cross over and be interested and expert in more than one thing. But will people take them seriously? There is a thin dividing line between genius and madness and the children of this decanate walk it. With their personal magnetism and electrifying charisma they are often under-used or under-rated, for people are afraid of what they don't understand. But then every so often they meet a disciple who is prepared to follow and back them for the visionary individual they are, and a star is born.

LIBRA–VENUS DECANATE ....February 10 until February 19/20

The charm that pours out of this Venus/Uranus connection makes for someone very cute and special. They possess a power to make things happen for, like New York, anything is possible when they are around. They can fall in and out of love at the drop of a hat with sudden but sincere infatuations taking over their sense and sensibility. They can find success not only on artistic merit but because they present and portray their ideas differently to the rest. They have a way of doing things that neither offends nor upsets, but stimulates and gratifies, as they have a certain *je ne sais quoi* that makes them mesmerisingly unique.

AIR

PISCES

RULER: Neptune, who can deceive and give false impressions but is also an imaginative force which can conjure psychedelic clowns out of colourless clones. Jupiter is the traditional ruler, making some Pisceans easier to understand and less diffuse.

LOVES: The twinkle of coloured lanterns on a Christmas tree or a scented candle flickering by a frost-coated window. Sophisticated surroundings and an elegant ambiance. Sensitive people.

LOATHES: The loud, the raucous and unrefined riff-raff – oiks of any description. Having to face facts, the truth or reality if it doesn't fit in with their idea of what's real.

NEEDS TO CULTIVATE: A much more honest approach to life where they take the rough with the smooth and don't keep sweeping things under the carpet. A more realistic view of people, because not everyone is as nice as they think.

NEEDS TO TONE DOWN: Reliance on anything which could become a crutch such as drink or drugs or any other substance that files away the harsh corners of life. Living in a dream world.

PISCES–NEPTUNE DECANATE ....February 19/20 until March 1

Being able to see the wood for the trees is hard for this fairy-tale cast, who floats like Titania and Oberon living in a midsummer night's dream world where nothing is as it seems. Because of the impressions and sensations they can pick up these people must be aware of their propensity for make believe, so whatever they feel or sense they must make sure it is not their imagination, for once the magic wears off they find the prince was a frog all the time! They change like a chameleon choosing a mood or image to suit any occasion: they can deceive or be deceived, they suffer from delusions and paranoia or use their imagination to create works of art. Their psychic energy makes them a candidate to be a clairvoyant, just so long as it is true spiritual guidance and not just wishful thinking.

CANCER–MOON DECANATE ....March 2 until March 11

The tenderness and compassion that seeps through this wonderfully watery combination shows someone who is pure and selfless. They truly care for others, the greater good of the globe and all that lives therein. They can be saddened by the hate and violence that intrudes upon universal peace and understanding. As a result, they want to take the blame and carry the problems of the world on their shoulders, but this is not possible and they must realise that despite their sincere spiritual wish to make the world a better place they must start with their own personal patch first. The love and harmony they extend to the human race can be misused and abused by crooks or beggars who see them as an easy touch. Equally, they must come down to earth every so often as they have no divine right to demand anything.

SCORPIO–PLUTO DECANATE ....March 12 until March 20/21

This is a most complicated character where only a few are allowed to see behind the mask. Don't judge this Pisces book by its cover for there are chapters written by Pluto and that means fate has a large stake in the story of their life. They may have to suffer in silence, experience a tragedy or trauma, but will emerge from it a better person – transformed and reborn. Because of the great spiritual empathy of Pisces and Scorpio they are able to cope, for they realise there is a reason for their sorrow but what it is they cannot explain. They just know that this existence is the final spoke in their karmic wheel, it is the last test and if they come through it then any suffering is ended forever. This person has the makings of a saint and it takes an equally sacred person to unlock their secret heart and befriend them.

WATER

21 MARCH

'You might as well say that I dream when I sleep is the same thing as I sleep when I dream,' said the dormouse conversationally. 'Would you like some more tea?'

'I've had none in the first place,' replied March 21 tartly. 'How about some cake?' asked the Mad Hatter solicitously, albeit timidly, because of course there was none. This tea party was a disaster. March 21 adjusted its long golden hair and wide blue sash and threw several cups and saucers onto the ground, which broke into small pieces. The dormouse scampered away, crying, and the other guests sat very quietly. This individual goes

to 100 per cent rage from a standing start and it's not lack of tea and cake that ruins the party, but temper. You might as well wrongly observe, as the dormouse might say, that being hungry can make you ill-tempered is the same thing as being ill-tempered can make you hungry. But in this person's case it often comes down to the same thing. They'd better get control of themselves or they'll begin to lose control of everything.

No fate is so firmly decreed or temperament so binding that things can't be changed by an act of will, and really and truly this is one of the easier ones to fix. You just have to admit it, then find a way to stop it. This problem manifests itself slightly more in women than men. It comes from tiredness, overpressure and a deep seated lack of self-confidence which means this person sees criticism or slight, particularly about weight and perceived lack of genuine, reliable friendliness.

Just relax. Wear white, the late March colour for luck and innocence and new beginnings. And if you can't wear white, wear jet jewellery. It's supposed to inspire the wearer with courage, hope, overcomes melancholia and maybe with this ancient and powerful reputation it's got as much chance of keeping you calm as anything else.

Never forget what a man says to you when he is angry.

(Henry Ward Beecher)

BODY

March 21 is prone to colds which adds to her general weariness. It's always been known that zinc supplements help, taken daily in conjunction with vitamin C to aid absorption, but up until now it's been a hit and miss affair, especially as it's unhealthy to take more zinc than the pharmacist prescribes. America now comes to the rescue with homeopathic zinc lozenges, soon to arrive here. Cold viruses link in, then attack human cells. Tests show that the lozenges successfully prevent the viruses from sticking to human cells. Apparently it's not an outright cure, but cuts the duration of the cold by half.

MIND

Rage comes to fertile ground. Classical music calms and wards it off. Choose single instrument music, piano or violin sonatas, rather than the more stirring big orchestral pieces.

DATESHARE

Gary Oldman, *British film actor.* **Timothy Dalton**, *film, stage actor, starred as James Bond.* **Matthew Broderick**, *film actor.* **Robert the Bruce**, *Scottish king, nationalist icon.* **Ayrton Senna**, *Brazilian racing driver, world champion.* **Johann Sebastian Bach**, *German composer, organist, Baroque music.* **Peter Brook**, *British stage, film director.* **Modeste Mussorgsky**, *Russian composer, Boris Godunov.* **J B J Fourier**, *French mathemetician.* **Ingrid Kristiansen**, *Norwegian runner, world record holder for women's 5000, 10,000 metres.*

March 22 goes for the feel-good factor at parties, suffering fairly rigorously from the feel-bad factor the next morning. Around Christmas and other festive occasions, hangovers are a plague. Acids in alcohol strip away the protective layer of the stomach causing indigestion and nausea. Plus your blood sugar level is reduced (hypoglycaemia). Eat a protein-rich breakfast, bacon and eggs, with toast and fruit juice to restore energy levels and blood sugar. If this is something you can't face, magnesium is reckoned to be a good hangover ameliorator, so start the day with milk and bananas.

MIND

Traditional March days of fortune are March 3, 5, 12, 17, 24, 26. Very specifically these are days when people with money worries can expect good fortune. And long standing quarrels will end in reconciliation and joy.

DATESHARE

Nicholas Monsarrat, *British writer, The Cruel Sea.* **George Benson**, *jazz guitarist.* **Chico Marx**, *Marx Brothers pianist.* **William Shatner**, *Star Trek's Captain Kirk.* **Stephen Sondheim**, *composer, lyricist.* **Sir Andrew Lloyd Webbe**r, *changed the face of 20th century musical theatre.* **Marcel Marceau**, *French mime artist.*

MARCH 22

There's a lot of leadership in people born on this date. Many are attracted, like to be directed by them, but with March 22 it only works if it's fun, because they can be arrogant and impatient. With some, the competitive side to their nature is so developed they become bored with, even resentful of those who refuse either to compete or agree with them.

Sometimes this makes marriage sticky and they may go through two, four even six marriages before he or she realises that breaking up is wantonly hurtful – and expensive – and compromise is the solution. Marriage, or at least a long term partnership, is necessary because isolated March 22 gets extremely set in its ways and dusty bachelordom or spinsterhood ensues, the gloss goes off the flesh, and loneliness settles in disguised as independence and a love of solitude. This can, however, be quite difficult, because sex is such a strong passion here, and these people are so adventurous that they can't help stringing along several partners at once, afraid that if they plump for one person they'll certainly miss out on something.

Many rise to the top of their profession, hiding their arrogance beneath a lovely, diffident-seeming charm. There's never a hint of anything but extreme honourableness, always immense sweetness of character. Find them in teaching and religious life, but also in daredevil pursuits, motor racing, flying aircraft, the armed forces where many end up in the Special Services.

Both sexes have a strong visual eye. They like paintings, architecture and photography, and often make extremely good home movies. Women adore primroses, cowslips, irises and roses and if they can, will heap them into vases. Most of the men are passionate about some sort of racing, horse or motor, as a watcher as well as a doer and you can find quite a few in betting shops or in the hospitality tent at Le Mans.

One nice thing about egotists:
They don't talk about other people.
(Lucille Harper)

23 MARCH

There's a touch of GS here, Giggling Syndrome as opposed to the sexually famous GSS, G-Spot Syndrome, which is more a search-and-find situation. GS happens mostly when March 23 is in her teens and twenties, when quite often she and her friends end up crying and writhing with laughter at nothing at all. It's just a bit of fun and makes other people laugh, which is great. The problem comes when March 23 absolutely knows it's going to

happen in church, in class, at the theatre, especially during ballet or opera, at important family functions, while being interviewed by any authority figure and in particular places which require you to be silent such as libraries, where this person will become snortingly insane with suppressed laughter.

A much more anti-social problem than giggling in the library is a tendency to giggle when something appalling happens to somebody else. This is not because March 23 is heartless, but a very familiar reaction to emotional stress, shock and just a strangeness of situation. There are plenty of ways to handle it, and if you feel you are liable to do this and are in a profession where such a reaction would make your work impossible, then immediately consult a doctor who can point you in the right direction. There are also expert counsellors who can help you understand how to control this troublesome and anti-social reaction.

Apart from this, people born today are remarkable for their infectious charm. They're the kind who walk into a room and light it up. Attractively lean, with good ankles and hands, there will be many eager partners drawn to March 23 not just because of the charm and the ankles, but the illuminating intelligence. This individual reads a great deal and likes to learn a great deal about subjects that interest him, so his talk is never waffle and companions usually come away from a few hours' companionship quite inspired.

The good life is one inspired by love and guided by knowledge.

(Bertrand Russell)

BODY

Generally speaking, March 23 people are the velvet fist in the iron glove when it comes to sex. Outwardly so cool, they luxuriate in sensuosity. PEA (phenylethylamine) is the chemical thought to be responsible for the falling in love 'rush' and it's found in both rosewater and chocolate. Natural oil of rose is expensive, but you only need a few drops in an almond carrier oil. For a turn on massage, smooth oil on a partner's back and firmly caress down from the nape of the neck to the buttocks and up again. Accompany this with a slowly eaten Whipped Cream Walnut.

MIND

Numerologically 23 is ruled by 5 (2+3=5) and the 5th card in Tarot's Major Arcana is The Hierophant. It indicates all that is best in 23. Capacity for profound human understanding, natural authority, rapid and accurate comprehension.

Italian cooking, the Mother of European Cuisine, keeps the heart and soul happy. Try Fettucine and Seafood Sauce (serves 4). Take 4 scallops, cleaned and cut in half, 225g peeled prawns, 225g mussels, boiled and shelled, 2 garlic cloves, crushed, pinch freshly ground chilli, 45 ml chopped parsley, olive oil, ½ glass white wine, salt and pepper. Cook, drain pasta. In a separate pan, fry garlic, chilli, parsley in olive oil for few minutes. Quickly add prepared seafood , fry on high heat for 3–4 minutes. Add wine, reduce sauce until glaze appears. Season mixture and pour over pasta.

MIND

To travel with friends is companionable only if they are optimistic journeymakers and can fit in and enthuse about the destination. A good holiday is one spent with people whose notions of time are vaguer than yours.

DATESHARE

Lawrence Ferlinghetti, *San Francisco beat poet, painter, author.* **Malcolm Muggeridge**, *writer, journalist.* **Bob Mackie**, *costume designer.* **William Morris**, *British pre-Raphaelite leader, painter, poet, designer soft furnishings, church decorator, Oxford Movement.* **Joseph Priestly**, *British chemist, oxygen discoverer, clergyman, philosopher.* **Steve McQueen**, *Hollywood film star, daredevil.* **Fatty Arbuckle**, *silent film actor.* **Wilhelm Reich**, *revolutionary psychologist, inventor of 'orgone accumulator'.*

MARCH 24

March 24 is a tremendous traveller and is often happier abroad than at home. A foreign way of life suits her temperament better, especially if it's in a hot country, because she feels the cold. And rain soaked dull grey streets, and indeed rain soaked deep green fields, depress her almost physically. If he wishes, he can become a fine linguist, often speaking three or four different languages well – once you've learned another it's always easier to go on to a third. But it's worth remembering that March 24 is not a natural linguist, so the languages are more a tribute to massive effort and single-minded concentration – well known qualities for late March people – than innate talent.

Psychologically this date is born to the easy going lifestyle of Italy. Find them idling in cafes in Venice or Rome, wearing an elegant hat to keep off the sun, reading a local newspaper and draining a glass of red wine or chilled beer. They've probably acquired a flat near the centre for next to nothing and they are earning their money in tourism, possibly in teaching or medicine, and in further flung countries, engineering, mining or surveying.

Find them also in the Middle East. The Gulf States attract them. Here they also learn the language and make a point of becoming friendly with people and their families native to this area, very much enjoying the courteous mien of Quataris or Bahrainis and the 'tomorrow will do' lifestyle. Sometimes they marry, settle down and never come back to England, except for visits. And when they do, they don't like what they find.

Just because they travel so much and are very independent, March 24 tends to cook extremely well. They will throw an exquisite pasta dish together in ten minutes out of apparently next to nothing, follow it with fruit and cheeses, something perfect to drink and provide one of the best evenings their companions have ever enjoyed.

What do you do if you find a blue banana? Try to cheer it up.

25 MARCH

Starglitter dusts the furry coat of this great hearted and cuddlesome person. Usually tall, with a big resounding voices, and an affectionate way with others, if anybody tries to be unkind, March 25 is as upset as the Great Bear star (Ursa Major) when it thinks it's lost its pup. These individuals can't bear horribilis behaviour. Neanderthal man and woman are anathema to this highly developed social animal. He will go out of his way to repair any unkindness done to another.

This makes working life painful because offices can be mean places. So although they are clever enough, unless they can alter the structure of work, and instil the idea of generosity one to another, they are better off in areas where they can do tangible good. This justifies a bit of interstellar scrapping. If it isn't possible, you can always pick out Ursa Major at work. She's the one who protects young colleagues, the vulnerable and the unhappy. She biffs the bully with her massive paw. She gets the shower put in the ladies' loo and prevents the canteen from completely closing when there's a night shift on. Everybody always remembers Ursa Major's birthday with presents, cakes and silly balloons on the Big Bear's desk.

At his freest and best, however, March 25 is happiest in a research laboratory, or working out in the open with animals or taking care of our environment. Charity gives him a purpose and teaching, social work, theatre, music, arts and crafts make this sparklingly furry creature dance to the lovely tune in his head and heart.

It goes without saying that they can be the rock of the family. Loath to flibbertigibbet about with different partners, they enjoy the monogamous life, sticking with the same partner for ever if they can. They play with their children and visit their dads, mums, aunties, uncles, grans and friends as many times a week or month as they can fit everybody in.

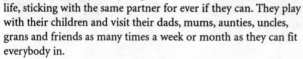

Come on babe, get with the beat.
(Baloo, The Jungle Book)

BODY
This person tends to eat fatty fried food and snack all day, which makes skin dull and does the same to the mind. Get into healthier habits. Try a cleansing drink to start the day, a cup of warm water with lemon. Helps purify the system and skin benefits. If you feel a virus coming on take a ginger bath, grating the ginger and then squeezing it through cheesecloth. Or add lemons, tangerines and oranges, cut into quarters to the bath, encouraging toxins to depart and enhancing the complexion with Vitamin C. Get into the country as much as possible and breathe fresh, clean air.

MIND
This date can get tense about family occasions, especially around Christmas. Best not to mind who does and who doesn't come, because this sort of tension ruins what should be a joyful, relaxed occasion for everybody.

DATESHARE
Steve Norman, percussionist, saxophonist, Spandau Ballet. **Ed Begley**, stage, film actor, **Elton John**, singer, songwriter, phenomenon. **Aretha Franklin**, gospel singer. **Gloria Steinem**, feminist activist, author. **Simone Signoret**, French film actress. **Paul Michael Glaser**, TV actor, Starsky and Hutch. **Béla Bartók**, Hungarian composer. **Arturo Toscanini**, conductor, classical music legend.

March 26 is a sensualist and a money-maker and most people can't work out how this intergalactic charmer finds the time to do so much of both. Both sexes seem positively shiny with natural luck, at least for a period of their lives. Their skin glimmers with health and some other luminous quality as if moonbeams are moisturized into it every night. Prospective partners come queue-hopping at the door. It's not unknown for this person to take two people home to bed. Or go from one lover to another and sometimes an especially beautifully cooked dinner to another one, which is taxing for Aries' slender waistline.

If they buy a house, it will rocket in price. If they open a shop, restaurant, café or club it will be a success. When March 26 approaches a bank manager or building society money man, the hand that bestows the cash belongs to a face wreathed in smiles.

It won't last, but for maybe ten years the good times roll. Watch for when the luck turns. Make sound investments. Keep strict ledgers. Some can be unworldly with their money even when the business is accurately efficient. Others go to the opposite extreme and tight as a well-tuned violin, never buy a round of drinks.

Most of the women and some men develop a money making sideline in collecting. Women favour the traditionally feminine, sneered at by some, old samplers and bits of lace. It's dressing up box collecting. But the rag of lace from a street stall, with its needle lace roses and point de neige spotted net is from Brussels and worth £600. Guys like models. And they'll be the ones to pick up a 7.25in gauge model of the Great Western Railway 14XX Class 0-4-2 side tank locomotive by I R Holder, for £25 at a house clearance and then discover this beloved toy from somebody's attic is worth £12,000.

The passion ending doth the purpose lose.

(Hamlet, *Shakespeare*)

27 MARCH

March 27 is so talented that fame could very easily come his and her way. They're the lilies in this particular patch of the universe, they toil not, neither do they spin, yet Solomon in all his glory was not arrayed as one of these. From teenage years everybody knows this is the one to watch.

It's an extremely intelligent date as well as clever, good looking, so on and so on. What rockets them into stardom is the Arian competitiveness. All talent needs an extra something to get itself noticed. Teenagers may form a pop group and very soon they've  got a manager, a recording contract and Chris Evans wants to be their friend. The girls, who are taller than average, shoot onto the catwalk without really trying. Soon they are winning the day in New York and buying a new bungalow for Mum and Dad in Catford.

Some become famous academics, many, ground-breaking scientists. Others win at sport. Or writing. Or very big business. It's a multi-skilled individual and there's almost nothing they can't do if they put their mind to it. Naturally not all will become famous, but in their hearts they know it could have happened. Especially when you think of the berks it does happen to. The Arian tendency to pull back may be responsible for this lack of momentum.

Excellent travellers, they may roam the world for a few years, but eventually, drawn by love of this country's loveliness, they come back and settle down very happily. Quite who with, however, may be more difficult, as March 27 is prone to falling in love, often at times when they are already happily married. Best for this date to get lots of love affairs out of the way, then choose a mate and try to stay put. Because the underlying sadness in their character easily comes to the fore when they think they have hurt others.

BODY
March 27 is prone to exhaustion. Foods rich in trace minerals like boron, and selenium may help you focus on a task in hand, and act as a natural upper. Fruits and nuts, high in boron, seem to speed up brain activity, pushing more energy into the system. Other boron rich foods include legumes and green, leafy vegetables. Selenium is found in beef. Folic acid, another booster, is found in broccoli, green leafy vegetables like spinach, broad beans, and various animal livers. Recommended by the government for women prior to and during pregnancy, folic acid also lifts your mood.

MIND
Everybody has a smidgeonette of superstition and everybody has returned to their house for something forgotten. Superstition says that when you get indoors, you must count backwards from seven in order to avoid ill luck.

DATESHARE
Mstislav Rostropovich, *Russian cellist, conductor, composer.* **Gloria Swanson**, *film star.* **Michael York**, *film actor.* **Sarah Vaughan**, *jazz singer.* **Michel Guérard**, *French chef, Nouvelle Cuisine inventor.* **Mies van der Rohe**, *American architect, designer.*

When will I, will I be famous?

(Bros)

BODY

March 28 loves a sweetly scented house. Old cabbage and fish pie odours genuinely offend and in particular the pervasive odour of cats, which owners often don't notice but everybody else does. Use an oil burner to perfume rooms. Buy the burners in any health food and department store. Drop an essential oil into the water container and light a small candle underneath it. Choose cedarwood, a woody smell, wonderfully soothing, which reminds you of old churches. (Alleged to be an aphrodisiac.) Lavender, the most popular of all the oils is wonderful, calms the fevered brow and restores energy.

MIND

In numerology those born on the 28th are ruled by number 1 (2+8=10, 1+0=1). The 1st card of the Major Arcana is The Magician, which brings with it all those talents for communication, magical companionship and diplomatic skills.

DATESHARE

Dirk Bogarde, *British film star, actor, beloved by most people, author.* **Neil Kinnock**, *British Labour party leader.* **Raphael**, *Renaissance master painter.* **Maxim Gorky**, *Russian author.* **St Theresa de Avila**.

This lovely person is disarmingly charming and you'll never catch March 28 indulging in snobbery. This is good, because some Arians do, especially if they are born into blue-blooded galaxies, when the conversation is almost entirely devoted to who their relatives are. Our birthday child is never lost for amusing conversation and it's rarely about him or herself.

What makes them special is the talent for listening. Genuinely interested in almost everything others have to say, March 28 is the one who finds out more about your mother than you knew. She will suddenly tell him about the love affair that never flourished twenty years ago, and describe in detail the sun-lit field where she and the departing lover exchanged a final farewell. He sees in her a beauty you as her child can't.

They mix with anyone, swapping opinions in the canteen about *Eastenders* with the same dexterity they use for a discussion about the next day's duck shoot in a Norfolk stately dining-room. Both sexes are recorders of human habits and fascinations, and in many cases their professions will be serving the public. Find them in the police force, the army, running a theatre company, a restaurant, or in the retail business where customers come in as much for the chat as the buy.

If the woman earns a great deal, or wins money, the first instinct is to buy presents for everybody and March 28 doesn't give any old thing just because it's expensive. She values her own birthstones, diamonds, blood stones and the haematite, an iron ore which is cut as a black, shiny gem when crystalline. Expect her to research and give you yours. Or a silk shawl in the same blue as your eyes. The men are just as imaginative and generous. Expect a hat which fits the size of your head – it's a very hatty date. Or a CD of your most favourite piece of music.

~

Serve the servants.

(Nirvana)

29 MARCH

March 29 is ruled by his nose. Often extensively aquiline, it may cause this person depression every time he looks in the mirror. If our protuberant creature simply suffers from a cosmetic problem there are remedies. Experts suggest you dab a darker colour foundation on the tip, then shade upwards, supposedly camouflaging. But this just looks as if you've got dark make-up on the end of your nose. Large noses are extremely distinguished, but if March 29 doesn't think so there are excellent doctors to provide the perfect shape.

No cosmetic surgeon, however, can stop him from sticking his proboscis into other's affairs. They sniff out trouble as fast as any space probe star, and just when you are absolutely sure nobody nose your secret, March 29 is beside you, nostrils quivering – waiting to be punched. In some cases, especially at work, pleasure in other people's business may be useful. Newspapers and television abound with people born on March 29 and the other sniffer dogs of the zodiac. He or she may rise to become the Great Detective. Or discover how to crack secret codes. Some of the best computer hackers are born on this day. International banks beware.

At home, Lady March 29 in particular always nose best. Her habit of lecturing people for their own good makes the level of optimism around her take a fast nosedive. She is an expert on every aspect of the present and eternally grateful to her favourite historical figure, Nostradamus, for delivering to her the future.

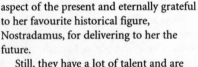

Still, they have a lot of talent and are often stunningly perceptive about other people's problems. The good ones, and most are really, do a lot of good, by solving them. What they also have is a nose for a bargain and there's nothing like going shopping with this person. You'll come home with something wonderful which has cost you next to nothing.

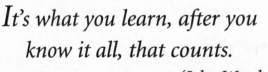

It's what you learn, after you know it all, that counts.

(John Wooden)

BODY

Many March 29 people swear by ginseng, which is thought to improve physical and mental endurance. There are several types of ginseng, but Siberian ginseng has proved to be suitable for most people. Co-enzyme Q10 is the nutrient that ignites and helps to sustain the body's energy production. It is also a valuable antioxidant, one of a group of vitamins and minerals that help to neutralise destructive free radical particles in the body. Q10 is particularly beneficial for Arians because it also benefits teeth, gums and eyes and boosts the immune system to fight the repeated infections to which you are prone.

MIND

This old traveller's weather predicting rhyme is for March 29 who loves to roam this country. Probably inaccurate, but endearing. 'Evening red and morning grey/Send the traveller on his way/Evening grey and morning red/Bring the rain upon his head.'

DATESHARE

Eric Idle, comic, writer, Monty Python member. **Christophe Lambert**, film star. **Jennifer Capriati**, tennis player, youngest US Olympic gold medal winner. **Billy Carter**, the president's peanut farming brother. **William Walton**, British composer. **John Major**, British prime minister. **Pearl Bailey**, singer.

MARCH 30

There's a magnetic force field around March 30. Most people can't resist the crackle of lightening which accompanies this person. It's simply more fun being with them than not being with them. Not necessarily born with physical beauty, they may spend their childhood pursuing ordinary delights without any seeming distinction. Then one day this magic child puts down her

butterfly net and sets out with a bigger one to trawl the skies, riding on stardusted wings until she reaches her chosen star.

And still this ram seems less than notable to those who can't see the soaring creativity which makes this person special. Whatever this individual does works. Both sexes make everything seem so easy, that again, others can't understand their success. Some will be painters, musicians, sportsmen, scientists and become household names. Others may not glitter on the world stage, but in their own locality they are well loved.

This is the person who makes things happen in your town or village. He or she may run local authority or state departments. If there is no theatre or the church needs repairing, they build and mend. If a specialist hospital is needed, both sexes campaign until it happens.

What they say at certain moments in life, other people will remember for ever because these are the shapers of others' destinies. March 30 is always on the telephone because someone has rung for help, maybe to solve an academic problem, ask the name of the author of a favourite book, what colour to wear to a wedding, and, of course, who to marry.

The glimmer about them is part sex appeal. They do not realise that the telephoners would like to be lovers, but settle for friendship because they know that's all they can have. March 30 mustn't hold on to these friends so tightly they can never be free to find someone who will love them back.

Please don't tease.

(*Cliff Richard*)

3I MARCH

March 31 is not a domesticated creature, will do anything to avoid housework. The men turn avoidance into an art form, a sort of psychological battle when they are young with their parents, and when they are adult with their partner. They use their sex appeal to get round those they are leaving to clean up.

March 31 walks in the door, takes off his shoes and leaves them in the corridor, in the middle, one at an angle to the other, for somebody else to fall over. He sits at the newly cleaned kitchen table with his beer and chocolate biscuits, then leaves everything and wanders away. He can't go shopping because he has brought work home. And doesn't know how to turn on the washing machine.

It's not lighthearted, although possibly masked with wit. This person doesn't like any form of housework and doesn't ever want to do it. Marriages or partnerships may break under the strain, unless those who love them understand it's a deep-seated prejudice. In love, he temporarily relaxes the rules, but another comes by who doesn't require domesticity and he leaves.

Miss March 31 has but a shadow of this complex. Most can't change plugs, more daffiness than an aggressive statement.

These are successful gamblers. Lucky people who fall on two feet. Many will be successful salesmen. Others are content to hold down a steady office/factory job, putting their energies into gambling. Happiness comes late in life with a first, second, third or fourth marriage. Many have late children, the men possibly in their sixties and seventies, and the woman in their late forties and early fifties, helped by science. It's mostly because they are procrastinators. But when they decide not to put things off all their plans succeed.

This day's strong convictions could take the religious path, or manifest themselves in Third World charity work. Changes of direction mark their life.

No man can be friends with a woman he finds attractive. He always wants to have sex with her.

(Nora Ephron)

They have to rise above the day, endless April Fool teasing. Since it starts at birth and continues into the departure lounge, there's lots of practice in tolerance and expertly masked feelings. Modesty is not an Aries characteristic, nor diffidence, but they have a quiet dignity which impresses others.

Sometimes they must start work very young and determinedly work their way up, often from shop floor to the top. Those with

little schooling are always conscious of it, so wise April fools must get an education at a later date, or grow chippy. Guard against resentfulness. There's a wet slither of self-pity beneath the dignity. Not to be mined.

Success and money may come quickly because they have a knack for spotting a need. Like a sponge which doesn't break into pieces or an iron which doesn't scatter white powder over your black jacket. Then the men, in particular find that having propelled themselves into the stratosphere, they have attained something they don't want. A different way of life beckons, a leap from salesman to archaeologist, from policeman to deep sea diver.

The women don't go in for such violent life changes, perhaps because their energies are diverted by children. This is not a steady marriage date, so they may be struggling along as a single parent with little time to put their librarian's pen down and tap dance off to Hollywood. Both sexes are also always held back by responsibilities to parents and relatives. This is the one who looks after everybody, and that doesn't mean money. For April 1 it means energy, love and time.

There's a psychic streak here. Lurking, but could be usefully developed. They really do 'see' a horse winning a race, a lost Rembrandt portrait in a junk shop, a box of jewels buried three hundred years ago in a village garden. Treasure-bearing moorland dotted with golden gorse waits for April 1.

Call me but love,

and I'll be new baptised.

(Shakespeare)

2 APRIL

Greedy in love, greedy for food and greedy for success. April 2 may appear to have the charisma of Miss Mouse, but don't be fooled. She gets a foot in the door and the next step is going to be a foot on your head. Older colleagues rush to help them. The peer group make a run for the door when they see Miss M lithsp her way over to the male boss, and ask pleath for his advice.

She'll answer your telephone, grab your work, your contacts and your boyfriend. And he will do the same. Naturally thin and often extremely good at very competitive sport. Mr Rodent usually has bags of doughnuts on his desk. He stokes himself with this jammy petrol all day, offering the fattening goodies to older fatter people, so that their abstinence and his hunger, their paunch and his tiny waist can be fully appreciated.

April 2 is promoted as fast as Triffids procreate. The girls hang about their older woman boss in the loo, enquiring sympathetically how she feels now her time is up. Nobody ever lands a punch on the tip-tilted nose. They make the boss's job by twenty-five, and do it brilliantly. April 2 is a sun-burnished Mars warrior. Everybody knows it.

Early rewards give them a chance to develop young, but not lose out on personal and family life because they are so busy. They grow up accompanied by success, and after 30 develop all the most generous aspects of the Aries personality. Spontaneity is their trump card. And romantic enthusiasm. Socialising is their chosen way of life. They fall passionately in love, have children they adore more than they adore their partner, and give parties where everybody is made to feel glamorous and wanted.

They also travel abroad with groups of friends. Everybody is welcome to stay on the Spanish villa's floor. Nights sparkle with fun and days with good food and better conversation.

And since my love
doth every day admit
*   New Growth, thou shouldst*
*   have new rewards in store.*

(John Donne)

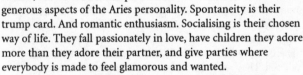

BODY

Many April 3 people adore having their head stroked by a lover. It's affectionate, calming, sexy, intimate and pleasingly attentive. Without scented oil, massage your partner's head as if you were washing his or her hair. Concentrate on the crown of the head and the point at the back of the head where the skull joins the neck (the occiput, an important shiatsu point). A 10 minute massage can release tensions and banish worldly problems. And since the brain controls sexual activity, this area is of great importance to lovers. The head massage quickly opens the body's gateway to erotic need.

MIND

Maybe logical 3 doesn't believe in Fortune. Just in case, here are April's Fortune days, 5, 9, 15, 18, 21, 29. These are the best days to fall in love and embark on new enterprises. Lucky too for gamblers and speculators.

DATESHARE

Marlon Brando, *film actor, icon.* **Washington Irving**, *19th century short story writer,* Rip Van Winkle. **Eddie Murphy**, *comedian, film actor.* **Doris Day**, *singer, film star.* **Alec Baldwin**, *stage, TV and film actor.* **George Herbert**, *British metaphysical poet.* **Leslie Howard**, *British film actor.* **Helmut Kohl**, *German chancellor, effected German reunification.*

APRIL 3

I f you want something organised, ask April 3 to do it. She's a list maker and a doer. In the local theatre production of Macbeth, she's the one who gets the paint free for the stage backdrop and persuades the artist who never speaks to anyone to paint it for free. He's never had such a good time in his life and loves the chips she brings at night while he's finishing the castle ramparts. She's a true Mars warrior, her shield, efficiency and imagination and her weapons, glib persuasion and charm. What she can't stand is people who say they'll do something and then don't.

In any place of work, find this person in Human Resources, where they run day release educational programmes with flair and keep up to the minute with latest government health rulings. If the office has to be reorganised, the lists come out, but everybody is consulted. Tact is another Mars weapon.

At home, this person is likely to be married. The list of prospective partners has been examined, and someone picked with the right qualities. There's nothing unromantic about this. They just crave simple happiness and abhor the expensive agony of divorce. Children will have labels sewn into all their school clothes. (She tried sewing them on ordinary clothes but the kids recoiled with embarrassment.) Books in the house are in alphabetical order and so are the CDs. In the medicine cabinet, nothing lies around for longer than the prescribed time.

Both sexes are excellent gardeners, preferring shrubs, because they are interesting and tidier than seeds, although a weakness is the poppy, a true Aries flower. They garden and they dream, pondering on a great ambition. Perhaps there's a book to write, or a new way of life to adopt? They're a 'change in mid-stream' date. The one who leaves farming at 32 for an advertising career. Or turns his back on factory management for teaching.

Sex is a momentary itch

Love never lets you go.

(Kingsley Amis)

4 APRIL

April 4 likes to use his hands. He's a gardener, a cook, maybe a furniture maker. Many do this as a profession, always happiest elbow deep in the workshop, kitchen or greenhouse. This day has psychic aspects for money so it's possible there will be a legacy or windfall. Clever Aries is excellent with investments on the stock market, property, or money put into London's West End shows. There may be sufficient funds to choose not to work.

So there's time to devote to a project. It may be cultivating a new single flowered, pale red rose, powerfully scented, disease free and flowering all year. Or concocting delicious dishes. Or designing a bed for children which rocks and plays them lullabies.

April 4 also likes to use those strong Mars hands to give pleasure  to a partner. This is not an inhibited person, and although the tastes are never for the too outrageous – dignified Mars doesn't dress up for the event – there's a deal of interest in sensuous pleasures. Aphrodisiac dishes will abound. The sex zones on the whole body which make touch and aromatic massage so stirring, will be investigated. The spine and back are Aries' vulnerable parts, but they are also the areas which give maxi pleasure. A little rub at the base of the spine can bring up a helluva shine.

Some Aries people often feel a deep sadness. It's not individual acts of unkindness which cause it, although that too, but an understanding of the passing of time and loveliness. They feel no worries about their own mortality, but grieve terribly for others. So much so that a few are better off not reading the newspapers or watching news on television, because disaster disturbs their equilibrium. If they stick to reading, creating, sex and music they will be happier, and while not forgetting our fleeting state, will have no cause to ponder deeply on it.

Abstainer. A weak person who yields to the temptation of denying himself a pleasure.

(Ambrose Bierce)

BODY

There are two spots about three inches below the waist, just above the buttocks, in the centre of the lower back on either side of the spine, which when pressed and stroked, trigger sexual desire and pleasant anticipatory warmth. Using the shiatsu method, press with the thumb until the pressure is quite hard. Then hold this for seven seconds. Release the pressure until your thumb is just resting on the skin's surface, wait five seconds, then repeat ten times. Or just massage gently with the finger tips, never on the spine, using drops of reputedly aphrodisiac sandalwood in a carrier oil such as almond.

☾

MIND

April 4 has a tendency to flirt with drugs and other addictive substances. This individual must be extremely careful about anything he takes. Whether it's alcohol or drugs, there's a tendency to overindulge and over-experiment.

DATESHARE

*Died: In New York, lovely Hollywood star, **Gloria Swanson**. Born: **Kitty Kelley** author unauthorised biographies, including of Sinatra. **Marguerite Duras**, French novelist, screenplay writer, Hiroshima mon Amour. **Muddy Waters**, blues singer. **Anthony Perkins**, film star, Psycho. **Arthur Murray**, dance instructor, dance schools. **Robert Downey Jnr**, film actor.*

Pimms is a great drink, a party drink, a festive occasion drink, a sexy experience in the right company and everybody should know how to mix one properly. For a jug (8–10 glasses), pour 240ml Pimm's into a large jug, plus 600ml lemonade, 600ml ginger ale, 120ml gin or vodka, ice cubes. Garnish with sliced cucumber, slivers of apple, very thinly sliced orange, slivers of peach or nectarines, one or two strawberries (to taste) and fresh mint leaves. It's wise to remember and we've all forgotten, that it tastes sweet, refreshing and summery, but it contains a helluva wallop.

MIND

Good gardeners can cure drooping plants with a few drops of the famous Bach Flower Rescue Remedy. Ten drops in a watering can applied regularly for two or three days revitalises a garden. Five drops watered into vegetables benefits crops.

DATESHARE

Judith Resnick, *US astronaut killed in Challenger accident.* **Algernon Swinburne**, *19th century poet, pre-Raphaelite group,* **Jean-Honoré Fragonard**, *French painter.* **Bette Davis**, *Hollywood film actress.* **Spencer Tracy**, *film actor.* **Gregory Peck**, *film actor, heart-throb.* **Herbert von Karajan**, *German conductor, Berlin Philharmonic.*

APRIL 5

Most Aries people are competitive. So much so, that some will try to win every game of chess they play with an eight-year-old. April 5 is competitive enough to induce you to be on his team, but never enough to introduce edginess. He'd rather somebody else won than that. What both sexes want most is to have a good time and give everybody else a good time.

They're the darlings of the zodiac. Like the lovely generous splash red poppies make in golden cornfields, this scarlet Aries poppy makes a similar splash in other people's lives. Laughter excites this person. As does the sparkle which comes to a group having fun.

They work to play. Most choose a sober profession such as law, accounting, engineering or something to do with money, where they know they can get on with things quietly day to day, without exhausting their creative energies. Because they can soar across social barriers, their choice of playground is immense. Find them in grand country houses organising the most terrifying game of murder in the dark. That is if you can stop the murder 'victim' cackling with laughter. In charades April 5 makes a saucepan into the most stylish makeshift hat. And their team, with its astonishing rendering of Nelson's victory at Waterloo, wins hands down.

Find them too, dancing in the most interesting clubs, with an assortment of partners which would make a Hollywood playgirl/boy envious. There's an electrocrackle of sex about their heads very similar to the pale light which shimmers across the night landscape and is gone just before torrential rain.

When, eventually, they have children, and these creatures aren't keen to settle down, they will play games until everybody drops. Then go and find the best stack of lollies in the world. Children adore their excitable inventiveness. Parents adore them for their sweetness of temperament and their virtue of never leaving anybody out of their plans.

The magic of first love is our ignorance that it can ever end.

(Benjamin Disraeli)

FIRE

6 APRIL

Frankly there's mystery to April 6. They don't know what they want and nor does anybody else. It's an unusual psychological duality, and it means this creature is liable to take one step forward and one step back. It's partly the fault of their many skills. At birth Good Fortune bestowed on them

 numerate and linguistic skills as well as creative and artistic ones. So the poor thing just doesn't know which direction to take.

Will I be happy? Will I be rich? Will I be famous? Will I be a doctor? Maybe an actor? Maybe travel? Maybe marry? Maybe not? Che sarà, sarà. It's hard for April 6 to settle down because the cake on the next plate always has more icing. The truth of the matter is that they are better off choosing more than one way of earning a living. A doctor can be a writer, a carver, an embroiderer and painter and an actor. A taxi driver can be a florist. A plumber can be a pop singer. Going for multichoice is best in this person's case.

It is essential that they try a lot of things, because otherwise their restlessness can become exhausting to themselves and others. At least one extensive trip to a foreign country is a good idea, preferably living in it for a little while. Learn the language, adapt to the customs. Be French for a year or two.

The women change their looks constantly. Some days blonde, some days red-haired. Sometimes they are the elegant, country type. Other times, they slink through life siren-fashion on the highest of heels. Younger men also change their style with their mood, from brooding pony-tailed rebel in long boots, to casually suited and clean shaven. It's all fun. There's no need to stay the same.

They need a sexual partner who is fond of acting, and can play different parts and take on different looks to suit the mood.

Older women make the best lovers because they always think they may be doing it for the last time.

(Ian Fleming)

BODY

April 6 adores chocolate. Try Chocolate Temptation to induce pleasure and thoughts of love. PEA (phenylethylamine) found in chocolate is the chemical responsible for sexual desire.

Take 100g plain dessert chocolate, broken in pieces, ½ tsp instant coffee dissolved in 2tbsp cream, 2tsps brandy, 1 large egg, separated, pinch salt. Melt chocolate plus coffee in heat-resistant bowl over saucepan of simmering water. Cool and stir in brandy and yolk. Whisk white with salt, until stiff. Fold in chocolate mixture. Spoon into large glass bowls and place in fridge for 2 hours. Serve in bed with biscuits and raspberries.

☽

MIND

Jet is an excellent stone for inducing love and curing ills and can still be found in the Yorkshire hills around Whitby. But it's particularly bad for Aries or Libra to possess. Give it to another star sign.

DATESHARE

Emperor **Charlemagne**. **Ian Paisley**, Northern Ireland political leader, Protestant clergyman. **Butch Cassidy**, outlaw. **Harry Houdini**, illusionist, escapologist. **Anthony Fokker**, Dutch aeroplane manufacturer. **André Previn**, conductor, composer, pianist. **Gerry Mulligan**, jazz sax player, composer. **Barry Levinson**, film director, The Tin Men, Rain Man.

FIRE

BODY

Grapefruit is an amazing medicine for the heart. It contains potent compounds that lower blood cholesterol and may even clean out some of the arterial debris known as plaque, possibly reversing atherosclerosis. In reducing blood cholesterol, grapefruit pectin is as powerful as the drug cholestyramine, according to some experts, although don't take up the grapefruit and drop the drug. For heart benefits be sure to eat the grapefruit pulp, including the membranes that separate the sections and the white interior of the rind. Grapefruit is very delicious, halved, segmented in the skin and grilled with a light topping of brown sugar.

MIND

Fortune says that money comes to April 7. Dreams of elephants, fish, farming, walking in a forest and bowls of peaches all mean that a windfall or a success in investments or business is imminent.

DATESHARE

Died: **Theda Bara**, *silent movie queen. Born:* **William Wordsworth**, *British 19th century Romantic poet, famous for daffodils.* **Ravi Shankar**, *Indian sitarist.* **James Garner**, *film and TV actor.* **David Frost**, *British TV host, political interviewer.* **Francis Ford Coppola**, *film director, The Godfather, Apocalypse Now.* **Buddha**.

APRIL 7

Flash, dazzle and wham, you're in the net. April 7, the people collector, whirls at the centre of a turning universe. They are the evening star, first to shine at dusk and in early dawn's flooding sun, you still see their brilliant echo. The only, even remote downer is that they must take care not to burn themselves out, or give too generous emotional support too widely in case they become exhausted.

It's unlikely. April 7 has huge stamina, establishes a clear space around him/herself from small childhood, and unless fate deals an unexpected blow, they're unlikely to trip. The capacity for inventive and logical thinking is impressive. Like many Arians, talented in both arts and sciences, they have endless career choices, but are most likely to choose a science related subject. Genetics fascinate them. Neurology draws them. The nature of our being, how we arrived where we are, preoccupies them.

But they love poetry too, one of the few days in the year who do, understanding the minds of those who write it. They want to change the world for the better – and they just may do it. Everybody needs the conjunction of circumstances to achieve such ambitions, but this person does all he/she can to bring it about. They are in the right place at the right time. They know where things are happening.

No wonder people want to be with them. Many would be lovers, few are chosen. The rest, including members of the opposite sex, have to make do with friendship. This individual doesn't differentiate between a best friend and a lesser one. All are equal. With friends in need, April 7 listens for hours, always helps. Class, race, physical good looks, intelligence, make no odds. He will not judge a person on any of these. But still, and here's the catch, they will marry, have children, live happily ever after, yet there is something unattainable about them.

'Tis better to reign in hell Than serve in heaven.

(Milton)

FIRE

8 APRIL

Some say the colour for Aries is white, others say red. April 8 is carnivorous cardinal red and you'd better watch out. Excellent at sport, many play at the highest level. And absolutely nothing gets in the way, not parents, loved ones, illness or politics. No weakness is allowed except in opponents, kicked aside as they run past without a backward glance.

As tough as the men, the girls apply Spartan rules when they have kids. The house is perfectly run, and impressive. April 8 hates muddle, and doesn't go for pastels, flowery things or lavish curtains which look as if they were nicked from the local hotel.

At work, no quarter is given. This creature is Mars and this is war. They'll pinch ideas, criticise opponents for being out of touch, fat, thin, nervous, too old, too young. All those ruses we know and hate and which are so astonishingly effective. This is a computer age advocate, joined at the nose to his screen, contemptuous of anyone who can't manage the whole programme, but sticks, snail like, to the word processor slow lane. They are usually perfectly dressed and if they can afford it, the men wear Paul Smith and the girls favour a little Chanel mixed with the season's hot Marks & Spencer's line. Naturally they always know what it is first.

April 8 loves her children, as do the men. But kids are really an extension of themselves and must excel. This person worries about her children not having enough of the right friends, right talents and it's all completely exhausting for the young ones concerned, and frequently for their teachers.

Don't imagine they mellow with age. At 70 both sexes will still be looking over your shoulder for somebody more interesting at a party. And they'll still ask who the other guests are before accepting a dinner party invitation. How do they get away with it? Power and money.

Men have always detested women's gossip because they suspect the truth: their measurements are being taken and compared.

(Erica Jong)

BODY

April 8 loves pets but becomes panicky when they have accidents or seem unwell. It's just as good an idea to use the famous Bach Flower Rescue Remedy for animals as it is for human beings. It comes in liquid form, a few drops to be taken in water, or cream, which keeps wounds supple, speeds up the healing process and relieves pain. Many vets use the liquid form to help animals overcome the shock of strange surroundings, especially after accidents. It can be dropped into water or put directly in the mouth and will not interfere with any other medicine or treatment the animal may be receiving.

MIND

Those who devote themselves to the social round, judging others only by their appearance and usefulness, will find themselves so judged and the struggle to keep up as time passes, becomes, in the end, overwhelming.

DATESHARE

Ian Smith, Rhodesian premier. **Betty Ford**, American First Lady, founded alcohol treatment centre. **E Y Harburg**, lyricist, 'Over The Rainbow', 'Can You Spare A Dime?', 'Finian's Rainbow'. **Franco Corelli**, operatic tenor. **Sir Adrian Boult**, British conductor. **Julian Lennon**, singer, songwriter, son of John. **Jacques Brel**, Belgian singer, songwriter.

BODY

Sometimes this date suffers from mild depression, occasional 'lows'. This can be helped, especially after drinking too much alcohol, by eating tomatoes or drinking the juice. A fat tomato sandwich is well known to be a tremendous comforter because tomatoes contain small amounts of serotonin, a substance found in the brain which helps to elevate the mood. Serotonin levels are often reduced during the winter months due to lack of sunshine and working under fluorescent or artificial lights. Increase exercise out of doors in daylight and eat other foods which contain serotonin: milk, cheese, oranges, soya beans, potatoes, root vegetables, brown rice, brown bread and wholewheat pasta.

MIND

In the Tarot's Major Arcana, the 9th card is The Hermit, who walks carrying a lantern and stick. Dominant qualities of this day include a healthy conscience, wisdom and understanding of others, and tremendous self-discipline.

DATESHARE

Severiano Ballesteros, *Spanish golfer.* **Hugh Hefner**, *Playboy founder.* **Jean-Paul Belmondo**, *French film star.* **Robert Helpmann**, *Australian dancer,* The Red Shoes. **Tom Lehrer**, *satirist, songwriter, performer.* **Dorothy Tutin**, *Shakespearian actress.* **Charles Baudelaire**, *French symbolist poet, 'Les Fleurs du Mal'.*

April 9 would love to be ruthless, rich and coveted by everyone. Yet deep in her generous psychology there's the red-gold ore of kindness, which prevents all that. And an undermining, but appealing, instinct for self-mockery, which prevents it too. In the cause of good, she will go into battle, Mars' armour burnished. In her own cause, it's more Marsipan and she retires laughing.

Laughter makes everything work for this person. Terrific mimics and stand-up comics, some are so good they make it a career. In the office – they often work in big companies or product producing factories – this wit is a fearsome weapon. Everybody laughs, but bosses get frightened. So less promotion than you might have expected for our competitive baby. Still, no matter. There's the work outing to look forward to, when everybody will laugh themselves sick. And what's more memorable? A lot of fun with mates, or an impressive discussion about next year's budget?

Most of them throw ambition to the wind early on. Home life, time to think and the value of small passing moments with children, pets and beloved relatives become more important. April 9 earns more money at home than by going in to work anyway. They plan family days with massive cook-ins, plenty to drink and the girl's flower arrangements are legendary. The men do glamorous things with fairy lights. If there are no children, these people are perfectly sanguine, indeed some make a choice to spend a childless life with their partner.

Some take refuge in the country where they live a life of unpolluted bliss, playing with animals. Horsey, doggy people, these ramettes. Favoured dog breeds are big, kind golden retrievers, for their intelligent eyes and gentle way with children and older people.

Not a date for an isolated house in remote countryside. Like their dogs, they need people, fun, love and chat and can become morose when lonely.

The measure of a man is what he does with power.

(Pittacus)

IO APRIL

They seem to be full of good feeling. She calls people 'Darling' and he says 'Sweetie'. April 10 is stardusted, toffee coated, tastes like sweet, fresh cream. Actually there's more manipulation than feeling. You are mad to give them your affection. Most of us are mad.

This date attracts followers at work who act loyally for many years. People will do a lot for April 10, work all night, give up holidays, fetch the dry cleaning, pour the scotch. Some of the gang even spend holidays with this ramette and his family. Then this most forgetful of meteors in the night sky, will shoot away in search of shinier friends. Everything forgotten.

People born today only really trust blood relatives and partners. They can't judge other people's personalities, quite enjoy flattery and can't see the oil slick behind a courtier even if it's a mile long. The person they love and listen to most is Mum, so if you want to influence April 10, get on Mum's wavelength. At work or at home, paranoia stalks them. An intense telephone conversation must be about them. If they could they would bug the phone. Some can. And they battle with neighbours about light restriction and the massive tree next door.

They can make a lot of money, but won't be spending it on the house, usually painted white, with convenience cupboards and lots of electronic equipment. It will be on presents for children and partners – they patronise the latter. Often expensive cars. Some are talented fine art and antique collectors. Always with an eye on future market value.

Money is also spent on healthcare, alternative medicine and health farms, which they adore and dream of in times of stress. In mid-life, these people may seek religion, which finally makes them happy. And different. All the underlying good qualities suddenly emerge, trust first, then appreciation of others. At this point April 10 may do something memorable.

BODY

April 10 suffers increasingly from a dire feeling of 'Oh what's the use?' In this creature's heart there is a feeling that all the effort is for nothing, because what has been achieved is now no longer interesting. While this person searches for his or her destiny, it's an idea to try taking the Bach Flower Remedy, gorse (Ulex europaeus). It will help this individual not only to decide another direction must be found for his life, but to search actively for the right one. After taking the gorse, both sexes should feel more optimistic and convinced that the new path will soon occur for them.

MIND

Share your feelings with your partner. Tell them that the goals you treasured, now no longer seem precious. Two heads are better than one and you will find the extra mental energy beamed on the subject energising.

DATESHARE

William Booth, Salvation Army founder. **Paul Theroux**, playwright, novelist. **A E**, real name George Russell, Irish poet, mystic, poet. **Max von Sydow**, Scandinavian film star, featured in Ingmar Bergman films. **Omar Sharif**, film star, bridge player.

You're all that I need.
I'll be there for you.
(Method Man)

BODY

Try dock leaves with mushrooms: wash and blanch young dock leaves. Drain, dry and brush both sides with olive oil. Place a cleaned mushroom in the centre of each leaf, season with salt, pepper and crushed garlic. Wrap the leaves around the mushrooms to make little parcels, and put in a greased baking dish. Cover with more blanched dock leaves, brushed with olive oil. Cook covered with foil for ½ hour at 350°F, 180°C or gas mark 4. Serve hot as an hors d'oeuvre or cold with pre-dinner drinks. Never pick plants you are going to eat from roadsides or front gardens.

MIND

It's a common temptation to relate to others as if you are the young one. But at a certain point in your life you must decide firmly upon adulthood, otherwise your fate is never in your own hands.

DATESHARE

*Died: **Dolores Del Rio**, Hollywood glamour goddess. Born: **Ethel Kennedy**, mother of President John Kennedy and Robert, and nine other children. **Oleg Cassini**, fashion designer. **Clive Exton**, British playwright, screenwriter. **Louise Lasser**, film actress.*

April 11's love of animals is central to her personality. She doesn't prefer them to humans, but handles animals well and just being around horses, dogs, cats and pigs keeps her optimistic.

Urbanites born on this day may take their dog to work. In the highest reaches of media, design and fashion, on both sides of the Atlantic, offices contain working dogs. Aries' preferred office pet is the West Highland white terrier, who manages the life with enormous charm, neither piddling in the publisher's handbag, nor farting in the features conference.

Most confine their animals to out of work, unless their work is with animals, highly likely for this date. Farming is an attraction. Competitive riding is ideal for such a combative psychology. Many combine breeding, training and running events for a lucrative career. Doggy Aries may also breed and train their preferred animal, the aristocratic English Setter. This individual acknowledges there is nothing to beat a long walk or ride in the English countryside with your dog or horse. Everything seems closer and your soul is at peace. And animals love you in an uncomplicated way.

Highly driven, exceedingly ambitious, these creatures remain childish. This is the first star sign of the zodiac year bringing many unresolved aspects to the psychology. Success beckons. Responsibility puts them off. At work, they do best with a powerful mentor, providing a settled backdrop for their juvenile lead, and helping assess other people, at which April 11 does not excel.

Relationships with same age partners are often difficult, and many find older partners, which brings great happiness to both. The artistic streak could take them far if encouraged by friends. Discouragement makes them over-react, give up, or even despair. A child himself, this creature understands kids and talks their language. They are also impassioned about wild plants, encouraging their preservation and the reviving of ancient medicinal and culinary uses. Expect nettle soup and dock leaves stuffed with mushrooms for lunch.

Grumbling is the death of love.

(Marlene Dietrich)

I2 APRIL

The joker in the pack, this creature laughs its way into people's hearts and their beds. And all the way to the top of a chosen career ladder. While some Aries are extremely tall, fine boned and good looking, not all people born under this star sign are so blessed. Many find laughter the weapon they need to get attention and please others. It usually starts at school, where this person entertains the class, diverts the bully with ferocious

playground jibes, and endears teachers, who goodness knows, need some cheering up.

This star-spangled laughter maker never plays dirty or uses cruelty to pin down a victim. It's more wit than ribaldry. The turn of phrase that others wish they'd thought of. An enviable verbal facility. Sales and marketing would die for this creature. City investors need someone like this to take the edge off the swinging money market. Advertising will pay a lot for April 12's slogans. Witty women do well here, because society regards them as a precious rarity.

April 12 likes money, but doesn't care greatly about acquiring it. At home, one room will probably be painted red (Aries colour) and other warm colours, but all done himself and at no expense. Not socially competitive, this creature just wants everybody to have a laugh, a good time and try to like each other.

The ram travels light and on holiday, when the plane is late and the hotel lavatory is blocked, rely on him to take it all well and keep others' morale up. They dislike the Moaning Minnies of the zodiac and will either avoid them, tease them out of it, or retire with them to the bar and get them drunk. A brave creature, always looking on the bright side of life. They are good friends, generous, tolerant lovers and no child of April 12 ever feels afraid for long, because their parent will solve the problem.

BODY

Travel sickness can be a plague to April 12, although neither sex lets it get in the way of going places. Ginger can be as good as any shop-bought travel sickness reliever. It has been renowned for its alleviation of sickness since ancient medicine began. Before buying, weigh the ginger root in your hand. The heaviest will be the freshest, containing the most moisture. Make ginger tea by grating a tablespoon of the root and leaving it to infuse in boiling water for five minutes. Also excellent for colds, to stimulate circulation and the Chinese use it for all rheumatic pains.

ॐ

MIND

Greed leads to a desire for power and to dictate to others. It denies the individual's freedom to develop according to the dictates of his own soul, to work and blossom unhampered and in doing so find inner peace.

DATESHARE

Andy Garcia, Hollywood heart-throb. **David Letterman**, TV entertainer, late night show magnate. **Alan Ayckbourn**, playwright, satirist, wrote Jeeves with Andrew Lloyd Webber. **Montserrat Caballé**, opera singer, cut record with Freddie Mercury. **David Cassidy**, singer, actor, The Partridge Family.

Ride time
as you would ride a river.
(Gerard Manley Hopkins)

APRIL 13

April 13 overdoes it on the alcohol front and Christmas, birthdays and parties are often ruined by appalling two-day hangovers. Sensitive stomached Aries should avoid red wine, whisky, brandy, rum, port, bourbon and other thicker, darker and sweeter drinks. The reason is that they contain more chemicals called congeners, which, along with ethanol, cause hangovers. Experts think that congeners in some way stimulate the pain receptors in the brain. Vodka, gin and white wine have the fewest congeners and normally produce the least severe hangovers. Take the precaution before a party of lining your stomach with a pint of milk.

MIND

Music is known to lower blood pressure, improve the memory and bring joy to patients in hospital. In German hospitals, music is used during minor operations to lessen the dose of anaesthetic. Doctors say Mozart works wonders.

DATESHARE

Gari Kasparov, *Russian world champion chess player.* **Frank W Woolworth**, *store chain magnate.* **Stanley Donen**, *film producer, choreographer, Singin' In The Rain with Gene Kelly.* **Samuel Beckett**, *Nobel Prize-winning playwright.* **Thomas Jefferson**, *American president.*

It takes time before April 13 stops blaming others for their own misfortunes. This is the child who is late for school because somebody 'deliberately moved his homework'. This is the adult who fails a job interview because of being the wrong sex, race, religion or just having the wrong accent.

April 13 is tempted to blame parents for everything about her life today. Doctors are dunces. Colleagues at work are out to get her. And the bank manager can't stand her personally. It's a mind set this dark star must exclude from the psychology, or unhappiness sets in permanently.

It's all part of the childish psychological streak, not wanting to grow up. But our lost lamb must find its own way, and not blame the shepherd. There's talent and more in April 13.

Music is a comforter. Many play an instrument well. Drums and trumpets are perfect Aries instruments, but their physical dexterity draws them to the piano and they have a powerful singing voice. If this person can be a professional musician, the music may solve all personal problems and many are so good, it will solve their financial problems too. Remember that E and F Major are Aries keys, bringing Pythagorian harmony, the basic musical structure of the universe and its singing stars.

Both sexes delight in running their own business, working at home by themselves. Redundancy and the sack hold no fear. There is a strong possibility of late acquisition of masses of money, made after a spectacular idea comes to fruition. Though not particularly psychic, April 13 must listen closely to the dictates of his psychology.

Domestically, these gentle companions give generously of time and energy and usually form partnerships for life. Childbirth ain't vital, and sans offspring they won't pine. Surprisingly there are powerful resources of strength to cope with an unfaithful partner, but hearts may stay broken for a while.

Let's talk about sex . . . It keeps coming up anyhow.

(Salt 'n' Pepper)

14 APRIL

If it could reach the sky, this decorative, decorating-mad lambkin would hang the firmament with fairy lights and bind the moon with silver balloons. Both sexes are the natural landscape gardeners, architects and interior decorators of the universe. Quite often they go into some aspect of this as a career. But even if they work in a shop, theirs is the best-wrapped parcel. Nurses born on this day can make the most frightening hospital ward a welcoming place.

April 14 doesn't need money to create beauty. In their hands the barest winter twigs and golden autumn leaves make an arrangement you'd spend £40 on in the local posh florist. What they do need is encouragement. Other less sensitive dates may get impatient with April 14's ideas, even dismissing them, instantly quenching the creative sparkle.

This individual likes to please others. They'll dress a new baby's crib so beautifully, the child won't want to grow out of it. Find them in tourism and retail, where pleasing is what you pay for. Find them also as style gurus, hob-nobbing with international snobnobs when they may become exceedingly precioso.

Gaiety is always pleasing and theirs is infectious. Many of them have the fetching slenderness and aquamarine eyes of the true Arian and of course they can run up a little something out of a length of material in a sale bin and look as if they've just come back from Bond Street. What's even more galling for the stouter occupants of the universe is that flirtatious April 14 can eat until the lambs come home and not put on an ounce. In fact food occupies them almost as much as sparkly things to tie on the Christmas tree. Our Marsipan sweetheart's favourite galaxy is the Milky Way, which is made of chocolate and of course we all know that the moon is made of her favourite brand of cream cheese.

The only way to get rid of temptation is to yield to it.

(Oscar Wilde)

BODY

It's particularly vital that April 14 is matched with the right partner, or unhappiness will ensue. Aries perfectly understands Aries. Taurus can be befuddled (too slow). Gemini, too sharp tongued and edgy. Cancer, too timorous and not quite smart enough. Leo will adore and financially back April 14. Virgo finds her embarrassingly unconventional. Laissez-faire, laid back Libra will delight in fantastic 14. Sensuous Scorpio, another Mars sign, will idolise 14. Mutable Sagittarius will throw money at the Decorator and probably go bankrupt. Acutely sensitive, allegretto brained Aquarius will adore 14's beribboned arabesques in the sky. Aries will break Pisces' heart.

MIND

The April 14 starlet has so much fun being creative. Give an oblong table the Rennaissance look. Drape it with a blanket. Cover with dark chenille, an Indian print or rug. This gets rid of legs, and looks painterly with still life-style fruit, dead hare and violin heaped on top!

DATESHARE

Sir John Gielgud, British actor, film and TV star, icon. **Julie Christie**, film star, stage actress, 1960s icon. **Arnold Toynbee**, British historian. **Loretta Lynn**, country singer. **François Duvalier**, Haitian dictator, known as Papa Doc. **Rod Steiger**, film and stage actor.

BODY

April 15 is very breast conscious, always worrying that her bosoms are either too small, or too large or in some way not quite right, like most other women in the universe in fact.

Before you resort to more serious medical devices, why not try these aromatherapy recipes for enlarging and reducing the bosom? To tone and enlarge: 2 drops geranium, 2 drops clary sage, 2 drops ylang-ylang, 2tsp camellia oil. This makes enough for about a week. Massage on at night. To tone and reduce: 1 drop rose, 1tsp jojoba. Jojoba emulsifies fat tissue, while rose is astringent.

MIND

To discover if you and a lover are suited, both must place a nut on the glowing embers of a fire. If they merely glow and smoulder, you will be happy together. If they burst or crackle, it will be all quarrels.

Airhead Aries encourages flibbertigibbet April 15 to chase the silliest ideas. This creature is like an adorable lamb, springing about in the meadow, racing after a dragon fly here and then getting lost and crying for its mama. There's always a 'tomorrow' for April 15 and it's always going to be big. Today is just a preparation for tomorrow and we don't bother with yesterday because we've forgotten all about it.

This is the person at work who has marvellous ideas which make everybody else squirm because they are impossible to get done. Should the heavens want a bit of fun, April 15 is promoted and then everything is hither and thither. Chasing the craziest of ideas, there's nobody left back at the coal face to get anything done, and 15 certainly isn't there because she's gone to Ascot to show off her new hat.

Some are inspirational, cutting through old ideas and traditional office 'no-manship', to revolutionise a business. But this almond-eyed creature, the windows to its soul, causes others many sleepless night and weary days. When 15 comes in the room and

says, 'Why don't we?' other star signs attempt to lemming it out of the window.

Amorous 15 loves to love and attracts partners as a row of lavender attracts late July bees. With much the same effect. Drunk on honey, the bees fall sated into surrounding grass, and dream of pleasure, until somebody treads on them.

This person does best making a late marriage, when the racing blood has cooled and their airstrip Aries brain has ceased to accommodate so many landings and departures. Some make steady parents in youth. Parent-love concentrates the brain, and those who have to handle the single parent role do so admirably.

Perfume is their passion and birds bring out their tenderness. Find an almost pet robin in their day garden and at night a nightingale sings in the rosy perfumed darkness.

> *A girl with brains ought to do something else with them besides think.*
>
> *(Anita Loos)*

16 APRIL

April 16 likes a quiet time and would prefer to stay in the house where he was born all the days of his long life. Many live in the country and have the deepest love for every hedgerow, and old rosebush in the village. This determined creature achieves her ambition, resists temptation to depart, except to study and train so that she can make a living on her return.

April 16 may choose the law, medicine, teaching or master plastering, but all fit with life where the first roots were put down and the last will be lifted. Sexy, agreeable Aries is the prized partner of the county, losing its virginity somewhere along the mid-teens in sun-baked local fields and woods where couples have gone to romance for hundreds of years. But adventurous 16 will probably lure a permanent partner from far away, brook no resistance and block any urgings to move elsewhere. Just a smidgeonette of a bully here, maybe?

They're readers and thinkers, good farmers and gardeners. They understand animals, ride to the hunt, know every inch of the river and can handle a boat with their eyes closed. And a good Arian's cooking is second to none in the county, country or galaxy. Expect delicate stews, with fresh herbs, tarts to tempt the toughest tastebuds, cheeses from France, sun dried tomatoes from Italy, finest Spanish olives and Turkish delight made with rosewater, so fine it kills the eater with pleasure, presented in scented boxes straight from the soukhs of Asia Minor.

Both sexes are excellent travellers, keen to see how other people live and many will take the trouble to learn the language if they are to visit often. They have a powerful appreciation of other people's national identity as well as their own. Many will become village or town 'elders', respected for their sagacity, honesty and in many cases, loved for the music they play on the church organ on Sunday morning.

Change is the free cosmetic that keeps you young.

BODY
When you've got too many strawberries and they're going off, here's a refreshing and new way to use them up. Strawberry Ice: Take 450g strawberries, washed and hulled, 175ml orange juice, 225g sugar, 4tbsp lemon juice, 2tbsp curaçao or any fruit cordial. Blend or beat until smooth, then sieve. Freeze in plastic container until nearly frozen but still soft. Take from freezer, empty into a bowl and beat hard, until smooth. Return to freezer container, cover and freeze again until firm. Serve in large glasses decorated with strawberries, or fresh sprigs of mint. Accompany with plain yoghurt.

MIND
In Tarot's Major Arcana, the 16th card is The Tower, indicating sudden rises to and obsessional preoccupation with success, but also awareness of impermanence and the need to change. Tarot is a signposter not a dictator.

DATESHARE
*Died: **Sammy Davies Jr**, comedian, member of Hollywood rat pack. **David Lean**, producer, director. Born: **Ellen Barkin**, film actress. **Kingsley Amis**, British author, father of Martin, Lucky Jim. **Spike Milligan**, comic, member of The Goons. **Merce Cunningham**, choreographer, dancer. **Charlie Chaplin**, British comic, silent films and then speaking, famous for trilby and walking stick, Modern Times, The Great Dictator.*

BODY

April 17 people need food to stoke their mental energies. Psychic's Rosy Meringue Delight: You don't have to be psychic to know this will pile on weight. Take 4 egg whites, 275g shredded coconut, 275g sugar, drops pink food colouring optional. Whisk egg whites stiffly until they peak. Fold in sugar and coconut. If you want pink, drop a little colouring in mixture. Grease baking sheet, line with rice paper, with teaspoon drop small mounds of mixture on baking sheet. Bake at 140°C/275°F/gas mark 1 for 50 minutes, until meringues start to colour. Place on wire rack and cool.

MIND

According to old colour lore, black means dignity; blue, friendship; green is for virility; grey for modesty; orange for health; pink for devotion; red for love; white, innocence; and yellow, high spirits. Wear them for the right impact.

DATESHARE

Nikita Kruschev, *Russian leader.* **Sirimavo Bandaranaike**, *first woman prime minister of Sri Lanka, elected to fill assassinated husband's place.* **Karen Blixen**, *Africa lover, author, Out of Africa.* **Clare Francis**, *round the world sailor, author, ME sufferer and campaigner.* **William Holden**, *film and stage actor.* **Lindsay Anderson**, *British film director, This Sporting Life.*

pril 17 may be a genuine, highly-gifted psychic. Not all people born on this day will have this talent, but when they do, it's the real thing. It's advisable to consult an established expert in this field so that you understand yourself and what you are dealing with.

There is a clear cut vision that comes to many and they must learn to interpret that vision. We aren't talking about dead relatives

floating about in the doorway and indicating where they buried their tiaras. This is another thing all together and fairly questionable. We are talking about an image of a building or place and an indication that something may be waiting to be discovered there. Maybe it's an old well in a famous writer's garden, with an unpublished manuscript tucked in an iron box on a ledge six feet down. Maybe it's a clear sense of somebody important you are about to meet, not long before you do. A sudden need to phone home, and you discover that Grandma has won £20,000,000 on the National Lottery. A certain knowledge that behind the mantlepiece there lurks an exciting discovery.

Or maybe it's a certainty that this particular aeroplane or train will not, after all be carrying you that day. And later you hear there has been an accident. With this kind of experience it's hard not to take note of all kinds of omens, superstitions, lucky stones and colours. But many people born on this date are strong minded and just stick to their interest in psychic phenomena.

Apart from this these people continue a perfectly normal life, often involved with money and accounting. And no, your high street bank manager born on this day doesn't take punts on the stock market with your money and put a safe load on his favourite horse. But he does get occasional flashes about a person, which he might or might not find useful and take notice of.

Shake and shake
The ketchup bottle
None will come
And then a lot'll.

18 APRIL

Angry, argumentative April 18 is really a pushover. The poppet of the universe. Gentle of intent, lover of choccy biscuits and generally having a good time. And, in many cases has the sort of brain worth much to a kidnap-happy extra-terrestrial bootlegger of special interest humans.

But oh, hist, who goes there? A neighbour who has built his garden wall too high, too low, too thin, too thick. A damsel who has let her perfumed bath water run down our darling's light socket in the living room beneath. Awful 18 will become so obsessed with this misdeed, it will entertain him for months. Years. Friends soothe, discourage the lawyer's letters, the telephone calls and threatened court action. But often to no avail.

Civilised, sexy April 18 should know better. But lets it get out of hand until everybody is on non-speakers and choosing their frock for the court appearance. What can one say? It gets worse as this creature gets older. Nobody wins and the cardinal rule for Aries anyway should be never enter into a dispute with a neighbour, because you live there and must surely want it to be peaceable.

Loneliness often accompanies this person, partly because he is slightly obsessive and works too hard to give time to a lover. And yet the world about her is beckoning with people desperate to become her companion. This is one of those days which attracts hordes of admirers into old age. In youth, both sexes will have been fairly outrageous bed hoppers, so they know that a powerful electromagnetic pulling power is theirs.

It may be that these disputes add the missing passion to their lives and take the place of time-consuming love affairs, where the interaction is not confined to threatening legal letters. But while there's life and laughter and willing admirers, this child of arguments should drop them and allow all that old generosity, sweetness and sense of fun to be uppermost once more.

Have you heard the one about the man who always wore sunglasses? He took a dim view of things.

BODY

Sleep is essential to this person, who may suffer more than most from nervous irritability and disturbing dreams. It is helpful to use an essential oil burner an hour before bed with lavender, sandalwood, rose, neroli, camomile and frankincense. Some scatter drops of lavender on the pillow or put drops on a piece of cotton wool and then place it in the pillow case. Camomile is generally regarded as especially helpful for disturbing dreams and should dominate all your blends. Try a herb tea before retiring. Camomile, lime blossom and lemon balm are effective. A relaxing lavender bath before bed may do the trick.

MIND

In numerology 18 is ruled by 9 (1+8=9) which means aggression and a wrong path taken. But the 18th card in the Major Arcana is The Moon, promising love, empathy, happiness and emotional understanding. Let The Moon rule.

FIRE

APRIL 19

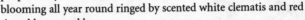

BODY

For April 19 every flower has significance. They all have meanings, some less than romantic. Red roses mean 'I love you'. Pinks say 'How lovely you are'. Tulips state 'By this token I declare my passion'. And violets insist 'Pure and sweet art thou'. So with these commoner gifts we're safe. However a bunch of daffs says 'I do not return your affections' and narcissus, worse still, 'You love no one better than yourself'. The paranoid and popular begonia warns 'We are being watched'. And straightforward basil declares 'I dislike you.'

MIND

You like to live in peace and a good atmosphere. Yet discord and upsets are bound to happen occasionally and when this happens you suffer considerable mental strain. Take the Bach Flower Remedy, agrimony (Agrimonia eupatoria).

DATESHARE

Dudley Moore, *comedian, film star, actor, musician, restauranteur,* Beyond The Fringe. **Paloma Picasso**, *lipstick entrepreneur, stylist, jewellery and perfume magnate, daughter of painter.* **Jayne Mansfield**, *comedienne, famous for wonderful bosom.* **Anthony Bliss**, *head of Metropolitan Opera.* **Lucrezia Borgia**, *Pope Alexander VI's poisonous daughter.*

April 19 may spend the days at a desk working out budgets, meetings and a company health policy, or nights stacking shelves at Tesco to earn money to pay for studytime. But what 19 dreams about are banks of yellow nodding foxgloves. It's no wonder that gardening is a passion for many late April people born at the time when nature crowds hedgerows with beauty and the perfumed cowslip dollops pale sunshiny colour over green fields.

Passionate gardeners are born all year, but April 19 likes brilliance. And wild flowers in the garden border. Theirs are full of yellow Welsh poppies, clumps of white and purple dead nettle and the luxurious golden rod. Splashes of red and purple everywhere, with modern roses blooming all year round ringed by scented white clematis and red tinged honeysuckle.

Wild in the garden means wild at heart. Pressure at work drives April 19 lupins for a few peaceful moments and this individual often throws career to the winds, plumping for less money and more time. They are happy living cheaply, finding work here and there. Both sexes long for an equally unmaterialistic mate. Together they will muddle along, raising kids without luxuries, but happy, healthy and always laughing.

Wealthy in affection, no visitor goes away uncared for, always happier than when he arrived. And usually with an exotic plant for his own garden or window box. If April 19 only has a window box, it will be a glorious creation. And there are flowers growing all over the kitchen.

If April 19 does get his or her hands on money, and fortune promises the likelihood by some accident of fate, friends must try to stop this person giving it away to someone they feel is more in need. April 19 needs persuading that money invested for a rainy day is a comforting thought, and even if they don't want it, their children or some other relative may in the future.

Don't go chasing waterfalls
Please stick to the rivers and
the lakes that you're used to.

(TLC)

FIRE

20 April

A pril 20 thinks a kiss on the hand may be quite continental, but diamonds are a girl's best friend. This Maserati of the skies is always chasing time, and since time waits for no man it's going to be a long drive. From earliest youth, both men and women are unusually conscious of encroaching age. They shore up their bodies with visits to the gym, and mental fitness with every alternative medicine you can mention. Investments are made for the future. Love is exchanged for commodities, diamonds maybe, or property. Divorce is a way of getting rich quick if you've married wisely and signed a helpful marriage contact.

Every moment of both sexes' lives must be packed with work, or fun. Friends are fitted in for half an hour, or cancelled because there's no time. Family seek a window in April 20's diary. There aren't enough hours in the day, too many are wasted in sleeping at night. Holidays are always a waste of time. And quality time with children means precious hours packed with activity, exhausting the child.

Yet April 20 has many spiritual qualities and though he may be driven, he can stop. Often this creature does just that when enough money has been accumulated to ensure a secure future. Then time takes on a different speed and April 20 learns the pleasures of wasting it. A second life now begins, where leisure is pursued and quality time with child, friend or partner stretches for days or weeks.

The same drive that was devoted to gaining, now goes into restoring an old building, learning new languages, how to judge a good painting or a horse and how to watch the sky change colour. In later life travel becomes a great pleasure and a great deal of time may be spent in leisurely journeys abroad. Time usually speeds up as you grow older, but in April 20's case it's the other way round.

Time is a gentleman.
  Pay him respect
    and he will wait for you.

BODY

Garlic (Alium sativam) is wonderful for your health, although its pungent odour on the breath makes it better consumed at weekends or during holidays. Unless, of course, you work at home or don't work at all, in which case eat it all the time. Cooked garlic lowers blood cholesterol and acts as a decongestant. It contains minerals, calcium, phosphorus, iron, potassium, thiamin, riboflavin, niacin and vitamin C. A garlic soup made from 50–100 cloves is an enormous help when suffering from the common cold. Raw, it contains powerful antibiotic qualities. Garlic also protects you from vampires, in particular Count Dracula.

MIND

When a lazy pattern of life reinstates itself, it assuages all relationships, allows for compromise and dreaming and makes things safe again between lovers, parents and children and old friends.

DATESHARE

Jessica Lange, film actress, The Postman Only Rings Twice. **Daniel Day Lewis**, British film, stage and TV actor. **Luther Vandross**, soul singer. **Ryan O'Neill**, Hollywood star, father of Tatum. **Adolf Hitler**, German Nazi dictator, author, Mein Kampf. **Joan Miró**, Spanish painter.

This is a sleepyhead. Many people find the idea of lying about in bed horrifying, but those born on April 21 regard sleep as a great sensuous pleasure. Not because they are neurotic, or want to escape, they simply like it. And naturally, it often makes them late, because they just can't get up in time.

People born on April 21 have a horror of early starts because of this. They say: 'Of course I'll be there at nine o'clock. What do you take me for?', getting cross with others who enquire if it's possible to be punctual. Then they are late, rushing in with flustered murmurs of the car/train breaking down.

Many individuals born on this day avoid corporate life. Usually very clever, they have a wide range of interests which have nothing to do with work and a horror of being bossed about by somebody less intelligent. For this reason, both men and women make excellent teachers, often at universities. And good personnel officers, where they will go to endless pains to look after people. Find them too in music and the arts. An April 21 person is a wow at running local theatre, or a summer concert. (There will always be enough loos. This day is sensitive to the physical needs of others.)

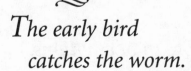

When it comes to sex, these steady creatures are extremely keen – on quantity. They patiently circle the planet of their affections, and will put up with crossness and bad behaviour, just as long as they share a pleasurable bed at the end of the day. This is not to say that April 21 is not an adept lover. Often starting their sex lives at a tender age, they are alert to the needs of their partner, preferring to give pleasure than take it. Most of the time.

When they are hurt, they say little, arguing that those who upset them are under pressure and can't help it.

The early bird catches the worm.

22 APRIL

T hese people would like recognition for their considerable talents, but often find somebody else takes their ideas and the kudos. April 22 easily creates superb projects, unwittingly causing jealousy among less gifted colleagues. Rather irritatingly, many of them just let things go, perversely content with a couple of sneers at the ideas-thieves. It would be better if April 22 made an effort and attempted some judicious secrecy, because it's fun to bask in your own starlight and stupid to content yourself with merely illuminating others.

Women born today make terrific leaders, in private and at work. Stunning at birth, they go on – sickeningly- to stun everybody at school. They can spot a window in the market, turn it into a successful business, play an important role in the local community, and combine it all with a family.

Both sexes are openly affectionate, which is good for family. Children never feel neglected. There will be stories, lullabies, dressing-up games and hide and seek. And when the school puts on a play, who oversees the costumes? Why, April 22.

However, beware a down side of this easy affection, the temptation to fall in lust with co-workers. Undiscriminating April 22 finds practically anybody fanciable in the right circumstances and gets into horrific jams, especially with other people's husbands, wives or lovers. There's no harm intended, just the pursuit of pleasure. It's just that April 22 doesn't think of the consequences, and anyway, they just can't help it. One whiff of temptation, and they're gone.

Weather plays havoc with this psychology. In cold and rain, they get easily depressed and extraordinarily resentful, almost as if they really think there's a being standing up there with buckets of water, specifically aiming to destroy their fun. Naturally it's not helped if social events they organise depend for their success on dry, sunny days. Try a more balanced approach. Make contingency plans for weather. For everyone's sake.

BODY

When you feel the world has got you down, try a soothing home-made scented skin cream, which will make you feel pampered and sexy, put your body at ease, and help you sleep. For silky, smooth, sensuousness, mix five drops of myrtle, ylang-ylang, patchouli, clary sage, neroli, jasmine or rosewood with 20ml camellia oil and 100ml spring water. Shake well. Alternatively use 100ml floral water, 20ml camellia oil and a drop or two of chosen essence. This mixture, like salad oil, separates if left to stand, so always shake well before use.

MIND

April 22 builds failure into his or her psychology because they are afraid of success. This may be a reason to let others pinch your inspiration. But success is fun. Don't let anyone tell you otherwise.

DATESHARE

Aaron Spelling, *Hollywood TV producer, father of Tori.* **Yehudi Menuhin**, *violinist, conductor, born 11.30pm in New York.* **Alexander Kerensky**, *Bolshevik revolution leader, held himself responsible for the killing of the Tsar and family.* **Jack Nicholson**, *film actor.* **Vladimir Ilyitch Lenin**, *founder Communist movement in Soviet Union.*

Love is an ocean of emotions, entirely surrounded by expenses. (Lord Dewar)

BODY

Problems of the flesh weigh down on April 23. By the age of 25, the eating and drinking catches up, and what was a 24 inch waist, has suddenly turned into a 30 inch one. Many individuals have been reasonable sportsmen, used to burning up the calories, so weight creeps up on them as a nasty surprise. Young people should cut down on chocolate snacks and endless packets of crisps. If they regulate themselves in their early twenties they can stay slim. Older people must stop pretending to themselves that their clothes have shrunk in the wash, and give up any snacks between meals.

MIND

You need to combat the stay at home tendency, which can transmogrify pleasure in domesticity to a fluffy slippers mentality. It's important that April 23 people don't get set in their ways and old before their time.

DATESHARE

William Shakespeare, *British Elizabethan playwright.* **Joseph Turner**, *British pre-Impressionist painter.* **Sergei Prokofiev**, *Russian composer, in trouble with the state, wrote the ballet* Romeo and Juliet. **Vladimir Nabokov**, *in trouble for writing* Lolita. **Roy Orbison**, *singer, songwriter, 'Pretty Woman'.* **Lee Majors**, *actor,* The Six Million Dollar Man.

---

ecurity is the chief ambition of people born on this day. They like the comforts of home – their favourite place. These individuals are sociable, sensible and jolly. They like going out and enjoy socialising with lots of people. Their idea of a good time is most certainly not being alone with their own thoughts.

What April 23 adores is a movie, followed by a get together with masses of drink, plates piled with food and good conversation. In numerology, this day is ruled by the number 5 (2+3=5) which means that theirs is an intellect which is powerful and gets bored easily.

This is the day of the great reader. Intoxicated by bookshops, April 23 always comes out with bag-loads to read. Their homes are stacked precariously with exciting booky promises. They are well versed in current affairs, hold strong opinions about European politics and have ideas which get to the heart of the matter. Nothing wishy washy and dreamerish about this big placid bull.

At work they are good with numbers. In fact some can turn into mouse potatoes and have to be lured away from their computers. Usually the promise of food or sex does the trick, because even the most intellectual and numerate April 23 people can't resist regular dips into fleshly pleasures.

They are dynamic in bed. No messing about and not much interest in folderols like honey on the toes and mince pies on the stomach. April 23 doesn't care about satin sheets, is faintly embarrassed by pink light bulbs (these people are very straight and think it makes a room look like a brothel) and would just as soon make love on the floor, with a pile of judiciously placed cushions. Of course, they will go along with a partner's starlight fantasies, because they are kind. But in general, those born on this date can't abide anything sticky or anything that hurts.

The right diet directs sexual energy into the parts that matter. (Barbara Cartland)

24 APRIL

April 24 people make terrific parents and unconventional lovers, because they resist any kind of cliché in their thinking. Nobody born today thinks others should behave in a certain way if it makes them unhappy. Good news for their tearaway kids. Good news for their love-life too because they have an open mind about everything. Not such good news for the parents of young April 24, who probably won't agree with anything their parents say, certainly won't do what they are told, and will probably drive teachers at school mad with their questions.

This is a day which questions everything, especially the status quo. At work, they can't understand why bosses are supposed to know less about certain parts of the organisation than the workers. As bosses themselves, they make sure that all managers mix with the workers, understand the business from the floor upwards and don't behave patronisingly to employees. They are also careful to maintain a healthy environment for people at work. Kind and fair, employees like them. Managers are frightened of what they will think up next. And it's likely to be no private offices, no company cars and everybody eating together in the canteen.

They throw a great party at work and at home. These are the people who shine at karaoke, dance brilliantly and often play in their own band. Some go on to make a career in showbusiness, where they will be known for their innovative style and infectious energy. On stage, everybody likes working with them because they are generous about others' talent, and always good for a laugh.

Many people born on this day are keen on sport, sometimes overkeen according to their long suffering lovers and friends, who have to listen and enthuse until tears of boredom flow. Their homes will be tapped into cable and satellite for the sport, and newspapers seized first for the sports pages.

BODY

April 24 people can suffer from physical tension, or simply muscle strain. They get this from sport, just horsing around, and moving through life fast. An aromatic bath may be the answer. It's not expensive, helps skin disorders, relieves muscular and other pains, and induces restful sleep. Some essential oils can be an irritant to the skin if you use more than three drops. So be careful of basil, ginger, fennel, orange and peppermint. Sandalwood is one of the mildest and you may safely use up to 10 drops in your bath. Sprinkle the drops after you have run the bath.

MIND

Most people born on this day are essentially kind, but some may get swept away and make more conventional people feel dull and even afraid. Terrifying others is never an attractive characteristic, and always rebounds on you.

DATESHARE

Barbra Streisand, American singer, songwriter, one of the towering talents in showbusiness. **Anthony Trollope**, Victorian novelist, favourite of British prime minister, John Major. **Jill Ireland**, married to Charles Bronson, died of cancer. **Shirley MacLaine**, actress, alternative thinker, acquirer of famous men.

Love your enemy ~

it will drive him nuts.

(Eleanor Doan)

BODY

Like most Taureans, April 25 has a tendency to put on weight and many of them diet too hard. Both sexes can suffer from low blood sugar, which of course makes them reach for the sugary doughnut – with jam and a cream filling. And icing on top. All this does, is make them fatter, more breathless, and more worried about weight-gain. Natural sugar is the solution when this craving comes, particularly for women at certain times of the month, or during the menopause. Try bananas and strawberries. Eat plain yoghurt, low fat please, with a little honey stirred in, but no strawberry jam.

MIND

This lover of the galaxy has a deep spirituality, but sometimes gets tired of being charming. Music is April 25's soul food. Try a little Mozart, or listen to Pavarotti's wonderful soaring voice.

DATESHARE

Guglielmo Marconi, *invented wireless telegraph in 1895, Nobel prize-winner.* **Oliver Cromwell**, *ruled England as Lord Protector.* **Ella Fitzgerald**, *jazz singer.* **Walter De La Mare**, *British poet.* **Al Pacino**, *film actor.* **Patrick Lichfield**, *celebrity photographer.* **Eric Bristow**, *world darts champion, 'The Crafty Cockney'.*

Whent April 25 sashays into a room, everybody looks. And this little bull likes it that way. They want to play the field and have their own way all the time. Most of the time, they can.

Both men and women born today have good bodies. But what really gets the opposite sex going is their come-to-bed eyes. They can turn a potential lover's stomach to water with a speaking

glance. They have hands like ballet dancers. Just looking at those hands gives their victims a dizzy sensation. Being touched by them is so pleasurable it should be against the law.

Naturally, such silky individuals think about sex much of the time. Sexy movies excite them and they want to act out the hottest scenes immediately. Their houses are full of sexy books, and sometimes, but you mustn't look, they have sensational magazines secreted in their office drawers. Both sexes have sensuous points on their bodies and go dreamy when they are rubbed. Behind the earlobes and the ankle bone are their secret erogenous zones.

Sex appeal gets you a long way up the career ladder, not by sleeping to the top, just by being glorious to have around. The problem is that people tend to fall in love with this creature and their admiration may be pestiferous. April 25 is brutally straightforward in these circumstances, not a creature celebrated for tact. Most prefer actions to words, are not great conversationalists. How others react to them is crucial, and compliments are relished, to the point of tediously repeating them to everybody. Beware vanity.

These gorgeous creatures are often tempted to the silliest self regard, always an Achilles' heel. While the puffed-up one is smirking at itself in every mirror and shop window, others are laughing up their sleeves. This apart, good looking Taurean April 25 is a pleasure to know. They make the world go with that much more zing.

The heart can do anything. (Molière)

26 APRIL

This nurturing sweetie-pie is everybody's ideal companion, just as long as you can stand experiment. Nothing ordinary is really interesting to April 26. They are a space capsule, always travelling farther and farther in search of new knowledge and new experience.

The women may insist on natural childbirth with some extra interest tacked on. Perhaps the idea will be to have the baby underwater? Or surrounded by flowers – lilies are a Taurus favourite and their sweet perfume would make a grand welcome to any baby. Some may want music in the labour room.

Males born on April 26 will harbour the same ideas which may not be in accord with the women in their lives born on other dates. But this adventurous dazzler finds it hard to take 'no' for an answer, and will try to persuade companions go along with their thoughts.

At home, the experiments continue, particularly with food. Many of these individuals become vegetarian and many grow their own vegetables and learn to make them into wonderfully appetising, original dishes.

Most people born on this date are too experimental to fit happily into ordinary corporate life. They can't see the point of rigorous rules and dislike authority figures. Find them running their own business, where they may flourish as inventors. But whatever they do, whether it be in the arts, or using the computer to earn their money, they find most corporate bodies eager to employ them as freelances, just because they *are* so original.

This birthday child often does best away from towns, settled in the country. There they can farm, or garden, and do what they like best, walk and marvel at beautiful nature. In local communities they can be invaluable, striving to improve the environment with money-raising, energy and devotion which will surprise those around them.

All April 26 people need regular solitude, without which they may feel overburdened and nervous.

BODY
This is the day that likes to experiment with food and makes its own wine. Nothing passes the lips of April 26, without this individual considering the effect it may have on the body. If you must indulge in wine-making, try this old recipe, traditionally valued for warding off fatigue, calming the senses and supplementing vitality and physical strength. Take 750g fresh peaches, 100g rock sugar and 1.8 litres of 45% clear alcohol. Place ingredients in a wide-mouth jar and leave to mature for three months to a year. Drink 20ml after dinner.

MIND
Some of the battier ideas entertained by this caring star may be unattractive to others. Don't equate their love of you with their compliance with some of your more unusual dietary suggestions. This is unfair.

DATESHARE
Eugène Delacroix, French Romantic painter. **Charles Richter**, seismologist, invented scale for measuring earthquakes. **Anita Loos**, Hollywood scriptwriter, Gentlemen Prefer Blondes. **A E Van Vogt**, Canadian science-fiction writer. **Rudolf Hess**, Hitler deputy, parachuted to England, imprisoned for life.

Intimacy is a difficult art. (Virginia Woolf)

BODY

Some Taureans suffer from sore gums, bad breath and less than brilliant teeth. Mostly because they are lazy and don't take care of their teeth. If April 27 wishes to wake up in middle age with his teeth in his head, there had better be a change of habit. Teeth need to be attended to at least three times a day. Use a firmish brush, not too hard, not too soft. Use floss. Use salt dissolved in hot water as a mouthwash. See the dentist regularly. Go now. Ask if your teeth need professionally cleaning. Oh, stop wingeing.

MIND

Emeralds are believed to calm fears and ease childbirth pains. If you can't wear them, put them by the bed. They are also said to protect chastity and dim when in the presence of a lie or broken promise.

DATESHARE

Coretta Scott King, political activist, wife of Martin Luther King. **Cecil Day-Lewis**, Irish born, British novelist, poet laureate. **Sheena Easton**, singer, songwriter. **Samuel Morse**, inventor of Morse code. **Edward Gibbon**, historian, author The Decline and Fall of the Roman Empire. **Pik Botha**, South African politician.

This is one of the gardening dates. Most people born today find great pleasure in planting things, whether it's in a garden, or a window-box.

All the Taurean sensual qualities are in the April 27 gardener. Both sexes love a riotous stretch of flowers and plants, all higgledy-piggledy. This creature feels that plants look good whatever their colour and is of the opinion that everything goes with everything. Don't expect this person to give much of a jot for striped lawns and perfectly weeded flower-beds. He quite likes weeds and will cultivate them as flowers.

April 27 will use kitchen refuse to feed the plants, and do some other fairly unorthodox things. These creatures swear by old remedies. They place banana skins in the soil around clematis, because old wives' tales dictate that clematis has a taste for banana. They may even tuck a mug full of cold lard into the earth by the roots of their roses, because, for many, it encourages growth. And there will be bunches of garlic discreetly hung near garden gates and doors, the traditional remedy to ward off evil. If they could, they would go the whole hog and use the family's waste to fertilise their garden, just as gardeners once did in the gardens of great houses. Please be warned. It requires careful, scientific control or the idea could result in something at best unhygienic and at worst – let the imagination run.

When you visit April 27, expect to be offered something to eat which has been home-grown. Dandelions are a favourite Taurus flower and indeed they make delicious (and pretty) salads; the leaves, and maybe a few flowers tossed with a vinaigrette. Or you may be given a bowl of nasturtium salad, peppery-tasting leaves and some bright red and yellow flowers. Why not? Supermarkets actually sell nasturtiums in the summer. Perhaps it will be dandelions next?

When a rogue kisses you, count your teeth.

(Yiddish proverb)

28 APRIL

This is a day where intellect, determination and physical attraction combine with devastatingly potent effect. April 28 is the stuff that heroes are made of – or anti-heroes if things go wrong. Either way these sterling creatures use their physical allure to get what they want, and show remarkable bravery if what they want or pursue requires sacrifice or heroism of any kind for a humane cause.

It has to be said, that some never, physically, go as far as shocking. Just enough to promise something that never actually comes through. In the course of public duty, that is. Privately, this hot frittata is a different matter.

When destiny calls, April 28 turns out to be a great negotiator, ruthless, charming and resourceful. If you want an historic building saved, or a lovely piece of countryside, or an old railway, here's your spokesperson. Big business just can't get round them. They look up every old law in the book, find financial support in the most eccentric corners. Don't bother to fight April 28 with the bit between its teeth.

Throughout their lives, other people have to fit in with this creature's strictures. As children and teenagers they already show leadership characteristics which make their parents and teachers admire them – and listen to them. As parents they can sometimes be overbearing, forgetting that others are not like them and maybe don't want to be. But April 28 always inspires admiration.

This individual needs to relax, and what pleases most is sex, and a brilliant financial deal, at both of which they can excel. In particular, they like the backs of their ankles stroked, which does amazing things to other parts of the body which are vulnerable to a sensuous flutter. And as far as money goes, they adore splendiferous fantasy games with lover and friends about how to direct their latest collection of mint-fresh currency.

BODY
Go on, admit it, like the Duke and Duchess of Windsor, and of course, the Duchess of Fergiana, foot massage transports you to the realms of delightful deliciousness. Furthermore, a feeling of bodily well-being comes from feet which are regularly massaged with aromatherapy recipes. Put two to three drops of scented oils into a camellia oil base, as instructed on bottle or ask health store assistant. Try peppermint for hot feet, myrtle for cold, cypress for smelly feet, and when recovering from any illness, any of the following oils naturally promote health: lavender, bergamot, lemon, neroli, and rose.

MIND
You need to calm the mind to concentrate. Seek half an hour's solitude each day, preferably in sun, or during the morning, in the open air, with green grass and trees around you.

DATESHARE
Lionel Barrymore, founder first acting family, author of We Barrymores. **Saddam Hussein**, Iraqi dictator. **Oskar Schindler**, Nazi Party member, saved over a thousand Jews during World War II, subject of film Schindler's List. **Odette Hallowes**, French Resistance fighter, British Special Forces agent, tortured by Gestapo, refused to talk. **Ann-Margret**, film actress, singer.

Assume a virtue
if you have it not.

(Hamlet)

The potato has a bad diet press, but some doctors recommend them for weight loss and to aid constipation. The American expert in weight and fertility, Dr E Flatto, extols their virtue in his famous book, Super Potency *(Thorsons) insisting that potatoes can in some cases, because they have zero cholesterol, contribute to an eating regime which can reduce high blood pressure. Whatever its effect on you in this area, this very ordinary vegetable is composed of 78% water, has more than twice the protein of human milk and one six ounce potato contains only ninety calories. But it's no good smothering it in butter.*

MIND

Some people have flashes of temper over piddling things, which leave them upset for hours, along with everybody else. This can be due to hormonal changes in both men and women. See your doctor.

DATESHARE

Michelle Pfeiffer, *Hollywood star, Catwoman, adopted a small girl.* **Andre Agassi**, *tennis champion, wears a hat to hide thinning hair.* **Sir Malcolm Sargent**, *British conductor, BBC Symphony Orchestra.* **Duke Ellington**, *jazz composer, pianist, bandleader.*

APRIL 29

April 29 is good fun, glamorous, with a strong image which often forms the basis for their profession. Most people born under this sign are blessed with excellent looks, regular features, strong bodies and fine eyes. Some may suffer from the old Taurean problem of early baldness, but most are philosophical about it – sufficient unto the day is the hair loss. Who knows if tomorrow it may come back again?

They are likely to become extremely rich, their income based to some extent on their looks, but mostly on their talent. While they adore fast living, flash cars and flasher houses, none of this goes to their head. At rock bottom they can live off little with enormous happiness.

At work they are punctilious, arriving on time, even much earlier, and going through the day with energy and brightness. Don't mistake the smile and the relaxed manner as pushover attributes. Low self image is not a component part of this person's stable psycheology. They know what they are worth, negotiate for more, and get it.

Extra dependable, many take positions of responsibility, sometimes succeeding in the travel industry, where whatever they organise always works out well. This is partly because April 29 thinks through what may go wrong, and pre-empts it. So he and she will check if the new hotel has actually been finished, if the hired car is roadworthy, if the swimming pool is properly cleaned, and the cook does what he says he will do.

It's a sexy enough date. They like it and they do it with good humour. What really matters to many of them is having children, though, and because they are responsible types, they will try to ensure that a child is born to a lasting relationship. Nobody can calculate the future though, and if this creature ends up a single parent, they will be remarkable in their ability to love and cope.

The bashful always lose.

30 APRIL

Aeroplanes make April 30 uncomfortable. They aren't afraid of flying, but arrive with tired eyes and swollen feet, generally feeling jaded. Many airlines devote time to helping their passengers but there are things you can do for yourself. To refresh eyes, take a cotton or silk scarf, soak it in bottled water (tap water in planes is not a good idea) and place it over your eyes. Tina Turner's travel guru, London and New York based Rajendra Sharma has also found that some female patients benefit from putting their shoeless feet in brown paper bags. No kidding, it has reduced their swollen ankles.

MIND
Small things make you unnecessarily mad. Sleeping policemen, being put on hold, the uncertain driver in front of you, another mound of socks to match together. None of these is worth a temper tantrum. Ignore the irritation.

D on't go breaking their heart. This nicely turned out pudding is liked by everybody and most people just want to gobble it up. But if you make April 30 sad, it will never forgive you, and you may regret such an action for the rest of your days. You may regret it because there is a fascinating side to this character which many remember all their lives, and to which they often wish to return even if it's just to talk.

April 30 is a day which knows where it is going, like a steady, bright satellite. A broken heart is one thing that does get in the way. When love goes wrong, this creature feels terrible pain, may sit alone for hours gazing at nothing, be unable to work or think properly and is sometimes so depressed a doctor must be called in. For those who hold this person dear, it's worth remembering that everybody born on this day has a taste for alcohol, and can often be coaxed out of unhappiness if you take round a wallop of champagne, a good video and then act the clown. (They have a simple sense of humour.)

Nothing has the same capacity to cause sadness, so it's best for creatures born on this day to establish a long-term relationship. Which won't be hard, because they are sexy, charming and usually intelligent.

While they are capable of making money, finance doesn't come high on April 30's list of priorities. Both sexes dislike greed in others, and get bored with the accumulation of material wealth. They think it vulgar. Nor are they likely to let ambition get in the way of their pleasures. No late nights and gritted teeth over work brought home here.

When faced with not having a job, they merely shrug their shoulders and pick up a book. Something will turn up is their philosophy. And it usually does.

DATESHARE
Alice B Toklas, *Gertrude Stein's partner, cook.* **Jill Clayburgh**, *film star.* **Joachim von Ribbentrop**, *Nazi foreign minister, convicted at Nuremberg .* **Queen Juliana**, *Dutch 20th century sovereign.* **Queen Mary II**, *British ruler with Dutch husband, William of Orange.*

Love means ∿ *never having to say you are sorry.*
(*Erich Segal*, Love Story)

May I

May 1 is not a morning person and sometimes just wants to sleep all day, pleasurable certainly, but a bringer of headaches and a depressing sense of time fleeting. Exercise gets the body going, even if it's just a brisk walk to the shops. Swimming is better if you can cope with the wet hair or the blow-dryer problem. Sleeping does no good if it's beyond requirements and time spent working in fresh air, even if it's just gardening, will give you that sense of well-being which comes from a body which is working at a proper rate of knots.

MIND

People do listen and act upon your advice, so it's vital to be extra responsible about what you say. It's so easy to ruin somebody else's relationships, even their life, with the wrong persuasive analysis.

DATESHARE

Rita Coolidge, singer, songwriter. **Glenn Ford**, film star. **Pierre Teilhard de Chardin**, philosopher, Jesuit priest, paleontologist, geologist, helped discover 'Peking Man'. **Steve Cauthen**, jockey, Triple Crown winner. **Terry Southern**, screenplay writer, Dr Strangelove.

These individuals are perceptive about others and enjoy helping solve personal problems. May 1 is patient and thoughtful at best, but some of these creatures use their perception unwisely, to browbeat others. These are the porkers of the year, who urge their advice on people and then show anger if that advice is not followed. Their attitude is: 'You've only brought it on yourself. You should have listened to me.'

You can find May 1 in all the caring professions. In youth they lunge for a career in psychiatry. Older people, especially women, train as counsellors when their children have grown up or as a second career, and sometimes espouse faddiness. The up side of May 1 is that he or she may be so convinced of another's fecklessness, that they pop round and sort out all the practical problems themselves. Which may be ideal for lazy people on the receiving end.

At party-time, they make stunning hosts, so good at catering  that they may choose it as a profession. In the hands of these people a table of food looks unutterably glamorous. They can do things with ribbons and balloons you wouldn't dream of. And they don't need to spend money to get the effect. It just magics out of the air. In the same way they will run up an outfit for themselves or a friend, seemingly out of nothing, and be the belle or beau of the ball.

When they are not advising others, this creature sometimes gets too involved in his own health matters. In general they have the good solid health enjoyed by Taureans, but some can suffer from a slow metabolism which makes them feel leaden in the mornings. And sometimes they wake in the night, worrying about an ache in the leg or the stomach, imagining dreadful things to come, when all that's wrong is an ache in the leg or stomach.

A great love is never returned. (Dag Hammarskjold)

2 MAY

These are peaceful people, revelling in the pleasures of social life. Ill-tempered disputes upset them. At work May 2 is the pacifier, calms warring opponents and asks the canteen to put more salt in the chicken casserole. Colleagues turn to them and always go away reassured and calmed.

In the home and the local community they do the same job. There may be rows with parents, brothers and sisters and children. May 2 understands that tempers must sometimes be raised, but our kindly creature always sets about smoothing the atmosphere afterwards.

This is a singing star, the beautiful voice reflects the music of the planets. Many have a guitar in their room, some play the piano and if they are not professionals on the international stage, they will often enjoy being involved in a local band, either pop or classical. Natural leadership, which is a characeristic of Taurus, comes out on this day. Find them managing the band, going places as a singer, a songwriter or even conducting.

While they are happy listening to other people bang on about their private lives, most May 2 people keep their own private life out-of-bounds. When they fall in love they don't want others to know, not because they are ashamed, but because they don't want interference. When they are ill, or somebody close is unwell, they have no desire to discuss symptoms with others, nor hear somebody else's medical solutions. Unless, of course, it's from a doctor.

Many Taureans have a problem with authority. They dislike it, look for the foolish side in their boss, and find it. This compliant sparkler, however is easy-going with bosses and authority, but may not take much notice of either.

Both sexes like to please others. They may do this by painting something for them, or embroidering a cushion. Others love to cook, reflecting their star sign's passion for eating.

Never let the sun go down on a quarrel.

MAY 3

BODY

May 3 might as well go the whole hog and use mouth perfume. In ancient love rituals, these were commonly considered a compliment to the intended. Why not now? Try one drop rose, and two drops bergamot. Add the oils to a 100ml bottle of spring water. Shake well. Or you could try a sweet, alluring lip balm, one drop rose, one teaspoon camellia oil. Store in a small, tinted glass bottle. On a more sober note, get your teeth checked regularly by the dentist, not only for a lover's sake, but to ensure you keep your teeth. Kissing with false teeth requires concentration.

MIND

Major keys in music are harmonious and seductive for Taureans. F Major (now what can that stand for?) is best for love. Try the Spring Sonata by Beethoven and the first Brandenburg Concerto by J S Bach.

DATESHARE

Golda Meier, *Israeli prime minister.* **Engelbert Humperdinck**, *singer, performer, sex symbol.* **Niccolò Machiavelli**, *Italian political theorist, author of* The Prince *and the idea that it's OK to use any means to achieve a desired goal.*

Sugar and spice and all things nice, that's what May 3 is made of. But they are trouble too. People born on this day like lots of sex with lots of people. Many are attracted to their own sex, or indeed either sex. Most are popular because they are such fun to be with, if a little unreliable as lovers.

Two-timing is a problem for these naughty things. They spend  half the time on the telephone hurriedly altering their plans so that one new partner doesn't clash with another. It usually means they have to have a fast car so they can speed about, like a bee zooming from flower to flower. And of course, they often get found out. A honey bee of this proportion will often find irate lovers on their doorstep demanding an explanation, and may frequently suffer personal attack from their victims. A bop on the charming little nosette is the mildest revenge. Frequently there will be May 3 clothes flying from the window, trousers with the legs cut off, and their telephone used to call New York's speaking clock and left off the receiver. A complicated love life can be costly.

Many May 3 people find they have to eat two dinners in one evening: an early one with their first amour; and then a later one with the second. This means that fat piles on, but it doesn't mean they stop doing it. Taureans love guzzling anyway, so if they must do it in the cause of love, well it's a good excuse.

Not surprisingly, these sultry creatures are such great kissers they should give classes. There's no clumsy groping, or lack of aim here. No wet-lipped squelchers. They go in for the sort of mouth to mouth contact which is practically as intimate as the sex act, long, pleasurable and enough to make the recipients' eyes cross. But not their legs.

A bird in the hand
∼ is worth two in the bush.

4 MAY

If this rotund creature had known you were coming, he'd have baked you a cake. Any excuse for getting out the mixing bowl and making the house drift with delicious, appetising smells. May 4 likes to cook; it's the best way they know of pleasing people. And of course, they always eat as they cook, because you must taste as you go along. Most stars born on this day turn to food for an expression of love, affection or just parenting, so their house will be stocked with coconut pyramids fresh from the oven, little fairy cakes covered in bright icing for children to delight in, and squelching, delicious, big-occasion chocolate numbers with chocolate butter cream topping and filling.

They put the same enthusiasm into their own personal recipe for love, concocting different ways of pleasing a lover and indeed themselves. For this creature, straightforward sex is not usually enough, although sometimes it's a necessity. Drinks by the bedside usually feature in their amorous nights of pleasure. Then there will be scented baths to play in together and a great deal of slow stroking and massage to feet, especially toes and the base of the spine – a favourite place for May 4.

Both sexes like money. So they strive hard to succeed at work

 and do well in big corporations because of their pleasing personality, often making excellent accountants and managers of big departments. All of this is, of course, to finance their private palace of enchantment.

Younger people born on this day are also extremely image conscious and spend a lot of money and time on clothes and the dressing of their usually luxuriant hair. As May 4 gets older, however, they sometimes find their love of food leads to the need to shop for clothes with elastic waistbands. But slenderness of body is not a prerequisite to enjoyment of life, and we are not talking mounds of fat here, just a certain appealing rotundity.

BODY
With these tastes nothing is going to persuade May 4 to lead a life of bean sprouts and boiling water with a squeeze of lemon. It's worth remembering that most women in the UK are size 16 and over anyway and most men are considerably larger round the middle than they admit to. Just watch the weight doesn't get excessive and enjoy yourself. Try this bedside drink with a kick, just to ring the changes. It's called Brandy Alexander. Mix one part crème de cacao with three parts brandy, one part cream and four ice cubes. Put in cocktail shaker with cubes. Shake well.

MIND
Both sexes dream of love with famous people. Recent surveys show that Princess Diana and Brad Pitt are top of everybody's dream lists. It's OK, but if they come each night, could get tedious.

A gourmet who thinks of calories is like a tart who looks at her watch.

(Henry James)

MAY 5

May 5 should beware their pessimism, because the world is much brighter than they sometimes think, and they are certainly cleverer and lovelier. This grumbler should take a look at his and her diet to see if anything they eat or drink could be contributing to the feeling of gloom. Alcohol for instance, makes some people absolutely tragic. Others are reduced to lethargy because they favour drinks with too many preservatives. And very sugary things like doughnuts and chocolate cake can taste good, but induce lethargy and lack of enthusiasm. In effect mild allergy to some foods can induce low self-image.

MIND

Moaning is really a form of self-indulgence and it's the grumbling, not the supposed lack of looks and talent ,which will put people off in the end. Stop looking at your reflection in shop windows.

DATESHARE

Tammy Wynette, *country singer, always moaning, five marriages.* **Michael Palin**, *British actor, comedian.* **Karl Marx**, *German political economic philosopher, author* Das Kapital. **Tyrone Power**, *film actor, heart-throb.*

May 5 has a complex psycheology. Nothing is what it seems with this space traveller. Blessed with physical attraction, like many Taureans, they are not convinced of their good looks, and like the Beast in the famous fairy story, they always see ugliness when they look in a mirror. Worse still, both sexes habitually check their reflection in shop windows, to see if it's still as bad as they think. These windows make everbody look awful, so their pessimism is confirmed. No amount of Beauty's persuasion will really convince the Beast in May 5 that everything is fine and that their looks are excellent.

Similarly they are always unsure of their talent. If they aren't wailing about awful hair and legs, they are moaning about schoolwork and how thick they are, or office work and how nobody rates them probably because they aren't any good. Fortunately for us all, in many cases May 5 secretly understands it's not bad looking and quite good at what it does, and much of the snivelling is fudge.

Both sexes take refuge in music and many in something arty. Some like to collect musical instruments but many will enjoy roaming the world looking for natural and precious stones, which they value for their beauty rather than their financial worth.

This individual's favourite colour is in the blue to deep green range. They like to wear emeralds, which traditionally promote learning and enhance self-confidence, and lapis lazuli which traditionally enhances every personality's emotional side.

When either sex has children their self-confidence suddenly comes to the fore. They make loving parents, forgetting reservations about themselves and throw great energy into entertaining their kids with toys and marvellously invented games. May 5 must watch, however, becoming over ambitious for his or her children.

It's not the wrapping
but what's inside it that counts.

---

6 MAY

Basically lazy in practical areas, these people always leave things for others to do, although they swear they will fix it themselves. The men are much worse than the women. In youth May 6 is a slob, their bedroom floor heaped with clothes and mouldy sandwiches. Like all Taureans, they are extremely interested in sex, so the walls will be plastered with pictures, some rather shocking.

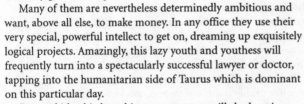

Their taste in music is for loud rhythm, with massive bass. Their social life, every night spent in a club, home at 6am and little sleep. Their sex life usually starts earlier than any parent would wish. But the upside of a May 6's teen and twenties sex life is that the bedroom suddenly gets tidied up.

Many of them are nevertheless determinedly ambitious and want, above all else, to make money. In any office they use their very special, powerful intellect to get on, dreaming up exquisitely logical projects. Amazingly, this lazy youth and youthess will frequently turn into a spectacularly successful lawyer or doctor, tapping into the humanitarian side of Taurus which is dominant on this particular day.

But, and it's a big but, this starry creature will shed copious quantities of the kind of dust you have to clean up. At home there will always be piles of paper on the floor and empty drink cans. Somebody else has to take out the rubbish. And at work, somebody else will sort out the computer, do all the minor detail checking, and if May 6 can get away with it, fetch and carry their cleaning and their coffee.

And yet, and yet, what you get with this disorganised creature, is a sweet time and a lot of laughs. These individuals are not unaware how much work they generate for others and they compensate for this with constant flashes of wit and mimicry which entertains the clearers-up while they work.

All women think they're ugly.

〜

Even pretty women.

(Erica Jong)

BODY

Sore throats plague people born on this day. Nothing serious, but hard work and exhaustion can set them off. Sometimes they find that travelling brings on the soreness too, so precious time is spent nursing this nasty condition. Everybody should check with their doctor, but most of the time it will not be thought a good idea to have tonsils out. Thirty years ago, doctors regularly whipped out tonsils. They aren't keen now unless it's clearly vital. Having a flu jab can sometimes help protect the throat from infection. Many also find relief from gargling with TCP or hot, salt water, or consult a pharmacist.

MIND

Your ideals are admirable, but all the world is not made up from chambermaids and chambermen ready and willing to couch your progress. And some lovers may just disappear because you are so much hard work.

DATESHARE

Orson Welles, film actor, director, screenwriter, pursued by both sexes. **Rudolph Valentino**, screen star pursued by every sex known to man. **Sigmund Freud**, Viennese founder of psychiatry, inventor of the Oedipus Complex. **Maximilien Robespierre**, instigator of French Revolution, guillotined.

BODY

Sometimes this person could really do with a clock round the ear. It might stop them drooping about, and worrying so unnecessarily. And worrying others too. Strongly recommended here is Rescue Remedy, one of the most famous of the remedies discovered by Dr Edward Bach, who searched the hedgerows of England and Wales in the 1930s for medicinal plants and gave us his marvellous Bach Flower remedies. Three drops in a small glass of water does wonders for some of his modern day admirers. Rescue Remedy can be bought in most health stores and may be given to pets to perk them up as well.

MIND

Most of you are blessed with humanitarian feelings and the talent to put ideas into practise. It's wise to remember that what's good for you may not be perfect for somebody else. And do perk up.

DATESHARE

Peter Ilyitch Tchaikovsky, Russian 19th century composer, conservatory teacher, created Russian ballet music for Swan Lake, Nutcracker. **Robert Browning**, British 19th century Romantic poet, Pied Piper of Hamelin. **Eva Perón**, actress, dictator's wife, subject of musical and film, Evita. **Susan Atkins**, murderess, Manson follower.

Such a serious space traveller this. May 7 is a spiritual creature, with a deeply non-materialistic view of his and her place in the world and a strong desire to create better surroundings for all the people in it. For many, humour is not a strong point and they abhor even the lightest mockery, deeming it merely cruel. So don't joke around with this reforming star.

Often deeply drawn to religion, most find it hard to go through life without a firm belief system, and once they discover it, they will try to convert others. In the nicest possible way. Some may be vulnerable to cults and should take care. Others, especially women, may turn to strong, firm and tough beliefs such as Roman Catholicism or Islamic Fundamentalism, finding the brashness of western culture offensive. Both men and women born on this day make great mentors in the arts and in life. It is given to them to change younger people's lives and open their eyes to new thoughts and this they do, winning wholehearted respect. Their selflessness is enormously attractive. Many are extremely talented and reach international fame – something that all Taureans love. This star sign feels validated by fame. There are some born on this day who are so self-critical that unless they become known, even in a narrower sphere for their talents, they doubt themselves and wonder if their skills are not just bullshit. In particular women feel this, that one day they will somehow be found out.

Overmodesty is irritating because others must constantly reassure you. At worst, it so undermines May 7's self-confidence that personal growth and talent can be suppressed. Some of the men are also overmodest. They judge less modest people too harshly, frequently underperform and throw away their talents by going for the easy option. Naturally some also suffer from a bad case of green-eyed jealousy.

An atheist is a man who believes himself an accident.

(Francis Thompson)

8 MAY

Venus is a ruler of this day and May 8 is someone who can't do without beauty. Usually beautiful themselves, they can be enormously vain about their best features, notably great hair and astonishing legs. May 8 will always be drawing attention to one or the other. There will be a lot of running hands through the rich mane, and with women a great deal of tossing hair. But why not? For these people it is an absolute crowning glory. Except of course, for those who are challenged in this department, as some bulls – not a creature famous for its hairy nature – are.

This person goes barefoot as much as possible in the house, and outside in the summer. The feet are lovely, the ankles superb and the rest is not left to the imagination. Women will wear skirts up to there and men dress in shorts, or else jeans so tight they show every sinew.

In private this individual campaigns for the environment and for beautiful buildings, which they like to visit. And they are tough  opponents, well able to hold a crowd with persuasive speaking. They are also good at raising money with a silky telephone manner and charmingly well-argued letters.

Many companies like to employ them, using these talents for persuasion to benefit the product. They may also flourish in the political arena, with the combined assets of physical good looks and plausible beliefs.

And they may make a great deal of money for themselves. May 8 is good at running his or her own business and if they are employed, quite often manipulate their redundancy or sacking (with money) so that they are free to pursue their own plans. Few of them are afraid of the isolation which comes with working for themselves. They just pick up the phone and call friends, and enjoy the time they now have to stop and talk and simply enjoy the rhythms of life.

BODY

This person is drawn to a vegetarian life, they find eating something with a face off-putting. This being so, they have strong stomachs, good digestion and few intestinal complaints. Nor is food poisoning much of a problem. They should ensure, when cooking for a family which might not want to be vegetarian, that some meat and fish is included, and that all the dishes made for others are as tasty and unfaddish as possible. A lot of people really don't want to be stuffed with veggie burgers. Beansprouts can be boring. And radishes and beans make you fart.

MIND

Some people born on this day swear by keeping a piece of rose quartz in their pocket for its mystical properties, which includes the ability to soothe and fire the imagination.

DATESHARE

Harry S Truman, US president, authorised use of atomic bombs against Japan in World War II. *Oscar Hammerstein*, opera impresario, built Manhattan Opera House. *Candice Bergen*, film actress, photojournalist, activist. *Peter Benchley*, novelist, Jaws. *Norman Lamont*, British chancellor.

It is better to be beautiful than to be good. (Oscar Wilde)

MAY 9

BODY

May 9 suffers from stress which means sore throats, fatigue and tired eyes, often from too much computer work. A change of diet can help balance the body which in turn may contribute to control of bad throats and blurry eyes. Have a salad a day, plus raw, steamed or lightly cooked vegetables. Change to camomile tea at work. (Many women magazine editors favour camomile.) Go for one serving of fish or poultry every other day instead of red meat. If you are vegetarian, use bean derivatives. Try to include grains in your diet, such as short grain brown rice, millet and basmati rice.

MIND

When your pulse rate rises, take ten minutes for this simple meditation technique. Close your eyes. Imagine you are on a sandy beach, barefoot in the surf as it froths in and out.

DATESHARE

Glenda Jackson, *British stage and film actress, politician.* **Carlo Maria Guilini**, *Italian conductor.* **James Barrie**, *Scottish playwright,* Peter Pan. **Pancho Gonzalez**, *tennis champion, winner of US Open and Wimbledon.* **Albert Finney**, *British film & TV actor.* **Billy Joel**, *singer, pianist, songwriter.* **George Lippert**, *German three-legged man, two legs from the right knee downwards. He walked using all three.*

May 9 is a good sportsman, plays hard and fair. Not so in the office, where they are often badly afflicted with *work rage.* You've heard of the road kind? Well these people favour head on collisions, drive roughshod over colleagues, attack other people's ideas and often steal them. What to do? Distance yourself, duck, find another job – or apply for theirs.

May 9 often gets so angry he or she start to talk to themselves. You can hear them muttering at their desk, puce in the face as the violent volcano stirs, bubbles, then erupts. They are convinced they are the only one really working and that everybody around them is a knave or a fool. Bosses born today feel that anybody who works for them is inferior, and *getting away* with something. Because they are  paying for somebody else's mortgage, they expect to be crawled to, and indeed get on best with creeps and creatures whose bellies are close to the ground.

At home they rant to their spouse, who must develop blind loyalty syndrome, because any contrary suggestion produces monster sulks. The male of the species calms down in environments they aren't used to. Take them to a lingerie department, hand them something silky and ask them to buy it while you pop off to the loo. They go nervously polite. Women are calmed by buying something nice, or gifts of jewels and having babies.

Fortunately work rage doesn't affect all May 9 people. Many do have a temper, but usually learn to control it in young adulthood, often with the help of parents who spot the tendency in childhood and stamp on it hard.

The upside to this fiery star is their courage. When there is a problem, or someone is in danger, May 9 will be the hero or heroine, showing resourcefulness, reserves of stunning humanity and leading others out of danger. They are tender with small children and make good playmates.

Patience is a virtue

Possess it if you can

Seldom found in woman

Never found in man.

IO MAY

In many countries a man's wealth is still calculated by the number of cattle he owns, and the Taurean sign of the bull indicates that those born under it will be financial accumulators. Fortune favours the brave, a talent which May 10 has in full, and which he and she may need, because their Tarot indicates that the 10th card in the Major Arcana, is The Wheel of Fortune, signifying reversal in fortune, gains and losses. Nothing is permanent except change.

These individuals focus on opportunities. Numerology helps, the 10th of the month is ruled by the number 1 (1+0=1) and by the Sun, which means they generally like to be first, but have well-developed, balanced judgment, ideal for making the right financial decision at the right time.

Both sexes understand that ill luck may be around the corner – for anybody. They enjoy their wealth, but invest it wisely. Many end up owning their house, the mortgage paid off. They lay-up resources in case of job-loss, or reversal at work which may affect their income. In fact they plan well for the future, take into account inevitable problems on the way, and so can cope when they come.

The women are immensely attractive. They adore children and make exciting, relaxed mothers, although some may not have a family, in which case they will develop a strong circle of friends, powerful interests and a happy way of life much admired by others. Nor do the men count parenthood as a necessity to fulfilment.

Both sexes are pragmatic, fast-witted and funny. And May 10's generous streak means that they have no need to court others for their success. They simply couldn't care less what people do, only liking them for what they are. And will while away the hours with neighbours, relatives and friends, chatting, drinking, eating and generally having fun.

BODY

May 10 loves to cook for people, especially little surprises you rustle up and hand round while everbody's chatting. They are ideal cooks for small children who really prefer nibbles anyway. Try making Old Fashioned Toffee, tough on teeth, but May 10 doesn't have many tooth problems: see it as a jaw firming exercise. Take 300ml condensed milk, 45ml golden syrup, a large pinch salt, put into a saucepan, stir continuously and bring to boil for 20 minutes until toffee becomes a firm ball. Pour into greased tin, leave until cool enough to handle. Cut into squares and finish cooling.

MIND

May 10 can have psychic powers. They have dreams which come true, hunches which are correct, frequently think of somebody who then unexpectedly turns up or telephones. Useful powers to develop rather than deny.

DATESHARE

Barbara Woodhouse, dog trainer. **Sid Vicious**, punk singer, bassist with Sex Pistols. **Max Steiner**, film composer. **John Wilkes Booth**, stage actor, Lincoln assassin, killed during capture. **Donovan**, singer, songwriter. **Phil Mahre**, alpine skier, three-time world champion.

Little things that you do ∼
Make me glad I'm in love with you. (Dave Berry)

MAY II

They are like the silvery thistledown mist that sometimes lies across the moon, enchanting, but like a fleeting pleasure, half known before it's gone. This is a very unusual psycheology. Those born on the 11th are ruled by the number 2 (1+1=2) and by the Moon. Not suited to the ordinary rules and regulations of the workplace, they simply don't fit in and feel odd in such surroundings.

They are not so much odd, as extremely creative with unusual thoughts which are often worth preserving for posterity. This is the day which brings forth some great and original artists. If they had fitted in, the creativity might have been lost and then the rest of the world would have been the poorer.

Left to their own devices, these people will flourish if they can earn a living by themselves and create their own community and their own way of life. Few other dates are gifted with such imaginative perception of the world, but they need calm surroundings. Their Tarot shows that the 11th card of the Major Arcana is Justice, a seated woman holding the scales in one hand and a sword in the other. This is the card of serenity, balance and harmony, which highly developed people born on this day will achieve with discipline.

There may be a petulant side to some of these creatures, which manifests itself in a string of grievances. They can pick quarrels too easily, especially with family and neighbours, and sometimes the ill-feeling, frequently based upon some imaginary slight, may last for life and cause a lot of people unhappiness.

Then the danger is isolation and those qualities which can light up the world with a peculiar radiance, will be dismissed as eccentricities. When this happens the fabulous ideas and stories woven by this creature become increasingly fantastic, but take on the unpleasant aspect of lies rather than luminous inspiration.

T rend is not destiny. (Lewis Mumford)

12 MAY

May 12 turns everything into a good time. They're the best people to go places with, always fascinated and fascinating, finding perfect places to eat, views to share, movies to watch, fun to be had. Most of them simply don't understand the word depression, although they are sympathetic with others, and this makes them ideal cheerers-up, which they do with goodwill.

These people are sweet in the workplace, always looking out for others, with just the spiciest note of debunking when they encounter the pompous and puffed-up. With this temperament, May 12 is not an especially good boss. Mostly they can't see why they should be giving the orders, and haven't the faintest notion why anybody should follow them. And in truth they don't really have an air of authority, only of reassurance, so people who work for them tend to run riot.

With friends, particularly of their own sex, they are faithful and will always rush to help, planning treats for their buddies, finding them presents, and generally wanting to entertain. With lovers it's a different matter. Kind and considerate, yes. Faithful, forget it.

It's a fact of life that this butterfly goes in for a sundance every time it flutters across anybody fanciable. At work they have to be prised out of cupboards where they have retired with someone for a cuddle. Colleagues are always taking calls from furious lovers who were meant to be meeting this individual somewhere and of course May 12 hasn't turned up. Everybody has to tell so many fibs for May 12, that eventually they get into a hopeless muddle, as indeed does the twinkling subject of their confusion.

They mean better than they do with love. But where their own children are concerned they do better than they think they will. This is the day which loves its children more than the partner who shares parenthood. It's just one of those things.

I never know how much
of what I say is true.

(Bette Midler)

The flitting way of life chosen by May 12 takes its toll, and occasionally they should sit still, take it easy, and review their circumstances. Trouble haunts them day and night – the best thing is to learn not to cause it, because better health follows.
Some Bach Flowers induce welcome calm. Collected by Dr Edward Bach from fields and woods they sell widely today in health food shops. Take two or three drops in a small glass of water. Pine (Pinus sylvestris) will go some way to alleviating guilt. Walnut (Juglans regia) is good for stabilising emotions and adjusting to new beginnings, of which this date has a lot.

MIND
The downside to promiscuity is danger to your health, and to others. It also addles the brain. Unless of course you are the poet Lord Byron or Mozart, in which case it seems to fire creativity.

DATESHARE
Emilio Estevez, filmstar, son of Martin Sheen. **Florence Nightingale**, British founder of the modern nursing movement. **Stevie Winwood**, singer, songwriter, Traffic. **Edward Lear**, maverick limerick writer, The Owl and The Pussycat. **Dante Gabriel Rossetti**, Pre-Raphaelite painter

EARTH

BODY

May 13 needs to watch the weight, and usually does so quite efficiently. Most people born on this day get to know what suits their body and what doesn't. Many become a dab hand at the quick, healthy sandwich for lunch, something they have made themselves and therefore know what has gone into it. Excellent slimmer's sandwiches include tuna, celery, nuts and cottage cheese filling on thin slices of brown wholemeal bread, or a delicious mixture of cooked chicken, whole berry cranberry sauce, with a little orange juice on the same thin, brown bread. Good health.

MIND

If you can't get out into fresh air and green countryside each day, the next best thing is to close your eyes and simply imagine that you are walking on a sunny, green hillside.

DATESHARE

Stevie Wonder, *blind singer, songwriter, keyboardist.* **Harvey Keitel**, *film actor, producer.* **Jim Jones**, *cult leader, The People's Temple, led mass suicide in Guyana.* **Bruce Chatwin**, *novelist,* The Songlines. **Ravi Shankar**, *spiritual leader of the Vedanta tradition.*

People born today are likely to live to great old age in happiness, health and mental alertness. May 13 creatures carry on shining when others fade, yet they often live hard and don't take particular care of their health. Although they have Taureans' large appetites, these time-blessed children possess more self-control than their star siblings.

They adore to eat, but stick to healthy, homemade sandwiches and honey rather than sugar. They like to drink, but not every day and not very often to excess. They may ride a motorbike, but not so fast and always with a good quality helmet. When they are tired, they put their feet up. And most of them have extremely relaxing hobbies, which fascinate them and always keep them busy.

Many Taureans are skilled with their hands. They play music, which is excellent for health. Why do you think so many great conductors are 80 and look 50? They like to carve, or paint. And many of the women are brilliant at textile design, sewing and tapestry or embroidery. Indeed, their houses are full of brilliant shimmering creations, which gives their surroundings magical calm. These are not the bungee jumpers of the zodiac.

From an early age May 13 makes sure to make and keep their money. They don't worry about work politics, don't have sleepless nights about who will win promotion. They just lie in bed adding up their possessions and working out the next financial move. Like counting sheep, it sends them into a peaceful and dreamless sleep.

Well, mostly dreamless. If they do encounter a midnight fantasy, it will usually be the pleasant flying and travelling kind, both of which are thought to be sex dreams. So they wake up refreshed.

Most of them end up owning their own unmortgaged house, having spent their life with one partner. If they have gambled a little, they mostly won more than a little. They're just lucky.

May you live ∾
all the days of your life.

(Jonathan Swift)

14 MAY

This heavenly dazzler is bright of eye, sharp of wit and has even sharper teeth. 'What big teeth you have Grandma,' said Little Red Riding Hood. 'All the better to eat you with,' said the Big Bad Wolf. And that sums up May 14. A wolf in sequins.

Charming enough to inveigle their way into any glamorous granny's bedroom, they always keep their eye on the goodies in the basket. Prospective partners with a car are better than those without and if Daddy's the boss, that's a plus factor too. This creature always prefers love in a palace to a hut, when all their lust will certainly turn to dust. It's not that they are completely money-grubbing and they're certainly not mean. It's just that they prefer having it all.

Many individuals, especially the young ones are clever with computers and any new technology. They pick up techno-changes fast. They dream up complicated programmes, sort out problems, and best of all, don't patronise those who can't. Both sexes are in great demand in every workplace. They can pick and choose, frequently working as emergency operators, called in for a few weeks to sort out staff and glitches, then off to the next hunting ground.

If you want to please, find them a new techno-toy. State of the art mobile phones always delight. They use them out walking, on the beach, in the ER, and if they could, during weddings and baptisms. They also like love on the phone. It amuses them at work to murmur sweet shockers, the telephone held between shoulder and ear, while they type into a computer. It's not thoughtlessness. It's the buzz.

When they give presents, it is likely to be techno-orientated. Both sexes adore computer games. Other whizzy things for the kitchen, garden and bathroom are favourite. Their ideal would be a toothbrush/telephone with tape recorder attachments. Techno gadgets of a more private kind are also welcome.

BODY

May 14 works so hard that sometimes physical love seems an exhausting challenge. The desire is there, but a falling off frequently follows. Just thinking about aphrodisiacs makes this creature feel good again. It's well known that, for some, chocolate is held to have aphrodisiac properties; and was thus held to be so valuable by ancient Aztec Indians that the cacao beans from which it is made, were used as financial currency. Another traditional aphrodisiac is coriander (Coriandrum sativum). Use one or two drops of coriander oil in an aromatherapy oil base in combination with citrus and other spicy essences, and massage the body.

MIND

You know what you want, and maybe that's good. But there is a tendency for people born on this day to be formulaic, which eventually bores them and others. Changing your mind is good.

DATESHARE

Jack Bruce, British bassist, Cream. **George Lucas**, film director, Star Wars. **Gabriel Daniel Fahrenheit**, physicist, introduced Fahrenheit scale for thermometers. **Otto Klemperer**, German conductor. **Thomas Gainsborough**, British 18th century portrait and landscape artist.

A little hush money ∼ can do a lot of talking.

MIND

The trouble with things is that your interest in them suddenly palls and then you wonder what you can do with them, and often end up just giving them all away.

DATESHARE

Richard Avedon, *society fashion photographer,* Vogue. **Mikhail Bulgakov**, *Russian author,* The Master and Margarite. **Mike Oldfield**, *British composer, instrumentalist, 'Tubular Bells'.* **Jasper Johns**, *Pop artist.* **Claudio Monteverdi**, *Italian baroque composer.*

Ruled by Venus, people born on this day are deeply concerned with their surroundings. They yearn for wealth, lust for possessions and easily feel insecure. Both sexes like to wear their wealth on their sleeve, delight in designer clothes, jewels and costly watches. They are the magpies of the solar system, filling their nests with bright things, including other people's, when greed may push some of these individuals to commit minor crimes.

They are the shoppers of the world, regarding each country they visit as a department store, in particular drawn to India, enjoying the sybaritic pleasures of Eastern perfumes, brilliant carpets and exquisite jewels. Some even marry, or start a business and settle down in their chosen foreign cave of treasures. When they do this, May 15 quickly learns the language and equally quickly make friends with the residents. They are not really subject to homesickness. Home to them is where the pleasures of the eye lies.

Many are extremely generous with their money and often with their possessions. Where greed is not so much to the fore, they will come to the rescue of friends and relatives in need, throwing all their resources at the needy one, knowing that with their charm and wit they can soon lay hands on more of the same.

Many marry for love, but must manage to combine this with espousing money and people born on this date often link up with

much older people who have already had the time to acquire wordly possessions. Such liaisons are usually successful, because May 15 has a naive, childish streak which benefits from the experience of mature lovers, and indeed, in work situations you often find this individual attached to an older and wiser mentor. The friendship is always genuine as well as beneficial. They may not choose a mentor who isn't loaded, but this being so, the emotional attachment is heartfelt.

If diamonds are a girl's best friend,
and a man's is his dog,
which sex is the cleverer?

16 MAY

May 16 makes a splash, likes a riot and is a fool for love. There are two main things for Mr and Mrs lemon meringue pie – sex and talk. The talk comes first, it's the meringue. Then you get to the sex, oodles of syrupy, delicious lemon cream. You can always spot a May 16 in any room. It's the person whose eyes are constantly darting across the assembly, looking for someone new to play with.

This is a fun day, but a rum day. Subject to enthusiasms, for people as well as ideas, these individuals simply get irritatingly sidetracked. They can be gazing deep into a new conquest's dilated pupils, talking of love, plans and even presents. (May 16 likes to give a lover something sparkly to remember them by, so if they are rich expect a diamond, and if they are poor, gold and silver ribbons.) And the next day, when there should be an after dalliance telephone call, they are in fact off somewhere else gazing deep into another wide-eyed faunette. These girls and boys can't help it.

These sybarites can be induced to stay a little longer by bribery of the senses. If a partner does something in bed that is new and exciting, then they will come back for more. Ration it a little, and like Sheherezade, who spun stories for 1001 nights to keep her husband from chopping off her head, and May 16 may just keep on coming.

They have extra-sensitive ear lobes and they like to have them stroked, kissed and maybe licked with little circular movements of the tongue. Try placing the tips of your fingers at the base of their throat, just where the pulse is and gently, gently stroking. Rub the vertebrae at the middle of the spine. May 16 are good lovers, swift and sweet, but they like to be worked on rather than working hard themselves.

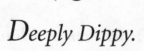

Deeply Dippy.

(Right Said Fred)

BODY

On an enchanted scented evening May 16 will be at their best. Both sexes adore the perfume of roses – blooming the day they were born – and their scent calms and excites them. Prepare rose water by adding drops of rose oil to a bottle of water, shaking vigorously. Pour it into bowls around the room, with some floating rose petals. Pick blooms from the garden (shop-bought have little perfume), and put a vase in each room. Use rose essence on strips of ribbon tied around chair legs, curtains and door handles, or draped over a warm radiator.

MIND

'He slipped four doves, whose wings were saturate with scents all different in kind … these doves wheeling in circles round let fall … a shower of sweet perfumery, drenching, bathing both clothes and furniture.' (Xenophanes, The Settler of Alexis)

DATESHARE
Liberace, singer, entertainer, much loved for his gorgeous stage clothes and the candelabra on his piano. Sadly died of an AIDS-related illness. **Olga Korbut**, Soviet Olympic triple gold-medal winning gymnast. **Janet Jackson**, sister to Michael, singer, songwriter. **Debra Winger**, Hollywood actress. **Christian Lacroix**, French fashion designer. **Gabriela Sabatini**, champion tennis player.

MAY 17

BODY

Lavender induces sweet sleep, calm and well-being, so for a change why not eat it? Talented May 17 should delight in Victorian lavender honey ice cream. Take 90ml lavender honey, 450ml milk, 125g caster sugar, 120ml double cream, a few drops vanilla essence and 5 egg yolks. Combine milk, honey, cream, vanilla and half the sugar; bring to boil in saucepan, stirring constantly. Beat egg yolks with remaining sugar until foamy, then strain boiling mixture over eggs, stir over hot water until smooth. Pour mixture into container and freeze. Just before frozen, take out, beat and replace in freezer.

MIND

Sometimes it seems a good idea to do nothing and nothing is good if it's surrounded by something. May 17 should guard against a tendency, however, to drift along in happy inertia, because later there will be regrets.

DATESHARE

Sugar Ray Leonard, *world welterweight, junior middleweight, middleweight boxing champion.* **Dennis Hopper**, *film actor, director,* Blue Velvet. **Birgit Nilsson**, *Swedish soprano.* **Ayatollah Khomeini**, *Iranian Shiite religious leader came to power after Shah of Iran.*

M any young ones live their lives as rock chicks and rockers, outrageous, party-obsessed and careless of tomorrow. Sometimes they are weighed down by the cares of the world – and the number of ear-rings in one ear – but generally they are decent, socially concerned individuals who want to change the world for the better.

May 17 is full of good intentions, but often fails to see them through. This doesn't matter, because their ambitions may be

unattainable and the sadness lies not in the wanting but the impossibility of their goals.

Many people born on this day find comfort in water. They long to mess about in boats, or dip their feet in a rippling river watching the willows stir in the current. (Willows are a Taurean tree.) But because life can't be spent splashing in the paddling-pool, many individuals choose a water sign as their lifelong mate, in particular Pisces, whose spirituality appeals to the finer side of this sensous beast.

Like most Taureans, this little number is good at making money and handling it. If the sensible side of their nature dominates, they are excellent accountants, made more excellent by the fact that they bother to discover what the businesses which they are handling are about. Or the characteristics and talents of their personal clients. (By now the multiple ear-ring situation has disappeared.)

Females born on this day have strong artistic talents. Their houses are usually interesting and splashily decorated, by their own hand. The men have similar tastes, often excel in carpentry and woodwork, sometimes becoming internationally successful furniture makers. Both sexes are happiest turning their talent into their livelihood, partly because they don't respond to corporate rules with any alacrity.

Privately both sexes are passionate and tend to stay with one partner for their whole lives. Ask them sixty years after their wedding day how they feel about each other and the radiance is still there.

I'd do anything for love ∽
But I won't do that.

(Meat Loaf)

18 May

These all-rounders can always find a project to make them happy. May 18 is one of the best adjusted days in the year. They are good achievers, often ambitious but can also make do with what they've got. Slimmer, too, than most Taureans, they are too busy with their hands, making things about the house, to need them filled with doughnuts and too busy with their brains thinking up new schemes, to yearn for a chocolate biscuit.

They rarely suffer from depression. Their Tarot gives the 18th card in the Major Arcana as The Moon, which represents a world of dreams and emotions, sensitivity, empathy and spiritual understanding. In the office they are honourable colleagues, resisting any temptation to curry favour. With nasty bosses these individuals keep their counsel, but won't go along with bullying or meanness. If these elements rear their ugly heads, expect people born on this day to challenge authority in a way that seriously endangers and probably scuppers the pompous, arrogant ass in power.

If things don't go well at work, it's not usually May 18 who gets rounded up into the redundancy net. But they may decide to take up the offer anyway and bunk off. Partners beware. The independent soul in this star may decide to take its glitter elsewhere once their surroundings seem compromised.

If this happens, May 18 usually finds it easy to get another job, but more likely will choose to get going alone. Who better to work for than themselves, and why should their talent go to profit somebody else? Capable of enormous hard work, they should find great success, but must monitor their relationship with the computer. The mouse potato lurks on this day, and a regular fifteen hours at a stretch narrows everybody's horizon.

But most of these scrumptious brandy snaps make delicious knowing, everybody's most sought after star with just the right crunch and sophisticated liqueur allure.

Body

This earth creature needs daylight and may suffer lethargy and headaches without it. Light is as much a nutrient as food and water, yet few realise how much is absorbed by our bodies and used in metabolic processes. Artificial light is inferior, lacking the full spectrum of daylight's ultra-violet rays and has been blamed for a number of ailments. The easiest way to sort this out is to make sure that each day, preferably before the sun has risen to the mid-heavens, you spend at least half an hour sitting and relaxing somewhere in the open, preferably with green grass and trees.

Mind

Don't be tempted to elongate your working day and start at 5 or 6am just to catch more computer time. The early bird may catch the worms, but who needs worms?

Dateshare

John Paul II, *current pope.* **Margot Fonteyn**, *wondrous British ballet dancer.* **Toyah Wilcox**, *singer, actress.* **Bertrand Russell**, *British philosopher,* Principia Mathematica, *Nobel prize-winner for literature.* **Nicholas II**, *last Russian Tzar, murdered with his family.*

All work and no play
makes Jack a dull boy –
and Jill a rich widow.

BODY

Bald people look great. Try to accept it. If you must attempt to combat a disappearing crowning glory, some men swear by lying on a slanted board for ten minutes a day with the head hanging down to encourage nourishment from the blood to reach the scalp. Once or twice a week, use mild shampoo containing natural ingredients such as seaweed or nettle extract. As a pre-wash conditioner add six drops of coconut oil, jojoba or almond oil and massage into wet hair and scalp. Wrap head in warm towel, (replace every fifteen minutes) and let the heat aid absorption for an hour.

MIND

Breathing exercises clear the mind. Breathe in and out slowly, count one, in and out again, count two. Count only on the out breath. If thoughts come crowding into your mind, push them aside and start counting again.

DATESHARE

Eric Burden, singer, The Animals, 'We Gotta Get Out of This Place'. **James Fox**, British actor, well-known for royal performances. **Edward de Bono**, British physician, developed concept of lateral thinking. **Lady Nancy Astor**, American-born politician wife of William. **Grace Jones**, Jamaican-American actress, androgynous icon. **Peter Townshend**, singer, songwriter, The Who. **Malcolm X**, African-American activist, assassinated.

The oddity about May 19 is its occasional psychic ability, a rarity amongst people born under the sign of Taurus. The child will have inexplicable perception flashes. Initially they may be dismissed, because these creatures are steady and sensible, the last type you associate with such capacities. Many hide their ability because it embarrasses them. Other, more highly developed individuals can develop their psychic capacities to a high degree, using them to help themselves and others. Some can even foretell problems, but usually, because libido is their energiser, they foretell love. If May 19 matchmakes for you, take it seriously. They're probably introducing you to your future spouse.

Cyprus and the Greek Islands are cradles for our far-seeing lover's destiny. They may also find what they seek in Ireland's fairy hills. Here they sense what ordinary mortals can't. The green beckoning smile of Ireland's Queen Mab, the voice of a lost oracle.

At work, most colleagues will not sense this power in the bull. Instead they just think it's luck. Luck can be a lottery win, a killing on the stockmarket, or, more often, a competition and a good horse. Stick with this guy or girl. Take their tip. Let the star shake some gold dust into your hand.

Less lucky creatures may be as bald and shiny as any crystal ball. That's only, of course, if you see it as less lucky. The high domed Taurean head looks distinguished with little hair, but many refuse to take this comfort and suffer bad bouts of 'baldophrenia'. Common symptoms include thinking you hear voices commenting on your lack of hair, looking in mirrors at the back of the head to check what's growing, nights devoted more to restoring cream than lust and unfettered envy of hairy people. Baldophrenics think their sexual advances are rejected because of no hair, forgetting that it's seductive air waves, not the hair waves, that matter.

Millions of angels are at God's command. (Billy Graham)

20 MAY

This is the day of the serial charmer, no creature in the universe is more charming. Both sexes are vigorous, funny and definitely good in bed and many have smooth, golden skin and thick, very touchable hair, which lovers dream about ever afterwards.

With romance, as with most other things in life, they have a touch which seems so sure that others gain confidence simply from just being around May 20 and not necessarily in their beds. Although that too. Essentially kind, these creatures of pleasure have difficulty with their own short attention span. Boredom sets in like a squelching cloud, and they just want to skip off and pursue a new quarry. But they truly don't like to hurt people's feelings, so spend hours devising plausible excuses to move on.

They really shouldn't bother. Nobody ever believes the story about not being good enough for a partner, or the one about an old lover who's come back out of the blue and must be attended to, for a short while, or their shadow will cast a pall over the current relationship. It just means that May 20 is a fickle fancier.

Kindness is nevertheless a trump card for our sweet, sexy May 20. They have good, close friends, sometimes with members of the opposite sex which they manage to keep platonic. Amazing for such a tactile star.

They adore their children, even if they have swapped the other parent for a new model. They see to the little ones' physical needs and will always be there when needed. And they try to get on with the separated partner, for the sake of the kids, and also because they retain affection for all ex-lovers.

If a friend is in trouble, this creature will also always come to the rescue, devoting energy and money to the problem. And solving it, even if it's to their own detriment.

BODY
People born under this sign often have a slow metabolism, the last thing May 20 needs when sex means a need for physical dynamism. Sometimes these people do wonder just how they are going to summon up the energy for the next amorous encounter, and consider whether a night in bed alone might not be more fun. If you can't, try a lemon bath. The essential oil is mainly produced in Spain, acts as an invigorating tonic and wipes away fatigue. Scatter a few drops in the bath once it's run. Traditional conditions benefited by lemon include cuts (it arrests bleeding), insect bites and stings, stomach acidity, rheumatism.

MIND
Excessive addiction to habit can become restricting. May 20 should avoid the tediousness of the same breakfast each day, the same clothes and music, the same place at lunch with the same workmates or friends.

DATESHARE
Cher, singer, Hollywood actress. Joe Cocker, singer. Socrates, Greek philosopher. James Stewart, film actor. Moshe Dayan, Israeli defence minister.

If you aren't going all the way, why go at all? (Joe Namath)

MAY 21

May 21 people are leaders. They are particularly good at borrowing money and handling it, so at work they are often employed to pull a company together and get it in budget. Men and women have none of the nervous reactions to finances, common to so many born on other days.

If they are in debt, they don't wallow, but work and trade their way out of it, thinking up brinkmanship, creative ideas, taking advice from the best, then modifying the whole cocktail to create a drop-dead plan. And amazingly, they manage to be good fun – at least for those they like.

This superstarette has a couple of problems. They can't understand others' lack of interest in what they do, dismissing them arrogantly as anoraks, and anoraknophobia, as you may know, means living in a narrow little circle where people are either deemed to be for you or against you.

These individuals are also unbelievably vulnerable to flattery and can't judge a person with a mile-long oil slick behind them as anything but wonderfully loyal, unless their dear old mum and dad have the wit to warn against them. It's worth remembering that Mr and Miss May 21 always listen to Mummy and Daddy. So really dedicated courtiers must pay a lot of attention to the parents.

Both sexes are often blessed with good looks which they maintain with careful dieting and exercise. Cellulite is a matter of life or death to these babes. They are always on the go because somebody has told them that sitting down promotes orange peel thighs. Find the men on the squash court and golf course, networking furiously while attempting to win – or lose if they are playing their boss. Younger men, proud of their 28-inch waists, lounge glamorously at the juice bar of a fashionable gym, sometimes organising team events against neighbouring villages or rival businesses.

BODY

Without sex May 21 grows depressed and physically unwell. These creatures adore having their feet stroked, a tickled toe and they're yours. Foot massage was practised by Indian masters of the erotic long before the west was out of woad. It's arousing, and rejuvenates the body's energies. Tired feet communicate their unhappiness to the rest of the body. Take May 21's foot, holding it under the ball, with thumbs resting on top, at the base of the toes. Exert gentle pressure, pushing the thumbs up towards the top of the foot. Then move gently and firmly outwards in a fan movement. Repeat five times.

MIND

They are fixed folk, shying away from emotional experience in unchartered areas. Yet May 21 genuinely needs fresh personal stimulus, something or somebody who has nothing to do with their work. This will bring great joy.

DATESHARE

Fats Waller, jazz pianist, composer. Harold Robbins, author of deeply sexual books including The Carpetbaggers. Armand Hammer, businessman, environmentalist friend of Prince Charles, promoted US/USSR and US/China trade. André Sakharov, Russian physicist, dissident. Mary Robinson, Irish president.

We are all in the gutter
but some of us
are looking at the stars.
(Oscar Wilde)

EARTH

22 MAY

This flirtatious flitter attracts lovers like ants to a strawberry jam sandwich. Indeed May 22 people can get so bogged down beneath the weight of their admirers that much of their time is spent avoiding them. Pretending helplessness, they may appeal to a gallant rescuer, establishing one of those sudden intimacies so characteristic of this air sign, then drop their newly devoted companion without a backward glance.

Some of these people have a steadier nature and will fall in love for ever, but if that happens they will boast about their lifelong commitment, drawing everybody's attention to it as a wondrous thing to be admired.

If they have children, they will take a dramatically patriarchal or matriarchal role, fiercely protective and supportive. They make good, caring parents but do prefer their offspring to be at the brainy, beautiful or eyecatching end of the gene pool.

If children don't come along, this person often surrounds him or herself with unusual pedigree dogs or perhaps 'designer' farm animals such as cashmere goats. Whatever they choose, there will always be something of the collector about May 22.

Some turn this talent for collecting into a profession and can be found working in specialist areas. Others use their flair for publicity to get on in the media, particularly advertising and newspapers, where their epic energy is greatly admired. Most of these will continue to collect in private – particularly something which is to do with numbers. May 22 adores categorising, making files and putting lists into computers. And, indeed, playing expertly with computers which appeal to their sometimes egocentric, directional natures.

Structures as well as figures fascinate them. Some may be trainspotter types, pursuing engine numbers and dreaming of destinations, or mapping waterways and the movements of the stars. Less commonly, other May 22 people introduce grand new artistic or philosophical structures to the world.

Whom we love best, to them we can say the least.

BODY

This individual is sometimes an on-the-hoof eater, cramming in bread and butter, chocolate biscuits, crisps and (no, honestly) pickles. In consequence, they frequently suffer constipation and stomach pains. Figs can help. For centuries the medicinal use of figs has been recommended to treat constipation, liverishness and to restore vitality. Japanese scientists at the Institute of Physical and Chemical Research in Tokyo have even isolated an anti-cancer chemical from figs and used it to treat cancer patients. Put the figs in a bowl of mixed dried fruit and snack on them, not the biscuits and pickles.

MIND

Concentrate on fewer projects at one time. This helps you plot the sequence of your actions and ensure that at the end of the day you don't collapse in a heap with everything only three-quarters done.

DATESHARE

Richard Wagner, opera composer, wrote music on favourite rug he also used for love. **Lord (Laurence) Olivier**, British actor, married Vivien Leigh, Joan Plowright. **Sir Arthur Conan Doyle**, British writer, Sherlock Holmes. **T-Bone Walker**, blues singer, guitarist. **Susan Strasberg**, stage & film actress. **Charles Aznavour**, French singer, songwriter.

S peed and a longing for change are the characteristics of this individual. They talk fast, often with a winning charm and adore making deals. They put the fizz into conversation, but so keen are they on winning points that 'fact' can sometimes become a dirty word and dishonesty a virtue.

May 23 should be extremely careful of this last characteristic. Sharp-witted May 23 often spots the shady area between truth and fiction and bamboozle colleagues, not always wittingly, but often with disastrous results. Frequently ignoring the maxim 'Neither a borrower nor a lender be', some openly regard banks and building societies as simply there to lend money, and they are remarkably good at getting it. Others are willing to put money into flash enthusiasms. At best, this makes May 23 a millionaire. At medium … infuriating. At worst … there's a problem.

Not always the most reliable lover, this individual has the sort of sparkling charm that can breach the toughest citadel and when they stay put there is no date in the year which provides a better companion. They are sexually adventurous, with a deep generosity to others. Almost nothing shocks them and they delight in theatrical bedroom games, taking champagne, chocolates, pots of delicious ice cream, strawberries and other  tit-bits to the love nest. In consequence, because of the frequency of their loving, May 23 people may put on weight as will any companion fed with doughnuts and chocolate biscuits during the intermission.

Part child themselves, they make excellent parents, spending time and using their imagination on their children's toys, inventing games and songs and generally creating treasured memories. This individual doesn't harbour unsuitable ambitions for his or her children, and can be relied upon to back them if schools complain.

Some people born on this date become great inventors, benefitting mankind. Most are glamorous, capable of inspiring personal affection and if they become famous, the general public will always love them.

Actions speak louder than words.

24 MAY

The psychology of this date is oddly self-effacing, a characteristic of Gemini, which is the sign of the Twins. Poor May 24 doesn't know what it thinks, can see both sides of the question and so adopts the irritating 'no you choose' habit. They convince themselves that letting others decide holiday destinations and which colours to decorate a room is a sign of generosity. But this little cabbage has tough leaves which hide an even tougher heart, often brimming with resentment at another's decision they secretly dislike. Worse still, when the wrong choice is made there may be days of sulking until a companion works a mindreading miracle, and changes that choice. So, when dining out with May 24, resist pleas to recommend, thus avoiding the hissed 'But you know I never eat eggs'.

 Those born today must antidote this essential laziness, cease procrastinating, and develop their problem solving skills. They are nature's transmitters, can bring a glow to a room as well as gloom, and in difficult situations May 24 will surprise everybody with resorcefulness and bravery.

These individuals are clever with their hands and brimming with creative intelligence. So when the lights fuse, or the video breaks down, when the roof is pouring water into every bedroom, the boat's engine has packed up and the car lights won't work, May 24 can usually fix it.

Similarly, if someone is sick, this person often shows extraordinary energy, devoting long hours to nursing and, perhaps more importantly, to thought about the symptoms and how to alleviate them. Not usually impressed by authority figures, in particular doctors, May 24 will read every book on cure and cause, not necessarily accepting doctors' diagnoses and always asking for another opinion.

Like all Geminis, those born today thrive in the company of others and should take care not to choose professions – writing, composing, some forms of research – which could isolate them.

BODY
Because of their quick movements and physical tension, people born on this day tend to suffer from back injury and strain. Do heed advice not to bend from the waist to pick up heavy items. Instead, crouch, pick up, then lift as you rise. Do find a chair to work in that supports your back properly, which doesn't mean you work with head poked forward. Do choose a flat, hard mattress, preferably with no pillows, or just one if you must. And if you can, try to lie flat on the floor for ten minutes each day. Better still, take a swim.

MIND
Sometimes dislike for authority can get out of hand. At best this results in infuriating confrontations – frequently your fault. At worst it can lead to legal wrangling, time-consuming letters and a general anger overdose.

DATESHARE
Queen Victoria, the 'Grandmother of Europe', a sixty-four year reign over the largest empire in history. **Priscilla Presley**, Hollywood star, widow of Elvis Presley. **Bob Dylan**, singer, songwriter, poet.

Isn't your life extremely flat

∼ With nothing to grumble at?

(WS Gilbert)

MAY 25

People born on this day must take care of their hands which could develop joint stiffness and even arthritis later in life. This is particularly important as many May 25 people rely on their hands for work, including, as we have discussed, cookery and decorating, but also music and writing. Bach Flower Rescue Remedy cream is especially good for stiff fingers, aching hands and any small cuts. Available from most health stores, it is made up from impatiens (Impatiens glandulifera), clematis (Clematis vitalba), rock rose (Helianthemum nummularium), cherry plum (Prunus cerasifera) and star of Bethlehem (Ornithogalum umbellatum).

☾

MIND

Sometimes what you fear most is a lessening of the creative urge which is so natural to people born on this day. Try listening to classical music. It's a great refurbisher of creative energy.

DATESHARE

Sir Ian McKellan, British stage & film actor, gay rights activist. **Josip Broz Tito**, Yugoslavian dictator, unified Yugoslavia. **Miles Davis**, jazz trumpeter, band leader.

May 25 people like doing things to please others and they have wonderful domestic skills. They often choose cookery as their way of being nice to people. This individual has all the lightness and passion for summery things which reflect his and her birthday, so expect each dish to look as good as it tastes.

Both men and women will develop skills for particular types of cookery at certain times in their lives. Younger individuals dream of India and the mysteries of China, spicing pieces of meat with cumin or ginger, the merest hint of coconut, and a touch of saffron for glamour. Vegetarians will concoct exquisite temptations, cucumber with yoghurt and a dash of black pepper, garnished with fresh mint leaves, swede turned into a heap of sunshine. The men may concentrate on puddings and  sweetmeats good enough to tempt an emporer's lack-lustre appetite. Expect homemade vanilla ice cream, strewn with crystallised violets, grapefruit crushed with ice and crème de menthe. Above all, expect this date to change his or her passions for cookery with the changing seasons.

Other domestic skills which dominate this day are decorating and sewing. May 25's ideal room will be rich in colour. When in doubt, paint a room yellow, is the maxim. But marvellous blues which reflect the changing sky and calm the soul are also a favourite. Expect pieces of embroidery to glow from chaircovers and rugs, with delicate flowers picked out on tables and bed linen.

Those born on this day have a powerful moral code, and while they may be generous with others who do not, do not expect them to waver in their own judgment of what is right and wrong. Where this moral sense is overdeveloped, some May 25 people can become tyrannical about other people's behaviour. In extreme circumstances this leads to an unforgiving nature and a desire to withdraw from the world, which can be difficult for family and friends.

You've heard of the three ages of man: youth, middle age, and 'you're looking wonderful'.

(Francis Joseph, Cardinal Spellman)

AIR

26 MAY

This date walks on the wild side and fears nothing. Dangerous, desirable and trouble all the way, few people can resist the magnetism of May 26. Yet it's a mistake to think this individual is sexually greedy. There is finesse in the flirting, secrecy in the erotic adventure.

May 26 will see someone at a party, form a connection with one glance, then turn away until at the very end they magically appear by the newly chosen partner, who has been secretly waiting – but unsure – for this moment.

So what is life like with this Prince and Princess of Dark Desires? Thrilling and agonising. Most do settle down in the end because they get tired of all the tears and pleading letters. And they do suffer some guilt. But they are innately unfaithful, always alert to the sudden lurch of interest in an attractive stranger, and always

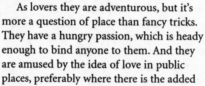

amused by their ability to catch a glance, hold it and trade on it.

As lovers they are adventurous, but it's more a question of place than fancy tricks. They have a hungry passion, which is heady enough to bind anyone to them. And they are amused by the idea of love in public places, preferably where there is the added danger of discovery. In fact this creature's ideal fantasy is a chance meeting on a train, naturally a European train with those high steps up to carriages which have curtained compartments. As the train rumbles through the night, the two strangers will kiss and wrap their bodies around each other. Then dawn comes. The train pulls into a far away station and one of them is gone …

Such wildness is romantic and appealing, but these characteristics can border on the anti-social, even criminal, and although many devotees will continue to admire, the reality and results of May 26's impetuous behaviour may be less pleasant.

BODY
May 26 is attracted to alcohol. Young people born on this day can drink, dance, drink again, stay up all night, then go to work fresh as a newly opened buttercup. They also have phenomenal concentration, so the indulgences of the night before seem to barely touch them. But as the clock ticks on this behaviour catches up. Some may find they are drinking to keep themselves going, and then drinking because they can't start without it. Control the alcohol intake before alcoholism hits. Remember, reformed alcoholics can't drink and who wants to grow old without the pleasures of chilled champagne?

MIND
Sometimes it seems that everybody wants something from you, that people won't leave you alone until you have satisfied them. Try to spend time alone. Be self-sufficient. It will steady your mind and clear it.

DATESHARE
John Wayne, movie star. **Peggy Lee**, singer, songwriter, 'Fever'. **Queen Mary**, 20th century British monarch who adored shopping, but sometimes forgot to pay. **Peter Cushing**, British actor.

If I told you you have a beautiful body,
would you hold it against me?

(David Fisher)

BODY

Although basically vigorous, these individuals may be vulnerable to allergies. In particular those who live in the country can suffer slight asthma because of crop burning or the widespread cultivation of rape, that virulent yellow invader of our agricultural land. Children are particularly vulnerable to asthma from rape (Brassica napus) and should be kept away from it as much as is practical. Sadly life in all major industrial centres promotes asthma. Not much you can do, except keep away. But one in twenty asthmatics is sensitive to sulphites used in food preservatives (E220-E227), particularly cheap wine, so it's worth monitoring alcohol intake.

MIND

In numerology the 27th is ruled by the number 9 (2+7 =9), which is powerful with other numbers. (Any number added to 9 yields that same number, eg 5+9=14, 4+1=5.) Power is only good if used wisely.

DATESHARE

Henry Kissinger, *German born US presidential adviser, Nobel Peace Prize-winner.* **Vincent Price**, *horror film actor.* **Georges Rouault**, *French Expressionist painter.* **Isadora Duncan**, *modern dance pioneer, strangled when her shawl caught in the wheel of her sports car.*

May 27 people are unusually single-minded Geminis, displaying none of the flibbertigibbet characteristics of their sign, remarkably clear cut about their aims and capabilities. Look for them in social professions where they have a responsibility to direct and help others and you will find excellent teachers, sharp-witted doctors and social workers who show immense understanding and patience with their cases.

Many have an oddly attractive and unusual take on the world, a sort of child's truthful eye, which helps promote that instant intimacy, valuable in any profession where power is wielded. Most are sufficiently modest to avoid pomposity, but some do have the Gemini self-seeking streak and can't keep it at bay. And you can't tease these individuals out of it. Another Gemini characteristic is inability to take criticism so this particular May 27 person will lack the self-knowledge common to most

individuals born on this day and unless something amazing happens, they remain convinced of their superior position in the universe.

Women born on this day make the most inspirational teachers, spend much time and energy bringing pleasure and understanding to their pupils, whether it be in a school or at work where they are in charge. Less professionally motivated women are always ready to offer solace to others in the office, and at home they are marvellous, funny and inventive wives, mothers and daughters.

Some men tend to provoke ultra-strong reactions amongst their colleagues, which they find puzzling, but in general can use this to the good because it means they are always listened to and their opinions never ignored.

May 27 is often a great reader and follower of the arts and much of their private time is devoted to these pursuits. Great personal comfort can always be found by these people in a piece of favourite poetry or music, and simply listening or reading always renews their spiritual strength.

Morality is simply the attitude we adopt towards people we personally dislike.

(Oscar Wilde)

AIR

28 MAY

Some people born today suffer lack of determination and over self-criticism. They have grand ideas, start extraordinary projects, but then, when obstacles arise, just give up. These problems can be rectified. May 28 people with a poor self-image may have been unhappy in childhood or lost someone close when very young. Perhaps they have never acknowledged their sadness. Sometimes it's hard to take a look at what makes you weep, but these things really are part of the human lot and once May 28 understands that tragedy comes to everyone, he or she will gain new inner strength.

These individuals have lots of original flair and may find that colleagues simply don't understand them. It's important to be able to put new ideas over fluently and to the right people. A little business training may come in useful here but if colleagues remain unimpressed and stuck in their corporate mud, May 28 should just move on. Some businesses are so moribund and self-congratulatory they will forever be blind to the fact that May 28 has something important to say. Remember this.

There's an inventor's streak in both sexes born on this day and a genuine problem-solver's talent. May 28 will take a fresh look at something run-of-the-mill, identify an area of profitable change, and go for it. Other people will then always mutter: 'Why didn't I think of that? It was so obvious.' But everybody has their chance.

Look for this individual in small breakthrough companies, such as mail order catalogues, design outfits, successful shops, rock groups. Find them also in the local community fundraising for church roofs and for charities, with enormous strength of purpose and effectiveness.

Socially May 28 is always the person who gives the theme party that works rather than the ones that are fantastically tedious and embarrassing. For this individual, everybody really does turn up wearing green, looking glamorous and feeling at ease.

BODY
A lot of people born on this day like to smoke and drink, generally have a good time and frequently fall into bed in the early hours of the morning without cleaning their teeth. Such careless behaviour costs future smiles and it's better to grow old with most of your body intact than drop bits along the way. A brush at the start and end of the day is not enough, which everybody knows really. Get a proper toothbrush, go to the dentist for regular check-ups, take the dentist's advice, look after your teeth and the smiles will look after themselves.

ॐ

MIND
Great loss and sadness is nobody's fault. It's just the way the world is constructed. There's no need to talk about your feelings, if that is not your way, but you must acknowledge them to yourself.

DATESHARE
Gladys Knight, soul singer, songwriter. **Dietrich Fischer-Dieskau**, wonderful German baritone and lieder singer. **Joseph Guillotin**, French physician and guillotine inventor. **Sondra Locke**, Hollywood star, ex-lover of Clint Eastwood.

I am the master of my fate,

I am the captain of my soul.

(William E Henley)

BODY

Quite surprisingly May 29 suffers from nervous fear, panics that seem to come from nowhere. Both sexes need to understand that such fear is based on their own disposition rather than a genuine material cause. The famous Dr Edward Bach addressed the need to find remedies for fear, and many other problems, in his travels through Wales and South England, searching for curative flowering plants and trees. Just two drops of Rescue Remedy in a glass of water will do much to calm the mind and ease the fluttering heart.

MIND

Nobody likes to imagine they have lived a life for nothing and with no result. There is a brilliant talent resting in you, and you will be deprived of great pleasure if you fail to search it out.

DATESHARE

John F Kennedy, *US president, assassinated in Dallas, Texas.* **Annette Bening**, *film actress.* **Latoya Jackson**, *singer, writer, sister to Michael Jackson.* **Charles II**, *British king, master of 39 mistresses, patron of the composer Purcell, credited with reviving British theatre, music and architecture.*

The roll-on-roll-off style of this star baby gives the word 'effortless' a new meaning. Like everybody born under this sign, Gemini's child is laden with charm and the kind of talent that smoothes paths. But May 29 people often prefer to lie about doing very little, merely *talking* about future plans.

As lovers they are often spoiled for choice, with natural good looks to boost their chances. Both sexes wait for an approach. They may see someone they lust after, perhaps make a telephone call and talk charmingly, but then leave the running to others. Such languidness can be very appealing, and many of May 29th's prospective partners think this character's lack of sexual energy and effort is down to good manners, nice behaviour in a rapacious world. But, hey, it's just inertia.

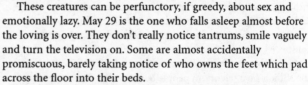

These creatures can be perfunctory, if greedy, about sex and emotionally lazy. May 29 is the one who falls asleep almost before the loving is over. They don't really notice tantrums, smile vaguely and turn the television on. Some are almost accidentally promiscuous, barely taking notice of who owns the feet which pad across the floor into their beds.

Nor are they domestically alert. Nothing houseproud here. Both sexes will drop clothes on the floor, leave the milk out, lose the bath plug, and let others sort out the consequences.

Work, however, brings out the lode star in them. It may be dormant, but when polished it burns with a fierce fire and May 29 people can become defenders of the corporate faith, the people who changes things. Up against it, there is nothing they respond to as well as a challenge and drawn to dramatic situations, they will find dramatic solutions. In these circumstances their lack of material acquisitiveness, sometimes unwordliness, stands them in great stead, and allows them to concentrate to good effect. Success brings generosity of spirit and it's worth remembering that changeable Gemini is always open to reform.

Sex is a conversation

~

carried out by other means.

(Peter Ustinov)

30 MAY

ay 30 is loaded with talent, but things come so easily to this character that they sometimes have trouble following them through. This character talks a streak, but quite often it's just simply painting grand ideas in the sky. They soon flit to something else.

This can be irritating to those around them particularly people whom May 30 has persuaded to come in with their future plans. It is important not to talk so much and concentrate on actions, because some of these ideas really are grand and could bring success.

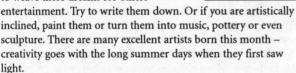

Some may just be dreamers, without the practical streak which can be a true Gemini characteristic. In this case, it's best to weave these dreams for others' entertainment. Try to write them down. Or if you are artistically inclined, paint them or turn them into music, pottery or even sculpture. There are many excellent artists born this month – creativity goes with the long summer days when they first saw light.

Remember that both sexes are often bedevilled by uncertainty about their own talent. All people feel this way. The successful among us acknowledge their feelings and get on with it anyway. The less successful allow themselves to be paralysed by it and frequently become bitter, even envious of others who aren't.

May 30 is usually quick-witted, with a rapid grasp of figures. Although they are not life's natural accountants, they understand control of the budget makes everybody less vulnerable to the dark shadow of financial worries. They may also use this talent to make money for others as well as themselves and can be very useful problem solvers in the financial area for friends or anyone whose business needs sorting out.

And when they have made their money, what does May 30 spend it on? This air sign loves to travel. They may also enjoy fast travel toys, their own aeroplanes, fast cars and of course big, beautiful motorbikes.

BODY

Fast-paced May 30 often gets run down. People born on this day should develop an interest in alternative medicine, because enthusiasm often develops into health-conscious habits. Whatever happens, it's wise to remember that trace minerals are important to well-being and without them you will feel very run down. Zinc, manganese and iodine are just a few. Zinc from carrots, peas and nuts. Manganese from wholegrain breads and cereals. Iodine from sea vegetables such as kelp and dulse. Also from seafood. Don't use extra salt in your food as a means of obtaining iodine.

MIND

When you have a really cracking idea, sit down with a sheet of paper and write how it would work, and why it is different. This stops you dissipating it with talk and helps in the execution.

DATESHARE

Peter Carl Fabergé, *Russian designer, goldsmith and jeweller to the Tzar and his family.* **Paola Fendi**, *Italian fashion designer.* **Mel Blanc**, *voice of Looney Tunes animation, Bugs Bunny and Porky Pig.* **Peter the Great**, *Russian Tzar, 6ft 8ins tall, designer and builder of St Petersburg, lived anonymously in Holland for over a year to learn western building techniques.* **Benny Goodman**, *jazz & classical clarinetist, band leader.*

Security is all mortal's chief enemy.

(Ellen Terry)

BODY

Many people born on this day enjoy physical exercise, in particular, dancing. If you don't, you should try it. Dance is better than psychotherapy, better than dieting, better than anti-depressants. Experts recommend it for promoting joy, easing stress and tension, toning up the body, honing the mind and fostering the most pleasurable of human contact. Michael Argyle, Emeritus Professor of Social Psychology at Wolfson College, Oxford says that anybody who involves themselves in dancing, whether it be Scottish dancing, disco, waltzing or Latin American, will find their fears slowly eased, their sex-life improved and their happiness enhanced.

૨૭

MIND

The depressive streak can sometimes haunt you. Make sure you get outside as much as possible, preferably somewhere green, where you can breathe the fresh air. Seek out water, always calming for the depressed.

DATESHARE

Clint Eastwood, *Hollywood star, heart-throb and alleged pushover for any nice, enthusiastic woman.* **Brooke Shields**, *Hollywood glamour puss, famous for her eyebrows.* **Walt Whitman**, *19th century poet, Leaves of Grass, free verse innovator.* **Joe Namath**, *football quarterback, model, actor.* **Rainer Werner Fassbinder**, *German master film director.*

Another day with strong sex appeal! So many of these summery people are just born for love and many of them find it with, earthy, cautious but emotionally true Virgo. May 31 often has a style that influences others, either in dress, speech or mannerism.

They are sure of what they want, and mostly pick partners for long-term love affairs. But there can sometimes be a deep-seated unhappiness which comes out in a depressive streak. As lovers they usually overcome this inner feeling of desperation, but should sometimes beware of the stardust in their eyes when they spot a new partner. It blinds May 31 to reality and they can be a pushover for anybody who fancies the idea of winning their heart.

People born on this day spend time thinking up treats for those they love. They adore sparkly things and like to buy them for others as well as themselves. Opals are the natural precious gem for this star sign, but some depressive May 31 people may not want a

traditionally unlucky stone. Amber may be a better choice, especially the lighter, clear amber, very near to orange, which is Gemini's favourite colour.

May 31st loves the gorgeous occasion. Expect both sexes to dress up whenever they get the chance. They will always prefer a lavish dinner to a picnic, champagne to a glass of chilled Australian white wine, velvet to jersey and high-heeled shoes to trainers.

Both sexes adore expensive perfume and frequently wear too much of it, particularly in bed, when they think an enormous squirt is all they need to launch the perfect night of love. Apart from this, expect May 31 to spend a deal of money on the bedroom. They think it the most important room in the house and will cover the bed in furs, silks and satins and put mirrors in places you wouldn't have thought possible.

Brevity is the soul of lingèrie.

(Dorothy Parker)

I JUNE

These individuals are extremely passionate about whatever they do, brave and experimental, in spite of inner doubts. This birthday provides the celebrated cook, the glamour goddess, the great romantic, and the top advertising executive.

The cook will specialise in something simple but exotic-sounding. They may rustle up frozen almond cream (made with 1½ pints of double cream, whipped, two egg whites, beaten until stiff,

caster sugar, pinch of salt, 4oz chopped toasted almonds and a large dash of Marsala, all beaten until stiff, then popped in the freezer for four hours). Or they may do something extraordinary with figs! There is always an innate sensuosity to whatever June 1 does.

The goddess purrs in silk, shows off her handspan waist and her shining hair. The god makes sure his credits are complemented by the tightest of jeans. The romantic looks on the bright side of life.

Most June 1 people escape the depression which plagues their star. Simply not understanding what depression is can be the best talent in business. Not easily intimidated, they think the best of colleagues and bosses, and have such sunny dispositions that everybody wants to promote them and they are never sacked. In particular this person shines in tense jobs such as advertising, or television, where success is based on those frail things, hunch and flair. If somebody rejects an idea, June 1 goes off and has another one.

This individual adores children, and is often happiest simply reading to them, singing with them and loving them. June 1 people may marry a few times, so there is a great chance they will have lots of children and step-children to care for. Quite a few won't marry and still have plenty of babies. Fertility is not usually this individual's problem, so much of June 1's life may be spent trying out different contraceptives with varying degrees of success.

If you can't say something nice, don't say it at all.

(*Thumper,* Bambi)

BODY

Both sexes born on this day have a sweet tooth. Many can't resist chocolate. June 1 should understand why craving comes so it can be resisted. There are several categories of chococraver. The first is the Sensuosity Snacker, someone who likes chocolate to accompany sex. Lots of sex equals lots of weight gain. Desperate desire equals a Michelin Man figure. Try peppermints. Try strawberries. Try keeping your mouth shut. The second is the Office Chocohog, who can't get through mid-morning conference without it. The third is the Weekend Wobbler. They indulge at weekends. It speaks for itself.

MIND

Tarot's card in the Major Arcana for June 1 is The Magician. Love Magic experts give this card the power of safe judgement in love matters. You will know when it's safe to trust a new partner.

DATESHARE

Marilyn Monroe, *probably the sexiest screen star Hollywood ever produced, sadly gave in to despair and died young.* **Brigham Young**, *Mormon leader, founded Salt Lake City, had seventeen wives and fifty-six children.* **Morgan Freeman**, *handsome, talented, stylish actor.* **Ron Wood**, *wild man of the Rolling Stones.* **Norman Foster**, *British architect.* **John Masefield**, *British poet laureate.*

There's something of the collector about this day, an unusual characteristic for the star sign. Perhaps it's the strong individualistic streak, combined with a pickiness and that restless energy which drives them always to look further for new delights.

June 2 may combine a love for travel with the collecting. But it is more likely to be home-grown. In some cases the collecting instinct is so highly developed that this individual becomes a successful dealer or even an expert in his or her chosen field. But it usually starts from small beginnings.

This individual has the magpie's love for pretty, often sparkling things, so the collection may be of Victorian and Edwardian glassware, which can still be found at cheap prices, yet respected enough to have its own gallery at the Victoria and Albert Museum. Or it may be precious and semi-precious stones, in which case June 2 can combine the collector's hunt while holidaying: in Scotland for quartz and amethyst; Wales for garnets; Cornwall for iron pyrites, (fools' gold) and in the Pennines for pretty green or white fluorite, which is often translucent in ultraviolet light.

It's not unlikely that June 2 may also become a people collector. They have complicated needs and many create a circle of lovers, all secret from each other, to answer the variety of demands. This pleases creatures born on this day, because they adore secrecy – it excites them – and will try to live their life laced with this clandestine commodity. Expect June 2 to confide in you, but swear you to silence. Expect private notes, or at work, messages on the e-mail that are coded so that only you understand.

Expect to get engaged to this character, but for nobody to know about it. Have a child and the event is not publicised. A wedding may be a secret adventure, suddenly dreamed up and accomplished.

It all adds up to an exciting life, full of surprises.

Few love to hear the sins they love to act.

(William Shakespeare, Pericles)

3 JUNE

June 3 is a great talker, which many people find relaxing as they don't have to do much themselves. People born on this day are often expert in their field and their talent for talking makes them great teachers, speech-makers, and excellent politicians.

Both sexes may be extremely idealistic, with a passion to make the world a better place and since they make inspiring leaders they are well equipped to achieve their goals. Apart from politics, find them in the army, medicine and the church, where they are inventive, brave and inspirational. Their talents can certainly bring fame.

At home, they are full of adventure and no family judges June 3 the boring relative they don't want to visit. On the contrary, this is one person everybody wants at gatherings, because this individual can makes things go with a swing. Women born today form strong friendships with their own sex, life-long best pals, who will bring them laughter and strength when they hit a rough patch. The men, too, are naturally sociable, and often very funny, in some cases so witty they can make a profession out of it. Both sexes make good club members, excellent at organising social occasions, dab hands at fundraising, and generally always welcome.

Just a few people born on this day tend towards vanity, with a domineering streak which means they don't so much want to lead as boss. They can become bullies, justifying themselves with all the disgusting self-pity common to this type. It's a moral duty not to look the other way, but to spot this type fast and slap it down before they become a complete pain and someone gets hurt.

June 3 hates to be ignored, to be made to feel they have no impact, and this may be the best way to handle difficult individuals born on this day. But beware a sometimes harsh reaction, disproportionate to the event.

BODY

Many people travel long distances to work, which pushes up the stress levels and exhausts them. Some relaxation exercises may help. First tense every muscle in your body, your jaws, eyes, arms, hands, chest, back, stomach, legs and feet. Hold the tension briefly, then silently say 'Relax and let go' and you breathe out … let your whole body relax … feel a wave of calm come over you as you stop tensing. Feel the relief. Gently close your eyes, take another deep breath, slowly breathe out and silently say 'Relax and let go'. For a few moments, let yourself drift more and more.

MIND

If you want to see who you'll marry, open the bedroom window and ask the new moon: 'I prithee, Good Moon, reveal to me this night to whom I'll wedded be.' You'll dream of your future spouse.

DATESHARE

Raoul Dufy, French painter, illustrator, muralist. **Tony Curtis**, Hollywood actor, famous drag performance in Some Like It Hot. **Suzi Quatro**, leather-clad singer, bass guitarist, songwriter. **Allen Ginsberg**, beat poet. **Josephine Baker**, dancer, devoted life to adopting children of various nationalities.

I wasn't really naked.
I simply didn't have any clothes on.

(Josephine Baker)

BODY

People born on this day work very hard, often at a computer and as a result they may suffer from eye strain, or simply tired eyes. It's important to get a computer with a properly contrasted screen, and to investigate the overhead lighting so that it doesn't bounce off the screen, causing glare. It's also important to get up and get away from the screen. Try to take a quick walk outside into the open air, preferably a place where green plants and trees are growing. Close your eyes here for five minutes to rest them.

MIND

There is a tender heart lurking in most June 4 breasts. Let it dictate your actions. Calculation and taking control may feel safe, but what the heart says is wise and often brings greater happiness.

DATESHARE

Dennis Weaver, *TV and film actor.* **Bruce Dern**, *film actor and father of Laura Dern.* **Oliver Nelson**, *jazz composer, alto tenor saxophonist.* **Joseph Smith**, *American religious leader and founder of the Mormon movement.* **Sir Thomas Mackenzie**, *New Zealand statesman.*

This character is nice to be with, always fun and seems a good sort. But you can't trust this bundle of contradictions as far as you can throw it. She says 'Darling', he says 'Darling', neither of them means it. Watch out.

Some make great lovers, often faithful and particularly careful parents. They are not flirts, except where it may help them to get on in either a career or up the social ladder. And when this is necessary they do it extremely effectively. But the moment they no longer need the object of their attentions, they simply don't bother any more, leaving their benefactor, now their victim, utterly bewildered.

June 4 women can rise far up the corporate ladder, using their quick Gemini wit to make fast, interesting decisions. Some become the worst kind of female executive, joined at the nose to their computer, working until midnight, a glass of diet cola by their side. They come home late at night even when there are small children, leaving someone else to tuck them up, and often show a condescending kind of boredom to their long-suffering house-husbands. The men are the same, except they have a greater tendency to pop down to the bar with a few mates, which makes them nicer people, if slightly drunk.

Those who escape these traits show the homely streak common to Gemini, and devote their undoubted energies to the domestic arts. But there is always, lurking just beneath, a little competitiveness. A slightly better carpet than their sister's or neighbour's is often the order of the day. Taller trees. A bigger garden, with brighter lupins.

When they are around those they consider their equal, however, they can be very charming. Firm competition often brings out the best in them, and with the saving grace of a strong sense of self-mockery, June 4 can flower into a sturdy and useful plant.

Never let a fool kiss you or a kiss fool you.
(Joey Adams)

5 JUNE

June 5 people are intensely idealistic and often seek expression in the arts. Many famous writers and painters have been born on this date. But for everybody who's name is known, there are many others almost as, in some cases just as, talented. And it's important for everybody to realise they just have to keep going, for the pleasure as well as the recognition.

Fortunately they are not materialistic, can live stylishly on less than most, so lack of funds won't necessarily prevent them from pursuing their passion, even if it doesn't earn anything. Either sex, for instance, can develop a capacity to put together a meal for a lot of people, with apparently no proper ingredients. Even better, because both men and women have a strong visual flair, they make the food look nice, which is three-quarters of the battle.

Similarly these creatures can make a house look brilliant with almost no resources but plenty of imagination. They pick wild flowers and leaves and turn them into an arrangement, which

women in Knightsbridge would pay a fortune for, and some actually take this up as an extraordinarily remunerative profession. They dress well for practically nothing and can turn rooms into theatrical extravaganzas with a few clever colour-combination licks of paint.

Because they are unusual, this individual may come across mockery from those less blessed with natural talent. This takes some handling. But June 5 should stick to their guns and never apologise for who they are and how they think. Nature didn't intend us all to be alike. Mockery is often born of the mocker's own timidity.

These people are sensitive with others and interested in their ideas. They are charismatic teenagers and grow up to be encouraging to young colleagues and their own teenagers or indeed other people's. You'll often find others' difficult adolescents come to live with June 5 for a bit, taking shelter for brief moments around personal crises.

> *All men*
>
> *have aimed at,*
>
> *found and lost.*
>
> (*W B Yeats,* Lapis Lazuli)

BODY

Sometimes you work so hard you forget to eat, then binge on rubbish. Remember baked beans – cheap, fast and healthy. Put beans with toast and you have the dietary equivalent of a good marriage. Separately neither is nutritionally complete; together the two complement each other to produce a nutritious whole. It's all down to protein and its constituent amino acids, the stuff of body tissues. Pulses are rich in the amino acids which cereals are weak in and vice versa. Beans on toast, easy on the butter please, provides an amino acid profile which closely reflects the body's own protein requirement.

MIND

Overwork causes loss of creativity. If you have a good run, the temptation, high on adrenalin, is to go on and on and on. But you pay for it with a great big low the next day.

DATESHARE

Federico García-Lorca, *Spanish, famous for bullfighting poetry and political comment, murdered by Fascist regime.* **Ken Follett**, *British author, Eye of the Needle.* **Margaret Drabble**, *author, editor of* Oxford Compendium of English Literature. **Tony Richardson**, *British film director,* Tom Jones, Loneliness of the Long Distance Runner.

BODY

Many people born on this day have indigestion and take far too much shop-bought medicine to cope with their heartburn, nausea, stomach aches and general feeling of discomfort and being clogged by food. This day is physically sensitive to pressure and the best thing to do is reorganise the diet. Drink warming, but light broths, homemade chicken noodle is perfect. Step up the fresh vegetable intake, especially root vegetables, carrots and beetroots. Stick to beans, wholegrains, small amounts of tofu and soyabean products, fish, chicken, pork and beef. Cut down on dairy products, caffeine, refined white flour and sugar.

MIND

There's no reason at all why you shouldn't hide your feelings, act the conventional citizen if that pleases you. Just don't let it exhaust you or make you ill, because deception can be wearing.

DATESHARE

Robert Englund, *film actor, Freddie Krueger in* A Nightmare on Elm Street. **Bjorn Borg**, *Swedish tennis champion, won six French Opens, five straight Wimbledons.* **Billie Whitelaw**, *British actress, Beckett interpreter.* **Alexandra Fjodorovna**, *last Russian Tzarina, wife to Nicholas II, murdered by Bolsheviks during Russian Revolution.*

This creature is fire beneath the ice, black lace beneath tweed suits. Scratch the conventional surface and find molten precious metal. But they are secretive and spend energy disguising their wayward, passionate nature behind a Mr and Mrs Ordinary Person façade.

People think they know all about June 6, then after years of dependability, perhaps as the local postman, or bank manager, they throw it all up one day for a grand and unsuitable passion. Or worse, still, commit an astonishing crime. Then everybody says: 'Who would ever have thought it?'

Sex always brings out the wild man and woman in June 6. Lovers already know that their partner is extra-hot to handle, will openly enjoy experimenting with clothes and sex toys. But never in any way that might harm. Those born on this day generally have a loathing for violence, even the pretend sort. Nevertheless, expect excitement, candles by the bath, athletic requests, provocative behaviour under the table during the most formal of occasions. Otherwise, for the most part, butter wouldn't melt in this hot little baked potato until the explosion.

At work they are careful to be punctual, apparently uninspiring and well-organised, a model of corporate co-operativeness. They are often given huge responsibility by bosses who secretly think they are dull. Then, suddenly, those who mocked June 6 for lacking that special spark, find themselves taken over and working for the object of derision. They will seize the company and make what didn't work sparkle with profit. They will relocate the workforce and streamline it, but never indulge in the ruthless psychotic behaviour common to other birth dates. They are not innate bullies and do not enjoy other people's discomfiture.

Less financially-motivated people will just plod along for a period of time, mowing the lawn, taking the dog to the vet, returning the videos on time. Then throw regularity to the winds and disappear round the world.

Still waters run deep.

7 JUNE

Because June 7 always seem strong, other people confide their woes in them. As these creatures are up-to-date with popular culture, they often have high powered, very commercial jobs. So they have a work force which relies on them for pay and their happiness.

While the going is good, this talented planet thrives at the centre of its satellites. But June 7 overestimates its strength and sometimes the sheer strain wears down body and spirit. They get run down. More problematically, June 7 may develop a tendency to depression, or a constantly nagging illness which undermines strength. Skin troubles may plague them.  Perhaps hay fever, or asthma. Nothing life threatening, just tiring.

Born with physical good looks, their natural stylish confidence may mean they look extra good even when they feel bad. So those satellites around the main planet have no idea that the ball of fire they regard as their strength is waning.

Working women born on this day should take care to avoid being overstretched. There are so many demands to be met. Cut down, or reorganise, before things get out of hand. Can you get someone else to help with the domestic load? Can you be less of a perfectionist, let things go? Dust and dirt never hurt anybody. You don't have to redecorate. Just stick some flowers in a vase and it cheers up the room. Stick the washing in a basket or behind the door for a couple of days more and nobody will care or even notice.

Men should be similarly careful. Give up being a workaholic before it gets to you. Don't go in for complicated jobs about the house. What both sexes are good at, is being attractive and good mixers. This is what people value you for, and this is what gives you a kick.

Stay intimate with people. This is another talent. But stay free.

BODY

A lot of people swear by the alternative remedy to stress, ginseng. In more than 1000 tests conducted over the last 30 years in China, Japan and Russia, including tests on Olympic athletes, astronauts and sailors going on long sea voyages, ginseng has shown its value by bringing support to the stressed body. Experiments with patients at the Institute of Biologically Active Substances in Vladivostok showed ginseng to have both tonic and stimulant. Ginseng instils a sense of well-being, helps to ward off anxiety, depression and irritability and has a normalising effect on the metabolism.

MIND

Change is a basic law of the universe and often problems can be resolved better by change than by attempting to solve them one after another. Remember that many problems just go away if you ignore them.

DATESHARE

The Artist Formerly Known As Prince, singer, songwriter, extraordinary entertainer. **Tom Jones**, Welsh singer, famous for women in the audience throwing their knickers at him. **Paul Gauguin**, French post-Impressionist, left family to travel to Tahiti and married thirteen-year-old girl. **Pietro Annigoni**, Italian society portrait painter. **Beau Brummell**, British dandy.

Too long a sacrifice
Can make a stone of the heart.

(W B Yeats, Easter)

BODY
These people limit their daily intake of food so much that they make themselves extremely tired and ill. They get distracted if they put on a few pounds, so intense about perceived perfection, that they may over-diet. They may adopt faddy eating patterns, only eating fruit, which plays havoc with their digestive systems, drinking too little liquid and cut out so much fat that they become listless and can develop depression. They lack confidence in their own ability to attract unless they look 'perfect' and should try to revise their too demanding attitude to their physical appearance.

MIND
People who can't find someone to love outside the office lack imagination and oomph and draw intense criticism. Look for a date amongst friends, rely on relatives, anywhere but the work environment.

DATESHARE
Nancy Sinatra, *singer, Frank's daughter, lovely, difficult and always struggling.* **Sir Francis Crick**, *British co-discoverer of DNA, Nobel Prize winner.* **Joan Rivers**, *comedienne, TV personality.* **Barbara Bush**, *US first lady.* **Robert Schumann**, *German romantic composer.*

Beauty and social graces are everything to June 8, which may irritate others who are less blessed. Gemini often has a slenderness of physique and charm which is enviable. But this difficult twinklet is an attractiveness-snob, and can spend too much time admiring itself.

Worse still, they spend rather too much time criticising others, especially their nearest and dearest. Young people born on June 8 take is so far that they don't want to be seen with their parents. Nor will they necessarily choose a partner with sterling qualities, preferring to drool over curly hair and remarkable blue eyes. It won't matter that there is little sign of a brain, just that the partner matches their own image. Naturally it's a problem if you want a conversation, and there's the rub, because June 8 is prone to boredom and is extremely cutting about anyone slower-witted than themselves.

Nicer people born on this day develop an amusing sense of self-mockery, always the perfect antidote to vanity. This, combined with their high intelligence, makes them wonderful company and much-desired lovers. These much-pursued individuals show generosity to other people's talents, but woe betide companions who haven't got much talent. They are likely to be on the receiving end of a devastating smile, then ignored.

June 8 can be an asset at work. Bosses often use them to raise money and make connections with other businesses because of their immense attraction. But they do tend to indulge in office affairs, and worse, get sick of these affairs quickly, leaving colleagues to handle an embarrassing situation. Neither men nor women born on this date seem to twig that everybody at work always knows about other people's sex lives, if the connection comes from work. And no amount of arriving separately, not talking to each other during office hours and disguising telephone conversations as important work calls will pull the wool over anybody's eyes.

~

Mirror mirror on the wall who is the fairest of them all?

(Snow White)

9 JUNE

This individual has a struggle with himself. Sometimes charming and helpful, other times ratty, catty and hysterical, there's no knowing which side of the June 9 personality will come to the fore. They bring trouble on themselves by their inability to sustain kindness, yet when they are in trouble they are remarkably brave. This is not a character which shows weakness under pressure, although the women are not above some judicious weeping to get their way, and the men can develop sudden, diplomatic illnesses.

At work, both sexes can be doggedly determined, although leadership of others is not their strong suit. If somebody puts them down, they work their way up again, with good ideas and application. Both sexes are not above the use of sex appeal to make their point, but whoever minded that? It brightens up the Christmas party and it's fun. This day rarely has more than a flirtation at work, so there's no risk of mockery or embarrassment.

At home, June 9 can be difficult, often so tired they fly into a temper at the slightest thing. This is difficult for children of people  born today, but children can put up with more than you think as long as their parents love them, and these individuals do love their offspring. The trouble is that they always want their kids to do well at school or in clubs – the pushy parent – which is hard on little ones.

Many individuals can become hypochondriacs. Women born on this day often have difficult periods and pregnancies, which set the stage for future worries about themselves. They may become frenzied about their children's health. Many men examine themselves each morning for signs of illness, or temperature, and take the slightest bug very seriously indeed. Some of these people have been known to keep a thermometer in their briefcase so they can regularly take their temperature during work breaks.

BODY

June 9 can get too anxious and work him or herself up into a state. Reach for those comforting and pleasant Bach Flower remedies, so popular today. If they don't help, it's still a nice idea that they were collected for our greater health from British fields and woods. Try rock rose (Helianthemum nummularium) for terror, panic, fright and nightmares or gentian (Gentianella amarella) for those who feel easily discouraged, or who feel self-doubt and anxiety at even the smallest delays and when tiny things go wrong. These remedies can be found in most good health food stores.

☾

MIND

There is so much talent in you, it seems a shame to jeopardise it with petulence. Try to be more consistent with other people, less suspicious, and you will find they return this attention with rewarding affection.

One may smile and smile ⁓ and be a villain.

(William Shakespeare)

AIR

BODY

June 10 takes everything to excess and should be careful about drinking too much, smoking and in some cases, taking drugs. It's tempting to accept drugs at a party or club, in order to impress, and then find you want more. Try to regulate the desire to put something in your mouth when you have nothing better to do. Food is also a terrific temptation and sugary things are the worst for this birthdate. Whole packets of chocolate biscuits can disappear at one sitting. Three doughnuts may leave the plate in a matter of seconds. Greedy June 10 eats fast.

MIND

In Tarot, the 10th card of the Major Arcana is The Wheel of Fortune, which indicates good times and reversal of good times. The plus factor is that bad times won't last either.

DATESHARE

Prince Philip, *Queen Elizabeth II's charming but ill-tempered consort.* **Judy Garland**, *lovely Hollywood actress, singer, dancer, sang 'Over The Rainbow' as Wendy in* The Wizard of Oz. **Maurice Sendak**, *children's book writer and illustrator,* In The Night Kitchen. **Robert Maxwell**, *British newspaper owner, charming, devious, fell off his boat and brought his empire down.*

The temptation for June 10 is to do everything to excess. Lovely, extravagent and generous, these little pumpkins are always looking for love and really have no idea about how to choose the right person.

This is because many people born on this day are ruled, body and mind, by sex. There's nothing wrong with that, except it can become a kind of drug, and people who this creature finds attractive will not always treat them well. Essentially June 10 is looking for a good time. And if they don't make love at least five times a week they feel bad. What's moonshine – and indeed sunshine – for, but love?

At work they dream of love. If they haven't got a lover, the first question they ask about a stranger is: 'Are they single? Are they available?' Quite often they can't concentrate on the job for thinking about sex, which is a way at least, of passing the time pleasurably. But June 10 never listens to advice about their love-life, frequently take up with the wrong person, and get let down more often than not.

This is a very physical creature, and when love comes, like Cinderella's pumpkin, it turns into a radiant vehicle for pleasure. But June 10 forgets that when midnight chimes, the magic may stop.

Those born on this date think underwear is more important than outerwear. Their drawers are always full of the most amusing knickers – for either sex, their bathrooms stocked with perfumed oils, and their beds are covered in gorgeously scented fresh sheets. Their fridges are packed with food for love, champagne, smoked salmon, chocolate yoghurt, honey and cream.

But when it comes to the more practical side of things, forget it. This creature would have baked you a cake if it had known you were coming, and if it knew how, but it didn't and it doesn't.

Love Changes Everything.

(Michael Ball)

11 JUNE

June 11 will have a lifelong battle with weight. They swear that they eat very little yet still pile on the pounds, and this may be true. There are those who only have to look at a strawberry tart and their buttons burst, while other, luckier dates can eat as much as they like and stay slender.

It's unfair. But then life is unfair. The trick is to cope. First, June 11 should consider if they have a medical problem (rare) or if it's really that they like to eat. Probably the answer will be the latter.

Then it's really a matter of not giving in to somebody's else's fish and chips. And those people who have children must avoid at all cost, nicking something from the leftovers on their child's plate.

Part of the problem with weight is that June 11 has an unreal idea of what life should be like. A grass is greener on the other side of the fence mentality. Many look very nice the size and shape they are, and will never attain the sort of skinny body you see in the movies – which anyway is frequently the result of diet pills. Unless June 11 is positively wedged in the door, it's wise to get used to it.

When his mind is not on fat problems, this individual is capable of academic brilliance. He and she were in the top section at school and today this cleverness is useful both at home and at work. The June 11 brain is capable of storing vast knowledge and the memory is excellent for minute detail.

As a child, this person – who probably came into the world dramatically – was always the ringleader, and so it is with adulthood. They are the leaders at work, reorganising with charm and efficiency. And in private they use this talent to create fun for those they love.

Eat, drink and be merry,
for tomorrow ye diet.
(Lewis C Henry)

BODY

Sometimes drinking herbal teas can take your mind off hunger, and anyway they make you feel better. Delicious teas are available in health food stores, so experiment. Parsley, lemon grass and hibiscus teas are diuretic, relieving fluid retention and cellulite. Parsley is a powerful diuretic herb and calming to the stomach. Lemon grass is helpful in the elimination of cellulite. Hibiscus is often an ingredient in commercial teas, along with rosehip. Both are a good source of vitamin C, provided you make the tea with water that has not come to the boil. Vitamin C is destroyed at 100°C.

MIND

You are excellent at talking your way out of a crisis and when a friend is in trouble you can help by speaking for them. You talk sense when others panic. You're a star.

DATESHARE

Jackie Stewart, *Scottish racing driver, three times world champion, winner of 27 Formula One races.* **Gene Wilder**, *actor, comic.* **John Constable**, *British landscape artist, painter of churches and haywagons.* **Richard Strauss**, *German composer, famous for operas.*

BODY

June 12 lives by his or her spectacular memory. Be careful to maintain it. Everybody knows that alcohol undermines the memory, but few realise that many foods can addle this precious asset. Overwork and overstudy can fuddle mental function. It's as if everything is wiped except the matter in hand. A poor diet full of chemicals and additives, excessive spices and caffeine don't do it much good either. Other memory reducers include refined sugar. Try malt as a natural sweetener and reach for fruit rather than sugary foods when you have a relentless sugar craving. Dairy allergy also reduces memory energy.

MIND

Fave saying for this individual is: 'If you want something done properly, you have to do it yourself.' Complete nonsense which often leads to appalling self-pity because this individual always – unnecessarily – does too much.

DATESHARE

Anthony Eden, British prime minister. **Brigid Brophy**, British writer, The Snowball. **Charles Kingsley**, British clergyman, writer, Westward Ho!. **Anne Frank**, Jewish girl who died in Bergen-Belsen concentration camp aged fifteen. Her famous diary was published after her death.

June 12 has a passion for making lists and rearranging things. Perfect if those around this creature want to be rearranged. Disturbing if they don't.

This individual is always on the move. If they don't change houses every few years, they think they've got middle-aged. Each time they swear is the last, and each time they see another perfect home they must have. This is expensive and disturbing for partners and children, unless June 12 can make the sort of profit to improve on the last buy. But all too often it's not a case of better or grander, just different.

This is the creature who drops in half-way through the cooking and redoes it. When the glasses are washed up, June 12 goes over them again, complaining that they are cloudy. Every book on the shelves is alphabetically arranged, with titles kept in a notebook so that borrowers can be asked to return them. There will be a first aid kit in the car, but only to be used in dire emergencies. This creature hates having to replenish the Walt Disney elastoplast and

reminds everybody it's not a toy, which of course, it is.

Most people born on this day have excellent memories, will remember a promise you made or an opinion you expressed days or even years ago, and if the promise is broken or the opinion changed, will query it. They pride themselves on not writing down telephone numbers and being able to remember directions. They think paperwork in the office is a waste of time, prefer e-mail to memos and letters. If they can there will be a rearrangement of the office furniture, of everybody's working day, and a new rota for lunch breaks. Sometimes their need to exercise petty power over others borders on the psychotic. The best thing is to ignore them, but if you can't, try a punch on the nose.

When I say 'Everybody says so', I mean I say so.

(Ed Howe)

I3 JUNE

Gemini is often prone to snobbery, but fortunately this individual is free of such petty little restrictions to the soul. They can soar in any society and are likely to be a great success, make heaps of money and live a pleasing life. When they do make money they invest wisely and with the greatest of ease and enthusiasm.

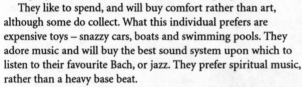

Men and women born on this date are never hamstrung by money. If they are born to it, they don't neurotically wonder if people only like them for it. They simply assume, rightly, that most people like them because they like most people.

They like to spend, and will buy comfort rather than art, although some do collect. What this individual prefers are expensive toys – snazzy cars, boats and swimming pools. They adore music and will buy the best sound system upon which to listen to their favourite Bach, or jazz. They prefer spiritual music, rather than a heavy base beat.

In private this bright star devotes energy to pleasing others. Presents are their joy. A leopard broach if you like cats. A mermaid rose if you like gardening. A silk rug to remind you of your travels. If a friend has money worries, June 13 will offer to help, and not necessarily ask for it back. If the debtor insists on paying back, they will accept with grace so there is never an awkwardness.

At work expect June 13 to pull the company out of trouble with an educated financial wheeze. They will be the one to collect for a colleague's present, arrange a birthday lunch, the office party. And they'll add a touch of their own brand of fun, a magician or a fire-eater. Something to make the occasion memorable.

It's important for June 13 to have a strong social circle, preferably a family. They are not happy alone for long and they don't work at their best in isolation.

BODY

This day has delicate skin prone to allergies, which are not major enough to be a health hazard, but sufficiently irritating to be a drag. You can go the route of proper medical investigation, but for many people born on June 13 this is too tedious. Instead, try to discover the causes yourself and eliminate them. Common skin rashes can be caused simply by a too abrasive washing power, or washing your hair with a heavily medicated shampoo. Some pop stars who have to wash their hair a lot don't use shampoo but stick to hot water with good results.

MIND

Some may warn June 13 that they are generous to a fault and should watch out for charlatans. Don't underestimate this good star. Generosity doesn't go hand in hand with stupidity.

DATESHARE

Fanny Burney, British 18th century novelist, friend of Samuel Johnson. **W B Yeats**, Irish poet and mystic. **Basil Rathbone**, British actor famous for his interpretation of Sherlock Holmes. **Dorothy L Sayers**, British detective novelist. **Martha Washington**, first US first lady, wife of George.

All happiness depends on a leisurely breakfast.
(John Gunther)

This is another day with obvious talent, and again the Gemini determination dominates. Take a pleasing manner, courtesy, a good body, add a touch of loner and a sprinkle of travel bug and you get the recipe for a popular dish.

Those born today have a problem with commitment, simply because they love to travel, often living in different countries and this doesn't lend itself to domesticity. There's a strong likelihood they'll be bachelors or spinsters because of this. But hey, this character won't necessarily think that's bad. Just as long as enough effort is made to keep a good circle of close friends going.

People born on this day can do without sex for periods of time, but again it's necessary to remain receptive. Because solitude doesn't suit.

Although June 14 makes an excellent parent, often becoming their adult child's best friend, many will be happy without children. It always means they are better off, for starters. And they can set up a business, or try financial speculation without worrying. The prospect of wealth is very real.

Money usually comes from personal interests. A talent for computers may bring success – it's where fast fortunes are  currently made. But this character needs to sit down, and concentrate hard on a window in this market. Fortunes can also be made in retail – Gemini's talent for pleasing people again.

Great cooks have been born on this day and we all know that a winning personality combined with a fetching recipe, say for walnut salad, something which catches the fancy, can put you amongst the current crop of high society chefs. Remember, nobody needs a high society background to learn how to please the moneyed and titled. In fact it's preferable not to have one, so that you can't feel bullied by the little signs of class these people swear by – because you don't know what they are in the first place.

Nothing ventured,
~
nothing gained.

AIR

15 JUNE

June 15 cuts a swathe through life like a meteor with a thousand sparks in its tail. When these characters pass by someone usually says: 'Who was THAT?' It's important to remember that although they are loaded with natural charm and their very own, custom personalised gravity force, 'more' is the third most dominant word in their psychology, after 'I' (number one) and 'You' (number two).

Good looks are usually given by the fairies at birth, but in cases where the wand slipped people born on this day are not shy about trying the entire range of beauty treatments currently available. And we use 'beauty treatment' loosely here, to cover lotions, alternative wonder workers and richly skilled and richly rewarded doctors with sharp knives.

Forever conscious of their effect on the opposite sex, or whichever sex is appropriate, and sometimes both, people born on this day work hard on their charm. And actually there is very little more pleasing than somebody who is immensely attractive and who wants to charm the pants off you.

Most people born on this day are quick-witted and amusing, again talents which they practise to make more perfect. This makes them successful in corporate life, where they are terrific to work for, but more important than this, they can ward of banks and attract money. This is an ideal sales and marketing executive, wonderful in any area of advertising, an insouciant entrepreneur who people can't wait to invest in.

So. What is the down side of June 15?

After a really good search, we can say that they may spoil other people, suffer from vanity (never actually overweening) and perhaps break a few hearts. And that's about it fellas. Because June 15 is usually in possession of a decent set of moral values and since their basic instinct is to watch the reactions of other people to themselves, they grow up to be sensitive to others.

BODY

Since this date is very interested in sex there are a couple of ingredients in a daily diet which do help and they might like to read about. Zinc is very important for both men and women. The processing of food removes zinc and a zinc deficient, junk food diet should be boosted by the addition of peas, nuts, whole grains, carrots, oysters and sunflower seeds. If you take zinc supplements do not exceed the recommended dose because toxic reactions are possible. Manganese is also necessary for a good sex life. Sources are nuts, cereals, vegetables and fruit.

MIND

Most people are more fascinating between the ages of 35 and 45, when they've won a few races and know how to pace themselves. Take your time about passing 45, and maximum fascination can continue indefinitely.

DATESHARE
Edvard Grieg, Norwegian composer, Peer Gynt, music incorporated Norwegian folk influences. **James Belushi**, Hollywood actor. **Xaviera Hollander**, Dutch brothel keeper, author, The Happy Hooker.

Whoever named it necking

was a poor judge of anatomy.

(Groucho Marks)

BODY

Many people born on this day worry about their health and tend to visit the doctor more than their friends. Yet doctors frequently don't have a solution for June 16, whose aches and pains often derive from spiritual upset. It may be best to develop an interest in alternative healing, which will fascinate this individual, if nothing else. They should consider trying some of the remedies suggested by the extraordinary healer Dr Edward Bach, now available in many health stores.

MIND

June 16 should avoid a tendency to morbid thoughts and pessimism. Concentrate on the fine writing and music you so enjoy and remember the generosity of spirit that inspired people to write these things for you.

DATESHARE

Stan Laurel, *part of the comic Hollywood duo, Laurel and Hardy.* **Tom Graveny**, *British cricketer.* **Katharine Graham**, *newspaper publisher.* **Adam Smith**, *Scottish economist, capitalist theorist, author,* The Wealth of Nations. **Erich Segal**, *novelist,* Love Story.

Rather quiet and certainly thoughtful, this character is struck by the beauty of the world and deeply aware of the vastness of the turning universe. Generally this individual is not interested in material things, although their naturally studious nature can mean they understand the world's money markets and some play the stockmarket extremely well. They may also make millions if they market their own interests, often utilising their computer knowledge or the simple inventor's streak which is common to Gemini.

June 16 frequently takes refuge in books and this is a birth date which resorts to poetry – often writing it very successfully – to express feelings. Sometimes when they read a familiar phrase they are so struck by its beauty they are reduced to tears. And similarly with music, which they often adore, they are so personally moved by its familiarity that it feels like they wrote it themselves.

Both sexes use poetry and music to woo a mate, and their burning soul means that they like to mate for life. Crossed in love they may pine to the point of illness. If things don't go right, they may choose never to marry and resign themselves to the contemplative pleasures of the bachelor state.

Both sexes like to spend time haunting old churches, where they light candles for all their friends and sit for hours enjoying the peaceful calm. Some may even be drawn to the religious life, which can suit their quiet desire to understand the workings of the world.

June 16 is ideally suited to life in the country rather than harsh crowded urban environments. They need the open spaces and skies and an ideal choice of profession for this birth date would be a country teacher or librarian. And for the slightly more sociable, the lure of a village post office and its involvement and service to community life may be overwhelming.

If you are afraid of being lonely, don't try to be right.

(Jules Renard)

17 JUNE

June 17 people make fine planners. Domestically they like to sit down a make a list, which they will then stick to, extolling themselves all the while for their efficiency and others' lack of it. But this means they are perfect to go on holiday with – if you can stand it. And why shouldn't you be pleased to accompany this star on its organised journey through the universe, never without elastoplast, the right money and a well worked out route?

In numerology, those born on the 17th are ruled by the number 8 (1+7=8) and by the planet Saturn, which carries a serious aspect. The number 8 straddles conflict between the material and spiritual worlds and those ruled by this number are often leaders of people, with profoundly held political or patriotic views and are happy to sacrifice a social life for the lonelier path of those who are born to change things.

Generally they make inspiring partners. Nothing is dull around June 17 and those who love them frequently take on their views. This individual also inspires fierce protectiveness. In some cases people will actually die for them. In other cases, companions will make every excuse under the sun and moon to exonerate beloved June 17 from every fault. Life can be difficult, because both sexes may fly in the face of society endangering those around them with their political, religious and artistic beliefs.

Less inspired individuals can be tricky because their wayward behaviour may be anti-social, bordering sometimes on the criminal.

As parents and lovers they are usually extremely caring, tender with anyone who is unhappy, or unsure, and tender too with people who are not so clever and prefer a life of simpler pleasures. June 17 love their children, whatever they do, and will usually be particularly attentive to elderly relatives and friends, and although this character may prefer the solitary life, others who need companionship will be looked after.

I love you whatever you do,

but do you have to do

so much of it?

(Jean Illsley Clarke)

BODY
Because of their strong nature, this person has strong desires and often little time and energy to control them. They may use alcohol or other drugs to keep themselves going, chain-smoke or on occasions simply eat in an absent-minded sort of way. In youth they exhibit extreme physical and mental stamina, but even the toughest mortal breaks down under such a harsh lifestyle. June 17 tends to regard natural born strength as a sign of starry immortality. But without care the body will rebel and then this particular date will then be agonised with frustration.

MIND
Try not to be so rigid about every aspect of life. If something about you inconveniences others, change it. Consider the 1960s Fijian cricketer, who thoughtfully changed his name from Ilikena Lasurusa Talebuhlamaineiilikenamainavaleniveivakabulaimainakulalakebalau to I L Bula. Sensibly.

DATESHARE
Igor Stravinsky, *innovative Russian composer*, Rite of Spring *provoked a riot at the 1913 Paris première.* **John Wesley**, *British religious reformer, Methodist church founder.* **James Brown**, *soul singer, songwriter, wildman.* **Barry Manilow**, *singer songwriter.* **Dean Martin**, *Hollywood actor, member of the Rat Pack, hellraiser.*

BODY

Gemini hands are sometimes vulnerable to aches and pains, general stiffness and rough skin, which comes with the hard work most people born under this sign inflict on their hands. A soothing hand massage helps fingers to stay supple, but more than that, it encourages your whole body to feel more relaxed and cared for. And some say that a hand massage helps them recover from mild illness. Use two or three drops of lavender, bergamot or rose oil in a base of two teaspoons of camellia oil, which does not oxidise and therefore your mixture will keep longer without going rancid.

MIND

Sometimes everything makes you nervous and each day seems a minefield. Most things aren't worth the upset. Put them in an imaginary briefcase, dump them by the side of an imaginary road – and walk away.

DATESHARE

Paul McCartney, *singer songwriter, the Beatles.* **Isabella Rossellini**, *daughter of Ingrid Bergman, star of* Blue Velvet. **Jeanette MacDonald**, *singer, film actress teamed with Nelson Eddy.* **Ian Carmichael**, *British comic film actor.*

JUNE 18

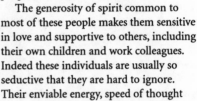

These are people pleasers. The good companion June18 puts others before himself, which may often be an attractive characteristic, but some women born on this day take their pliability to the point where they are a pain in the back pocket. Constantly taking decisions for other people is tiresome in the extreme.

The generosity of spirit common to most of these people makes them sensitive in love and supportive to others, including their own children and work colleagues. Indeed these individuals are usually so seductive that they are hard to ignore. Their enviable energy, speed of thought and the quicksilver charm in communicating these thoughts, so characteristic of the best of Gemini, see to that.

This super sparkling dish comes lightly frosted with stardust. But greedy admirers beware, June 18 is short on patience with flatterers and twitterers, who will probably find that the embarrassed subject of their admiration has zoomed off. In fact this creature is as shy as a tiger with a full stomach and shrinks into the undergrowth away from the spotlight of stardom. It's worth remembering this at work, because the role of team member will always be preferred to team leader.

Speed may be a characteristic, but this doesn't mean that punctuality results. June 18 thinks time is on his or her side and nothing surprises this creature more than exactly how long things really take. People born today are ruled by the planet Mercury and can therefore move very effectively from one place to the other. But they dally with diversions on the way and are then astonished to be late.

These individuals don't much like solitude and are happiest messing around with crowds of friends. They are also extremely good with their hands, so messing about in boats with crowds of friends will keep them happy, or any other creative group activity, such as flower arranging, building theatres or commercial design.

I'd rather keep my mouth shut and be thought a fool, than open it ∼ and remove all doubt.

(Sir Denis Thatcher)

19 JUNE

June 19 works too hard. Amusing, sweet and clever, this character finds it almost impossible to relax, can't get to grips with the concept of doing nothing. But human beings are meant to do nothing at least some of the time.

At home both sexes are always on the go, inducing appalling guilt in more indolent companions. If they could lighten up a little bit, this puritan work ethic can be extremely useful, especially if June 19 wants to run an independent business.

This creature is beloved of bosses all over the land. You can find them working late everywhere, the only person left in a brightly-lit office, with a sea of dark night around them. They will devise clever

schemes, logically constructed and practical. They will steer projects through impossible deadlines with their above-average stamina and concentration.

But in most cases, June 19 would be happier running his or her own business, where the results of Herculean energies bring personal benefit. Why bother putting so much into somebody else's company, when the only reward is at that company's discretion? This psychology is particularly suited to working at home, or starting up on his own, because June 19 doesn't suffer from isolation – indeed very often actively enjoys time spent alone. And, although those born on this day do have the troubled streak common to Gemini, they are particularly self-aware and have learned to control it.

Because this creature is unhappy with idle hands, quite complicated hobbies are popular. Nothing delights them more than amateur archaeology, sleuthing Anglo-Saxon village sites and Roman roads, birdwatching with carefully kept records, or indeed a strong and useful campaign for the environment. If you don't want a road built where rare orchids grow and you do want the river to be clean enough for baby trout to survive, this is the person to have on your side.

BODY

If you can't relax by lying down, try cooking, which is enjoyable, productive (important to June 19) and soothing. Learn about the ancient properties of so many fresh ingredients and you will make things taste delicious and do some good. Did you know, for instance, that garlic not only gives food spin, and scares vampires, but also, eaten raw, acts as a powerful antibiotic? Other traditional therapeutic qualities attributed to garlic include keeping hearts healthy by lowering blood cholesterol and acting as a decongestant. A garlic soup made from 50–100 cloves is an enormous help when suffering from the common cold.

MIND

Avoid stress because it will induce negative feelings about your very considerable talents. Make sure you attend sufficiently to your surroundings at home, because living in an attractive place is particularly important to your well-being.

DATESHARE

Salman Rushdie, British novelist, The Satanic Verses, sentenced to death by Islamic Fundamentalists for blasphemy against the prophet Mohammed. **Kathleen Turner**, tall Hollywood star, Romancing The Stone. **Paula Abdul**, singer.

When a fellow says 'It ain't the money, but the principle of the thing' ~ it's the money.

(Frank McKinney Hubbard)

BODY

This individual is vulnerable to upset stomachs, making him or her nervous of travel, or indeed, just going out. Observe key hygiene rules in the kitchen, to ensure that you are eating safely. Keep all work surfaces scrupulously clean and wash all utensils and chopping boards after they have come into contact with raw meat, poultry or eggs, to prevent cross-contamination. Wash hands before preparing food. Wash all fruit and vegetables. Leave washing-up to drain. It's more hygienic than using a tea-towel, although a dishwasher is best. Remember to defrost the fridge regularly and don't overload it or leave the door open for long.

MIND

Sometimes the sense of unreality is so overwhelming it causes a range of reactions from nerves to panic attacks. Try a few drops of Rescue Remedy in a glass of water. Many people swear by the calming effect.

DATESHARE

John Goodman, *American actor who makes fat sexy.* **Jacques Offenbach**, *French operetta music and cancan composer.* **Jean-Marie Le Pen**, *French ultra-right politician.* **Cyndi Lauper**, *singer, songwriter.* **Lionel Richie**, *singer, songwriter.* **Catherine Cookson**, *British popular romance writer.*

There may be magic in the eyes and hands of this character, but is it the black sort or the white? Sometimes June 20 is irrational and emotional and in both sexes there's an underlying instability which most grow out of in adolescence. But if they are mishandled in childhood – not loved enough – the crackle in the air around June 20 becomes as dangerous as a faulty electric cable. They wear charisma like a tailor-made cloak. No man or woman can resist the magnetic force field and nobody can feel neutral about this person.

At work they may seduce their way to the top. Both sexes use flattering trickery to get on, happily doing Christmas shopping for a boss, much better and more imaginatively than he would. Both sexes will also enhance the personal diary of anybody who can help them get on, procuring treasured theatre tickets, delivering and fetching clothes from the dry cleaners. If they could sit on the lavatory for their boss, you know they would.

At parties they flit from one to another, their eyes constantly flickering towards the door in a desperate search for someone they are afraid to miss. Yet all the while June 20 is the one with the magic and the sadness is that uncertainty, that old instability of judgement, makes them unaware of it. Once master of these personal powers, however, they make exciting leaders with a force field everybody wants to get inside. In this situation, the almost visionary powers of this individual radiate.

June 20 is ultra sensitive to emotion and extremely empathetic. Sometimes they use these qualities so well that they really do seem to create magic. Their generous character traits usually mean they use these powers to do good. But a few are born without concern for others, and this may emphasise the dark side of their star. These people can be destructive.

In the battle of existence,
Talent is the punch;
Tact is the clever footwork.
(Wilson Mizner)

21 JUNE

This is another highly sexed date, but there is nothing frivolous about these individuals and they seek a mate with similar intellectual tastes to themselves. June 21 likes to hang out with close friends, happiest sitting in a pub or club, drinking, flirting and above all talking, far into the night.

Revolutionary thinking is a powerful characteristic. The Tarot is important here, because the 21st card of the Major Arcana is The World, which shows a goddess running, and holding energy-giving rods. She has unlimited power, and in her lies truth. Those born on this day are famously seekers of truth, will not accept conventional ideas until they be re-examined, and may strive to live their own lives by a new set of truths.

Some people show extreme bravery and strength of purpose, whether they simply choose to live in a way others condemn, or to overturn corruption and tyranny. An unfortunate few can be tedious, spotting non-existent problems, and being so studiedly unconventional that everybody gives a sigh of relief when they are gone.

Their sensuosity can also be a pain in the metaphorical bum. Not everybody wants to spend the whole time talking about sex, then doing it, then talking about it some more. And not everybody wants to experiment, preferring to make love in the old, pleasurable, ordinary ways that have delighted humans since the stars first sparkled down on them. June 21 can't understand this and is given to outbursts about other people's prudery.

They are at their best working in teams, where their energy and direct thinking make them excellent leaders. In a more creative, solitary life, they can be extremely content and self-confident. They are often not so good in areas where they have to deal with other people's problems. They can be dictatorial and get nasty if those in their care, for instance, fail to take their advice.

BODY

The intense work ethic of June 21 often produces tired eyes, especially working on a computer. Take care of your eyes by looking at colour, in particular go out and look at the colours in nature. Walk through the countryside, or into a garden and study the flowers. Yellow, orange and red are warming and stimulating. The flow of blood to the eye is activated by studying these colours. Green is harmonising, which is why you feel good near lush vegetation and trees. Blue, violet and magenta are relaxing. All of them de-stress your nervous system and make you see better.

MIND

Counteract your flashes of anger by taking a few moments away from any stress which is revving the mind. No need to walk away, just think yourself away to a favourite place with happy memories.

DATESHARE

Gerald Kaufman, British Labour MP. **Benazir Bhutto**, Pakistani president, first woman to head a Muslim country. **Françoise Sagan**, French novelist, Bonjour Tristesse. **Jean-Paul Sartre**, French existentialist thinker, refused Nobel Prize. **Prince William**, son of the Prince and Princess of Wales.

Our task now ꝙ
is not to fix the blame for the past,
but to fix the course for the future.
(John F Kennedy)

BODY

Food related allergies can be a plague for this date. If the allergy is severe a doctor should be consulted. Minor allergic reactions can be tracked at home. Bad digestion, water retention and irritable skin can easily result from the delicious take-away meal, if the restaurant is using too much monosodium glutamate. Chocolate causes rashes and headaches in some people and so can tomatoes. The list is endless and very personal. Watch carefully what you eat and any consistently bad effects. If it's a favourite, cut it down slightly until you reach a tolerance level, if there is one. Otherwise, eliminate.

MIND

It's very easy for this person to feel low, and the best cure is creativity. Ideally choose to work with colour or music, both of which have well-recorded soothing, healing powers for both mind and body.

DATESHARE

Meryl Streep, *Hollywood actress.* **Erich Maria Remarque**, *German-Jewish novelist,* All Quiet On The Western Front. **Bill Blass**, *American dress designer and society darling.* **H Rider Haggard**, *British novelist,* King Solomon's Mines.

JUNE 22

Romantic June 22 often gets carried away by a need for intensity. They fear boredom unless something amazing is happening most days. Such ethereal creatures always delight in surprises, often unconsciously demand them and lovers frequently try too hard to please. June 22 may be a thrilling sex bomb, but partners know that their blow-hot, blow-cold birth date, born on the Gemini-Cancer cusp, can have the attention span of a tadpole.

Some provide their own adventures. The entertainment industry nourishes their thirst for theatrical life and provides the highs and lows which give this drama queen a buzz. In the countryside, expect to find fireworky June 22 sorting a major community project. (Most don't like minor occasions; only those with the Canceremini solitary streak.) Some people have a logical streak and those who do like to organise such things as voyages or expeditions, where there's just a smidgeonette of danger.

Food will be planned carefully, nothing heavy, nothing starchy, but delicacies cooked with fruits and unusual spices.

Don't be cross if June 22 gives you a lump of rock for your birthday rather than expensive toys. Don't chuck it in the garden. Put it on the mantelpiece. To this individual a piece of quartz found on the beach is lovelier than any man-made thing. And cheaper. June 22 ain't a big spender. But beyond that, this imaginative creature takes pride in knowing where, in every country, certain semi- and semi-semi-semi-precious stones can be found lying about for the picking. In Scotland there'll be amethysts on your beach and sparkling pieces of fools' gold in Texas.

Some of these characters suffer bouts of depression which may be lightened by the affection of friends and a new enthusiasm. Those with acute feelings of sadness frequently flirt with professional magic and magicians, which is fine, but they should beware their natural attraction to the occult, which can sometimes prove overwhelming.

Don't Go Breaking My Heart.

(Elton John)

WATER

23 JUNE

Fitness is important to June 23 and they are usually active and, especially in later life, look after themselves well. Many adore outdoor sports and other sociable activities in the fresh air, particularly, because they are a water sign, the pleasures of swimming in the sea, or rivers and lakes. They should take great care to check with one of the many guides published that the water they are bathing in is clean. Walkers and tennis players must also be sure to wear a high factor barrier cream and sunglasses with properly formulated lenses for maximum eye protection.

This is a lover's birthday. June 23's whole life is devoted to romance and there will be a lot of it because this individual starts early and finishes late. Added magic is given to this date because it is often celebrated as Midsummer's Eve.

Expect this child to have idealistic playground passions, not to be discounted. A child's heart can dream and be broken just as

powerfully as an adult's. These early loves will be cherished life-long memories, the adored one often encountered again in old age with sweet affection.

Most prefer to show off their love, so secret affairs and adultery are a turn off. Heart on sleeve, June 23 is vulnerable to jealousy – love's twin – and may become obsessive.

Don't take chances with this big heart. The aggression that accompanies their jealousy comes from June 23's propensity to attack when threatened. If they are unlucky in love, expect fireworks at least, maybe a stream of telephone calls. At worst, they may go through wallets and hangbags, checking up on the defaulter.

Open hearted June 23 adores gossip. They care about friends and their talent for advising on problems is usually kind, perceptive and helpful. But this little plum sometimes gets its nose too far into others' affairs and could get it squashed.

June 23 is not, however, so romantic that work takes second place. They are well organised, and straight-dealing team members. Work flirtations may be a weakness. Love in the office often backfires and everybody else always knows more than you think and certainly more than you'd wish.

Our romantic often takes lovers on a magical mystery tour of the arts. Financially blessed people shower their squeeze with beautiful things. They are also devoted to making a comfortable elegant home and since no labour saving device has yet been invented that can match any rich lover, grab a wealthy June 23 and hold on.

MIND

A broken heart makes life wonderful five years later, when you meet your old lover in the lift, now fatter and braying 'long-time-no-see'. If your heart hadn't been broken, you couldn't relish the glorious relief.

DATESHARE

Alfred Kinsey, sexologist, author, Sexual Behaviour in The Human Female. **Duke of Windsor**, abdicated as Edward VIII to marry Wallis Simpson. **Empress** 'Not tonight' **Josephine**, Napoleon's wife. **Alan Matheson Turing**, computer inventor. **Ray Davies**, British singer, songwriter, The Kinks.

I'm gonna wash that man right out of my hair.

(South Pacific)

June 24 is often careless about health and gets so involved in current activities that regular health checks are forgotten. Such intense people often suffer from digestive problems, particularly because they snatch at food and sometimes snatch at a little too much alcohol or even drugs to keep them going. These people should take time out to set a sensible eating pattern for themselves and stick to it with the same devotion they give to their work. Some form of yoga is extremely helpful and should be carried out regularly. It will clear the mind, balance and re-energise the body and soul.

MIND

Examine your work and lifestyle and consider from time to time whether you can't see the wood for the trees. Music is a great healer and will help you get in touch with what you really want.

DATESHARE

Fred Hoyle, astrophysicist, philosopher. **Jeff Beck**, blues, jazz and rock guitarist, The Yardbirds. **Lord Horatio Herbert Kitchener**, British General World War I. **Jack Dempsey**, world heavyweight champion for eight years.

JUNE 24

June 24 is allergic to leisure. They are often so taken up by work that they can't talk or think about anything else. First in at their desk, last to leave and happy to volunteer for Sunday rotas, this individual makes the lightning leap up the corporate ladder look like kids' play. They long for the aphrodisiac of power and think any lack of it such a turn off that terminal tantrums result if promotion passes them by. Bosses often just give in because they can't face the consequences.

Companions frequently complain that June 24 is an ideas-pincher. He or she may encourage their victim to go home, then work late on their own presentation and deliver it before the competitor has had time to start the day.

The most sophisticated types are excellent at original thinking and can put into practice ideas that nobody else would dream of trying. This is partly due to their exceptional technical ability. In science, they are inventors. In other businesses they are strategic planners.

Less self-confident people can be brazen bullies and underminers of others. The female executive of this type sits at her computer from morning to night, counting the minutes others spend on personal telephone calls. She can't make time to get to the hairdresser, or the dentist so she has awful hair and teeth. The male executive also has tooth problems.

The nicest June 24 character has a talent for sensitivity. The more spiritual may be drawn to religion and make fine leaders in this field, using their enormous energy to improve their surroundings.

These people have a great need to be alone, which is partly why they like to work late. Family and friends must understand this need and allow them regular periods of isolation. It's an interesting birth date, with a marvellous potential for good – and not so good. The choice is always theirs.

*Tomorrow
~ is another day.*

(Gone With The Wind)

25 JUNE

This individual is lucky in love, but changeable. One minute in pursuit, the next bored – pursuit and seduction are the essence of their sexuality. It's part of the June 25 sizzle. They think that nobody is unseduceable except when approached by an inept lover. Which this desirable creature is not.

Fun to be with, their greatest promises are best ignored for a few months until they have decided to stay. And they will only stay when the timing is right for them, when they are tired of the endless succession of different heads on the other pillow and the piles of unwanted CDs which played a brief part in some forgotten flirtation. They may also have a definite notion about when they should settle down. It's usually quite a conventional decision, not difficult for the eagle-eyed to spot, like when July 25 reaches 30, can afford to buy a house, discovers the first grey hairs, and that their waist size is three inches larger than it was at nineteen.

Because this date is often greatly attached to its parents, when a father or mother dies and leaves an emotional gap, June 25 often yearns to fill that gap with another love and dreams of a new future promised by the birth of children.

June 25 is an exciting lover, full of passion and a flattering need for instant gratification, but there's little taste for, or talent for niceties. No elaborate games here; no strawberries and cream eaten off naked skin and not much champagne in the bath. But after the event, it's different. June 25 adores post-coital bingeing and lovers already languorous with sensation can expect more pleasure with endless varieties of chocolates, delicious oysters and pieces of lobster, maybe slices of papaya, all served in the tumbled sheets. Expect all this to be accompanied by a powerful drink, such as whisky sour on the rocks.

BODY

If you are often tired and your skin is muddy, it may be that snatched meals of fast, or prepared food have left you low on zinc. Low levels of zinc can be caused by the contraceptive pill, steroids, cigarettes and alcohol. Trials have also shown that using zinc supplements can be as helpful as some antibiotics in treating skin conditions such as acne. But for ordinary run-downess and not brilliant skin, just try eating more zinc-rich foods. Look for it in mushrooms, eggs, mustard and brown rice, which contains six times more zinc than the polished white variety.

MIND

This individual should try to be aware that people are not like a pack of cards, to be constantly reshuffled. Many lovers could make perfect life-long partners and a chance lost will usually come again.

You have to kiss *an awful lot of frogs before you find a prince.*
(Graffito)

BODY

This birth date can celebrate the number of its summers with a gorgeous choice of seasonal fruit, one golden key to well-being.

Some fruits, particularly pineapple and papaya, are rich in enzymes that assist our digestion and can help us absorb other nutrients. So if you need to absorb more iron from your food, simply serve the meal with fruit rich in vitamin C such as papaya, pineapple or citrus. Try to eat fresh fruit that is in season. Juices are fine, but the pulp and skin are discarded and of course this is a perfect source of extra fibre.

☾

MIND

June 26 should practice putting himself in somebody else's shoes, keep trying to imagine what others want. Others have a different view. Both sexes beware your doctrinaire tendencies, particularly with children and elderly parents.

DATESHARE

Georgie Fame, singer, songwriter. **Claudio Abbado**, conductor. **Colin Wilson**, British writer, The Outsiders. **Willy Messerschmitt**, German aircraft designer. **Peter Lorre**, Hungarian-American film actor. **Laurie Lee**, British poet, writer, Cider With Rosie.

Passionate June 26 puts people before things or work every time, but such is the power of their convictions, that those they love may find themselves endlessly bossed about. This individual has the empathetic Cancerian sweetness of character, which is so utterly disarming that most lovers turn a blind eye to the odd flash of dictatorship. This is not good for June 26. It's better for them to learn an early lesson in the knack of controlling this hectoring side to their nature.

June 26 unleashed will dictate the kind of television programmes watched by all the family, including adult members.

There will mad bans – on certain kinds of books, or music and maybe even food. If things get truly out of hand there'll be bonkers banning of certain friends, neighbours, even relatives and in some cases countries which can no longer be visited because of a supposed offence. A few of these individuals refuse to go abroad at all, suspicious that foreigners with their foreign languages are somehow conspiring to confuse them.

Yet, and this is a big yet, few people are as enchanting to travel with. Some individuals born on this day have a rare capacity to listen to another's heart. Let them take you to the Scottish Highlands or the Welsh cliffs and you will never forget their companionship and the sudden way the light burnished rockfaces, more intense, more beautiful because they were consciously willing a singular delight into your soul.

Many people born on this day do well in corporations, keeping their peculiar powers to themselves. They often have a flare for organising institutions and frequently tap into the talent with money which is another characteristic of their birth sign. This person is not usually afraid of money, willing to borrow or lend, on practical terms. If you borrow, be sure to give it back, because some of these individuals aren't picky about strong-arm tactics.

Be thou familiar, but by no means vulgar.

(Hamlet*)*

27 JUNE

These are very direct people and can be difficult company for those who are uncomfortable with too much reality. But they are the salt of the earth, the people who everybody turns to when they need help. June 27 often shoulders the burdens of a family that other members can't face, and they do this cheerfully. Usually physically and mentally strong, they can manage to live a full life themselves alongside whatever duties they may have to others.

June 27 has a strong creative streak which often manifests itself in domestic skills. They can be inspired cooks and gardeners, taking infinite care with the more delicate side of both pursuits. This person is more interested in sliced peaches soaked in orange juice with a dash of brandy, than a lengthily planned rabbit and game stuffed cassoulet. There will be violas, pansies and columbine straying through the borders in their garden, rather than towering conifers and azaleas.

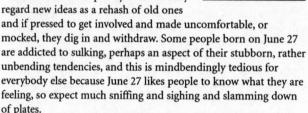

Steadfast in everything, this individual is a traditionalist and while perfectly alert to modern ideas, neither sex is seriously interested in contemporary fashion. They regard new ideas as a rehash of old ones and if pressed to get involved and made uncomfortable, or mocked, they dig in and withdraw. Some people born on June 27 are addicted to sulking, perhaps an aspect of their stubborn, rather unbending tendencies, and this is mindbendingly tedious for everybody else because June 27 likes people to know what they are feeling, so expect much sniffing and sighing and slamming down of plates.

These can be problem characteristics in some areas of corporate life, but this individual does very well in traditional types of business such as banking, transport and other industries which serve the community. In a local area or country village, this is the bank manager or postmistress, or policeman and woman upon whom the healthy and successful structure of ordinary living depends.

BODY

Sometimes this person just can't get to sleep because their mind is still racing with the tasks of the day. Experts suggest that you try to wind the body down an hour or so before you go to bed. For instance, try to stop working an hour earlier and if necessary start working an hour earlier at the beginning of the day. Avoid strenuous exercise before bed. Turn off the news. Cut down on tea and coffee during the day and don't drink either during the evening; some people cut both out after 4pm and say they sleep better for it.

MIND

People who successfully break their habits have one thing in common – they desperately wanted to break their bad habits. They made choices and sacrifices to get a life without the monkey on their back. Are you?

DATESHARE

Helen Keller, educator, overcame being deaf, dumb and blind. Isabel Adjani, French film actress. Sally Priesand, first American woman rabbi. Charles Stewart Parnell, leader of the Irish Nationalist Party, imprisoned for policy of violence in 1881. Charles IX, 16th century King of France.

Many people quit looking for work ∼ when they find a job.

(Vincent T Foss)

BODY

June 28 sometimes eats indiscriminately and this frequently leads to indigestion, heartburn and a chronically unsettled stomach. Pay more attention to your own body and a little less to everybody else's, and these problems can be solved. Avoid overeating, then try to cut down on dairy products, fast-food which contains additives and preservatives, and sugary treats. Instead try to introduce more fibre into your diet of the sort contained in oats, brown rice and beans. Add sesame oil, which contains vitamin E to lightly steamed vegetables and cooked salads. Drink a measured amount of hot tea and broths to help digestion.

MIND

Relax so much that you allow yourself to feel pleasurably dimwitted. It's a joy that often goes uncelebrated. Stay in bed until midday. Lie in the bath reading. Swing in a hammock in a country garden.

DATESHARE

Henry VIII, *whose six wives mostly came to unhappy ends, Composed 'Greensleeves'.* **Jean Jacques Rousseau**, *Swiss-French 18th century philosopher, educational theorist, thought toys were bad for children.* **Mel Brooks**, *comedian, actor, film director, Blazing Saddles.* **Gilda Radner**, *comedienne,* Saturday Night Live. **John Cusack**, *film star.*

June 28 is usually a joy to be with, both at home and at work. They are generous minded, quick to compliment others and equally quick to foster other peoples' talents. This star sign is noted for its perception and people born on this day are blessed with many of the Cancer virtues. In any kind of work or community activities this individual will shine at organising, drawing the best out of people, and overcoming difficulties with charm. Many are talented with money. They can frequently make money seem to go further than others do, yet they are usually safe hands with financial affairs, rarely having difficulties with a budget.

Quick to love, this individual is often extremely romantic and will shower a chosen partner with attention. They are good listeners and most of them are astute where other people's feelings are concerned. Some born on this day, however, may not be blessed with quite the same talent for assessing other people so they may make wrong judgements in their relationships. If this happens too often, June 28 can take betrayal too much to heart and the result is a dangerous temper. All people born under this sign may have a streak of aggression which they can sometimes find hard to control. Romantic betrayal may be the raw nerve here and often leads to long periods of resentment and sometimes enmity.

Because these people are good money–managers and leaders, they enjoy travelling and do so with imagination. They frequently like to go off the beaten track and avoid package tours, preferring to plan their own itinerary which allows them to see more closely how other countries live. June 28 will take care to find out about local customs and interesting places to see and some have a talent for learning languages which they see as a necessary courtesy to the natives of whichever country they are visiting.

*P**eople who are sensible about love are incapable of it.***

(Douglas Yates)

29 JUNE

If there's something to worry about then people born on this day will find it. It's always an Achilles' heel for June 29 and causes so much more upset in the life of our birthday child than is necessary. Sometimes these people get the measure of it and use their worries as an armour against the future – if they fear the worst in every possible way then they can always be pleased if things turn out better. And they won't be surprised if they don't. But often they take the Eeyore stand to such a gloomy degree that people around them lose patience.

The plus side to vulnerable June 29 is a brilliant capacity to think through all possible eventualities, and this makes them invaluable planners. Their memory is usually phenomenal, which means they can be relied on and can't be tricked, but will also drive others insane by reminding them of what they said some time before which is contrary to what they are saying now.

Sometimes this sense of foreboding is shot through with a brilliant capacity for humour and a natural raconteur's timing. Then, suddenly June 29's worrying psychology becomes the perfect basis for humour – all the best comics have a strain of pathos and self-mockery within their best jokes. They like making people laugh.

While this individual also tends to be hypochondriacal, their bags and briefcases actually rattle with bottles of pills and thermometers – just in case- most of them are capable of great bravery. And nearly all refuse to follow rules and etiquette too closely, deeming them fatuous in the face of the sterner issues of fate. Stick with them and they'll queue jump for you, bargain prices down for a cash payment, complain about awful hotel rooms and rotten service and stick two fingers in the air at the least whiff of snobbery or discrimination, especially if it masquerades in the disguise of reason.

A person must try to worry about things that aren't important, so he won't worry too much about things that are.

(Jack Smith)

BODY

Fatigue can be your problem and with it, the urge to boost energy with a sweetie binge. Chocolates, ice cream and fatigue lead to more chocolates, ice cream and more fatigue. Experts agree that natural, white sunlight keeps body functions working at the healthiest physiological level. Without it our nervous system makes adjustments which can cause fatigue and depression. Try to spend thirty minutes a day out of doors, before 10am, or after 4pm, to avoid unnecessary exposure to ultraviolet rays, and preferably where there is green grass and trees. Protect your eyes from sunlight reflected off reading material.

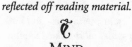

MIND

Self-confidence is gained by knowledge rather than hunch and the best way to gain it is from books. Reading induces calm and a new independence will bring a refreshing balance to your life.

DATESHARE

Susan Hayward, *actress.* **Mike Tyson**, *youngest world heavyweight boxing champion in history, convicted of rape and sentenced to six years.* **Lena Horne**, *singer, film star.* **Winston Graham**, *British writer, Poldark series.*

It's a sexy date and most people want to get off with June 30. This individual has been attracting people since early childhood, and some can be irritatingly accustomed to adulation. Some say that these are 'magic' children and certainly, in many families they will have been a favoured child.

Passionate lovers, June 30 can resist the blandishments of others – for the most part – and there will be a lot of them to resist. Many may seek out equally attractive partners, but others quite deliberately look for character qualities rather than physical beauty, and will stay put for life.

Great beauty in childhood and adolescence often induces social laziness and lack of personal development. Some have relied so strongly on their natural allure that they become quite dull adults, often painfully surprised when other less richly endowed people take centre stage because they are basically more interesting.

Nevertheless, many June 30 people prefer to downplay their own gift of natural attraction and develop as many talents as possible because they want people to like them for who they are and what they can do, rather than what they look like. While this individual frequently has a talent for acting or some form of entertaining, very often the creative flair which is common to this birthday comes out in artistic skills.

At the very least there is a good eye for style. Men may become photographers and the more practical members of that sex can excel in design technology or simply maintaining beautiful machines such as classy cars or antique clocks. Women born on June 30 are frequently able to run up a dress, or put a look together, in a matter of moments for very little expense. At the other end of the spectrum, both sexes can be found in the class zone of the style market, maybe in design, but also the media which records that market.

How little we should enjoy life if we never flattered ourselves.

(Duc de la Rochefoucauld)

I JULY

July 1 people are charming, effervescent and many have a facility for money-making, particularly in computers and gadgets. They can brilliantly invent new programmes but with easy generosity often use their talents to help less confident colleagues. Sometimes July 1 is cocky, but more often displays adroit self-deprecation, a necessary political talent in the work place. A mistake may be made if these individuals are so convinced that clever actions speak louder than words, that they fail to claim their successes. There's always somebody else who will.

Sensitive to nuance, professionally and in private, people born today are often lost for the right word. They must rely on actions when they can't think of something appropriate to say and this may make them seem slow to comprehend. A verbally skilled potential lover should best look elsewhere, unless prepared to sacrifice fascinating conversation for the chance to be paired with a millionaire. But July 1 people should be wary of romancing passionate talkers because love easily sours into criticism and an undermining mockery which will hurt them.

Nevertheless, they are natural party people, often arriving with unusual flowers and exquisitely chosen presents. (This date thinks

a dozen roses are dull. Instead, because July 1 people adore a mass of colour, expect armfuls of cobalt irises.) If any social occasion seems to flag it will be this quiet creature who has a flash of inspired showmanship, turns into an extrovert for the moment and leads the crowd. Often tremendous dancers, they can also make the clumsiest partner feel like candyfloss on the dance floor. More than that, July 1 people, with their exceptional physical and mental co-ordination, often become professional dancers, musicians and sometimes international sporting stars.

Sadly the Cinderella syndrome dogs some Cancerians born on this day and they can be tempted to indulge in maudlin unhappiness for no other reason than they feel a bit low after having a good time.

Haste makes waste.

BODY

If insomnia is a problem, try a tisane of sophorific lettuce leaves. Remember some people quite naturally need less than eight hours sleep a night and try to work out what you feel best with. If you find that bed at midnight and getting up at 6am works for you, or if you constantly wake in the night, but don't feel the worse for it the next day, then clearly that is your natural ryhthm. The best thing is to cease worrying about the eight hour concept. Like most other things, it's just a general measure, not a specific. If, however you are always exhausted because of lack of sleep, then combine the lettuce leaf drink, which works for some, with a few drops of lavender oil sprinkled upon your pillow.

MIND

The best love partners for July 1 are born between February 21 and March 21, and between October 21 and November 21. Best days of the week for marriage are Monday (for health), Tuesday (for wealth) and ultra-lucky Wednesday.

DATESHARE

Princess of Wales. **Carl Lewis**, US athlete, gold medallist in Olympic track and field events. **Dan Ackroyd**, film actor, Ghostbusters. **Gottfried Wilhelm Leibnitz**, German philosopher. **Charles Laughton**, British stage actor. **Debbie Harry**, singer, Blondie. **Leslie Caron**, dancer, film star. **Genevieve Bujold**, film star.

This is the shopper's birthday, at its most fun the person who just likes nice things, but more seriously, July 2 people are often knowledgeable art and antique collectors.

This individual is unhappy in ugly surroundings and sometimes thinks the key to happiness is extravagance. It's also the sociable side of buying that attracts. Auction houses, car boot sales, garden fêtes, street markets and department stores are gossipy places, like a daytime party.

Both sexes are naturally drawn to precious and semi-precious stones, the one to wear them and the other (men) more to give them. Special Cancer stones include the moonstone, which is reputed to balance moodiness and amazingly enough relieve stomach aches. But the lovely soft pearl is perhaps the best natural reflector of the shimmering depths of this dreaming star.

Dreaming or not, however, the more practical side of their nature means that July 2 people gravitate to money and power. If they can't make it for themselves, they marry it. For those who do go this route, such personal and material motivation will naturally mean they are extremely sophisticated sexually, skilled in seduction and often devastatingly attractive.

July 2 reads a great deal about sex, talks sexy, which they often regard as foreplay, and play all manner of pleasing games. Look in the cupboard and you'll find a strip poker board big enough for several people to stand on, with a silver dice shaker. Let them know you've seen it and they will issue an immediate invitation.

Essentially warm-hearted, they adore children. Flighty ones may see a baby on the arm almost as a crucial accessory. But most make loving parents. This date frequently has a big family, four or more children. Their chronic hypochondria may reflect genuine health problems and if this causes difficulty with conception, either sex must guard against desperation. Highly motivated July 2 has a determined streak which helps fulfill their longing.

No sex ∽
is better than bad sex.

(Germaine Greer)

3 JULY

Those born on July 3 are introspective and interested in how others tick, both powerful characteristics of the crab. Psychiatry, poetry and scientific philosophy may be their passion and many happily pursue these interests, showing no real need for wordly success. Some may have sufficient talent to become famous in the creative arena, but will usually be attracted to the cutting edge of new ideas, rather than traditional areas.

At work, July 3 listens to woes, usually giving good advice and acting as peacemaker and problem-solver. Unfortunately, they may be so empathetic that they become overwhelmed by others' miseries, so a measure of self protection is advisable if there is a resident fountain

of tears in the office. Equally unfortunately, some also suffer from a nosey-parkerish need to know and should resist reading memos upside-down on colleagues' desks.

These individuals are intensely stirred by the beauty of Nature, need little money and are often sparing in their appetites. Love must be based on shared interests and they are passionate, committed and rarely unfaithful. They keep careful watch over their partner's and any children's health, diet and happiness, but can also be tiresomely faddy, imposing barmy opinions on their unfortunate nearest and dearest. Because they don't adore eating, or have a flutter on the lottery, or flirt with as many people as possible, means they can't imagine why others should.

Single July 3 people could easily become hermits and must remember, or be reminded to keep in touch with family and friends. They are capable of showing astonishing bravery and bringing immense good to the world, make excellent physicians and can be found in organisations which work for the care of mankind.

Those who are less dedicated to the good of others have extremely good taste and make their homes lovely, choosing pale, watery colours, shimmering pearly-whites. Walking into their houses is like taking a step inside a delicate, alluring water lily.

BODY
They have fine, delicate skin, subject to spotty problems in adolescence. Some potions from the chemist may work, but it's best not to use too much. It's often disappointing, no miracles here, and some of the creams may set up their own reactions. Experts are divided in their advice and of course it's different for each individual. But too much hair washing with harsh, chemical shampoos is often the culprit for acne. Just hot water can be best for hair and skin.

⟳

MIND
Big heads often mean big talent. While the average brain weighs 1,400 grams, Oliver Cromwell's and Lord Byron's were 2,200 grams each, Otto Von Bismarck's 1,900 grams. But not always. Dante Alighieri's was 1,420 grams.

DATESHARE
Franz Kafka, author, The Trial. *Tom Cruise*, US movie star. *Tom Stoppard*, Czech-born playwright. *Ken Russell*, British TV & film director, Women In Love. *Leoš Janáček*, Czech-born composer. *Jean-Claude 'Baby Doc' Duvalier*, Haitian dictator, succeeded his tyrannical father. *George Sanders*, film actor.

The Kingdom of God is within you.

BODY

Ginger has always been popular in cooking for its extraordinary fragrance, but it is also well known for very many medicinal properties. Some swear by cooked ginger as a cure for the common cold. In Chinese medicine, a herbal brew of cinnamon, ginger, dried tangerine peel and Chinese liquorice – mmm, delicious?- is used for added energy, to improve poor circulation and to give the digestive system a boost. Add equal amounts, 3–4 grms each, to 0.75 litre water and simmer until the liquid is reduced by a third. Divide into three portions and drink two to three times a day.

MIND

The tender crab has a hard shell and a far from straightforward approach. But people respond best to tenderness and an honest mind, and you will certainly be confused about people if you make snap judgments.

DATESHARE

Guiseppe Garibaldi, Italian unification leader. **Eva Marie Saint**, film actress. **Tokyo Rose**, propagandist traitor. **Gina Lollobrigida**, Italian film actress. **William Byrd**, English Elizabethan composer. **Thomas Barnado**, Irish philanthropist, founded homes for abandoned children.

The eyes are the windows of this individual's soul, so expressive that others sometimes shy away from vulnerable July 4. This person cannot easily dissemble, so won't get on in industries where flattery is the main currency. Best to avoid a career in newspapers or television where July 4 may imagine the request 'Give me an honest opinion' needs an honest answer.

Professions which demand exact skills are best. Good at teamwork, this sociable personality may enjoy a life in the army or medicine. July 4 has a skill for entertaining and pleasing others and this, combined with a meticulous nature, may mean that working in retail or tourism is ideal.

Those born on this date frequently dislike being alone. They are naturally sociable, excellent club members and always welcome to join the crowd. Some have a strongly developed idealistic drive to serve the community and will defend either groups of people who come under threat, for example the homeless or the countryside, even historic buildings with absolute dedication. On occasion they may behave too aggressively in pursuit of a cause, but will usually listen to advice and stop short of fanaticism.

Debate about issues delights this date, but they tend to squirm at talk about personal feelings. On the sociable side, they are happiest entertaining a houseful of guests to a memorable dinner, with gorgeous, infectious gusto. And then having them stay to a huge, late breakfast, laced with some sort of fascinating alcoholic

pick-me-up, possibly their mother's secret Bloody Mary recipe.

Slow to give their heart, they are sometimes unpleasantly snobbish with individual strangers, but can be relied upon never to forget their mother and father's birthdays. In fact this person uses the family to road test all potentially serious partners and will fade out at the first intimation that a lover is either unhappy with this situation, or is failing to make a suitably warm impression.

Want a thing long enough and you don't.

(Chinese proverb)

5 JULY

T hose born on July 5 often have excellent skills in the kitchen, cooking and choosing wines with grace and enthusiasm. Naturally sensuous, these people enjoy the consumption as much as the preparation, so of course they usually have a battle with their weight.

They may also go into food or wine as a profession, where they frequently find success, particularly because they have an innovative flair which naturally gets them noticed. Some people born on this day use this flair and response to natural pleasures to develop expertise in recording these delights. Many paint. Others use a camera. Some like to write. But the subject is usually pleasure.

July 5 people do best as freelancers or running their own business. They are not at their best playing politics and are not usually ambitious enough to supress their social life for the good of somebody else's corporate outfit. This individual won't happily work through lunchtime unless it's for personal benefit, and they have to leave work promptly at the end of the day because they're meeting friends for a drink. Regular visitors to the same chic place to be seen, these people make a point of getting to know the staff, often becoming personal friends. Either way it ensures excellent service and that gratifying feeling of belonging somewhere. July 5 adores being part of the furniture in a place where he or she can watch smart money drift by, casting envious and curious glances at them.

Needless to say this cool birthday person makes a terrific nightclub owner. Theirs will be no ordinary gaff, but decorated with the latest computerised gadgets and toys for dancers to play with when they need a break, and gorgeous sofas and chairs to lie on while consuming iced lemon in a tall frosted glass.

When July 5 runs the show, the energy and inspiration can be extraordinary and very attractive to others, particularly mavericks with similar tastes.

BODY

July 5 will always think there is something one can eat to cure most ills ,so especially for this mildly gluttonous creature it is recommended that a handful of nuts should be eaten at least five times a week to provide dietary fibre, reduce high blood pressure and cholesterol and generally halve the risk of heart attacks. Nuts are rich in polyunsaturated fat (many nuts give us valuable oil), protein, carbohydrates, vitamins (particularly E), and minerals. One hypothesis is that vitamin E prevents the oxidation of cholesterol. It should be born in mind that nuts are high in calories.

MIND

Laughter improves our sense of well-being. San Francisco medics say intensive laughter over four weeks reduces the need for painkillers, although not the pain you cause, by doing this, in everybody else's arse.

DATESHARE
Jean Cocteau, French novelist. **Phineas T Barnum**, circus founder, showman, promoter, brought Jenny Lind (The Swedish Nightingale) to American public. **Cecil J Rhodes**, British empire builder, premier of Cape Colony. **G J R Pompidou**, French president.

Eat, drink and be merry,
       for tomorrow ye diet.
                    (Lewis C. Henry)

Both sexes can suffer from urinary tract problems and should always consult a doctor. Minor disturbances can be remedied by avoiding alcohol, tea and coffee, all fizzy drinks and concentrated orange and lemon squashes. Instead drink plenty of water, alternating this with barley water and the occasional cup of herbal tea made from camomile, or rasberry leaves, available at health food shops. Avoid commercially bought bath essences or oils. Some people find great comfort however from natural oils and aromatherapists recommend dropping four drops of bergamot and two drops of lavender, or six drops of tea tree oil into the bathwater.

MIND

July 6 works and worries so hard that they lose the talent for relaxation, some even feel uncomfortably useless if they take time to chill out. This attitude dulls the mind.

DATESHARE

Dalai Lama, *Tibetan religious and political leader.* **Andrei Gromyko**, *Soviet foreign minister.* **Bill Haley**, *rock and roll star.* **Sylvester Stallone**, *macho film star.* **Candy Barr**, *stripper and poet.* **Nancy Reagan**, *first lady to President Ronald Reagan.*

July 6 spends a great deal of time talking abut the inner workings of his or her mind, sometimes perceptively and sometimes as if they were talking about another person altogether. So July 6 will often say something like 'I'm the sort of person who always keeps a promise' or 'I always remember a good deed', unfortunately, an observation which is rarely true.

Poor memory is sometimes a problem for this individual, particularly with the males who can never remember where they have put keys and wallets. Both sexes can make a habit of failing to settle their bank account so that cashpoint cards are swallowed, usually on Saturday night when extra money is particularly vital, because somehow there wasn't time to get to the bank on Friday.

Generally this date tends to worry about finances more than is necessary. So much so that they leave bills unopened because any demand for money always seems too great. Watch out therefore for the telephone to be cut off and the electricity too. It's worth remembering with the latter that some electricity boards make a point of cutting the electricity off just as their office is closing on Saturday in order that the luckless and lightless punter has sufficient time over the weekend to consider the error of their ways and have a few major rows .

Other people born on this date are free of this problem-provoking behaviour and merely careful with their money, or in some cases, clever with it and can make excellent investments in property and a killing on the stockmarket. Some go to the other end of the spectrum and become inveterate gamblers, frequently extremely lucky as this is a particularly optimistic birthday to have.

In spite of this strong, very personal and perhaps inward psychology, this person is often blessed with a true sweetness of character and can attract loyal affections in others.

Drink to me only with thine eyes,
And I will pledge with mine.

(Ben Johnson)

7 JULY

July 7 is unconventional, even intimidating on first meeting. Quite often their verbal dexterity is disquieting for more conventional, less self confident types. They just take a bit of knowing, but it's worth it, because these individuals have a fantastic talent for bringing happiness.

They see far beyond what others see, and are completely devoid of snobbery, taking people as they find them and never demanding something which a companion is reluctant to give. Ruled by the moon, this creature likes to delve deep into his and her own psycheology, and do the same with companions. No shadows are left unlit, no secrets unprobed, difficult for those who enjoy keeping secrets.

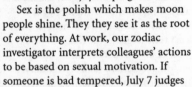

Sex is the polish which makes moon people shine. They they see it as the root of everything. At work, our zodiac investigator interprets colleagues' actions to be based on sexual motivation. If someone is bad tempered, July 7 judges him or her to be temporarily deprived of passion and if they are permanently bad tempered then they must have a serious dearth of romance – which needs fixing. So this creature sets out to fix, questioning, probing and, of course matchmaking. It can be irritating. But when July 7's judgement is correct, a lot of people are grateful for some help.

When July 7 becomes a boss, they usually manage to put away their addiction to other people's sex lives and use the swift Cancer intuition to remarkable effect when making deals, seeming to know what the opponent is thinking before they know it themselves.

Moonshine babes are pretty challenging lovers. They suggest things most people have never heard of. At the conventional end of the sex-adventure spectrum they adore making love in water. A swimming pool will do, but something natural is better – the sea or a crystal spring in some secret valley. The unconventional end is impossible to describe in a family birthday book.

Curiosity killed the cat.

Women born today may not be, physically, the star-spangled conventional figure-of-eight, but under the well-cut jacket, many hide their secret and perfect bosom. These babes may walk in the modest shadow of the moon, but they glimmer with promise. Great breasts are as much a Cancerian characteristic as the Pisces drown-in-me eyes and Taurus's solid waistline.

Many also have smooth, creamy skin and flat stomachs, at least in youth, attractions shared by both sexes. Many men born on this day are noted for their evenly textured skin and slender waists and hips.

Gratifyingly, we don't have a preener here. They are more interested in mind than body, and wish everybody else could keep their attention focused on the brain rather than elsewhere. So strong is the intimidating willpower of this creature, that many find themselves, unwittingly, doing what they are told by July 8.

In private there is almost no self-doubt. Many like to travel long distances, and certainly not with package tours, which are far too conventional. Some will take off to see the world for a year, working their way across continents, or seek a job abroad for a few years, before moving on. There are no obvious nerves about taking up a new way of life, none learning new languages, or fitting in. Nor is there homesickness. It's a pragmatic date and those who love this person must quietly accept that they rarely look back and that includes on their nearest and dearest. Fortunately July 8 quickly makes a new place look like home, which is certainly comforting if they are carting children about. They know that a home is where it smells good and even the dullest little space will soon be perfumed with a warm, herby fragrance. In winter they keep an open fire if they can, partly for warmth and partly for the delicious smell of woodsmoke.

Freedom is not for the timid.

9 JULY

This is a psychic date. Some less developed individuals simply have astonishing hunches, sudden starry bounds from A to Z without really understanding why. Others, better endowed with this ability should not deny it, but accept that the coincidences in business and personal life and the strange perceptions are a sure indication of this talent.

July 9 goes out on Saturday night sensing that they will meet someone who is their destiny. And they do. Women know they will get pregnant before anything physical has happened. Both sexes may decide on a whim not to travel, then discover that their train or aeroplane has subsequently been involved in an accident. And many sense that a loved one has met with accident or death long before they are told.

If twins are born on this day, this psychic capacity is frequently doubled. Twins have long been the source of study because of their heightened capacity to communicate with each other when they are apart. But with July 9 it will almost seem as if there is a psychic telephone line between them, and between themselves and the rest of the world.

Naturally this comes in useful at work, particularly because this creature is an original thinker, like many Cancerians, and dreams up unusual projects which are seen through with ease and the help of this heightened perception. Outside work, their sixth sense is as natural to them as the five senses are to the rest of us.

It usually makes them lively and confident and above all curious. Where others fear the unknown, July 9 doesn't really because he or she already has a perception of it. On the practical side it gives them the confidence to invent gadgets, or go for an idea which only later seems startlingly obvious to everybody else.

They are also persistent people. If they can't sort something out straightaway, they go back and try again until they can.

On a clear day

~

you can see for ever.

BODY

Both sexes have a tendency to experiment with alcohol, drugs and some of the more outlandish experiences. Sometimes they think these things heighten their perceptions, and this may even be true for a limited time. Young people born on July 9 are physically strong and can withstand quite a bit of drinking and other excessive behaviour for a period. But any kind of drug always undermines the body and mind in the end, especially as this creature has an addictive nature. They will be happier and clearer of head and heart if they get hold of this message sooner rather than later.

~

MIND

People born today shouldn't give in to anxiety. Bad things don't happen all the time, and if they do, July 9 won't necessarily sense it. In general these perceptions are simply there to aid a choice of action.

DATESHARE

Tom Hanks, prolific Hollywood star, Oscar winner. **Oliver Sacks**, neurologist, writer, The Man Who Mistook His Wife For a Hat, Awakenings. **Barbara Cartland**, British novelist, proponent of virginity. **O J Simpson**, sportsman, film star, centre of famous murder trial, found not guilty of murdering estranged wife. **Edward Heath**, British prime minister, conductor.

WATER

This quiet individual is generally extremely self-sufficient and knows his mind from an early date. July 10 has creative talents which may be developed and become a career. In particular, theirs is an impressive writing talent, although they are not extrovert talkers.

They may not be overly forthcoming with their opinions. But when asked, their opinions are well informed, logically thought through and may be powerful enough to swing a political vote or win the applause of a crowd. In the local community, July 10 may become a force for improvement, but all executed while remaining a pillar of respectability. Either sex can be good at raising money, great at thinking up original methods of doing so, but it's not they who actually organises the ER party in aid of the theatre roof. This can cause the willing workers, people born on other days, to

respond less enthusiastically to July 10's next very brilliant job-creation scheme to support charity.

Many July 10 people are happiest away from urban centres. They are susceptible to noise and get over-anxious about urban problems such as dirty air and the dustmen not turning up. Outside towns they may start businesses which derive their inspiration from the countryside, making furniture or textiles to distribute not only through chain stores but mail order catalogues. And many people born on this date thrive in the rural tourist industry.

Both sexes like to cook. Their tastes veer away from red meat and dairy products, towards vegetarian dishes and they develop passionate enthusiams for growing their own vegetables and for alternative medicine based on herbs. It's usually the men who like to cultivate rare vegetables, growing six kinds of tomatoes, from little cherry ones to the more unusual white and yellow types which can be raised from seed. The women are more interested in experimental cooking with edible wild plants many of which have medicinal virtues.

*Dawn comes slowly,
but dusk is rapid.*
(Alice B. Toklas)

II July

The psychic in July 11 is very dominant. Tall, dark handsome strangers, short fat rich strangers, they always know in advance they will meet them. They know where they will marry and when they get pregnant, instinctively, they know which sex to expect. When July 11 goes house hunting, neither sex can help judging the house by the atmosphere. They trot round the rooms and garden sniffing like a psychic bloodhound and if the coast isn't clear the owner could offer the property for 25 pence and this creature wouldn't take it.

Although neither concerned nor bothered by ghosts, they don't usually want to share a home with one. Some do get quite fond of an ephemeral resident, but usually it's because they're a relation. What is disconcerting about this individual is that they can put their hand on a patch of skirting and find a hidden box which has maybe lain there for years. Or they dream there is a manuscript hidden on a ledge in the well in the garden, when there is no well. But later it's discovered and so is the manuscript.

Some July 11 people may consult professionals about their psychic powers and go on to develop them, either as a hobby or professionally, even learning the skills of exorcism. Most are reasonably pragmatic souls and tend to keep quiet about their divining skills, partly because it gets boring when people continually seek their advice.

July 11 has a capacity to make people feel safe. Both sexes bring reassurance to the workplace. Find them advising colleagues, always careful, never gossipy. They may rise extremely high in any field because of their psychic talent, few colleagues ever realising that this creature knew a deal would be made before it was even thought about.

In private they are especially good with the sick and can make everything feel better again, bringing optimism with them as they enter a room.

BODY

Sometimes caring for others can become overwhelming and July11 finds that his or her powers are not only depleted but that they have taken on some of another's woe. There are good Bach Flower remedies to help this. Centaury (Centarium umbellatum) works for those who have difficulty in saying no, and have become exhausted with neglecting their own interests. Chicory (Cichorium intybus) for those who are over-full of care for those close to them and have begun to feel self pitying and angry that others don't conform to their commands.

MIND

What July 11 needs more than most is light relaxation which requires almost no thought. This creature will really benefit from a few hours of sitting in front of the television with a glass of good red wine.

DATESHARE
*Died: **George Gershwin**, great American composer. Born: **Giorgio Armani**, Italian fashion designer, perfect men's clothes. **Yul Brynner**, film star, fascinated a generation. **Robert the Bruce**, Scottish King. **Nicolai Gedda**, Italian opera singer. **Bonnie Pointer**, singer, Pointer Sisters. **Mark Lester**, film star, Oliver!. **Gough Whitlam**, Australian prime minister.*

Love is like the measles;

we all have to go through it.

(Jerome Klapka Jerome)

This is the day of the impressive thinker. These quiet people don't shilly-shally, but come to the point after due consideration, and even if others don't go along with July 12, most people agree that they always shed a new and interesting light on a situation. Nor does July 12 take the conventional route to his conclusion. Indeed, they dislike clichés so much that they shy away from those who use them.

Many rise high in public affairs, because they speak well, but also because they have another valuable quality – consideration for others. Endless trouble will be taken to listen to and consider advice and, if necessary, a great deal of time spent on research and in particular the effect that any decision may have on others around them. Some may find themselves involved in rethinking a company's future, a redirection, or even a merger. These are not people who will easily reach for mass redundancy or sacking. Wisely they are aware of the old saying 'So you sow, so you shall reap' and they will look for cost-cutting in other areas rather than simply reducing the number of people.

Other June 12 people can be found in government, or local government, where their thoughtful, often spiritual approach is always valued. This individual can be an excellent mentor, to the same sex as well as the opposite. Highly-sexed and emotional, the mentoring gets mixed in the pot with lust and love and sometimes everybody ends up confused. This is a difficult relationship to escape from completely unharmed.

Fortunately, in many cases, the relationship, often with an age gap, can work. Initially based on admiration – July 12 loves to teach about life and about sex – these mentoring love affairs are a nice mix of protectiveness and affection. The sparkle of stardust stays. Just occasionally the story turns into Pygmalion, when these people develop bossy and hectoring tendencies with gentler people.

Do unto others ⤙ as you would be done by.

13 JULY

This birthdate's child is full of woe, never comes across a good thing without looking for the bad thing that goes with it and is often such a worry-bore that others get caught in the crush as they make for the door. When this happens, he or she is deluged in self-pity.

And yet, they're the sweetest, kindest people, full of talent and perfectly clever enough to have an excellent, long and happy life. What they don't realise is that pessimism is more a phobia than a reality, a mindset you can choose to change. It's no more true that disaster is waiting around the corner than a stroke of fantastic luck, but you're a lot more fun to be around if you think it's the latter.

Women are the worst offenders here. They worry if someone's a couple of minutes late. They go into hysterics every time they get a bill and imagine imminent bankruptcy. They're obsessed with global warming, the problems which supposedly can be caused by eating beef, if their lover really does adore the size and shape of their bosom as he says he does, or is he just trying to be nice in the face of enormous odds, or perhaps in their case, enormous oddities?

Men worry about hair-loss, the shape of their chin, the size of their car and whether the small pain in their diaphragm is terminal and in which case, how long they have got to live.

Nip it in the bud. Or, if the misery mania is in full flood, nip it anyway. And the way to do this, for July 13, is to step up your sex life, take more time off, and concentrate on the physical pleasures of life. The afterglow of lovemaking puts everything in a rosy light. So more of it ensures more rosy light and the world and the universe seeming a better place.

Laugh ~
and the world laughs with you;
Weep, ~ and you weep alone.
(*Ella Wheeler Wilcox*)

BODY
Feelings of anxiety may be fostered by too many hours spent working in artificial light. Natural, full spectrum, white sunlight keeps the bodily functions working at a minimal physiological level. In the absence of full spectrum light, the autonomic nervous system has to make too many adjustments, which manifest themselves as fatigue, the desire to binge on sweet fast-food, irritability, gloom and mood shifts. Spend half an hour each day out of doors, preferably walking, which is calming to the mind and induces fitness in the body. Clear your mind of all preoccupations. Let the pleasure of the rhythm of your steps take over.

MIND
When you feel a worry rising to your lips, bite it back. Left unexpressed, many forebodings do actually go away. A spoken anxiety somehow becomes tangible. Just being cheerful is often the best cheerer-up.

DATESHARE
Harrison Ford, film star, who gets rid of his anxieties by building fences at his ranch. **Sir George Gilbert Scott**, British architect. **Wole Soyinka**, Nigerian playwright, first African to receive Nobel Prize for Literature. **Cheech Marin**, US comedy film actor, Cheech and Chong. **John Dee**, astrologer to Queen Elizabeth I. **Sidney Webb**, British socialist economist, co-founder of Fabian Society.

T his is a lucky birthday. July 14 is one of those people who goes through life boosted by sudden strokes of good fortune. They may be buying a house, a rival is offering more, but the seller likes July 14 best because they share the same passion for stock car racing. Our man with the star-studded destiny gets the property. Or, popping out of a movie for some cokes, and finding a lost purse on the floor, which contains several hundred pounds, they hand it in. The owner of the purse turns out to be a millionaire looking for someone honest to manage his business and, bingo, our Cancer child immediately steps on the ladder to wealth and position.

We've all heard such stories. We know it does happen. But be alert. Chances slip away fast – and you have to believe in them- so seize the moment. Because chance is a golden seam in July 14's psychology, they are open to new ideas and emotions. Both sexes question established traditions in big companies, not out of destructiveness, but knowing that a fresh eye picks up old problems, too long accepted and just put up with. Nor is Cancer

keen on intricate hierarchies, thinking too much energy goes into furnishing posh offices. With July 14 about, there will be open plan, little rank-pulling and no talk of 'proper channels'.

Privately our lucky star may seize a few more chances of love than most. There could be several serious affairs or marriages and, be warned, quite a few children. One or two of these kids may come along as a surprise and July 14 is likely to have at least one excessively talented offspring. Both sexes adore children, and since their winning streak stays with them all their life, watch out for sparks of excitement which will help provide financially for kids born to July 14 in later life.

BODY

If you suffer from indigestion, it may be because you eat too fast. Many July 14 people wolf things down, often while they are on the move, and then wonder why they suffer from stomach cramps. Grapes are traditionally thought to be soothing to the stomach – and far more slimming than snacking on chocolate biscuits and cheese sandwiches. They are also thought to be helpful with viruses.

MIND

The temptation for July 14 is to sit back and wait for something to happen, and this person is confident that it will. Laziness diminishes everybody's chances because you're simply not around in enough places to maximise the luck.

DATESHARE

Lino Ventura, *Italian screen and stage star.* **Terry Thomas**, *British comic film actor.* **Ingmar Bergman**, *Swedish film director,* The Seventh Seal. **Jerry Rubin**, *long-haired, bearded, vegetarian Yippie leader and author.* **Joe Sacramento**, *at 601 pounds one of the fattest men in the world.*

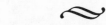

Character is destiny.

(Heraclitus)

15 JULY

The mystical psycheology in July 15 is very powerful and shows young. Luckiest people born on this day have parents who understand the dream side of their child, and bring him or her up to understand that there are some activities, places and ways of life that truly do not suit July 15. With all birth date psychology, the variant is huge from one individual to another. And there is always a wide element of choice in the path you take. But some characteristics are like a shimmering thread, a fine line between balance and sadness, so it's helpful for July 15 to know early on what brings a shadow to the soul.

Most of these individuals need solitude. Children need somewhere to go by themselves. Adults do better in the country, particularly by mountains which inspire this dream star. A karaoke office party, an inter-departmental seminar on budget keeping and a girls' night out at a strip club will simply make July 15 feel embarrassingly different. There's nothing wrong with not being like other people. Most people aren't. But this gentle creature too often wants to be what it can't be.

The women can make a home look good on minimum money, concentrating on pearly paint washes, beautiful materials and paying great attention to the way everything smells. Noxious stinks make them shudder. They prefer the scents of summer which greeted them when they were born, roses, jasmine, carnation and lavender. They will be more interested in

possessing a flower jug which belonged to a grandmother before World War II than a dishwasher. And they are perfectly happy to leave dust lying about, particularly if it's the starry kind.

The men share the same attitudes. Both may have musical talent which can become a profession. Both need to find a way of making a living which is highly individualistic, although running a shop is wonderful for many because of their natural sensitivity to peoples' needs.

BODY
Cancer's delicate stomach plagues July 15 and it may be a good idea to eat more garlic. (Encourage a partner to experiment with you, so as not to let the solution come between you.) The sulphur based compounds of garlic help to maintain a healthy cholesterol level, assist the functioning of the immune system and help keep infections and stomach bugs at bay. Regular consumption of garlic is also said to reduce the risk of stomach cancer. Many have found its use helps to keep eyes and skin clear. If the odour of garlic worries you, chew a sprig of parsley – nature's own breath deodoriser.

MIND
Don't bore people at dinner parties or anywhere else with your psychic experiences. Wait until you're asked. Some people have a positive aversion to the subject – and there are other things to talk about.

DATESHARE
Brigitte Nielsen, film actress. **Linda Ronstadt**, singer, songwriter. **Rembrandt Harmensz van Rijn**, Dutch 17th century painter. **Julian Bream**, British classical guitarist. **Inigo Jones**, British 17th century architect. **Iris Murdoch**, novelist and academic.

The best thing
others can do for us
is to tell lies.

July 16 is a prey to love and nothing seems right with the world unless they are consumed by greedy desire. This is OK when people born on this day are very young, but it can get in the way in middle age. Although in old age the spring in this creature's step is what keeps him and her entrancing, while others are content to wind down.

Because they are clever and very good planners- and because somebody senior fancies them – July 16 may zoom up the career ladder fast. But no amount of golden promises, company cars, expensive lunches and company-funded holidays will divert this individual from dropping everything to follow a gorgeously beckoning opportunity. However unwise.

This is the Lothario at work who every female colleague longs to kiss. He never lacks for coffee and biscuits and just a flash of his even teeth makes women shiver pleasurably. It makes no odds to him if a girl is married, or going out with his best friend. He plays around, always leaving people wanting more – except when the involvement is with the boss's daughter, when the solution is usually to marry her.

The female version suffers from Marilyn Monroe syndrome. Too needy for new pleasures, too intent on provoking, she is only saved from being thought a slut by her moon-radiant beauty.

Never mind. July 16 is a sex-bod and that's the way it is. In any close encounter with this jewel, expect the most expert lovemaking. Cancer has extra sensitive skin, so ever conscious of the pleasures of stroked flesh, this person excels at 'effleurage' which is a massaging movement where you glide your palms across the skin, putting body weight behind the movement. And 'petrissage', where the balls of fingers and thumbs move in a circular motion to soothe any muscle tension along the spine. (Do not massage the spine itself.)

Habit is the chloroform of love.

17 JULY

This person has close friends, valued as much as family. July 17, a neighbourly creature, always in and out of nearby houses, is famously the semi-detached star of the zodiac. He won't work or socialise singly but moves about as part of a constellation.

At home there is absolutely no risk of any marriage with July 17 turning into a nuclear family, because both sexes always ask everybody round, and are constantly feeding and nurturing the hordes. Life with this creature is a constant party, which they actually often throw to get things done. In their own home, important to anybody born today, decorating will be done by a group of mates, rewarded by several glasses of wine and maybe tiny homemade Scotch eggs. July 17 likes finger snacks.

At work, if anything needs rearranging, this person rounds up colleagues and it's fixed in a trice. Either sex enjoys an excuse to work at weekends. The men in particular are almost certifiable shopophobics and Saturday and Sunday hours spent at the office mean that their partner will have to do it all.

Sadly, a honeymoon with July 17 may be overcrowded, but any objection will be met with a four star rated sforzato tantrum. Our strongwilled, firmly contoured tomato rolls over anything that gets in the way and anybody who gives it the pip.

Women born on this day are quick witted and extremely funny. They aren't fussy mothers, don't insist on absurd rules for their children and as a result bring up reasonable adults. Some of the men may suddenly change their life, and not always for well thought out reasons. If it's for someone else, they set too much store by them and endanger the relationship. If it's a result of thoughtful research – July 17 is talented at spotting the window for a successful new venture – then they usually find that out of change something extraordinary comes.

BODY

There's a lot of partying and a lot of hangovers in July 17's life. But since Cancer people like natural remedies, here's a juicy way to deal with them. Hangovers are caused by the toxicity of excess alcohol and dehydration. Banish them by flushing alcohol from the system with plenty of liquids and raise energy levels with quick nourishment. Try the following combinations in the juicer to replace vitamins B1 (thiamine) and C, which are depleted by alcohol. Half a large pineapple plus 1 mango, or 2 large carrots, 6 kale leaves and quarter of a cucumber. Both recipes make one 230ml glass of juice.

MIND

Although crowds are not to everybody's taste, it's one great way of living and it would be a disaster if you change it because someone close wants you to him or herself. You will find it stifling.

DATESHARE

Donald Sutherland, American film actor. **Diahann Carroll,** singer, actress. **Phyllis Diller,** comedienne. **Earl Stanley Gardner,** mystery story writer, Perry Mason.

All you have to do is call
And I'll be there.
(James Taylor)

BODY

This good-looking date should ensure that skin is protected from sun. July 18 people burn easily, but sun is not really good for any skin at all. There are two types of sun ray you should protect your skin from, the UVA rays, responsible for stimulating the production of the pigment melanin, which is the skin's natural protection against sunburn. UVA rays are most closely associated with skin cancer. The second type, UVB, age skin by damaging collagen and elastin, the suppleness and elasticity of the skin. Don't go below a Sun Protection Factor 15.

MIND

Your natural talents are so tremendous that it's really a duty to develop them and not allow fads and wrong judgment colour your life. It's easy to tell sensible from silly if you really want to.

DATESHARE

*Died: **Jack Hawkins**. Born: **Richard Branson**, British businessman, Virgin empire owner, adventurer. **Nick Faldo**, British golf champion. **Nelson Mandela**, South African president, anti-apartheid leader, head of ANC. **Yevgeny Yevtushenko**, Russian poet, dissident.*

Women born today are Cancerominously romantic and this tendency should not be encouraged, or they will spin forever through the universe, gazing down at the world through their rosy-tinted aura. Little girls get all the usual good fairy gifts, good looks, wit, talent, sweetness of nature, but then the bad fairy popped by later and counterbalanced all of this with a wedgette of vain gullibility.

They think lovers and frocks and even new jobs grow on trees – for them. Because they reap so much personal praise they often expect the best of everything, and more difficult, they expect somebody else to get it for them.

July 18 window shops for life. Then a partner, or friend, or even child, clinches the deal. Anything without an accepted, conventional style makes them shudder and they suffer from trainspotteritis at the mention of any outdoor activity involving fresh air. These girls have more earrings in an ear than anybody else. They could be persuaded to go to a club with a bathbag on their head, if the persuader had a glib enough tongue. The worst kind of man takes them for a ride.

If July 18 could but listen to sense their life would be easier, and better, too, for advisers who spend endless hours advising, while this creature revels in the attention. When she does take sense on board, the most delightful independent butterfly emerges, more eye-catching than anyone else around.

The men are not quite so subject to enslaving others, and even become other's slaves. And they are certainly more practical and able to do things for themselves. But at home, in any financial area or anything to do with property they are prey to bad influences from others on the make. And in the office, they are vulnerable to the worst kind of flattering toad. Everyone's nature can be modified. These are only general guidelines. Don't let the gullible factor bring you down.

*She who has never lov'd,
has never liv'd.*

(John Gay)

19 JULY

These people have great influence over others and can be found at the apex of power. They are seldom, however, the ones to actually exercise it. The subtle, empathetic nature of July 19 is better suited to advise and help. They lack the blistering roar of the leader and a naturally sympathetic cast of mind makes it almost impossible to do anything nasty.

This does not prevent them from advising somebody else to take drastic steps. Women find this role rewarding. It comes through marriage or the conventional personal assistant relationship so many develop with a powerful boss at work. They understand the need to provide physical comfort, to find the exact kind of tea, the perfect cut to a ham sandwich, the only shade of nail varnish in town. And of course they know who will be welcomed by their master, mistress, husband or lover and who won't.

July 19 may spend hours reading papers, researching in libraries or interviewing specialists in order to come up with vital answers for a conference. Most of them thoroughly enjoy this, fascinated by learning. Naturally they also enjoy the wealth and power, glamorous receptions, television interviews and the sheer fun of having the prime minister on the telephone.

In all their dealings, July 19 remains discreet and never misuses his power. Nobody is personally favoured or worse, excluded by this master of the key to the charmed circle, in a fit of willful meanness. They stay tactfully in the background behind other advisors, simply because the personal relationship means taking extra care.

July 19 must ensure there is sufficient time left for a personal life. If the powerful one is a domestic partner, it is vital for everybody's happiness. It's never the right time to get pregnant, so do it anyway. If it's a friendship then our summertime babe must have his or her own life. You can't live through another and overdependent people lose their attractions.

We can learn from history that nobody learns from history.

BODY

Swimming is perfect exercise for people born in the hot months when slipping into cool water is more desirable than anything else. Exercise in water is disarmingly easy. Just try this simple pulse-raising walk on the spot routine for a few minutes and you will start to feel pleasantly agile and put your heart rate up. Stand, feet apart, chest deep in water and bend your right knee so that the right heel is lifted and your weight is over on the left. Now shift your weight back to the other foot, allowing your arms to move as if walking. Do it for seven minutes.

MIND

Repeated deliberation and procrastination brings fresh doubts and scruples and thereby humiliation, because one shows oneself unable to act. After a matter has been thoroughly pondered, it is essential to form a decision and to act.

DATESHARE

Edgar Degas, French Impressionist painter, concentrated on ballet dancers. **Natalia Bessmertnova**, Russian dancer, escaped from Iron Curtain to make successful career, helped by Anton Dolin in London, Paris and New York. **Ilie Nastase**, Romanian explosive world tennis champion, original terrible brat of the courts. **A J Cronin**, novelist, The Citadel. **Gilbert Sheldon**, 17th century Archbishop of Canterbury, builder of Sheldonian Theatre at Oxford.

WATER

People born on July 20 may be extremely good at sport and retain a lifelong interest in it. Their empathetic nature makes them spectacular at team sports or any other physical activity, such as boating, pot-holing, climbing or even exploring, which involves a close working relationship. In youth, days are spent messing about in playing fields and water or on horseback. These people are nearly always amazing with horses, showing no fear and forming an instant bond.

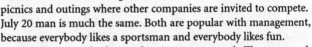

Both sexes love to dance and can do it for most of the night. In career terms this little crabette with just the hintiest flicker of the lion's tail – Leo days are coming shortly – keeps her sporty hobbies. She will run an office team and organise summer picnics and outings where other companies are invited to compete. July 20 man is much the same. Both are popular with management, because everybody likes a sportsman and everybody likes fun.

Many have a wide choice when it comes to work. They are good with words, fast with ideas and unusually visual. Plus a lot can sing well. Some flit from job to job, stepping from one career to another allied area. They make good agents, excellent publishers and being the first water sign, anything to do with water always attracts. Money has its attractions and most will acquire plenty. But they don't seek to display wealth, so the old tracksuit and trainers stay favourite and their posh clothes consist of matching well-cut suits and classy shoes. Not a person with a pigtail on top of his head and black nail varnish.

Most houses are furnished discreetly and usually painted white or pale shades of peach and blue for bedrooms. There will be wall charts of birds and mushrooms, perhaps butterflies and insects, all mirroring July 20's outdoorsy style and interests. If they have children, they'll all go blackberry and mushroom hunting.

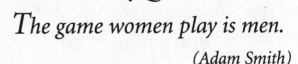

The game women play is men.

(Adam Smith)

21 July

July 21 is intensely conscious of its surroundings, whether it be in the countryside or the deepest city. The eye is good, sees everything with the appraising detachment of a painter. Many express themselves best working in some visual area, such as set design or shop window dressing, where they usually win the annual Christmas festive design award. But quite a few with an aptitude for mathematics and sales, may enjoy working in banks or marketing departments. Wherever they go there will be flowers and plants, always something to please their senses and those of their colleagues.

The girls adore clothes. Find them at work in intense discussions about the exact shade of orange right for a weekend's car trip to a neighbouring village's flower festival. They can make plans for a wedding last a lifetime and fortunately you will never get a hint of those particular fondant shades of turqoise, pale pink and yellow which haunt such occasions.

Many of the men are even more stylish dressers, genuinely handsome and with impeccable taste, especially in shoes, of which they have so many that most partners have to train themselves not to fall over them at night on the way to bed. Neither sex cares too  much about money, although many people born on this day land a financial windfall later in life. What they like is a loving partnership, healthy, happy children and a serene life, the accent on beauty.

Both sexes excel in the garden. Neither are they so fussy that others can't lie about drinking cans of coke and scattering newspapers. Favourite plants include the common buddleja, butterfly bush, (*Budleja davidii*) which comes in shades through lavender to deepest mauve, burgundy and creamy white, flowers all summer long and throws out such seductive honey fragrance that the air around it is busy with butterfly wings. Amongst roses they adore the oddly blueish Blue Moon hybrid tea, powerfully lemon scented.

How do you get an elephant into a matchbox?
Take all the matches out first.

BODY

Delicate, dry skin on the hands which sometimes cracks is a common problem for July 21, made worse because they like to paint and do things about the house with their hands. Contact with household cleaning materials, paint, glue, insect sprays or highly perfumed soaps can cause this chronic skin condition. Avoid these substances to see if this helps. Zinc, found in seafood and seeds aids skin healing. Take it in in multi-mineral formula with a multi-vitamin for six weeks. Sunflower and pumpkin seeds help to heal and moisturise skin. Try taking one tablespoon of Essential Balance Oil daily, available from good health stores.

MIND

Sometimes you feel hurt because a lover fails to understand what you want. It's because you haven't told them. July 21 plays this maddening mindreading game as a love test, but others can't always pick up the right message.

DATESHARE

Robin Williams, comic, Disney star, Dead Poets Society. **Isaac Stern**, violinist. **Jonathan Miller**, British intellectual, opera producer, television producer, author, distinguished medical practitioner. **Cat Stevens/ Yusef Islam**, singer, songwriter, Moslem. **Ernest Hemingway**, author, follower of the bullfight, Nobel Prize-winner. **Carl Reisz**, British director, The French Lieutenant's Woman.

From a very young child July 22 is fascinated by travel and longs to discover the world. They use their good ear and interpersonal skills to help them learn several foreign languages and by their early twenties these jolly creatures will have either worked for a few weeks abroad or be planning to do so.

Quite a few of the girls train in catering or nannying, skills which are always in top demand in foreign countries. The British nanny abroad can choose her ski resort, whizzing down star-frosted slopes with Prince Charles and his equerries the Lords Rosenstein and Guildencrantz, and the summer at any beach resort of her choice.

Both sexes may be drawn to the backpackers' trek through New Zealand and Australia, earning their way by sheep shearing in the former and cattle ranching in the latter. Many later go back and live in these countries, in love with the landscape, the weather and the niceness of the people.

July 22's rooms are crammed with trophies from their travels. They go to parties wearing embarrassing kaftans and the acidic chemically dyed colours of the rug on the floor were carried back from China. There will also be a lot of African wooden heads and Indian elephants. They are completely passionate about cultural identity, praising the traditional Kenyan Masai warrior's nomadic way of life and the virtues of using cow dung to line the roof and walls of family huts – such an environmentally friendly use of the animal's end product. And what a pity that the women, whose job it is to spend half their lives up to their elbows in it, are becoming more attracted to western brick and roof tiles.

Their cooking is usually flavoured by the last trip, so when you encounter a thickly sweet curry laced with coconut, you know it's authentic. In restaurants July 22 always speaks to waiters in their native language.

Right at the evening star and straight on 'til morning.

23 JULY

I solation is bad for July 23 people. They seek its sweetness but get sad when they are lonely. It's a psychology which usually has two sides to most emotions and the one wars with the other. What is good for this mysterious star is a deep loving relationship, which allows for the need to be alone, but when another is near at hand. The sun needs its moon. Some July 23 people may have difficulty achieving this because they are shy, convinced that nobody will want them.

Fortunately their precious, wistful charm and dreamy vision is a

magnet to those who want to share their life. This little violet lures lovers simply by its beauty, so that when plucked the perfume can be enjoyed. If they don't acquire a lover, and many choose to remain single, then it is essential for this creature to establish good friends.

For many, work is their life. There they are valued for their loyalty and thoughtfulness, will rarely find themselves sacked because others rely on their generosity with time and energy. In small projects the dreamy psychology also works well because it contributes an unusual overview.

Either sex may pursue a specialist interest extremely successfully. Jewels lure them – emeralds and pearls are their gemstones – and so does anything redolent of an ancient culture. Roman coins fascinate them, still easily picked up in the Thames. You may find both sexes on archaeological digs in places such as the gold-working centres in the Ecuadorian highlands, where excavating is still in its infancy.

Back home this interest may develop into something the family can share, when July 23 goes metal detecting and treasure hunting on every holiday, usually with astonishing results. And very often, their finds are of such value that something extremely saleable and a subsequent fortune is discovered almost by accident.

I know who I was when I got up this morning, but I think I must have changed several times since then.
(Alice In Wonderland)

BODY
July 23 likes dairy food and pastries and can't understand why the weight piles on. How can a custard tart or two mean a new pair of trousers? This creature usually thinks of nuts as a treat too, yet eaten carefully they will help you slim and reduce your cholesterol level. And they are just as filling as a custard tart. Nuts are rich in polyunsaturated fat, protein, carbohydrate, vitamins – particularly E – and minerals. It has been found that a handful of nuts a day could halve the risk of heart attacks, possibly because the vitamin E content prevents the oxidation of cholesterol.

MIND
In difficult times it's best not to awaken enmity by inconsiderate behaviour, easy to do when you're not happy. Best to let things pass when you disagree with them, not castigating others if they are wrong, but not being duped either.

DATESHARE
Died: **Montgomery Clift.**
Born: **Michael Wilding,** Shakespearian stage and film actor. **Raymond Chandler,** thriller writer, scriptwriter, The Big Sleep. **Graham Gooch,** England batsman and captain. **Woody Harrelson,** film and TV star, Cheers (dumb blond). **Haile Selassie,** Ethiopian 20th century emperor, deposed.

BODY

These people can be mixed up and should try to maintain, or reintroduce some balance into their lives. Sensitive bodies do not function optimally without regular times for sleeping and eating. Women with babies and young children cannot help odd sleeping patterns, and often fail to get the balance back later. July 24 should try to eat and sleep at regular times in the day for one week. During this week, he and she might try half an hour's walk, always at the same time, and a specific few moments, again, at the same hour, to sit down and think for fifteen minutes or read.

MIND

They want big families, but like the rest of the world, some have starter difficulties. Fantastic work rates and stress can undermine conception. You can't give up the job, but you can mentally poke fun at stress-provoking neanderthal creeps.

DATESHARE

Linda Carter, *TV actress,* Wonder Woman. **Amelia Earhart,** *pilot, first woman to fly across US and back.* **Zelda Fitzgerald,** *beautiful wife to writer Scott Fitzgerald, became a drunk and was hospitalised until her death.* **Robert Graves,** *British poet, novelist, I Claudius, mentor to beautiful young women.*

You can't help liking July 24 who is attractive to other star signs because he is the leader. But people born on this day must balance their unusually volatile nature. Born on the Cancer-Leo cusp, the combination of crabby scuttling sideways and leaderly leonine bounding forwards causes tensions in the star-lit chamber of their complex psychology. One minute a plan is going well for these people. The next is devoted to stamping and the banging of doors.

People born on this day are charmingly decisive, but carry others along with their enthusiasms on the wings of empathy and communication. Mostly they run alongside their companions, rarely out in front. Teams work well for both sexes, where they initiate original work practices, with everybody's help. They are usually open to suggestion, even criticism. Some individuals go overboard for the more extreme Harvard work theories, but this is generally harmless and can be indulged a little.

You'll find quite a few in charities, where they keep things going without adopting the frequently drab – which denotes appallingly respectable – appearance, apparently mandatory in some such organisations.

July 24 women have the sensuous Cancer streak, but the Leo broad sweep. They make places feel right, fast. This lady will fill her garden, and anybody else's with stunning lavender in shades from white through pale and dark lavender blue to pink. Honeysuckle perfumes the air all year round. Everything has two functions, visual and scentsual. Male gardeners do the same, but devote themselves a little more to multifunctional inventions about the house. They adore the idea of a stool that unfolds into a magazine rack. And they are fascinated with alternative ways to run a house, such as solar heating.

Most true Leos can't be bothered with such fiddly ideas. Their vanity requires a bigger stage. But once July 24 perfects something, you nearly always find that everybody else is keen to do just the same.

The premature ejaculator's favourite orgasm battle cry is 'I'm coming. I'm sorry.'

(Jerry Rubin, Mimi Leonard)

25 JULY

Danger, sex, travel, intellectual brilliance and money are keys to this creature. Their ideal is not a life spent in rural contemplation. (Nobody about to admire them.) People are drawn to July 25 and enjoy allowing him or her to take over. Tag on behind them at airports or ferry crossings, because NO ENTRY means SHORT CUT to this creature and you will find you have jumped the queue.

If there's a problem which needs solving, they sort it. The

slightest hint of danger? They enjoy any challenge which utilises their leadership skills and fast reflexes, and their natural vanity is titillated by admiration. Most retain a courteous attitude towards authority figures, if only to be expedient. They are not lawless, although both sexes drive too fast, and irritatingly, won't let anyone else take the wheel.

They get to play at sex games a little earlier than other star signs, but since this master of the universe is one of the goodies, nobody gets hurt and everybody has fun. It's a good idea, even in adulthood, for them to keep these secrets – but hard, because he's an amusing gossip, and she is too keen on being seen to be more informed than her companion, to keep a secret.

Men and women born under this sign are often tall and good-looking and do well in corporate life as well as starting their own business, because they really don't have a problem with fitting in with, changing, or running work structures. Find these diplomats of the solar system in the Foreign Office, commanding a sub, heading an advertising agency, newspaper group or, indeed a charity.

If July 25 does get involved in any charity fundraising, they will drum up quantities of money, as indeed they do in any walk of life. Both sexes do throw it around a little, but neither sex is frightened of it and most know how to invest carefully.

BODY
July 25 suffers from back problems. Backs flare up under stress, when you least expect trouble and could most do without it. So adopt a lifestyle which is kind to this vulnerability. Even with care, you may get trouble, but less so. Regular workouts can do wonders. Make sure the regime is planned by a professional who is fully informed about the back problem, and check credentials. Swimming is wonderful for backs. Try to use a chair at the office which is specially constructed for backs. There are plenty of them about. And get a hard mattress or sleep on a futon.

MIND
July 25 is very directed and can be snappy with others who seek to change the subject to another which bores him or her. Since this day can be so incredibly charming, it's so much better to control irascibility.

DATESHARE
Louise Brown, first test-tube baby. **Arthur James Balfour**, British prime minister, Balfour Declaration created Jewish state. **Maxfield Parrish**, painter, illustrator. **Omar Khayyam**, Persian poet, mathematician, astronomer.

I want to do with you
  What spring does
    With the cherry trees.
      (Pablo Neruda)

FIRE

It's important for women and men to understand their face is their fortune. Essential oils penetrate through the skin to the dermis, and travel through the interstitial fluids, the bloodstream and the lymphatic system. You can effect a remarkable change by applying a treatment oil each night before bed. Apply with gentle, upward strokes and leave on while you sleep. Beautifying Blend for Normal Skin: Mix 2 drops ylang-ylang, 2 drops rosewood, 2 drops lavender, 2 drops sandalwood, 10ml jojoba, 15ml camellia oil, 5ml rosehip seed oil. (Rosehip seed oil is excellent for dry or mature skin, not suitable for greasy, blemished skin.)

MIND

To gain success, July 26 is prepared to slim, have plastic surgery, give up drinking and smoking and generally horsing around. Fine. But there is no reason why everybody else should, and anyway, that'd be more competition for you.

DATESHARE

Mick Jagger, lead singer Rolling Stones, won fame, fortune, women, keeps on rocking. **Salvador Allende**, Chilean Marxist president, assassinated. **Aldous Huxley**, British novelist, Brave New World. **Blake Edwards**, film director, The Pink Panther. **George Bernard Shaw**, Nobel Prizewinning Irish playwright. **Carl Jung**, Swiss psychologist, psychiatrist.

JULY 26

The golden necklet of fortune is clasped around children born on this day. These self-made men and women find it easy to gather riches. Simply hold out your hand and the pearls which make up the Milky Way will slide down the sky into your grasp. Most fortune and position is gained more or less conventionally. Both sexes quickly rise to the top of their chosen industry with a combination of hard work, flare and enormous dedication. So much so that many people, rightly, accuse July 26 of narrow interests, because they eat, drink and sleep their work.

Career women born today are impressive public speakers, usually tall, make friends easily and inspire positively canine admiration. They choose the male sex for their henchmen. This leaderene likes – desires – masculine talents she misses in herself. She learns from them power mongering, judicious brutality and studious aggression, then maybe allows one or two the privilege of escorting her on business functions. But a July 26 babe is not interested in sex outside her own marriage. In fact she's often too tired for more than a kiss within her own marriage.

The prime interest of both sexes is the commercial uses of lust. Many run media and creative businesses. Their skill is the cutting-edge of public life, to be at the centre of affairs, manipulating them if at all possible.

Adoring followers and dazzled bosses should beware the golden spikette in this lion's tail. They always said they were just in it for the money and they meant it. Once proper money is in their grasp, this individual lopes off without looking back. Theirs is not attachment to business, only the benefit. Others who are emotionally attached can be hurt by such desertion. But in the end, July 26 is working for family. Securing its future, which includes parents, is the prime drive. The rest is having lavish fun and probably never working again.

I've got a long felt want.

(Eric Morecambe)

---

27 JULY

This person is a good host, so brilliant at dreaming up great wheezes to entertain others, that many companions forget the formidable brain lurking beneath the wit. Which is exactly what July 27 wants.

It's a shrewd creature, capable of profound thinking, but while he is doing so he likes the sound of music and wine corks popping. Both sexes are fabulous cooks, with a taste for experiment which never seems to end in disaster. When July 27 mixes rose petals with crushed fresh ginger and chicken pieces marinated in rosewater, all stir fried in sesame oil, it will be a success. He puts purple pom-pom chive flowers into coleslaw, instead of onions. Everybody murmurs praise. Other birth dates can't pull this off. That's the way it goes and it goes July 27's way.

And when the party is over and friends sit with a last glass of chilled wine, discussing who got off with who, this individual mentally puts the finishing touches to the plan he was working on. It's a Leo characteristic. Doing two things at once, the one benefiting from the other, because while July 27 is cooking she can concentrate on thinking.

So we have creativity, versatility, a creature bound for the top or at least to get what it wants in life. The downside may be that where love is concerned, inspiration is taken and pleasure is given, but the heart stays untouched. Out on the bleached grasses of the Masai Mara, the lion hunts and usually wins, but is itself notoriously difficult to hunt and catch. And that's the way with love.

There's always a spin off too. July 27 will have a long, startlingly provocative telephone conversation with a lover – lust on the phone pleases them- but they are also testing the range of their mobile as they murmur. The good news is that they tend to marry for life and make great parents.

BODY
July 27 people are blessed with luxuriant hair. Both sexes frequently keep it long and take good care of it. Naturally, fab hair adds to physical attraction, first used to allure, and then in lovemaking. The Kama Sutra acknowledges the eternal fascination that a woman's hair has for a man, stating that among the lessons she must learn, her duty is to 'dress the hair with unguents and perfumes and braiding it'. In the author Vatsyayana's time, long hair would have graced the male sex too. He instructs stroking a lover's shoulders and chest with handfuls of silky hair. Try it. Short hair? Grow it.

MIND
July 27 often adores gardening from early youth, largely to do something practical while thinking. Plant rosemary, mint, thyme and basil, aromatic plants which please the senses and have that attractive duality – invaluable culinary uses.

DATESHARE
Christopher Dean, *British Olympic gold medal-winning figure skater.* **Peggy Fleming**, *world champion figure skater, Olympic gold medallist.* **Anton Dolin**, *British ballet dancer, co-founder London Festival Ballet.* **Hilaire Belloc**, *British writer.*

She offered her honour,

he honoured her offer,

and all night long

it was honour and offer.

BODY

Leos have a great mane of hair. Some, however, may develop a physical condition which alerts them to take care. Hair loss in both men and women can occur as a result of poor circulation, acute illness, surgery, radiation, skin disease, sudden weight loss, iron deficiency, diabetes, thyroid disease, drugs such as those used in chemotherapy, stress, poor diet, vitamin deficiency and pregnancy. Some hair is lost as the seasons change. Male hair loss may be hereditary, or due to hormones and ageing. Most women lose some hair two or three months after childbirth, due to hormonal changes during pregnancy that prevented hair loss now changing again.

☾

MIND

Friendship is extremely important to this wild creature. Value it for the trustworthy structure it brings to your affections and for the warmth and the welcome. Don't put it away for love, which often substitutes indulgence for fair play.

DATESHARE

Jacqueline Kennedy Onassis, *late stylish widow of President John F Kennedy.* **Beatrix Potter**, *British author,* Peter Rabbit. **Gerard Manley Hopkins**, *British poet.* **Mike Bloomfield**, *rock blues guitarist.* **Sally Struthers**, *film actress.*

The thing about snobbery is that it's amusing if it's not serious. Indeed it has often been the subject of bestselling wit, circulation-boosting magazine articles and soaringly successful TV series. But when it's for real, Cinderella's coach turns to a pumpkin and so does July 28 if she's not careful.

You don't have to be born into a titled family to be a snob. In fact many of these people find snobbery offensive, although let's not kid ourselves that this is the norm. Anybody, from any walk of life, can be a snob. It's just an extension of 'I am better than these people, and my friends are classier than theirs'. People born today do have this tendency. It's tiresome, and in some cases appallingly embarrassing.

It's just about OK for July 28 to joke about 'anoraks' and people with zerobubble. It's not OK when this creature tries to prevent family and friends from falling in love with or just knocking around with individuals they disdain. In particular it's not OK when July 28 is pointedly rude and puts someone down, which is another strong tendency.

All of this arises from the competitive streak which is common

to most Leos and the basis for much of their creativity. This same streak can give rise to malicious behaviour and jealousy, even sabotaging others, so it's important that this child, who in numerology is ruled by the number 1 (2+8=10, 1+0=1), understands that the desire that those ruled by 1 have, to be first, needs to be measured.

The 1st card of the Major Arcana is The Magician, who symbolises intellect, communication and information, as well as magic. A potent weapon in anybody's hands.

When these individuals hold steady control of all their diverse and shifting emotions, there is nothing to stop them achieving what they wish and rising to the most inspiring heights in whichever is their chosen field or interest.

A lover is like a traitor: you can expect to be turned on by either.

(A F G Lewis)

29 JULY

Everybody born on this day takes delight in the opposite sex – or indeed their own – with tremendous abandon. Money is extremely important to July 29 and when they get it they spend it grandly on lavish holidays, fast cars and impressive presents for a lover. Nobody is more generous in love than this individual. He or she will work day and night to support their darling and be happy to spend too much money on them.

At some times in their lives, love and career can become incompatible. July 29 falls in love to such great depth that his office desk may be empty for weeks, with just a coating of stardust he brushed from his winged shoulder as he flew by. He can just dump the job and may travel across the world to follow the babe who has his heart and it's to be hoped that any employer will show patience, because July 29 is a high flyer and worth waiting for.

Intoxicated as these space rangers are by love, it's not surprising that they can zoom through the universe from one delicious docking procedure to another without much heed for anybody else's feelings. With some it gets to be such a habit that they don't settle down until middle-age or even later. Either sex may marry someone a great deal older or younger, and in both cases this versatile, resourceful, emotional creature chooses right and makes it work. Naturally this can mean a late family.

Since both the men and women are physically vigorous, they can just as easily swirl a child around in their fifties as their thirties. It's likely to be more than one child, because this is generally a very fertile date. But if a baby doesn't come along in the normal way, it will arrive by another route. Babies are attracted to this bright creature, like moths to a light.

Champagne to your real friends.
Real pain to your sham friends.

FIRE

JULY 30

BODY

If it was safe, July 30 would lie in the sun all day. This sun-lover should always use a powerful protection cream. But it's worth noting that medical experts now say that incidence of melanoma is ten times higher in the rainy north of Scotland than in the sunny Mediterranean. And melanoma occurs more frequently on parts of the body rarely exposed to the sun, such as the back and feet, than areas like the face and hands. Nor does ultra violet therapy increase the risk. So judiciously enjoy the sun and discourage others from treating it like a contagious disease.

MIND

Sometimes you can be rather relentless in pursuit of your own interests. A rich interest in yourself may also encourage you to show no interest in others, which manifests itself in forgetting everything they have told you.

DATESHARE

Peter Bogdanovich, film director, The Last Picture Show. **Kate Bush**, singer, songwriter. **Paul Anka**, singer. **Emily Brontë**, British novelist, Wuthering Heights. **Arnold Schwarzenegger**, film star. **Daley Thompson**, British Olympic gold medal-winning decathlon champion. **Henry Moore**, British sculptor.

This is a sporty day and indeed, July 30 excels in all physical pursuits, such as dancing, riding, swimming and athletics. Where they don't do it, they delight in watching .

People married to July 30 men resign themselves to life without Saturday afternoons. Practically every traumatic life event takes second place to Match of the Day, or anything that is remotely categorisable as sport. Some July 30 men have been known to conceal a radio beneath their pillow so they can listen to Test cricket from the other side of the world. During the most intimate moments between woman and man, a favourite batsman hits a six and they cry out 'YES' – rather puzzlingly to a companion – not at the right time during those moments.

The women go in for less extremely passionate interests, but nevertheless many are keen athletes and swimmers, and a growing number regularly attend football and rugger matches.

This person can have a curiously idiosyncratic habit with words, which others around find catching especially if July 30 is in any position of authority, and many are, because this is a leader's birth date. Club owners, team leaders, newspaper editors, television producers and factory managers all employ a customised mode of

address to anyone around them, from the girl on reception to the head of sales and marketing. Varieties include, to both sexes, 'Doll', 'Lover', 'Chuck', 'Matey', 'Lovely One', and to girls only, mostly anyway, 'Sweetie Bottom', 'Petal', 'Pretty One', 'Sweetbriar' and 'Babe'. There's no offence meant and they do it as much at home as at work or in team sports. You can often tell where they've been, because their colleagues start to do it too.

Many individuals born on this day are too busy to worry over-much about the niceties of decor in their houses. Functional is what they like, nothing challenging. Rich July 30s hand the job over to an interior decorator. Poorer ones plump for safe and pleasing creamy white.

A gossip is a person with a keen sense of rumour.

FIRE

149

3I JULY

Some people born on this day have a psychic gift, unusual in a Leo, and because they are often temperamentally unsympathetic to this area of the psycheology, the gift may be surpressed. This is as foolish as it is to ignore any talent. Spot the tendency early in youth with the usual signs – thoughts of someone you haven't seen for a long time, the telephone rings and it's them, or, with children, second guessing their opponent in snap to an unusual degree.

It will rarely develop to its full degree in people born today, but sensible individuals hone their psychic talent and make use of it. July 31 is particularly interested in money. Both sexes get over anxious if they feel they haven't got enough, or can't treat themselves, or somebody they love, to something they feel they deserve. Yet July 31's clever hunches are often famous, and particularly useful in making deals, laying bets on horses or even just having a go in the lottery or at bingo. Never use it to take a big risk or when you feel desperate, because these emotions will muddy the clarity of your talent. But if you stick to little things, you will be pleased at what comes your way.

Both at work and in private July 31 is characterised by marked generosity of spirit. This, coupled with great charm, makes both sexes sought after companions, lovers and colleagues, although they can make it hard for unpleasant bosses, because another marked part of this psychology is an extreme sense of honour. Anyone transgressing is likely to be taken to pieces very thoroughly, and without fear.

If such confrontations result in the departure of this creature for another job or way of life, so be it. These people, more courted by the world than courting, have no difficulty finding other jobs, changing careers, or establishing a completely new, enjoyable way of life.

I have three pets which answer the same purpose as a husband: a dog which growls every morning, a parrot which swears all afternoon and a cat that comes home late at night.

(Marie Corelli)

BODY
Leos are great animal lovers and July 31 in particular is a doggy sort of person. People born on this date often have iron constitutions and new medical research now shows that pets actually contribute towards good health. Latest studies have established that stroking or cuddling an animal reduces health risks by lowering heart rate, blood pressure and cholesterol levels and boosting immunity to illness. Even watching goldfish reduces blood pressure by up to 15 per cent. Medical workers at Buffalo University, New York, have discovered that when dog owners solve mathematical problems and give public speeches, their heart rate and blood pressure rises less than when non-doggy people do the same.

MIND
In numerology, those born on July 31 are ruled by the number 4 (3+1=4). People ruled by four are opinionated and argumentative, and although they make good leaders there is a vulnerable side to them which emerges when exhausted.

DATESHARE
Jonathan Dimbleby, British journalist, broadcaster. **Lynn Reid Banks**, British novelist, The L-Shaped Room. **Geraldine Chaplin**, film star. **Hank Jones**, jazz pianist. **Maximilian II**, Holy Roman Emperor.

AUGUST I

They have a natural eye for design, and what they wear today, is what everybody will be wearing tomorrow. August 1 is fascinated by style, clothes, music, writing, all the cultural things. No day is boring to them because they only have to look about them to see something which takes their fancy to the point of fascination.

Either sex should work in a profession which uses this visual dexterity. Then they can combine an unusual degree of pleasure with what frequently turns out to be an unusual degree of earning power. Small children show this talent young. Three- and four-year-olds roll ankle socks down to their shoes, because having them pulled up is a no-no at the local nursery. Not much older than this and they are advising their parents, with a sure touch, about the decoration of the house.

When it comes to painting a room, many August 1 people's motto is 'When in doubt, go for yellow'. The men may carry this colour through into different rooms, varying the shades from yellow through amber to terracotta. Women frequently experiment with the lovely duck egg blues and turqoises found in Chinese

porcelains and lovely silk rugs. Everything is done for next to no money, which is good, because next year, or even next month, they may change the whole shoot.

In the office, these are the people whose dress code gets up the noses of the frowstier reaches of management. The male August 1 wears perfect jeans with a perfectly fitting T-shirt, and maybe the odd one or five earrings. But the jeans will be yellow or red and the jacket which goes over everything, washed-out peacock. Girls born on this day are lanky in brilliantly coloured PVC, with long legs *sans* cellulite.

This enviable grace and ability to eat doughnuts without putting on an ounce may not last for ever unless some care with diet is taken.

Women are never disarmed by compliments. Men always are.

(*Oscar Wilde,* An Ideal Husband)

BODY

August 1 should have beautiful objects around, which simultaneously bring a sense of well-being. And preferably inexpensive, since generous Leo prefers to spend hard-earned money on travel and taking friends out to dinner. Find their houses crammed with vases of sunflowers and bowls of lavender pot-pourris (Leo flowers). Find fascinating rocks picked up while travelling and used as ornaments. What to another is just an old pebble, is to August 1 an exquisite piece of rose quartz, whose properties include arousal of awareness of the beauty of nature, creative inspiration, absorption of harmful vibrations, enlivening of the mind and hastened recovery from illness.

MIND

These people unwittingly make others jealous. It's just something they generate in the air. The fault lies in the feeler, not the felt about. August 1 should be prepared for this. A little steeliness is recommended.

2 AUGUST

Ultra-creative, blessed with good looks and often extremely long legs, August 2 goes in pursuit of three goals: love, money and children. With all three achieved, both sexes remain content to pass up other interests or temptations. If they have to drop one, it will be money, because although this individual likes money, wants money, he also knows how to live well without it. Both sexes are enormously resourceful when financially deprived, can make a home look grand with a couple of twigs and their own imagination, and put a meal together whose originality, deliciousiocity and inexpensivity is breathtaking.

Children are at the centre of this birthday's heart. They want lots of them. And when they do have them they spend hours playing, dressing-up in silly clothes and generally making small people happy. When the children grow up and leave home, August 2 isn't really sad, because he and she have done their job and they reason that if a child stayed with them for ever it just wouldn't be good for him. While they are growing up, August 2 is very helpful with schooling and guidance, but not at all interested in having successful children as a good reflection on them. Surprisingly, many of these creatures are not devoted grandparents, preferring to love mostly from a distance while they get on with other things.

This day suffers from the hypochondriacal streak common to lions and lionesses. A temperature is always a fever. A headache a migraine. A stubbed toe is a broken toe. Pop down to the supermarket with them and they quickly wander away from your trolley, scurrying to the medical shelves and vitamin remedies which they read with gullible fascination and then buy and try.

So naturally if August 2 has any difficulty conceiving children there's a great deal of turmoil. There are many options to explore and brilliantly kind doctors to consult, and the goal should be achieved.

BODY
If you are plagued with chickweed, take advantage and cook it, as it is a healthy meal for August 2. (Don't confuse it with the inedible mouse-ear chickweed, Cerastium fontanum.) Chickweed tastes like cress, was grown in Tudor vegetable gardens and sold as a vegetable on market days until the turn of this century. Smells wonderful while cooking and very good fresh in salads and sandwiches. To cook, wash it well and cut off straggly bits. Don't add any extra water, but do add a pinch of salt, a knob of butter and chopped shallots or chives. Simmer gently until tender – about 8 to 10 minutes. Something to surprise and amuse the palate, which costs nothing.

MIND
Since you are one of the strongest, healthiest days of the year, anxiety over a possible illness may be more a tendency to worry than something that's really there. Check with your doctor, then try to relax.

Don't take up a man's time talking about the smartness of your children; he wants to talk to you about the smartness of his.

(Ed Howe)

BODY

August 3 is a great traveller, socialiser and worker. Parties and computer time often mean tired, itchy eyes. Try a soothing compress. Make up a 100ml bottle of floral water, using lavender, neroli, geranium or camomile, and soak two pieces of cotton wool. Squeeze out the excess liquid and apply the moist pads to your eyes. Lie down for at least 20 minutes. A compress soothes the eyes of contact lens wearers (remove them before applying the compress), and is also good for after-party eyes, when smoke has irritated and inflamed your eyes and possibly given you a headache.

MIND

Can you pass a shop window without glancing at your reflection, go straight from work to dinner without getting undressed, just changing your shoes and cleaning your teeth? You've got vanity in hand. (And you'll be on time.)

DATESHARE

Martin Sheen, *film star,* Apocalypse Now. **Tony Bennett**, *singer, entertainer, started career as a singing waiter.* **John Landis**, *film director,* Blues Brothers. **Terry Wogan**, *Irish TV personality, BBC interviewer, radio broadcaster.* **Rupert Brooke**, *British war poet, symbol of gifted youth destroyed by World War I, although Brooke died before he actually reached the battle zone.*

AUGUST 3

Most Leos are vain because there's lots to be vain about. But August 3 can take vanity to new heights of self-indulgence. Frankly it's amazing anybody sticks around to continue heaping the praise. But these people have enormous sweetness of character. They are intelligent, brave and make excellent captains and captainesses of industry as well as racing drivers. They are also maxibubble lovers and companions, kind to old ladies and dogs and not at all embarrassing dancers.

The one problem is that whenever they go out, it takes ages to get through the front door because they can't decide what to wear. And when they have decided, they change it. And when they reach the finally settled stage of attiring themselves for the evening, they demand comment and praise in sufficient depth to render a companion, who has so far been unable to get to a mirror, demotivated and half-naked. Car journeys to balls and clubs are taken up with discussions about how August 3 looks. Social events may frequently be reviewed later on the basis of the right outfit worn, the right hair, and why.

If August 3 is male, his female companion needs to be extremely patient, but should also point out that so far he has failed to notice what *she* is wearing. Men born today will then instantly leap to offer praise, mortified by their own self-preoccupation. If August 3 is female, then her companion should adjust his impatience and assuming they will always be late, adjust all clocks half an hour forwards.

It doesn't make August 3 late for work, surprisingly. And here the vanity often just shows as perfectionism. Find this birth date in the ranks of air hostesses, advertising executives, in any kind of travel business, tourism and catering where their perfectionism is invaluable. In the retail trade, they may often own their own shop which will be spectacularly attractive and extremely efficient, with unusual and desirable products.

Thank you for giving me the pleasure of giving pleasure to you.

(Ashleigh Brilliant)

4 AUGUST

This is a birthdate when the Leo potential preoccupation with privilege and snobbery is turned upon its head. August 4 people always side with the underprivileged, the poor against the rich, worker against employer. In short this baby has revolutionary tendencies. He or she will mock established systems, hierarchies and social cliques. They are dangerously upsetting to puffed-up social toads and if they seduce a partner from a blue blood background, fitting in will not be the aim. Disruption is the game. Handle with care.

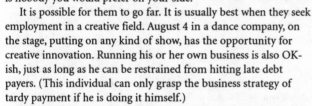

Nevertheless, there is no one funnier, or more attractive. They remind others what a simple addiction to right and wrong is like, how uncomfortable it can occasionally be. And there is nobody you would prefer on your side.

It is possible for them to go far. It is usually best when they seek employment in a creative field. August 4 in a dance company, on the stage, putting on any kind of show, has the opportunity for creative innovation. Running his or her own business is also OK-ish, just as long as he can be restrained from hitting late debt payers. (This individual can only grasp the business strategy of tardy payment if he is doing it himself.)

In big corporations they may also rise because of their natural leadership and facility to stay with the cutting-edge of contemporary thinking. But the slightest attempt by those in high places to double-cross the workforce, and appallingly true pieces of gossip about the company chairman's misuse of the company helicopter to entertain the company chairman's mistress will zip its way into everybody's computer screen.

By forty, most August 4 people will be well established, likely to own a home, maybe a couple of cars, a caravan. Even the most rebellious individual has a flare for money-making. But then this person may throw it all up and simply walk away in search of another life.

BODY

The women do suffer from cellulite. The men, only rarely. Here is a solution female August 4 can use and male August 4 can tell his friends about. Scrubbing is thought to be one of the best ways to prevent cellulite and it can also help eliminate it. One of the best recipes is the ginger juice rub-down. Grate one large ginger root, then squeeze the gratings through a cheesecloth. Dip a warm, moist scrubbing cloth in the juice. Ginger is both a stimulant to the circulation and a potent purifier. (Ginger can cause burning or irritation, so test before using it all over.)

MIND

Get into the country. Breathe fresh, clean air, take hikes, wash your face in cold water. Eat simply. Learn about purification from the earth by existing in harmony with nature.

DATESHARE

Queen Elizabeth, *the Queen Mother, as old as the century.* **Knut Hamsun**, *Nobel Prize winning Norwegian novelist, Hunger.* **Sir Osbert Lancaster**, *British writer, artist, cartoonist.* **Percy Bysshe Shelley**, *British Romantic poet, friend of Lord Byron, drowned at twenty-nine.* **Mary Decker Slaney**, *US middle-distance runner, held world records at 1500 and 3000 metres.*

Work is the refuge of people who have nothing better to do.

(Oscar Wilde)

Chronic fatigue may be a problem for these individuals, partly because they do too much, and partly because we live in a polluted environment full of pesticides, food additives and car exhaust fumes. Some people are genetically more vulnerable to a combination of these factors than others.

Symptoms may include sleeplessness, clumsiness and muscle pains. Naturally, consult your doctor. Dr. Charles Shepherd, adviser to the ME Association and an expert on fatigue, suggests that three 500mg capsules of evening primrose oil each day can relieve some symptoms. Sufferers may improve with multi-vitamins, vitamin C and ginseng. Gingko biloba can also bring relief.

MIND

Straighten out your attitude to others' money. Other people's – banks – get tired of the 'Let's be happy and live within our means, even if we have to borrow the money to do it with' philosophy.

DATESHARE

Loni Anderson, American comedienne. **Neil Armstrong**, US astronaut, first man on the moon. **Miriam Rothschild**, Britain's leading expert on fleas and campaigner for 'wild flower' gardens, friend of Prince Charles and inspiration for wild flowers at his home, Highgrove. **John Huston**, father to Angelica, Irish-American film maker, African Queen, The Man Who Would Be King. **Guy de Maupassant**, French novelist.

AUGUST 5

Those born on August 5 have the gift of enormous stamina. Add that to the tremendous talents bestowed on this individual and you have the recipe for a life of fulfilled ambition. But beware, both sexes have a violent temper, a tendency to flare up and shout, and with some men, to hit people. It's a good idea to curb it early, or the way to the top could become a rapid U-turn.

August 5 is a charismatic lover. The tendency to make an extravagant gesture is disarming. And if they haven't got the money, they will be extravagantly thoughtful. Rich creatures born today, can whisk you off in their private jet for lunch in Vienna, take in a Holbein at the Kunsthistorisches Museum, an apfelstrudel at the café where Sigmund Freud, struggling through his daily strudel, invented the Oedipus complex, then back in time to catch a surgeon kicking in the ER casualty department door.

Poor ones can tell a partner they are beautiful in six different languages. And give them a foot massage, which is certainly more stimulating than strudeling. According to the theory of reflexology, foot massage has beneficial effects on other parts of the body. A man takes each of his partner's feet in turn, massages them, then holding each foot behind the ankle with one hand, slowly rotates it with the other. This creates warmth and pleasure in the pit of a woman's stomach. When women do it, exactly the same effect is caused in men. Give or take some differences.

The psychology of this individual is rooted in the home. They paint and decorate their homes in the golden colours of the sun, in some cases to such gorgeous effect they have been found guilty of gilding the loo. Nothing is

ordinary. The cushions of the finest duck-down, the air perfumed and the armchairs are the kind that elongate into luxurious chaises-longues.

It is only possible
to live happily ever after
on a day-to-day basis.

(*Margaret Bonnaro*)

6 AUGUST

Some people are made to create beautiful gardens. There's nothing stuffy about the lawns and flowerbeds that August 6 makes lovely. No little snobberies about not growing flowers at all. No exclusion of a rose because she is a hybrid. Nor will this gardener faint dead away if he finds a gladiolus.

Both sexes generally ignore the U and non-U list of garden plants because they feel that anybody who gets incredibly het up about whether a flower is socially acceptable has probably gone lupins. But it's true to say that August 6 likes to make a garden not only pleasing to the human eye and nose, but pleasing and useful, to all the other creatures who live in it.

They charm butterflies to stay for a while with gorgeous bushes of purple and blue fragrant buddleia. And intertwine roses with honeysuckle, so powerful that bees and wasps, becoming drunk on the nectar, lurch away to doze in the grass, exactly in the path of bare human feet. Cherry trees and vines provide humans with something to pick at, but also sweet things for robin redbreasts and thrushes to steal. There will be plums, some for us and some for the squirrels. And apples for blue tits to swing on and the tiny, dull brown but musically endowed dunnock to peck.

Both sexes like to entertain in their garden, when it will seem strewn with recumbent figures, lying about on cushions and dreamily consuming more chilled wine than you would have thought possible for any human being to do. There will be swinging seats for adults to play on and paddling pools for every age. And elaborate tents to keep the sun off, made from silks, laces and velvets and any old pretty thing, all sewn and safety pinned together that morning to look like the summer garden palace of an eastern potentate. Of course, if you've just got the one window-box, it's more of a challenge.

You know what charm is: a way of getting the answer yes without having asked any clear questions.

(Albert Camus)

BODY

This gorgeous concoction makes guests feel as if they're in a country garden, even if they're not. Le Grand Dessert Troisgros: 600ml vanilla ice cream; 300ml strawberry sorbet; 300g strawberries, 12 plums, 500g pears and 500g peaches, poached in syrup, sugar and water, flavoured with vanilla; raspberry syrup, made from jam with a squeeze of lemon or lime to freshen; double cream. Place vanilla ice cream in centre of shallow round dish. Crown it with sorbet. Arrange fresh and poached fruits around outside and pour the syrup over the top. Pipe the outer edges of the plate with whipped cream and serve with petits fours.

MIND

August 6 makes the garden gorgeous, or a window-box, or pots in the backyard, because it's one of the best ways you can find of being nice to other people. While pleasing yourself.

DATESHARE

Sir Freddie Laker, airline owner, famous for exquisite gardens at country home. **Alfred Lord Tennyson**, Victorian poet laureate, The Lady of Shallot. **Andy Warhol**, pop artist, film maker, publisher, gossip monger. **Robert Mitchum**, film actor. **Alexander Fleming**, Scottish Nobel Prize-winning discoverer of penicillin.

BODY

Now the spotlight is on neurological science, there's a great deal of depressing talk about the decline of brainpower in forty-somethings. Surprisingly, aspirin may have a key future role in treating dementia and even Alzheimer's disease. Cases of vascular dementia are caused by small blood clots sticking in the arteries within the brain. The destruction of brain tissue by such clots eventually leads to loss of intellect. In theory, an aspirin a day should reduce or even prevent this. Aspirin reduces the stickiness of platelets, the smallest type of blood cell, which play a major part in blood clotting.

MIND

In numerology, those ruled by the number 7 enjoy travel and excitement, but may be indecisive. In Tarot, the 7th card in the Major Arcana is The Chariot, which suggests success, talent, efficiency – and a poor sense of direction.

DATESHARE

Mata Hari, *gorgeous spy, double agent, exotic dancer famous for the allure of her stomach, made a noble show of bravery at her execution.* **Louis Leakey**, *British archaeologist and anthropologist, discoverer of remains of early man, author,* Human Origins. **Ralph Bunch**, *US statesman, Nobel Peace Prize winner, negotiated Arab-Israeli truce.*

AUGUST 7

There's a curious side to August 7. An urge to seek out information especially where there are obstacles to doing so. Sometimes it's just gossipy intruding. Sometimes it's what goes into the making of an investigative journalist, a policeman, a VAT bat, or one of those sweet customs and excise lads who think

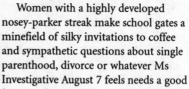

that all middle-aged lady travellers have a packet of cocaine in their bathbag along with emergency anusol.

Women with a highly developed nosey-parker streak make school gates a minefield of silky invitations to coffee and sympathetic questions about single parenthood, divorce or whatever Ms Investigative August 7 feels needs a good ferreting. Failure to comply can induce pushchair rage, the victim mercilessly trapped against playground railings and threatened with a Johnson's Wet Wipe.

The men go into 'human resources', a fab opportunity to read everybody's secret file and add some thoroughly fair, unhelpful comments.

More rounded individuals use the questioning urge to general good. Both sexes can be relied on to keep an eye on nearby old people. Kindly, they will pop round to help with a garden, or mend a broken window. And if they don't see one of these neighbours for a day or two, they will investigate to make sure nothing is untoward.

Similarly if a neighbouring child is in need, August 7 volunteers a tactful rescue. Other people's children frequently come to stay in their house for short periods. And elderly relatives live very happily beneath the same roof, because this individual enjoys the rough and tumble of big family life where age and youth complement each other.

Many people born on this day excel at public speaking. Pillars of the local council, or, maybe editors of local newspapers, they will not let a beautiful meadow be dug up for housing or an old building crumble away until there is nothing for it but to turn the site into a lucrative car park.

Once I make up my mind, I'm full of indecision.

(Oscar Levant)

FIRE

8 AUGUST

These people don't know the meaning of 'depression', which makes them perfect candidates for a career in politics and any other competitive profession. If August 8 loses a deal or a battle, he thinks it through carefully and of course he's sorry. But his attitude is simply to take a few lessons from the failure and play the game more subtly the next time.

A lot of sportsmen claim this birthdate and both sexes are naturally athletic, likely to be tall and long limbed and *very* strong physically. Their frequent solution to work fatigue, or indeed a lost deal, is to go and have a game of tennis or golf. Both sexes play good golf, the women realising today what extraordinary opportunities there are for networking as they walk the course.

Highly sexed, they choose their partners judiciously. Most will prefer to associate with someone who is both wealthy and influential, putting beauty, wit and trendiness well down the shopping list. They love easily and they stay faithful. And just because they are sexually charged, both the men and women, can make a success of marriage to, say, a much older partner. Just as long as the older partner is loaded.

This is not at all cynical in the end. Because August 8 may be drawn by the marital opportunity to step up the social ladder, but genuine devotion follows, bringing joy to all. In truth this individual is essentially kind, with a deep sense of honour, and if he can do someone a good turn, he will. If he causes hurt, he is mortified, yet puzzled because, lacking the habit of introspection, he can't quite work out how it happened.

Although some August 8 people will stay very happily childless for one reason or another, both sexes make excellent parents. The women may have to spend some time as a single parent, which they accomplish with grace and courage. The right man usually comes along.

*My belief is that
to have no wants is divine.*

(Socrates)

BODY
You start the day fresh, but by mid-morning your mouth is dry and irritation has descended. Try blaming breakfast. Some nutrients have drug-like qualities, causing mood swings and fatigue. Carbohydrate snacks are commonly taken for energy boosting. They bring a rise in the brain's level of serotonin, a powerful chemical associated with mood, sleep, aggression, sexual behaviour and appetite. Sometimes the pick me up works in reverse. In extreme cases ankles can swell, vision blurs and there is an overwhelming urge to lie down and sleep. So much more is known nowadays about the allergic affects of food. Check with an expert.

♦

MIND
Music is the perfect enhancer for August 8. It creates a feeling of well-being, enhances creative thinking and you will find that as you listen, something or someone you have been trying to remember will come back to you.

DATESHARE
Keith Carradine, *film actor, singer, songwriter.* **Leonide Massine**, *Russian choreographer, Firebird, Rite of Spring.* **Isabel Allende**, *Peruvian novelist, niece of assassinated president.* **Dustin Hoffman**, *Hollywood star.* **Nigel Mansell**, *British Formula One world champion, 21-times grand prix winner.*

These are extremely persuasive individuals, with buckets of reassuring charm. August 9 is clever, serious and innovative, with a genuine desire to make the world a better place. You will very often find them in medicine, science, teaching and writing where they may become famous for new breakthroughs. If they turn to the visual arts there will be murals, or sculptures for public places and hospitals, maybe stations, which are primarily constructed to give enjoyment, not to shock. August 9 is a jolly person whose artistic view is not ultra-challenging – neither better nor worse for that.

Both sexes may be drawn to medicine from an early age. If this is so, how lucky they are to pursue a career to which they are dedicated. It will be cruel and pointless for anybody around them to try to put them off. Far better to discuss if a teenager wishes to end up as a GP, or a hospital specialist. The former doesn't necessarily come second to the latter. And then, which particular speciality fascinates them. At present it looks as if virology and the study of the brain are going to be areas of high hospital employment in the 21st century.

The men's reassuring manner helps them lead others. They make audiences listen, and that also means children in a school class. August 9 makes science lessons as fascinating as *The X-Files*, social studies as enchanting as Disney's *Beauty and the Beast*, and literature something to enjoy and be proud of. Kids will always remember this individual, and in adulthood look back with grateful affection.

The women are as likely to be a surgeon as a hairdresser, but when babies arrive, hairdresser may be a more practical alternative. Surgeons regularly work all night. If it's a hairdresser's, or any kind of service shop – perhaps a beauty parlour or a baker with ovens at the back – August 9 will make it very special.

She who hesitates is won.

(Oscar Wilde)

10 AUGUST

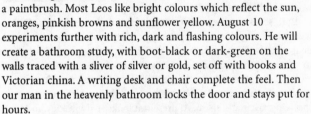

August 10 is domestically creative, likes to spend hours decorating the home and further hours reading about exotic ideas. Either sex may have a brilliant career, probably in something that involves current trends and technology, but what they like to spend their hard earned money on is a designer chair, or new lace for the windows.

The men may be tough at work, masters in memo land. But when they get home, they throw their clothes on the floor, change into a tracksuit and take out a paintbrush. Most Leos like bright colours which reflect the sun, oranges, pinkish browns and sunflower yellow. August 10 experiments further with rich, dark and flashing colours. He will create a bathroom study, with boot-black or dark-green on the walls traced with a sliver of silver or gold, set off with books and Victorian china. A writing desk and chair complete the feel. Then our man in the heavenly bathroom locks the door and stays put for hours.

If not a dark-green bathroom, it will be a lipstick-red hall with so many coats of high gloss varnish that it looks like a Chinese lacquered box. Or perhaps, for a bedroom, that shade of lavender which looks grey, blue and even pink depending on the light and the time of day.

Although August 10 aims to earn pots of money, he won't be spending it on decorations. This guy squanders his money on designer clothes (his own) and sometimes for a girlfriend. Sometimes he dreams of a flash car, but this is not gadget man. He's more Degas than Daimler.

While Ms August 10 is not so hot on do-it-yourself paint effects about the house, she has a good eye. If she can manipulate it, this creature would prefer to be sitting on a stool directing somebody else's efforts with multiple praise and cups of tea.

BODY
August 10 dreams vividly and is concerned about their meaning. The slightly superstitious nature of this psychology makes both sexes nervous in case these dreams foretell future events. Although some psychic characters may experience foretelling dreams, even these are only metaphors of what is to come. One of the commonest dreams for either sex, happy with their partner, is of parting and divorce. This is not an indication of anything about to happen. It's probably your subconscious reminding you how fortunate you are. Such a dream could, however, indicate concern about the delicate nature of another partnership, perhaps at work.

MIND
For those August 10 people who take their clothes off as they walk in the front door and leave them in a scattered trail through different rooms. You're not at work now, babe. Who's picking up after you?

DATESHARE
Rosanna Arquette, *Hollywood comedienne, Desperately Seeking Susan.* **Ian Anderson**, *rock singer, flautist, songwriter, Jethro Tull.* **Norma Shearer**, *film actress.* **Eddie Fisher**, *popular singer.*

It doesn't matter ~
if you're rich or poor,
as long as you've got money.

AUGUST 11

Rescue Remedy may be the answer to August 11's prayer. You can buy it in most health food stores and a lot of people swear by it. Just a few drops in a glass of water can calm the fevered brow. Put together by Dr. Edward Bach in the 1930s, Rescue Remedy contains impatiens (Impatiens glandulifera) for impatience and agitation accompanying stress; clematis (Clematis vitalba) for spaciness, rock rose (Helianthemum nummularium) for terror and panic; cherry plum (Prunus cerasifera) for fear of losing mental and physical control; Star of Bethlehem (Ornithogalum umbellatum) for mental and physical trauma. You can use it for animals, plants and children too.

৪১

MIND

The trouble with people who habitually suffer from random anxiety is that it's fantastically dull for the rest of the population who have to reassure them. Too much seeking of reassurance and you won't find.

DATESHARE

Claus von Bülow, *businessman with wife in coma, murder conviction overturned.* **Arlene Dahl**, *film actress, in cosmetics business.* **Angus Wilson**, *British writer, satirist.* **Enid Blyton**, *British childrens' writer, creator of Noddy and Famous Five.* **Alex Haley**, *African–American writer, Roots.* **Hulk Hogan**, *TV wrestler, icon.*

If August 11 isn't careful, the streak of anxiety murmuring through this psychology, will grow into a torrent. It *is* something that can be controlled. Spot it first when the child is more than usually nervous about cuts and bruises, stinging nettles and wasps. So nervous they refuse to go out to play unless covered from head to toe. The male of the species is not quite so prey to 'what-iffery' as the female, possibly because male colleagues and friends would find it odder than women do. However, at work, men who were born on this day may be amusing bosses and funny colleagues to work with, but this is the guy who worries and worries about the effect on his eyes of working with a computer. It's worth worrying about, of course, because nobody is really informed about the possibly bad effects. But it's not worth days of upset.

August 11 worries about his car. What if it's stolen? Will the company insurance pay? Will he get another one now they are doing away with perks? He writes a brilliant memo. What if, he asks himself, the boss thinks it's too strong? He worries about a friend's drinking habits at lunchtime, and, what if somebody important thinks that he is encouraging it?

Women can be much worse. Money plays an important part in their Leo star sign, but with August 11 females it can assume a negative dominance. Bills terrify them so much that they

sometimes leave them unopened. Although they can afford to splash out, they will choose cheap clothes from a market stall. Redundancy is particularly hard for this day because it seems that every nightmare may come true. In truth, this situation often brings out the best in people and in the face of any mishap both sexes show extraordinary resources of imagination and courage, and in changing their lives, lose their fears.

T o fear love is to fear life,
and those who fear life
are already three parts dead.
(Bertrand Russell)

I2 AUGUST

People born on August 12 may have some years of wildness in youth, but at heart they want to settle down and live a traditional life. This doesn't mean that after a misspent youth, this individual turns his attention to stripey lawns. But with rather more emphasis on the traditional, spiritual necessities of life, they become involved in helping to run and maintain a community in a way that has always brought pleasure. They are naturals for the parish council and any kind of involvement in the Christian church. Many will work within the church, some taking orders. In other religions, both sexes play the equivalent roles, understanding yet again, the need most communities have for a structure which reflects a combination of old and new ways. At its best, August 12 adopts a civilised way of life.

Some of them, however, get right out of hand. Swap the even overview for a passion for romantically whimsical traditions. They insist on candlelight in order to see the world how people once saw it. There will be cooking in straw boxes, spinning and weaving, which always results in something appallingly unwearable – they must see this- and a version of early English folk dancing that's infinitely more embarrassing than watching important company directors shimmy like they did at the office party.

A gentler version of this results in enthusiasm for natural childbirth and babies arriving under water, which female August 12

does with stoic expertise. As the baby grows up, he will not, of course, be watching television. Neither sweetie nor dangerous sugary thing will pass rosebud lips before the age of five, and she will be the only little girl at school who doesn't have a Barbie doll. August 12's kids often have a late career start, because they have to spend most of their twenties lying in front of the television with Mars bars and popcorn.

The good news ～
is that Jesus is coming back.
The bad news is that he's really pissed off.
(Bob Hope)

August 12 places store by his dreams. Favourite subjects for the nineties are angels, cherubs and heavenly pastures. Dreaming of angels may be a sign of forthcoming peace and prosperity. But sometimes, such a dream is indicative of concern over judgement for one's conduct on earth. Cherubs: indicate your positive feelings about children, or possibly an anxiety about the lost innocence of your own childhood. Heaven: means either you aspire to reach the heights of ambition, that you probably aim for contentment and peace or, more prosaically, that you have realistic expectations of a better job.

MIND
Only those who really love you will fully share your interests, so treasure them even if they reject bits and pieces of your dream. Assume that your children will eventually disagree, although they may change their minds later.

DATESHARE
Mark Knopfler, *British lead guitarist, singer, songwriter, Dire Straits.* **Cecil B De Mille**, *Hollywood director, The Ten Commandments.* **Norris McWhirter**, *co-writer, co-creator of* Guinness Book of Records. **Tsarevitch Alexis**, *heir to the Russian throne, son of Tsar Nicholas, executed by Bolsheviks.* **George IV**, *British king.*

AUGUST 13

BODY

People who drink milk may be less prone to strokes. A group of 3000 men has been monitored for twenty-two years. Overall calcium intake did not alter the risk of stroke, but only 3.7 per cent of the group who drank half a litre of milk every day had the most common type of stroke, compared with 7.9 per cent of those who drank less.

One explanation is that extensive milk drinking arose from thirsty exercise. So the big milk drinkers were fitter. A not unimportant factor. (Perhaps the conclusions might have been more useful if they'd done the study using rice pudding?)

MIND

With a healthy body and mind, nature deals you a fine hand at cards; and with a steady will, you learn to play the hand well.

DATESHARE

Fidel Castro, *legendary Cuban revolutionary dictator.* **Alfred Krupp**, *Nazi weapons maker.* **Sir Alfred Hitchcock**, *British-American film director,* Rear Window, Psycho. **Archbishop Makarios**, *feared Greek-Cypriot president.*

August 13 always looks on the bright side of life, which is pretty astonishing since enough rotten things have happened to this indivual to make him relax his hold on sagacity. This powerful psychology may revolutionise a way of doing something and he or she is often suspicious of other, clever people. But they have an innate empathy with others who have had a rough time, and while not wishing to discuss it, do what they can to help.

Girls born on this day are good managers, preferring to run institutions such as schools and hospitals, rather than be involved

on the corporate ladder. Good-looking but retiring, Ms August 13 always thinks other women are more glamorous than herself, and the slightest thing – an unacknowledged greeting – merely confirms this. She may devote herself to the welfare of others, caring for elderly relatives, maybe even running an old people's home. She does it well. She is much loved. She avoids the silly internal power games and politics you get in such life-and-death institutions, always the trustworthy one people can appeal to. She may not marry and if she doesn't, she doesn't mind.

Both sexes will encounter powerful love affairs in youth and much later in life. These will work out well, fitting into their chosen lifestyle. If children come, August 13 is happy, but without them, this creature resolves to accept the situation and turn his or her attention to other things.

The men born today are frequently so individualistic that they are drawn to roam over the wild wastes of the world, perhaps in an explorers' team or climbing mountains. There's no point in trying to convert either sex to a more conventional mind set. They're not interested in silks and satins, their eye is on the sunset behind other horizons, or simply changing things so that vulnerable people around them are safe.

Grow old along with me!
The best is yet to be ↩
The last of life, for which the first was made.

(Robert Browning)

14 AUGUST

A ugust 14 people reflect the characteristics of the decade. Those who swung in the sixties and seventies may have dumped the 'Do your own thing' philosophy, but still carry its imprint. Scratch a 50-year-old accountant and you'll find he or she knows all about 'chilling' and why people who liked Lulu last time round were embarrassing. Both sexes probably wore bronze satin shirts.

They still harbour a touch of the free spirit credo, don't get married, don't possess anything, don't get hooked, don't get a career, just light in and light out. Some secretly still feel this way, which can be bad for them, because older lions aren't happy without a secure companion. Leos are fixed, which means they are intrinsically loyal and prefer a life which is financially secure, with children and a nice house. The rolling stone time for them was out of character, but this easily bewitched individual maybe never came out of the incense clouds to keep a proper job, stick with a love affair or bring up their children with stability. With their credo of kindness, live and let live, August 14 swingers of both sexes are perfect in any profession where they in some way care for a lot of people. None better to run a club, a hotel or a charitable institution. And they're fantastic dancers.

Eighties babes and boys are different. August 14 was the space magpie, collecting mobile telephones, designer clothes and false nails. Both girls and men went for the fast buck and even the highest-flying women thought it was interesting to discuss the right lipstick shade. All this appealed to the taste for extravagance. Just spending money is a turn on.

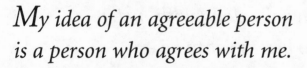

Nineties August 14 is changing his priorities. Both sexes want to get rich quick, so that they can stop work and devote themselves to the finer things of life: family, reading, music and films, love of the countryside and just messing about in boats.

My idea of an agreeable person is a person who agrees with me.

(*Benjamin Disraeli*)

BODY
August 14 is attracted to alternative remedies – very nineties. Both sexes love travel, finding their own ways to handle minor afflictions which come with flying, train journeys or driving. An easy favourite to cure blocked sinuses, common to travellers, is to put a drop of eucalyptus oil on fingertips and press very gently above the nose up to the hairline. Make sure when you buy the oil that it's the pure, essential oil, usually found in small, dark glass bottles. Adulterated, or synthetic oils may have an unpleasant effect. If eucalyptus is too strong, dilute it in a carrier such as almond oil.

☾

MIND
The strong heart of August 14 will always be troubled if its urges are thwarted by contemporary fashion. It's important for this lion to know exactly what makes him happy and then go for it.

DATESHARE
Magic Johnson, US basketball star, HIV positive, US Olympics 'Dream Team' member. **Steve Martin**, popular film star, comedian. **Danielle Steel**, bestselling 'bonkbuster' novelist worldwide. **David Crosby**, singer, songwriter, guitarist, The Byrds and Crosby, Stills and Nash. **John Galsworthy**, British author, The Forsyte Saga.

Drivers often suffer from bad backs, general cramp and dehydration, made worse because they won't drink so they don't have to stop for the loo. Getting the seat right is important and some doctors suggest using a pillow behind the back and adjusting it so that the back, neck and head make an easy, continuous, straight line. General cramp comes from sitting in one position and gradually getting too rigid, with fingers gripped round the wheel. It's much better if you have a non-alcoholic drink and go to the loo, because getting out and walking, however brief, exercises the limbs and relieves physical tension.

☾

MIND

This is such a generous, jolly person, he sometimes wonders if he isn't complicated enough. But the fact remains that August 15 is envied by most for such a harmonious approach to life.

DATESHARE

HRH Princess Anne, the Princess Royal, a woman who finds horses more attractive than many courtiers. **Napoleon Bonaparte**, whose charming heart and desperate leadership inspired France and wiped out the cream of a generation. **Menachim Begin**, Israeli prime minister, Nobel Prize winner for stabilising homeland with diplomacy towards Egypt. **Nicolas Roeg**, British film director, Performance. **Gianfranco Ferré**, Italian fashion designer.

AUGUST 15

Women born on this day are Ms Houseproud. Their home is their council chamber and all that is decided within is accomplished under the great, luminous eyes of August 15. Most prefer to do everything themselves, because they are better at it and why pay for somebody else to get it all irritatingly wrong? This girl may take a passing interest in contemporary style, but she ain't led down the path of fashion and fad. She likes clean

lines, but can't see the point of living in a place so bare you'd be afraid to put a coffee cup down. She likes white, but can't see the point of only having it – because who wants to play safe?

August 15 woman is so sure-handed that decorating may become her profession. She'll be the one to win an award for the Christmas windows in the local department store, and she'll be the one asked to do-up a display house on a new housing estate. Either sex has a horror of frilly things and flounced curtains and it's most unlikely you'd find one of those white and gilt bedrooms with satin covers on the bed in the house.

While August 15 is as ambitious as any other Leo day, these people may not devote themselves to big careers in big business. The women in particular want to have children and stay around to look after them, so part-time work will do. They have lovely musical voices, and anything to do with the telephone is just up their street. Many of the men may similarly prefer part-time, or freelance work. Most individuals born today like to travel, and may choose driving and tourism.

They are ambitious for a happy family, well-balanced children, and a comfortable life. And with everybody around them heading for divorce, August 15 heads off heartbreak, and like goose grass, stays put where he or she is thrown.

*I'm a self-made man.
Who else would help?*

〜

16 AUGUST

Men born today may be eternally naughty boys. The women grow out of it. Many people who share an office with the male August 16, wonder how he gets away with everything. He doesn't *seem* to work. Sharp at the end of each day he is gone to meet friends, and usually a luscious girl, in the nearest bar. If he is meant to work later, the old jacket over the chair trick comes out and, surprisingly, senior employers fall for it.

Most mornings, this robust huntsman has to swallow doughnuts and ham rolls at his desk in order to soak up the hangover. His telephone constantly rings – it's girls who need a tender word. Our star emerges from his alcoholic eclipse, a twinkling eye on the new work experience girl, whose appreciation of the workplace he will shortly enhance when he shows her round the stationery cupboard.

These bad boys often make good. There's something about the cut of the shoulders – usually sporty – that makes people laugh. Something catchily joyful about his enjoyment. So it's no surprise when management invest in Mr Zest. The natural leadership comes to the rescue, and the show-off streak means he'll enjoy planning major projects in impressive detail, while making love to the latest beauty.

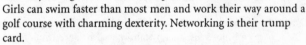

Both sexes are sporty. Some professionally. The strong shoulders, arms, powerful legs and excellent eye of the lion are perfect for competitive sport. And they look good on the cricket pitch. Girls can swim faster than most men and work their way around a golf course with charming dexterity. Networking is their trump card.

Nobody gives a party like August 16 can. It will be somewhere romantic and extraordinary, ideally in a Channel Tunnel train carriage, or an empty hairdressers' with its mirrors, low lights and adjustable chairs to lie on. People remember August 16's parties, because that's where they meet and fall for at least one love of their life.

I don't want any yes-men around me. I want everybody to tell me the truth, even if it costs them their jobs.

(Samuel Goldwyn)

FIRE

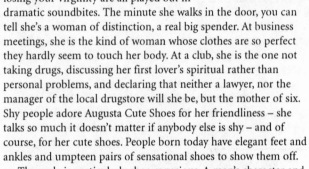

These guys and girls run the show and call the shots. Others sometimes become discouraged by the ease with which August 17 removes their favourite toy, and then plays Mr Absolutely Amazed. 'I'm absolutely amazed that you mind about moving your desk, me borrowing your mouse.' But because this sun-kissed peach is essentially kind and fair – unless it's absolutely against their best interests – everybody else is eventually allowed to get a juicy bite.

August 17 women are *appassionata*. Success, failure, love, sadness, childbirth, losing your virginity are all played out in dramatic soundbites. The minute she walks in the door, you can tell she's a woman of distinction, a real big spender. At business meetings, she is the kind of woman whose clothes are so perfect they hardly seem to touch her body. At a club, she is the one not taking drugs, discussing her first lover's spiritual rather than personal problems, and declaring that neither a lawyer, nor the manager of the local drugstore will she be, but the mother of six. Shy people adore Augusta Cute Shoes for her friendliness – she talks so much it doesn't matter if anybody else is shy – and of course, for her cute shoes. People born today have elegant feet and ankles and umpteen pairs of sensational shoes to show them off.

The male is particularly shoe conscious. A man's character and worldiness is judged by his footwear, more damningly than for women. Girls in red slingbacks are spirited and sexy, in trainers, sporty and sexy, sleek 'n' sexy in boots, seductively country fresh in wellies. But there are men who have lost a deal because they wore suede shoes, lost a job because they came to lunch in brown ones, lost a girl because of their grey suede hush puppies. August 17 will never let his shoes make an independent statement. They are exquisite, maybe two-tone, maybe shocking, but they're under control.

In my beginning is my end.

18 AUGUST

August 18 people have that sunshine coating which makes Leos gleam among the glum. However, a reservation in their character, an edgy attitude makes them more challenging than many – more Creamy Cheese Cake Frost for party-time than Apricot Glaze.

Sometimes their original thinking works well, when others are receptive – and clever – enough to go along with them. These inventive creatures do have to spend time searching for their thought twins, spinning along the universe on the same electro-magnetic waves. Often, however, both sexes grow discouraged and flit away from urban environments to plough their own furrow, take over the village post office and generally use their unusual mindset to create an attractive, but different way of life. Certainly different from friends' lifestyles.

The great thing about this child, who wears a coat of many coloured sun rays, is that either sex is fantastically resilient. They weather the hardest hits the world can deliver, loss of loved ones, money and position, stay down for a little, harbouring their resources, then use the experience to help others and themselves understand a little more about destiny. Many become counsellors where they are extremely effective and not prone to faddiness. If it's running the post office they prefer, then this little shop will be the

jolly centre of village life, a place to pause and chat, where you know you'll meet friends.

Girls born today make any place they go look wonderful, all done on talent not expenditure. Animals come running to them and many women will work with animals, either farming or breeding and in some cases, racing. Most men have similar talents and may also turn to a career with animals. Either way, when August 18 lives in the country, the house will be full of dogs, rabbits, baby hedgehogs, maybe the odd singing canary while Old English bantams snick-snack about the back door looking for grubs.

BODY

Creamy Cheese Cake Frost is culinary stardust. Piquant. Unusual. Delicious. Take 170g cream cheese, 30ml evaporated milk, pinch salt, 5 ml vanilla essence, 450 g icing sugar, sifted. Beat the cream cheese with the milk until smooth, add salt, vanilla and sugar. Creamy Frost between the two cake layers, a scrumptious filling, and even more delicious when lightly spread across the cake top and down the sides. Tiny fairy cakes coated with Creamy Frost suddenly sparkle. For a change add coffee or rich dark chocolate.

❧

MIND

In the end no-one gets away without their own personal piece of suffering. If you choose to live, then try to do it with grace and enjoyment, even if there's only despair at the core of your being.

DATESHARE

Patrick Swayze, *film star.* **Rosalyn Carter**, *US first lady.* **Roman Polanski**, *Polish film director,* Chinatown, Knife on The Water, *his wife Sharon Tate was murdered by the Charles Manson gang.* **Robert Redford**, *actor, director, tireless worker for children's charities.* **Shelley Winters**, *Hollywood actress, comedienne.*

He's a distinguished man of letters.
He works for the post office.
(Max Kauffman)

AUGUST 19

You can't beat August 19 for sensuosity. Their sense of smell is very powerful and they enjoy being beguiled by aromatic oils. August 19 has a spot in the middle of the spine, which, when rubbed, turns either sex into a creature dazzled by pleasure. Just rub it and he or she is yours, like the genie of the lamp, and all your wishes will come true. Put a couple of drops of aromatic oil into a carrier such as almond oil, then smooth gently around the middle of the back, avoiding any pressure on the spine. Try cedarwood oil, an alleged aphrodisiac, and patchouli.

MIND

You have extraordinary powers to inspire love and must value them and never take them lightly. Nor take lightly other people's generosity towards your idiosyncrasies. Life will deal you good cards.

DATESHARE

Bill Clinton, *US president, Rhodes scholar.* **Willie Shoemaker**, *very small and very great jockey, Kentucky Derby winner.* **Gabrielle 'Coco' Chanel**, *Parisian clothing designer, socialite, perfume maker.* **Jill St John**, *film actress, sadly died of cancer after brave battle.* **Ginger Baker**, *rock drummer, The Cream.* **Comtesse du Barry**, *French mistress to Louis XV, guillotined.*

They need a lot of love and if they have that, then let the rest of the world go hang. August 19 men and women go hunting for love in the most seductive and charming way. Perhaps you're out of money for a parking meter? This creature will be there, slim, smiling, and the moment is full of laughter. You're out of milk? The guy down the road with the devastating eyes has some to spare and he'll come round later.

Accidental meetings are not absolutely accidental. They look for the opportunity. But then the first date may turn into a twenty-four-hour round-Britain car drive, perhaps a visit to the sea and paddling, maybe they'll show you their beach hut, maybe they'll take you to meet their parents.

With this creature most people know immediately that the affair will be something big. Sex is urgent and funny, not necessarily calculated or ultra-professional, but the fiery emotions behind the sex are what carries people away.

August 19 should be careful when they first fall in love not to bunk off from work or their studies. This shooting star wants to link up with its new companion and sweep him or her away, far across the world, with no thought for practical things like income, or where you are supposed to be tomorrow, or where you might stay tonight. But Fortune smiles on this person. Bosses and teachers are usually quick to forgive, maybe remembering a similar intoxication they once felt many years ago.

Both sexes are different in the moonlight. By day they mostly just enjoy themselves and treat others with affection, although at work they turn into towering pillars of confidence who can grasp a situation, push a deal through or persuade the workforce to turnabout apparently effortlessly. Moonlight drives them wild with a longing to be caressed and concentrate on only one thing.

Sex between a man and a woman can be wonderful – provided you get between the right man and the right woman.

(Woody Allen)

20 August

There are deep psychic forces at work here, which often manifest themselves in childhood as maybe a particular fascination with the past or an understanding that there are certain houses and places which have a good feeling – and others which do not. Children born on this day into a deeply conventional family may have difficulty with this gift because family members won't – and won't be inclined to – recognise it.

Perhaps for many August 20 people this won't matter terribly, because their psychic capacity remains largely undeveloped, with just a few shadowy hunches which seem compelling to this creature, but in general don't matter very much. But a side-effect of this fine tuned ultra-awareness is that they can act as an empathetic magnet to other people with problems and August 20 may find himself overloaded with confidences but in some way duty bound to help. The people he or she is helping are often very damaged and act as an undermining energy drain on this individual.

By the time they have reached their late teens or adulthood, many people with a strong extra perception have discovered it and since children and teenagers are independent creatures, a lot have experimented, and read up the subject. Out-of-body experiences, for instance, are not uncommon in teenagers. Many keep it secret, partly because it's a valued private experience, and partly because, can you imagine explaining it? Sadly, quite a few people find that they 'grow out' of this capacity. At a certain age it gets harder and then it's gone.

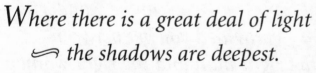

Sensible August 20 people seek out experts, well-known with checkable credentials and affiliated to a professional body. This enables them to examine their talent within a controlled environment. It's very important that these people don't get into the hands of occult groups or irresponsible people who are attracted to psychological manipulation.

Where there is a great deal of light ∽ the shadows are deepest.

(Goethe)

BODY

August 21 loves to dream and can usually control the good ones so that they go on and on. Dreams put them in a good mood and they wake up happy and refreshed. Some have a favourite dream subject, which they claim to induce by thinking hard about it just before sleep.

And many swear by the 'problem-solving' dream. You go to bed with a problem, the brain solves it for you while you sleep. August 21 favours dancing dreams, which indicate joy, youth, victory and general humdinger attractiveness. Flying means the savouring of new excitements.

MIND

Those born today can ensure wedding day good fortune. It's lucky to enter the church right foot first (stumbling is considered an evil omen). A smile between bride and groom meeting at the altar means a happy marriage.

DATESHARE

Princess Margaret Rose, *younger sister to Queen Elizabeth II, wildly beautiful in youth and gave up the love of her life because he was divorced and the British monarchy wouldn't accept it.* **Count Basie**, *bandleader, pianist, composer arranger.* **Aubrey Beardsley**, *British illustrator, Yellow Book, died at 25.* **Janet Baker**, *British concert mezzo-soprano.*

They start their adult life with an attractive, apparently reckless, wildness. And since this individual is blessed with good looks, long legs and charismatic smile, the wildness is irresistible to other people. August 21 girls are the kind who dance naked, or wearing very little, in perfectly stylish places of

entertainment, to get themselves through college. The boys clean skyscraper windows to admiring glances from beneath.

Some dance their way with ease through the rest of life. They need a change? It comes along. A new, prettier house. There's one. After an initial immense career success, they may not all stick with it, but somehow or other August 21 always finds a pleasant way to earn a living.

These individuals are unhappy when they don't have a steady partner and are truly convinced that one marriage is much the same as another, so why upset everything? Once their children are grown up, however, they are happy to renew old friendships and have a whale of a time. August 21 travels the world with friends, stays with them for weeks in the country or other countries, spends his or her time at the theatre, in restaurants or just making clever lunches and dinners. This whole sign is one of the cooks of the zodiac and they usually can't bear somebody else in their kitchen.

They do have the 'what if' tendency. They are postphobic – letters never come, maybe they're lost. Burglars are a constant worry, even with the most sophisticated devices, and August 21 would be happiest living on bare boards with no furniture or any ornaments. If they are town-bred, they tremble through the countryside, especially women, wincing at rivers supposedly full of pesticides. Every plant is a stinging nettle. It's hard to resist the temptation to tell them you saw an adder in the garden. If they are country-bred, they think all townies have pollution-related asthma.

I went on a diet, swore off drinking and heavy eating, and in fourteen days I had lost exactly two weeks.

(Joe E. Lewis)

FIRE

22 AUGUST

August 22 is one of the nice guys or girls of the year's birthday people. Children are usually good at sport, taking quite naturally to swimming, horse-riding, football, rugger, cricket, hockey, netball and any other competitive activity you can think of. This creature is made for competition and a natural winner, but plays fair and loses with grace.

Either sex may find that childhood sporting injuries come back to plague them. Back problems are common as are joint injuries. Expect sore knees, stiff wrists, wonky elbows and maybe the grasp in one hand isn't as good as it was since the stunning cricket catch they made at 17 which broke an index finger, or the time when somebody accidentally thwacked the hand that held the hockey stick.

August 22 may not play so much as he gets older, but gentler pursuits, reading about it and watching programmes will always be a source of the purest pleasure. Many women ski well – helped by their long legs. When they take ski holidays it's always fun, not least because of the dressing-up and partying. August 22 likes sport partly for the fun and socialising.

Ms August 22 is usually keen on marriage and a lot of children. If she gets the children without the marriage, she will be a tough act for any other adult to deal with.

Opinionated, independent and in many cases easily able to make her own way in the world, authority figures such as teachers and social workers may find themselves on the end of a lecture and a wagging finger. The father of the children and his family should mind their Ps and Qs too. She will be fair, for the sake of the children, but criticise her or try to double cross her and by golly, Miss Molly, this lady can be awkward. Ms August 22's children often grow up like her and certainly admiring her.

The most popular labour saving device today is still a husband with money.

(Joey Adams)

BODY

Many August 22 people are susceptible to summertime allergies, which include hayfever type symptoms, running nose, sore eyes and sneezing. This is due to all sorts of pollutants, including pollen. There are some allergy inducing pollutants, a group of hydrocarbons given off by household products containing solvents, for example some paints. If you are decorating, use water-based or low-solvent paints, glues, varnishes and wood preservatives. If you must use oil based products, keep the lid on the tin as much as possible to prevent hydrocarbons evaporating. Better still, enjoy the sunny day and put off decorating when high levels of pollution are forecast.

MIND

Contrary to drawing-room chatter, destiny is never entirely in each person's hands, nor can you plan your life or your career. You can have a go, of course. You only control how you deal with destiny.

DATESHARE

John Lee Hooker, blues, jazz and general singing idol of all generations including the nineties. **Dorothy Parker**, humourist, writer, journalist. **Leni Riefenstahl**, German woman director Nazi propaganda movies. **Ray Bradbury**, science-fiction fantasy writer, Fahrenheit 451. **Claude Debussy**, French Impressionist composer.

AUGUST 23

BODY

Too many hours at the computer can bring 'screen blurr', which is an extremely good natural reminder to take remedial action for your eyes. The antidote is to place your thumb in front of your eyes in line with a distant object. Keep eyes concentrated on the thumb, but noticing without changing your focus how blurry other things are in the distance. Pick a distant object, then zoom your focus into it and observe how blurry the thumb appears relative to it. Look closely at the thumb, noticing how clear it looks. This exercise promotes quick focusing of the eye muscles and helps relieve strain.

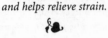

MIND

In numerology, August 23 is ruled by the number 5 (2+3=5) and by planet Mercury, ruler of Virgo which starts tomorrow. A cusp creature, you share Virgo's speedy thinking, attraction to exciting people and strength of purpose.

DATESHARE

River Phoenix, *Hollywood star, tragically died young from a drug overdose.* **Louis XVI**, *French king, husband to Queen Marie Antoinette, taken to guillotine in French Revolution.* **Keith Moon**, *rock drummer with The Who, tragically died young from a drug overdose.* **Shelley Long**, *American TV and film comedienne, Cheers.* **Queen Noor of Jordan**, *wife to King Hussein.*

This is another lucky date. August 23 people tend to swing through life, getting a few things wrong here, solving them there. But the clouds that overshadow some of their days are small, with lavish silver linings. Somehow or other this individual always seems to be able to lay his or her hands on just enough money to sort out their latest need. Thanks to enormous adaptability in the job market.

Firstly, they aren't fussy about choosing a career, as long as the surroundings are nice and the money's OK. They may often arrive in a job via friends or relatives, happy to have an opening found for them and a helpful senior eye kept on them. They are therefore attractive to older would-be mentors who like an enthusiastic pupil who can see the point of a chain of command. Many therefore end up inheriting or taking over a business just because they have been loyal.

Both sexes may have a flare for technology which makes them particularly useful, especially as they are privately interested in it and will have state of the art equipment at home. Even elderly men and women born on this day have a facility for computers and can understand how to manipulate them with greater ease than others who are half their age.

They fall in love easily, or maybe it's lust? August 23 often can't tell the difference, partly because they are suckers for other people's good looks, adore lots of uncomplicated sex – they like having the base of their spine rubbed – and they are too kind to say 'no'. This may lead to periods of intense juggling with several partners on the go. The women will try to fix up unwanted admirers with girlfriends. The men may simply decide that the telephone bill is absurdly high, pick one partner, propose to her and shoo the others away.

Easy come, easy go.

24 AUGUST

This creature embodies all the alluring qualities which make so many of their admirers want to murmur 'Come live with me and be my love'. The best kind of cusp cocktail, there is fire in the heart, lightness in the wit, and a steadiness of concentration which can impress the cleverest people in the land. In effect, August 24 catches Leo's last brilliant rays, twists them round a cocktail stick and slips the golden wand into the luscious dark velvet of their psychology.

The women are much pursued, not least for their mystery. She doesn't try to be mysterious. On the contrary, she is bright, witty and can sometimes be the gorgeous focal attention of a party. But for all the friendliness, there's that feeling you just can't grasp her. Many of the men are very similar and give even their closest loved ones a prickly sensation, foreboding of loss, even when there's absolutely no indication of anything but happiness. You are always trying to hang on to August 24 and always glad you have a firm hold because somebody else is trying to lure them away.

Many people pursue some kind of academic career, or at least research. They are clever, yes, but what takes them onwards is dedication to a subject and pleasure in isolation, which of course ain't easily accomplished in open plan offices.

Ms August 24 likes to make her house cosy, with lots of affordable collectibles she has picked up here and there on her travels. She favours Italy, in particular the south with its stinging heat and the dusty white light. She brings back terracotta pots and bright scarves which she puts on shelves and hangs on walls.

Males of the species don't care so much about their surroundings and can be quite stickily conservative with anybody who wants to cheer them up. But he too likes to decorate the place with personal mementoes.

~

Should I stay or should I go?

(The Clash)

BODY

Lady 24 adores aromatic oils and uses them for baths and hair and every purpose she can imagine. She's a girl who is made for motherhood and can expect quite a few pregnancies, not all planned and very possibly either from different fathers, or a second batch of babies several years after the first. Slightly faddy about health matters, she should avoid any unconventional alternative medicines during pregnancy and certainly give up many favourite aromatherapy oils. In particular don't use basil, cloves, cinnamon,hyssop, juniper, marjoram, myrrh, sage and thyme, peppermint and rosemary. And don't take any essential oils internally during this time.

MIND

In numerology 24 people are ruled by the number 6 (2+4=6) and the 6th card of Tarot's Major Arcana is The Lovers – great powers of affection and decisiveness, with an unfortunate tendency to sentimentalise.

DATESHARE

George Stubbs, *horse painter, friend to the aristocracy.* **A S Byatt**, *headmistressy writer, Possession.* **William Wilberforce**, *philanthropist, abolitionist.* **Gerry Cooney**, *heavyweight boxer.* **Deng Xiao Ping**, *Chinese leader Communist Party.* **Jorge Luis Borges**, *Nobel Prize winning poet, Labyrinths.*

EARTH

174

AUGUST 25

You always feel you want to watch where August 25 is going, because it's bound to be interesting and you may want to follow. These people are at their best when they don't cultivate this aura to the point where it's divisive. A few schoolgirls practise excluding games, pointedly stopping a classmate sharing a lunch table, or not inviting her to their parties. And of course boys do it too.

Both sexes can take this habit into adult life and the workplace, where they may actively encourage – though difficult to pin down – little outings to bars with one or two colleagues left out. Since August 25 is always the invited one, the charmed circle leader, he sees no reason to change. Unless it's put to them in the name of kindness, when there will be a great deal of sighing and loud complaints followed by an invitation given in bad grace and ten times as embarrassing and hurtful as the previous situation.

Less than brilliant behaviour such as this usually mediates against promotion, but not always. Everybody has come across the baby-faced game player boss. Usually these individuals fall hard, without the slightest idea why. If a patient and respected senior friend does criticise, then self-interest and embarrassment at being detected may induce August 25 to change its ways.

The good side of this capacity to make people feel privileged just by being with you, is that August 25 is brilliant at running small businesses, often paying little to staff, but keeping everybody going on the petrol of loyalty, praise and creative group thinking. If they run a restaurant – many are fab cooks – where the plates don't match because they can't afford to buy them, it will seem to be the stylish thing to do. And if there's cheap lino on the floor, then lino will be the most fashionable restaurant flooring of the moment.

I don't care to belong to any club that will accept me as a member.

(Groucho Marx)

EARTH

175

26 AUGUST

People born today often value their friends, of either sex, more than family or lovers. Capable of depths of feeling, they are serial fallers in love/lust. In many cases it will be somebody close to home, a friend's partner, a friend's brother or sister, because they are quite mentally lazy and feel safer as part of the social patchwork. What makes August 26 sad, and others too, is that he and she just can't help falling out of love again.

They dream of an endless partnership stretching through the future. Some achieve it. But many simply veer off. In the end, they

prefer to spend time with close friends, sometimes living with a bunch of people or family. Often they simply enjoy life alone, as do many more people each year in this country. But both sexes try to stay friendly with ex-lovers and many succeed extremely well. When August 26 has children, there is no sudden falling out of love. The children are at the centre of their universe. They will move mountains to be with them, earn money for them, making any sacrifice needed. They talk to their children endlessly about every adult topic in the world and very much want them to enjoy the pleasure of books. Children born to such parents manage very well within what is usually a split family and grow up happy, well-balanced and charming individuals.

At work this person is an excellent colleague and responsive team member, often extremely generous about another's talents and will frequently help that person and contribute to their success, rejecting thanks and shrinking from the spotlight.

August 26 may be elusive, but being such magical people, there are moments spent with this soaring meteor when the satellites who can bear to be near feel they will be taken up in the flight. And nothing is ever quite the same again. It's just that they are more desired than desiring.

They lose least ~ who have least to lose.

Many August 26 people are prone to exhaustion and when they are run down can be prone to all sorts of minor infections. Potent baths help relaxation and stimulate circulation, a common Virgo problem. Ginger is a traditional Japanese remedy for fatigue, thought to speed up metabolism. Grate one large ginger root, then squeeze gratings through a piece of cheesecloth. Add juice to a hot bath and soak for 20 minutes. A more extraordinary sake bath – but good – is prepared by adding 2 litres of the rice alcohol to bath. Soak for as long as possible. Makes skin soft and smooth.

MIND
People will be attracted to you and it is not their fault. It probably won't be possible to give the devotion they require, but kindness, not emotional rejection, is the best course.

DATESHARE
Died: **Charles Boyer**, glamorous French matinée idol. Born: **Prince Albert**, German consort to Queen Victoria, died young and left her heartbroken. **Peggy Guggenheim**, much pursued, took refuge in her art collection in Venice and found happiness. **Christopher Isherwood**, author, muse and lover to the poet W H Auden. **Guillaume Apolinaire**, French writer, poet, artist. **Albert Sabin**, virologist, live polio vaccine developer.

AUGUST 27

BODY

This Orange and Raspberry Sherbet is perfect for our masterchef of the universe, such a wily dark red it seduces eye and taste. Take 450g raspberries, 2 large oranges and 30ml honey. Juice or blend raspberries and oranges. Put mixture in bowl stir in the honey. Pour into shallow dish and freeze until almost firm. Remove from freezer, break up with fork and mix until fluffed up. Put back into freezer until firm. Remove dish from freezer ten minutes before serving. Serve with garnish of grated milk chocolate, raspberries and scattering of pink rose petals (washed and dried on kitchen paper).

MIND

It's difficult to be alone with August 27 and this can be frustrating for partners and children. Sometimes this creature also hides behind the jolly crowd. Give someone who loves you some private time together.

DATESHARE

Died: **Gracie Allen**, *Hollywood sex bomb, comedienne. Born:* **Pee-Wee Herman**, *actor, TV series, children's idol.* **Tuesday Weld**, *film star beauty, ex-wife of Dudley Moore with one son by him.* **Ira Levin**, *novelist, Rosemary's Baby.* **Mother Teresa**, *Yugoslavian Nobel Peace Prize winning nun, founder of Missionaries of Charity, idol of many round the world.* **Lyndon B Johnson**, *US president, popular nice guy.*

August 27 likes to be surrounded by a great many people and is at his happiest planning their entertainment, cooking for them and just generally sitting chewing the fat. In youth they live in groups – a new family of adopted siblings. In adulthood they want lots of children. Find this character living with assorted relatives, friends and their children, who August 27 relates to as his own. This baby is the grape in the universe's fruit bowl, firm, sweet and comes in clusters.

It is natural for both sexes to work in areas which directly benefit the community. They are drawn to social work and hospitals, where they bring an aura of comfort and gentleness. People who are sad find a ready ear but never someone who is content just to listen and sympathise. Virgoans like solutions and this character is no exception. He won't take inertia lightly, and anybody who thinks there is a permanent shoulder to sob on will receive a swift rapette on the knuckles.

Both the men and women are master cooks. It's their gift to others, but also their passion. Find them watching television and reading a recipe book, dreaming of quick, exquisite dishes. They think that the way food looks is as important as the way it tastes.

When the women have children they encourage them to join in the cooking. There will be lots of chocolate cake mix to lick with

fingers from bowls, small plates of toffee made by tiny hands and delicious dark red strawberries dipped in the kind of dark and shiny chocolate sauce that looks as if it was directly scooped from the midnight sky.

There are usually so many people to take on holiday that August 27 can only really afford to take off for the seaside around Britain. Find them all barefoot on those endless yellow Norfolk beaches building castles to die for in the sand.

What are we doing here? We're reaching for the stars.

(Astronaut Christa McAuliffe)

28 AUGUST

They exude sex appeal, sometimes so powerfully that August 28 wishes it would go away, but in later years when it does, they wish it hadn't. This individual gets on his star-spangled motorbike and when he speeds into town knocks everybody for six. They could wear a paper bag over their heads and it wouldn't diminish the magnetic field force.

Blessed with slender, sinuous good looks, these usually dark-haired conquerors of the night often have their eye on other things than love. Clever too, they'd as soon discuss a new project in weekly morning meeting without admirers fawning to agree. And they dread being told to pair off with a colleague and work out the details. It always ends with attempted hand-holding, sometimes in a furious rumpus and rarely in romance, because August 28 truly madly deeply does not want to have an office affair. What happens when it's over but you've still got to work with an ex-lover, while they glare across the room – or sob? Most probably he or she has a steady partner anyway, waiting to meet for dinner.

Nevertheless, sexuality is not entirely an unwanted cloak. They can spend whole days sitting at their desk thinking about last night and the night to come. Spot them gazing into the distance in a golden haze of contentment. Both men and women enjoy complete surrender to lust. The female is easily aroused by stroking the insides of her wrists, and delicate skin at the backs of the knees. And the men give in to pleasure as deft fingers stroke their hair and broad shoulderblades.

Many of these people are seriously creative. Find them as soloists in classical music or rock bands, and in the sort of graphic design departments which churn out award winning CD covers and advertisements. They'll decorate your house with original murals, and play a child a lullaby on their 17th century violin.

BODY

Give in to the delights of this famously sexy cocktail traditionally named Between The Sheets. For two, take 55ml fresh lime juice, caster sugar, 55ml white rum, 55ml brandy, 55ml Cointreau and fresh mint. This alcoholic wallop is slightly sour. Moisten the rim of two large chilled cocktail glasses with lime juice. Dip rims of glasses into sugar. Set aside. Pour remaining lime juice, rum, brandy and Cointreau into a shaker. Add a few ice cubes, shake and then strain carefully into each glass. Garnish with mint. Savour slowly through the sugar.

MIND

If your sex appeal is really a burden, then get rid of it. Eat a bag of doughnuts a day. Don't have your hair done. Wear crimplene trousers and talk about your illnesses all the time.

DATESHARE

Johann Wolfgang von Goethe, poet, playwright, Faust *and some of the most moving love poems ever written.* **Ingrid Bergman**, *devastated a generation of men with her clear-eyed, well-bred sex appeal.* **Charles Boyer**, *devastated a generation of great-grandmothers with his sloe-eyed French come-hither.* **David Soul**, TV actor, Starsky and Hutch.

I'm at the age where food has taken the place of sex in my life. I've just had a mirror put over my kitchen table.

(Rodney Dangerfield)

Latest health thinking is that a pet dog is more effective than other therapies. Stroking them brings down high blood pressure, relieves stress and some experts think makes you mentally alert. Country life addicts may prefer a bounding creature who takes them for walks and to meet the neighbours. Dalmatians are out-going and friendly, neither shy nor hesitant and free from nervousness and aggression.

Townies might choose a Yorkshire terrier, happier in an urban environment, but with the spirited, even disposition and air of neat importance most people find fetching. Some people even take them to work, convinced it helps calm office politics.

MIND

In numerology the 29th is ruled by the number 2 (2+9=11, 1+1=2). In Tarot, the second card of the Major Arcana is The Priestess, shown seated on her throne. People born today have intuitive powers.

DATESHARE

Died: film star, hardman **Lee Marvin**. *Born:* **Rebecca de Mornay**, *screen star.* **Michael Jackson**, *superstar, rock singer, songwriter, fab dancer, animal lover.* **Richard Attenborough**, *film director and actor.* **Elliot Gould**, *good-looking American film star.* **Charlie Parker**, *be-bop king, sax player, composer.* **William Friedkin**, *film director, The French Connection.* **John Locke**, *empirical philosopher, Essay on Human Understanding.*

AUGUST 29

This is another Virgo sex shuttle, although August 29 is more romantic than the bearer of pure animal appeal. The women have that attractive distracted look which often comes with short sight and they frequently keep a dog as silky and bounding with enjoyment as themselves. For Lady Virgo, the black labrador is perfect. It will protect her, be an intelligent and friendly companion, and attract the right kind of man. She likes sporty men who know how to handle a horse and a gun and when she has met him, Ms August 29 will want to ride and hunt with him.

Many girls gravitate to the country if they were not already bred there. Some will farm, becoming expert by training if not already so by birth and heritage. Our farming darling is well organised with an extensive knowledge of crops, a firm refusal to use environment endangering pesticides, and she can sort out a cow with a labour problem as well as the vet – if she is not actually the vet.

This individual has such taking ways that the whole of the county is round for her hand in marriage. Many enjoy blood sports, so no townies need apply for an interview with her father. Indeed she hasn't much time for urban culture and thinks her citied schoolfriends are misled into a horrifying existence based on terrible raw Japanese food and warm, sweet wine.

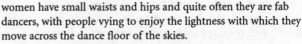

Both sexes shine like the evening star at any country dance. Both the men and women have small waists and hips and quite often they are fab dancers, with people vying to enjoy the lightness with which they move across the dance floor of the skies.

The men may suffer from hayfever in high summer and some are allergic to cats. Most of the girls have mild rashes on their hands, largely due to the rough work they do.

A politician is someone who will double-cross that bridge when he comes to it.

30 AUGUST

This birthday girl walks in beauty like the night. Another breathtaking Virgo babe. And the men are as impressive. The drawback, especially with the women, is a slight nervousness, fractious reactions to normal events. Some read too much into another's actions and the simplest words get loaded with the wrong significance.

So there's a rather tedious amount of cajoling and explaining required by these women. If a friend has bought a new frock, for instance, but says she doesn't think August 30 will like it, immediate affront is taken, when in fact the dress is a straight stone-coloured linen shift down to the ankles which curvy Virgoans usually do reject. They like to show off their often neat waist, flat stomach and lavish bosom.

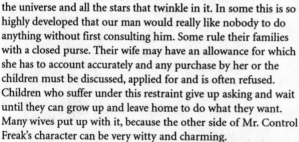

The men don't make quite so much commotion, but deep in their autumnal psychology there is an urge to control the universe and all the stars that twinkle in it. In some this is so highly developed that our man would really like nobody to do anything without first consulting him. Some rule their families with a closed purse. Their wife may have an allowance for which she has to account accurately and any purchase by her or the children must be discussed, applied for and is often refused. Children who suffer under this restraint give up asking and wait until they can grow up and leave home to do what they want. Many wives put up with it, because the other side of Mr. Control Freak's character can be very witty and charming.

In any place of work, both sexes exercise their talent to organise extremely well, making good team members and observant bosses, always the first to congratulate and pick out for praise. Both sexes also make brilliant doctors. Fired by a desire to help humanity, they leave no avenue unexplored to cure a patient and will personally spend nights by a bedside. Coming home late from work is a problem.

BODY

August 30 slaves so long over papers and often at the computer that he or she can suffer from burning or red eyes. Possibly this is shortness of oxygen and eye-dryness, lack of tears. Try yawning, loud and long, as if you are a hippopotamus. Make a big yawning sound and then do it all over again. This stimulates the tearducts, which distribute liquid over the cornea and help calm the redness. Then, tighten the shoulders, staring with wide open eyes. Now yawn again and blink. Blink hard every three to five seconds, it reduces the burning feeling.

MIND

Some quite ordinary stones bring you luck. Virgo's favourite is the cornelian, which is traditionally given the powers to strengthen family love and unity, helps to raise low spirits and minimise melancholia.

DATESHARE

Died: **Charles Coburn**, *Hollywood tough guy.* **Lindsay Anderson**, *film director, famously grumpy.* *Born:* **Mary Godwin Shelley**, *daughter of Charles Godwin, wife to Percy Bysshe Shelley, author,* Frankenstein. **Raymond Massey**, *stage and film actor.* **Joan Blondell**, *actress.* **Shirley Booth**, *film star.*

A man with an empty desk is a man who hasn't got enough to do.

BODY

The high fliers can get weighed down by their responsibilities and the irascible ones, made more so by overeating and drinking, should temper their procrastinophrenic reactions to any suggestions for a healthier lifestyle. Both can be helped in some measure by the famous Bach Flower remedies, discovered for us by Dr Edward Bach earlier this century. Travellers will find them helpful too in times of deadline stress and the simple difficulty of living in a community where they were not born. Rescue Remedy has been found to help nervousness, anxiety and the stress arising from bereavement, great fright, hysteria, arguments, speeches, exams and job interviews.

☾

MIND

Don't exercise too much control with your children, or expect them to reflect your own ambitions. This is common to people born today, and it's a common source of unhappiness between father, mother and teenagers.

DATESHARE

Caligula, *Roman Emperor with an unfortunate dominating manner and cruel streak.* **James Coburn**, *graceful, lithe, Hollywood star of cowboy movies.* **Richard Gere**, *another Hollywood idol admired for his sinuous body and lithe walk.* **Van Morrison**, *Irish singer, songwriter.* **Alan Jay Lerner**, *lyricist.* **Itzhak Perlman**, *Israeli violinist.* **Sir Bernard Lovell**, *radio astronomer.*

This is another birthdate who can make a good career in medicine. People born today run spectacularly successful general practices. Patients get in to see doctors without having to wait for too long. Records are never lost. And August 31 is a dragon about meticulous diagnosis, so there will be no dismissing of symptoms as neurotic in order to close the surgery down and get onto the golf course. The deep spirituality which is part of this person's psychology makes them extremely empathetic to anybody in trouble and our white-coated star will scan the universe with all its hidden knowledge to come up with a solution.

In medicine, August 31 may specialise in diseases of the pancreas and immunology, both areas of vulnerability for Virgoans and so there is an innate sympathy with these afflictions. This individual is very likely to make a fortune with some discovery which may benefit mankind medically or in some area to do with pharmaceuticals. The chemistry set was the child August 31's favourite toy, for girls as well as boys. Some react against this component of their psychology and become pill phobic, reacting with insultomania at any doctorly suggestion that they lose weight and change their lifestyle.

This creature is very fond of its food and drink and would not consider taking even one glass of wine less, or cooking with yoghurt instead of cream. In fact their ideal pudding is strawberries and cream with lots of brown sugar. And since it's almost impossible for August 31 to become addicted, it's possible to

understand why they like to be in charge of their own lives.

Although most crave a family and to settle down in their own home – they are sometimes too stringent with their children- a few have explorer lust. They may live abroad, taking up posts in far off places as journalists or as researchers helping a local population learn new farming and engineering techniques.

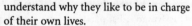

When a patient is at death's door, it is the duty of the doctor to pull him through.

(*Finley Peter Dunne*)

EARTH

I SEPTEMBER

Many of these people take a long time to grow up, some still regarding themselves as too immature to make decisions when they are past forty. Often extremely charming, this golden-fleshed but tough-skinned purple plum trades on its toothsome appeal for longer than most because it has always been cherished and lovingly handled. Some indeed, may go through the whole of their life Virgo intacta.

Many men can reach high places, driven by the force of their ego, untramelled by the world's seductions and penalties.

Marriages and love affairs drift away into space like discarded space capsules. Politics is ideal for this gorgeous reclining addition to the fruit platter of the universe. He will be thoroughly organised, a harsh opponent,but if someone takes a proper bite they will find the flesh bland, lacking the subtlety that comes with a more vivid recollection of the tree that bore him.

Women who remain untasted all their life do so by giving in to the temptation to put off any action until tomorrow, which is, after all, another day.

Nevertheless, life not always being fair, our plum-bums have a lucky streak. They often scoop large sums of money in later life, then enjoy gold bath tap luxury and other exotic toys favoured by this diamante-studded darling. Now September 1 women, and daughters they hardly know, slide into designer outfits and devote themselves to A-list partying, with a quick prayer that they won't ever again meet anybody they used to know.There may also be late romance and kids, although both sexes will somehow manage to relate to a child as their friend and not as a parent.

This person suddenly switches careers and spotting a window founds a new business, possibly in rejuvenating cosmetics or something sparkly-dangly, and makes pots of gold. Or they write a novel, an instant success, and bingo, Pundit Virgo September 1's face is all over television.

A gold rush is what happens when a line of chorus girls spot a man with a bank roll.

(Klondike Annie)

Most people born on September 1 have vivid, prophetic dreams, reflecting a flicker of the psychic flame common to many Virgos. The women are likely to be extremely fond of dolls and dolls are a favourite dream, indicative of enjoying being coddled. Other common September 1 dreams include the millionaire dream, an omen of good fortune, and the naked in a public place dream, which can express fears that people see through you, sometimes indicates desire for sex, and sometimes reflects this person's awareness of the role he and she adopts, choosing not to fit in but instead assert their individualistic enjoyment in rebelliousness.

☾

MIND
People born on the 1st are ruled by the number one in numerology, and in Tarot, the first card in the Major Arcana is The Magician, the key to September 1's meteoric and successful flight through life.

DATESHARE
Lily Tomlin, film star, comedienne. Seiji Ozawa, handsome, charming Japanese conductor. Gloria Estefan, singer, songwriter, film star, survived near fatal accident. Barry Gibb, Australian singer, songwriter, Bee Gees. Yvonne de Carlo, film star. Edgar Rice Burroughs, British author, Tarzan. Rocky Marciano, undefeated world heavyweight boxing champion, died in plane crash.

BODY

Pets are excellent for September 2's physical health, mental balance and as a source of vital affection. Canaries reduce high blood pressure in their owners as do goldfish. The cat is good, but doesn't give enough. Medical experts recommend a dog to promote balance and healthy well-being. It's important to pick the dog to suit your lifestyle. Cocker spaniels like country life and bring enormous pleasure with what The Kennel Club describes as a 'merry nature, with ever-wagging tail'. Jack Russells are good for towns. Anything small with bows on its head, will only make you feel shih-tzuphrenic.

MIND

Because natural beauty brings great pleasure to September 2, it's good to have flowers in the home. Pots of growing lilies or any other sweetly scented plant bring more joy and visual reassurance than you can possibly imagine.

DATESHARE

Director **Joseph von Sternberg**, discovered and cast Marlene Dietrich in his hit film The Blue Angel. **Keanu Reeves**, Hollywood star born in Lebanon. **Russ Conway**, pianist, songwriter. **Alan Drury**, writer, Advise and Consent.

September 2 people are gifted with special powers of concentration common to Virgo. Like mice, information technology enthusiasts are never happier than when they are procreating new IT crackshots exactly like themselves. The girls are as talented as the boys and both make a very good living, either in one company's project development, or as trouble-shooting freelances hired to retrain the workforce, and then depart after a few weeks.

The latter's ability to make a great deal of money, while flitting like a bee from one corporate flower to another, underlines the loner side of September 2, the desire to be independent, neither beholden to nor admiring of conventional authority structures. They dislike hierarchies, mostly because their personal experience of top executives is on the pathetic side as they try with gentle desperation to instruct a man or woman in charge of millions of pounds worth of company and staff, and thousands of pounds worth of personal equipment, how to turn on the computer. And then the basics of how to use it without shouting for an underling every few minutes.

It's hard for these whiz-kids to retain any IT (Inner Tranquility) skills in the face of such challenges, and indeed you can often hear the rising emotion in the instructor's voice. Miss Technosqueak is usually beautifully dressed, the leather trousers, white silk shirt type. She is so full of nervous energy, she doesn't come in fat sizes, and always has love on the other part of her mind. She can't fall for any man who is unable to  match her skills and so she lusts after a fellow computer nerd, squeakily offering to get his coffee and sandwiches and discuss his latest, brilliant theory. Sadly, this gentleman is so unwordly he's more the sort to blush when 'tools' flash up on screen than give in to the urge to caress her microsoft skin.

To speak ill of others is a dishonest way of praising ourselves.

(*Will and Ariel Durant*)

3 SEPTEMBER

This is a remarkably tolerant person. September 3 will go along with others' plans for long periods, only slightly modifying them. But they are watchful. In many cases this person is the best kind of partner to have, either in a career or at home, because they understand and support, always with an alert eye. At work they may rise to high places, although more frequently in tandem with another. Many women start off as personal assistants and end up owning equal shares.

Many will unexpectedly become main breadwinner for the family, because a partner is studying, needs to take a lesser paid job as a step to a better future, or just because of illness. If the breadwinning role becomes permanent, the women in particular have reserves of strength and intelligence and meet the challenge, admirably and without self-pity.

Like many Virgos, they have a greatly developed capacity for friendship, keeping best friends from school until old age. But, since they are always looking, always open to the delights of new people, many friends will be made as they go along, other parents met through school, co-workers in some local charitable scheme, or maybe a neighbourhood theatre group. And in old age, they often start all over again, forging fresh friendships and new starts just when life seemed to be narrowing.

Surprisingly they are not so tolerant with their children. Often over-determined about academic achievement, they can be

surprisingly fussy about food and mealtime etiquette. Both can be areas of volcanic tension build-up for children, so anybody who has an influence with September 3 should get them to temper this behaviour.

Both sexes take tremendous spiritual pleasure from water and it's ideal if they can live by it. But since having a house with a sea, river or lake view may be hard, boat holidays or long walks by water are the next best thing.

He's the kind of man
who picks his friends – to pieces.
(Mae West)

This secretly sensuous creature adores to be massaged. And their favourite is a silky stroking of the face with some gentle aromatic oils. Begin with fingers at the base of the neck and sweep up to chin and then outwards under the jaw towards the ears. Pause and return to under the chin. Now stroke up, around bottom of the lips, don't touch the lips, then up and outwards towards the cheekbones, then up to the temples, slowing the movement and increasing the pressure slightly. Hold the pressure for a moment at the temples, then glide the fingers back to beneath the chin.

MIND
In Tarot, the 3rd card of the Major Arcana is The Empress, who symbolises Mother Earth and native, creative intelligence. Find in The Empress stability, steadiness, charm, wit and grace. The downside is a few irritating affectations.

DATESHARE
Died: **Frank Capra**, film director. Born: **Charlie Sheen** (Carlos Estevez), film star. **Memphis Slim**, blues musician. **Valerie Perrine**, Las Vegas showgirl, film actress. **Pietro Locatelli**, Italian composer. **Alan Ladd**, British film actor, famous for being extremely short.

BODY

Given their love for giving pleasure, here is a recipe using lettuce, both a delicious soup and reputedly aphrodisiac, too. In ancient Egypt, the god Min was responsible for procreation and his sacred white bull was fed copiously on lettuce to increase sexual potency. In the Nile today, the men still believe lettuce promotes fertility. Cream of Lettuce and Fennel Soup: Take 55g butter, 4 chopped shallots, 1 clove garlic (chopped), potato (peeled, chopped), 3 heads fennel (chopped), 1tbsp chopped chervil, 1.1 l chicken stock, ½ tsp sugar, pinch ground nutmeg, salt, black pepper, 90ml double cream, chervil sprigs.

MIND

Feed the mind and increase sexuality with this delicious meal. Cook butter, shallots and garlic for 3 minutes. Add potato and cook 5 minutes. Add lettuce, 2 fennel, chervil, cook for a further 5 minutes. Add stock, sugar, nutmeg, salt, pepper, bring to boil. Lower heat, continue to cook for 20 minutes. Cool, liquidise, return to heat. Serve with cream, fennel garnish and chervil.

DATESHARE

Jesse James, western outlaw, shot by own gang. **Anton Bruckner**, Austrian composer. **Mitzi Gaynor**, singer, dancer, film star. **Dawn Frazier**, Australian Olympic swimmer.

There's no urge here to grasp money, babies or fame from fate. Many September 4 people just like to look around a tableful of friends, for whom they have cooked a delicious meal. It's not that this individual isn't clever or ambitious, they're certainly the former, although more rarely the latter. It's just that both sexes learn early to savour the moment. Many have experienced childhood bereavement of some kind, or seen money problems destroy people they love. What's important to our steady wren is the peacefulness of passing days.

Ms September 4 is often a brilliant student. She chooses to work from home, earning quite frequently a great deal of money from writing, painting, maybe music or sewing. She does this to help in the care of children or elderly relatives, but even without these, she'd mostly think the office environment was unpleasant. These are often in the over a hundred thousand pounds a year category, so don't sniff at the home-worker. The men feel the same. Conventional jobs structures seem irrelevant.

Because September 4 appears to be so strong, people are drawn to his house, to discuss ideas, to eat, to party and just absorb some of the affectionate atmosphere. There's no curb on drinking alcohol, red meat or cigarettes, but visitors will find that this person abhors drugs so don't even consider importing anything. If anybody does persist, there will be a dangerous, forceful flash of temper, shocking, unpleasant but effective.

Rooms which belong to this birthdate are nearly always decorated by their own hand and very idiosyncratic. The Virgo dark colours will be there, indigo, blackest violet underpinned with dark-green, or sensational burnt-orange. There will be beautifully embroidered cloths on the wall, some made by September 4. The silvery mirrors reflect smoking perfume. Favourite scents include geranium (*Pelargonium odorantissimum*) which enhances balanced joy, and orange sweet (*Citrus aurantium*) which makes you feel frivolous.

There is no spectacle on earth more appealing than that of a beautiful woman in the act of cooking dinner for someone she loves.

(*Thomas Wolfe*)

EARTH

5 SEPTEMBER

These people benefit in youth from the companionship of either a dog or a pet pony who gives them affection and instills in any child a sense of responsibility for the care of another living thing. A Welsh cob or Shetland have perfect steady temperaments, although they may nip just like any other horse. There is a sixth sense about these little horses which communicates with the child's own, as yet undimmed sixth sense, and most people who have been lucky enough to keep such a pet never forget the intense pleasure and moments of such deep communication they can never be repeated.

A horse is happy to share its stable, let you lie on its warm body and maybe talks back. A horse makes a child look at the landscape in a way no adult can teach, one that is never forgotten. Some people's psychology is so bound up with the horse, that they keep the connection in adulthood, working with them, or at least, winning a lot of money on them.

For this is another birthday where chance dominates, in this case with a stream of lucky breaks. A dull bequest of jewellery turns out to be worth tens of thousands. The house September 5 bought goes against national trends and almost doubles its value. The lottery and bingo seem made for this creature. And they're the one who wins the new car competition on the back of the cereal packet.

Lucky in money, OK with love, this individual may have some problems with his working life. There is natural talent, but neither sex is pushy and others always seem to slide past and take the bacon. September 5 has to fight a strong sense of being unappreciated, and with it, a tendency to wallow in self-pity. Fortunately, just as everything is getting on top of him, along comes another stroke of luck. And bingo, the sky is clear again.

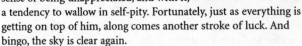

'Curiouser and curiouser'
cried Alice.

(Lewis Carroll)

BODY

Some people born on this day suffer from skin rashes, especially in high summer or when it is very cold. Sensitivity to foods like milk, eggs, peanuts and potatoes is common, so try removing these foods. Use non-dairy soya or rice milk, low in saturated fats. Essential fatty acids found in sunflower seeds, linseeds and oily fish are vital for healing. Add two teaspoons of Essential Balance Oil, made from organic linseeds, pumpkin and sunflower seeds, to food every day. As the oil is organic and unrefined, it must not be heated and is best kept refrigerated. It can also be applied to the skin.

MIND

In Tarot, the 5th card of the Major Arcana is The Hierophant. This card has good qualities of intuition, human insight, thoughtfulness and appreciation of the beauties in life. Power over things unseen controls the luck factor.

DATESHARE

John Cage, *American modern composer, immortalised the dreaming beauty of suburban gardens and children off to early morning school.* **Raquel Welch**, *Hollywood star.* **Freddie Mercury**, *lead singer, songwriter of Queen, tragically died of AIDS, mourned by the world.* **Joan Kennedy**, *long-suffering wife to Edward Kennedy.* **Christopher Nolan**, *disabled Irish boy writer, Under the Eye of the Clock.* **Louis XIV**, *French Sun King, seventy-three-year reign at the end of which he said with some satisfaction 'Apres moi, le deluge'.*

SEPTEMBER 6

Those born on September 6 are usually blessed with extreme good looks, wit, charm and sexiness. The women have the delicate rounded legs characteristic of Virgoan pins, with excellent ankles, small feet, but full thighs big enough to plague their owner. They have good waists, shining hair and excellent hands. The men have strong silky hair, but beware – some may start to disappear in the late twenties.

A few are athletically proportioned, still on the slim side, with square shoulders. But, sadly, most men rarely reach six foot tall and many don't grow much beyond five foot eight inches.

Nobody else of course ever cares about the height of this man because he is so attractive and brimming with Virgo maxi-bubble that it doesn't matter. But it matters to him and in youth he will study all sorts of crackpot medical reports about foods and drinks to make you grow taller.

Miss September 6, being extremely fond of food, similarly studies masses of slimming literature and buys bagloads of slimming pills and teas. Usually nothing works and she looks great anyway.

This preoccupation with looks often leads to a career in the fashion industry, cosmetics, hair or health. At the top end of the market, both sexes will hang out in the most luxurious health farms, polishing and pruning for their next publicity drive. But find them working there too, the genius massage therapist, the magician with skin and the person who cooks exquisite food, apparently containing no calories at all.

Within a 'safe' environment such as the looks business, these people flourish. But if they leave to work elsewhere, or even start a family, September 6 sometimes finds that whereas before he or she could rely on their planning ability, now things may go astray in spite of the greatest care. They are subject to the downside of chance, but fortunately only in patches during their life.

You must suffer to be beautiful.

7 SEPTEMBER

Many people born under the sign of Virgo are like sleepwalkers. They move carefully, tentative feet, metaphorical hands out in case they fall. And those around hush up in case they startle them. Both sexes reach maturity late. Often they feel they don't really understand what's going on until their mid or even late twenties. At school they sometimes did well and sometimes badly without the faintest glimmer of an idea why. Their beauty, often black-haired and astonishing, or red-haired and equally astonishing, seems not made for touching.

Love is not the key, but it helps. Though September 7 easily loses his or her virginity early, they hardly noticed. Then a Pisces or Aquarius flashes into their life and the earthling's chill heart smoulders and breaks into flame. These creatures still have a rather experimental approach to sex, that is before the intoxication sweeps them away. And 'I don't know what you're talking about, but why not?' Pisces, and 'What a good idea' Aquarius, are perfect partners, rather liking suggestions of love in the freezing water of a Welsh mountain pool.

September 7 soon wants more, a relentless pleasure hunt which may drive some lovers briefly round the dark side of the moon. Then come-hither Virgossamer kisses set pulses racing all over again. This individual's sworn by seductobite is two fried eggs, medium soft, eaten with salt, black pepper, tabasco sauce and good cold champagne. Enjoyed in bed, it certainly works.

Business colleagues have no glimpse of Virgolden boy's volcanic heart. They only see the precise colleague, with polished shoes and dynamic project suggestions, who apparently doesn't perspire into the elegant jackets on even the hottest day. As in sex, so in career. The late blossom is breathtakingly Virglamorous when it comes.

Unlike most people born near this date, September 7 has too much on his mind to care much how the home is decorated. She will not be doing many flowers.

His idea of oral sex is talking about himself.

(Lin Field)

BODY

September 7 is psycheologically geared to music, in particular compositions written in D Flat Major such as Debussy's Claire de Lune, quite a lot of modern rock and Gregorian chants. Both sexes work best with their favourite pieces helping them along. The music sharpens concentration, improves memory, rejuvenates problem solving capacities and lifts the mood. This isn't just quasi-mystical guff. Medical experts clearly document this to be the case, and furthermore they have proved that listening to Mozart or Bach can reduce pain, can sometimes be used in part instead of anaesthetics for minor operations and calms the cardiac pattern.

MIND

Try this at daybreak. Born Again Virgin kick starts a good mood. Take 350ml tomato juice, 15ml Worcestershire sauce, Tabasco, black pepper, ½ tsp celery salt, 10ml fresh lime juice, ice cubes. Serves two.

DATESHARE

Queen Elizabeth I, 16th century monarch. **Buddy Holly**, singer, songwriter, killed in plane crash young, but enough time to write a bunch of greats. **Chrissie Hynde**, British singer, songwriter, The Pretenders, 'I'm Special'. **Edith Sitwell**, Bloomsbury poet, sister to Osbert. **Peter Lawford**, film actor, connected with Kennedy family. **Grandma Moses**, primitive painter, patchwork artist, started career aged 67, lived to 101.

BODY

Better educated people live longer, according to new researches in North Carolina. Good news for September 8 who is likely to return to some form of higher education at any time in their life. Findings show that 65-year-old women with less than eight years' schooling are expected to live until 82, while those with more education live a further seven years. Researchers think this may be due to greater independence, which tends to lengthen lifespan; greater mental agility, which does the same; and of course better educated people seek better medical attention. September 8 is a longlived date.

ॐ

MIND

The sudden reverses in your life can be extremely dramatic, hard for others to follow or accept. Hard for you to accept if the roles were reversed and only the most devotedly self centred person could ignore this.

DATESHARE

Died: **Jean Seberg**, *exquisite French actress, memorable as Joan of Arc.* **Dorothy Dandridge**, *Hollywood cutie. Born:* **Peter Sellers**, *comic actor genius, friend to the royal family and most of the talent of his generation.* **Siegfried Sassoon**, *British World War I poet, essayist.* **Richard The Lionheart**, *heroic British monarch.* **Patsy Cline**, *country singer, songwriter.* **Antonin Dvorak**, *Czech 19th century composer.* **Hendrik Frensch Verwoerd**, *South African political philosopher, founder apartheid, Hitler ally, anti-semite.*

Ceptember 8 is an extraordinary mixture of characteristics and may be almost a completely different person at different times of life – more so than most people born on other days. Conventional in childhood they may not shine at school or indeed throughout their education. It's part of the late starter Virgo nature. But then by the mid or late twenties this creature suddenly gets an idea, understands exactly how it's going to work and steams it towards a brilliant conclusion.

This can be in a job, or setting up an independent money-making operation. Or it can be a resolution about having a family and how to run it. Either way, those who previously saw September 8 as an extremely frivolous person, the dance until breakfast of sausages and doughnuts, up again to go out to lunch, tennis, sleep, out again to go dancing sort, will be amazed. And slightly disappointed because this individual drops friends from a former era for the kind who fit more readily into his new life.

Although one of the roles taken is that of protector of the people, another adopted not many years later can easily be scourge of the same people. Ambition and the discovery of money changes many convictions. Extreme kindness and fairness are replaced by resentment of employees, and constant suspicion that plots are being hatched and resources heedlessly drained. There will be rules about using both sides of pages in a notebook, reusing envelopes. Memos float down instructing the turning off of lights, the brief use of the telephone, the answering of calls after just three rings, new restrictions on sticker pads.

Then suddenly there is another volte-face. Some threat looms and causes September 8 to change again. Either sex may throw up everything and change career. Or work as a team with colleagues

and underlings on terms of newly forged lifelong affection. They're mysterious people. You can't tell which way they'll jump.

To know, know, know him, is to love, love, love him.

(The Teddy Bears)

9 SEPTEMBER

Few people born under the sign of Virgo show the generous spirit of the star sign so seductively as September 9. The girls use their strong powers of concentration to get on at school and in their first jobs or higher education. Where once people might have said they were good, but plodders, their deeper brilliance begins to show as they mature. In this case earlier than other Virgo days.

Brilliant, charismatic, rich partners may be drawn to September 9 as mentors because of the honest, trusting nature and intelligence of these Virgolden girls and boys. Soon those mentors, having showered gold and silver, and September 9's favourite amethysts, denoting freedom from nagging worries, and pearls, denoting calm, find that their moment is past. No one is discarded. Others merely take over as escort to the empress or emperor.

Partners who have been loved even briefly by these creatures never forget that magical time and in later years, happily ensconced

elsewhere, simply the name of the lost one brings mistiness to their eyes.

The girls may try several successful ways of earning money, perhaps first in medicine where they are well suited with their nurturing instincts. Then into some form of retail, or publishing. And then into public life, with a powerful hobby as a sideline – painting in particular – which may dominate over all in the end.

The men follow a similar pattern. Expect to find them in some aspect of law, or in a public service where a knowledge of law is necessary. These are the guys who work hard to maintain the environment, but never with politically correct zeal. September 9 is never a dull do-gooder.

Expect more than one important love affair. Even several marriages. Expect a late child or two, some being born to September 9 at 50 plus. (That includes women! The natural or aided way!)

She was another of his near Mrs.

(Alfred Mcfote)

BODY

September 9's pleasure in marriage, even if there have been several, helps them to live a longer, healthier life. Surveys have shown that if you are married you have less chance of dying from strokes, cancer and heart disease. Divorced and single people are, by conrast, 30 per cent more likely to suffer from chronic conditions such as bronchitis, arthritis, diabetes, peptic ulcers, back problems, gallstones, skin complaints, hypertension and even varicose veins and migraines. Why? Medical experts say it's possible that people who live in a close relationship mutually activate and stimulate the immune system. It has been demonstrated that married people even catch fewer colds.

MIND

September 9 is vulnerable to strong colour which can lighten and stimulate with almost as powerful an effect as a glass of champagne. Crimson lake, Chinese turqoise, ambers through to burnt sienna, platinum and silver is the right palette.

DATESHARE

Otis Redding, *wonderful soul singer, 'Dock of the Bay', seminal, died young.* **Captain William Bligh**, *cruel captain on HMS Bounty, became victim of the mutiny.* **Michael Keaton**, *film star, Batman.* **John Curry**, *Olympic gold medal figure skater.* **Chaim Topol**, *Israeli actor, Fiddler on the Roof.* **Arthur Rackham**, *Victorian illustrator.* **Leo Tolstoy**, *Russian novelist, War and Peace.*

SEPTEMBER 10

DATESHARE

Amy Irving, American movie star. **Karl Lagerfeld**, German fashion designer, one of the greatest contemporary influences on style. **Margaret Trudeau**, wife of Pierre, novelist. **Mungo Park**, Scottish surgeon, explorer. **Stephen Jay Gould**, paleontologist, writer, Bully for Brontosaurus. **Robert Wise**, film director, West Side Story, The Sound of Music. **José Feliciano**, singer, guitarist, songwriter, blind from birth.

September 10 is addicted to luxury. They read recipe books for pleasure, dreaming of spicy prawns with delicate watercress. At night they nod to sleep cogitating over the extra touch of brown sugar needed to transform a chicken chorizo. And in the morning over coffee and home made croissants, they take important decisions about ice cream sundaes.

Marble is their favourite bathroom decoration. The dark brilliance of malachite underpins the colours of this Virgo's exotic soul. White lace might be welcomed by the girl, but the woman will choose mysterious, sea blue. Men prefer dark, gentlemen's club library colours. Everywhere old mirrors glimmer their soft light.

The bedside reading material of both sexes contains cooking, decorating, travel, gardening and some antique collecting thrown in. They like Victorian china, but may be drawn to the historical feel of old coins or domestic implements.

Many make a good living, catering to big business, running shops or restaurants, because they are meticulous, with that beckoning, alluring taste which attracts customers. Others who go into teaching professions, suitable for this controlled and concentrating person, may become very rich when they set up independent schools or coaching colleges.

Some seek life abroad where their teaching abilities and amusing conversation attract influential and generous friends. Find this toffee dipped earthling ensconsed in its own little palace a stone's throw from the markets in Marrakesh, rose petals strewn on the courtyards and barefoot exquisites stepping forward to serve iced goblets of aphrodisiambrosia. Lesser sybarites settle down and raise their kids, learn the language, fit into local business, build large houses and watch their children grow native to the adopted country. September 10 ain't the homesick kind.

At home, in less exotic locations, it's wise to remember that even in age there's an aura of glamour about September 10, which makes people look up when they enter a room and want to hear what they have to say.

To travel hopefully is a better thing than to arrive.

(Robert Louis Stephenson)

II SEPTEMBER

There is just a trace of the psychic in September 11, found in the most domestic of these creatures. Generally people who have this gift will not develop it sufficiently to use it continuously and confidently, but will come to rely on it as an accepted prop which helps them sort out their daily life.

It's usually men and women who live a life at home, often in the countryside who manifest the psychic talent. Those who care for animals in the fields, for the land, and for forest and water listen to songs in the wind heard by no other. Those who nurse a baby to this wind song understand that it speaks of what is past, and what or who may be to come. People who work in big cities generally can't hear a thing.

Some September 11 people who shine in the media or arts are vaguely aware of this gift, which is sometimes responsible for brilliant hunches and lucky breaks. They too try hard to listen. Their best bet is an empty art gallery or church, where the creativity and thoughts of others swirl into particularly potent atmosphere. Or failing that, a walk in the blackest early hours of the morning clears the mind and opens it to other awarenesses. Put the mind on an imaginary star-lit golden bough and you may unwind the winding path.

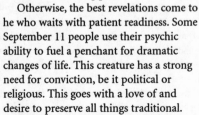

Otherwise, the best revelations come to he who waits with patient readiness. Some September 11 people use their psychic ability to fuel a penchant for dramatic changes of life. This creature has a strong need for conviction, be it political or religious. This goes with a love of and desire to preserve all things traditional.

Both sexes often hold strong religious views and become involved in their chosen church's social life. This brings them great happiness, especially in later life when a new friend is met there.

Where law ends, tyranny begins.

(William Pitt the Elder)

BODY

The humble potato, boiled and eaten without gravy, butter, mayonnaise or salad dressing, can bring you vitality, inner health and a slimmer body. There's a natural tendency to Virgobesity with September 11, and it's easier to side step it young. Potatoes also help with constipation, which somewhat afflicts these individuals. It acts as a natural broom in the intestines, sweeping out the toxins. It also has zero cholesterol, so that high blood pressure may come down on a potato intensive diet. And really, best of all, potatoes leave you with that full-up feeling. And a six ounce potato only contains 90 calories.

MIND

In Tarot, the 11th card of the Major Arcana is Justice. The card with the seated woman, scales of justice in one hand, sword in the other, underlines September 11's preoccupation with a proper system of good and evil.

DATESHARE

*Died: **Jessica Tandy**, Oscar winning star of* Driving Miss Daisy. *Born: **Jessica Mitford**, one of the famous Mitford sisters, author, socialite, social protester. **Brian DePalma**, film director,* Scarface, The Untouchables. ***Herbert Lom**, Czech actor. **D H Lawrence**, poet, painter, novelist, controversial views about sex.*

BODY

Drink often goes with the gambler mentality and certainly in youth September 12 likes nothing more than to throw him or herself into a black hole of alcoholic bubbles, and emerge next morning a little dreamy but otherwise apparently unharmed. On nights such as this, our Virgo wild child can be seen drunkenly burning money just for a bet, or to light someone's cigarette. There is a tendency towards addiction here, so lay off in your twenties or you won't be able to touch a glass of champagne in your sixties. A cold compress with a few peppermint drops added is remarkably effective for hangover headaches.

MIND

If you have to choose between manipulative charm and bullying manipulativeness, you'd probably take the pleasanter route. If you must devote yourself to reprehensible desires, at least make it as amusing as possible for others.

DATESHARE

Died: **Anthony Perkins**, *haunting Hollywood star of Psycho. Born:* **Maria Muldaur**, *country singer, songwriter.* **Maurice Chevalier**, *French film star, singer, 'Thank Heaven for Little Girls'.* **Jesse Owens**, *Olympic gold medallist sprinter, long jumper.* **Louis MacNeice**, *Irish playwright, poet.* **Henry Hudson**, *explorer Arctic circle, sought Northwest Passage, died tragically adrift in small boat with young son.*

They spend much time in the pursuit of money. Yet September 12 is always missing golden opportunities to collect up the minty bits. He's the kind who lets fortunes drift through his fingers on madcap schemes. But when all seems lost and somebody else's floor is paved with the fallen gold, suddenly there's a turnabout of fortune which may favour this creature.

It's true that September 12 is money-grabbing in the worst possible way and will go in for the most cynical means of collecting it. He will spend months courting a distant elderly relative in case there is some money to cough up at the final splutter. But there's so often an *up* side to these actions. The elderly person will enjoy amusing companionship when she might otherwise have been lonely. And this kid is fun. There's an electromagnetic crackle wherever she goes. Days at the races, visits to stately gardens and maybe just down the pier for some cockles and a spot of palm reading all have the extra-treat feel to them and strangers will smile and start to talk to her.

The other up side to September 12 is that he's a good loser, but when he wins everybody else benefits. This little Virgopod can't resist buying everybody presents, enjoys the pleasure of actually throwing the money away. Fortunately, those who benefit when he or she is in the money are usually happy to provide emergency finances when they are not.

September 12 always has plans. They may start a touring theatrical company, convert a ruined church into a club, found a catering empire based on twenty ways with the baked apple. They think bank managers are simply money-lenders and most of these high street toughies quake in the face of another financial trapeze act, and an irresistible Virgoing over. Their plans often work, bringing happiness and quite a few pounds to all.

To be ignorant of one's ignorance is the malady of the ignorant.

(A B Alcott)

13 SEPTEMBER

There's a work addiction here. September 13 may have a more physically loving relationship with his or her computer than with any human partner. These are extremely directed stars, capable of assimilating complicated technical formulae and spotting a problem. Maybe trained engineers or scientists. Others just slide down the Milky Way to stardom because their luminous beauty, talent or the intense rainbowness of their shimmering aura makes them recognisable to the world.

This symmetry loving creature always tries to create order where there is chaos. 'Random' isn't a word that exists in the ideas files. In office buildings this person, usually the male of the species, can get out of hand, starting to issue the absurd sorts of housewifely orders you find in Japanese and American companies, where staff are asked to wear a particular colour of suit. If somebody issues a memo that no posters are to be stuck on the wall without written permission from office 345 on floor 27b, or that taking lunchtime sandwiches at your desk is a sin, it's going to be September 13. Female executives don't go in for this because housework isn't such a novelty to them.

Bewitching, yes, but they spoil it all by examining every coffee cup that somebody else washes up. Immediately after lovemaking they start to tidy up. They practically brush their teeth between kisses. And exquisite little provocative wispy silk undie numbers will be regimented in neatly closed bedroom drawers too terrified to slide open with ease.

Because their powers of concentration are extraordinary – they can do at least three things at once – both sexes elevate this skill to almost magical dimensions. Others' impetuosity is anathema. Theirs is the right way. But Virgo consistently overdoes things, gets too tired for superhuman concentration feats. Then September 13 is puzzled and not a little shaken to find he is as others. All of them are a pushover for chocolate!

BODY

The aura is said to be the life-force or magnetic field that surrounds all living things – as well as substances. The word is derived from the Greek avra, meaning breeze, because it is said to be continually in motion.

Psychics describe it as a rainbow-coloured emanation, radiating two or more feet around the body, ovoid in shape. It is said to shimmer and alter in colour, depending on our health and state of mind. If September 13 gets too wound into the largely negative world or monitors others' activities for neatness and obedience, their aura will become muddy-coloured quite quickly.

MIND

Some are born with sufficient psychic powers to see a person's aura. Others need training. If you sense your own aura is muddying, try a drop of juniper oil – a psychic cleanser- on your forearms.

Punctuality is the thief of time.

(Oscar Wilde)

Children can enjoy aromatic oils as much as adults, but they have different preferences, more floral and citrus, and it's important to use half suggested quantities for children under twelve. No more than two or three drops in the bath. For children under seven, dilute the essential oils in a few teaspoons of vegetable oil or a tablespoonful of full fat milk before adding them to the bath. This will reduce the possibility of neat essential oil being rubbed into the eyes. Essential oil of lavender is an excellent remedy if added to the bath of a fractious child shortly before bedtime.

ᏚᎪ

MIND

On his travels, September 14 collects stones and rocks which bring him calmness. Coral is helpful for minor illnesses and brings the soothing vibrations of the sea. Jade is a lucky charm to ensure safe journeys.

DATESHARE

Maria Callas, *great opera diva, famous love affair with Aristotle Onassis, which reputedly ruined her voice.* **Sir John Barbirolli**, *conductor Hallé Orchestra.* **Georges Seurat**, *French Pointiliste painter, bathing scenes.* **Julie Harris**, *film star, TV actress.*

SEPTEMBER 14

At their best, people born on September 14 are tremendous party-givers and general planners of fun and great holidays. Although both sexes will hold down a very good, conventional job, frequently something to do with the law or money, they aim to save enough first to find a decent place to live, then, to have a good time.

The true Virgorama of their pleasures seems never ending. There'll be parties in ruined castles with fireworks and cauldrons of the finest venison stew. There'll be bathroom cocktail dos with drinks called Whirlpool Sensation and Pull The Plug. And fancy-dress items where everybody has to come as a squid.

These individuals like to move around in a crowd, so the richer ones will take a villa in Spain with a swimming pool, then fill it with friends and friends of friends. Plus relatives too. September 14 take their mum and dad wherever they go, because everybody gets on with everybody. So one golden summer, Grandpa will be paddling with his little granddaughter while pink fleeces the darkening green and indigo night sky. Somewhere over the valley Moorish music murmurs – edgy, primitive – while cards are played on the terrace, and people saunter back from the bullfight. Another summer, when there's not so much money about, more or less the same bunch of people will be building award-winning sandcastles on the miles and miles of yellow Norfolk beach, hunting for

samphire and sea lavender in marches, and for tiny crabs which grip stick ends pushed into soggy sand.

September 14 likes to drink, have lots of sex and lots of babies. The girls adore mothering. Breast-feeding gives them pleasure and their babies sleep the damp, heavy, dreamy sleep of small people who have been played with and laughed with all day. At night their mother puts her nose into their cots and scents the lovely baby smell of new mown hay. And so does Daddy September 14.

You can be my bodyguard

and I can be your long lost pal.

(Paul Simon)

15 SEPTEMBER

They like money and they can't help spending more than they should. They like sex and it gets them into trouble. They like work and that gets them into trouble as well. In the few moments between, they worry about their health and have more pills and health books in the house than the Biggleswade poisoner who wanted to give his victims different coloured potions until he had gone through all the shades of the rainbow.

If this individual can, he and she chooses some form of work that involves travel. If they can work on planes and trains, boats and cars, then they are happy. Of course it can mean they don't get home much. But September 15 usually takes her partner to most places. Unless, of course, they are the secretive sort born on this day, in which case constant travel fits in with their desire simply not to have everybody know what they are doing or where they are. Some of these have a liking for the I'm-only-passing-through existence. Prospective partners be warned. They aren't easily reformed.

Most equate status with the amount of money they are paid and how much they are seen to spend. It doesn't do to reward them with kindness or a better title, because resentment just builds until there is a show-down. Women, in particular, who still suffer from unequal pay, object. Expect genuine trouble if this situation gets out of hand, including industrial tribunals, and not just for themselves. September 15 are on the alert for their sisters.

The trouble with sex is that these individuals often can't tell the difference between lust and love until after the main event, and when they want to walk away the other partner may hurt sufficiently badly to start sending round several hundred takeaway pizzas. But for the most part, September 15 lives a happy and long married life.

Nobody goes to that restaurant
any more.
It's too crowded.

BODY

Fast eating and indigestion are two characteristics of September 16. Upper digestive tract symptoms like indigestion or acid reflux may be a sign that we are not producing enough acid, rather than too much. Ridges on your nail often denote poor digestion caused by low acid secretion. Chew food really thoroughly and never drink too much with meals as this dilutes acid and slows down digestion. Avoid tea, coffee, sugar, chocolate and artificial additives. Ask your doctor's advice about hydrochloric acid tablets and digestive enzymes which are known to aid some. Food combining is also thought to be helpful and there are many books available.

MIND

Sports experts with a fascination for peculiarities may like this cricket bag of odd names: J W Box, Middlesex wicket-keeper. P A C Bail, Cambridge Blue 1986. W L C Creese, played for Hampshire. A Chance, played for Shrewsbury. C H Cort, played for Warwickshire.

DATESHARE

Henry V, *immortalised in Shakespeare's play, conquered the French at Agincourt.* **David Copperfield**, *illusionist, TV star, showman, magician.* **John Gay**, *British writer, The Beggar's Opera.* **B B King**, *blues guitarist.* **Nadia Boulanger**, *French, much loved piano teacher, conductor, musical mentor to nearly all the greats today.* **Lauren Bacall**, *exquisite wife to Humphrey Bogart, author, actress.*

Many September 16 people may not be born with conventional good looks, but are physically and mentally attractive in their own way. They are often extremely tall and big-boned, the men well over six foot and the women not far behind. Some grew tall and bulky early in life and with it came some clumsiness, which may mean that in early adulthood they are shy and choose to wear loose clothing and big boots so as to hide their size. But as the years fine them down they realise that tall and broad is good.

Nevertheless neither sex is likely to be a maxi-bubble extrovert and nor do they want to be out all the time clubbing, pubbing and generally exhausting themselves. Even when a measure of self-confidence has come, they can still find themselves looking sadly at the thinner members of their group and fantasising about tiny waists and midriff baring tops, with tight jeans and skinny sweaters.

Maybe because they are so large they are extremely gentle with small children and animals – and never use their bulk to frighten. Many are seriously intelligent, reading widely and keeping up with current affairs. They make a thoughtful and balanced contribution, very much the problem solvers of the galaxy.

Male September 16 people are excellent with mechanics and foreign languages. Both sexes have quiet diplomatic skills, invaluable in any work where they deal with others' welfare, either a public entertainment project or in the higher reaches of human resources. This trustworthy star does not gossip, and never reveals a confidence.

However, the men may not be as enthusiastic as they might about others' success. Women don't suffer this envy blip.

Both sexes are devoted to faithful marriage and the careful raising of children. Whether they be Muslim, Hindu, Jew or Christian, they are thoughtful parents, never sticking to hidebound conventions, and so they're often the ones other people's troubled children turn to.

The heart can do anything.

(Moliere)

17 SEPTEMBER

September 17 people are honourable and always look for the best in others. They are the first to praise and be generous about friends' success, and the first to offer help when it's needed. Most people born on the other days of the year would give their right arm to have this person on their side.

This lucky creature has almost no streak of depression in its psycheology. They are very clear-cut about what they can and can't

do and rarely take on so much they feel overburdened, because they possess an extremely logical equation in their minds between things to be done and the time there is to do it. Sometimes at work this sensible attitude may irritate over-pushy bosses or colleagues, but our steady star refuses to let him or herself be panicked into volunteering for anything which they know will drive them round the bend.

Many people born today have strong religious beliefs and will be extremely involved with their local church and the community. Good team workers with a developed social conscience, their training may make them extremely useful in volunteer work or with charities. And since they are witty, pretty and gay (in the jolly sense, although they may be gay in the modern sense and jolly too) nobody they deal with is patronised. Neither the old, the sick, nor the habitually drunk will be made to feel lesser people because they are old, sick or drunk, although September 17 takes a vigorous attitude towards addiction.

There's another streak in their psycheology which indicates that some may be single parents, at least for a time. (Although late romance and permanence are promised.) Either sex manages brilliantly to keep a good job going and bring up the kids. Fortunately many September 17 people work in jobs such as teaching and areas of social work where hours can be made flexible, but if not, then big business must make allowances.

Make war upon

this bloody tyrant Time.

(William Shakespeare)

BODY

Tired eyes plague this individual. Fortunately there's much that can be done. Avoid alcohol, caffeine and sugary desserts and try to stick to vegetarian food for at least two days in the week. Sugary foods affect glucose tolerance, which affects the ciliary muscle, the focusing muscle of the eye. So it's important to eat complex carbohydrates, fresh fruits, vegetables and a minumum of red meat. Try breathing exercises to help. Breathe in. Breathe out. Pause. Do this from ten to fifty times. Research on shallow breathing shows that not enough oxygen reaches the eyes, which leads to impaired vision.

☾

MIND

In Tarot, the 17th card of the Major Arcana is The Star, a card which shows a naked girl pouring water from a pitcher. In her lies a promise of the good things of life, but also dreariness of overwork.

DATESHARE

Ann Bancroft, *legendary Hollywood beauty, seducer of Dustin Hoffman in* The Graduate. **Sir Francis Chichester**, *solo round the world sailor.* **Frederick Ashton**, *dancer, choreographer, Covent Garden guru.* **Stirling Moss**, *British champion racing driver, sixteen Formula One wins.* **Roddy McDowall**, *stage and TV actor.* **Hank Williams**, *country singer, songwriter.*

This is another of those ice cream sundae people, completely gorgeous, gone in a minute and you often regret you ever set eyes on them. Little yum-yum sits about waiting to be noticed. An exquisitely presented dish, she knows she's bad for you, especially when her consumer is the married kind. But who's fault is it? Nobody has to pick up the spoon.

The women are not career-minded. Find them squishing about in dress shops and hairdressers patronising plump people with thin hair. The lady's face is her fortune, which with so much unemployment about is as good a way of making it as any other. She sets her sights on rich older men who will be astonishingly grateful just to be near anything so scrumbublious. Find this 20-year-old Virgoette on the arm of a 70-year-old. She looks good in black and hopes the chance to wear it comes along soon. She's a serial marryer. If her husband sticks around, our lady of the golden brow may simply take over his business assets and turn herself into a terrifyingly astute power goddess.

Both sexes have a daffy streak, but their lucid psychological toughness wells up when opportunity knocks. Many of the men are equally decorative, but on first acquaintance strike one as a bit of a mezzoninny, with several choices for a happy landing but can't make up their mind which one. They usually get it right in the end, however, so live tolerantly with it now and you won't pay later.

Always find these good time kids where the beautiful and witty want to be. Sexual predators, they are generous with their bodies – rubbing the base of their spine makes them fizz – they give pleasure as well as take. But may not come back for more.

They are passionate collectors, buying old Odeon-style lighting or sixties paper chairs just before they hit big time prices. Worth watching.

∽

Don't step on my blue suede shoes.
(Elvis Presley)

19 SEPTEMBER

Time is this creature's enemy. Firstly, September 19 can't get up in the mornings, mostly because they have been up most of the night. Such creatures come out to play with the stars and are best employed during this quiet time, then go to bed with the sun. They make good film makers, night shift workers, club owners, hostesses and bouncers, TV editors, astronomers and hospital workers, because there, at three or four in the morning, they are always happy. It's the intensity of the night they love, the fresh night air and a sense of the world sleeping.

Forced to work by day and sleep at night, they can train themselves to manage. But most will be unpunctual at the very least, because the hours of the day seem shorter than those of the night and time is always catching up with them. If they have a task to complete in the night, it will be done by morning. In the day, it won't be done by nightfall.

Naturally the women adore motherhood because it gives them a chance to stay up at night, feeding their baby when the universe is still and the two of them are at its centre. Such an intensely romantic creature quite often has stars in its eyes for only one partner and will never believe anything bad of them. If they marry somebody who loves night partying, travelling at night or somebody who works in the theatre which opens mostly at night, the marriage will amble along in complete happiness.

Music and poetry are important to this satellite as it traverses its course. Some may compose works of great beauty. Others feel spiritually refreshed when they read words such as these: 'Shall I compare thee to a summer's day? Thou art more lovely and more temperate: Rough winds do shake the darling buds of May, And summer's lease hath all too short a date.' (William Shakespeare)

If it weren't for pickpockets I'd have no sex life at all.

(Rodney Dangerfield)

BODY

Since September 20 is keen to keep his brain sharp and prides himself on his memory, here is a little test which will (a) tell him how good he is and (b) give her something to practise with, thus improving that memory. Here are some number sequences.

38147; 013825; 7958423; 51739826; 163874952; 9152438162; 15284673183.

Read the first sequence (38147) out loud at a steady rate. Now close your eyes and repeat the numbers in the correct order. Progress through the sequences until you start to make mistakes, then continue until you are always inaccurate. Most people can manage to remember six- or seven-number sequences, so you can judge immediately how you compare with the average.

MIND

Too much work makes September 20 a frazzled star. Vitamins B1 (thiamine), B12 (cobulamin) and C can help. Juice 6 kale leaves, 2 tomatoes, 1 celery stalk. Take with a piece of cheese (for vitamin B12).

This sharp-witted creature goes in for self-improvement. Many September 20 people left school with poor exam results, or none. But this may have been a problem of timing, not dimness. Many thought school dull and found it hard to concentrate when the sun was shining outside and loafing around in the shopping centre beckoned. But then they get onto a training scheme or take a job with day release at the local tech and everything changes. He or she can suddenly see the point, mostly because it's a more adult environment and the learning is for something. Many a magnate and top executive comes up this way. And many a famous writer.

Sometimes it was just the self-doubt which lurks in many Virgos which held this striking space traveller back. A little learning is not at all a dangerous thing. Only those who want to keep education to themselves tell you that. Knowledge is pleasure. Knowledge is power. It's one way to make a fortune, and to attract the opposite sex. It gives you something to talk about, makes you an accomplished traveller and brings confidence.

Both sexes make excellent late starters. Many men and women who have been made redundant find themselves easily able to re-train and thoroughly enjoy the next step in their lives. A lot of women go back to some kind of learning when their children are old enough for them to look for work.

All of this happens to September 20 because they are exceptionally open-minded to new ideas, a characteristic which is invaluable in the workplace and domestically. You'll never hear them say 'I'm not interested' without even listening. And they always listen to others with attention. Indeed, it's just because they are such good listeners that these creatures are always socially in demand and, of course, popular with children who need somebody to listen to them almost more than anything else.

Excuse me, I didn't recognise you. I've changed so much.

(Oscar Wilde)

EARTH

21 SEPTEMBER

September 21 is a worrier. In childhood he and she heard parents despairing about bills and, like most children, took it more dramatically than the situation deserved. The frightened child becomes an adult who never wants to experience this. Unfortunately, unless your name is Lord Borace Bleepfurgle and you inherited snoodles of money – and some September 21 people are and do – then, along with everybody else, money worries come.

It's just that this creature has to fight bigger bogeys when it comes to unpaid bills and carnivorous bank managers. Others regard Mr B M as Mr Piggy Bank. September 21 thinks he's the headmaster. Fortunately the strong side to their psychology means that they usually get over this, mostly because everybody else is having to.

The women worry about not being promoted and general unfairness at the office until they understand that much of management has spinach for brains and what gets you up the ladder is quite often straightforward brown-nosing. Men's noses are bigger than women's so they are better at it. Then, when they have a big desk, they worry about why the staff don't like them and sing a lot of karaoke at staff Christmas parties in order to curry favour.

These lovely creatures, because September 21 mostly are, should try to master this tendency, partly because it wearies companions. And frankly, blessed with humour, brains and a natural capacity to

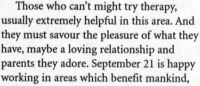

attract the opposite sex, be grateful. Thank the kind fairies who delivered the good bits and ignore the bad fairy's gift.

Those who can't might try therapy, usually extremely helpful in this area. And they must savour the pleasure of what they have, maybe a loving relationship and parents they adore. September 21 is happy working in areas which benefit mankind, when she can forget herself in the efforts to create greater good. Or else seek a passionately involving hobby such as gardening, walking or amateur dramatics.

Try to please everybody.
That's the formula for failure.
(Howard W Newton)

MIND
You frequently dream of falling. There are two interpretations. The one you pick says it indicates fear of failure at work or some inadequacy. The other is an omen for sexual excitement and falling in love. Choose the second.

DATESHARE
Died: **Walter Brennan**, *Hollywood classic comic and actor. Born:* **Stephen King**, *horror writer,* The Shining. **Shirley Conran**, *novelist, mother to clothes designer Jasper.* **Larry Hagman**, *JR from* Dallas, *director.* **Girolamo Savanorola**, *Italian philosopher, excommunicated, executed.* **Sir Allen Lane**, *founder of Penguin publishing empire.* **H G Wells**, *novelist, high liver,* The Invisible Man.

BODY

Many September 22 people have to travel long distances and look good within hours of arriving. Wash hair before travelling and to stay fresh keep cleaning your teeth, perhaps each time you go to the loo. On arrival, wash hair again, one shampoo. If it's to look natural, towel-dry it, then run fingers through the hair in one direction, twisting the hands in on the hair, so that it is pulled round the fingers, rather as if they were rollers. Do this until the hair dries naturally with the warmth of your hands. This gives the hair bounce and encourages natural movement.

MIND

In Tarot, the 22nd card of the Major Arcana, is The Fool. On some cards he's stepping over a cliff. He represents instinct and will freely followed. This is a spiritual card, indicating enthusiasm untainted by greed.

While September 22 doh-se-dohs about the sky, Rome burns. This person is dance mad in youth, in middle and old age. They're good at it and may win sparkly medals. The main concern is who'll be their partner and what to wear. And why not? Most of them, spurred by the puritan work ethic, slave all day at their studies or over a computer or maybe doing what many do best, keeping customers happy at the supermarket checkout point.

If dancing takes over as a lifelong hobby, they work hard at the day job, because what they do at night is expensive and extremely competitive as well as pleasurable. What they don't have much time left for is whether the ozone layer is thinning, and anyway if they were to worry, it would mean giving up mass hair spraying with the aerosol can, vital to professional dancers and so conducive to more ozone layer thinning. There are more sequins in female September 22's life than stars in the firmament and this creature is convinced that like each grain of sand, God has counted every one.

All born under this sign have this capacity to throw themselves into a passion, but September 22 is more singleminded than most. It may just as well be fishing, where the male dreams all day of river banks. Or flying aeroplanes, driving fast cars, or stock car racing. Or even gardening.

It's a good life for both sexes. They may turn their interest into a terrifically successful and enjoyable career. There's always a demand for specialist shops, new books to be written, clubs to be run. The social life is usually excellent, full of like minds. You can meet a future spouse here knowing you'll have interests in common. The elderly always have friends to meet and somewhere to go. And children join in, playing with everybody else's kids. Just don't expect a coherent conversation about politics.

~

I can't control myself.

(Troggs)

23 SEPTEMBER

This lovely creature, fair of face, full of grace, looks set for a good life. Blessed with an astute brain and the powerful child of early autumn's sex appeal, their only need is to stay true to themselves. The earthling's compliant nature means that they may sometime abandon their ambition in the face of super persuasion. Young September 23 must listen to his or her heart and not the sensible advice of loving but misguided parents.

Quite a few may find that while they want to be writers, or join a pop group, or be a footballer, mum and dad say go for safety in the local bank or accountancy. But September 23 is not a natural

librarian, nor will he or she be happy sitting behind a glass panel serving people money with a smile. And many secretly think accountants are pompous know-alls, living off the backs of other's inspiration. So there may be some early career changing as they switch back to their heart's desire.

Many older people see themselves in the young September 23 and will move heaven and earth to help. They bring out the generous in most people and return that generosity. Many shine out in later life, rising to the top of their chosen path and shed an irridescent light all around. The women may fall out with their parents temporarily, but soon make it up. The men take longer, only because they are less family conscious than their female counterparts.

Most of the girls eventually long to have children. Some may give up ambition to raise them, happy that at least they tried. Most men continue. Both sexes can find fame and fortune, and live in grand houses, often in other countries. Only some may suffer from delicate health, which could interfere with conception for the females. Successful help is at hand, but if no children come along, September 23 woman manages without looking back.

BODY

These people have lustrous hair and it's nice to keep it that way. For an incredible shine, take some sweet almond or other nut oil, add jojoba and the essential oils of your choice, then massage through your hair, paying particular attention to your scalp and hair ends, especially if your hair is long. Pile hair on top of the head, cover with a towel and leave on for 30 minutes to one hour. Wash with very mild shampoo. Try this once weekly and you will get a lustre that ordinary conditioners don't manage, because aromatherapy benefits the roots of the hair.

MIND

September 23 is a pushover for chocolate, especially in smart boxes. Buy one for yourself. It may seem somehow sinful, but that's just upbringing. What a simple formula for such a lot of pleasure.

DATESHARE
Romy Schneider, *Viennese film star, actress.* **Bruce Springsteen**, *rock star, film songwriter.* **Ray Charles**, *singer, songwriter, blind, beloved.* **Julio Iglesias**, *singer, hearthrob, supposed womaniser, bit of a disappointment.* **John Coltrane**, *jazz guitarist, saxophonist, composer.* **Frank Cupka**, *Czech abstract painter.*

Don't worry kid,
    the wages of sin is birth.
                (Derek Walcott)

BODY

Eating for comfort is a big problem with September 24, especially as being seriously overweight is statistically associated with high blood pressure, arthritic knees and other disorders. Follow former chancellor of the Exchequer, 64-year-old Lord Lawson's example. When prime minister Margaret Thatcher made him unhappy he tucked into favourite golden crispy roast potatoes, shepherd's pie, real mayonnaise, Hollandaise sauce, treacle tarts and single malt whiskies. He left the job, cut out sugar, butter, cream, starchy food, fat, a bottle and a half of wine a day and took more exercise. Now he's slender and his arthritic knee is better. And he's written a bestseller about his diet!

MIND

A really good book takes your mind off yourself, gives you a glimpse into another magic world, where your woes don't exist. It also sharpens the brain. You've no doubt seen Jane Austen on TV. Why not read her?

DATESHARE

Svetlana Beriosova, *Russian ballerina, took refuge in England and Paris.* **Linda McCartney**, *musician, photographer, vegetarian entrepreneur wife of Paul.* **Jim Henson**, *Muppet and Miss Piggy creator.* **Anthony Newley**, *actor, author, lyricist.*

September 24 people are usually very physically attractive, but devastatingly vulnerable to love's pain. Both sexes will be able to go to work through it, but come home and shut themselves away, almost paralysed with agony.

This creature must get over her plight. For her, upset entrenches itself, making it hard to try love again. If unrecovered September 24 goes through life without a loving partner, they can get difficult and sour and very lonely. These delicate individuals must arm themselves against permanent damage by keeping eyes and ears open to the beauties of nature. Take long walks in the green countryside. Let the sea soothe you, in particular the vast reaches of sky, sunset and sunrise which always lift the heart for late September people.

To counteract the bitterness of love's pain and make them brave enough to try again, this creature must keep green about her. In ancient lore it's the colour associated with earth and growing things and was thought to cure sadness and all love's afflictions. Try keeping bowls of green fruit about the house and green plants. Use a green throw on the bed. Fortunately it's a favourite for many born today. Try it on your walls. For opulent (curative) brilliance, paint a room dark bottle green with maybe a hint of gold splatter. High gloss varnish brings a shimmer, like malachite under a shifting sea sparkling with flashes of sun. In living rooms and bedrooms, dusty pale greenish shades are elegant and soothing and make a perfect backdrop to paintings or wall hangings.

Wear green. Green silk underwear makes you feel glamorous and unusual. A dark green coat is mysterious but controlled. A pale green linen shirt is apple fresh. Use fresh green herbs in your cooking, mint for joy, rosemary for digestion, thyme to keep your head clear. And scent your pillows each night with a sprig of lavender leaves tucked into the case.

Confidence ∼ is the best proof of love.

(Maria Edgworth)

25 SEPTEMBER

This seemingly respectable person very frequently has seduction on his mind. They say that the average man thinks about sex every fourteen minutes during his waking hours and that about sums up both sexes born on September 25. Lissom and brown limbed, these men and women exude an aura so pink you would think even the densest people could spot the candy floss ring around their heart.

Fortunately people born on this day are extremely kind hearted – otherwise they'd be unbearable. At work they put themselves out to help colleagues of either sex and do it discreetly. Well, fairly! Expect just the odd person you might not have chosen to confide your most intimate secrets in to be confided in with your most intimate secrets. Still, this birthday person is a great dancer and who's nit picking?

The male can also tend to undercut colleagues, especially

women, so a little nit picking here might be worthwhile. He's extremely adroit and usually thinks nobody has noticed, except the recipient. September 25 relies on the fact that he's such a good guy anybody who hears her complaining will put it down to the time of the month, or some other ruse for blaming the victim for the perpetrator's crime.

During an important meeting, the victim should remember that male September 25 may appear to be taking copious notes, but what he's really thinking about is how most of the people round the table would look without clothes. And who would be amenable to suggestions of love in the lavender bed. The victim should ask some complicated questions, in rapid succession with a show of admiration, directly related to his work area. Hey presto! The inattentive streak in this person's psychology will let him down.

The girls don't do anything as low down and dirty as undercutting colleagues. They are extremely brainy and beautiful, very physically self-confident and have tattoos in wonderful places.

Delay is a great procuress.

(Ovid)

The basic massage strokes to arouse a partner, popular in France, include effleurage, tapotement and cupping, and petrissage. With effleurage you glide the palms across the skin, putting some body weight behind the movement. With tapotement and cupping, you first drum the fingers, very lightly on sensuous spots, shoulder blades for instance, then softly bring each hand down with fingers together and thumbs folded in – cupped. Petrissage involves moving the balls of your fingers or thumbs in a circular motion to soothe away any muscular tension down the back. (Do not massage the spine itself.)

MIND
In numerology the 25th day of the month is ruled by the number 7, (2+5=7). In Tarot, the 7th card in the Major Arcana is The Chariot, symbolising flair and talent, but also a lost route.

DATESHARE
Michael Douglas, Hollywood film star, heart-throb to many, confessed sex addict (cured). **Pedro Almodovar**, Spanish satirical film director, Women On The Verge of A Nervous Breakdown. **Christopher Reeve**, film actor, Superman, paralysed in tragic riding accident. **Wendell Phillips**, explorer. **Cheryl Tiegs**, model, film star. **Sir Colin Davis**, British conductor. **Heather Locklear**, actress, model.

BODY

It's an exhausting life. Those keen to try the latest energy fad should brew a cup of Kombucha tea. This humble fungus from Russia is said to prolong life, bestow energy, and strengthen the immune system. Float the culture on sweet tea, then leave to ferment in a warm environment for eight days. The resulting liquid, utterly revolting-looking but tasting like scrumpy cider, is supposedly rich in anti-bacterial acids, B complex vitamins and a powerful detoxifying agent, glucuronic acid. It makes another culture while it's stewing which you can use for more tea and give a bit away to friends.

MIND

September 26 dreams a great deal, often of visits to the doctor followed by extraordinary adventures. The first doesn't mean you're ill, just that you should take more care. The second indicates that you can look forward to some good news.

This is the toffee apple of the constellations. Sweet and fresh underneath, but rolled in molten sugar so hot it could burn a chunk off the moon. The protective sheath of toffee acts as a sticky kind of armour for this old softy. But most people want to bite a chunk out of September 26 so it's probably best for this date to remember that toffee apples who seriously want their hearts to stay intact keep better tucked away in the fridge.

It's always a problem when sex appeal seems to have been ladled on to a person who isn't innately driven by sex and is often flummoxed by the whole thing. Best solution for both sexes is to choose a reasonably monogamous way of life, thus protecting themselves from the confusion of passing dates.

Because of their alluring image, these guys do well in fashionable areas. They could be the editor of *Tatler*, a supermodel, youth television presenter, clothes designer, pop star, dancer and any other area which benefits from glitter. No, the head is not turned, because they are not toffee all the way through. Nor do they get stuck into one trend, so they do well. Often, they are the emotional anchorman or woman for others. The person who sees the business is run properly and that people are civil to each other, plus work in proper conditions.

Children are drawn to September 26. They trust them more than other adults because this individual understands the concept of fun and playing. Neither he nor she sidesteps a child and shoves them onto somebody else to entertain.

They won't necessarily have children of their own. Those who have difficulty can find medical intervention helpful. But many throw their desires to the wind and choose to stop worrying. Other people's children can always do with an extra adult to be friendly with and to help guide and nurture and that's what usually happens.

A mind of the calibre of mine cannot derive its nutriment from cows.

(George Bernard Shaw)

AIR

27 SEPTEMBER

September 27 usually has strikingly good manners which, as we know, maketh man and wo-man too. Like most Librans they are also blessed with open faced good looks which attract many to their side. Unfortunately, most people born on this day have a psychological duality, on the one hand they enjoy striking success, on the other they usually do something to mess it all up.

Both sexes enjoy early promotion. They have all the characteristics of a high flier, swooping through the universe like a Damon Hill-manned space capsule. Excess is their enemy. Perhaps it's alcohol for which they have an extraordinary liking. Maybe early sexcess goes to their heads, choosing partners for lust who are so deeply awful they badly affect September 27's career prospects. Or perhaps it's unreliability. Whatever it is, just when the limelight is full on them, they blot their copy-book.

None of this is ever written in the stars in such permanent black ink it can't be unwritten by those who heed the warning. Some quell the temptation to throw themselves into an abyss of self-indulgence. Others have powerful and indulgent bosses.

In private, the story is much the same. In college or at school, they are just about to be made captain of cricket or netball, or head girl/boy, when temptation comes roaring out of the black hole and they're caught smoking, insulting the headmaster's grandmother or

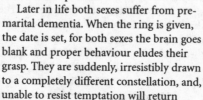

wandering too far into the undergrowth with a sexual partner.

Later in life both sexes suffer from pre-marital dementia. When the ring is given, the date is set, for both sexes the brain goes blank and proper behaviour eludes their grasp. They are suddenly, irresistibly drawn to a completely different constellation, and, unable to resist temptation will return home reeking of strange perfume or with their tights in shreds. Fortunately they are blessed with the gift of the gab. September 27 can and does talk him/herself out of most sticky situations.

Love is a transitive word.

BODY
Honey is a booster for the immune system, spinach boosts energy and is full of beta-carotene, being tested for its anti-cancer properties. And strawberries contain disease fighting anti-oxidants. Try this delicious Spinach with Strawberries and Honey Dressing. Take 170g fresh spinach, torn into bite size pieces, 170g hulled strawberries, sliced, 1tbsp sesame seeds, 1 small red onion thinly sliced. For the dressing: 2tbsp balsamic vinegar, 2tbsp rice vinegar, 4tbsp honey, 2tbsp Dijon mustard, salt and black pepper. Wash and dry spinach. Whisk dressing ingredients. Add to spinach and toss. Dress with strawberries.

MIND
Lapis lazuli is the precious stone favoured by late September and it's good to have this exquisite blue/green mineral around with its golden flashes because it is thought to be one of the stones which bring happiness and fortune.

DATESHARE
Died: **Gracie Fields**, *British movie star and singer. Born:* **Louis Auchinloss**, *short story writer, novelist.* **Meat Loaf**, *rock singer, biker.* **Jacques Thibaud**, *French violinist.*

BODY

Frigidity comes to many from time to time, perhaps the result of illness or tiredness. Fear, stress and anxiety cause the testosterone level to diminish, so why not try these essential oils which combat anxiety: neroli, rosewood, pine, patchouli, lemon, jasmine, clary sage and bergamot. Put a few drops in any massage oil, or in the bath. And later slip a piece of cotton wool with one or two drops in your pillow at night. Other relaxing essential oils which can help include rose and lavender, which bring relief from stress.

Fear may be lessened by massaging rose or rosemary over the solar plexus area.

MIND

A house that heaps evil upon evil is sure to have an abundance of ills, it didn't just happen. Indeed it took a long time for things to get so bad and they came about because they weren't stopped earlier.

SEPTEMBER 28

This person isn't really interested in any form of corporate life and seeks to find spiritual and personal happiness in natural things. Many September 28 people are happiest working on a farm or as a forester, anywhere in conservation. They are sociable enough, but shy away like deer if approached with too great a noise and turn into a ball of prickles if anyone tries to coerce them into another way of life.

Air sign people sometimes can't do without each day spent in the open enjoying the vast reaches of the sky. The light that they love is the light of the sun and the moon and stars, not the artificial sort that comes with business and offices. The sound they like best is not music, but the sweet soughing of wind in the willows. Most Librans are drawn to water and will be excellent boatmen and women.

Don't persuade this creature to come inside and conform. He won't care about money, unless of course he can make it by growing things. Landscape gardening is the perfect choice for this individual. In the pinks amongst her fragrant borders, she is violeted by attempts to make her understand current events, watch television or read newspapers. Let her be.

This being said, neither sex is a wallflower when it comes to love. There is always an attraction about those who don't value money or the scramble up the social ladder. Those who can adapt to September 28's way of life, will find recuperative recreation in tranquillity. Much of the time there will be a party of sorts in this Libran's garden, because they like a good time. And when kids come – lots of them usually – they will be raised with love and affection, but without possessiveness. Children born to this person grow strong limbed and happy, firmly directed against meanness, abhor bullying and always ensure the best for their fellow man and woman.

They went at it hammer and tongues.

(Mary Schafer)

AIR

29 SEPTEMBER

I f they are not careful, people born on this day become the very worst kind of hypochondriac. You measure it by the amount of suffering inflicted on other people and boy, do they inflict.

When it comes to worries about mortal contact with illness-inducing situations, nothing outstrips the male sex. Most girls fret about their bad backs, period pains, headaches, inability to conceive, overability to conceive, broken nails, lank hair and cellulite with more or less the same intensity. But with male September 29, it takes on cinematic proportions.

They are the first to turn to the *Daily Mail* health pages. Just reading them makes them ill, hearts breaking in sympathy with obsessive reportage about others' non-specific syndromes. Thermometer in mouth, they wonder gloomily why their temperature is dropping. It's because the profoundly bored thermometer has itself slipped into unconsciousness. Male September 29 is what he reads. The sun is dangerous. He can't go out. Meat is dangerous. He doesn't eat it. Water is contaminated. He can't drink it, or swim. Ice lollies are a health danger. The humble chocolate bar lurks to eliminate his teeth.

Worst professions for extreme male hypochondria include journalism, television, advertising, taxi driving, art history, telephone switchboard operator, teaching and social work. Anybody who marries them has to have a medicine cabinet which is so full of bottles it regularly falls off the wall. Wives must also be prepared for him to rise early and perform a series of warding-off-disease rituals, including gargling with salt water, running, cold showers, vitamin pills, standing on the head, cotton knickers hand washed in anti-allergenic soapflakes, specially constructed breakfast cereals and several minutes devoted to worrying about the cancer inducing properties of his portable telephone. Advice? Ignore the first lot and throw the telephone away. He'll be grateful that you've saved his life! Although this may not be the first reaction.

After silence that which comes nearest to expressing the inexpressible is music.

(Aldous Huxley)

BODY
Since you're so preoccupied with your problem fate, why not cheer yourself up and read the tea leaves? The ritual associated with this doesn't include teabags. Make tea in a pot. Don't strain it. Drink the tea, until a teaspoonful of liquid is left at the bottom. Hold the cup in left hand and move three times in a circular anti-clockwise direction. Invert the cup in a saucer. Now read the tea leaves at the bottom of the cup. If it's a boot you see, take it as lucky. This gives protection from either physical or mental hurt. A cake means a feast, a camel means travel and a ladder means promotion.

MIND
Most of us have aches and pains, but they're not so much a sign of illness as just the body tweaking itself. How sad to be morose when you are well. Put others' sanity first.

DATESHARE
Emily Lloyd, British film actress. **Admiral Horatio Nelson**, British naval commander, defeated Napoleon. **Lech Walesa**, Polish president. **Sebastian Coe**, British mile runner, Olympic gold medallist. **Greer Garson**, film actress. **Anita Ekberg**, film actress, big bosoms, sex symbol. **Stanley Kramer**, film director, High Noon.

BODY

It's OK to eat fresh veg and fruit grown in the garden and some wild plants. Here's a list of what you shouldn't eat because they are poisonous. Autumn crocus (Colchicum autumnale), *foxglove* (Digitalis purpurea), *ivy, laburnam* (Laburnam anagyroides), *lily of the valley* (Convallaria majalis), *lupins* (Lupinus), *bulbs, daffodils* (Narcissus), *hyacinths* (Hyacinthus), *cut flowers, monkshood* (Aconitum), *seeds, castor oil plant* (Ricinus communis), *rue,* (Ruta graveolens) *yew* (Taxus baccata), *horse chestnut* (Aesculus hippocastanum), *and hemlock* (Conium maculatum) – *obviously.*

MIND

But for a healthy mind and body you can eat the following: horseradish and safe mushrooms, including morel, puffballs, field mushroom, cep, chanterelle, wood hedgehog, oyster mushroom. Make a horseradish sauce and dip the mushrooms in it. Delicious.

DATESHARE

*Died: **James Dean**, Hollywood actor, died in a car crash at the age of 24. **Simone Signoret**, French actress. **Orson Welles**, Hollywood great, Citizen Kane. **Roy Kinnear**, British comedian, in riding accident on location. Born: **Euripides**, Greek ancient philosopher. **Truman Capote**, social observer, writer, In Cold Blood. **Deborah Kerr**, British film star. **Angie Dickinson**, TV star. **Victoria Tennant**, stage, TV film star, married Steve Martin.*

SEPTEMBER 30

This is another extreme day. September 30's undoing will most likely be either food or drink. In youth they are excellent sportsmen, Librunners who burn every calorie, eat what they like and stay slim. The après sport bit usually includes lots to drink and fortifying plates of chips. Then the running stops and speed of acceleration switches to the waistline.

The women cotton on faster than the men, not a statement of sexism, but women are usually more weight-conscious and young male sportsmen usually need greater quantities of food and drink to stoke their performance. Accept that the rest of your life will be a lifelong struggle with indulgences of too much flesh. Better, however, than not struggling and the costly business of having to book two seats every time you get on an aeroplane. Very fat people also find that the ladder to social and career success very often won't bear their weight.

The other problem with September 30 is a heightened sense of indignation which frequently turns them into women's or men's lib-rettes. Pushed, they can even grow into ornery full time fattists. It's a good idea to get hold of this urge and squash it because people born on this day tend to make such issues highly personal, misinterpreting others' intentions and generally turning what may be innocent into mayhem.

If these individuals can keep extremes at bay, channel the energy elsewhere, they will find success in whatever field they choose. Blessed with portable talent they will hop from one big job to another, often in the financial area. Redundancy holds no fear for September 30. They flourish by themselves, earning more money than ever before and achieving greater happiness.

Nor will they have, where love is concerned, the old psycheological dichotomy common to September. Little sex bombs they may be, but they generally keep the explosive nature of their feelings confined to one person, seriously serially monogamous.

Jack Sprat could eat no fat
His wife could eat no lean
And so between the two of them
They licked the platter clean

AIR

I OCTOBER

People born today are galactic thinkers with such precision to their thinking it's likely they may discover or invent something which benefits all mankind. Whatever their fate, October 1 are planets around which smaller stars circulate.

Many have demanding sexual tastes. Both sexes are charmed by feet and shoes and often own up to thirty pairs. They wear them to bed. Both sexes also slip into each others clothes for the thrill of it. (Rod Stewart wears girls' knickers under tight pants and there's nothing odd about him.)

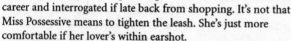

This little pumpkin is not as imaginative about a lover's need for freedom, as about personal pleasures. Lovers could find themselves nagged to stay in, discouraged from pursuing a career and interrogated if late back from shopping. It's not that Miss Possessive means to tighten the leash. She's just more comfortable if her lover's within earshot.

The male of the species is usually more possessive than the female. They hark back to the ideal woman praised by Sheikh Nefzawi, author of *The Perfumed Garden*, an ancient Indian erotic manual. 'She speaks and laughs rarely and never without reason. She never leaves the house. She has no woman friends, gives confidence to nobody and her husband is her sole reliance. If her husband shows his intention of performing the conjugal rite, she is agreeable to his desires and occasionally even provokes them.'

Difficult, because today this jewel would probably be diagnosed agoraphobic. October 1 desires extreme domestic stability because they are frequently work addicts, happy to fight lower down and dirtier than others. Combined with a precision brain and inventive originality they will make heaps of money and win fame. It's just that they don't want hassle when they get home.

What they do want is to watch a great deal of television. Many will be working in TV or allied fields and even if not, it's October 1's way of relaxing.

Everybody winds up kissing the wrong person goodnight.

(Andy Warhol)

BODY

Books like The Perfumed Garden *and the* Kama Sutra *show that 2000 years ago men had no problem with the concept of a woman initiating sex. Yet today some men still find it difficult to accept when a woman makes the first move. Even then, with shy men, the* Kama Sutra *suggested a simple kiss which delicately indicates desire without seeming pushy –* The Kiss That Kindles Love.

This is done to a sleeping partner (or pretend sleeping). It's a desire kiss, straightforward in meaning, but lightly so. The 'sleeping' partner can then choose to awaken or snore on.

MIND

In numerology those born today are ruled by the number one. These people have masses of drive and pep and are born leaders, although they may be slightly overpowering to others. Don't let frustration get you down.

DATESHARE

Walter Matthau *(Matuchanskavasky), born New York, legendary comedian and actor, film and stage.* **Laurence Harvey** *(Lerushka Skikne), adopted British nationality, born Lithuania.* **Julie Andrews** *(Julie Elizabeth Wells), actress.* **Jimmy Carter**, *American president.* **Richard Harris**, *stage, film actor.* **Stanley Holloway**, *stand-up comedian.* **Randy Quaid**, *film star.*

OCTOBER 2

The erudite side of Libra comes out strongly in October 2. Be they academics or train ticket inspectors there will be a streak of expertise and knowledge which is always a delight to companions.

Many of the women are walking textbooks on country matters. They can tell you that there are 5,000,000 pairs of robin redbreasts in Britain and imitate the soft oo-roo-coo call of the pearly rock dove with its emerald collar. Find wallcharts in their house illustrating edible and poisonous mushrooms and expect to go picking in dew-soaked fields at dawn. (Nothing is more enjoyable.)

Children adore being with them because the hedgerows and fields hold no fear. There's no shouting when you put something edible into your mouth. She teaches nettle wisdom, those that sting and others, like the red and white deadnettle flowers which taste of honey at the base (check for insects) and can be candied. With this creature it's fun to pick the young leaves and shoots and bounce off home to cook them like spinach, tossed in butter. More important, October 2 tells kids what's poisonous. The lovely bluebell, graceful delphinium, wild lupin and golden marsh marigold will make you very ill. October 2 creates safety through knowledge, not hysteria.

Most men are the same. They are the ones at work who research the history of the business, the local history of buildings and churches nearby. Ask him anything about cricket or football and he can tell you when and where scores were made and matches won and that the famous playwright Samuel Beckett was the only Nobel Prize-winner to play first class  cricket – for Dublin University against Northamptonshire in 1925 and 1926. You have to dig it out of them, but it's worth it.

If you want something done, get October 2 to do it. They'll find out more, work out the right way, and they'll enjoy every moment.

I never know how much of what I say is true.

(Bette Midler)

3 OCTOBER

O ctober 3 is a born parent. If this creature doesn't have its own children, others will discover they make the perfect godparent, beloved teacher or mentor. Unlike so many people, they seem to talk the same language as children. Catch them involved in intense bits of nonsense which delight both equally. They can play endlessly and find as much pleasure in what they are doing as their small companions. Watch this Libretto enjoy his cornetto with the same gusto as his childish playmate, both getting as sticky as each other.

This person never takes the opportunity when a child – or adult for that matter – enters a room, to tell it something. They are not forever instructing, 'Can you put the milk bottles out? Empty the dishwasher? Tidy up your toys?' They don't dress children in white cardigans and shirts and then harass them if a drop of orange ice lolly gets onto it. They don't have food fads where children are concerned. They don't stop them watching television because it means they won't read. They let them watch television and then do a lot of reading with them because both find it fun.

Much of this is because October 3 remembers as a child that he or she just wanted to lie in the grass and look at the sky. Or idle pleasant hours away dreaming. And somebody was probably always after them to be up and at it. Naturally capable of being competitive, they don't regard competition itself as vital to character building.

Both sexes therefore make excellent teachers, children's club organisers and such occupations as theatre productions are always the most fun and successful. Any sport they get involved in, particularly teams, create a brilliant atmosphere. They make the best kind of social worker, observant, responsible, intelligent and never giving in to hysteria or fads. And always giving that secure feeling of being on a person's side.

The hand that rocks the cradle is the hand that rules the world.

(William Ross Wallace)

BODY

Kids will like to make these with you: Double Chocolate Drops. Take 110g butter, 170g caster sugar, 55g plain chocolate, melted, 1egg beaten, 200g plain flour, 1 level tsp salt, ½ level tsp bicarbonate of soda, 2tbsp milk. Icing: 55g butter, 45g plain choc, melted, 170g icing sugar. Grease baking sheets. Cream sugar, choc, butter, beat in egg, add remaining ingredients for biscuits, stir until smooth. Drop teaspoonfuls of mixture onto baking sheet, 3cm apart. Bake at gas mark 6 for 10 minutes. Icing: cream chocolate, butter, beat in sugar until smooth. Let biscuits cool and ice each one.

MIND

The trick is to stay open-minded and not allow ageing to make you so mentally respectable you forget that children's eyes are sharper, their laughter often dirtier, yet with all of this they have a kind of searing innocence.

DATESHARE

Chubby Checker, *rock and roll singer, started the twist.* **Eddie Cochran**, *singer.* **Eleonoro Duse**, *Italian beauty, muse to lover playwright D'Annunzio.* **Pierre Bonnard**, *marvellous French Impressionist, capturer of innocent pleasure.* **Emily Post**, *shaped American modern manners.* **Gore Vidal**, *playwright, critic, novelist.*

BODY

Platinum person needs lots of energy and a trim figure to stay effective. It's important that this person doesn't go without breakfast, teeth sharpened for their first encounter of the day. Without breakfast you risk a severe drop in blood sugar levels by mid morning which can cause bad judgement and sugar cravings. Choose either one slice of wholemeal toast with 1tsp low fat spread and one medium glass of apple or orange juice; or a 30g serving of low-sugar cereal (Rice Krispies, Weetabix, Special K or Kallo Puffed Rice) with 110ml semi-skimmed milk. Serve with 50g strawberries.

MIND

Listen to your conscience when it pricks. It's no use half listening to the pricks and then getting angry with other people. When people do this it makes matters worse and them look absurd.

DATESHARE

Died: **Bette Davis**, *Hollywood gal with the big eyes. Born:* **Susan Sarandon**, *comedienne, film star.* **Sir Terence Conran**, *furniture designer, restauranteur, bon viveur, bon marryeur.* **Anne Rice**, *novelist,* The Vampire Lestat. **Buster Keaton**, *good looking silent film comedian.* **Charlton Heston**, *film star, always remembered for the greatest chariot race on the silver screen.*

OCTOBER 4

This megastar has a platinum heart and an eye for money and advancement. Most drop their old friends and lovers on the way up Jack's beanstalk to the riches in the sky, which they are going to steal from some slow old giant. He may wake up to October 4's threatening presence and shout 'Fee fi fo fum, I smell the blood of a nasty little crumb', but it won't make no odds. All the golden eggs and the goose will be gone.

This is the worst side of October 4. Fortunately they're not all like that, although most have a sliverette of this hardest of precious metals where their emotions ought to be. At best the male of the species seeks out a rich man's daughter and marries her for her father's money. He reasonably loves her, but loves her father more and is chosen over her brothers to run the family business. Sometimes the honourable side in every Libra is so dominant, that our ambitious hero divides the business up fairly between all siblings and everybody lives in harmony for ever more. Sometimes he prefers to admire himself in the mirror, repeating ten times each morning 'Aim for the top' and shoots his cuffs.

Platinum woman is just the same, in no way softened by her sex. If there's family money about she will try to oust her sisters. If she makes the money herself and they need it, she certainly won't be giving them any. Ms Platinum Knickers only values newly minted friends, usually for their social power. She marries one man after another en route to the centre of things. Libra is prone to several marriages.

Most individuals can avoid these extremes. In many cases their drive to amass a fortune is beneficial to those they work with and to their family. Watch what they do and copy them and you too can be in clover.

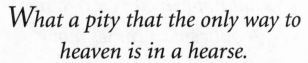

What a pity that the only way to heaven is in a hearse.

(Stanislaw Lec)

AIR

5 OCTOBER

Always in a muddle, October 5 usually can't find her keys. This clever, loving creature was born to be happy and often is, between worrying and losing things. At work both sexes can rise high which is a help because then a secretary runs their diary and finds their wallet. The mind is sharp, the recall for figures or a phrase said at a crucial meeting last year, perfect. They have excellent ideas by the hundred-fold. And they're so deliciously charming it seems to others that they are dusted all over with chocolate milk flake.

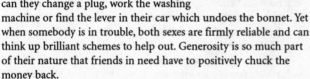

But ask them to get an aspirin out of a child-proof bottle and they wail with terror. They can't remember anybody's name and they can't work the video. Nor can they change a plug, work the washing machine or find the lever in their car which undoes the bonnet. Yet when somebody is in trouble, both sexes are firmly reliable and can think up brilliant schemes to help out. Generosity is so much part of their nature that friends in need have to positively chuck the money back.

Utterly impractical male October 5s make loving husbands if they can find their way to the church and haven't forgotten the wedding ring. Although when it comes to their own children, these men suddenly become sensible and handy. Miss Flapper October 5 may do extremely well at work and is often the breadwinner, so it doesn't matter that she always pushes a door when it says 'pull'.

Many will become successful in some creative area, although surprisingly they can be brilliant at budget keeping and making money. Some feel so upset by other people's reactions that they put themselves out to be more practical and capable. But they are really happiest in a situation where they provide the flair, the flowers, the laughter, even the money to live on, while somebody else switches things on and does the bottle opening.

What happens if you dial 666?
A policeman comes along
upside down.

People born today may suffer from a variety of summertime hayfever. Quite often it's caused by photochemical smog, a complex mixture of pollutants, which can form in hot sunny weather. It is caused by the action of sunlight on certain gases of which motor vehicles are the main, but not the only source and can contain pollutants blown over from elsewhere in Europe. What to do? Avoid strenuous exercise at this time. Children with asthma should be able to take part in games, but they may need to increase the use of reliever medicines before participating. Don't light bonfires and avoid using a bicycle.

☾

MIND
Someday you may be able to stand on the moon, look down through a quarter of a million miles of space and say, 'There certainly is a beautiful earth out tonight.' So let's save our lovely world from pollution.

DATESHARE
Louis Lumière, French chemist, movie camera projector inventor. **Bob Geldof**, rock musician, actor Live Aid benefit organiser, autobiography Is That It?. **Horace Walpole**, historian, novelist. **Donald Pleasance**, comedian, film actor. **Steve Miller**, singer songwriter. **Glynis Johns**, star of Mary Poppins and many others. **T P O'Connor**, Irish Member of Parliament. **Vaclav Havel**, Czech president, writer. **Denis Diderot**, French 18th century philosopher.

AIR

BODY

Some people seem to be born to fat families, families who divorce, or live unhappy lives. Others seem to bloom as they go along. Research shows that children of divorced couples are more likely to end up divorced themselves, and furthermore tend not to remarry. Negative effects may be due to low expectation of success and hence low commitment. The same goes for eating disorders. Children see parents with a problem and themselves develop an unbalanced approach to food. Not that you should always be blaming your mum and dad. There's such a thing as free will, after all.

MIND

Life is a series of discoveries and collisions with the future. It's not a resumé of what has gone before, or that's not the bit that interests us. What excites us is that which is to come.

DATESHARE

Thor Heyerdahl, *Norwegian adventurer who sailed the* Kon-Tiki *raft across the Pacific and Atlantic.* **Carole Lombard**, *film star married to Clark Gable, died in an air crash aged 33.* **Janet Gaynor**, *film star.* **Britt Ekland**, *Swedish film star, married to British comedian Peter Sellers.* **Le Corbusier**, *Swiss master architect.* **Helen Moody**, *eight-times Wimbledon champ.*

All October 6 people have a talent for harmonious surroundings. The strong artistic eye means that most are aware of the psychological effects of colour from a very young age and every place they inhabit will benefit. The proper colours for each star sign are: Aries – white, Taurus- yellow, Gemini – red, Cancer – emerald green, Leo – golden yellow, Virgo – pale blue, Libra – violet, Scorpio – russet brown, Sagittarius – orange, Capricorn – brown, Aquarius – dark blue, Pisces – white.

Ancient law says Librettos, violet, are not best mated with white, Aries and Pisces. Brilliant red Gemini is best, although sensual October 6 gets on with most people .

Because colour matters, they have strong views on the right shade to wear and decorate with. This is a date which makes a

career out of designing places for people to work, worship and live in.

Most Librans will not choose to surround themselves with white, to them a negative. Ruled by Venus, this individual's psychology is healthy, orange, passionate, pink and violet, but with a balanced sense of dignity and harmony, purple. And then there is a lot of frivolity, a sudden tendency to burst into song and dance routines, very engagingly, yellow.

This is only the basic palette for October 6. In general he or she will paint rooms to live in with soft browny pinks, a range of yellows and lilac through lavender. If it's a workplace, then conservative individuals may choose steely blue for endeavour and dark green for virility. But the jollier ones will go for orange, the colour of intelligence, yellow again for high spirits and lighter shades of turquoise/green for brilliance and candour.

It even affects the food they eat and how it's presented. Most people born on this day are ravishing cooks, their menu plans an unrivalled Libretto for the universe's musical stars to accompany with their Pythagorian tetrachords, sounds which engender the harmony of our world.

*What do you call
a lazy Stegosaurus?*

A Stegosnaurus.

7 OCTOBER

This little piglet went to market, which is a pity because if it had stayed at home there would have been enough money to eat roast beef. As it is, there isn't any left and when October 7 discovers that his credit card has been cancelled he'll run screaming all the way home. He never looks to the pennies and so the pounds don't take care of themselves.

This is a lucky money date as far as acquisition is concerned. They work hard to get or win it. But they never make cost and expense correlate. Maybe Good Fairy Fortune muddled her spells, giving fortune and profligacy in equal measure instead of the less problematical 'pleasure in spending'.

Flaring, meteor-brilliant October 7 must meet a nice, self-controlled Taurus or Aquarius, with a talent for helping money grow. If somebody else controls the purse strings then all will be well. This creative person can get on and be brilliant untrammelled by finance.

So what is the psychological streak that gives him such a hard time? Perhaps it's that common Libran duality, where acumen is combined with daffiness. Or maybe our star finds some parts of the universe too frightening to traverse. Both sexes are dreamers, multicoloured rainbowettes, can't stick around in bright light but need to bowette out and find a shadier place. And of course the pot of gold at their finger tips magically disappears before it gets to the bank.

The women don't understand that charge cards equal real money. If a builder comes round October 7 has to be tied hand and foot to stop her asking for one or two little, three or four, extra bits here and here and here. Builders are always so obliging and you forget you have to pay. The men can't open bills. They think loan sharks are magicians who find gold coins behind people's ears. But they make great and often grateful lovers.

Change is sometimes good for change's sake.

BODY

This person has a vulnerable back, which may pull or hurt at any moment. Partly it's the physical tension, with maybe some weakness thrown in. It's vital to understand the back problem and learn to balance it, because October 8 often finds that medical people aren't much cop. Firstly, it's essential to have a flat, hard bed. Many choose a futon to sleep on, excellent for their back. If partners object to sleeping on the floor, tell them it's an earthier experience this way. Then it's important to have proper high-backed comfortable chairs, both at home and at work.

MIND

It's an easy stride from bossing friends and family to strangers. Best stop now, because this makes you seem foolish in the eyes of a world which doesn't care to be ordered about on its days off.

DATESHARE

Damon Runyan, writer. **Sigourney Weaver**, film star. **Chevy Chase**, comic, TV, film actor. **Klaus Kinski**, Polish film star of enormous talent. **Paul Hogan**, leathery weather-beaten film star, Crocodile Dundee. **Juan Peron**, Eva's husband, Argentinian dictator. **Ray Reardon**, Welsh world snooker champion.

October 8 has a magnetic personality and while this may be an advantage in work, it's pretty damn awful for the nearest and dearest at home. Intellectually and emotionally high powered, smooth of conversation, usually dripping with typically devastating Libran charm, this individual can't understand why the spouse, relatives and children don't jump to it just like the secretary and underlings do.

Quite often of course our would be and already established magnate works so late they aren't in the house very much, which is sadly a relief to everybody at home. Children sigh when they hear the key turn in the lock. They jump out of October 8's very own most comfortable armchair, pretend to be studying their homework, put away plates of chocolate biscuits and turn off the television. The harassed spouse is probably reloading the washing machine, having cleaned up the kitchen for the umpteenth time and observed how the spaghetti Bolognese sauce has cooled into congealed lumps of fat.

If the family doesn't do this, October 8 bursts in and says 'Turn the television down. What's this rubbish you're watching? This place is a mess. Why are you eating chocolate biscuits? You'll get fat/spotty.' First words to spouse usually are, 'You're not still doing the washing/ironing are you?' and 'I'm completely exhausted.'

Both sexes' idea of conversation at dinner parties is to wait for a pause and then talk about themselves. Neither usually bothers with anybody who won't contribute to their career. Magnateic personalities think people who don't work are odd and most of their own employees must be pretty stupid or they wouldn't be doing their jobs. Newspaper editors are all like this. And some television producers, men and women who work in the city or run shopping chains. Explorers. Agents. Chefs. Politicians, both national and local. Tease them unmercifully and don't give in or this person's heart will freeze over with complacency.

How often you and I
had tired the sun with talking
and sent him down the sky.
(William Johnson Cory)

9 OCTOBER

Here's an interestingly psychic birthdate. October 9 is particularly tuned in to the vibrations of place. Early in childhood, this person will find precious objects while just playing games. Into this child's hands will apparently fly flintheads from the back garden dropped thousands of years ago by an early British hunter. It is she or he who picks out the Roman figurine from the builders' rubble. Others may search but October 9 puts his hand in the right place without thinking.

As treasure seekers, diviners, explorers, archaeologists and anybody to do with the ancient world or mining engineering, they are therefore invaluable. And may make a fortune. Both sexes are helpful if you want to know the right place to build your house, or the right house to buy. If there are bad or good vibrations, October 9 can tell you, which is useful because when there are particularly bad feelings about a place most birthdates will eventually pick them up. And you don't want to have gone to enormous expense and then find yourself haunted.

The psychic talents which belong to this individual don't extend very much beyond place. They aren't interested in auras or other's well-being in the curative sense, although people born on this date are sensitive and kind. In any career they are usually quite successful because of their highly developed personal warning system. But both sexes are really more taken by their own outside interests. A passion for walking is common. And for history and architecture.

As lovers you can't beat them. Ms Psychic knows exactly where her partner needs tickling and kissing and she will go to any lengths to make sex as glamorous, perfumed and exotic as possible. (Check her underwear, almost never pristine white, but shades of violet, blue and pearl grey silk.) The men like to make love to music and usually feed an overexcited partner with a spectacularly arousing dish before spectacularly arousing them in other ways.

All you need is love.

(The Beatles)

O
ctober 10 should be nicknamed 'The Cleaner'. With the sharpest acumen and most resourceful of imaginations, it is often people born on this date who are called in to help out when a company is in trouble. These people were born to be rich. Love of money does not dominate Libra, but it certainly comes out here. If the right amount of money is not paid for the job this individual feels emotionally affronted and will either not take on a task or very quickly leave. There is no room in his or her mind for sentiment or enthusiasm.

If you ask the women, for instance, to save an ailing magazine, dress shop, local theatre company or stately home, they will only do it for good money and will then exercise a ruthless cost-cutting budget. Nevertheless they do have sufficient amounts of natural flair and very often succeed in paring everything down so that the creative side has room to grow. Both sexes can be increasingly found in investment, banking and accounting.

The men make excellent business partners. Indeed one of their commonest demands as a reward for work is a partnership. But this is the day of partnership and anybody lucky enough to find an October 10 will probably make their own life a success and found a permanent friendship.

Most of the women are similarly suited to partnership, both personally and professionally, and it is these women who often go into business with a husband or lover, or even son and daughter, extremely successfully. Some, however can be fanatical about professionalism, instigating goals almost impossible to achieve and developing a relationship with their computer which can be described as joined at the nose. When this happens October 10 woman will not go home at night and stops taking lunch so that she can stay Siamese-twinned with her beloved. It's an unfortunate human/machine partnership which turns her into just another computer geek.

At every summit you are on the brink of an abyss.

11 OCTOBER

This is an adorable person. Although not necessarily gifted with the usual stunning October good looks, this creature is loaded with allure. Both sexes are also flighty. This is the Librarian whose glasses you must take off first before you understand how beautiful his eyes are.

Her slender attributes may be covered in a regulation overall, needing a voyage of discovery. Like a banana, October 11's outer covering may have some blotchy imperfections, but underneath is the creamiest of pure sweet flesh.

The women in particular can easily become an addiction – for others. Helen of Troy was born today and when her intoxicated lover Paris stole Helen away from a perfectly OK marriage, hundreds of brave soldiers died and the noble city of Troy was destroyed. So don't underestimate the devastation this woman may bring if anything goes wrong.

Many of the men have a similar effect, although fortunately not quite so drastic. The trouble with both sexes is that they love deeply. But they also go off the boil and switch to another, always trying to be tactful. But since tact doesn't mend broken hearts, keep your wits about you if you fall for this day. October 11 knows its sexual power but you can hang on if each day brings with it sufficient variety.

Concentrate on what this October creature favours most – sparkly things, food and entertainment. They adore diamonds, which traditionally bring fortune while also symbolising innocence. Men wear them in ears and wrist-watches, girls favour a diamond studded belly button. Other good fortune stones which please include blue and sparkling gold lapis lazuli and the fire opal.

Take care of their health, which with October 11 can be delicate. Entertain them with music and dancing and the theatre and let them sleep in a bed which smells of roses and you should be able to hang onto them.

*She's got diamonds
on the soles of her shoes.*
(Paul Simon)

Kissing is a tonic for everybody, but it's made nicer with sweetly scented lips and mouth, rather than the usual slug of toothpaste or breath freshener. For a mouthwash, take 1 drop rose oil and 2 drops bergamot, add the oils to 100ml bottle of spring water, shake well. For scented lip balm try 1 drop of rose, 1tsp camellia oil, store in a small tinted glass bottle. Follow this up with perfumed underwear. Add 10 drops of your favourite oil to a 1 litre bottle of spring water, shake well, add to the final rinse. Do not tumble dry because the fragrance will evaporate.

MIND

Jewelled Tiebacks. Thread small beads on lots of separate strands, with some bigger ones in contrasting sizes. Twist them around each other to make braided cord, leaving enough extra tassel length where cord comes together for a velvet ribbon to tie across, beginning tassel.

DATESHARE

Luciano Pavarotti, *Italian tenor, made opera famous and popularly acceptable to people all over the world.* **Aleister Crowley**, *The Great Beast, British satanist, black magician, author, nasty piece of work.* **Ralph Vaughan Williams**, *English composer.* **Edward VI**, *only son of King Henry VIII, died at 15.* **Susan Anton**, *model, actress.* **Ramsay MacDonald**, *Scottish statesman, first British Labour party prime minister.*

OCTOBER 12

This creature is a universal home decorator. Mostly it goes wonderfully right, but sometimes wonderfully wrong and so sensitive are they to criticism that even their best friends are afraid to tell them. They need maximum time to pursue this passion so often choose a profession with short-ish hours. Any kind of teaching is good. It's probably one of their subjects anyway. Others may work on the land, in shops or with definite and regular hours in public transport and the post office. Nothing will work out for this person if they choose to go into a profession where they never get home until 9.30pm.

Always a long-term planner, October 12 already has an eye on making presents for Christmas, probably on October 12. The girls get enthused, making every other birthday in the year exhausted by the too-early contemplation of another merry yo-ho-ho-ing. But ever since she was a little girl, this creature has made pipe cleaner dolls for her aunts and tooth-destroying toffees for uncles. The grown up version of this may be jewelled curtain tiebacks, and maybe they'll look ravishing and just like you'd bought them at Harrods. And maybe not.

The men usually decide to paint a vital room four days before the festive season begins, staggeringly unaware of the tension this decision brings. They are methodical beyond the dreams of organisedness. Some even bore a pencil size hole in the middle of their brush, so that indeed a pencil can be inserted through the

handle, thus balancing the brush on a jar so that the bristles hang clear in white spirit. Others forget to tell people when they have painted a banister so that you walk away a different colour from when you arrived.

Both sexes are convinced that only idle hands and minds let the Devil in, and so they will bring up their children and encourage everybody else's to make everything they can about the house.

The Devil finds work for idle hands.

13 OCTOBER

Although they are born on the supposedly unlucky number 13, these individuals are another of those lucky types who don't know the meaning of depression. At least as far as they are concerned. They are immensely sympathetic to others who do because they have plenty of imagination.

This is a reassuring day to be with. He seems to know exactly where he is going and what he wants and has no truck with trend addicts. Find this day in the City or in something similar, solid and honest. Just occasionally the resolute cheerfulness combined with slight thickness means this megadope is always asking what is wrong with someone who is clearly upset or ill several weeks after everyone else has cottoned on. To give them their credit, however,

 megadope is the doughnut with the huge heart of jam, and when he or she feels they haven't been sensitive towards another in need they make up for it with immense kindness, giving lots of their time without a thought.

As lovers they may be charmingly diffident, the men more than the women. Yet they go for the ultra-glamorous partner and in some extraordinary way, very often succeed where other glossier creatures fail. This is because October 13 has those dependable qualities a glamour cat needs, swamped with admiration and glittering promises. Very probably October 13 is more conservative in its lovemaking than other dates – can't really see what's wrong with the missionary position not very many times a month. Again quite a few partners find this a relief.

But they're not always brilliant parents. Most Librans understand children's need to make at least some of their own choices. October 13, while never reading a book him or herself, can become hectoring where a child's reading is concerned and is likely to ban television, while sitting in front of the box himself for hours.

Sometimes the bell swings the bellman.

BODY

October 13 loves the sweet smell of a scented room. Not everybody likes the smell of incense. In summer time try the extremely heady smell of white tobacco plants (make sure they are the perfumed ones) crowded into a window box. Plant too many and open the window to let the perfume invade your room. These flowers also cut extremely well. Open fires with bunches of lavender and apple tree logs thrown on them are also great for scent and cleansing the air. As is your old real Christmas tree, made into logs which flood everywhere with the delicious odour of burning resin.

MIND

In Tarot card number 13 is Death. Not to be taken literally, it signifies new beginnings, the leaving of past mistakes behind, an end to the bad times and a start to the good times.

DATESHARE

Margaret Thatcher, *British prime minister for eleven years, first woman to hold the job, first Conservative party woman leader.* **Lenny Bruce**, *social satirist, stand-up comedian.* **Paul Simon**, *singer, songwriter, guitarist, 'Gracelands'.* **Yves Montand**, *French actor.* **Lillie Langtree**, *mistress of Edward VII, actress, Jersey Lily.* **Cornell Wilde**, *film star.*

BODY

Lack of iron causes exhaustion and anaemia, leaving the body prone to infections. Iron is vital for making red blood cells and is involved in energy and enzyme production, which helps to protect cells. For some people iron supplements are extremely effective. Poor diet, too much tea, coffee and alcohol blocks absorption of iron from food. Egg yolks, pork, spinach, sesame seeds, sunflower seeds and whole grains like brown rice are all good sources. If you decide to take iron, also take one gram of vitamin C daily with your iron tablet to aid absorption. Too much iron can become toxic. Check with your GP.

MIND

This person is gregarious but like many sociable people needs periods of time to him or herself. If this is denied, they become bad tempered. A spot of reading or listening to music alone does wonders for the soul.

DATESHARE

Died: **Errol Flynn**, Hollywood idol, sexual adventurer. **Bing Crosby**, wartime crooner 'White Christmas'. Born: **Hannah Arendt**, political scientist, philosopher, The Human Condition. **Ralph Lauren**, respected clothing designer, for men too. **Roger Moore**, film and TV actor, James Bond. **John Dean**, convicted Watergate conspirator. **Cliff Richard**, enduring rock singer, actor, songwriter. **Katherine Mansfield**, New Zealand short story writer, member of Bloomsbury Set. **Isaac Mizrahi**, fashion designer.

nother baked beans lover, but with a little problem. October 14 is not keen on athletic sexual behaviour, except at the very beginning of a relationship when some extremely aeronautical suggestions may be made. The trouble is, mostly for the men, that they quickly go off sex with a new partner. In fact after novelty has worn off they would rather have a plate of baked beans.

It's easier for women because they can always pretend and October 14 is an extremely good actor in this department. He and she have to be to counteract the lack of enthusiasm. It's difficult for would be lovers, because October 14 is often blessed with the usual fine-boned Libran good looks and oodles and boodles of charm. They make lighting a cigarette for a partner almost as exciting as the sex act, unfortunately for the lit-up one, the sex act doesn't necessarily follow.

This Libran duality can cause problems with love affairs and marriages. When there are sex problems the best thing to do is acknowledge and act, seek counselling and if necessary accept this is just the way you are going to be. It's wise therefore that October 14 lives with someone for a period of time before finally settling down and going for commitment. This gives the partner time to understand what is going to be lacking in life. In many cases they will accept it for the amusement of just being with this individual.

Away from domesticity they should find success and happiness. Their charm and intelligence takes them a long way at work. They develop multiple skills, and if sacked or made redundant, can rely on their own resources to find even more amusing work. And their urbane humour makes them popular.

Both sexes also have an adventurous streak. Find them riding on horseback and trekking through far away lands, then writing brilliantly about it and being published to sensational applause.

What's purple and hums?
An electric plum.

15 OCTOBER

Very camp is this creature. A zebra in sequins. Most of the time he just likes dressing up and hanging out in bars and clubs and the same goes for the girls. He's the boy with the spikey blue hair, five earrings in one ear and lime green knee boots. He says 'Oh Hooray' a lot, and 'Jolly good show' and can't dance in time. Often not the marrying kind, it's not necessarily out of sexual preference, although that preference may be somewhat of a mystery. Just when you were absolutely sure he preferred blondes with muscles, he turns up with a brunette in a bottom high skirt.

The girls are similar, often dark and wild with black and blue nail varnish and all sorts of leather outfits, which other stars of the zodiac couldn't squeeze into. They live in groups and in truth, their preferences are not pin-downable and change from year to year. But it's unlikely they will turn into the marrying kind until very much later in life.

Many go into arty professions where everybody is paid 12p a year until they are 35, so this is probably a good thing. The pram in the corridor is not a burden they can tolerate. When success comes at a later age, they don elegant linens, chuck the earrings, and bingo, they're fashionable, responsible members of society with mortgages, children and curtains.

They don't like country life in early adulthood, but later may become great contributors to the local community. This is not a townie creature who visits green fields, but one who lives there and gets on with it. They are the ones at 50 who run school fêtes and dos in the church hall, giving hours of their time to painting the scenery for the Christmas pantomime. In towns, they fit in extremely well, in spite of their daring looks, with any corporate set up. They are not really rebels.

When a man is tired of London he is tired of life.

(Samuel Johnson)

BODY

Take care to eat properly, ensuring that there is enough zinc in your diet. Apart from the famous aphrodisiac qualities attributed to zinc-rich oysters, the mineral is found in nuts, fruit and other seafood. Without it there may be spottiness. It's vital for sexual health and to counteract tiredness, for both sexes. Men who lack zinc find sexual function impaired and the number of spermatozoa is known to be related to the zinc content of seminal fluid. Since 2.5mg of zinc is lost in every ejaculation, a constantly tired sexually active man should consult a doctor.

MIND

October 15 is one of those rare people who can choose and control her dreams. She often chooses to float in a warm swimming pool, which she knows is a sign of future prosperity.

DATESHARE

Friedrich Nietzsche, German philosopher. **Virgil**, Roman poet, 'The Aeneid'. **Oscar Wilde**, tragic, brilliant, homosexual writer, persecuted for his love affairs, The Importance of Being Ernest. **Sarah Ferguson**, Duchess of York, now divorced from Prince Andrew and referred to by bad people as the Duchess of Fergiana. **P G Wodehouse**, novelist, playwright, creator of Jeeves, inspired by young World War I soldier, killed in action soon afterwards. **Mario Puzo**, writer, The Godfather. **Arthur Schlesinger**, historian, writer, **John Kenneth Galbraith**, economist, presidential advisor.

AIR

OCTOBER 16

When October 16 overdoes it, both sexes suffer from aches and pains. Warm herb baths can often help. Grated ginger soothes aching legs and joints. Lavender reduces anxiety, gives general pain relief and induces sleep. Sake lessens pain of sore knees and sports injuries. Add 720ml to water that is just above skin temperature. Parsley soothes anxiety, restlessness and irritability. Rosemary is for general pain relief. Rock salt relieves pain in joint and tendons, back and shoulder muscle aches. Garlic is also a general pain reliever. Steam 3-4 peeled cloves to remove smell, rinse, wrap in gauze, fasten and add to bath.

MIND

To ensure wedding day good fortune for yourself or another, remember it's ill luck for the bridegroom to turn back once he has set out for the church or registry office. Anything left behind must be fetched by a friend.

DATEHSHARE

Peter Bowles, actor, famous for To the Manor Born. **Günter Grass**, German author, Tin Drum. **Terry Griffiths**, Welsh snooker player, world champion. **Angela Lansbury**, Murder She Wrote TV star. **Max Bygraves**, singer and entertainer.

October 16 people can be remarkably intolerant of others, considering that they usually choose to express themselves in clichés. This is the person who boasts that he or she 'Doesn't suffer fools gladly'. Everybody else nods and wonders what they mean, when frequently they are the fools. It's just that October 16 has a high an opinion of him and herself.

They are excellent at entertaining, but constantly chant that irritating refrain, 'If you want something done well, then you have to do it yourself'. Then they whine with appalling self-pity 'Why do I have to do everything myself?' In fact self pity is the basis of many clichés. And self-regard. Neither of which is attractive. If you hear someone say 'Why does it always have to be me?', 'I'm the sort of person who likes to thank people properly', 'People are only out of work because they can't be bothered to find work', 'I've got a long memory', 'I don't forgive easily', and 'A friend in need is a friend indeed, and invariably wants to borrow something', then it's likely to be October 16 muttering on. Turn a deaf ear.

Apart from this, and as long as it's not your mother-in-law or dreadful, moralising, self-centred brother, October 16 is OKish at heart. If they carry on like this, they really won't get far in offices. Nor will they be the person everybody wants to invite to the party, certainly not to help decorate for it or clear up. 'If you want something done properly . . .' combines evily with other people's hangovers.

If this person could only jettison his and her sense of righteous indignation and look outwards to the magnificent things other people are doing, they would stop it and automatically become so much more attractive to others, that they would find their life instantly enhanced. And the invitations flooding in.

Next to entertaining talk,
a thorough-going silence
manages to impress most people.

(Sharlot Hall)

AIR

17 OCTOBER

O ctober 17 is born with all the indications that he and she will live a long and happy life, full of love, friendship and moments of great good fortune. Venus, the ruler of Libra, smiles on this startlingly easy-going person and most people remember October 17 with pleasure.

Some can be taxing husbands and wives, demanding a high standard of perfection about the home and about their spouse. But it's not really a downside as they do the decorating themselves and are fond of arriving home with wonderful new frocks, shirts, coats, bags, gloves and hats for their best beloved. Their taste veers towards elegant, rather than wild, so if the best beloved's is more wild, it's probably best to make a gentle adjustment in taste and keep the peace. There's nothing wrong with high heeled shoes rather than sneakers, and a well cut jacket flatters shoulders better than a track suit top.

Because if you don't there will be quarrels and sadness in the house. Many October 17 people have a highly developed sense of justice and a desire for peace. Some pursue a successful career in the law. Others thrive in local government, teaching, social work or the great art of running a library. Good Librarians run a place which welcomes obstreperous children and old ladies and calms

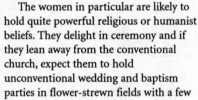

everybody down with a generally good time.

The women in particular are likely to hold quite powerful religious or humanist beliefs. They delight in ceremony and if they lean away from the conventional church, expect them to hold unconventional wedding and baptism parties in flower-strewn fields with a few ancient Celtic rites thrown in. They look to the Moon for solace and like to make love in moonlight at some quiet spot under the night sky. Many will conceive a baby this way, born of love and moonlight. These moon-begot children grow up serene and to be peace seekers.

A man in the house
is worth two in the street.

(Mae West)

BODY
Although this person rarely suffers from depression, they do have delicate health, vulnerable to kidney infections and sore gums when stressed. Indeed, they can be extremely prone to stress, partly because they are so perfectionist and because they work so hard to make everything right. October 17 usually recovers well when he or she pays attention to their body's plight. But if they plough on things will just go from bad to worse. So it's vital that people born on this day take time away from stress to relax. Many are naturally at home in the countryside where they enjoy growing things.

MIND
Sometimes it's hard to relax. Perhaps it will help to try one of the famous Bach Flower remedies? Elm (Ulmus procera) is for those who over-extend themselves. Oak (Quercus robur) is for those who are brave, determined and steadfast.

DATESHARE
Rita Hayworth, tragic and beautiful screen goddess, Gilda. **Montgomery Clift**, film actor. **Sir Cameron Mackintosh**, British musical theatre impresario. **Arthur Miller**, American playwright, Death of A Salesman, married briefly to Marilyn Monroe. **Evel Knievel**, motorcycle daredevil. **Pierre Antoine Baudouin**, French 18th century painter.

ctober 18 women are so bursting with creativity they could open a shop just to sell their brilliant ideas and very often do. Like most Librartists their psycheology is so marinated with talent that everything they do seems not only exquisite, but startlingly simple to do. This Libran Christmas will, for instance, be like something out of a magic treasure cave. And she'll do it for

next to nothing.

Everywhere she goes she collects old bits of jewellery, beads and sparkly materials, velvets and shiny gauze, keeping them all in boxes and bags of goodies so gorgeous that children who like dressing up are driven wild with excitement. The tree will be decorated with glittering jewels that look like drops of purest crystalline ice beading. Underneath, swags of rich velvet hold the presents as if they are something magical from of Aladdin's cave.

There are pearls glimmering across mantlepieces and woven into holly. And everywhere the scent of fresh pine. Sometimes she makes things to give away, but only usually if there's no money to buy presents. October 18 is generally too modest to imagine anyone will actually want anything she has made. Nevertheless in her hands a papier mâché bowl made by sticking strips of newspaper to a blown up round balloon, with flour and water paste, then painted and varnished with rich colours will be a delicate thing of beauty.

The men are just as talented, just not quite so flamboyant and secure in their taste. Many are expert with wood so expect precious carvings as a Christmas or birthday present. But both sexes born on this day may also develop expertise in beautiful things that other people have made. In which case expect them to have, or even deal in brightly coloured Mason's Ironstone junket bowls and plates and pink and delicate mauve lustreware cream jugs from the 19th century. And expect to be given them. October 18 is a generous date.

I had too many keys
that opened too many doors
in too many places.
(Jessie Tarbox Beals)

19 OCTOBER

There's no doubt that October 19 is a lucky date. This is one of the most likely people to win the National Lottery, or any other competition for that matter. So instead of sneering, just get going. Some of you can almost make a living from minor wins, let alone the big ones.

Generally speaking the best bet for a win is during your own birth month, that of Gemini, which is so sympathetic to Librettos and around every full moon. Ignore sceptics. Apart from the financial kind of luck, people born on this day are also subject to other pieces of good fortune. They do well in almost any chosen career, but often find that they have just left a company two or three months before that company folds. The house they decide

not to buy turns out to have extensive dry rot which the unfortunate new owners only discover six months after they move in.

On the very day they decide to go to the races rather than clean the car, somebody walks into their life who will be pivotal to them. They pick up a piece of paper with a telephone number lying on the pavement and when they dial it, they meet the love of

their life. And so on. October 19 spend some time saying 'Just fancy that' to others' chagrin. Although few people envy this cheerful soul, because his or her luck means that others may find some too.

There's nothing magical about this winning streak. Indeed it's partly due to the constant effort this person makes in life. He may accidentally turn up for a job interview on the very day when somebody has walked out and a replacement is needed immediately. But it has to be said that she is always writing and turning up to find work. They just make a point of being in the right place at the right time.

What's luck got to do with it?

BODY

Many people born today have sensitive skin, nothing much, but the itchy rashes which seem to come from nowhere are irritating. Some may be sensitive to foods like milk, eggs, peanuts, and potatoes. Use non-dairy soya or rice milk, which is low in saturated fats. Essential fatty acids found in sunflower seeds, linseeds and oily fish are helpful. Many sufferers are low in vitamin C and minerals such as zinc and iron, so try adding one drop of multi-vitamins and minerals to food each day. Include live low fat yoghurt in the diet to aid digestion.

MIND

Luck means celebrating, which means a great deal to drink. Don't become addicted to alcohol. It could ruin your future parties because alcoholics have to watch everybody else celebrating with a glass of champagne.

DATESHARE
John Le Carré, British *novelist, author,* The Spy who Came In From The Cold. **John Lithgow**, *film star, stage actor.* **Simon Ward**, British *matinée idol.* **John Profumo**, *British War Secretary, resigned over the Christine Keeler and Stephen Ward scandal.*

For Librans these people are unusually indecisive and can be irritating to those who have to help them make decisions. In particular the women drive their companions round the bend because they never know what they want. This dark aubergine with the squashy inside gets into a really half baked mush when the temperature rises ever so slightly. She genuinely can't tell if she'd like to go swimming or take in a movie. She has no idea if she'd like an orange ice lolly or a Magnum, or if she can be bothered to pay £1 for the latter. Or if it's silly.

And so it goes. Out to dinner, her companion has to choose, and then she picks at the lobster because she remembers she doesn't like it. The pudding trolley comes along. She can't decide on chocolate cake or the crème brulée. She has the cake, he has the crème brulée. She eats his.

It's all born of a desire to please, but this is no way to do it. 'No, you choose' people are hard work for others. The conventional rôle of the sexes can mask the problem for women. When it comes to men it's more difficult. Male October 20 can't decide between one job or another, often accepts both, much to the irritation of the party he finally lets down. He can't decide whether to holiday in Israel or Edinburgh, both having their own thing going for them. He can't decide whether to make a move on his girlfriend, driving her round the bend and on to further excesses of low necks, green bras and skin-tight trousers.

And out of two or even more girls, he can't decide which one to marry and often ends up proposing to all three or four. This can be the eventual cause of multiple injury to October 20 man, and indeed to the girls involved when they find out what he's been doing, yet again.

I never forget a face, but in your case I'll make an exception.

(Groucho Marx)

21 OCTOBER

Charming, persuasive October 21 is more interested in a grand chase across the skies, his chariot in sparking pursuit of a fleeing space capsule. But when the thing that was so desired is netted, the chariot wheels around and drives away. Or worse, leaves another, lesser huntsman to net the prey.

We've all met and fallen for Mr and Mrs Fancy Tongue. And we've all watched in horror at work how, when the field is won,

some other colleague has to wind up a deal, often starting from scratch in the knowledge stakes. Mr Persuasive watches from sidelines, observes an inevitable cock-up, then maybe saunters back and with a quick and expert flick of the whip, puts things right.

What both sexes should know, is that the rest of the world long for them to stay in charge. People want their charisma, to see the star glitter sparks spin from their chariot wheels. Don't want to be put in the charge of a sergeant at arms.

We're going away from Libra now and soon we'll meet Scorpio, but this shying away at the last moment is a true Libran characteristic, which sometimes even disturbs its owner. The urge to leave when something is not quite finished. In love this is a problem for those with easily given hearts, because October 21 hunts down his target and then shys away, bored. Indeed, boredom in love is one of the emotions that most worries both sexes born on this day. They long for the all embracing love which will drive them on forever, the true romantic, burning fire, and they listen with increasing dread for the first breath of boredom to come creeping in on the wind.

Many do find their one true love and stick with it. Others go off to travel the world restlessly, and there, far away in some exotic corner, is the love of their life, waiting. Then they never come back.

An imaginary epitaph for Hitler:
Here lies a man who hated men.
We wish his mum had felt the same.

The psycheology of this date is truly romantic, all for the quiet life. They are lovely men and women, whose sheer enjoyment in doing their chosen thing is immensely infectious to others. This can make October 22 a leader in his or her own way.

If they move house to another town, or to the countryside, friends will follow and set up house nearby. What October 22 wants is to enjoy his own version of a good, quiet life and to give that pleasure to those he loves. Frequently, this person will work like a slave in the early adult years to get enough money to enable him or her to do just this. They set up businesses in comparative youth, build them up and sell out at 38 in order to retire. Most of them very resolutely never work again, although they may just take on the odd consultancy task.

October 22 has a powerful sense of what is right and wrong and keeps a sharp eye out in his local community to see if he or she can help. Neither sex will be the one to oppose a homeless hostel in their road, or a home for the insane. They don't value property prices more greatly than people's happiness. Nor do they consider their home some sort of fortified castle. Once they have made their

fortune, anybody can come knocking for help, will be taken in, housed for a short while and every attempt made to solve the problem. This is one of those dates which gives refuge to other people's troubled adult children and lonely relatives.

The women will content themselves with their own passions, dog breeding, riding, or growing things. Quite often they will be extremely successful at this and almost accidentally make more money and a second career out of it. When their children leave home they don't feel bereft, simply seeing it as a passage in life and find something else to do.

BODY

A lover of natural remedies, October 22 should try the lemon. Long heralded as a diuretic, and astringent, a good gargle for sore throats, a lotion for sunburn and a cure for hiccoughs, the lemon is a tonic throughout the world. In India the common morning drink is two tablespoons of lemon juice and two of honey mixed with an ounce of water. A little over a tablespoon of lemon juice daily prevents scurvy because of its vitamin C content. Lemon juice is an antioxidant, which is believed to ward off ageing. Pectin is also found in the pulp and lowers blood cholesterol.

MIND

Folklore says that October 22 is traditionally a day when losses can be regained, business expanded and the achievement of cherished ambitions attained. Wear red, the colour of success, and your dreams may come true.

DATESHARE

Derek Jacobi, *Shakespearian actor, film star.* **Timothy Leary**, *LSD poet, 1960s guru.* **Doris Lessing**, *author,* The Golden Notebook. **Catherine Deneuve**, *French actress, film star.* **Jeff Goldblum**, *actor, comic,* Jurassic Park. **Dory Previn**, *actress, songwriter, ex-wife to André Previn.* **Lord Alfred Douglas**, *Oscar Wilde's lover.*

I just want your extra time
And your ～ kiss.
(The Artist Formerly Known As Prince)

23 OCTOBER

Poor October 23 suffers from Paradise Syndrome. It's a mysterious new affliction which affects the supremely talented and successful. 'You get it,' says PS sufferer millionaire rock star Dave Stewart, 'when your world is going absolutely fantastically well and you feel so inspired you think you must be ill. Everything you have possibly wanted to do in life, you can do, so you think there must be a catch.'

Nonsense, rubbish? Nonsense, of course it's not rubbish. It's that feeling when you are extremely happy, that everything's too good to be true, and like poor Adam, just one bite of the wrong golden apple and it'll be Paradise Lost. October 23 is very blessed, half meteorite, half peachette with no stone for a heart and it's the squishy side of his and her nature that lets him down. This person just can't believe his luck and thinks it must all go away as quickly as it came, even if in reality it's been a long time coming.

At work we know she'll make ludicrous sums of money out of an original idea, from marketing tomato ice cream to, in her hypochondriacal case, chic hip medicine flasks (popular with the ancient Chinese). Outside work she'll marry another fantastically rich, exquisite person and they will live happily with the number of children they long for – or not – and everybody's mother, sister, dad, granny, brother and auntie set up with swimming pools for life.

But the PS symptoms persist. With money there's a tendency to throw it away, tempting fate. There'll be absurd extravagances October 23 knows are foolish and doesn't really want, like £2000 spent on a too-skimpy-for-her/him Jasper Conran jacket and dress. And £50,000 on flowers for her birthday do. With friends there's a tendency to lend too much. With lovers there's a tendency to give too much, like a gold card, no strings.

~

Somewhere a queen is weeping.
(Jimi Hendrix)

'OCTOBER 24

O ctober 24 is unusually saddened by the ending of summer. They adore the warmth and light of mid summer, which brings out a gaiety in them sometimes quenched by shorter, darker days. Some actively hate the turning colour of leaves on the trees, almost willing them to stay green for that much longer, like a child who doesn't want Christmas to end.

Over-preoccupied with the weather, this creature feels the cold badly and has a tedious tendency to complain about draughts and lack of heating in other people's houses. They've always got one too many sweaters on and in the middle of the deepest cold, unpeel their layers to find long silk thermals.

Cusp people always have an internal conflict and October 24 is no exception. Fortunately, the sociability of Libra combines well with the equally sociable instincts of Scorpio, and indeed you get a double whammy with these people, always out until dawn, then apparently fresh at their office desks by 9am. They like to drink and eat and you can normally find them at the epicentre of having a good time. But the underlying self-discipline of this individual means that even while they're blowing up forty balloons and telling jokes, their deepest psychology is preoccupied with the latest work plans.

An organised bunch, they aren't comfortable with the latest 'hot' desk system operated by some innovative companies, where staff don't have their own desk but settle each day for what they can get. This person suspects it's simply a bosses' ruse to get the staff to come in earlier and earlier in an effort to bag the best desks and avoid the isolated one in the dark corner with bad lighting and a computer with a tendency to crash. Nevertheless, both sexes come in earlier than most. They abhor unpunctuality and their own lateness at the start of the day makes them feel uncomfortable for the rest of it.

Shall I compare thee to a summer's day?

(Shakespeare)

25 OCTOBER

October 25 is as luscious and alluring as a whole bush of blackberries, but you get scratched *en route*. Glittering with sex appeal, silky of hair and skin, Ms and Mr Blackberry (*Rubus fruticosus*) play hard to get. Suddenly their diary is booked. They ignore dates who try to court, 'forget' to return telephone

calls and flirt with everybody else. There'll be no kissing on the first date, and it's all a mysterious challenge for would-be lovers.

Persist in pursuing this fatally floriferous fruticosus for the fantastic fun you will have. October 25 is slow to respond, suspicious that potential lovers may not mean what they say, which is not the same thing as saying what they mean. Once plucked they're the source of sensuous inventiveness, wild suggestions and juicy with love and laughter. But this person needs an armour of prickles, because more than most both sexes suffer the pain of love, which can put them off their work and general pleasure in living for months. Even years.

In any kind of work, October 25 shows a driving force and energy which takes both sexes as far as they wish. Their organised minds suit them to big producer industries, such as cars, electronic goods and drug manufacturing. Conscious of status, they hiss like a snake – the Red Indian name for October people – if somebody gets their title wrong, or impinges on their department. But this individual takes endless time to help others with generosity and honesty, never gossiping, never sneering. And they are so shocked by office rage and bullying that they will sort it out fast and efficiently, or refuse to do another stroke.

Money comes to fruticosus like flocks of hungry birds to a blackberry bush, and both sexes can be careless with it, leaving purses lying about, spending without counting the cost, and giving lavishly to siblings and friends. Remonstrated with, they smile, 'You can't take it with you.'

Once bitten, twice shy.

OCTOBER 26

People born today adore feasts and fun. In the summer, just the word 'picnic' cheers them up. Like Ratty, there's only one thing they like better than rowing their boat to a place where the wind drifts through the willowy tendrilled river bank and that's planning their picnic basket. October 26 always takes too much. There will be a pork pie with an egg running through it. Several packs of Scotch eggs. Cold chicken legs. Sausages. A cold bacon and egg quiche. One chocolate cake, one fruit cake and some strawberry tarts. Cream optional. Fairy cakes with yellow and pink icing. Doughnuts squidging with jam. Plain and milk chocolate for nibbling at. Nectarines, peaches, bananas. Packets of crisps. And Penguin biscuits.

No amount of rowing will burn off all these calories and sometimes October 26 gets so fat the boat just sinks under him. Which means, we're afraid, a lifetime of dieting. At which this person is, frankly, not good. The first thing to do is get the weight parameters right. Ignore tables which show people of 5ft 9ins should weigh 8½ stone. Get the goal weight into proportion. Ms Snacky Eater should remember that the majority of women in this country are size 16 plus which may not be a comfort when you look at some of them.

Both sexes should avoid those plump people white lies. 'I'm big-boned.' 'I hardly eat anything.' 'These trousers shrunk at the cleaners.' 'I'm normally a size 12 (the girls)/32ins waist (the boys) but this shop makes them very small.'

New research shows that to be slightly overweight is not really a health problem and you can have just as much fun plump as you can skinny. If weight is going to be a lifelong battle for October 26, let the battle be confined to one psychological area only, leaving the rest of your time free for other more interesting things.

Outside every thin girl there is a fat man trying to get in.

(Katherine Whitehorn)

27 OCTOBER

Some people born today are such perfectionists and so argumentative it rather drives others round the bend. You say the air is chilly. They say it's rather warm and they're going to open a window. You say that the Russian Czar, Peter the Great, kept his unfaithful mistress's chopped off and pickled head in his bedroom and October 27 argues that no, it was the Czarina's lover's head. Actually it was both. Their bedroom was packed with pickled heads.

The trouble is that October 27, bitten with the bug of pointing out mistakes, couldn't bite back a correction if he or she tried. This star can't easily exist in a matey constellation because it must explain so many things to all the shimmering companions that they simply shimmer off.

Some make good teachers, historians and other cloistered academics, their noses – and this date has a long one – so far in the air, that ordinary mortals are fortunately left alone. But the habit of correction also comes out in older people born on this date. And teenagers. Someone might say: 'I was such a skinny child.' October 27 might reply: 'Oh no. The kids at school always called you Porker.' Teenagers feel the need to correct their 'senile' parents out of a sense of across-the-generations superiority.

Fortunately Scorpios are excellent at finding mates for life, so there's someone at home who loves and admires them and it doesn't matter that everybody else wishes they would stay there. Fortunately, again, many escape this extreme and simply delight in a good memory. They will never give spaghetti to a child who has disliked it all its life. Nor roses to a woman who prefers lilies. Nor ties to a man who prefers sports books. These romantics are thoughtful companions valued for their knowledge, which never impinges, and for their interest in others, which is supportive, not corrective.

Curses are like young chickens,
they always come home to roost.
(The Curse of Kehama, *Robert Southey*)

Scorpios are extremely creative and like to make things to decorate the autumn house and presents for Christmas. To make a Moss and Flower Basket: Line the bottom of a basket, with dip at front and handle, with plastic. Using mossing wire, cover outside of the basket with sphagnum moss. Fill with clusters of dried hydrangea – painted here and there with kid's pink or red paint, or any colour you wish. Use other dried flowers, small roses, small pieces of moss. Fill spaces with pine cones, dried seedheads and cinnamon sticks. Tie a wired ribbon bow round handle. Add drops of essential oil for fragrance.

MIND
The best conversation shifts attention from ourselves, our own feelings and our own desire to shine in imparting knowledge and wisdom, to other people's thoughts, feelings and experience. Knowledge in this situation is best used for pleasure and not personal aggrandisement.

DATESHARE
Dylan Thomas, *Welsh poet. Under Milk Wood.* **Sylvia Plath**, *poet, The Bell Jar.* **Roy Lichtenstein**, *pop artist.* **John Cleese**, *comedian, Fawlty Towers, part of Monty Python team, film actor, author.* **Fran Liebowitz**, *writer, comedian, Social Studies.*

BODY

Everybody secretes substances called pheromones, responsible for individual body scent. No two people smell alike, but there are racial similarities, possibly due to diet. Scandinavians and Japanese prefer floral perfumes, disliking animal fixatives such as civet and musk. Experts believe it's because their diet is mainly fish. High dairy consuming Dutch, plump for light floral fragrances, whereas mutton and garlic eating Muslims prefer rose perfume. Citizens of the Far East and tropical countries, where food is highly spiced, prefer heavy animal-like scents with plenty of fixatives. Scorpios prefer woody and famously aphrodisiac cedarwood, sandalwood and frankincense, extracted from the gum of a North African tree.

MIND

Lucky October days for 28 include 15, 18, 21, 24, 26 and 28 which presage well for the regaining of losses, expansion in any business or money-making enterprise, and the achievement of cherished ambitions.

DATESHARE

Joan Plowright, stage and film actress, married Sir Laurence Olivier. Nicholas Culpepper, herbalist, mustard inventor. Jonas Edward Salk, inventor of Salk vaccine to combat polio, saved many modern lives. Bill Gates, established Microsoft, worked on inventions in garage. Auguste Escoffier, French chef, restaurateur. Julia Roberts, film actress, Pretty Woman. Evelyn Waugh, author. Francis Bacon, 20th century British painter.

This dark star has a luminous sensuosity which draws others to him. They're people magnets, tactile individuals who like to show affection and regard with a light touch to the hand or shoulder, always delicate. Nothing intimate. Quite often the starlets who cluster to this creature with its rich pink aura, betokening a balanced mind and joyful spirit, would like something more than casual regard. But although October 28 is wildly sexy and exciting, unless either sex is unmarried and looking for a mate, there's no chance of anything more than the mildest enjoyable flirtation.

Find an unmarried one, however, and the sizzle is yours. October people are psycheologically controlled and usually avoid affairs at work. Everybody knows what's going on as if by osmosis. One of you comes to work wearing yesterday's clothes. Any preference shown causes resentment. Lack of preference causes resentment in the lover. Scorpio knows that sex runs through any

office like a silver seam and both sexes with their discerning observations know how to mine that seam between others to their advantage. What they don't want is somebody mining the glimmer of silver between them and a partner.

Utterly work directed in youth, they aim for the top, particularly in the media. But anything to do with transport or water also suits them. Scorpio in charge of a waterboard doesn't let the water dry up and tell his or her customers not to have baths. Scorpio in charge of vehicles doesn't allow dangerous sloppiness.

Scorpio in charge of your heart wants a lot of adventurous sex. Love in a boat, the back of a car or on top of a washing machine amuses them. And love where you could be discovered! In a lift perhaps. On the beach. In an unoccupied box at the theatre. Lovers of October 28 need strong nerves. But after the wedding bells, October 28 makes a fine husband or wife, always loyal, faithful and thoughtful.

Everything we look upon is blest.

(W B Yeats)

29 OCTOBER

October 29 adores food, wine and having a good time. Hours are spent planning feasts to entertain friends and family, scouring the best food shops, searching for the nicest restaurants. So much so that this scrumbublious creature would be better off turning professional foodie.

Neither sex lets food take their mind off work. That's not October 29's way. They have the usual massive concentration and determination of most Scorpios. And they have an inventive streak at work, which makes them doubly valuable, seeing as they do, a better way of doing things than the accepted and wasteful route. Nevertheless, when they're tucked up in bed at night, or just want something to read while watching television – characteristic of this day – it will be a recipe book.

There are no fads here. This creature doesn't put on extra pounds, or not many, so their cooking is the indulgent sort. Chocolate cheesecake, or the famous Robert Carrier's asparagus, rocket and French bean salad with parmesan curls. Any talk of healthy cutting back on delicious dairy foods makes October 29 Danish Blue. To both sexes, strawberries are naked *sans* cream and they have a sneaking conviction that yoghurt is a boring substitute. Or no substitute.

All of this makes both sexes party people. Never happier than with a good-time crowd to feed. Indeed there's usually a houseful at number October 29. What this person likes best is for guests to stay over, then start the party again with a walloping brunch.

None of this means that October 29 imposes food ideas on others, especially children. As teenagers they prefer to graze, resisting the set family meal with its frequent tensions. (This is why they prefer the non-nuclear massive gathering for meal times). With children and teenagers, 29 is always careful to let them pick what they want. Both sexes simply cook up a selection of tempting things and leave them lying around.

BODY

Quickie Cheesecake. Take 450g cottage cheese, 150ml double cream, 225ml milk, 2 eggs separated, 4 tsp powdered gelatine, 1tbsp lemon juice, grated lemon rind, ½tsp vanilla essence, pinch salt, 225g sugar. Heat milk and sugar in pan, stirring until sugar dissolved, pour on to beaten egg yolks, stirring, then back to pan, add salt, stir until back of spoon coated (don't boil.) Cool custard. Dissolve gelatine in lemon juice, add custard, lemon rind. Sieve cottage cheese, stir in vanilla, custard, refrigerate for 30 minutes, stirring frequently until just beginning to set.

MIND

Crust for Quickie Cheesecake. Take 225g crushed digestive biscuits, mix with 100g butter. Press half on to base of tin. Whisk egg whites stiff, fold in whipped cream, stir into cheese mixture, pour in tin, top with remaining crumbs, chill until firm.

Things always look better ⤳ on a full stomach.

Try this test to see how sexually creative you are.
Do you have: 1: A sense of adventurous playfulness?
2: Willingness to experiment and risk hazard of failure?
3: Strength to start all over again? 4: A tendency to view problems from an unusual perspective? 5: A capacity to rearrange things in new ways that please better. 6: Willingness to let some areas stay unresolved for a while? 7: Capacity to ignore stereotypes in favour of new approaches? 8: Capacity to challenge conventional truths?
9: Ability to fantasise?
10: Tolerance for differences?
No need for jealousy if you do.

MIND

Best partners for love are –
Taurus/Scorpio, fantastically faithful and gorgeously generous. Cancer/Scorpio, instinctive understanding of each other's dreams. Virgo/ Scorpio, comforting familial happiness. Scorpio/Scorpio, destined for each other. Capricorn/Scorpio, permanent business and love partnerships. Aquarius/Scorpio, a united front.

DATESHARE

Diego Maradonna, *Argentinian soccer star, Player of the Decade.* **Grace Slick**, *singer, songwriter.* **Richard Sheridan**, *Restoration playwright.* **Charles Atlas**, *body-builder.*

OCTOBER 30

Beware jealousy, the green eyed god and plague for October 30. It's an insidious voice often masquerading as reason and common sense. This is a real problem emotion for Scorpios. Remember the poisonous arachnid, the scorpion who hides in your discarded pyjamas on a Spanish bedroom floor, then swipes you with its tail thus ruining a holiday at very least. The Spanish scorpion isn't jealous of others' love lives. It's just doing what comes naturally. At worst, October 30 is jealous and also doing what comes naturally.

Most people born today have enough charm and balance of personality to refrain from jealousy's worst excesses. It just flickers a green glance occasionally, when someone else is promoted, or looking forward to their wedding day, or has landed a windfall or just given birth to a baby. 'There's no need to go on about it quite so much' snarls 30 to itself – or out loud, not quite managing the happy congratulations given by other days. Nevertheless, friends recognise this characteristic and people born today are often tagged with the 'Old so and so will be furious' snort of laughing criticism.

Others can get into genuine difficulty with envy. They may try to unsettle somebody else's love affair with unfounded gossip, or blemish their reputation in the boss's eyes. If you hear yourself saying 'Isn't she too old for the job? Too faddy? Didn't he mess up badly over that deal in Basingstoke? Wasn't there some talk of a broken heart in France?' you know you're letting jealousy get the better of you, even if you pretend to yourself that you're just making a couple of helpful points.

Second children, especially those with a younger sibling and in particular with a more than ten years younger brother or sister, are the most vulnerable to jealousy. Best to excise it from your psycheology. It makes you see the world in the wrong light.

Make me pure, Lord: Thou art holy;
Make me meek, Lord: Thou wert lowly

(Gerard Manley Hopkins)

WATER

31 OCTOBER

This is another finger wagger. October 31 has difficult relationships with parents and when this creature has its own children, there are difficult times. The trouble is that opinionated October 31 sometimes can't see the other side of the coin. There's a great deal of 'I'm just an ordinary person and I may seem dull but my views are my views, take it or leave it'. And of course, neither this hapless individual's parents or children can easily opt to leave it.

In teenage years they curl their lip at practically everything their parents say. Basically both their mother and father seem embarrassing and October 31 wishes they would stay out of sight. While this may be normal, poor October 31's mum and dad have to put up with it when the child becomes a man or woman. They'll find they're banned from smoking or maybe from leaving their fishing gear or their knitting about.

As a parent, October 31 is a great banner of television, so their children spend 24 hours a day prone in front of the set during their twenties which means a late career start. Sliced white bread is usually off the menu. As is reading comics, getting up late and playing pop music. If they get hold of power at work, they start banning straightaway. Nobody is to eat at their desk. The men mustn't wear suede shoes. You should answer the telephone after three rings, never put up posters, maintain a clear desk, not chew gum.

And yet, October 31 has the sweetest, most romantic nature and can be a memorable companion. Compassionate, it seems, with everybody but close family, they adore the countryside and love to walk. Companions see things they never noticed before, and return enchanted by October 31's tactful, gentle and enthusiastic observations.

Many are also tremendous performers, actors and musicians. Some find fame. Others shine in local theatre where their foibles are tolerated for their talent.

Man is born free,
but is everywhere in chains.
(Jean-Jacques Rousseau)

BODY
Being bossy doesn't stop these creatures from being sensational lovers with a sensuous passion for having the inside of their wrists stroked in bed, and out of bed for studiedly romantic occasions. Both sexes prepare imaginatively for dinner with a lover. A Chinese meal is favoured, the room scented with jasmine. Make jasmine water by adding two drops to a large bottle of water, shaking vigorously and filling little Chinese bowls. Before setting the table spray the cloth with a mist of clove oil in water. Afterwards, diluted rose oil in water or camellia oil (safe on most skins) is perfect for scented nipples or anywhere else.

MIND
Magpie spotting is good and bad according to the traditional ditty: One's sorrow, two's mirth, Three's a wedding, four's a birth, Five's a christening, six a dearth, Seven's heaven, eight is hell, And nine's the devil his ane sel (own self).

Protective, possessive November 1 adores his/her children and must look to their safety in the garden. Many plants are harmful if small children stuff them into their mouths. Discourage them from doing this with anything, until properly taught the many plants which are safe. What isn't safe: foxglove, ivy, laburnum, leyland cypress, giant hogweed, mistletoe, horse chestnut, wild privet, rosy periwinkle, umbrella tree, daffodil, narcissus, hyacinth, tulip bulbs, monkshood (aconitum), cut flowers. Lily-of-the-valley, lupins, rue, yew, spurges (euphorbia, autumn crocus, cherry laurel, oleander, angels' trumpets and leopard lily. And of course, woody and deadly nightshade, and hemlock.

MIND

For Christmas or partytime, create shell candles which look beautiful in groups. Collect shells with flattish bases from a beach, or buy non-endangered ones. Fix wick to base of shell with florists' putty and pour wax in shell. Leave to cool.

DATESHARE

Died: **Phil Silvers**, Sergeant Bilko. *Born:* **Victoria de Los Angeles**, *Spanish soprano.* **Alexander Alekhine**, *Russian-born French world champion chess master for a record eighteen years.* **Umberto Agnelli**, *Italian industrialist, Fiat chairman.* **Stephen Crane**, *war correspondent, novelist,* The Red Badge of Courage, *died aged 28 of tuberculosis.* **Gary Player**, *South African golf player, champion British Open and Masters.*

NOVEMBER I

You see them in the sky, shooting across its dark reaches, straight and assured. There's usually a lot of money riding on November 1's enterprises, but there's no re-entry problem with this cute character and it always finishes the job trailing glory and financial success for itself and companions. Money comes early to this person. But if it doesn't come early, it will come just a little later.

November 1 has no problems with money, either emotional or practical. Scorpios are controllers and planners. And November One is intent on being Number One. Except in unusual circumstances, they don't lose the money, but make it grow and spend it on fun.

This individual truly has a taste for grandeur, big houses, flash cars, rolling stripy lawns cared for by an expert gardener. At the vast end of fortune, there's a Picasso in the drawing-room and William Morris tapestries in the bedroom. And a Wendy house in the garden, complete with electric lighting and a porcelain dolls' tea service. Both sexes sometimes give big parties for some people they don't know, and when it gets this lavish, November 1 will be unhappy. But they always have someone they love, who loves them back to turn to.

Ruled by tough Mars and intellectual Pluto, Scorpio is a sexy beast, but not a wanderer. Except in the mind, when quite astonishing fantasies may be occurring about their immediate companions. They like sexy books, films and magazines too. And some may collect very rude art. It all adds up to an exciting, stable relationship, although there is a tendency for this space traveller to try to confine its lover to the home and smother them with possessiveness.

The downside to such giants among men and women is that neither sex can really tolerate the pygmies. They can't easily understand why everybody doesn't achieve their level of success, and judging those who don't as creeps, may behave with irritating arrogance.

With my mind on my money and my money on my mind.

(Snoop Doggy Dog)

2 NOVEMBER

This is one of the nicest stars in the zodiac. November 2 is clever, loving, modest and generous-minded. They're the edible seaweed on the beach. The succulent grape beneath the chocolate coating. The dolphin who plays around your boat, delighting everyone with somersaults and skill, and saves you if you fall in.

So is there a fault? The answer is that where judgement of others is concerned they aren't entirely watertight. This water sign can't judge a leaky vessel and thinks that everybody who smiles means well. Bad for their love lives or their business career, unless they speedily wring out the soggy areas of their psychology.

Passionate November 2 lets seducers walk all over them, lending money they can't afford to those with no intention of giving it back. Time and again the ill-fated tempter returns and for a few sensuous favours and promises gets this individual with a squelch for a heart to give up his or her home, car or just time spent caring for the undeserving wretch.

At work they get stabbed in the back and front and because of this, do better by themselves. Redundancy is no worry for this person who has portable skills and talent and can make pots of money working for employers who behave well to a freelance they would kick if employed. Working at home is good for this creature's self-confidence, because they learn to walk away from unpleasantness. There's always somebody else waiting to throw money at November 2.

Many have strong religious feelings, but if not, will espouse some cause which they feel must benefit mankind. Find them in charities, which they run expertly. Or working with the homeless or drug-addicted. Or more adventurously, in some far away country where they can teach money-earning, medical and food-growing skills to a local population rather than simply give out aid.

One can never speak enough of the virtues, the dangers, the power of shared laughter.

(Françoise Sagan)

BODY
November 2 drinks a lot, but not to the addiction level. Neither sex has an addictive personality on the whole. Hangovers are a problem. Television chef and bon vivant Keith Floyd recommends this cure: stir lemon juice with an egg yolk, add a dash of horseradish sauce, a shot of vodka with Worcester sauce and a dash of consommé mix in a cocktail shaker. If you don't dare, try taking 100mg of B complex vitamins and 2000mg of vitamin C before leaving, again during the party, then take more B complex and C with a multi-vitamin and mineral tablet before bed.

MIND
When you are a freelance it matters a great deal about returning telephone calls, even more so than it has before. People who don't bother to call back, either in companies or not, don't deserve the breaks.

DATESHARE
Shere Hite, sex writer and researcher, put new light on men's and women's orgasms. **Ken Rosewall**, Australian tennis champion. **Said Aouita**, Morrocan Olympic gold medallist, 1500, 2000, 3000, 5000 metre runner. **Benvenuto Cellini**, Italian Renaissance sculptor. **Marie Antoinette**, tragic French queen, wife of Louis XVI, beheaded by rebels, famously said 'Let them eat cake'. **Luchino Visconti**, Italian film director, Death In Venice. **Aga Khan III**, Muslim ruler, world's richest man.

BODY

Cellulite and rough skin are the enemies for plump and thin knees, turning things of beauty into an embarrassment. Men can suffer cellulite too, but the knobble is more likely. Body brushing is the latest rage. Take a long handled brush, sweep strokes up from ankle to knee and from knee to thigh always brushing towards the heart. No oil is necessary, but if you want to try something ginger juice is good, prepared by grating one large ginger root, then squeezing the gratings through cheesecloth. Ginger is both a stimulant and potent purifier, but may irritate, so test before using.

❦

MIND

Ancients believed that the backs of the knees are an erotic zone, and this sensitive area stroked in a circular motion, or just gently tickled is dynamite for November 3. Only to be done by intimates.

DATESHARE

Dolph Lundgren, *blond film hunk from Stockholm.* **Roseanne Barr**, *film and TV actress, star of* Roseanne. **Anna Wintour**, *American* Vogue *chief editor, daughter of British newspaper editor Charles Wintour.* **Roy Emerson**, *Australian tennis champion, Wimbledon winner.* **Charles Bronson**, *film star.* **Yitzhak Shamir**, *Israeli prime minister.* **André Malraux**, *French novelist, fought in Spanish Civil War.* **Larry Holmes**, *world heavyweight boxing champion.*

NOVEMBER 3

November 3 often chooses to be the power behind the throne rather than the glittering star. Many women marry famous men and devote their lives to a husband's career, often proving more useful than any paid adviser. Both sexes are acute foible observers and can spot a flatterer better than the flatteree, who probably enjoys being told that he/she is wonderful, beautiful, marvellous and utterly brilliant.

November 3's motto is 'actions speak louder than words' and they can't abide sayers not doers. They are also extremely financially astute and may be found in youth in some form of accounting, which skills come in useful later. Generous minded, they never feel jealous of their boss or spouse, always supportive and congratulatory. But woe betide the interloper who tries to usurp their influence.

Silky serpentine Scorpio isn't having that. At first they praise, to throw everybody off the scent, and may even appear to take the newcomer under their wing. Then watch out for the colliding star technique. There'll be nothing left of the rival but a few fluttering sparks, but amazingly the victim will still think 3 is their friend, such is the secretive skill of this person.

Outside of this, and it's not a problem for relatives and friends, they usually acquire a great deal of money and then devote themselves to spending it. It's a good-looking individual with a great body. Vain November sweethearts constantly point out their best features and tubby lovers must expect their own expanding waistlines compared to November 3's neat dimensions. This is the girl or man whose waistband never crumples and whose shirt and blouse buttons never strain over too much flesh.

The men have excellent shoulders, broad and thin, the girls have sexy knees and a bosom to die for. A lot of cash is spent on clothes. Look out for bare midriffs showing off golden delicious tummy buttons. And the sleekest of tight trousers for both sexes.

You were once wild.
Don't let them tame you.

(Isadora Duncan)

4 NOVEMBER

This is one of the homemakers of the year, unusual for Scorpio who often prefers an urban, party and work environment. November 4 needs green fields and trees and can sometimes suffer from stress-related illnesses confined to inner city life.

In particular, being a water sign, they should try to live near water. The sparkle on the surface soothes their souls. In particular, this creature thrives near the sea. Walking on beaches, watching the tide ebb and flow and searching for rocks and pretty shells is what many like best. But if that's not possible, it's a good idea to have a fountain in the garden. (Some even have one in the house, which makes an exceptional talking point.)

Essentially family people, they don't much like work and are better off taking a part-time job, or one that relates to other human beings, such as social work or teaching. If they must work, all the Scorpio concentration of mind and determination is brought into play, and they try to make as much money as they can early, putting everything into investment, so they can bunk out of work life in mid life and devote themselves to their own interests.

November's child has a vividly coloured home. Best colours for Scorpio are shades of russet red through orange to brown. Best colours for water people are blues through to green. According to the lore of colour, the first mean serenity, humour and nurturing. Blues have varied meanings: friendship and frankness for bright blue; truth, sincerity and earnestness for dark blue; innocence, virtue and steadfastness for light blue.

There's likely to be a blue bathroom, with shell decoration and pieces of pretty rock in November 4's house. And a blue coverlet in their bedroom, or that of a child, for serene nights. And there'll be blue flowers everywhere both inside the house and in the garden.

BODY

November 4 adores his or her own wedding anniversary and the presents that go with it. So here's the traditional present list. 1st: paper. 2nd: cotton or linen. 3rd: leather. 4th: silk. 5th: wood. 6th: iron, or chocolate. 7th: copper. 8th: bronze. 9th: pottery. 10th: tin or aluminium. 11th: steel. 12th: silk again, or linen. 13th: lace. 14th: traditionally ivory, but imitation now because ivory endangers the animals it's taken from. 15th: crystal. 20th: china. 25th: silver. 30th: pearls. 35th: coral or jade. 40th: rubies. 45th: sapphires. 50th: gold. 55th: emeralds, 60th: diamonds. 75th: diamonds again.

MIND

If you don't like the way you are living, change it. November 4 is seriously unhappy, even ill, with the wrong lifestyle. Resist temptation to think about some nebulous future time. Try to work out when you'll make your move.

DATESHARE

Robert Mapplethorpe, enfant terrible *photographer, died young.* **William of Orange** (later William III), *Dutch prince married to Mary, daughter of James II.* **Loretta Swit**, *TV actress, Hot Lips Hoolihan in* M*A*S*H. **Kate Reid**, *film star.* **Pauline Trigere**, *fashion designer.*

The trouble with wedlock is there's not enough wed and too much lock.

(Christopher Morley)

NOVEMBER 5

BODY

Blueberry Pie. Buy shortcrust pastry. Take 700g blueberries, 2tsp lemon juice, ½ tsp grated lemon rind, ½ tsp ground cinnamon, ½ tsp ground nutmeg, pinch of salt, 175g sugar, 25g plain flour. Mix flour, sugar, cinnamon, nutmeg, lemon rind, lemon juice. Line pie dish with half the pastry. Put in blueberries with half the mixture, add rest blueberries, then rest of mixture. Dot with butter. Place rest of pastry on top, dampen edges, pinch together with underlayer. Brush top lightly with milk. Bake at 220°C, 425°F, gas mark 7 for 45–50 minutes until pastry is golden brown. Serve hot or cold with cream.

MIND

To calm rage at lack of recognition, try taking one of Dr Edward Bach's famous natural remedies. Cherry Plum (Prunus cerasifera) was especially designed by the doctor in the 1930s for inclination to rage and losing one's temper.

DATESHARE

*Died: **Jacques Tati**, Parisian actor, film star, comedian. Born: **Sam Shepard**, playwright, film star, stage actor. **Vivien Leigh**, film star, married to Laurence Olivier, Scarlett O'Hara in Gone With The Wind. **Art Garfunkel**, singer, songwriter, Simon and Garfunkel. **Tatum O'Neal**, film actress, married John McEnroe, divorced. **Elke Sommer**, German film star. **Ike Turner**, singer, songwriter, Tina's ex. **Bryan Adams**, Canadian rock singer, songwriter. **Joel McCrea**, film actor.*

The Blue Belle of the zodiac, November 5's spiritual life is dominated by colour. This psychic creature takes blue as the main ingredient for life, being the shade of sky and sea. Neither sex is blue bonkers but they do have strong opinions and as this sometimes nasty-tempered bluefish can turn into a Bluebeard if opposed, those who love either sex should take their ideas on board. There are others, after all: those who won't have green in the house and early presenters of breakfast television were all instructed to wear pink, so this person isn't alone in his or her colour preference.

Many become designers and home decorators, slipping their favourite colour into other people's lives. When November 5 was

little he or she probably dreamed that their guardian angel visited them on shimmering blue wings. Certainly it's the colour of the mother of Jesus Christ, Mary's traditional dress.

Once you understand November 5's preference, its implications are everywhere. A bit of a blue stocking, she will put a blue pencil through any inferior work, and slave late in the office until she's blue in the face. Both sexes pine if another is the boss's blue-eyed boy and if their talent goes unacknowledged both may get the blues so badly they have to seek counselling.

Scorpio's personal ambition is usually to form a lifelong relationship and settle down. Both sexes long for children but since this is not an especially fecund day there may be conception trouble ahead. If medical help isn't forthcoming, November 5 throws a blue fit and gets his 'n' her way. The usual result with medical help is a bonny baby. And of course, if it's a boy, it will be a boy in blue. And if it's a girl, yes, you've guessed it, it'll be a girl in blue. Just the suggestion of a pink nursery would send November 5 into a pink fit.

A verbal contract isn't worth the paper it's written on.

(Samuel Goldwyn)

6 NOVEMBER

Marry for sex, repent at leisure, should be a warning to November 6. This sugar-coated starlet spins head over heels with passion and half the time can't tell its brains from its feet. Everybody looks up when she shimmies into the room – in his case leans meaningfully against the door. Everybody wants to get on the back of November 6's space motorbike and be taken for a ride past all the other envious stars, twinkling and blinkling to attract November 6's notice.

Once people have spent some time in this individual's bed, they find they actually never want to get out again. The only way to resist this person's siren allure is to tie yourself to the mast like Jason and his fellow seamen. The trouble with our imaginative sex bomb is that they are so romantic themselves that frequently all common sense is eclipsed by a few exquisite presents and murmurings of 'You are the most wonderful thing in the world'. And they like marrying people. All the attention, compliments and partying simply goes to their heads. If they don't marry, they move in with new lovers. Fewer presents, but just as risky.

What to do? If they can get their brains out of their red high-heeled shoes, or black suede shoes, November 6 people should try working very late most nights so that they go home to bed alone, too exhausted to ask anyone to come over. These exceptionally gifted people do well in large companies – they're such a pleasure to have around and everybody secretly lusts after them. It gives them a natural head start although this may be under-endowed-with-sex-appeal-ist.

Their burgeoning career brings them stability and better judgement and a good income is often an anti-instant marriage weapon. Otherwise it just means that they keep having time off work to get married, their colleagues have to save up for expensive wedding presents and everybody lays bets on how long the latest union will last.

BODY

November 6 should try this Should I Marry This Person Test. 1. Do we spend all the time making love? 2. Do my friends get on with him/her? 3. Have I read a book since we met? 4. Do I know what my lover feels about my career, my parents, animals, getting drunk? 5. Do I think my lover's perfect? 6. (For women) Does he watch football on television a lot? 7. Take the wheel in my car? 8. (For him) Does she comment on my driving? 9. About me watching football on television? Only 2, 3 and 4 should be 'yes'.

MIND

Acting on impulse is supposed to be charming, but where love is concerned heedlessly fast decisions can be disastrous. If Romeo hadn't been so impulsive, he would have properly checked Juliet and found she was alive, thus avoiding tragedy.

DATESHARE

Died: **Gene Tierney**, cinema idol. Born: **Sally Field**, film, TV actress. **Maria Shriver**, TV journalist, member of Kennedy family. **Mark McCormack**, founder of International Management Group, sports and entertainment conglomerate. **James Ramon Jones**, author, From Here To Eternity.

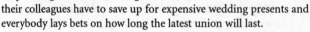

'No wise fish would go anywhere without a porpoise,' said the Mock Turtle. 'Why, if a fish told me he was going on a journey, I would say "With what porpoise?"'

(Lewis Carroll)

BODY

Are you getting enough iron? Low intake causes loss of concentration. 1. Do you eat meat, fish or poultry 3 times a week? 2. Drink three glasses of red wine each week? 3. Have citrus fruit with meals three times a week? 4. Sprinkle raw bran on cereals? 5. Drink tea or coffee with or immediately after main meals? 6. Constantly go on low calorie diets? 7. Regularly take heavy exercise? Score: 1: yes = 4 points, no = 0 points. 2: yes = 4, no = 0. 3: yes = 0, no = 4. 4: yes = 0, no = 4. 5: yes = 0, no = 4. 6: yes = 0, no = 4. 7: yes = 0, no = 4. High scores indicate enough iron. Low, eat more iron-rich foods and consider taking a supplement.

MIND

When abroad, it is still good advice not to drink the water, not necessarily because it's contaminated but because it contains sufficiently different minerals to upset a stomach. Drink bottled water or cans of coke, brush your teeth in bottled water and avoid ice in drinks.

DATESHARE

*Died: **Steve McQueen**, cinema idol, dare devil. Born: **Marie Curie**, physicist, discovered radium. **Captain James Cook**, British explorer, navigator. **Leon Trotsky**, Russian revolutionary, political philosopher, assassinated in exile in Mexico. **Albert Camus**, French existentialist, The Myth of Sisyphus. **Konrad Lorenz**, Nobel Prize-winning Australian animal behaviourist. **Billy Graham**, evangelist. **Joni Mitchell**, Canadian singer, songwriter. **Joan Sutherland**, Australian opera soprano.*

NOVEMBER 7

November 7 likes to take risks, and fortunately he is well-balanced enough to judge when it's necessary and when it's too dangerous. They may take a punt on a deal or purchase in their work, or even a risk in their chosen partner. But it usually works out because this person has weighed all the odds. Most people like November 7 just because he chances his arm. But they're glad that luck is with him or her.

Both sexes may start up their own business, but while they have spotted an obvious opportunity in the market place, no move is made before a great deal of research. Some of these creatures make a splash and find fame when they stick out their neck to back an invention or a hunch. Others content themselves with enterprise. Some may even have a mid life career change, but hard work and foresight usually pulls it off.

Scorpios are on the whole extremely attractive to other people. Most go for long-term partnerships although some buzz like a bee from flower to flower, eventually settling with one lifelong partner. In matters of love, November 7 will also take risks. They may marry someone from a different culture or religion or class. There are always potential problems here. Different ways of doing and seeing things. Sets of parents and friends who don't entirely understand each other to begin with. In the end the mixing of culture enriches everyone.

Being great travellers their opportunity to meet someone very different with whom they might spend their life is enhanced. Scorpio is attracted to Italy and Greece, homes of an ancient culture which appeals to the intellectual Pluto in them and the wandering propensities of Mars. This may simply bring great happiness, or introduce them to an international life, trading between their adopted country and country of birth. Whatever happens, November 7 enjoys his or her expanded horizons and lives in contentment.

*If I keep my good character
I shall be rich enough.*

(Platonicus)

8 NOVEMBER

Mostly it's the women born on this date who sacrifice too much for love. Like the Little Mermaid, they give up what is most important, independence and self-esteem, or in other words career, for husband and family. Sadly, this often goes unappreciated and November 8 can find herself *sans* love, *sans* everything. Mermen also have a tendency to throw over a career for love, but not quite to the same extent. Nothing to do with innate sexual difference, merely that convention accepts and blindly applauds a woman's sacrifice.

Fortunately the world is not lost and November 8 has a good head on its shoulders and can re-establish him or herself. But the wild, reckless over-self-sacrificing side to this psychology must be controlled. Keep your fate in your own hands. Make sacrifices for your children if necessary, but remember when they are grown and flown that they didn't ask it of you.

Many individuals born on this day pursue their needs with a powerful concentration, once they start again. They have more drive and insight than many other days and a fantastic imagination which inspires them. In the right circumstances they soar across the universe way out in front and unchallenged by competition.

All should avoid addictive behaviour, either to being martyrish, to alcohol, drugs (prescribed or not), and even money-hoarding. Some privation in youth and early adulthood makes them unable to acknowledge better finances and like the Royal Family, they may continue absurd penny-pinching when the bank account is bulging.

Either sex can be teased out of miserliness because their rational minds are always open to home truths. Then there will be great pleasure in spending, especially on art, furniture, and music. And on presents for others, because when this people-pleasing date realises that expansiveness brings joy, then that is what they do. As for alcohol and drugs, they can be diverted from them too.

Bitterness can eat you up, but it can't fuel you.

(Benazir Bhutto)

BODY
The chakras are sources of sensuous energy. The Kama Sutra *describes the chakras as centres of energy which occur at seven points in the astral body which yogis believe surrounds the physical body. Six chakras are located along the equivalent of the spine in the physical body, while the seventh crowns the head. Sexual activity is one way of arousing the awesome energy known as kundalini, which lies dormant, depicted as a coiled serpent, at the base of the spine in what is known as the Muladhara chakra. Ability to arouse and control the kundalini is believed to be a means of achieving and directing orgasm. Study yoga.*

MIND
Collecting charms delights November 8, for their beauty and meaning. Little silver 4th century Christian charms can still be picked up, but less rare and cheaper are Roman coins which can be wired to a bracelet.

DATESHARE
Margaret Mitchell, *novelist,* Gone With The Wind. **Alain Delon**, *French film heart-throb.* **Bonnie Raitt**, *singer, songwriter.* **Rickie Lee Jones**, *singer, songwriter.* **Kazuo Ishiguro**, *Japanese novelist,* The Remains of The Day. **Christie Lee Hefner**, *Playboy publisher and president, daughter of Hugh.* **Christian Barnard**, *South African heart transplant surgeon, novelist, biographer, playboy.* **Herman Rorschach**, *Swiss psychiatrist, invented the Rorschach ink blot test.*

WATER

Getting ahead in a difficult profession requires faith in yourself. You must be able to sustain staggering blows and unfair reversals. November 9 understands early there is no reliable code for beginners, only that you know your strong cards. And don't play the juvenile lead, invariably misused.

Many creatures born today, with moderate talent, but with great inner drive will go farther than people with vastly superior talent. This inner drive is itself a talent, something you are born with and which no one can teach you to acquire. There are two things which November 9 must learn straight away. The first is to value this drive. Let no one persuade you to downgrade it in your secret psychology. And the second is to respect other people's greater talent, even if they are less successful than you, and learn how to promote it and them.

Truly self-confident people surround themselves with talent. Its marvellous light will illuminate your own success and you can be the vehicle for a shyer man's or woman's genius.

November 9 make great agents and impresarios as well as performers, not simply in the theatre and entertaining but in every walk of life. Both sexes are self-confident, generous towards others, both privately and publicly. They don't patronise. They do see the flatterer coming, but understanding why the flattery is there, don't harm. To some will come fame. To many, recognition and, of course, money.

Some use their drive away from the work place. They enjoy the patriarchal or matriarchal role, founding dynasties, looking after relatives and friends. Theirs is usually the house where everybody meets to discuss a mutual interest or hobby fired by November 9's enthusiasm. Whether it be trainspotting, sport, history, music or politics, people born on this day and their families will never be isolated and their long life is mentally vigorous, packed with new thoughts and experiences until the day they choose to retire to heaven.

*I am not sincere,
not even when I say I am not.*

(Jules Renard)

10 NOVEMBER

Try though they may, November 10 has a superstitious side which won't go away. He or she may obtain a double first in mathematics and logic, they may be a captain and captainess of industry, or just a solidly sensible worker on the frozen pea section of the local factory, but they still won't bring branches of white may into the house in case it causes a death. No party can contain thirteen people. And one magpie makes them frantically look for its pair, usually and fortunately nearby.

Naturally it's all old wives' tales. But who actually chooses to walk under a ladder? How often have you thrown a pinch of spilt salt over your left shoulder for luck? And do you teach your children to turn the empty boiled eggshell upside down bash it in with a teaspoon so that witches can't sail away in it? What about blowing out all the birthday cake candles in one go and then making a silent wish with the first cut? A spoken wish, of course, doesn't come true.

Otherwise level-headed November 10 maintains a fascination with the ancient lore of all the countries they visit. Just a few become obsessed with omens and lucky days and won't take a decision on the wrong day. Nancy Reagan was one of these, not a November 10 person, but other days in the year can suffer from this too. But strong-minded November 10 is an unusual Scorpio in this regard. Most Pluto ruled people pooh-pooh the whole thing and wouldn't dream of telling a child not to wear his vest inside out or he'll be pixie led.

There's a psychic streak in November 10 which encourages this interest – a strong sixth sense which they listen to early and use very like others use the gift of the gab or a talent for mechanics. And then again, it's fun to remember old traditions.

Cross fingers.

BODY

Luckiest stones of all for Scorpio include the aquamarine, carbuncle and magnetite. Aquamarine is a water gem, its name taken from the Latin which means 'sea water', reflected in its bluish-green colour. It's lucky for seafarers, brings harmony to marriage and good fortune. It should be worn with the carbuncle, a deep rich crimson variety of garnet which possesses the attribute of hope. It is also meant to protect its wearer from disease, becoming dimmed when an infectious person approaches. And it protects the traveller. Magnetite's properties include preventing baldness and it invests its owner with wisdom and intuition.

☾

MIND

Avoid growing the following flowers with unlucky messages in your garden or window box: dahlias (rejection), foxglove (shallowness), bugloss (mendacity), anemone (desertion), African marigold (boorishness), French marigold (jealousy), blue lobelia (dislike), basil (animosity), pink, white and red geraniums (doubt, indecision, duplicity).

DATESHARE

Sir Richard Burton, Welsh stage and film actor, married to Elizabeth Taylor. **John Northrup**, aeronautical engineer. **Sir Jacob Epstein**, sculptor. **Mike Powell**, US long jump champion. **Roy Scheider**, film star. **Donna Fargo**, singer, songwriter. Earl of Essex, **Robert Devereux**, adventurer, favourite of Elizabeth I. **William Hogarth**, social satirist, painter.

BODY

A miniature Christmas tree is an absolute delight for small children to have in their bedroom. Take a small tree. Any kind of garden-centre conifer will do. Tuck a piece of red velvet round the pot, using small safety pins to secure, or some gold or silver wrapping paper, using glue or sellotape. Plus a wide wired ribbon tied in a bow. Let children add some glitter stars for good effect with a little of the scatter glitter you can buy from any stationery shop. Decorate the tree with tiny bows, strings of small glass beads or tiny cheap pearls. Maybe a few chocolates shinily wrapped.

MIND

When the work is done, the children in bed and the night is quiet late on Christmas Eve, play a CD of Christmas carols, pour a long glass of champagne for your partner and wish them Happy Christmas.

DATESHARE

Demi Moore, film actress. **Jonathan Winters**, comedian, film TV actor. **Bibi Anderson**, Swedish film actress. **René Clair**, French film maker. **General George Patton**, US World War II tank commander. **Daniel Ortega**, Nicaraguan Sandinista revolutionary president. **Fyodor Dostoevsky**, Russian novelist, Crime and Punishment, The Brothers Karamazov.

November 11 takes great pleasure in home and garden building and likes to spend a great deal of time in do-it-yourself and furniture shops and garden centres. And they are fabulous at making everything attractive. The men seem to be able to make anything work, from rewiring a house, to instituting eye-level washing up machines and pedals on the fridge freezer because handles destroy the design. The women turn the fridge freezer into a thing of beauty by covering it with gorgeously coloured oil paint, then sticking perspex over it for wipeability.

Both sexes are avid catalogue readers and shoppers, sitting up in bed and turning down corners of desirable pages. Both understand that it's self-confidence and a good eye, not money, which matters. November 11 would no more employ an interior decorator than they would a substitute lover for their mate.

Both sexes will work near home. Find November 11 in a country town or village rather than the great urban centres, at least after early adulthood. Commuting is their nightmare and the women want to be near the children. Some prefer to work at home, relishing their own pace and lack of need to kowtow.

Scorpio is good with money and finds a pleasant niche in the local bank, building society, maybe insurance or accounting where they rise as high as they choose, always keeping their amenable character. Mostly it's because they're dreaming about painting the downstairs loo lipstick red.

Christmas and parties are a ball for November 11. They adore the cooking, the planning, the entertaining and making things look different. And they make it fantastical fun for children with projects which involve bright colours and glitter. Always careful to leave sherry and a mince pie for Father Christmas at midnight on  Christmas Eve, when the world's animals are given the gift of speech, November 11 says hush, can you hear them chatting?

Never eat more than you can lift.
(Miss Piggy)

I2 NOVEMBER

There are times when November 12 gets weary being cheerful all the time and just keeping going. Stars born on this day are the ones who keep the world turning. They are always called upon to help out. Always chugging to the sick bed with a homemade chicken pie and then taking away the washing. And yet, this good-looking creature radiates with luminous glamour, looks good in the most rubbishy old clothes. It's just that they can't see their own glamour and tend to concentrate on the dull bits.

They have a peculiar way of thinking. Always telling the bad news first, they sometimes even hold back the good news. Not out of perversity – although there is an Eeyore tendency here. It's just that when good luck comes and fortune smiles, November 12 isn't sure that it's here to stay, doesn't like to celebrate in case it whisks away like uncatchable thistledown.

Yet of all the stars born in the zodiac this is one of the most romantic, with a capacity for empathy and feeling that far outstrips most. And although their deep psychology won't easily admit it, they have a fetching, catching capacity for joy. This is, of course, why others turn to them for help. November 12 is a joy bringer.

Blessed with psychic talent, they often sense what is to come, which can be a burden. But they also have fair warning of who they are to meet, and when the right life partner comes along they are expecting them. This avoids that old problem of wrong timing when the right mate disappears because you were otherwise occupied and didn't realise until it was too late.

In any kind of work situation, November 12 should be wary of others overusing and overdepending on their kindness and fixer talent. But this is easily avoidable because they have a strong character and know how to decline tactfully without hurting.

Knock knock.   *Who's there?*
Toby.   *Toby who?*
Toby or not Toby,
that is the question.

BODY

When care for others gets overwhelming, November12 might try a Bach Flower remedy which seems to have been planned by Dr Edward Bach in the 1930s just for them. It's Red Chestnut (Aesculus carnea). A typical state of mind that needs help is the overpowerful energy link between two individuals.

Symptoms include excessive concern and worry, fear for the safety of partners and children, over self-sacrificing, interpreting lateness as a potential indicator of an accident, although knowing this to be untrue. After treatment, sufferers report feelings of positive thoughts and security, plus a surge of courage and level-headedness.

MIND

Train yourself to think of the positive aspects of a situation when negative thoughts come. Do not imagine the worst that may happen, but accept that a desirable and pleasant result or situation is really here to stay.

DATESHARE

Auguste Rodin, French sculptor. **Grace Kelly**, Princess Grace of Monaco. **Neil Young**, Canadian singer, songwriter, guitarist. **Nadia Comaneci**, Romanian gymnast, Olympic gold medallist. **Charles Manson**, cult leader, convicted of Sharon Tate murder. **Booker T Jones**, singer, songwriter. **Alexander Borodin**, Russian composer.

BODY

Rosehip Syrup. This delicious vitamin C-rich syrup was made by grandma during World War II. Take 3.8 litres of water, 1.5 kg ripe red rosehips and 1kg sugar. Boil 2.5 litres of the water. Slice hips, put them into water. Reheat to boiling point and skim. Cook for 30 minutes, strain through a jelly bag, then boil remaining pulp in rest of water. Cool for 30 minutes, strain. Combine two liquids, boil until reduced to about 1.5 litres. Add sugar, bring to boil. Cook to syrup, then cool. Pot, seal, store in dark cupboard.

MIND

Wild Rose (Rosa canina) may be the ideal Bach Flower remedy for serenity seekers. It gives back a feeling of inner freedom and flexibility, the ability to follow life's inner laws and joyful vital interest in surroundings.

November 13 needs tranquillity to balance the fast pace of his life. If he doesn't get it unhappiness and exhaustion will ensue. Both sexes find music a great peace bringer, in particular choral music, jazz, blues and other pieces of classical music, in particular written in D minor and C sharp minor. These include the ever popular Moonlight Sonata by Beethoven (C minor) and many of the piano concertos by Mozart and Brahms.

It is now well known by doctors that simply listening to music can reduce high blood pressure, reduce pain and improve IQ and memory, so its curative effect on 13 isn't surprising. Neurological reception for music is mostly located in the right brain (speech is in the left) and the limbic system, which governs much of the brain's emotional responses.

To combat low self-esteem, which is sometimes brought on by working for large corporations and caring too much about what others think of you, get out into the countryside. People born on this day are great thinkers and walkers. They like to pass hours just looking, spotting rare plants, birds and, of course, being a water sign, river and sea plants, birds and fish. Most become expert in one of these areas, which gives them endless delight.

November 13 likes to collect flowers and press them in the old family Bible, just like his or her grandmother did. And what also amuses them is hunting for wild, edible berries and nuts and even wild plants which can be made into delicious dishes. (Never from hedgerows because of car fumes and

always check on pollution levels of seas and rivers.)

A walk with this person turns into an exciting forage for wild strawberries, cob nuts, blackberry patches and if you are lucky, the delicious and freely-growing blueberry. Children adore mushrooming with 13, taking out early morning baskets, finding fairy circles, jumping in and out and wishing, then coming back to make a delicious breakfast.

If you always do what interests you, then at least one person is happy.
(Katharine Hepburn)

14 NOVEMBER

S hyness sometimes makes this little silvery fish lurk under a stone, which is a pity because he who lurks loses the world. November 14 has enormous potential, all the usual Scorpio organisational talents and capacity for massive concentration. But their self-image is often zilch. They prefer to serve rather than be served and this can be irritating to friends.

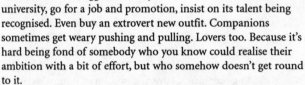

Too much time is spent by others persuading November 14 to come out of hiding and show its gleaming scales. This creature has to be egged on to try for university, go for a job and promotion, insist on its talent being recognised. Even buy an extrovert new outfit. Companions sometimes get weary pushing and pulling. Lovers too. Because it's hard being fond of somebody who you know could realise their ambition with a bit of effort, but who somehow doesn't get round to it.

Many do come out and when they do, dazzle all around not just with their talent, but a swift sense of humour and the kind of startling honesty which sees how a situation can be changed when others have long accepted its inconvenience. They're the kind who invent a childproof pill bottle which isn't also adult proof. And an iron which doesn't scatter white flecks all over clean clothes.

November 14 is much happier when he or she can realise their talents, because hiding away may be safe, but also makes you resentful. They are just as hesitant in love, which is odd because they have all the Scorpio slim, attention-grabbing good looks. Would-be partners have to make the running and must demonstrate their lack of flightiness because November 14 certainly doesn't want her heart trifled with. A powerful love affair and secure marriage or partnership makes those scales positively flash with iridescence and finally this person can forget whatever happened in his or her childhood – often a divorce or illness – which made them withdraw.

Keep a stiff upper chin.
(Samuel Goldwyn)

BODY
Sensitive November 14 suffers from mild rashes, puffy eyes, feet, insomnia and other symptoms which may be due to food intolerance. In the fifth century BC, Hippocrates was aware that a significant number of people reacted adversely to certain foods and needed instructions to avoid them. Ask your GP to help. Some sufferers react to gluten, the protein part of flour, or are intolerant to lactose, milk sugar, which possibly affects half the people on earth. Often those sensitive to aspirin are also sensitive to foods which contain salicylates, such as almonds, apples, apricots, peaches, prunes, oranges, tomatoes, tangerines, cucumbers, cherries, grapes and raisins.

MIND
Tarot's Major Arcana has the 14th card as Temperance. Obviously this can refer to excessive modesty, which is negative. Plus factors include powerful flashes of understanding and a humorous undermining of the egotistical.

WATER

NOVEMBER 15

This fixed water sign likes to think of herself as a bootlegger, wild, free, piratical, invading the firmament with new and revolutionary ideas. And this is one side to November 15. But this creature is also the buttered bun of the universe, homely, satisfying and just the same as it always has been.

A strong regard for convention keeps November 15's feet firmly on the ground, makes the unconventional side more interesting. Interesting rather than disturbing, which means that people born on this day can innovate in a way that pleases, making change insidious and acceptable. In the style arena this makes them courted and popular. Nothing is done without an eye on the human being who is going to buy their services. Nor which will hurt the workforce if November 15 is the boss. Both sexes get rid of slouches. But apart from that they abhor the employment market's new fashion for cruelty.

And yet, and yet, there is the moment in every November 15's life when both sexes do something spectacular that nobody else would dare to even dream of. Like a fantastic firework, they draw the crowd's eyes. It's the bootlegger psychology coming out and let nobody try to get in the way, or they will be roughly swept aside.

In private November 15 keeps the two sides of his psycheology.

A safe, loving environment is what both sexes prefer. But when it comes to love they'll fight as dirty as the next person, ramming their way through obstacles, sweeping rivals aside and devastating the desired one with charm. Theirs is always the big gesture, the engagement party where this person stalks in and hijacks the lover they don't want to marry another. The Christmas family do where November 15 arrives to charm a disapproving family with gifts and gift of the gab until the fair one's mum is practically pleading with her prospective son- or daughter-in-law to name the day.

Why are women so much more interesting to men than men are to women?

(Virginia Woolf)

16 NOVEMBER

B y day November 16 works methodically hard, and has a conventional image which belies the glossiness of the night creature who goes out on the town to conquer. In youth,

both sexes live for fun and romance, regarding the day job as there to finance what good times happen to this star under a friendly nocturnal sky. A walk in the moonlight, a talk in the moonlight and maybe even a tumble in the moonlight is what November 16 aims to get. And, dressed to kill, they do. Those who share an office with ordinary-seeming November 16 might fail to recognise their colleague as the succulent and sensuous Moonlight Tomata every night-clubbing guy or dame wants a slice of.

Both sexes may know how to have fun, but they have a deep psycheology and their goal is not so much fun as self-realisation. Ambition is one preoccupation. Personal happiness and security another. On a more complex level November 16 wants to resolve feelings about why we are here. This may involve religion. Or the study of history and psychology. Or perhaps a decision to live in the countryside and commune with nature. Whatever is chosen, it's certain that by mid life, this creature will have developed an overview of how life should be lived, which they probably want others, in particular children, to adopt.

Be alert here. Children and partners don't necessarily like these and there may be trouble ahead, unless November 16 keeps extremely flexible.

There's a natural talent here for modern technology which brings mountains of money, and employment where bosses court these people, particularly because they have oodles and snoodles of charm and a nice way of explaining technology to less confident people. All this fits in well with the quest for life's meaning, because work can be set up at home. Redundancy is a plus factor here and probably brings great happiness.

All animals except man know that the ultimate of life is to enjoy it.
(Samuel Butler)

BODY
People born today like swimming in natural water. Check pollution levels on the coast, lakes and lochs, and in particular, the rivers. Scientists say that toxins produced by blue-green algae in dozens of Britain's rivers and reservoirs can pose a high risk to swimmers and windsurfers as outbreaks of seasonal algal blooms begin to reach record levels. Britain's new Environmental Agency has no powers to force landowners to put up warning notices even at popular swimming or paddling spots. Last year rivers affected included the Great Ouse in the east Midlands, the Tamar in southwest England and the Ash, a tributary of the Thames.

MIND
You think the human pregnancy (267 days) goes on for ever? Try being an African elephant (640 days), a rhinoceros (360 days), giraffe (450 days), porpoise (360 days), horse (337 days) cow (280 days) or orangutan (275 days).

DATESHARE
Frank Bruno, British and world heavyweight boxing champion. **Sir Oswald Mosley**, British Labour Party minister, fascist leader. **Agnolo di Cosimo di Mariano**, Florentine Medici portrait painter. **Tiberius**, Roman emperor, general. **Burgess Meredith**, stage and film actor. **Paul Hindemith**, composer. **Eddie Condon**, dixieland swing guitarist. **Lisa Bonet**, TV actress.

The trouble with people born on this date is that they like to think things over for such a long time that opportunity sometimes passes. A truly dazzling job comes along which means they'll have to take a chance. It's nice to be asked, they think, but isn't life more pleasant staying where they are in a nice desk with a view of the river? More friendly frog than dynamic scorpion, November 17 needs friends and lovers to push, push and push again. But this so secretive creature frequently fails to tell even its nearest of any offer, so nobody knows when it's time to put the pressure on.

In their deepest psycheology, a lot of people born on this day would almost prefer to miss opportunities and sigh over them later, than take the chance and take the risk. It's a 'I would have been good at that' not 'I am good at this' date. Yet when they do venture into new experiences, this engaging froglet is transformed into a prince or princess. And everybody around says 'I knew it all along'.

Find our amphibious creature breast-stroking through the shallows of any bureaucracy, filing, filling in forms, answering the telephone and being kind to everyone. And when they take that froggy leap, find them almost anywhere in the glittering heights

where their tolerance and ability to tread water make them popular and invaluable to any industry where deals are done which need delicacy and intuition rather than fireworks and cut and thrust.

November 17 is popular for its shining honesty, although they do have difficulty with white lies. They can't tell them and so when others say they feel fat or they're having a bad hair day, November 17 gives them seriously good unwelcome advise. Some become professional advice givers, a solution lengthily explained for everybody else's curtains, pregnancy and car maintenance. They mean to be helpful. It makes them unpopular.

Twilight is not good for maidens;
Should not loiter in the glen
In the haunts of goblin men.

(*Christina Rossetti*)

18 NOVEMBER

I t's not what you achieve, it's how you come through that matters, should be November 18's maxim. It's largely true, but this creature is maybe dense about the stiff upper lip, sometimes so stiff it prevents them from having a proper conversation. They aren't good at introspection, the men worse than the women. Most female November 18s tend to run themselves down, laughing at their own misfortunes in an unwittingly bloodcurdling way. As in, 'I've been caught for drunken driving and my lawyer says it's possible to go to prison, which will serve me right.' True. But when sympathy is expressed November 18 rebuffs it.

They have a hard time at work because they often don't notice the bloodletting and this makes them seem hard. In fact they can have a hard time in life unless they get in touch with their inner self pretty fast. Because otherwise they can feel isolated, not quite knowing how it happened.

Most are physically attractive in youth, although they never believe it. This is the girl who when told she's attractive demurs that her toes are appalling. And the man who knows pale trousers don't suit his sturdy legs but wears them anyway. Others often let themselves go, almost deliberately rendering themselves unattractive, a sort of challenge to others. Many do like them for their bravery, terrific sense of humour and straightforwardness. But if November 18 has money or power, there's always a tendency to suspect others of liking him because of it.

The lesson to be learned here is that if you can't understand and like yourself, it's difficult to accept that others do. November 18 is excellent with animals, rides and cares for horses well and handles dogs with tremendous skill and affection. They may meet partners through this kind of mutual interest, which acts as a base for lifelong happiness, and which automatically sorts out many of the natural hesitations of this individual.

BODY

November 18's tendency to take a glum view of himself can often be eradicated by a Bach Flower Therapy remedy researched for us by Dr Edward Bach before the last world war. Pine (Pinus sylvestris) is good for people who over-discipline themselves and harbour self-dislike. If your symptoms include using apologetic turns of phrase, self-blame, droning on about your own limitations and considering oneself a coward at heart, then it's possible that Pine can sort this out. Claims for it include the acquisition of greater understanding of self and others and calm ability to accept faults but not cling to them.

MIND

If you think you're thick because a teacher tested you and found you had a low IQ, here are a few others who also scored low. Nicolaus Copernicus, founder of modern astronomy, Rembrandt and Miguel de Cervantes, author of Don Quixote.

DATESHARE

Linda Evans, TV actress, Dynasty. **Louis Daguerre**, French photographic inventor, daguerrotype. **Ignace Paderewski**, Polish pianist, then president. **George Gallup**, public opinion analyst. **Johnny Mercer**, lyricist, singer. **Don Cherry**, jazz trumpeter.

Beauty is in the eye of the beholder.

A marvellous nova such as November 19 flares with conspicuous brilliance, but unless it conserves its energies may be here today and gone tomorrow. Fortunately, soundly sensible Scorpio has a naturally conserving nature and most understand early their inclination to fatigue and take steps to remedy it. It's important for all November people to watch their health. Naturally strong, with enormous powers of concentration, November 19 can work all night, then be at his desk again by 9am, apparently sparkling.

But not every day. And the short term remedies of alcohol and caffeine will simply further exhaust them. Both sexes suffer from a kind of adrenaline withdrawal hangover. One simple remedy is a good night's sleep, a tremendous curative as every parent who has nursed a sick child knows. The next morning the world is washed in an optimistic light and the brain is fresh and sharp again.

Another is not to put so much into work that there is little private life left outside. Remember that many bosses aren't grateful for sacrifice and in today's rough employment climate, may not even notice. What does stand you in good stead is being fresh enough to give a contribution that is desired.

Burning the candle at both ends is another Scorpio temptation, because they are sensuous beasts and also never feel tired at the actual time. So although November 19 is almost never happier than when at a good party, try not to go more than once a week during working hours and preferably keep party-going to weekends.

Talking of parties, Scorpio gives a great one. Preferably with a mate as co-host. They're not happy hosting alone. Less interested in the decorations than other signs, what this individual does is plan the party list to include people who get on together or who seem likely to when they meet. They work hard at introductions making sure that everybody mixes, nobody feels left out and all are happy.

What little sense I once possessed Has quite gone out of my head.

(Edward Lear)

20 NOVEMBER

This kind little asteroid which orbits not far from Mars has a two-tone character. It will pull all the stops out to help another and if anybody is sick or in need, then November 20 will be there toiling in the house to keep it sweet, placing flowers on tables and cups of tea at the elbow. Cross November 20, however, and there can be an appalling row. Over-influenced by Mars, this person must be discouraged from going into battle quite so much over trifling things, because it's a waste of time and that vital quality Scorpio sometimes lacks, energy.

As neighbours they become incensed by too-tall trees, walls that need mending and noisy cars. Then storming Scorpio quite loses his Pluto sense of balance and starts to write notes, make phone calls and complaints to everybody's general discomfort. No quarrels should ever be instituted in the place where you live and November 20 must be discouraged by partners, relatives and friends.

They adore running things and can be found on committees working generously, if cholerically, with their time. Most people put up with it because of the good they do, murmuring darkly about barks being worse than bites. Partners rarely suffer from this creature's temper. While November 20 rages at work, he or she goes home a pussycat to make the spouse a cup of tea and sort the washing. Nor will children and elderly relatives suffer unkindness.

November 20 should watch their driving, shopping and their relationship with doctors. Many drive too fast, muttering and shouting. This results in rows, usually on the way to a do. In supermarkets, they're prey to trolley rage, using their vehicle to ram the ankles of those who linger too long over the ice cream cabinet. And they are convinced they know more than the doctor, especially if the white-coated one is either a different sex or younger. Exercise is a great calmer for November people and should be taken regularly.

Unfortunately, sometimes people don't hear you until you scream.

BODY

This asteroid suffers from haemorrhoids. Always check with your GP. Then you may try this traditionally soothing aromatherapy recipe. Add 10 drops of lavender oil to a large enough bowl to sit in, or to 2 inches of warm water in the bath. Mix thoroughly and sit for 10 minutes or so. Or you can try treating piles with 10 drops of cypress oil to a bath, known to soothe some cases in just days. Lavender water may be taken to work or while travelling, and a pad of cotton wool moistened with this lotion may be used during each visit to the bathroom.

MIND

A Mars day is 24.6 hours long and its maximum temperature is 80°F on the equator at noon. It is the most likely planet to bear life, with a sparse atmosphere of carbon dioxide and traces of water.

DATESHARE

Nadine Gordimer, South African writer, Nobel Prize-winner. **Robert Kennedy**, attorney general, brother of President Kennedy, assassinated. **Sir Samuel Cunard**, Canadian-born shipping line founder. **Maiya Plisetskaya**, Russian ballet dancer. **Alistair Cooke**, British journalist. **Bo Derek**, film star. **Barbara Hendricks**, opera singer. **Kon Ichikawa**, Japanese film director, The Burmese Harp.

November 21 never gets mean at Christmas or any other festival. Never moans about the buying and eating and doesn't ruin anybody's good time, either at work by making people stay long hours, or at home by making people do what they don't want to. They serve as many drinks as people can healthily cram into themselves – unless they are driving – and don't recycle presents to elderly relatives. They remember that Christmas celebrates Jesus Christ, give to charity, remember those who are unhappy at this time, give thanks in church for the passing year and pray for another good year to come.

MIND

Little baskets, sprayed gold (or not) and crammed with sweets, make adorable presents for small children and pretty tree decorations, hanging among the fir branches. Tie the handles with small pieces of tinsel or thin ribbon.

DATESHARE

Goldie Hawn, *film star, comedian.* **Marilyn French**, *author,* The Women's Room. **Mariel Hemingway**, *film actress, model.* **Tina Brown**, *British editor* Vanity Fair, New Yorker. **Oliver Goldsmith**, *poet, historian, writer,* The Vicar of Wakefield. **François Voltaire**, *French philosopher, poet, writer,* Candide. **René Magritte**, *Belgian surrealist painter.*

NOVEMBER 21

This is one of the entertainers of the zodiac. Devoted November 21 ought to work in a profession which involves pleasing people, because whatever he or she does, neither sex can help making things good for other people. There's an extraordinary generosity in their spirit and it never ceases to amaze other less-generously endowed creatures. Yet this person is nobody's fool.

They don't show their cleverness, however, and others have to try hard to discover it. There's a certain amount of playing the fool, both at work and outside it, which makes the solid brain belonging to this creature even harder to discover. Maybe it's shyness, which November 21 suffers from. Or maybe the misplaced modesty this creature entertains with such devotion, failing to understand that if you resolutely don't show your talent, refuse to display your capacities, then others will think you haven't got any.

Naturally, this makes it hard to gain promotion and there's a deep streak in this psychology of not wanting responsibility for someone else's business problems which may also be the cause. It's best for some of these people to start their own business, or become freelance, to get round this feeling. Then, because they benefit from their every action, November 21 shines, makes money and feels good about him or herself.

At Christmas or any other family occasion, they push the boat out. There'll be glittering tinsel, balloons and the soft glow of Christmas tree lights on silver and gold material twisted across the mantlepiece and under the Christmas presents. Rudolph the Red Nosed Reindeer always visits November 21's children, even in adulthood, and usually grown ups and grandma too. He knows what to bring the children because they've all either posted their letters to Father Christmas or sent them up the chimney, which is often a more efficient way of getting a letter to the Saint who cares for all the world's children.

Happiness is not a state to arrive at, but a manner of travelling.

(*Margaret Lee Runbeck*)

22 NOVEMBER

November 22 is long-lived. Good fortune frequently comes late in life. Right from the start this luscious autumn blooming Michaelmas Daisy is busy establishing its roots in all aspects of life. Charming, decorative Mr and Ms Michaelmas D has singular determination and usually gets what it wants. And what it wants is appreciation, an acknowledged place in society and as big a patch, nay the whole garden, as it can manage.

Terrific property speculators, they buy and sell luckily, end up owning their own place and with luck a few other places, maybe even abroad. Ancient European cultures appeal to these fine minds and you usually find November people favouring Spain, Italy or Portugal for a summer home. It's not the sun they go for, with their pale skins the sun can be a problem, but the healthy, relaxed way of life and idea of a two cultures outlook. (Proud November 22 speaks the language of his adopted country.)

November people aren't flirtatious flitters, at least not once they've settled down with their desired partner. They want lots of children, quickly establishing a colony. If not they adopt or foster, working wonders with needy children.

Before all this happens, some choose a period of isolation while

they slave to achieve money and goals, because they have no intention of missing out on family life later by sacrificing themselves to the office. Watch them at work. The Michaelmas Daisy is invasive and will undermine most plants, except for the great sturdy many-thorned modern rose, probably the chairman in this case. And the tough, perfumed buddleia who attracts every species of butterfly, in this case the chief accountant. Every other flower had better watch out or November 22 will have their patch for his own.

Should such behaviour bring about their own vigorous weeding, this creature is undeterred and will spring back again just as vigorously in another place, or even the same place.

I like the way you laugh
The way your body touches mine.
(David Cherub)

BODY

November 22 likes sex so much they can be a bit of a sex bore. Are You A Sex Bore? 1: Are you clever with sexual innuendos? 2: Do you think you have a right to sex? 3: Not having it makes you ill? 4: 'No' means 'Yes'? 5: There's something wrong with partnerless people. 6: Do you think having a baby on the way means you're sexier than those who don't? 7: Tell everyone about your conquests? 8: Always turn a kiss into an invitation? Answer 'yes' to all of these and you're a sex bore. Pick a friend, answer for them. See who agrees.

MIND

Lucky stones for November include the charming rose quartz, which arouses awareness to the beauty of nature, inspires creativeness, absorbs harmful vibrations, enlivens and stimulates mental ability and hastens recovery from illness.

DATESHARE

Died: **Mae West**, 'Come up and see me sometime', movie queen. Born: **George Eliot**, British novelist, author Middlemarch, Mill on the Floss, born Mary Ann Evans, assumed male name in order to be taken seriously. **Billie Jean King**, world champion tennis player. **Boris Becker**, world champion tennis player. **Jamie Lee Curtis**, film star, daughter of Tony. **Sir Peter Hall**, British theatre, film and opera director. **Benjamin Britten**, British composer, conductor. **Charles de Gaulle**, French general, president during World War II, symbol of French Resistance.

NOVEMBER 23

They are like those delicate spiders' webs which glitter with dew in the early morning and make dawn fields look as if hundreds of tiny stars have fallen overnight. Put out your hand to catch them and everything is gone but a damp patch and a nasty bit of mush. November 23 can spin the most radiant stories. They have breathtaking plans, iridescent charm, but often it all comes to nothing but, well, just a damp patch and a nastyish leftover.

In early life this addiction to bullshit is often convincing. But as November 23 ages, companions who've heard it all before head for the door. The odd thing is, this perfectly clever creature never really grasps that others have sussed him. Or maybe she prefers to live in dreams.

They are kind and loving. But these can be dangerous people, only really happy living in a fantasy and only really happy with others who go along with it. It's particularly problematical for children who do go along with dreams and blame all other adults for upsetting Darling November 23 by not taking him seriously.

Nevertheless, this individual does hit lucky patches. If they can consolidate this luck – and many can – then November 23 makes a deal of money, which is important to all November people. Someone else should be in charge of their money. That way they can be helped to hang on to it and not throw it all away on another possibly hopeless wheeze.

Both sexes are laden with charm and sex appeal practically comes out of their ears. Many may find themselves attached to older (in spirit at least) and richer partners, which is ideal, for then the wildness of their impracticality hardly matters and the glowing nature of their dreams adds an extra dimension. Nearly all November 23 people have an eye for excellence and can amaze everybody by spotting rarities in piles of dross on market stalls.

A little inaccuracy saves a world of explanation.

(C E Ayres)

FIRE

24 NOVEMBER

This child of November should try not to work so hard. While other stars come out at night to have a good twinkle, November 24 stays on in the office, hiding her light behind a computer. Bosses may adore her, but she should remember that this puritan work ethic narrows your life eventually until there's little you can either think about or talk about except the job. A bore for others.

Loyal November 24 gets put upon. Others leave her to finish their projects while they slip down to the wine bar. Then they take the credit, flashing around the office boasting about their brilliance.

Lighten up November 24. Take time off. Go get a new hairdo and have your teeth done before you have left the last time you saw a dentist so far behind that one day you wake up with an abscess, or worse, with all your teeth falling out of your head.

Away from work, both sexes get into a routine too easily and miss so much excitement because they are too careful, actually too lazy and set in their ways to try new ideas. November's child has a lurking sense of time passing, yet always seems to be at the mercy of time rather than the other way round. House-proud women should try just leaving a little mess around. No visitor ever really enters and assesses the dust quotient and if they do, why should

you care? Break your house-cleaning routine, put on a pair of glamorous shoes and some bright red lipstick and go out on the town.

Where children are concerned, November 24 makes an excellent if too attentive parent. And sometimes when grown up children want to leave, the gap they then leave may break November 24's heart. This is sad for many star signs, but November 24 is particularly fond of travel and if they take the new, now childfree opportunity to up and off, they may find new happiness.

I'm tired of saying 'How wonderful you are!' to fool men who haven't got one half the sense I've got.

(Margaret Mitchell)

BODY

Routine gets November 24 down to such an extent that they may not feel like facing another Monday morning. Energy is undermined by a one sided demands and a feeling that somehow nobody else will do what has to be done. The answer lies not in others' greater efficiency or willingness, but a change in oneself. Try the Bach Flower remedy, Hornbeam (Carpinus betulus), designed by Dr Edward Bach for this condition. After Hornbeam, many report clear minds, an instant attraction to variety, pleasure in breaking routine, spontaneity and confidence that one will be able to master tasks even if they appear too burdensome.

MIND

Weekends are a special time for hardworking 24. They want them to be spectacular and look forward to them. Wear lucky weekend colours, ie for Sunday, traditionally orange through to rust and for Saturday, mid- to dark-blue.

DATESHARE

*Died: **George Raft**, movie star specialising in gangster roles, famous for spats. Born: **Frances Hodgson Burnett**, British children's writer, The Secret Garden. **Laurence Stern**, British novelist Tristram Shandy. **Henri Toulouse Lautrec**, French painter, low life savourer, crippled. **John Knox**, Scottish religious reformer. **Baruch Spinoza**, Dutch philosopher. **Scott Joplin**, ragtime composer, pianist. **Geraldine Fitzgerald**, film actress.*

November 25 people like always to be making something beautiful – for nothing. Try this Golden Bay Leaf Wreath ideal for Christmas, or any other winter party. Maximum impact for minimum effect. Make a twig wreath base with florist's wire. Pick several handfuls of bay leaves – other leaves in pretty shapes with a similar firmness will also do. Glue the bay leaves onto the twig base with the leaves all pointing in the same direction. When wreath is covered, spray with gold paint. You can attach gold sprayed pine cones or acorns to the wreath with wire and tie on bright ribbon.

MIND

Sometimes November 25 is so resourceful and creative that other less gifted souls resort to envious mockery and criticism. It's worth remembering that anyone can criticise, but few can create what they mock.

DATESHARE

Died: **Gerard Philippe**, *Parisian screen heart-throb.* *Born:* **Tina Turner**, *singer, entertainer, film star, icon.* **Wilhelm Kempff**, *German pianist, composer.* **Cathryn Grant Crosby**, *film star, TV actress.* **Karl Friedrich Benz**, *German 19th century automobile inventor.* **Augusto Pinochet**, *Chilean dictator, overthrew Allende.* **Joe DiMaggio**, *baseball player, American sporting star, married Marilyn Monroe, places flowers on her grave each week.* **Paul Desmond**, *jazz composer.*

NOVEMBER 25

This lovely supernova takes pleasure in other's happiness and pleasure in its own brilliant capacity to provide it.

November 25 is unusual, so creative it's not true and had really better be employed in some area where both sexes make clothes, do hair, decorate houses, manage travel or give parties. As children many of them feel a little out of it because they don't really want to be a doctor or a lawyer, or work at the till in Sainsbury's or the local bank.

They want to paint everything red and have a good time. Excellent cooks, they will theme a party on a colour, or cook one nation's food, making Japanese evenings, or African evenings. Christmas, Easter, birthdays and summer dos are their ideal, with everybody roped in to help and having as good a time with the preparation as the final enjoyment.

You want a new hat? Let November 25 make it for you, costing nothing and looking better than anything bought. A wedding dress? Let them design something so silken, flattering and delicious you'll be the most scrumulicious bride ever.

It's important to remember that both sexes have this talent, and although some areas may be less conventionally acceptable for the men than the women, it's a pity that kind of judgement stops male November 25 from expressing such talent.

Most of these individuals also have a talent for flirtation, which leads them up all sorts of exciting forbidden alleys. They like to marry and they also like to propose marriage. And they also like to have sex, without which many go into a sad decline.

While children are important to this creature, many of those who have none will not grieve overmuch, as it frees them up to indulge in a genuine passion for travel of the most dedicated kind. Two weeks in Menorca is not their idea of travel. More six months in Kenya – many November people are particularly attracted to Africa.

Happiness is a way-station between too little and too much.

(Channing Pollock)

26 NOVEMBER

This is one of the nicest and luckiest people of the year. November 26 was born with a silver horseshoe in his mouth. Then the kind fairies dolloped on both sexes good looks, creative talent, intellect and leadership. Just one thing they forgot: judgement of others. Because November 26 is so well-meaning they judge all others to be so.

Most of these creatures want to earn their money by bringing some good to the world, so find them in teaching, medicine, the police force, social work and any other of the caring professions. Shiningly honest, this creature's silver horseshoe takes them right to the top, where they wipe out old practices, in particular empire building which November 26 has no time for at all. Anybody who likes to run a clique anywhere near November 26 had better watch out. This individual regards cliques as the dumping ground for failed and difficult people and will wipe them out.

Expect them to consult others before reorganising, run everything with a fair hand and stamp on the very first whiff of bullying. Expect them also to be visionaries, in many cases achieving an ambitious goal which can sometimes change history. Some will achieve fame this way, others local fame. Both sexes adore being well-known. They like the doors that open for them and the privileges, but never abuse them.

Unlike many who rise in the world, November 26 never forgets old friends or relatives. There will be new friends. Most of these individuals retain the capacity to make new friends well into old age and this is a very long-lived date.

For many there may also be a late romance or late marriage and children born in late middle age. November people are not fantastically faithful and always keep an eye open for new attractions, new sexual possibilities. Naturally this leads in later years to complicated relationships and lives, which November 26 rather savours, although others near them may be hurt.

Conversation means being able to disagree and still continue the conversation.

(Dwight MacDonald)

BODY
November 26 is fantastically sensuous and adores food, so one of the sexiest experiences is to combine the two. Shop bought ice creams get boring. November 26 is a Crème Chantilly person and here's recipe for Chantilly Sex. Beat 290ml double cream until thick, then fold in stiffly beaten egg white with 25g icing sugar and a few drops of vanilla essence. This should be stroked along the thighs of November 26 (they're that sort of date) and then licked off.

☾

MIND
Massage reaches to the very heart, creating sensuous moments to share. It also makes you clear-headed, light-hearted, laughter comes easily and the mind is suffused with a sense of well-being. Use a citrus essential oil in an almond oil carrier.

DATESHARE
Died: **Rachel Roberts**, *American screen star. Born:* **Cyril Cusack**, *Irish poet, film star, stage actor.* **Bruno Hauptman**, *kidnapper, killer of Lindberg baby.* **Charles Schulz**, *cartoonist creator of Charlie Brown and Snoopy.* **William Pitt** *the Elder, statesman.* **Eugene Ionesco**, *Romanian playwright.* **Samuel Reshevsky**, *chess grandmaster.* **Rich Little**, *impersonator, comedian.* **George Segal**, *sculptor.* **Earl Wild**, *pianist.*

November 27 loves to eat – and cook. Here's the ideal 27 recipe, something gorgeous to pick at, which always keeps this creature happy. Raspberries In Chocolate Cups. Take 225g raspberries, 150ml double cream, 25g icing sugar, 175g plain chocolate, 15g lard. Heat chocolate with lard until smooth, stirring occasionally. Put out paper cases, hold at angle, drizzle half mixture until inside is thinly coated. Chill for 30 minutes until set. Repeat with remaining cases until thickly set. Gently peel cases, stand on chilled serving dish. Mix raspberries, cream and sugar and fill cases. Chill.

MIND

Lucky days for November 27 include 3, 5, 7, 9, 14 and 22. On these days sufferers from sorrow or trouble will feel a little spiritually lighter, profitable plans are set in motion, and people fall in love with the right person.

DATESHARE

Died: **John Carradine**, *American screen star. Born:* **Jimi Hendrix**, *rock, blues guitar, singer, writer, lover, icon. Died aged 28.* **Bruce Lee**, *Chinese martial arts film star, icon, died mysteriously at 32.* **Anders Celsius**, *Swedish astronomer, inventor of temperature scale.* **Giovanna Fontana**, *Italian fashion designer.* **Caroline Kennedy**, *daughter of President Kennedy and Jackie Kennedy.* **Alexander Dubcek**, *Czechoslovakian president, perestroika innovator, great political icon.*

NOVEMBER 27

November 27's love for food and sensuous indulgence can get both sexes into trouble. Especially when you combine it with their perennial lack of judgement. This is the girl who gets taken out to dinner and eats everything from everybody else's plate. Unsuspecting companions visit the loo and return to find the prawns in their cocktail and the strawberries in their tart depleted. At cricket matches they'll eat half a friend's hot dog when there's a particularly good six batted and probably finish off the can of coke.

They are the Goldilocks of the firmament, stars who come out to nibble the Milky Way, pinch a bit of the Great Bear's porridge and gobble up the whole bowl which belongs to the Great Bear's pup. Apart from this food nicking tendency, November 27 is a delight, but this aspect can be irritating and could mean both sexes have to cut and run, just as Goldilocks did when she jumped out of the Three Bears' window and scuttled off into the woods.

At work, this individual is often inspired, staying late at night if necessary and wrapping up deals with great dexterity. (Don't leave a box of chocolates on your desk when November 27 is staying late or they'll all be gone in the morning.) Fortunately this individual is extremely sociable and doesn't make a song and dance about staying late if it's not necessary.

They make loving parents, although toddlers should gollop down their sausage and chips before ever-loving and expanding

mum starts picking just a chip or four and maybe half a sausage or the whole one. No November 27 parent gets irate about school work and their children are not driven to over-study or over-achieve. While this mother or father wants the best for their child, and they are sticklers for thoughtfulness towards others, they won't push children to achieve. Certainly not so that their excellence will reflect well on November 27 as a parent.

A foodie and his money
~
are soon parted.

28 NOVEMBER

This golden eagle in gold lamé is impressive, popular and probably going to be a millionaire. But he always overdoes it and goes on doing so all his (and her) life. Unlike so many others born around this date our noble bird may be stylish in action, but at rest and socially he has no sense of style. Like the wonderful conductor Sir Simon Rattle, November 28 people are exquisite on the podium, but socially they can wear the most embarrassing clothes.

People born today are often entertainers, in particular musicians, so their odd sartorial habits don't matter. Most November 28s are extremely creative, both professionally and privately and are to be found in country towns beavering away bringing pleasure to neighbours and friends. Some reap wealth and fame, when you can spot them coming in and out of airports wearing spangly shoes and imitation leopard-skin bowler hats. If they do, expect flash cars with, you've guessed it, imitation leopard-skin interior covers, baths with gold taps and ornate beds dressed in shiny satin-look black.

November 28s with slightly less creativity flourish well in conventional offices because bureaucracy has no fears. If you have to sign sixty forms in triplicate, they will do it without moaning. Just a few well placed jokes. At seminar weekends, however, watch out for the casual clothing, massive twinkly brooches for women, bright yellow v-necked sweaters for the men.

Such sartorial unconventionality goes deeper than clothes. Their unusual eye helps spot windows in the market, another way to make their millions. This is the guy who launches a fashion wellington boot with a small heel in all colours, with frogs' eyes on the toes just like the ones four-year-olds wear. The woman who opens an antique shop specialising in psychedelic  clothes and furnishings and creams the market. They live to a great age to enjoy the proceeds of their imagination, probably marry more than once and have several children.

~

Fine feathers make fine birds!

BODY
Careful diet (and money) keeps November 28 sexy until a great age. Long-lived races eat fresh food and November 28 should take a leaf from their book. Uncooked foods transport oxygen and oppose putrefaction. They are vitalised with living enzymes to aid digestion. Cooked starch, refined sugar and animal proteins tend to ferment. Many fast foods use animal fat or cooking oil that has been heated to a high temperature and kept there. The oil is often black and the same oil is frequently used day in and day out, so obviously it's not as good for the body as a quick, fresh green salad.

☾

MIND
Calm is vital to this date and classical music helps bring it. Most health experts now know that classical music balances mind and body. Works in B flat major and A minor suit Sagittarius best.

DATESHARE
Died: **Rosalind Russell**, *Hollywood sex goddess. Born:* **Alexander Godunov**, *Russian ballet dancer, film star.* **Anton Rubinstein**, *Russian pianist.* **Randy Newman**, *satirical songwriter, singer, film composer.* **Paul Shaffer**, *bandleader, keyboard player, personality on* David Letterman *Show.* **Nancy Mitford**, *writer,* Love in a Cold Climate. **Claude Levi-Strauss**, *French structuralist.* **Alberto Moravia**, *author.* **Rita Mae Brown**, *feminist, TV actress.* **Friedrich Engels**, *German communist movement founder, co-writer of* Das Kapital.

*When it comes to love,
November 29 sometimes loses
the thread. It's sometimes a
Sagittarius characteristic to be
more desired than desiring, but
that's no reason to get bored
half-way through. These
theatrical people should set the
stage for love in their own
bedrooms, decorated in
brownish-pinkey tones with a
dash of orange, Sagittarian
colours which also directly relate
to traditionally appropriate
shades for sex. Put the mobile
telephone next door. Lack of
sexual concentration plagues
this person, who can't resist
finding out who's ringing at the
most awkward moments. And
remember that a consistent
rhythm during lovemaking
usually banishes the blues.*

MIND

*Before going to bed, chant
'Matthew, Mark, Luke and John
Bless the bed that I lie on'
which traditionally keeps away
evil spirits and ensures good
health. Naturally, avoid this
when sliding seductively under
the cover to join a lover.*

DATESHARE

Died: **Natalie Wood**, *screen
beauty in mystery drowning
accident.* **Cary Grant**, *screen
star, handsome devil.* Born: **C S
Lewis**, *poet, author, critic,
children's writer, the Narnia
books.* **Jacques Chirac**, *French
president.* **Monsignor
Lefebvre**, *Roman Catholic
traditionalist.* **Busby Berkeley**,
*Hollywood director,
choreographer.* **Gaetano
Donizetti**, *Italian opera
composer.* **Petra Kelly**,
*beautiful, dangerous German
Green Party leader.*

NOVEMBER 29

Many November 29 people have a powerful innovative streak, which combined with good looks can be devastating. Yet there's something of the space bully about this date which must be watched. Fortunately most men and women sail along, successfully hunting fame and fortune in their golden armour, remarkable for their honourable, often religious intentions, rather than the disquiet this sign can sometimes bring.

It's an extremely good-looking date, usually tall with long limbs and flowing red-gold hair, a glittering catch for other less glamorous stars. And they age well, still velvety with sex appeal at seventy or eighty years old. Sagittarians such as this rarely get caught in today's ageist job market trap, because they look so good and seem to retain a noble wisdom which others admire and need. But if they do find themselves without regular employment – they are particularly good in the money business – finding freelance work is no problem.

The powerful unconventional side which makes them able to cut through paperwork and devise time-saving schemes has a gentler side which is extremely attractive. Both sexes can tell original stories to children and adults so well that if they write them down, they may well get published and establish a brilliant career. This is also the person, however, who can invent the shower which easily adjusts to the right water temperature, rather than too hot or too cold.

Idealism makes them easily led. The women may get swept away by political correctness and the men have a persecuting zeal for fairness, which makes them quarrelsome, especially in local affairs and politics. Those who don't completely agree may be treated as the enemy. The power of their conviction sometimes leads them not only into bad judgement about others who disagree, but also about those who apparently do agree. November 29 can't easily spot the ill-bringers of the universe and may trust someone whose over-frequent smile hides a black heart.

*Things are more like they are now
than they have ever been.*

(President Gerald Ford)

30 NOVEMBER

November 30's head is so far in the remotest galaxies that many of them have a problem with re-entry into the earth's atmosphere. Sagittarians are not noted for their dreaminess, being more practical. But not this gossamer projectile. Others try to catch them, hang on to them, but especially in youth, November 30 just shimmers away to dazzle somewhere else,

slightly unaware of the effect they have on others. Which is sometimes problematical, because this individual leaves a trail of broken hearts.

Some feel that November 30's unawareness of their effect is deliberately studied and that this ball of fire knows it scorches but doesn't much care. Certainly November 30 is fairly promiscuous, either physically or mentally, likes to devastate with charm, then walk away and then ask with shocked innocence, 'What did I do?' And certainly November 30 will be the first to insist that someone they have hurt is completely unhurt, when their victim is actually using friends as a life-support machine.

Whatever the rights and wrongs, in youth, you can't pin this creature down. Both sexes will simply smile dreamily and turn away to another interest. This doesn't apply in their chosen profession of course, quite often one allied to money or advertising. Fuelled by customary Jupiteronian ambition, they are not so vague when it comes to self-interest.

Many are excellent sportsmen and women. The hunter in them makes them run like a shooting meteorite and they play ball games as if their feet were shod with Mercury's wings.

This date seems to have all the talents. And yet, with many there is an underlying sadness, a feeling of time passing and the need to search for an explanation for their life, or even a justification. This usually takes them on restless travels, sometimes long sea journeys and more regularly on long walks over hills and fields where they find comfort and some calm in Nature.

Somewhere on this globe, every ten seconds, there is a woman giving birth to a child. She must be found and stopped.

(Sam Levenson)

BODY

November 30 delights in pregnancy. Women feel touched with grace and disappear into dreams of the child to come. They should resist giving up work because their sense of disconnection could turn into isolation. Aromatherapy can help overcome November 30's quite bad nausea and fatigue, the latter being difficult to get rid of when the pregnancy is over. Essential oils are quickly absorbed by the skin because of their small molecular structure, then quickly absorbed into the blood stream, travelling though the whole body via the blood vessel network. Use only citrus oils, geranium, lavender, neroli, patchouli, sandalwood, rose and rosewood.

MIND

This person is always being given presents by admirers. Furs, jewellery and yachts from those who come courting, but these should be returned by both sexes when one doesn't know the giver well, etiquette experts insist. You can keep the knitted toilet-seat cover.

DATESHARE

Winston Churchill, British prime minister during World War II, writer, painter, bon viveur, Nobel Prize-winner. **Billy Idol**, singer, songwriter. **June Pointer**, Pointer Sisters. **Virginia Mayo**, film star. **Jonathan Swift**, satirical writer and political commentator, poet, Gulliver's Travels. **David Mamet**, playwright, screenwriter, director. **Gordon Liddy**, Watergate conspirator. **Andrea Palladio**, Italian neo-classical architect. **Terence Malick**, film director, Badlands.

ecember 1 has a major Cinderella Complex, but don't for a moment think this is one of the servile human phobias. It has more to do with massively erotosensitive feet, a passion for exotic shoes and flagrant unpunctuality which often works to their benefit. Unfairly. Both sexes make others wait for meetings, personal and work, but when they do happen, they're usually so momentous that December 1 benefits greatly. In effect, they make an occasion out of anything, frequently benefiting by breaking all the rules, particularly those laid down by fairy godmothers. And they are so flamboyantly physically attractive that any residual resentment is overcome.

Take no notice of the office junior who constantly complains that the boss is making her or him do all the work, generally putting them down, and trying to block their talents. The manipulative little devil simply has it in for the immediate boss, wants to win sympathy and get as many colleagues as possible to give them a leg up. Very soon, that boss will have been heaved out for mistreating Ms or Mr Cinders, who will now occupy their job.

Very soon Ms and Mr Manipulator will be the overall boss, may have married the chairman's son or daughter and they'll have a large company car which won't be turning into a pumpkin. While some people born on this date do have a kind heart, it has to be said that the majority don't particularly connect with most of the

human race, with the exception of their spouse (possibly, but often only while this person is more attractive, rich and useful than the next partner coming along) and their children.

Unfortunately, even with children, Cinderella Complex women rarely put their manipulative instincts aside and will always try to get sons and daughters to do something for them, in some way take care of them, as if they were the child and the child the parent.

Beauty is only sin deep.

2 December

They are like Ariel in Shakespeare's *The Tempest*, creatures of the air whose natural element is freedom and flight, yet who are somehow trapped. December 2 is one of the most joyful of Jupiteronomous sky dancers. Iced with star-glitter sugar this creature casters doubt on his or her abilities and always feels burdened, even if there's hardly a responsibility there. If there truly is none, most December 2s will fabricate one.

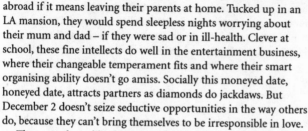

They have a greater innate sense of responsibility than most sky babes. Neither sex will be happy to take off and live abroad if it means leaving their parents at home. Tucked up in an LA mansion, they would spend sleepless nights worrying about their mum and dad – if they were sad or in ill-health. Clever at school, these fine intellects do well in the entertainment business, where their changeable temperament fits and where their smart organising ability doesn't go amiss. Socially this moneyed date, honeyed date, attracts partners as diamonds do jackdaws. But December 2 doesn't seize seductive opportunities in the way others do, because they can't bring themselves to be irresponsible in love.

They may dance like the Devil, who was after all God's chief angel, but all the while they'll be wondering if they ask their dance partner back for the night, whether they'll be lumbered. Both sexes are likely to marry more than once, only settling down in later life. Many will be burdened by too many children as a single parent. Sooner or later a partner turns up to help, but meanwhile this individual does her brave best.

In the end there's not a lot December 2 can do about invisible shackles which stop him from soaring towards the horizon. It's emotional ties, not money or work, that hold you, and it's possible to be free only if you want to be. In truth, if December 2 didn't feel trapped, he'd be lonely. And loneliness is something they greatly fear.

> ### 'Marx spots the -ex.'
> (Groucho Marx, on entering a restaurant where a previous wife was present)

BODY

Music is essential to this star sign's well-being. It helps clear the mind to concentrate on realities rather than muddled fantasies. December 2 should listen to music regularly, especially if involved in creative writing, logical work, or if suffering from stress, headaches or anger. Medical experts say that listening to music regularly enhances creativity and language skills. It also sharpens memory, some mathematical calculations, improves physical reflexes, certainly reduces blood pressure and in some cases regulates heartbeat. Studies also show that intensive listening to Mozart appears to raise the IQ, and in Germany the composer's work is being used in hospital pain-relief clinics as a substitute for drugs.

MIND

Long fingers denote a critical and analytical mind, not easily swayed by impulse or moved to do things in a hurry. Short fingers are in general a sign of a more impetuous nature.

DATESHARE

Sir John Barbirolli, British conductor, Hallé Orchestra. **Maria Callas**, great opera diva, love affair with Aristotle Onassis. **Monica Seles**, naturalised American tennis champion. **Julie Harris**, stage and film actress. **Otto Dix**, German post-expressionist painter. **Roberto Capucci**, Italian fashion designer. **Nikos Kazantzakis**, Greek novelist, Zorba the Greek. **Georges Seurat**, French painter, pointilliste.

DECEMBER 3

December 3 has good hair, infrequently lost in either sex. Keep it shining and healthy with a steady supply of protein and minerals. The B complex vitamins, notably pantothenic acid and vitamin B12, together with zinc and selenium are important for hair growth and preventing hair loss. Pantothenic acid in the form of panthenol is often added to shampoos to encourage shiny, manageable hair. Dog breeders often give their pets cod liver oil for glossy coats – and this can do the same for humans. Increase levels of essential fatty acids in the diet. Vegetable oils in cooking promote healthy hair.

MIND

In Tarot, the third card in the Major Arcana is The Empress. This indicates the mentor, the nurturer. There are the balanced qualities here, including love for family and loyalty. Beware vanity and a conviction that others are stupid and less gifted.

DATESHARE

Ozzie Osbourne, heavy metal singer, Black Sabbath. **Zlata Flipovic**, Bosnian child writer, Zlata's Diary, A Child's Life In Sarajevo. **Katarina Witt**, East German very beautiful figure skater, world champion, Olympic gold medallist. **Joseph Conrad**, Polish-born British novelist, Heart of Darkness. **Jean-Luc Godard**, French film director. **Anna Freud**, psychoanalyst, Sigmund's daughter. **Anton Webern**, Australian 20th century composer.

December 3 is an extrovert airhead who really doesn't know the meaning of the word 'depression', and most mornings wakes up feeling good, his first thought being breakfast. That's not to say that December 3 is unaware of the evils of the world. It's just that the good outweighs them. You can probably catch either sex in the bathroom singing their favourite song, 'Always look on the bright side of life, te tum, te tum, te tum.'

This is one of the mentor dates in the year. Both sexes take younger people under their skylark's wing. Some are swept along by a spurt of powerful ambition to realise their talents in early life, particularly in the academic field, anywhere to do with research and the area of computer and high-tech development. Both sexes have a facility for computers, the women as innovative as the men. But unless they reach a position of influence quickly, December 3 may wallow in the shallows of power rather than reaching the beach unless he is given a push by a senior hand.

Whether it's as boss, owner, or manager, December 3 has a particular dignity which goes with intelligent lack of neurosis and the kind of generosity that comes with a talented and enviably envy-free Jupiterite. In youth you won't find them griping about the older generation. In age, they don't bemoan young people's spelling, manners, pop music, morals, taste in clothes and all that jabberwocky which middle-aged and elderly people have gone on about since Adam and Eve acquired the first middle-aged spreads.

In private both the men and women find pleasure in simple things. They like cooking, carpenting, gardening, singing lullabies to children, driving too fast and eating ice lollies. They also like to walk in the countryside, sometimes alone. December 3 needs regular periods of solitude, not so much to think, but not to think.

Being bald ⁓
is an unfailing sex magnet.
(Telly Savalas)

4 DECEMBER

December 4 is a bit of a bruiser. They sail the skies in a stolen vessel in search of treasure and maybe fame. Sometimes this Robin Hood star is wrapped in the golden cloak of generosity. Other times he runs up the skull and crossbones and other ships in the sea of stars should take care. Take a wide berth.

This creature is most successful as a self-made businessman or woman. Although they may rise high in companies, theirs is the kick-over-the-traces tendency. They can't see the point of an empty desk policy and they certainly can't pussyfoot about while Human Resources slow coaches hum and haw.

Ms Robin Hood is just as impatient as men who are born on this day. And prone to violent flashes of temper with maybe the odd swear word, although she never means to offend and always apologises. They just can't bear jobsworths. And they're impatient with those who drone on about how it has always been done. Give her her own set-up and she's like a fireball, rushing here and there, seeing to everything and making a success of it.

This lady very easily combines childbirth with money-making and she's a jolly mother. No fads here about not eating chocolate and not watching television. But equally  she encourages self-discipline and her kids are some of the nicest to be with. The male of the species is a less perfect parent because most of the time he's not there and when he is, he can't understand how children dare to disobey his daft, sometimes outdated rules.

Less powerful creatures born on this day may have a problem with making up their minds and can go in for irritating chops and changes, but like their stronger co-stars still won't brook much guidance or interference. There's a tendency with both sexes to be coercive with those who disagree, sometimes happy to merely shout down the opposition.

Power corrupts and absolute power corrupts absolutely.

BODY

Lavender oil is a great calmant and good for those who lose their temper because they can't get to sleep. It reigns supreme in skin conditions, particularly acne and is a super sedative and pain-killing essence. Spray on pillow or place a piece of cotton wool with four or five lavender drops on it inside the pillow case to stop insomnia. Aromatherapists use it for boils, colds, coughs, flatulence, insect bites and stings, migraine, muscular aches and pains, pre-menstrual syndrome, sinusitis and as an air freshener. Its balancing action is best suited to those suffering from hysterical states of mind or wildly fluctuating moods.

MIND

In Tarot, the 4th card of the Major Arcana is The Emperor. He brings this individual worldly brilliance, energy and at its best, balanced domination. But again there's some roughness to be controlled and dangerous violence just below the surface.

December 5 needs to conserve energy and watch out for aching bones and even arthritis. Copper is useful here. Many arthritis sufferers maintain that a copper bracelet reduces aches and pains and even reduces inflammation of the joints. This may be because traces of copper dissolve through the skin and are absorbed into the bloodstream. Most supplements contain 1–3mg and a balanced diet should provide the rest.

Excess copper, however is harmful. Tap water from copper piping may produce high levels in the body, causing nausea, depression and even heart disease. Run tap water for thirty seconds before using the water to clear residual traces.

MIND

Handwriting is significant for December 5, who uses it in every creative aspect. Equal spacing between lines means mental equilibrium, little spacing indicates economy and avarice, wide spacing indicates generosity and prodigality, and unequal spacing a versatile, artistic nature.

DATESHARE

Walt Disney, *great animator, producer of Disney movies, founder of entertainment empire.* **Little Richard**, *rock and roll singer.* **Christina Rossetti**, *pre-Raphaelite poet.* **Otto Preminger**, *film director, Bonjour Tristesse.* **José Carreras**, *Spanish tenor.* **Fritz Lang**, *Austrian film director, Metropolis.* **Joan Didion**, *screenwriter, A Star Is Born.* **Phillip K Wrigley**, *chewing gum manufacturer.*

DECEMBER 5

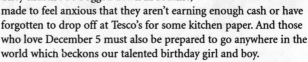

December 5 has a wild, original streak. They are exceptionally creative storytellers, musicians and general entertainers and on no account must they be discouraged. Envy is a problem for December 5 – other people's. Jealous colleagues, family and friends seek to dampen December 5's firework brilliance, pretending concern for their safety and their future and advising caution. Caution is to December 5 as water is to fire.

Those who love this passionate creature must protect and encourage. They mustn't be bogged down in routine, made to feel anxious that they aren't earning enough cash or have forgotten to drop off at Tesco's for some kitchen paper. And those who love December 5 must also be prepared to go anywhere in the world which beckons our talented birthday girl and boy.

Left to their own devices the women in particular get things done very rapidly, with absolute conviction that what they have produced will work. Sadly, in more conventional areas they fail to understand that others are not so capable and may become impatient, often failing to explain carefully. Some men may not be so directional – more tangential and by Jupiter, they can get themselves into all sorts of sticky situations as a result. Particularly financially.

Naturally many December 5s won't reach world fame, but will always be bewitching in whatever sphere they occupy. Their private lives may be complicated however. Because this person has great stamina they can exhaust all around them, especially lovers and spouses. Marriages and love affairs follow thick and fast, indeed some December 5s get a taste for change and aren't very reliable in matters of love and sex.

In particular those who like to travel may disappear abroad for years, flitting around the world, leaving a trail of ex-partners and children. And although December 5 feels great affection for all, neither sex's style is particularly attentive and those left behind should prepare themselves for long silences with the occasional telephone call.

Come back to me in dreams,
that I may give
Pulse for pulse, breath for breath.
(Christina Georgina Rossetti)

FIRE

6 DECEMBER

Sagittarians are naturally the centre of attention. They enjoy it and if they feel on the edge of things, they make sure they get back into the middle. December 6 is one of the storytellers of the universe, a star who attracts other members of the galaxy to him or her. Any member of a group which contains December 6 will be utterly charmed and full of laughter.

Their centre-stage behaviour is helped by the extreme good looks which often bless this day. Many are long-limbed, tall with magnificent hair and golden colouring. Because of their height and natural fitness, they make excellent sportsmen and women, often professionally. Brainy December 6 keeps another career in tandem, often a business with some form of product. In sport they are addicted to speed, running like the wind, swimming like a shark and throwing a cricket ball faster than the eye can see.

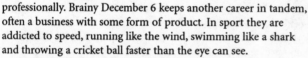

Addiction to speed is a characteristic in all things. December 6 likes to do things double-quick, and that includes jobs both at work and at home. The maxim of this person is that routine stuff should be completed extra fast so that enjoyment can begin.

This is the day of the avid collector, particularly coins which he hunts for in rivers and around ancient sites. It's not their value which attracts – many old coins aren't that valuable anyway. It's the romantic idea that a Roman once held the self same coin in her hand.

Romantic in action and thought, December 6 often searches for inspiration abroad. Africa and Asia draw them and many will stay all their lives, taking a local partner. If they return after some years, expect their home to have a foreign flavour, their cooking and also their style of present-giving. African beads rather than scented candles are their preference, and Indian silk rather than a box of chocolates.

The best pleasures of this world are not quite pure.
(*Johann Wolfgang von Goethe*)

BODY
Sensuous 6 likes to have its back stroked, is crazy about massage with perfumed oils and easily seduces other stars in the zodiac with his or her own talent for effleurage and the famous bedtime cat stroke. With effleurage, use the whole of the palm of the hand, plus the fingers for an exciting simultaneous sensation. Stroke down from centre shoulder blade, past waist to the buttocks, then over and down to thigh tops. With cat strokes, use each hand in turn, in the way that a cat sharpens its claws, perhaps adding a stirring trail or two of your fingers along a partner's body. Meeeeioow!

MIND
Many aromatic plants mimic the aroma of sexual secretions, in particular sandalwood, which contains aromatic molecules similar to those present in semen. Oil of sandalwood, claimed to be aphrodisiac, may therefore be an inspiring choice for intimate massage.

FIRE

December 7's full house needs feeding, and this day always finds a quick way to do so. Try Tomato Ice. Take 800g tomatoes, 1 small onion, sprigs of marjoram, lemon juice, salt, black pepper, 2 teaspoons sugar, lots of mint. Peel tomatoes, onion, chop roughly. Put into blender with marjoram, lemon juice, blend to purée. Season with salt, pepper, add sugar to taste. Turn into freezing container, freeze for 4 hours until solid. Remove from freezer, leave at room temperature for 15 minutes before serving. Pile crystals into individual glasses, garnish with mint and serve as soon as possible.

MIND

Sometimes heedless December 7 goes in for the slow jilt where love is concerned. They are emotionally lazy and like to let things work out for themselves, but in the case of an overeager, unwanted lover, this is cruel.

DATESHARE

Died: **Joan Bennett**, *British film star, stage actress. Born:* **Avril Chomsky**, *linguistics theorist, author,* Language and The Mind. **Richard W Sears**, *mail order merchant,* Sears-Roebuck. **Joyce Carey**, *British novelist,* The Horse's Mouth. **Ellen Burstyn**, *TV and film actress.* **Willa Cather**, *novelist,* My Antonia. **Tom Waits**, *singer, songwriter, film actor.* **Giovanni Lorenzo Bernini**, *Italian Baroque architect, sculptor.*

DECEMBER 7

December 7 loves the world for what it is, not what it ought to be and is therefore one of the most contented people of the year. They expect, and get, a great deal of happiness. And they'd like a great deal of money to follow suit. Very often this happens because December 7 is so tolerant, broad-minded and humorous that somehow the world wants to reward this naturally affectionate creature.

These people really don't seem to make much effort but always hit lucky. Others strive, December 7 merely attends, a starry magnet for all good pleasures. Both sexes love material things, but their good design eye is critical of gracelessness. Bright colours abound in private and work – they may be involved in the decorating business, or with something visual. But this is not a date which favours flash cars or tinkly chandeliers. In style they often prefer contemporary items with a 1996 feel, having little of the nostalgic longing for times past. The time present is what they prefer.

December has maxi-tolerance for others' foibles, religions and culture and zero tolerance for prejudice, which is one of the few things which can arouse this centaur to boiling rage. They will take up a cause in this area extremely effectively, but are not at all prey

to political correctness, which they find funny.

They may choose work which involves travel, speaking several languages and always fitting in to any country. Find them in the tourist industry where they delight in attending to other people's pleasure. Most December 7 women enjoy homemaking, even if they work. Natural mothers, many are likely to give birth in their forties or later and the male of the species may find himself a father at seventy.

No matter. This is a long-lived day. Their house is usually full of guests, neighbours, relatives and friends and any child born to them is in for a good time.

What kind of cat swims under water?

An octopus.

8 December

December 8 flings herself at life and success, winning hearts carelessly, then throwing them away. She takes risks, maybe drinks too much, shows off too much, a heavenly dazzler who so carelessly courts danger that she may plummet to earth in all her radiant beauty. Leaving nothing but a piece of cold stone.

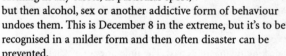

It's as if all the gifts of the gods, except balanced judgement have rained down on December 8's head. Both sexes are as bad. The men are handsome in youth, eye-catching in any career, in particular sport, but then alcohol, sex or another addictive form of behaviour undoes them. This is December 8 in the extreme, but it's to be recognised in a milder form and then often disaster can be prevented.

Teenagers born on this day are loaded with looks and talent and charm which gets them their way. They think they are immortal. But only the planet who rules their sign is immortal and Jupiter has seen men achieve greatness too fast only to fail young. Fortunately December 8 is sufficiently self-aware to understand this Achilles heel, especially if pointed out. Most are willing to take advice, be guided and so they skirt the danger, free to develop their talent without risk.

This day has tremendous vision and honourable qualities. They are sexually supercharged, trailing lovers like discarded diamond chips in their wake. Unusually lucky, they may make a fortune very fast. But even when they have their own children, they still behave like children themselves, right up to and beyond the age of ninety-nine.

Like all December people, this is a long-lived date, with a lot of luck scheduled for their old age.

> *I apologise for boasting,*
> *but once you know my qualities,*
> *I can drop back into a quite*
> *brilliant humility.*
>
> *(Christopher Fry)*

BODY

December 8 has sex-sensitive spots at the base of his or her back which are best left alone unless you can handle a riot. But they're proud of them and nearly always issue invitations to press them or stroke them and see. For women, the trigger points are about three inches above the cleavage between their buttocks, two points about two inches apart. For men there are three of these fast triggers in a vertical line just above the cleavage of their buttocks. Just rub these master points, over jeans will do, and you can be certain that 8's concentration will waver.

MIND

People who gossip unskillfully will find they get themselves talked about extremely unattractively. Confine yourself, if you must gossip, to people you don't know and aren't likely to. Otherwise it always comes back and hits you over the head.

DATESHARE

*Died: **Martin Ritt**, Hollywood screen star. Born: **Mary Queen of Scots**, beautiful royal rival of Elizabeth I, addicted to loving the wrong man, abdicated, imprisoned for sixteen years, executed. **Sinead O'Connor**, Irish singer, songwriter. **James Galway**, Irish flautist. **James Thurber**, humourist, cartoonist, The Secret Life of Walter Mitty. **Sammy Davis Jr**, singer dancer, film star, member of the Rat Pack. **David Carradine**, film star. **Kim Basinger**, film star. **Jim Morrison**, singer, songwriter, poet, The Doors, died of drug overdose. **Diego Rivera**, Mexican painter, muralist, revolutionary.*

BODY

Eating odd foods at odd hours, especially fast food, sometimes encourages cystitis, mostly a feminine complaint, but men get it too, particularly those with prostate or urethra problems. Medical help should be sought. Flush out kidneys with copious quantities of camomile tea or just plain warm water. Avoid coffee, tea and alcohol. Diet should rely on alkaline-forming fruit and vegetables. Eat quantities of yoghurt each day, about 700ml, or try acidophilus tablets (yoghurt bacteria). Aromatherapy consists of warm compresses over the lower back, massage and aromatic baths. Helpful essential oils include bergamot, camomile, cedarwood, eucalyptus, juniper, lavender, pine and sandalwood.

MIND

Tarot's Major Arcana gives this day The Hermit card. He walks with a lantern in the quiet night, meditating on the meaning of the world. He may also bring isolation, which causes December 9 unhappiness and should be avoided.

DATESHARE

John Malkovich, *stage, film actor, director.* **Beau Bridges**, *film star.* **Lee J Cobb**, *film star.* **Joan Armatrading**, *British singer.* **John Cassavetes**, *actor, director.* **John Milton**, *poet, 'Paradise Lost'.* **Kirk Douglas**, *film star, producer, stage actor.* **Dame Judi Dench**, *British TV, film, Shakespearian actress.* **Douglas Fairbanks Jnr**, *film actor.* **Elizabeth Schwarzkopf**, *German opera singer, lieder singer.*

DECEMBER 9

S ometimes December 9 just can't get out of bed. In fact you'll find many of them curled up while the midday sun tries to get in through a window and wake them. But they aren't lazy. It's just that this is an owl person. They fly at night. And if they could, and some can, they'd work at night.

The owl really gets going as the day starts to end, and in fact this is the reason why so many work late, because it's the time when they feel most alert. Nightbirds hunt their prey in the dark and it's no different for December 9 who can leave work at nine and slink into a club, making all heads turn as they walk in. In youth, many of these watchful creatures dance and flirt and then go back to work. Find them in the computer business where late hours are a must and in television or films where it's normal to work through the night. Or the police force, armed services or even politics.

Jupiter's little owlette is a nice guy or girl. They may like to eat  hamburgers at 4am but they don't in general take drugs or drink much. But anybody interested must be prepared to keep them company. If December 9 has to get to work early, he can do it. Unpunctuality is not a characteristic and some become extremely indignant if others keep them waiting for more than five minutes.

In private the owl keeps up his and her habits in later life. Both sexes will read or watch television and videos through the night, or just potter about waiting for the exquisite freshness and beauty of the dawn. Naturally they make good parents because getting up in the middle of the night comes easily.

And like the owl, who can see backwards, one invaluable characteristic of this date is their extraordinary vigilance and sensitive perception about what makes others tick.

. . . the night is thine;
And I am desolate and sick
of an old passion.

(Ernest Dowson)

10 DECEMBER

Of all the star signs, Sagittarius suffers most from Pinocchio's Nose. Neither sex can resist the temptation to fib. They start with a small one about the importance of having this or that relative. Then the lie grows and grows, just like Pinocchio's nose. And the trouble for December 10 is that he can't remember what he said in the first place. And the good thing for December 10s of both sexes is that they don't always terribly care if they're found out.

Mostly the lies are to do with love affairs, when other stars really have to be prepared to take much with a pinch of salt, and just concentrate on enjoying the moment. Lady Nose Problem will insist that she's a qualified cook and that her father owns an estate in Portugal, that he was a champion Channel swimmer and that she's been riding since the age of five. But most people born today do cook well, and this sign of the centaur does like  horses and rides them well, so there's some truth in all of this. The men also find something to enhance themselves in others' eyes.

More rarely they lie about old partners, insisting love affairs are over, when the answerphone is packed with old flames' messages. When tackled, both sexes argue glibly that they are just friends with old lovers, but you can bet anything in the world that this particularly sexy date is neither keen on nor capable of that kind of friendship. Look in Mr Nose Problem's bathroom cabinet for the tell-tale emery boards, and in the larder for the slimming soup packets and camomile tea bags. Check out Ms NP's medicine cabinet for the razor and her wardrobe for the Ralph Lauren men's pants.

Some work lies are irritating, but a lot of successful people of both sexes lie so December's tale that they were once a film producer doesn't stand out here.

It is a double pleasure
to deceive the deceiver.

(Jean de La Fontaine)

BODY
December 10 likes the high life and by their late twenties it's beginning to show. Try the 3 Day Slimmer's Miracle and lose 2kg! Make up the amount of cocktail given below and have a glass for breakfast, lunch and supper or, if you prefer, have smaller glasses and include one for tea. Eat nothing else, but drink as much water as you wish. (Diets are for healthy people, so check first with your doctor.) Take 2 eggs, 1 tablespoon vegetable oil, juice of 2 large oranges, 570ml cold milk. Whisk all ingredients together until frothy. Keep in refrigerator during the day as the mixture is best well chilled.

MIND
Tarot's Major Arcana gives this day The Wheel of Fortune card. It's the card of change, the card of opportunists, but also for a person who spots the right moment to act and reaps a massive reward. Also denoting impermanence.

DATESHARE
Kenneth Branagh, *British multi-talented actor, film star, director, writer.* **Emily Dickinson**, *19th century poet.* **Ada Byron**, *Lord Byron's daughter, Countess of Lovelace.* **Dorothy Lamour**, *Hollywood glamour puss.* **Edith Randall**, *astrologer.* **César Franck**, *Belgian-born French romantic composer.* **Morton Gould**, *composer.* **St Francis of Assisi**, *Italian saint for all animals, poet.* **Thomas Holcroft**, *British 18th century playwright.*

December 11 sometimes believes that he or she has inherited ill health. Mostly it's nonsense. Alleviate this state of mind by taking one of the Bach Flower remedies especially designed by Dr Edward Bach to cure this feeling. Wild Rose (Rosa canina), is for people who murmur 'It's in the family' about minor ailments or depression. And for those who bore others by failing to turn up to events. (The frantic manager-type may be a nervous reaction to the same set of preoccupations.) After taking Wild Rose people report a more outward-looking approach, feelings of joy, strength and hope.

MIND

Lucky precious stones for this day are topaz, amethyst and sapphire. The amethyst is a supposed remedy for headaches, the sapphire gives protection from ill wishers and guards chastity. And the topaz traditionally averts asthma and encourages faithfulness.

DATESHARE

Christina Onassis, *one of the wealthiest women in the world, died tragically young.* **Alexander Solzhenitsyn**, *Nobel Prize-winning Russian author,* The Cancer Ward. **Jean Racine**, *French playwright.* **Hector Berlioz**, *French composer.* **Naguib Mahfouz**, *Egyptian Nobel Prize-winning author,* Wedding Song. **Susan Seidelman**, *film director,* Desperately Seeking Susan. **Robert Koch**, *Nobel Prize-winning biologist, isolator of tuberculosis bacillus.*

DECEMBER 11

Dec_ember 11 is susceptible to colds and things and my goodness don't they go on about it. Many born at this dark turn of the year have a tendency to go down with things, but Sagittarius recovers quickly and nearly always goes on to live an exceptionally long and vigorous life. As does this little jam tart. It's just that they like to go all sticky when their pastry isn't perfect.

And maybe they also have a taste for being looked after. In

particular male December 11 needs pampering to a high degree, even when he's well. He sees himself as a racehorse and his partner as the owner/stable girl, there to provide him with protein-enriched, healthy, slimming foods, and constant exercise followed by rub downs. If he performs well, December 11 also expects a sweet treat and a great deal of nuzzling. Not surprisingly quite a few business magnates who behave like this are born on December 11.

Girls born today take a lot of time off and talk endlessly about which stage their particular bug has reached. They ruin dinner parties and children's outings by virtuously declining to go at the last minute because others 'won't thank them' when they catch whatever it is. In summer they talk darkly of nuclear reactions to wasps and are always searching for ants in their pants. Really and truly it's best to keep December 11 away from the country because they think it's packed full with danger. And if they stepped on a cow pat you'd never hear the end of their worries that Mad Cow Disease might have travelled through their shoe and up their leg to the brain.

Travel is a problem for December 11 because they think they're going to get ill and often do on plane, car, boat or train. But when they're not discussing all of this, and can be diverted with a good bottle of wine, they are imaginative and fun.

How many beans ⟿ can you put in an empty bag? One. After that it isn't empty.

I2 December

L ike the evening star, you always notice December 12 first. When 12 lopes into people's lives – it's a long-legged star sign – everybody wants them to stay. They're coated with the glimmering sauce of sex appeal, so let's not pretend the attraction is for great brains or niceness. Niceness and brains never caused this stir.

Only very old ladies and gentlemen can bask in their forcefield of seduction, untouched by the frenzy of the heart and the pull at the pit of the stomach. Of course, they are very often unfaithful, playing the dark fields of the night sky like a brilliant footballer, always up for sale and looking for another potential buyer. December 12 often experiments with people to see how long it takes to hunt them down.

In particular, they flourish in politics and local government, partly because of their verbally persuasive powers and partly because they genuinely adopt a strong, do-gooding line. Vanity may be their weakness, but this doesn't prevent them from excellence and the idealism which is characteristic of Sagittarius. Their search for the true meaning of life can be inspiring to others and thus attractive in itself. But the besotted must never kid themselves that this creature will find the true meaning of life lies in love for another.

Nor is there much nostalgia here. They are upturners of old systems, believing that nothing that has been done the same way for years can't be immediately improved by change. So if they manage a business, expect them to insist on computer literacy. Beyond that, if it's a vacuum cleaner business then all staff, including clericals must know how to assemble the product.

This is also a dogs and horses star, preferably big dogs and horses. Some may breed both, others may race them. Either way, their great pleasure is to wing their way at speed through the countryside accompanied by their animals.

Watch sex. It's the key to success and the trapdoor to failure.

(Michael Shea, one-time press secretary to HM the Queen)

BODY
Some stars are sexual hunters, the rest are prey. Are You Jupiter's Huntsman? Tick 'yes' where appropriate. Do you 1: Feel intrigued when a member of the opposite sex ignores you? 2: Fail to return telephone calls? 3: Ditto thank-you letters. 4: Inveigle others to shop for you? 5: Ditto taking your clothes to the dry cleaners? 6: Do you queue jump? 7: Find complete strangers attractive enough to contemplate how love with them would be? 8: Have you ever gone out with more than one person at once? 9: Made love with more than one person? 10: Drive too fast? Four ticks or more? You're the huntsman.

MIND
Country lovers should try to birdwatch only those winged creatures whose sighting brings good fortune. Doves are a happy omen for love and happiness, a cuckoo singing on the right means prosperity, gulls promise a safe journey and swallows promise a birth.

DATESHARE
Died: **Tallulah Bankhead**, *witty actress, muse to Sir Noel Coward. Born:* **Jean Marais**, *French early cinema star.* **Frank Sinatra**, *Old Blue Eyes, US singer, songwriter, icon.* **Dionne Warwick**, *singer.* **Emerson Fittipaldi**, *Brazilian racing driver, world champion.* **Tracy Austin**, *tennis player.* **John Osborn**, *playwright.* **Edward G Robinson**, *post-box-mouthed gangster film star.* **Edvard Munch**, *Norwegian expressionist painter.* **Ed Koch**, *New York mayor, personality.* **Cai Qi Jiao**, *Chinese poet. 'Drunken Stone'.*

Here's something simple and glamorous for Christmas-loving December 13 to make: Gorgeous Napkin Rings. Take plain or dark green, red or blue painted napkin rings and using a permanent ink gold felt-tip pen, decorate them with stars. Twine ivy and flowers around napkin, winding cord over stem and tying on the underside to hold in place. Wind gold paper around napkin, then tie with wire edged crimson and gold ribbon. Paint wooden acorns gold, the type used on roller blinds, and attach them to both ends of a length of gold cord. Tie cord round napkin, finishing off with an ivy leaf tucked into it.

((

Lucky stones for 13 include aventurine, which traditionally encourages independence, creativeness and tones down temper. Also chrysocolla, which helps psychic development, and chalcedony which is good for inducing cheeriness and mental peace.

Jane Birkin, British singer, society's darling rule breaker. **Curt Jurgens**, German cinema heart-throb. **Dick Van Dycke**, American singer, film star, dancer, longest legs in history of cinema, Disney star. **Laurens van der Post**, Dutch-South African writer, philosopher, Lost World of Kalahara. **Prince Karim Aga Khan IV**, spiritual leader of Ismaili Muslims. **Gustave Flaubert**, French novelist, Madame Bovary. **Heinrich Heine**, German-Jewish romantic poet, Book of Songs. **Christopher Plummer**, stage, film, TV star.

DECEMBER 13

This is one of the most practical people of the year. December 13 takes enormous pleasure in any kind of do-it-yourself. Both sexes make many items about the house and garden and will do the same for others, which frequently takes them into a profession where they may decorate, garden or design for everybody else's pleasure. Naturally, their good looks and charm help here. And a sympathetic psychology which convinces customers that December 13 will make their life, their house or their person a little lovelier.

For some this is the way to wealth. For all it's the way to personal happiness and saving money which is one of December 13's bugbears. Not natural shoppers, they resist paying good money for something they could make better themselves. Where money does come their way, this person will often give a great deal of it away to needy relatives, friends and charity, in particular those which care for the homeless. Because, for December 13, the home is the castle and so both sexes have a horror of not having one.

Most form steady partnerships. Not as flirtatious and flittery as other December people. But nearly all are addicted to good looks and secretly would like their children to be attractive as well. Some of the men may go into sales and marketing, which they excel at with their brand of persuasive charm. Most of the women prefer more technical occupations, excellent with their hands and with computers. But all who work out of the home long to get back there each day and maybe finish the shelves or a piece of embroidery.

When it comes to family occasions – Christmas, holidays – this individual can be coercive, especially the women, insisting that all members celebrate together or go on a trip which is no longer suitable for certain age groups. Occasionally intense rows may develop on these occasions when others beg to differ.

I prefer the word 'homemaker' because 'housewife' always implies that there may be a wife someplace else.

(Bella Abzug)

14 DECEMBER

December 14 suffers from the Eeyore Complex where money is concerned. They aren't natural misers, like some other birthdates. If they had oodles and boodles neither sex would worry and they'd make everybody else around them comfortable. But when cash is low December 14 fears that another bill will break the bank and they'll end up homeless.

In truth this state of mind can be induced when there really are sufficient finances. And it's often brought about by somebody else, partner or child, buying themselves a present or running up the telephone bill. Then Ms EC roars 'You didn't need that shirt/to make that telephone call last twenty minutes'. What's worse, she then mentions not having her hair done for forty years and all the times she's resisted buying something for herself. By this time everybody is reduced to desperation and children are in tears.

It is a complex easily transferred to work. Spot both sexes issuing instructions to reuse envelopes and putting a lock on the photocopier. It's Ms and Mr EC who stick those paranoid little notes on telephones saying they're not to be used before 3. 30 pm. Unchecked both at work and at home this can get right out of hand, so irrational that others begin to give December 14 a wide berth.

Properly controlled it does nobody any harm and actually does good to save money and run the accounts properly. Most workers will probably not end up in positions of terrifying power because it would disturb them and they are happiest in a cosy niche just making things work around them.

This otherwise generous minded creature, who naturally does his or her own cooking and sewing and home decorating, is the nurse of the universe. Anybody sick – relative, friend or neighbour – will be cared for. Either sex will be first in the door with chicken soup and a little piece of freshly made cake.

Money is what you'd get on beautifully without if only other people weren't so crazy about it.

(Margaret Case Harriman)

BODY

Glamorous, almost effort free and inexpensive, try making Sashimi, the world-famous Japanese speciality. Take 400g filleted raw fish. For the sauce, 100ml soy sauce, 2 tablespoons grated horseradish. To garnish, radishes, watercress. You can use one type of fish, but it's nicer if you mix the fish. Tuna, sea bream, sole, halibut, octopus and squid are most commonly used. Cut fish into strips about 3. 75cm long, 2. 5cm wide, and 0.75cm thick. Arrange on serving plate with garnish. Either stir the horseradish into soy sauce in separate bowl for the dip, or make two bowls for people to mix.

☾

MIND

Money worries afflict us all, but they're not so bad if you can think positively. Try Mimulus, (Mimulus guttatus) one of the famous Bach Flower remedies specifically made up by Dr Edward Bach with the purpose of controlling hysteria about bills.

DATESHARE

Died: **Myrna Loy**, Hollywood glamour goddess. Born: **King George VI**, 20th century king, held morale together during World War II. **Shyam Benegal**, Indian film director. **Paul Eluard**, French poet, hero World War I. **Stan Smith**, US Wimbledon tennis champion. **Patty Duke**, film, TV actress. **Christopher Parkening**, classical guitarist. **Rosalyn Tureck**, world famous pianist. **Lee Remick**, film star, TV actress. **Gerard Reve**, Dutch novelist, The Language of Love.

There's a delicious pleasure in picking wild sorrel leaves and making them into a perfect summer dish. The lovely lemony flavour of sorrel leaves makes a distinctive difference to summer cooking. They are good eaten raw in sandwiches, salads and known to walkers as a thirst quencher, simply chewed straight off the plant. In The Shepherd's Calendar *John Clare* says of sorrel, 'The mower gladly chews it down, and slakes his thirst the best he may. ' Put some sorrel leaves inside mackerel with a knob of butter and bake in foil. They are also delicious cooked in butter and put in omelettes.

MIND

This individual is amused by traditional weather omens and they are as true as most forecasts. Even meteorologists warm to 'Thunder in spring / Rain will bring.' and 'Winter thunder / A summer's wonder.'

DATESHARE

Don Johnson, TV, film actor. **Michael Bogdanov**, theatre director, **Dave Clark**, singer, Dave Clark Five. **Nero**, psychopathic Roman emperor, fond of playing the violin while Rome burned. **John Paul Getty**, oil tycoon, billionaire, collector of art and women. **Maurice Wilkins**, New Zealand Nobel Prize-winning molecular biologist, worked on DNA with Watson and Crick. **George Romney**, 18th century society portrait painter. **Alexander Eiffel**, French engineer, constructed Eiffel Tower.

DECEMBER 15

There is an unusually hesitant side to December 15, who is blessed with numerous talents but can't acknowledge this. The girls in particular are absolutely beautiful, but never enjoy their beauty because they can only see the ugly bits. Constantly checking in mirrors, the glass in shop windows and even their reflection in other people's sunglasses, poor December 15's glimpse of herself only confirms her worst fears – that she looks appalling. This women asks 'Mirror Mirror on the wall, who is the fairest of them all?', knowing it will be Snow White. Being a kind person, she has no desire to distribute poisoned apples, but rather takes the knife, or hires a doctor to take a knife to herself.

Every newspaper and magazine advert for cosmetic surgery is scanned. But it's not a good idea for December 15 to have cosmetic surgery. The condition is in their heads and they'll always see something wrong – both sexes suffer from over self-criticism.

Nothing is easy for this Space Traveller, who senses pitfalls beneath every triumph. However this often makes them try harder and almost in spite of themselves, succeed faster than companions.

Nevertheless, such reservations can hold December 15 back in his or her chosen career, which is a pity when the reservations are phantasms.

And it makes them vulnerable in love, sometimes overgrateful and too quick to accept a partner just because they've been asked. Fortunately, if this individual has children they take the utmost care to guide them away from similar reactions.

December 15 finds solace in books, paintings and music. (Watching television often makes them feel ugly and unsuccessful.) Their sense of social isolation is sometimes discomforting, but frequently this disappears when they seek physical isolation in long country walks. Marvelling at the beauties of nature, they are soothed and comforted.

In rivers the water that you touch is the last of what has passed and the first of that which comes: so with time present.

(Leonardo da Vinci)

16 DECEMBER

T his lovely creature is a joy bringer, one of those whose presence quietly makes other stars feel good. December 16 is softly coated with the star-dust of generosity, a talented Sagittarian who is sufficiently self-confident to seek the best in others and praise it. Yet few can take advantage of this Jupiterette. They are nobody's fool and won't be milked for praise by those whose psychology is too hungry for it. So moaners beware, because startlingly, December 16 is liable to turn away and talk to somebody else, or simply put the telephone down.

These are the wanderers of the universe, space capsules who must always be on the move, and although they will stay in one place for sufficient time to build a career, they aren't a long server. Job hopping is more their style, perhaps because some secretly feel that if they stay too long, somehow they'll be found out.

Many learn to play a musical instrument early – music is important to this date. Some will go professional, but all will find their life enhanced both physically and mentally. Find them running clubs with the best music in town, working in bands and some even flourish as DJs. Others like to dance, and everybody who knows December 16 knows that a waltz in slow time with them is the equivalent of several bottles of champagne and a passionate encounter with someone else.

Some of the men are also the best kissers in the land, which as every woman knows, is one of the most attractive talents a man can have. Slobbering is just not 16's style. And nor is bad breath. Nor do they bang their teeth on the kissee's, bump into their knees and tread on their toes. All the women are good kissers, but it has to be said, women don't have to be so skilled. You can judge a man's character by he way he kisses, which can't be said for Ms December 16.

Dreams and visions
are infused into men for their
advantage and instruction.
(Oneirocritica, 2nd century AD)

BODY

Without knowing it, December 16 communicates sexual attraction to others by scent. Pheromones are the name for the perfumes produced by one person which provoke a response in another, and December 16 has lots of them. (Except for 16s who are on the Pill, which robs the body of its special sex scent.)

Many essential oils have ingredients which mirror these pheromones and it's pleasurable to use them in scented mouthwashes and lipbalms. For mouthwashes, add 1 drop of rose and 1 drop of bergamot oil to a 100ml bottle of spring water. Lip balm is good made from 1 drop rose in 1tsp camellia oil, stored in a small tinted glass bottle.

MIND

While December 16 mostly resists the temptation, there is always a moment in anyone's life when congratulations and praise don't come instantly to the lips. Still, it's always better not to have said 'Not another one' when someone tells you they're pregnant.

DATESHARE

Jane Austen, *novelist*, Pride and Prejudice. **Sir Noel Coward**, *playwright, bon viveur, socialite, actor, composer.* **Liv Ullman**, *Norwegian stage, film actress.* **Ludwig van Beethoven**, *great German composer, pianist, deaf when he died.* **Margaret Mead**, *anthropologist who had three anthropologist husbands, author,* Coming of Age In Samoa. **George Santayana**, *Spanish poet, novelist, philosopher,* The Life of Reason. **Arthur C Clarke**, *science-fiction writer, screenwriter,* 2001.

Some December 17s suffer from water retention, a problem as old as time, particularly for women. There are various teas on the market in health food stores which can help. Try to cut down on salt which makes the body retain water, and alcohol which acts as a diuretic at first, but then encourages fluid retention. Celery and watermelon juice are believed to improve the condition. Juice a 20cm section of fresh celery with a quarter of a small watermelon, seeds removed. The juice is said to flush toxins, promote urination and increase vitality. Citrus fruits are thought to help some sufferers.

MIND

The Bach Flower remedy, Holly (Ilex aquifolium) was designed by physician Dr Edward Bach particularly as an antidote to negative feelings such as envy, jealousy, suspicion, undermining impulses and all states showing a need for more appreciation.

DATESHARE

Tommy Steele, *rock and roll, skiffle singer, stage, film actor, British cockney icon.* **Ford Madox Ford**, *novelist,* The Good Soldier. **Walter Booker**, *jazz player.* **Erskine Caldwell**, *football player, gunrunner, author,* Tobacco Road. **Peter Snell**, *New Zealand Olympic gold medal-winning runner.* **Paracelsus**, *German 16th century alchemist, physician.* **Sir Humphrey Davy**, *British chemist, electrochemist.*

DECEMBER 17

I t's a rare Sagittarius who suffers greatly from envy, usually dismissed by their noble nature. Unfortunately December 17 has a life-long battle which results in some people judging this creature as two-faced, because one side of them is generous and nice, and the other is not. It's down to that streak of self-doubt in the psychology that many Decemberites suffer from.

Both sexes are massively competitive and often can't cope with a rival's success or even a friend's. The men just can't bring themselves to congratulate even a close buddy if he makes lots of money, or has any startling leg up in studies or career. Jokingly they try to touch their friend for money or advancement. But it's only half a joke, because deep down they feel they're owed a favour, which causes resentment. But less than gracious December 17 in this kind of mood just can't see it.

If either sex loses a job, when a friend rings to comfort them and show solidarity, December 17 people can't stop themselves from suggesting that the friend's job also isn't safe. They may say, 'Naturally you know that so and so has been moved into that job to unseat you. I just thought you should be warned.' And when someone has been offered a big job, what's December 17's reaction? Why, the instant response is, 'Oh they tried to recruit me for that.' Naturally they regret it, thank goodness, because this is December 17's saving grace. Much of the time they strive and succeed to allow others their pleasure. It's just that many have that uncomfortable feeling that they're not where the excitement is.

The good side to December 17 makes them marvellous mentors, giving time and energy to young talent, both at work and outside it in clubs and acting or theatre groups. The bad side makes them resent the pupil who becomes more successful than they've ever been and who wants to break away and become independent.

Man is only a reed, the weakest thing in nature; but he is a thinking reed.

(Blaise Pascal)

18 DECEMBER

Many December 18 people have great joy in their surroundings. They were made for parties and celebrations. They were also made for summer sports, particularly watery ones, picnics and all the other good things that go with June, July and August. Weddings always make both sexes cry. The men like cricket. And both sexes adore dressing up for fancy events.

They make good style journalists and creators, always with an eye to novel ideas which bring amusement. It's December 18 who plans fabulous firework displays with a barbecue for forty beforehand. At weddings their speeches are packed with appalling jokes, but nobody minds. Both sexes have to be discouraged from taking their clothes off in restaurants and at parties. And in particular from feeling tempted to streak at the Oval or Wimbledon.

Jolly December 18 is the good sort at work who asks everybody down to the pub and institutes a work darts match, or a lovely legs competition for men. And he or she's the one who starts a collection for sick workmates or somebody who's been unfairly or even fairly sacked. They don't blame. Just help.

Many do have trouble reaching career heights because they aren't motivated to give everything up for vaulting ambition. As policemen they are happy to stay on the beat, where they feel the real work is done. Nearly all have such strong outside interests anyway that they can't abide the idea of staying late. And often can't abide staying in any job at all for very long because they want to travel, or maybe just go and live in a new part of the country.

Women born today have slightly less of the rolling stone about them, preferring to settle down and bring up children without too much change. But if they must, they take a sanguine view of any move, believing that somehow everything will turn out for the best. Which it mostly does for December 18.

~

Life itself is the proper binge.

(Julia Child)

BODY

Travel sickness plagues this travel-loving person who learns to control it by trial and endeavour. Don't curl up in the car seat or slump in the aeroplane. Don't read, but keep your eyes focused on a distant object out of the window. Keep one window open in a car, or at least a crack, and get out and take walks if you can. This Chinese wrist massage is a favourite for travel sickness. The point lies between the two tendons, two inches up the inner arm from the wrist crease. Massage for a couple of minutes or apply light pressure with fingernail or end of pencil.

℮

MIND

A short first finger, often found in December 18, denotes disinclination to take responsibility. Its owner neither wishes to be pinned down nor be put in a position where either sex has to pin down others.

DATESHARE

Brad Pitt, Hollywood hot property, Interview With The Vampire. **Keith Richards**, British guitarist, singer, songwriter, Rolling Stones icon. **Ray Liotta**, comedian, film star, actor. **Betty Grable**, film star. **Steve Biko**, South African student leader, murdered by police. **Steven Spielberg**, film director, producer, Jurassic Park, Schindler's List. **Willy Brandt**, Nobel Peace Prize-winning German chancellor. **Paul Klee**, Swiss painter. **Christopher Fry**, playwright, verse plays, The Lady Is Not For Burning. **Joseph Grimaldi**, British clown.

Sore eyes can plague December people, in particular as a result of coughs and colds. Always see a doctor. Some natural remedies are effective. In Sicily they use slices of tomato to reduce red swollen eyes, covering the eyes for ten to twenty minutes. Another useful remedy is the cold compress soaked in an infusion of marigold flowers (calendula officinalis) and placed over the eyes. Effective eyewashes for mild infections also include an infusion of strong camomile tea cooled to skin temperature, or a cooled infusion of eyebright (Eurphrasia officinalis) and rosewater. Rest and eat bran, green leafy vegetables, sea vegetables and take vitamin B complex.

MIND

Tarot's card for this day in the Major Arcana is The Sun, which, while it promises adventure and success and maybe even fame, can also indicate the blindness and vulnerability of vanity and stultifying pride which brings narrowness.

DATESHARE

Beatrice Dalle, *screen beauty, stage actress.* **Richard Leakey**, *African expert, anthropologist, environmental fighter,* The Making of Mankind. **Sir Ralph Richardson**, *Shakespearian actor.* **Leonid Brezhnev**, *Soviet premier.* **Jean Genet**, *French playwright, novelist, philosopher,* Querelle. **Edith Piaf**, *French chanteuse, strangled husky voice.* **David Suskind**, *Hollywood film producer.* **John Candies**, *mathematical child prodigy, twenty figure calculations in head.*

DECEMBER 19

Love is always on December 19's mind. Discombobulatingly candid about their pleasure in changing partners, many December 19s kid themselves that their honesty makes breaking hearts OK. The 'But I did tell you no strings' line is always to the advantage of the speaker. The poor recipient agrees out of desperation, hoping that somehow December 19 will change. The only thing that changes this person is a child, or acquiring such an enormous amount of money they have to be serious.

Otherwise this Archer takes a shot at what he or she fancies and Cupid's aim is often accurate. (Fortunately December 19 doesn't have the same sort of fat bottom.) This date will have a glorious time with Aries lovers, where the sex is Jupiterious and where these two can develop a terrific platonic affection. Not so hot with Taurus who doesn't understand December 19's love affair with language and ideas and would rather have a curry. Sex between Gemini and December 19 will be all spangles and feathers. But not so hot with Cancer. The domesticated crab wants Sagittarius to stay at home for a heated discussion about which colour to paint the bathroom, which won't interest the wilder Archer.

If December 19 goes for a Leo partner, everything promises excitement and even a permanent future. Both signs are equally passionate travellers, both leaders, never clingy and ruled by strong intellects. And both are prepared to live cheaply with just their mutual amusement to keep them warm. While Virgo and December 19 could get on for a while, this pairing is best avoided because apart from a love of change, they have nothing in common. Nor are Scorpio partners ideal, tending to trail far behind.

Those December 19s with a narcissus tendency will be happy with their own star sign, less so with careful Capricorns but make such discoveries with marvellous Aquarius that they can afford to ignore a disastrous temptation from Pisces who is altogether too wet for our airy friend.

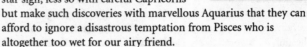

Happiness is
having a scratch for every itch.
(Ogden Nash)

20 DECEMBER

This lovely child of Christmas brings more to the mortal world than it understands. Like the Three Wise Men, December 20 comes to others bearing gifts whose richness can never be bought. This is an old soul, one who has lived before and brings back from another world wisdom which can't be learned in one lifetime. Most of them endure a career rather than throw themselves into one. They are talented enough to do anything, but content themselves by earning money by whatever is at hand.

December 20's main job seems to be to conserve, encourage and in some way enlighten those about him. Not done consciously, but naturally. Most will become extremely knowledgeable about their interests, formally educated or not. Most will also read and write and feel that there are never enough hours in the day to complete their intense interests and the tasks they set themselves.

Marvellous fathers, most December 20s pass on dignity and fairness to their own children, with a gentle love of the countryside and acknowledgement of each man and woman's value. Ms 20 is slightly more practical than her male counterpart, soothing herself with household tasks such as bottling fruit and traditional skills of homemaking.

In public life they will be concerned with some form of education, very likely setting up centres of learning, or making sure that all children, however underprivileged or damaged, get a greater chance in the world. Usually great linguists, but never showing off their intellectual talents in any area, either sex may choose to work abroad, often in dangerous countries and to their own disadvantage. But they never mind. If danger threatens they shrug and leave it to fate. A small house or even a room is all the home they need. And although pleasure-loving and certainly naturally aesthetic – they may have a stunning painting or book collection – it's no matter to December 20 if he or she loses most of their worldly possessions.

Murmur a little sadly how love fled.

(W B Yeats)

BODY

December 20 adores making small things for Christmas, much more than buying them. Try Traditional Christmas Tree Decorations. Gold or silver tassels from furnishing departments make lovely decorations, especially if you attach fake pearls, tiny beads or a single sparkling drop earring. Tie on tree with thin wire or silver embroidery thread. Thread an assortment of beads on to strong thin florists' wire or cord, mixing artificial pearls with different shaped glass beds, anything light and spangly. Hang a few short lengths of the beads off the main string and leave a wire loop at each end for fixing to tree.

MIND

Find this person with a dog or cat, neither pedigree, but sharing a close and loving relationship with their master or mistress. December 20 talks to animals for hours and others around them know that whatever is said between them is important.

DATESHARE

Died: **Bobby Darin**, *Hollywood heart-throb.* Born: **Kiefer Sutherland**, *film star.* **George Hill**, *director,* Butch Cassidy and The Sundance Kid, The Sting. **Jenny Agutter**, *actress, dancer,* The Railway Children. **Irene Dunne**, *film star, stage actress.* **Bob Hayes**, *US Olympic gold medal-winning 100 metres sprinter.* **Uri Geller**, *Israeli psychic, paranormal, once bent Katharine Hadley's spoon from behind kitchen door.* **Kim Young Sam**, *South Korean president.* **Peter Crisscoula**, *rock musician,* Kiss.

December 21 should burn essential oil of frankincense in an oil burner while reading or relaxing as this oil is particularly beneficial to coughs, colds, laryngitis, bronchitis, dull skin and mild depression caused by short dull winter days and lack of natural light. Frankincense (Boswellia thuifera) is extracted from a North African tree and along with myrrh was one of the first gum incenses to be burnt in ancient Egyptian temples. It was brought to Bethlehem at Christmas by the Three Wise Men. It deepens breathing which helps meditation and clear thinking.

MIND

Superstitious December 21 takes note of old rhymes like this wedding ditty: 'Monday for health, Tuesday for wealth, Wednesday the best day of all; Thursday for losses, Friday for crosses, Saturday for no luck at all.'

DATESHARE

Florence Griffith Joyner, American triple Olympic gold medal-winning sprinter. **Jane Fonda**, film star, stage actress, writer, political activist. **Frank Zappa**, songwriter, composer, died of prostate cancer. **Chris Evert**, world tennis supernova, triple Wimbledon winner. **Heinrich Boll**, German Nobel Prize-winning novelist, Billiards At Half Past Nine. **Phil Donahue**, American talk show host. **Joseph Stalin**, Soviet dictator, sociopath. **Benjamin Disraeli**, Victorian prime minister, author. **Kurt Waldheim**, Austrian president. **Anthony Powell**, author, Dance To The Music Of Time.

DECEMBER 21

I f December 21 could live abroad in a warmer climate they would. They may love Britain, but they're not enamoured of its climate and find its politics and mean emotional attitude tiresome. This date would like to inhabit a place where people like and admire each other, where there's a lot of laughter and sitting about under trees looking at the view. Winter chills them to the bone and the lack of light depresses them.

Fortunately this is a moneyed date. The financial promise here is enormous and probably allied with a job or some form of business contact abroad, so their wishes may be fulfilled. Content to live with one partner in faithful bliss and happy enough to raise children if they come along, December 21 usually develops into a passionate gardener, and dreams all day long, in office blocks and factories, in palaces and theatres, of getting back to the garden.

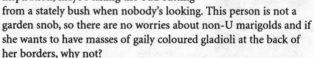

All year long December 21 plans and enjoys. Weekends are for travelling Britain to visit other people's gardens, seeking inspiration, maybe taking the odd cutting from a stately bush when nobody's looking. This person is not a garden snob, so there are no worries about non-U marigolds and if she wants to have masses of gaily coloured gladioli at the back of her borders, why not?

Other powerful passions with this date, and there will be many, may include railway history or memorabilia, antiques, and some form of sewing, in particular patchwork and tapestry. The antiques are most likely to be something pretty, china or porcelain, maybe a few curiosities such as commemorative pottery, which December 21 has inherited from elderly relatives and kept initially for love and memory before developing the collector's passion.

This date has rather a delicate constitution, frequently suffering from aching limbs and sometimes both sexes feel that they almost act as fly paper to any bugs around. Fortunately they shake temporary ailments off quite fast.

O pen your heart
~
and let the sun shine in.

22 DECEMBER

Born when the world is celebrating childhood and doubly welcomes the infant's arrival, this baby's first impressions are dazzling and December 22 yearns for dazzle ever after. However steady this shining star, and December people are some of the most conservative, they all like sparkly things.

People born around this time are true money-makers. It's not luck but judgement. And hard work. Extremely good with numbers, this is the person who conceives a system for beating the National Lottery or predicting the stock market. Both sexes watch company reports, investing just before shares begin to rise. Generosity is not their trump card, so they'll not share this information.

Seriously rich December buys him or herself a large house with all the trimmings. They don't like to swim, but have a pool because rich people do. Swanky cars don't give them pleasure, but they buy a whacking Mercedes, install a chauffeur and are then rude to him.

Expect to see December 22 swathed in diamonds, the women positively clanking and the men's watches crammed with as many sparklers as possible. And there are glittery things all over the house. Chandeliers clink and flicker on exquisite silvery mirrors, the light bouncing off cut-glass everywhere. Both sexes are showy and go on being showy until they're 99.

The women are great homemakers, but men born on this date can't put up a shelf that doesn't immediately fall down and if they go up a ladder *they* immediately fall down it.

Not really party people – they're too shy – December 22 adores going to smart restaurants just as long as the decor is sumptuous: red velvet, low lights, white linen tablecloths and gleaming silver is their ideal. Seafood is their indulgence, lobster the first choice and maybe oysters, although December 22 is worried that their aphrodisiac effect may kick in while they are still at the table. Waiters beware. This bellowing person sends back everything, even peas if they're too big.

Self-love is often unrequited.

BODY

December people find relaxation in cooking, at which, surprisingly, they are a whizz. Often extremely experimental and unconventional. Try Lavender Rice Pudding. This can be made with mint, bay, thyme or lavender. Take several sprigs of lavender, preferably fresh from the garden. 290ml cream, 140g caster sugar, 55g pudding rice, 860ml milk, 2 beaten eggs, pinch salt. Put rice and milk into saucepan, with lavender, bring to simmer until the milk has been absorbed and the rice is still crunchy. Beat in eggs, sugar and pinch salt, transfer to low oven for 20–30 minutes. Serve with slender biscuits of your choice.

MIND

Fortune's lucky December days include 6, 12, 15, 18, 25 and 28, all of which promise joy and an abundance of good things acquired, be they beautiful paintings, objéts d'art or culinary indulgences. Plus news from abroad and brilliant successes.

DATESHARE

Helmut Schmidt, West German chancellor. **Jousef Karsh**, Canadian portrait photographer. **Chet Baker**, jazz singer, trumpeter. **Pierre Etaix**, French actor, director, writer. **Jose Greco**, American choreographer, flamenco dancer. **Jorma Kaukonen**, lead guitarist, singer, songwriter, Jefferson Airplane.

DECEMBER 23

Ambition fuels this quasar of the skies. Imagine a spotlight which shines with the brilliance of all the lights in New York and you get a picture of the energy output of this fearsome creature, who emits the energy equivalent to a thousand galaxies. In every area of work the air crackles around them and strangers ask 'Who was that?' Other stars must take care around Quasar 23 because they will not only be outshone, but their light will be absorbed by this rapacious creature.

Although some are humane, most are too driven to bother with niceties. Watch them at meetings, apparently listening and joining in, but behind those opaque, wintery eyes you can see the mind sifting, calculating something to their advantage. Weakness is anathema to them. If a colleague is sick or in need, December 23 simply runs round him, even uses it against him. Hear December 23 murmur to a boss 'Do you think so and so can cope with this project? Is his/her health up to it?' Meaning he can't and it's not.

Both sexes are attracted to the very energetic young or the old and powerful. The young bring energy, sometimes sexual. The old bring them position and contacts. Marrying the boss seems an obvious course of action to an individual who rarely falls hopelessly in love.

As leaders they are coldly impeccable. Others follow but don't love them. When December 23 walks into the work washroom everybody scuttles off, avoiding any casual conversation at all costs. When December 23 questions a colleague or underling either sex will remember exactly what was said. Theirs is a photographic memory and you'd better watch out. Find them in the armed forces and at the highest level in business, politics, industry and commerce. Less carnivorous sharks born on this day may play a great part in local authority politics or running a hospital or school, efficiently but never emotionally.

There is a garden in her face
Where roses and white lilies grow.
(*Thomas Campion*)

24 DECEMBER

orn to celebrations, this glittering star on top of the tree has been partying ever since. Good humoured and kind, they'll make any occasion special and scatter their money about like clouds of golden confetti. If 24 isn't in charge of the office Christmas party, he should be because nobody else does it as well. Both sexes put the swank into celebration and the zing into swing. And people born on this day dance like a dream.

Many December birthday children are gloomy, but somehow the changeling December 24 zoomed down to earth with a Capricornucopia of personal gifts as rich as those brought by the Three Kings to Bethlehem. They can sing or play a musical instrument, often so well they may become professional. Many are great sportsmen. Decorative themselves, they make their surroundings attractive with just the flick of a finger. These are the family members who hold relatives together and always come up with a positive solution. And like many others born around this time, they cook like a dream.

When it comes to sex it's a different matter for December 24. There's nothing sweetly friendly about their passion. They fall hard, can easily become addicted to the love of their life. And can't be bothered with the folderols of courtship and lovemaking which puts them at a disadvantage when in competition with others who can. Love is often the undoing of this Christmas Eve child. No day suffers the pain of a broken heart more agonisingly or for greater lengths of time.

In some cases a broken love affair is so powerful an influence that they may throw up their life and work and move far away or even abroad in order to start again. But the image of their lost love remains branded on their hearts and any lover who follows must accept that December 24 holds a flame – or maybe a flicker – forever in memory of whoever cruelly betrayed them.

I believe that sex is a beautiful thing between two people.

Between five it is fantastic.

(Woody Allen)

BODY
Here's a folderol worth bothering with to entertain a lover. Chocolate Fruit. Take 375g selected fruit, anything hard enough to be dipped without squishing. Grapes, cherries, strawberries, apricot halves – or even nuts. 100g plain dessert chocolate, 100g caster sugar, 50ml single cream, pinch cream of tartar, oil. Heat sugar, cream, cream of tartar, stirring, then bring to boil and continue until mixture is golden brown. Melt chocolate. Dip one half fruit in caramel and other side in chocolate. Place on oiled tray to set. Take to bed with a bottle of champagne and expect a sweet sensation.

MIND
Everybody loves and loses love. If, like Heathcliff, you let this ruin your life, you are closing the door to other joys and taking a decision to live in the past. Cherish the memory but move on.

DATESHARE
*Died: **Rossano Brazzi**, Italian film star, matinée idol. Born: **Nostradamus**, French astrologer, prediction maker. **Howard Hughes**, film maker, recluse. **Ava Gardner**, film star, married Frank Sinatra who loved her all her life. **Emanuel Lasker**, German world champion chess grandmaster. **Matthew Arnold**, British poet. **Robert Joffrey**, New York choreographer.*

BODY

December 25 is a bit of a spoiled baby where love is concerned and if there's the slightest hint of boredom, or if a lover simply doesn't want to go along with every whim, may disappear into the horizon in search of another, juicier squeeze. But bouncing from one new love to another is exhausting and this individual can get low and lethargic with tiredness and too many changes. It's best to ask what advantage is there really in another new partner and having to go through all the courtship again. And what advantage there is in breaking hearts. The answer may be 'none'.

☾

MIND

This individual enjoys dreaming. Flying birds, however, warn of fear at being confined in a relationship as may the riding horses dream. Riding denotes a powerful sexual relationship, but if you hold onto the mane it indicates sexual discontent.

DATESHARE

Died: **Charlie Chaplin**, *great comedian, film star, director.* **W C Fields**, *great Hollywood comic actor, misogynist.* **Charles Pathe**, *picture empire founder. Born: Traditionally,* **Jesus Christ**. **Sissy Spacek**, *Hollywood film star.* **Hanna Schygulla**, *Polish film star, stage actress.* **Annie Lennox**, *rock singer, The Eurythmics.* **Helena Rubinstein**, *Russian cosmetics maker, socialite.* **Quentin Crisp**, *writer, eccentric extraordinaire, The Naked Civil Servant.* **Anwar Sadat**, *Egyptian president, Nobel Peace Prize-winner for peaceful agreement with Israel.*

It wasn't the stork who brought December 25, but Father Christmas who dropped the baby off while delivering the presents and collecting his glass of sherry and mince pie. Christmas babies are special, touched with moondust and sung to sleep by angels with shimmering blue wings. There are lots about at this time. December 25 people may not get a separate birthday, but what a fantastic birthday they do get. After all, it's the birthday of the year and not surprisingly December 25 is one of the jolliest of the year.

This succulent mince pie is sometimes hard on the outside, but by golly taste the squashy centre. Sugar and spice, fruit and all things nice. Very moreish, this creature, and will probably have to spend part of its life fighting off hungry mince pie addicts. They're so good-looking that creams and cosmetics aren't usually necessary, although this individual adores bright things and quite often the women wear a lot of colour on their face. It's a darkly sensuous date, so watch out for the women with bright red lipstick hanging about the mistletoe and the dark haired men with the burning eyes who use their glamorous birthday to claim a special kiss.

In youth this individual is drawn to travel, drawn to the sophistication of New York and the wide open spaces of America's mid west, and indeed Canada's vast mountains and lakes. Find them also in New Zealand and Australia working or studying for long periods. Both sexes may easily emigrate to warmer, cleaner places where they expect a freer life.

December 25 is a lucky person to employ and he's lucky if he starts his own business. Heaven wants to shower good fortune on both sexes. There's usually a little present of money round every corner – a rise, a win on the horses, a deal – and they are superb at spotting a bargain.

All I need is room enough to lay a hat and a few friends.
(Dorothy Parker)

26 DECEMBER

Christmas children are special and this Boxing Day baby is no exception. They arrive to such a welcome, are made to feel so special that these established good feelings stay with them for the rest of their lives. Those who are welcomed warmly from an early age learn to make others welcome. People born today are people pleasers in the best sense. They enjoy others' happiness, especially if they have helped create it. But they don't need to please to feel wanted.

Self-confident Boxing Day has an individualistic streak and both sexes may seek a change of direction in early adulthood. All December people can be spectacular at making money if they so choose, because a characteristic of Capricorn is ruthless mental organisation and dedication. Boxing Day may choose to make his or her money young, working morning, noon and night. Then give up conventional work, marry, raise a family and live happily ever after.

But the change goes the other way too. Many flit from job to job, even country to country, certainly from person to person. Then the Capricorn urge to settle suddenly dominates and making a late start in the career market, they quickly become successful and choose a mate. Most December 26 people want children badly. Many only have to look at their spouse and a baby is on the way, but when this doesn't happen they fret. Immediate, expert medical help should be sought. Time-wasting has no value here. It may cost a lot, but December 26 is willing to throw money at this problem. And with luck and dedication the desired bundle should soon be in their arms.

This individual likes to collect antiques and some may treasure hunt, usually with interesting results. Financial gain isn't the motive behind collecting or rooting for buried treasure. They are more interested in the beauty of their collection and the history of their finds.

Ruin seize thee, ruthless King.

(Thomas Gray)

BODY
Low levels of iron in the body can cause pregnancy difficulties and may also be at the bottom of tiredness, anaemia and muscle fatigue. Iron is lost in blood and women can lose a significant amount during menstruation. Best sources for iron are bread, fortified breakfast cereals, beans, nuts and green leafy vegetables. Liver and kidneys are rich in iron and the body absorbs more easily from meat sources. Signs of deficiency include pale skin, poor vision, indigestion and tingling in the fingers and toes. Iron needs rise dramatically during pregnancy as the growing baby takes up almost half a mother's daily iron supplies.

MIND
Handshakes reveal more than you think. A soft hand denotes an easy conscience. An elastic but firm grip points to honest and honourable intentions. An iron grip may indicate strength of will, but also lack of intuition.

DATESHARE
Died: **Jack Benny**, *film star, comedian.* **Howard Hawks**, *Hollywood star. Born:* **Phil Spector**, *record producer, friend of The Beatles.* **Steve Allen**, *TV and film actor, pianist, songwriter.* **Richard Widmark**, *film and TV actor.* **Maurice Utrillo**, *French painter of pretty villages.* **Thomas Gray**, *18th century British poet, 'Elegy Written in a Country Churchyard'.*

DECEMBER 27

This person is not what he seems. Mysteriously beautiful, these stars who watch the turning of the year may choose to shine, or cloak their dark and fiery nature in subterfuge. December 27 goes in disguise and sometimes even those closest don't really know what they are thinking. Both sexes are in love with secrecy, and sometimes, themselves confused about their own identity, should be extremely careful to avoid the wrong side of the law. There's a fascination here with get-rich-quick methods and that may include criminal behaviour.

More generally, December 27 is ambiguous and will develop this side of his or her nature to tantalise others. They may delight in copying the opposite sex, more usual here with girls than boys. But if Lady 27 does wear men's clothes, she makes a hauntingly handsome youth, her femininity easily discovered because this vain creature adores cosmetics and wouldn't be without her perfume. The men simply cultivate a disturbing slenderness and have

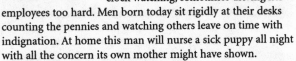

luxuriant hair, often worn in pony-tails, that could grace a shampoo ad.

Curious reversals are part of their nature. At home the women are often tremendously talented painters or textile makers, embroidering fantastic patterns in gold and silver thread, worthy of a king's ransom. At work, she stalks across the floor, hard-faced, clock watching, sometimes driving her employees too hard. Men born today sit rigidly at their desks counting the pennies and watching others leave on time with indignation. At home this man will nurse a sick puppy all night with all the concern its own mother might have shown.

Some play at philandering, yet deep down they're stable family minded people and can show disconcerting sudden flashes of respectability in the middle of quite enjoyably shocking occasions. Others will make a pile of cash with the breathless determination of a miser, then throw it all away on a good cause, usually requesting anonymity.

Learning about sexuality is an invaluable preparation for living.
(William H Masters)

EARTH

28 December

ecember 28 is an optimist. For him tomorrow is always another exciting day. If things don't work he walks away. Cool as any precious metal mined from the earth, Capricorn's element, this meteorite sticks its blazing tail in the air and cocks a snook at other citizens of the universe. Unlike the meteorite, however, neither sex is likely to burn out.

Some are too dippily optimistic. There's always another pipe dream project. Through rose tinted eyes the high street bank manager seems a piggy bank waiting to be raided. Entrusted with other people's money they kindly try to increase it on crackpot ideas. And probably lose it. Somebody else must be in charge of this Saturnoddle's finances, especially as they are easy prey to manipulation. Innocent of this 'talent' themselves, they couldn't spot a manipulator if she sat on December 28's head.

However, most undippy, charming December 28s glimmer in a spangly coating of natural gold dust which brushes off on everybody else. It's a lucky date to have around. In sales and marketing they up the profits, shine in the army, make breathtaking deductions in the police force. While decorating, they put their hand behind the chimney piece and find a box of rare Charles 1st coins.

Jolly December 28 has wide interests and sex is only a small part, although they are extremely partial to having their fingertips nibbled during lovemaking. Or not during lovemaking. Passionate about music, they love architecture and will take long building-viewing walks, if possible accompanied by a dog. Dogs and December 28 go together. Canine friends are optimistic too and don't sulk or brood, which suits this individual. And dogs always want to play, and so, really, does this person. Mostly they can't be bothered with big dogs, too much work, running about and mess for slightly lazy December 28. For them, the charming, liquid-eyed spaniel is the best companion, although some of the women may go for a small, decorative shih-tzu.

BODY

A bit of a stick in the mud this one. Are You Stuck In The Mud? For both sexes. 1. Would you paint a room bright red? 2. Dye your hair red? 3. Stand on your head if somebody bet you couldn't? 4. Wear green underwear? 5. Try out body jewellery? 6. Drink champagne in the bath? 7. Spend the night on the beach with a partner? 8. Slip into the Savoy Hotel in London just to go to the loo? 9. Give your partner a whole body massage – or even a half body massage? 10. Which half? Judge for yourself.

MIND

You only know the present. The future only matters when it becomes the present and the past cannot be altered. What you do in the present, each day, shapes everything. So make it important.

DATESHARE

*Died: **Sam Peckinpah**, Hollywood director. Born: **Denzel Washington**, Hollywood film star, stage actor. **Dame Maggie Smith**, stage and film actress. **Nigel Kennedy**, British violinist, composer. **Lew Ayres**, film and TV actor. **Hildegarde Knef**, German film, stage actress. **Joan Ruddock**, anti-nuclear campaigner. **Earl Hines**, jazz pianist, composer.*

Dear God: I know you will provide, but why don't you provide until you provide?

(A Jewish prayer)

Couch potatoes take heart. New research reveals that watching television uses up 20% more energy than lying in bed. And in calorie burning terms TV is just as good for you as more cerebral activities such as reading or writing. Watching TV uses up around 93 kilocalories an hour, the same as other sedentary activities, compared with 77 kilocalories expended while lying motionless. In reality most of the energy goes on associated activities like getting up to put the kettle on. Even extremely light physical activity such as walking at half a metre a second uses up 131 kilocalories, marginally better for you.

MIND

Those whose careers lie in the medical field are engaged in the maintenance of the structure of the human body, one word for which is :
OSSEOCARNISANGUINEO-
VISCERARTILAGININER.
Found in Headlong Hall *by*
Thomas Love Peacock.

DATESHARE

Ted Danson, *TV, film actor,* Cheers, Gulliver's Travels. **Jon Voight**, *film, stage actor.* **Mary Tyler Moore**, *American actress, stage entertainer.* **Marianne Faithfull**, *pop singer, songwriter, author, girlfriend of Mick Jagger.* **Pablo Casals**, *Spanish master cellist, anti-Fascist.* **William Gladstone**, *Victorian prime minister.* **Gelsey Kirkland**, *ballet dancer.* **Madame de Pompadour**, *French mistress of Louis XV, powerful political influence.*

DECEMBER 29

December 29 is relaxing to be with and those born on other days in the year seek her out. This gentle creature perfumes her house and keeps it warm and pretty and when others are with her, she just potters about. One of the least likely to put pressure on another human being, there's a peaceful rainbow-tinted aura about both sexes. But neither wants to talk a great deal about the deep problems of life so don't expect December 29 to encourage or welcome a great, squelching self-analytical occasion. Mostly they flit off to another room and take up their embroidery or turn on the television. This doesn't mean that people born today are insensitive to others' need to talk. If it's necessary, they will. But to them quiet companionship is the loveliest enjoyment.

Hassle and bustle at work don't suit them and at the worst can cause headaches and stomach aches, pressure symptoms for someone whose delicate stomach plays up during crises and often while travelling. Nor, for this reason, are they often good at exams, although many overcome the problem and fly high academically.

Work in the environment is best for them, or anything which doesn't involve crowds and office politics. Charities are full of them, and many become high-flying doctors, but December 29 won't be the one hosting a society ball. Glitter and social climbing are anathema.

It's probably best for this creature to make an office at home. It works very well, because there are always plenty of commissions and as they like to toil through the night with only the stars for company, then sleep late in the morning, regulating their own money-earning habits can be ideal.

More than one serious partner will probably enter December 29's life, partly because their social shyness and reluctance to keep trotting out in the evenings makes some lovers feel restricted. Eventually a soulmate turns up to share their haven. They are passionate about blue flowers.

Flowers in a city are like lipstick on a woman – it just makes you look better to have a little colour.
(Lady Bird Johnson)

30 DECEMBER

One of the sweetest people of the year, but so often this luscious cabbage underestimates herself and feels less glamorous than the flashier lettuce. And yet, in truth, too much lettuce sends most people to sleep, which you certainly can't say of December 30. The cabbage is a versatile valuable and its substantial properties come to the fore in money-making, surprisingly for this child of Capricorn who isn't particularly interested in riches.

Promotion seeks out our steady satellite, from people who are grateful because Capricorns have a habit of saving the day. In a crisis, December 30 forgets her self-doubts and hastens to suggest and then bring about positive solutions. Most Capricorns can work through the night and then the next day and she is no exception, although none of them can go on forever and must be warned about their habit of trying to do without sleep entirely.

Perhaps the key to December 30's psychology is their preference to remain a satellite rather than take centre stage. Many make excellent personal assistants and advisers, genuinely generous about others' success. Naturally this makes them very desirable mates for other ambitious days and many successful couples who run their own outfit have one December 30 in the pair, advising, steadying and steering the other to further brilliance.

The downside of this is that December 30 often makes a pushy parent, perhaps wanting to shine in their kids' glory too much. Competitive with other mothers, Ms 30 gets whacky about other mother's child-rearing methods, especially if they seem unconventional and produce brilliant kids. Watch out here for the yearly pantomime role and best costume competitive rage, children's birthday party over dressingitis which includes the matching bloomer, dress and hairband tendency and GCSE dementia. It's only over the children that both sexes lose that sweetness and why do it when the kids and you will be happier without all that aggravation?

Stay as sweet as you are.

BODY

Many female December 30 people get Saturnervous about their breast size. Are they too small? Too big? And what to do about this. Best to avoid the temptation to seek the surgeon's knife because bigger bosoms – or smaller ones – ain't a solution to the crisis in the psyche. Have it done if it's purely for vanity. Try these gentler aromatherapy recipes for bosom enlargement and reduction. Enlargement. Take 2 drops oil geranium, 2 drops clary sage, 2 drops ylang ylang, 2tsp camellia oil, mix and massage into breasts. Reduction. 1 drop rose, 1 drop jojoba in carrier oil.

MIND

To catch one's garments on bush or briar while gardening or walking promises good luck and monetary gain. To attract good fortune, always cut the hair at the new moon. If tights or stockings come down it means a lover is thinking of you.

DATESHARE

Ben Johnson, Canadian world record sprinter, stripped of Olympic gold medal after use of banned drugs. **Rudyard Kipling**, British Nobel Prize-winning poet, author, The Jungle Book. **Tracy Ullman**, British comedian, singer. **Carol Reed**, British film director, producer, Oliver, The Third Man. **Patti Smith**, singer, songwriter.

BODY

Are You A Saturnoxious Advice Giver? 1. Do you interrupt others half way through a sentence? 2. Insist on getting your word in edgeways? 3. Find you can never remember other people's names? 4. Take over the cooking without asking and automatically add more spices, turn down/up the heat? 5. Take over a project and automatically redo it? 6. Argue people down? 7. Feel unappreciated? 8. Insist on driving? 9. Automatically assume if the washing machine breaks down that it's somebody else's fault? 10. Think others' sickness is malingering? 11. Pooh-pooh another's fatigue as weakness? Answer 'yes' to more than six and you should modify your Saturnoxious ways.

MIND

December 31 adores odd fact collecting. Here's one about their own planet. Known since ancient times, Saturn is the only planet with rings. Galileo spotted it through the first telescope, but it was only finally described correctly by Christian Huygens in 1659. Its diameter is 75,100 miles.

DECEMBER 31

Perhaps this day is Saturnervous, coming to earth as he has at the turning of the year, but the nervous behaviour doesn't reveal this creature's best side. There's a Saturnoxious need to demonstrate superiority to other dates and a galaxian capacity to describe his feelings in clichés. Favourites include 'I don't suffer fools gladly', making assumptions that she is not a fool and everybody else is. Then there's 'If you want something doing well you'd better do it yourself'.

In the kitchen and on work projects December 31 believes that 'Too many cooks spoil the broth' which ensures that nobody offers to help, after which they complain 'Do I have to do everything myself round here?' Martyrs to punctuality and Saturnoxiously early rising they murmur at latecomers and sleepy heads: 'The early bird catches the worm. I've been here for an hour', or 'up since 5.30'. They interrupt others with 'Don't mind me' and then take over the conversation. And on meeting someone more attractive than themselves, they cry 'Handsome is as handsome does'. In the face of another's success they shake their heads with 'A flash in the pan'.

It's a sad fact that all of this complimentary commenting on their own behaviour gets up other people's noses. Unless December 31 can control herself, party invitations are a rarity and so is promotion at work, because others can't stand the advice

saturation which goes with this creature's presence. This is a pity, because while kindness is not their strong card, they are often very clever and can make a stunning contribution.

Not that it matters to strong-minded, personally convinced December 31. In fact it just goes to prove what fools most people are. Fortunately their dark, comehither good looks make them sufficiently attractive, so there's always an admiring companion at home for them to murmur at 'Two's company, three's none'.

He is about as useful as a one-armed paperhanger.

I JANUARY

January 1 is a natural child of change, not surprising since he is born on our first day of the new year. To this person there is always everything to look forward to and mistakes which went before are to be forgotten. Both sexes may learn from these mistakes, but they're not hot on learning, preferring to ignore. No change in circumstance holds much fear for these creatures. They listen to their very developed instincts and their timing is usually perfect, but even if it's not, there's always another chance in the life of January 1.

As bosses both sexes can be irritating, enthusiastically and thoughtlessly reorganising. When employees raise objections to coming in dressed in yellow and standing up during meetings, this person chants his mantra, 'People don't like change, but it's good for you.' Still they are always easy-going if change is imposed upon them, so management courts them.

Most January 1 people have a hefty streak of the psychic which acts as their guiding light, sniffing ill will as it comes in the door and the sweeter perfume of good will. Many are devoted to astrology and consult an astrologer about journeys, financial and marital decisions, and job changes. Care is taken about the house and garden not to harbour objects which bring ill luck and many avoid wearing green or living in green painted rooms.

Sexually, this earthy person is addicted to love in the open air. Sun-warmed grass, a bed of soft leaves – all of this is extremely alluring and a ramble frequently includes a pause for passion under the poplar tree. You won't get caught by a passing policeman because Capricorn's psyche acts as an early warning system.

All their life the psyche brings special opportunities. Many collect art or antiques with a special advantage over others. Others travel widely with their families. Fabulous festivals blossom in their path and dangerous journeys are avoided because the psyche says 'no'.

My wife Frances has beautiful hands. Someday I'm going to have a bust made of them.

(Sam Goldwyn)

BODY

This person likes to make love all night and pursues his and her Saturnalian tastes until a great age. Both sexes choose their mates passionately, lavish them with presents and many decorate their bedrooms with the favourite lucky Capricorn colour, violet. Capricorn have bodies spectacularly dotted with erogenous zones and can become instantly aroused if the backs of their knees are stroked even in the most public of places. Watch out for their wrists (especially the inside), their forearms, the base of the throat and – particularly with the men – the shoulder blades. Wise to avoid touching unless it's in privacy with love in mind.

MIND

When love goes wrong, beware. January 1 harbours enmity for life and can be a bitter opponent. Best birthdates for a mate are from April 21 to May 21 and between August 21 and September 21.

DATESHARE

Died: **Groucho Marx**, main star of Marx Brothers. Born: **E M Forster**, British novelist, Passage To India. **Sir James Frazer**, anthropologist, author, The Golden Bough, seminal collection of folk and ethnic myths and their meanings. **J Edgar Hoover**, American head of FBI, hated, feared, instigated communist hunt. **J D Salinger**, American author, Catcher In The Rye. **Carole Landis**, Busby Berkeley dancer.

JANUARY 2

*January 2 is fascinated by
haunted places and likes to
motor around Britain ghost
spotting. At Oldstone Hall in
Devonshire locals insist the
ghost of Laura Dimes still
haunts her ruined bedroom.
Forbidden by her parents to
meet her secret husband, Laura's
riding hat was spotted one
morning in the pond, close to
the bank. Bizarrely, Laura's
dead body stood bolt upright,
directly beneath the hat. More
generally, Cornwall's Bodmin
Moor is one of Britain's most
haunted landscapes. There are
skeletons driving ghostly
carriages, people who vanish in
a strange mist that descends and
remote spots brimming with
horrific feelings of timeless
melancholy.*

MIND

*In Tarot the 2nd card of the
Major Arcana is The Priestess.
She brings an awareness of
otherwordly secrets, gentle
reserve and a hatred of gossip.
Bad qualities include edginess,
untrustworthiness, a hard heart
and laziness.*

DATESHARE

*Died: **Jack Carson**,
Hollywood actor, icon. Born:
David Bailey, society
photographer. **George Blanc**,
French chef. **St Therese of
Lisieux**, had visions of Jesus
Christ. **Isaac Asimov**, science
fiction writer, The Foundation
Trilogy. **Renata Tebaldi**,
Italian opera singer, soprano.
Yuriy Grigorovich, Kirov and
Bolshoi ballet master.*

A bit of a Capricornflake, this person frequently backs out of a project, a house buy or even a marriage at the last minute and makes everybody around her nervous. January 2 was blessed with all the usual good fairy gifts at birth. The good looks are magical. The brain fast. The charm snaps, crackles and pops. But January 2 just can't make up her mind.

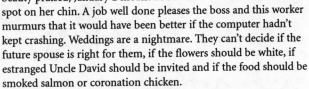

In part it's the Eeyore tendency common to many winter people. Her beauty praised, January 2 moans about the spot on her chin. A job well done pleases the boss and this worker murmurs that it would have been better if the computer hadn't kept crashing. Weddings are a nightmare. They can't decide if the future spouse is right for them, if the flowers should be white, if estranged Uncle David should be invited and if the food should be smoked salmon or coronation chicken.

Best men born on this day, bridegrooms, and worse still, fathers always tell deeply Capricorny jokes in wedding speeches and then worry for the rest of the day that they weren't funny enough. Many do manage to control the flakey side to their nature, and then a little doubt can be useful, keeping them watchful as they rise up the ladder. Best places for an ambitious January 2 are some form of politics where their industry, sharp wits and honesty marks them out, the armed forces, police force and for the arty ones, the theatre, design and architecture.

But where marriage or living together is concerned, this can be an unreliable date upon which to hang your hat. January 2 men can be found whispering 'My wife doesn't really understand me' to a long-legged person in a secret bar. And the girls easily come to the conclusion that they've hitched themselves to a falling comet. This star is always convinced that there's a lusciouser shade of blue in another part of the night sky.

Why did the policeman cry?

*Because he couldn't
take his panda to bed.*

3 JANUARY

Born in the dark days of winter, January 3 dreams of long summer days and breezy nights. His greatest delight is to sit in the garden amongst night-scented jasmine and entertain friends to good food, wine and laughter. Essentially a romantic, this Capricornflower has the kind of green fingers which could make both sexes professional gardeners. Even without a garden, there are window boxes crammed with pink and white petunias, and little balconies where multicoloured convolvulus climb. Even without a window box, great blowsy amaryllis blossoms decorate the window sills.

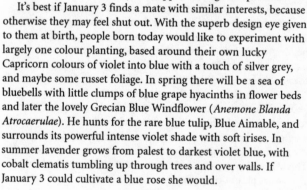

Although January 3 works in a responsible job this date is not over ambitious. He doesn't shirk responsibility or promotion, but does disapprove of the trappings of power and others' interest in them. But what both sexes do is think about their passion for planting while at their computer. Find plant catalogues in their desk drawer and expect them to lull themselves to sleep reading the latest season's bulb booklet just dropped through the postbox.

It's best if January 3 finds a mate with similar interests, because otherwise they may feel shut out. With the superb design eye given to them at birth, people born today would like to experiment with largely one colour planting, based around their own lucky Capricorn colours of violet into blue with a touch of silver grey, and maybe some russet foliage. In spring there will be a sea of bluebells with little clumps of blue grape hyacinths in flower beds and later the lovely Grecian Blue Windflower (*Anemone Blanda Atrocaerulae*). He hunts for the rare blue tulip, Blue Aimable, and surrounds its powerful intense violet shade with soft irises. In summer lavender grows from palest to darkest violet blue, with cobalt clematis tumbling up through trees and over walls. If January 3 could cultivate a blue rose she would.

Let the winds of dawn that blow
Softly round your dreaming head
Such a day of sweetness show
Eye and knocking heart may bless.
(W H Auden)

BODY

Lavender (Lavendula officinalis) originated in the mountainous regions of the Mediterranean. The Romans used it to add to their bath water and the English name came from the Latin lavare, to wash. English lavender is often regarded as the finest in the world. The best essence is distilled from the flowering tops, but it is present in the leaves as well. Spike lavender (Lavendula spica latifolia) is the most useful for respiratory disorders. Aromatherapists use it for skin conditions, particularly acne and burns, for insect bites and stings, muscular aches and pains, pre-menstrual syndrome, as a sedative sleep inducer and to balance body and mind.

MIND

What blue flowers in your garden mean: love-in-the-mist, uncertainty; hyacinth, devotion; forget-me-not, remembrance; harebell, resignation; cornflower, delicacy; clematis, intellectuality; Canterbury Bell, faithfulness; bugloss, mendacity; thyme, domestic virtue; violet, modesty; Grecian windflower, estrangement.

BODY

Raspberry Cream Capricornetto. Take 400g raspberries, sieved icing sugar, 2 eggs separated, 125ml double cream, lightly whipped. Sieve raspberries (frozen will also do) or put into blender. Sweeten to taste with icing sugar, beat egg yolks and 25g icing sugar until thick and creamy. Whisk egg whites until they form stiff peaks, then gradually beat in 50g icing sugar, a teaspoon at a time. Gradually whisk egg yolk mixture into this, then fold in raspberry purée and cream. Turn into container, almost freeze, remove and beat smooth, then freeze again for at least 4 hours. Serve in cones.

MIND

In Tarot, the 4th card in the Major Arcana is The Emperor, bringing wisdom, farsight, emotional steadiness and generosity towards others. There is also impatience with those who don't follow advice and even a bullying streakette.

DATESHARE

Sir Isaac Newton, British mathematician, discovered gravity under apple tree. **Jacob Grimm**, German writer of folk and fairy stories with brother Wilhelm. **Louis Braille**, French inventor of reading system for the blind, lost own sight at three years old. **Jane Wyman**, film actress. **André Masson**, French symbolist-surreal painter, sculptor. **Floyd Patterson**, world heavyweight boxing champion. **Grace Bumbry**, opera singer. **Carlos Saura**, Spanish film director, Blood Wedding.

A real problem solver this one. And a terrific cook. What better than to have a misery solved by January 4 and then be stuffed with a Capricornetto of delicious home invented ice cream. These people are great with children and teenagers, everybody really. It's a genuine capacity for good living.

Lovely January 4 is never so pushed for time that a telephone call can't be returned or a thank you letter written. They understand that time is the great luxury and that it expands or contracts according to your temperament and not the clock. For this reason, people born today seem to get more work done in offices or at home than other days. Maybe it's because they value time so much they don't waste it, knowing that to savour a moment is better than to let it drain through fingers into the sand.

Make no mistake. Gentle they may be, but not gullible. Like most people born now, they can spot ill intentions a mile off, and aren't above dealing a crushing blow, mentally or physically.

Natural happiness comes to them with a life spent in a crowd. They like big families, lots of friends and neighbours, cats and dogs. (They have a passion for thoroughbred cats at the Siamese end of the gene pool.) The best kind of work for this person is dealing with people. Teaching is ideal and since they excel at sport, and can make it fun for children of all ages, this is another talent to throw into the pot.

Sex is usually an easy come, easy go affair. Past lovers always remain friends and a January 4 wedding will be crammed with old admirers who genuinely wish well, but in secret regret this person is not marrying them. It's rare that they fall hopelessly in love, but when they do and the love is thwarted, this broken heart doesn't easily mend.

I won one game in a row.
(Viktor Korchnoi, chess champion)

5 JANUARY

In matters of love this gilded creature can be a real Saturnuisance. Both sexes shimmy about the night sky causing hearts to beat. A crook of the finger and the star they are hunting melts with love. Here's the Saturnuisance bit. January 5 is only interested in playing the great sparkler-studded night blue field and doesn't care for victims who've turned into molten mettle in his/her hands. They like the chase. They are the dangerous hunters with their jewelled bow and arrow in their hands and the poisoned dart of love in their belt. Willing victims mean nothing.

Worse still, January 5 doesn't worry about chasing married people and best friends' partners. It adds interest. Sexually, they're addictive. Wonderful, generous lovers, they ply their quarry with food and wine, all laced with heady compliments and deft caresses until the seducee bounds into their bed. In the 60s this was a one night stand person. Today they take care that sex is physically safe, even if mentally about the unsafest thing you could do.

January 5 does well at work. The seducer's charm, toned down, is heady stuff for bosses and colleagues. It oils deals, and makes working on their projects the coveted job.

Find them in film, television, theatre and any local amateur entertainment. Rich enough not to be tempted by money, they may eventually choose a well connected partner, then make charming,

inattentive parents. The only members of the opposite sex who can hold them are those who refuse to sleep with them, but become friends.

January 5 adores them, quietly lusting but never openly, afraid they'll lose this most valuable relationship. Others of their own sex find them faithful, generous friends and they are attentive relatives. The nuisance factor for others involves giving advice to avoid January 5, and mending broken hearts.

Apart from all this, they're great fun, full of decorating ideas for Christmas and parties and make every occasion go with a bang.

All really great lovers are articulate and verbal seduction is the surest road to actual seduction.
(*Marya Mannes*)

BODY
Perfume makes love more exciting. Always choose essences that are safe on skin, and only apply absolutely harmless substances to more intimate parts. Diluted rose oil is perfect on the nipples. To scent pubic hair subtly, apply a little neroli to a small, soft bristled hairbrush (kept specially for this purpose) and brush through. Use dilute vetivert on thighs, jasmine around your waist or on the navel and sandalwood oil for the inside thighs. Myrtle brings heat to wherever it is applied and can be used intimately. No more than 2 or 3 drops to a teaspoon of fatty oil.

MIND
Rubies are Capricorn's lucky gemstone, repelling ill luck and giving insight and mental power. Said to grow paler when misfortune threatens. Catherine of Aragon, first queen of Henry VIII, was warned of her decline from royal favour by the ruby she wore.

DATESHARE
Robert Duvall, film TV actor. **Diane Keaton**, film star. **Konrad Adenauer**, West German chancellor. **Umberto Eco**, Italian author, The Name of The Rose. **Alfred Brendel**, international concert pianist. **Jimmy Page**, guitarist, songwriter, Led Zeppelin. **Raisa Gorbachev**, Russian wife to Mikhail. **Juan Carlos**, Spanish 20th century king.

January 6 takes great delight in her surroundings. It's possible she sees everything in brighter colours than others. It's certain that Nature's beauty takes her breath away. This can be tedious to others who don't have a feel for plants, trees and birds, because January 6 people have a tendency to lecture about their favourite subject, and are startled to find others lack the same interests.

It can also be challenging to those who don't want to eat fritters made from oyster mushrooms which curl their way up deciduous trees and can look pretty disgusting. And certainly don't want to feast off an accompanying Burdock salad. But that's just the way things are. This creature sees Nature as a veritable Capricornucopia of edible goodies and if you forget prejudice, what she cooks is delicious. Unusually she may also use fruit, herbs and spices in flower arrangements and decorations.

With January 6, addiction to Nature gets out of hand if she works in a city centre during the week. Both sexes flourish when more relaxed about the countryside and living there is ideal.

Both sexes are computer literate and many flourish in design, much of which can be done at home, ideal for 6 whose allergy to bureaucracy sometimes induces fairly bad behaviour in offices. The freelance life is best. While they aren't necessarily good at self-promotion, and worry about where the next job is coming from,

this is no different from the rest of the world. The advantage is that work always comes to this talented person and they don't have to worry about office politics, which makes January 6 nervous.

Many have a religious leaning, which brings them great comfort, but must watch the proselytising side of their nature. Nagging isn't the best way to induce others to adopt ideas, in particular children, who rarely want to follow in their parents' footsteps and must be left to go their own way.

And the Lord God planted a garden eastwards in Eden; and there he put the man whom he had formed.

(Genesis)

7 JANUARY

This is one of the most enthusiastic dates of the year, a peach to work with, fall in love with and have either as a child or parent. January 7 always looks on the bright side of life and the bright side of people. They have the self-confidence which comes with being multi-talented and are rarely tempted to gossip. They never criticise others in order to build themselves up, aware that it's always the praising of others which attracts the rest of the world to their side.

This isn't a pushover peach, however. Both sexes are extremely tolerant about other's foibles, culture and religion, but they aren't tolerant of laziness. Their credo is that a job that's worth doing is worth doing well and things left half done will drive them to impressive temper flashes. January 7 rises high in any organisation, because of the hard work, the optimism and the loyalty. And because, with the methodical, logical thought processes common to this star sign, they are often up to the minute on latest scientific and technical inventions.

Our peachette is also one of the most attractive birthday people of the year, usually dark and svelte, but whatever shade of hair and colouring, fine eyes and in both sexes, unusually beautiful, long eyelashes. Not at all given to philandering – they prefer to mate for life – January 7 is nevertheless deliciously flirtatious and there will always be a crowd of hopeful admirers, any one of whom would give their eye teeth to leap into this Capricorn's bed.

Anybody who does make it into the peachy bedroom will find that love is taken seriously. Both sexes have extremely erotically sensitive bodies and respond to caresses on the rib cage just beneath the bosom for girls and on the equivalent ribcage spot for men. A little pressure from the thumbs just behind the ankle bone will also send Ms and Mr Peach into fruitful transports.

When the world turns
completely upside down
We'll live among wild peach trees,
miles from town.

(Elinor Wylie)

EARTH

BODY

Sometimes natural remedies can alter a hypochondriacal Paradise Syndrome mindset. Of the 38 Bach Flower remedies, heather (Calluna vulgaris) was made for January 8. Heather relates to optimism and the soul qualities of empathy and readiness to help. It will balance the personality of someone who relates to the world as a 'needy child' and indulges in excessive worrying. Heather will also help to firmly underline a sense of one's own talent and the proper enjoyment of recognition for achievements fairly won. Those who take it report that they become better listeners, more sympathetic to others and feel they are radiating strength and confidence.

༄

MIND

Lucky January days include 3, 5, 11, 19, 22 and 25. These are the days which are good for business transactions – except speculation. Extra luck comes to achievements on the sports field. These dates are particularly fortunate for young people.

DATESHARE

Died: **Terry Thomas**, *British actor, comedian. Born:* **Solomon Bandaranaike**, *prime minister of Ceylon, assassinated for advocating western medicine.* **Elvis Presley**, *rock and roller, film star, icon, died at 42.* **David Bowie**, *singer, songwriter, film star, art collector, painter.* **Shirley Bassey**, *singer, 'Hey Big Spender'.* **José Ferrer**, *film star.* **Wilkie Collins**, *author,* The Woman In White. **Stephen Hawking**, *Cambridge physicist, cosmologist,* A Brief History of Time.

January 8 is laden with talent and good looks and capable of earning phenomenal sums of money. Also capable of inspiring mass love-ins, being famous and very probably owning their own private jet. So why, oh why, is this Saturninny moaning and generally squelching about like a half-set jelly?

The answer is that the very successful birthday boys and girls who arrive here on January 8 suffer from the Paradise Syndrome. Sufferers have class, money, success and all the time they're wondering if anybody really likes them for themselves, how long they can go on being successful, and if they've got a temperature. Whatever their talent, people born on this day should get realistic about why people like them. The truth is, people do like them for their fame and popularity. They probably also like January 8 because they're good at netball and have a nice laugh, so it's really unrealistic to keep asking if people would like you just as much if it was an ugly laugh.

The streak of hypochondria and anxiety is a powerful influence here. Over consciousness of possible illnesses may be so burdensome that professional help should be sought. Fortunately these extremes are uncommon. In fact the tendency to pessimism may be painful but it's sometimes a useful antidote to the swollen head. January 8 may fear that he or she will be 'found out', but the fact is they're extremely good at what they do. It's not a flash in the pan, but based on talent.

Although they are rather inward looking, these individuals are capable of enormous generosity and intelligence. Deeply empathetic they may work for mankind's greater good. And faced with a real rather than imagined challenge, they can become inspiringly brave.

All of these individuals need solitude. While it is necessary to know they can go back to family, lovers and friends, too much socialising can genuinely disturb their spiritual balance and make them unhappy.

This world exists as a sheen of dew on flowers.
(Isumi Shikibu)

9 JANUARY

These people live a long, mostly lucrative life with much of the excitement coming in the middle years. January 9's star burns up brighter as they pass to their mid-thirties and by the time they have reached their fifties, most of these shimmery individuals have got their heart's desire.

Many long to travel and spend their early adult years working and living abroad. Saturn is drawn to Germany and Austria, can't resist the mountains for skiing and the cakes. And many love the music. Find them also enjoying a brief stay in Hong Kong or far away places like Vietnam where they are mostly attached to the travel industry. With their exceptional attention to detail and pleasure in giving pleasure, they shine in any tourist industry. Abroad, they always learn the language.

It's not so much money that January 9 desires, although that too, but recognition. This is where a late career change comes in, usually successful. With their tough physique and enormous capacity for concentration, they can become ruthlessly ambitious, hard for partners and family. Expect divorces and broken love affairs for both sexes. Lovers must 'fit' their style and get by in January 9's chosen social element.

The women are gentler, and although some may stick in the office all hours looking for advancement, many grow tired at a certain point, and ease up the pace. Many men continue their ruthless ways into old age.

What saves them is an essential niceness, which means they won't harm others unless pushed very hard, and always try to help others. It's a mentor date for both sexes. Expect them in mid life to be surrounded by young admiring talent, eager to copy every move and learn their trade.

January 9's problem may be that he or she don't see their children enough, which may cause lasting regret when the little ones have grown and flown. Nor do they give themselves enough time for relaxation and laughter.

I'm suggesting we call sex something else,

and it should include everything

from kissing to sitting close together.

(Shere Hite)

BODY

Sometimes January 9 works so hard that both sexes go off sex. This can be hard to talk about, given our social climate where many feel they must pretend to be permanently sexually ravenous. If hard work gets in the way of loving there's no need to worry. This is common. Give up the idea of active sex for a little while and concentrate on relaxing with your partner. A massage purely for the massage's sake is ideal, using essential oils that combat anxiety: neroli, rosewood, pine, patchouli, lemon, jasmine, clary sage or bergamot. Fear may be lessened by massaging rose or rosemary over the solar plexus areas.

MIND

Sapphires are a beneficial stone for this birthdate. Wear it with turquoise to enhance its traditional powers which are said to ensure mental health, strengthen and stimulate resolve, give the wearer a brave heart and generally act as good omens.

DATESHARE

Richard Nixon, US president, implicated in Watergate scandal. **Joan Baez**, folksinger, songwriter. **Lee Van Cleef**, film actor. **Mitch Mitchell**, rock drummer, Jimmi Hendrix Experience. **Gracie Fields**, entertainer, comedienne. **Judith Krantz**, novelist. **Rudolf Bing**, opera director, Edinburgh Festival founder.

JANUARY 10

This remarkable space traveller is an old star, possessing wisdom which comes with one who has made a long journey through time. With every January 10 there is a strong feeling that they have lived at other times, conventionally known as old souls. Even as a child, January 10 shows an unusually balanced, nurturing personality. If an adult is unwell, they will toddle up and caress the sick one, tenderness showing in their childish eyes. They adore myths and legends, and left to play in a corner by themselves, make up their own fantasies and generally enjoy their own thoughts.

In adulthood, 10 is clever and logical. Both sexes take an overview. They are exceptionally generous and sensitive towards others and show none of the petty envies and jealousies.

Old souls are a delight because they contribute so much. At work they are both ambitious and nurturing of others. Found in creative professions, medicine or jobs where they can do good, 10 is a persuasive speaker both privately and publicly. And uses charm to get her way.

But don't try to push them around. Born knowing what they want no amount of coercion makes any difference. Indeed if they suspect a manipulator they will become stubborn, uncooperative and quite frequently simply walk away, disconcerting to those who misinterpret 10's balance and nurturing side for weakness.

Where love is concerned they feel deeply and appreciate every tiny act of kindness shown by a partner. When they find another old soul as a mate nothing will part them. Even if that person is married and can't leave, there will be a connection between them more powerful than most can fathom. But beware. With ordinary partners January 10 is loving, but when things don't seem to work out, they're very easy come easy go. Why worry when there are always plenty more available lovers to choose from?

It was so cold last week, my grandma's teeth were chattering and they weren't even in her mouth.

EARTH

11 JANUARY

Such a worryboots this person. And sometimes it gets right out of hand. January 11 is a genuine shimmer-dusted high wire star. Others believe in his talent and a capacity to pull things off most people can only dream of. Others will follow his moral lead and even be inspired by this straightforward and honest creature. But then anxiety sets in like a nasty dose of acne. It won't go away and if January 11 lets it, things get silly.

High wire stars are essentially daring, as is this creature. They can't spend their time worrying about burglars and if they've left the tap on in the top bathroom so that it will flood and bring all the ceilings down. But this star does. It's a strange contrast in the psycheology which can make life unnecessarily uncomfortable. And if it does get out of hand, people born today can devote more energy to anxiety and futile worrying than they do to having a good time, working properly and falling in love.

This person is a prey to all the latest fad worries. She is so concerned about pollution that sometimes she hardly dares go out, will certainly never swim even in the cleanest natural water, won't eat sausages with even the freshest and safest beef in them, and finds going abroad a nightmare of imagined illness, strange insects and dirty water.

In particular the down side of this, apart from grounding our star, is that it irritates other people who immediately have to rush to reassure. Doctors get tired of January 11's constant visits. Other nervous dates don't want to have January 11 round in case the worries are catching. And there's altogether too much looking up of diseases and other problems in reference books.

A little worry is an OK thing and usually results in good old-fashioned responsible behaviour. A lot of worry is gruesome for this creature.

'Where should one use perfume?'
a young woman asked.
'Wherever one wants to be kissed,' I said.

(Coco Chanel)

January 12 tends to be a little coercive, often attributing his failure to others. A swanky little planet, fast on the draw with criticisms of stupidity. They should try to grasp that when people always feel they have to defend themselves, nothing very innovative gets done. The worst offenders go through work or love partnerships like a reckless card player rifling through his hand and throwing the latest choice down on the table without thinking.

Fortunately this challenging behaviour only severely afflicts a proportion of January 12s at the extreme end of the psychological gene pool. Most control it, but impatience is common with this sky racer and both sexes really ought to get hold of their short temper and irritation. Nevertheless January 12 is heaped with marvellous gifts, including a sparkling intelligence, seductive charm, courage, leadership and in-your-face sexiness. Ms Slightly Snappy can put a project together in Saturnanoseconds. Whether it be in the clothing

industry, where they reap a Capricornucopia of success, or in more rigid professions like the army or police force, everybody knows that if you want something doing from scratch in an impossibly short time, ask January 12.

Money is attracted to this creature like a swarm of summer wasps to sweet scented lavender. Some adore spending. Buying gives January 12 as much pleasure as sex, or any other sensuous indulgence. But actually they're greedy for all pleasure. An ideal day is buying a pair of shoes which they may very easily instantly wear to make love in (true!), and continue to wear while they rustle up a great dish to serve guests the self same evening. Without tiring.

Friends, lovers and children need to watch what they tell January 12. Both sexes are natural raconteurs and can easily reduce a roomful of listeners to delicious laughter. But today's embarrassing confessions and experiences are grist for tomorrow's entertaining anecdote. They're shameless really, but you can't help wanting to be with them.

'You'd be a good dancer but for two things.'

'What are they?'

'Your feet.'

13 JANUARY

This missile has strong passions. January 13 chooses a goal and goes straight for it. Our knight in steel armour has a list of ambitions that will be realised come what may.

With love he has a clear idea who will suit. And it won't be a gentle, dependent partner. Their lover must say boo to all geese, except of course the golden one. January 13 picks a partner of any race, creed or colour, unconcerned if they are different from his own. But they need a co-star with the same pleasure in laughter, success and most important of all the same desire to change things. What they don't like is stupidity. Capricorns admire their own IQs and judge many others to be less clever than themselves. It's a tendency which can be wearing to friends and family, because our nose-in-the-air knight is always correcting other's grammar and pointing out mistakes.

Most January 13s achieve their ambitions to own a house, wear great clothes (very vain), belong to the right clubs and have children. But beyond all material ambition, there's something else deeply desired. This missile wants a mission, nothing to do with work or family.

Many do discover the secret plans waiting for them alone in the firmament, finding on the way a measure of fame, which every January 13 hugely enjoys. The search is not a vain one for self-gratification. Many follow religious beliefs, finding a sense of belonging made more important by work in the community. Others may improve conditions for local children by running sports clubs or organising music festivals. Or they may start to collect or preserve something which is endangered. Perhaps a vital railway is to be closed, or a historic building threatened with demolition to make way for a car park. Or a river needs cleaning up.

Once January 13 has adopted his chosen cause he is a terrorist to the lackadaisical. It's a star who really can change things.

Don't be agnostic – be something.
(Robert Frost)

BODY
January 13 adores unusual recipes. Both sexes are excellent cooks. Pashka (the Russian name for Easter when this famous desert is served). Take 400g fresh cream cheese, 200g unsalted butter, 200g caster sugar, 4 egg yolks, drops vanilla essence, 400g mixed chopped sultanas, glacé pineapple, cherries, angelica, almonds. Sieve cheese, cream butter, beat in sugar and egg yolks until mixture is light and fluffy. Add cheese, vanilla and blend, stir in fruit and nuts. Line colander with muslin, fill with mixture. Put plate on top and bowl under colander to collect whey. Leave in fridge for 12 hours. Turn out on plate before serving.

MIND
Good cooks such as January 13 put on weight and dieting is often undermined by sugar craving. If you can stop thinking about sugary things you're half way there. Nibble radishes. Oriental medicine says they take the mind off sweet desires.

January 14 may suffer allergies, in particular the running noses and sore eyes which accompany hayfever or caused by general air pollution. Driving when pollution is high can bring this on. Avoid using your car at these times if it does not have a catalyst fitted. (Unlikely with L registration or earlier.) Vehicle idling produces more pollutants, so cut down on the use of a choke and if you are stuck in traffic, switch off the engine. When filling tank, try not to overfill or spill petrol and always park in the shade to avoid fuel evaporating from your car. Bicyclists should wear a mask.

MIND

Tarot's card for this date in the Major Arcana is Temperance. It shows that people born today are capable of more balanced lives where controlling their own impulse to flight, and may lead them to discover valuable truths about life.

DATESHARE

Died: **Humphrey Bogart,** *Hollywood star, icon. Born:* **Faye Dunaway,** *film star, singer, author.* **Albert Schweitzer,** *German Nobel Peace Prize-winning philosopher, missionary.* **John Dos Passos,** *novelist, USA.* **Trevor Nunn,** *Royal Shakespeare Company director, film director. Joseph Losey, film director, The Servant.* **Cecil Beaton,** *society photographer, artist, stage designer.* **Jack Jones,** *singer.* **Bebe Daniels,** *film star, World War II Medal of Freedom winner.* **Berthe Morisot,** *French Impressionist painter.*

JANUARY 14

There are always some people in every star sign whose tendency is to live alone. With January 14 there's a strong dislike of commitment. They may dream of finding the right person and settling down, but both sexes often prefer it to be kept in dreams. Many just don't want to wake up each morning to the same person. Shy of taking on financial responsibility, both sexes do like to spend money, but although they are terrific present bringers and treat providers, they mainly prefer to spend it on themselves.

Commitment at work may also be problem. Capricorn's unbending cynicism encourages them to think of others as fools and that goes for bosses too. Fortunately sticking with one job isn't fashionable in the late 90s, and January 14 is temperamentally bang on to benefit. They flit, maybe spending two years here, eighteen months there. While there they stay at work all hours, with a phenomenal production capacity, in some cases openly contemptuous of other mortals who go home on time. Ms 14 is particularly devoted to long hours and may be contemptuous of other women who go home to lovers and families. You can spot her because of her bad teeth and dull hair – she has no time for the dentist or the hairdresser.

If this Capricornflakiness about not sticking around overdevelops, employees may sheer away to find a solider, stay-around star, tired of leaping after our mountain goat. It's often better for this creature to set up her own business, because then at least she'll stay interested in it.

January 14 may be a good present giver, but not an attender at family occasions. At Christmas nobody knows what January 14 will do until the last minute, just as likely to stay home alone as to turn up glittering with desirables. The exception they make is for their own children, who become the centre of January 14's world, and whom they love and raise with total commitment.

Who says I am not under the special protection of God?

(Adolf Hitler)

15 JANUARY

This lovely laughing comet is a delight and one of the wittiest people of the year. They're the tomatoes of the universe. Round, attractively coloured, delicious as a snack, a main meal or even as a pudding, their versatile rotundity (yes, there's a weight problem here) will never be left on the shelf, nor would want to be.

As everybody knows, or should know, wittiness is twenty times more attractive than perfect skin and juicy sexuality, and January 15 attracts others with his sense of humour. Hers too. Both sexes could become professional laughter makers.

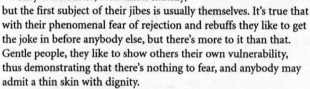

They tease others, sometimes harshly, but the first subject of their jibes is usually themselves. It's true that with their phenomenal fear of rejection and rebuffs they like to get the joke in before anybody else, but there's more to it than that. Gentle people, they like to show others their own vulnerability, thus demonstrating that there's nothing to fear, and anybody may admit a thin skin with dignity.

January 15 thrives in conventional settings. They like teamwork and the armed forces, medicine, teaching and the police force are ideal. The humour they bring, and with it, wisdom, means they can usually rely on promotion.

Naturally you can expect these people will have a happy home life. Partners can laugh away their worries and fears. Children are happy near January 15. Elderly relatives are soothed by the laughter, which makes them feel young again. And the humour never gets in the way of lovemaking, just means that all sorts of astonishing experiments can go on without anybody getting too serious about it.

This creature may or may not make money, but he is not overly materialistic and chooses happiness over vaulting ambition. They particularly enjoy making things for and planning a family Christmas or Easter, just as much as any soaring work success or clever international deal.

If you're not allowed to laugh in heaven, I don't want to go there.

(Martin Luther)

BODY

January 15 adores kids and can always find them something fun to do. Christmas Tree Cards are extremely easy, encouraging the idea of generous effort for another and saving money. Four-year-olds upward can do this, providing you work with them and control the paint spray. Read safety instructions carefully. Buy or pick a fern, spray a thin layer of spray adhesive on underside, position on piece thin cardboard, press gently to ensure complete contact. Spray silver or gold paint over fern, direct spray towards centre to give 'glow' around tree. Remove fern, glue on base cut from metallic paper. Edge card with braid. (After this tired children sleep well.)

MIND

Affectionate mockery is fun. Sometimes cruel mockery is equally funny. The difference is that the first brings pleasure and the second hurts. It's too easy and the temptation should be avoided.

DATESHARE

Lloyd Bridges, film actor, father of Jeff. **Martin Luther King**, American Nobel Peace Prize-winner, civil rights leader, assassinated. **Joan of Arc**, French soldier, saint, burned at the stake. **Gamal Abdul Nasser**, Egyptian president. **Molière**, French playwright, Le Misanthrope. **Aristotle Onassis**, Greek shipping magnate, married Jackie Kennedy. **Hugh Trevor-Roper**, British historian. **Maria Schell**, Viennese film star.

They have good minds and while they have no great ambition to seize fame and power, sometimes it's thrust upon them for their remarkable problem-solving abilities and capacity to communicate ideas. Indeed, January 16 is the communicator's day, not a typical Capricorn talent, but very dominant here.

As children January 16 people may not all be conventionally brilliant at school, but a good teacher can spot their outstanding talent if they look hard enough. What they are is 'different'. Sometimes both sexes feel so 'different' it upsets them. They have a deep need for their talents to be acknowledged. But generally this creature learns to make use of her other, original view of the world, and turns this freshness to her advantage.

Those around this individual soon understand that this is a special psychology with farseeing qualities which are extremely useful in sorting out difficult situations. At work, January 16 is never involved in gossip, but can manoeuvre her way through politics with dexterity and often puts a stop to unpleasantness. He abhors bullying and sabotaging, feeling tremendous contempt for those who indulge in them. Our Capricorn baby is sufficiently

talented not to need to undermine others, and in spite of early self-doubt, he knows it.

Most are animal lovers and will own as many as is practical if they live in the country, where a good number of 16s are at their happiest. But their kindness is not confined to animals. Friends or relatives in need find shelter with 16 whose idea of fun is to live in an extended family. Expect to find in their house somebody else's grown up child who's staying for a few months, a spouse's brother or sister, mothers- and fathers-in-law and anybody else who comes along.

Naturally, this means that January 16 doesn't have heaps of money. If they need more they can make it by freelance, often writing or designing, sometimes house improvement of some sort.

The way I see it,
if you want a rainbow,
you gotta put up with the rain.

I7 JANUARY

They are interested in food and drink. They like to cook for others and entertain, because January 17 is a people pleaser. They adore partying, can stay up all night and will travel miles for a good time. This individual is exceptionally slender in youth and can eat anything. But by their early thirties the lavish lifestyle is beginning to show. The waist is no longer 23 inches (28 for men) and there are little rolls of plumpness where there was once taught flesh.

This eventually rotund person will have a life-long battle with weight and is always scanning the shelves in Boots for another slimming drink or biscuit. The women suffer more than the men because that's the way of the world. Hear them say they only have to look at slice of chocolate cake and the inches pile on. Their credo is 'a moment on the lips, a lifetime on the hips', but apart from this sometimes too intense preoccupation, and days of lettuce leaves and water, January 17 usually reverts to delumptious ways and wolfs a packet of chocolate biscuits.

Mother January 17 is vulnerable to the guzzling-left-overs syndrome. Instead of binning the sausages and chips left by her children, she gollops the lot so as not to let the food go to waste (but to waist).

Nevertheless, they are good companions both at work and in private, although some have too great a tendency to control their environment and fear change more than they need. In such cases anxiety results when change does occur and 17 should remember that most things come right in the end, especially if they relax a little.

This individual is likely to have several other talents, which should not be left to lie dormant. Many have fine singing voices. Others are exceptional sportsmen and women, both of which talents bring harmony and balance to young and old. And often provide an excellent and jolly source of social life.

The flesh is aye fairest that's farthest from the bone.

BODY
There's a variety of activities such as body brushing, mud packs, massage and manicuring your nails, keeping thoughts away from food and hands occupied, which might otherwise be rooting in the fridge for a fattening snack. Manicuring nails makes both sexes feel good, especially afterwards, because dirty ragged nails and hands are an absolute turn off to some. File nails with an emery board to a smooth round shape. Stick hands in bowl of warm soapy water for three minutes. Pat dry with towel. Push back cuticles with orange stick. Massage in rich cuticle cream. Leave on for a few minutes, then wipe off excess cream. Buff nails to a soft sheen.

MIND
January 17 should take note of the following unlucky dates around the time of their birthday. (These are only signposts. Nothing will necessarily happen, especially if you take care.) They are January 2, 7, 10, 15, 17 and 21, all times when money problems may emerge.

DATESHARE
James Earl Jones, *film star, stage actor.* **Muhammed Ali**, *world heavyweight boxing champion, Olympic gold medallist.* **Joe Frazier**, *world heavyweight boxing champion, Olympic gold medallist.* **Moira Shearer**, *film star, ballet dancer.* **Vidal Sassoon**, *revolutionary hairdresser, celebrity.* **David Lloyd George**, *British prime minister.* **Al Capone**, *Chicago crime boss.* **Konstantin Stanislavski**, *Russian born stage director, founder of 'method' acting.*

JANUARY 18

MIND

Youthful marriages for January 18 are often a mistake. Successful love comes with maturity. Best long-term, harmonious partners are likely to be born between April 21 and May 21, or August 21 and September 21.

DATESHARE

Cary Grant, film star, idol. **Kevin Costner**, film star, sex bomb. **David Bellamy**, botanist, writer, broadcaster. **Danny Kay**, film star, actor, singer. **Oliver Hardy**, half of Laurel and Hardy duo. **John Boorman**, film director, Deliverance. **Tommy Sopwith**, aeroplane designer, Sopwith Camel. **A A Milne**, children's writer, creator of Winnie the Pooh, Tigger, Piglet, Owl and Eeyore and father of real-life Christopher Robin. **Baron de Montesquieu**, French political philosopher, statesman.

P sychic tendencies are not so common in Capricorn people. Theirs is usually a logical, tough mind, unreceptive to this otherwordly talent. January 18 is the exception. They get psychic flashes from early childhood. Coincidences are continuous. They sense what a friend or even stranger is going to do next. Most of us experience thinking of a person only to find that they are on the telephone. For January 18, this experience is so frequent they are almost never surprised.

It's a delicate talent to nurture. Some may find it frightening if they are prey to foreboding, but most of January 18's 'flashes' are positive. Many racing enthusiasts born on this day, whether it be horses, dogs or cars, find their 'hunch' bets keep them in pin money at least and sometimes phenomenal cash windfalls. Naturally friends watch them closely.

Some of the psychic supernova's capacity is born of a psycheological capacity for observation of surroundings and people. They read the signs. Of course, nobody knows for sure exactly where some of the 'messages' may lead. Always open to interpretation, they nevertheless give January 18 a head start.

In any kind of work they can almost smell a bad deal and a bad person. Colleagues and bosses watch January 18 closely and always take note. That they do well in the police force or investigative work goes without saying. But you can find them flourishing in

any industry which requires that you're spot on about what's happening.

In private January 18 uses her capacity to listen to her heart, so she's lucky in love, avoids danger and silly harmful people and usually knows when she's going to get pregnant before there's been anything physical. They know if they are pregnant the moment they've made love. They pick up immediately if they have met the love of their life. They know if a place is lucky for them. And they can 'see' the dangers that lie ahead for any of their offspring.

What is a forum?
A two-um, plus two-um.

19 JANUARY

A t school January 19 was always told off for gazing out of the window, but it would be a bad thing for this creature if he stopped doing so. On one level, gazing and thinking and dreaming is what this creature is all about. This is how to find peace of mind and mental rest, a fact which any child can tell you, but many adults have forgotten. This contemplation isn't vacant. Both sexes' minds are working, but they're working far away.

Both men and women can be unconventional and may want to travel for some years before settling down. Many may choose to live abroad. Often restless with their environment, January 19 seeks change. Many indeed become addicted to change, rejecting their background and sometimes even old friends and family. But this is usually when they are receiving too much advice, which January 19 sees as nagging. People born today are extremely original thinkers and don't want to be like everybody else.

In some cases a powerful sense of otherness makes them unhappy for a while and even bullyable, especially in childhood. But the otherness and the dreaming strengthens their drive and resolve and they will eventually find their feet. Although dreaming can get them through a lot of mundane jobs, this creature's strength lies in an unusual vision. Many take off to found their own empire and successfully realise the vision. It's not a fantastically money-minded date, although quite capable of reaping huge financial rewards. Without money, however, this disarming charmer quickly adapts, living creatively on very little.

These seductive solo stars seek like-minded lovers and won't tolerate somebody who gets their thrills from discounts. Both women and men loathe shopping and a relative who wants to discuss curtain prices is soon shown the door. Others are drawn to January 19 because he and she welcome friendship from all sorts – snobbery is anathema to this wandering star – and because of their peaceable companionship.

> Customs officer: 'Have you anything to declare?'
>
> Oscar Wilde: 'I have nothing to declare but my genius.'

BODY

Essential oil of rose is one of the most potent perfumes used in ancient love magic rituals, either to procure the interest of a new lover or pep up flagging desire. Originally from Persia, the oil was used on wedding nights and although it's expensive – it takes 81kg of damask roses to make 30ml – one drop is usually enough to produce tingling nights of pleasure. Use almond oil as the base. Touch a drop to your forehead and if you are feeling adventurous, on the nipples. (The nipples in either sex are erotically sensitive so both men and women can do this.)

MIND

Many January 19 people have distinctive handwriting, usually with well-spaced words and letters which show their generous natures, self-confidence and open-heartedness. Avaricious and mean minded people cramp the writing. Exaggerated spacing indicates irresponsibility.

DATESHARE

Sir Simon Rattle, conductor City of Birmingham Symphony Orchestra. **Julian Barnes**, author, Flaubert's Parrot. **Phil Everly**, rock and roll singer, Everly Bothers. **Edgar Allen Poe**, poet, journalist, short story writer. **Paul Cezanne**, French painter. **Janis Joplin**, singer, songwriter. **Dolly Parton**, country and western singer, film star, big bosom. **Michael Crawford**, film star, musical comedy actor, Phantom of The Opera. **Stefan Edberg**, Swedish tennis star. **Richard Lester**, film director, A Hard Day's Night.

EARTH

January 20 is one of those people who can do several things extremely well, which often irritates duller starlets who can't. By moondust, by stardust, this is the streetwalker of the Milky Way, pleasing to all, successful in every chosen pursuit, possessed by nobody. Worse still, both sexes are discombobulatingly sexy.

They can sing and paint, they are terrific sportsmen and women, often exceptional writers and worse still again, good businessmen and women. It's sometimes judicious for January 20 to hide some of their light under a bushelette so as not to make others sick with envy. Remember, this is the creature who saunters unescorted into a party and all eyes of the opposite sex swivel upon them.

And they're nice with it. Plus honest, decent and clever. Less gifted starlets can take some comfort because understandably, some January 20s are very vain. There is also a tendency to baldness amongst the extremely-hairy-in-youth males, and another tendency for our glittering sweetheart to become extremely rotund after years of swallowing caviare, champagne, chips, chocolate cake and other titbits offered them by drooling lovers.

Some of the men even run two partners simultaneously for many years – even on occasion two wives – in which case they often have to eat so many carefully cooked dinners and lunches that they swell to portly proportions. No matter. A stout and sexy January 20 is often worth several slimmer people, with equally slenderer seduction appeal. They're larger than life and enormous fun to be around.

The children of both sexes adore them, and with January 20 there will be a lot of children born on all sides of the blanket. Ms 20 has more leadership in her little finger than most and may become famous for her work. If not, much admired. Whatever happens, they walk, play tennis, swim, sing, have a ball and everybody, except for those whose hearts are completely tuned to green cheese, wants to be with them.

Extreme skill in many things is considered to be a deadly sin.

(Hilaire Belloc)

21 JANUARY

You can't get a handle on this soar-away bird. January 21 is unpredictable, multi-talented and needs to fly his or her own course, untrammelled by advisors and freeloaders. They are like storm petrels: brave, neatly designed, fast of flight but very private and better spotters of opportunities for life enhancement than most other birds.

The storm petrel follows great ships, picking up food and living sometimes by others' wits. And this is often what January 21 does, at least at the start of adult life, attaching itself to a mentor, acquiring know-how, then flying away to establish its own empire. Many have an excellent design eye, and excel in music, painting and writing. If they make careers in these areas, they institute a new way of seeing things. Whatever happens, when January 21 takes a job, however mundane, she always brings special vitality, changing it to make everything better for the company and those around her.

Spot January 21 giving advice both at work and at home. In particular the women seem to draw others to them, always full of reassurance, praise and comfort. They want the best for everybody and will often put themselves out both in terms of energy and even financially to help. When January 21 has children, it is her house that is full of their friends, because they find her delightful to be around and unfailingly interested in whatever they do. Moreover, when they get to teenage years, this woman praises their achievements just as much as her own children's.

Because they are so idealistic, many people born today will work in areas which can do the community some good. They may found special schools, or promote young people's music. They are frequently found at the heart of a worthwhile enterprise. Yet neither sex suffers from the do-gooder's coercive desire to make others agree. Theirs is the view that conversation and ideas are at their best when founded on civilised disagreement.

*Caveat Emptor
(Let the buyer beware).*

(*Latin Motto*)

BODY

January 21 is interested in health and tries to manage his or her own well-being with a combination of good doctoring, attention to diet and exercise and some alternative medicines. Many are attracted to the use of perfumed essential oils, believing that these oils bring great benefit both physically and mentally. Around the house, or at work if at all possible, they will use essential oil burners to promote good feelings for themselves, friends and family. Favourite everyday oils include cedarwood with its distinctive woody smell, like freshly sharpened pencils. It promotes calmness and erases nervous tension. Eucalyptus stimulates the nervous system and promotes a clear head.

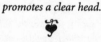

MIND

Sometimes January 21 feels weighed down by other's problems. It's important not to allow the empathetic side of their nature to absorb too much woe and they must learn sometimes to kindly keep others' distress at bay, avoiding over-exposure.

DATESHARE

Died: **Cecil B DeMille**, *producer, movie mogul.* **Ann Sheridan**, *Hollywood siren. Born:* **Christian Dior**, *Parisian fashion designer, perfume maker.* **Geena Davis**, *Hollywood film star.* **Paul Scofield**, *Shakespearian actor, film star.* **Telly Savalas**, *bald TV star, Kojak.* **Cristobal Balenciaga**, *Spanish master fashion designer, perfume maker.* **Jack Nicklaus**, *golf champion.* **Placido Domingo**, *Spanish opera singer.*

AIR

January 22 is an extremely tactile and flirtatious starlet, not at all the PC sort and so should avoid those who are. For the rest of us, 22 promises an interesting dangerous liaison. This is the man who meets a lovely stranger and says 'Marry me or have dinner with me'. And this is the girl who sleeps with someone on her first date because, why not? They often fall in love at first sight. They particularly like making love in dangerous, discoverable places such as the Royal Box at the Royal Opera House. If anyone's going to be found in flagrante at work, it'll be January 22.

❧

MIND
Tarot's card in the Major Arcana for 22 is The Fool. He symbolises wisdom, although there are more negative impulsive aspects. In this case they rarely bring harm unless our moonbeam goes right over the outrageous top.

DATESHARE
Kyle MacLachlan, *American movie star.* **Ann Southern**, *film star.* **John Hurt**, *stage, film star.* **Linda Blair**, *movie star.* **André Marie Ampère**, *French physicist, electrical units inventor.* **Beatrice Webb**, *early educator, social reformer.* **Lord Byron**, *great romantic poet, scandalous lover.* **Grigory Rasputin**, *Russian monk, therapist, attached to court of Tsar Nicholas II.* **Sergei Eisenstein**, *great Russian film director, Battleship Potemkin.* **Jerome Kern**, *musical comedy songwriter, composer.* **George Balanchine**, *Russian ballet choreographer.* **Sir Francis Bacon**, *essayist, philosopher.*

JANUARY 22

Wherever January 22 goes he makes an impact. Whatever he does, people watch with interested admiration, although some envy January's child, touched with magical moonshine. Others have to strive, but there was lightening at this creature's birth and they attain goals faster. Some have a problem with the jealousies of other less fortunate people who can't understand why it's easier for January 22. Some may even have to ward off nastiness – particularly at work – from those who want to denigrate and hold back this gorgeous moonbeam.

And this is where generous-minded January 22 must be watchful. If they were Cinderella they'd try to be nice about the ugly sisters and, once married to the prince, go about finding the awful pair good loving husbands. Yet there are those who will bring genuine harm to January 22 – out of envy – and so a spot of realism is practical.

Money is also a problem for January 22. The women aren't the natural shoppers of the universe and find money matters bring them down. Many prefer the man in their life to pay the bills and would be therefore better off marrying money. But since this shining sweetheart is not at all grabby, she won't try to fall for the guy with the fat wallet and usually finds herself with a much more interesting, but poorer, life-long companion. If they can, the men will give their money away to grandma or their needy brother.

All are interested in natural beauty. Expect to find natural rocks and shells, or pieces of strangely shaped wood in January 22's house. A lump of sparkling quartz is more interesting than a Meissen figurine, a piece of natural wood more fascinating than any man-made artistry. Because of this, both sexes and their children will wander over beach and hill, stopping to murmur at the beauty of a shell or wild rose. It may not make them wealthy, but certainly healthy and wise.

All rising to great place is by a winding stair.

(Sir Francis Bacon)

23 JANUARY

January 23 is the person others copy. From childhood they do things just that little bit different, the ones who can make school uniform seem stylish, the ones who are so good at football that smaller boys watch with shining eyes. And all their life this goes on right until very great old age.

It's a hard quality to define in January 23. But the cadence of their voice, the idiosyncrasy of their speech, the way they decorate their house, or the way they take the lead in the local drama society are all noticeable and somehow you find others talking like them, walking like them and using their catch phrases.

At work this is extremely noticeable, especially if January 23 rises high. They run their department or their business like a club which it's a privilege to join. There are no cruelties or acts of spitefulness with this person, and they see to it that others don't indulge. Endlessly helpful to colleagues, generous with their time, money and talent, this sugar plum can be easily out-witted and defeated by tough hunters with a nasty streak, and when that happens January 23 never plays dirty back. Instead they just pack their bags and go and set up business elsewhere, usually with enormous success.

Many like to travel and work abroad. They are drawn to old civilisations – this is the most civilised and mature of all the year's people – and may find happiness and inspiration in Far Eastern countries. If January 23 can't afford to travel, they will read about it, look at pictures and travel in their minds. Always open to new ideas, this creature develops a brilliant line in varying, foreign-influenced cookery. Or else January 23 takes fashion tips from abroad and modifies them to suit home life. They prefer to make clothes rather than find them in shops, which is why their style is so original and powerful.

Not every woman in old slippers can manage to look like Cinderella.

(*Don Marquis*)

BODY

Japanese or Chinese cooking fascinates this person, for its ease, style and healthiness. Try this Chinese Ornamental Raw Fish Delight. Take 400g plaice fillets, 1 tbsp sesame or soya oil, 2 tbsp sherry, 2 tbsp soy sauce, 2 spring onions, 200g small peeled frozen prawns, salt and freshly milled black pepper. Skin plaice, cut into narrow strips 5cm long. Thaw and wash prawns. Chop spring onions finely, put into shallow dish with remaining ingredients. Add fish, toss in mixture, leave 10 minutes. Mix in prawns, then arrange on pretty serving dish. Decorate with watercress, and or tiny florets of lightly cooked broccoli

MIND

Beware sexual predators or any other kind of predator. Many people want to be like 23 and certainly to appear as talented. This individual should guard against those who try to capture them for their talent rather than themselves.

DATESHARE

Died: **Alexander Korda**, *movie mogul, founder of British film.* **Paul Robeson**, *legendary black singer, political activist. Born:* **Humphrey Bogart**, *Hollywood film star, style icon.* **Jeanne Moreau**, *French actress, famous for skinny, husky sexiness and extraordinary mouth.* **Chita Rivera**, *Anita in West Side Story, world never recovered.* **Princess Caroline** *of Monaco.* **Anita Pointer**, *singer, one of Pointer Sisters.* **Edouard Manet**, *French painter.* **Stendahl**, *French novelist, The Red and The Black, made into movies, TV series.*

BODY

Stress can make you ill, lose concentration and see the world askew. Get somebody else to answer this for you. The Stressophile Test. 1: Is it always somebody else's fault? 2: Are you often late? 3: Do you lose your glasses, pen, wallet, keys, notebook, socks, telephone book, visa card, sense of humour, ear-rings or book more than once every two weeks? 4: Suddenly fly into red faced rages? 5: Think other drivers are inadequate? 6: The boss is a half-wit? 7: Think others are often too needy? Four ticks or more? It's not your surroundings but you that needs an overhaul.

MIND

If successful, this traditionally fortune-producing rhyme, could provide a stress-free rest of your life. 'Holly tree, O holly tree, Let much wealth come to me.' Say it to the tree while clasping it around the main stem.

DATESHARE

Neil Diamond, singer songwriter. **Daniel Auteuil**, movie star. **Michel Serrault**, French movie star. **Sharon Tate**, film star, married Roman Polanski, Manson murder victim. **Edith Wharton**, novelist, Ethan Frome, **John Belushi**, Hollywood comedian, film star. **Nastassja Kinski**, film star, daughter of Klaus. **Desmond Morris**, anthropologist, writer, The Naked Ape. **Hadrian**, Roman Emperor, ruled 21 years. **Frederick the Great**, Prussian ruler. **Ernest Borgnine**, film and TV star. **Maria Tailchief**, ballet dancer.

This is a shy creature. The dragon fly of the universe, January 24 hovers near for a fleeting moment, all iridescent blues and greens. Reach for her and she's gone in a second. Many Aquarians are more desired than desiring and this is one.

Although some slightly tougher individuals may do well at work, pioneering breath-taking projects, provoking a popular response and making whacking sums of boodle, many find high-powered environments too pressurised. They do better working alone, or occasionally joining a company of people, then disappearing to recover. Stress is a problem for the dragonfly, and when suffering from it her poor wings lose their lovely shimmer.

With love, January 24 can be difficult. Many can't tell the difference between love and lust; OK for them as they frequently prefer lust to love. But others fall for them, which this flittering creature – of both sexes – finds difficult. Irresponsibly, they blame the poor afflicted one, with little self-exonerating cries of, 'But I said it was just for fun and I was going away in two weeks.' So in their twenties and thirties there will be quite a few broken hearts around and it serves them right if a fed up desertee sends them twelve dozen bunches of rhubarb.

Many may marry and live happily ever after. But if a marriage or partnership doesn't work then 24 lights out faster than most. Some of the girls are happy to live singly, finding happiness in friendship, homemaking and a packed social life. Boy dragonflies do the same.

Expect to find this individual happily living abroad, where people accept their solitary mystery. Others will withdraw to far away places in the British Isles, where the lovely surroundings, slow pace of life and interest in natural things make them happy. All 24s are excellent with animals and if they can, find a life spent near them and caring for them, the best way to fulfilment.

I've told you for the fifty-thousandth time, stop exaggerating.

25 JANUARY

Like all Aquarians, this golden bird is more pursued than pursuing. Too clever to let vanity go to her sparkling head, her only problem is heedlessness. Half the world seems to want to capture her, maybe with the intention of shutting the door of the gilded cage. Captured she may even stay for a while, laughing and entertaining, bewitching with her cleverness, beguiling with her foresight. But then the resonance of the night recedes.

And around this bright creature the starlit or moonlit dome sparkles, suddenly seeming to disdain her capturer. Suddenly January 25 takes fright and is gone, leaving a lot of sadness in her wake. Both sexes are the same. To would-be lovers they seem a fantastic discovery. It's astonishing that somebody so come hither isn't tucked up in a long term relationship. But there's a reason for everything and with this winter child it's boredom and an easily sparked interest in something or somebody new.

This is one of the few unutterably glamorous creatures of the night sky who makes truly platonic friendship work. Although they may be ignoring the secret lusts of a 'friend', the relationship is usually worth the desirer's self-discipline, because then at least they know that January 25 will always be available. At work, find them in the media or tourism, where their charm takes them to high places and smooths the path for original thinking and deals. Bosses love them because their charisma is such that others want to throw money at them, ideal for January 25's employers.

Some stay with a partner for life, but most are serial mankillers (or ladykillers). Only children can command their total commitment. Often this individual finds himself as a single parent, but January 25s make terrific fathers and mothers and their offspring grow up as balanced as the scales of justice. While this person may be an earthquake in romantic love, a child's needs keep them steady.

The woods are lovely, dark and deep,

But I have promises to keep,

And miles to go before I sleep.

(Robert Frost)

AIR

BODY
January 25 is slightly psychic, but naughty with it and likes to wander about the British Isles frightening himself and companions by ghost spotting, at which both sexes are remarkably good. Favourite spots include Elton Hall, Cambridgeshire, haunted by a gambler's ghost who would kidnap and kill guests for the money in their wallet. Or the dark and dangerous grounds of Belvoir Castle, Leicestershire, supposedly haunted by three witches, executed for murdering the sixth Earl of Rutland's two infant sons, also rumoured to appear. January 25 is more likely than most to find a ghost so only the stout-hearted should go with them.

MIND
Long first and second fingers indicate intuitiveness, yet controlled by reason. A long third finger indicates a gambler and a risk-taker. A long fourth finger points to personal magnetism and the gift of leadership.

DATESHARE
*Died: **Ava Gardner**, screen goddess. Born: **Jacqueline Du Prez**, international cellist, tragic early death from MS. **Virginia Woolf**, novelist, To The Lighthouse. **W Somerset Maugham**, short story writer, novelist. **Robert Burns**, Scottish poet, songwriter, died young. **Corazon Aquino**, president of Philippines, unseated Marcos. **Eduard Shevardnadze**, USSR foreign minister. **Wilhelm Furtwängler**, German conductor, Berlin Philharmonic. **John Calder**, publisher, critic.*

We need full-spectrum, white sunlight to keep healthy. Its absence makes the body's nervous system adjust, which may manifest itself as fatigue, a desire to eat sweet, fast 'culprit' foods, irritability, mood shifts and blurry vision. January 26 should spend thirty minutes each day out of doors – without glasses or lenses, which block natural sunlight. Do this before 10am or after 4pm to avoid unnecessary exposure to ultra-violet rays. Looking at certain colours can have particularly beneficial effects. Yellow, orange and red are warming and stimulating, activating blood flow to the eye. Green is harmonising and balancing. Blue, violet and magenta are relaxing.

MIND

Don't put your money on the horses on January 2, 7, 10, 15, 17 or 21, when there may also be other financial losses and general shortness of cash. Good days for cash flow, deals, lucky wins or investments, include 3, 5, 11, 19, 22 and 25.

DATESHARE

Paul Newman, film star, bottled sauce entrepreneur, charity worker, icon. **Eartha Kitt**, kitten-voiced cabaret singer, film star, stage actress. **Jules Feiffer**, New York social cartoonist. **Stephan Grappelli**, jazz violinist. **Roger Vadim**, French film director, married Brigitte Bardot, then Catherine Deneuve, put them both in movies. **Nicolas Ceausescu**, Romanian dictator, executed. **Grantley Dick-Read**, famous obstetrician, Childbirth Without Fear. **Anita Baker**, jazz singer

These girls have great legs and so do the guys. It's just that you can't see so easily with men. January 26 is unusually tall for a winter child, and it's all in the legs. In youth they may seem merely gawky, but this is one of those days who suddenly takes off its ankle length skirt, shakes out a mane of heavy Aquarian hair, puts on her high heels and dances away leaving everybody devastated.

There's a strong sex drive to this sprite of the sky, a rush of hot air you might say. But it's not obvious. Watch our Aquariana, her

brow furrowed over the computer, snap at a colleague who's bunged up the computer printer and you would never believe this fearful double bass is the hussy who spirals all night on the club floor surrounded by admirers. Watch Aquarius guys adding up the figures in the accounts department. See how carefully they lay their knife and fork, precisely side-by-side in the canteen and you'd never guess that at home there lies waiting a powerful motorbike which January 26 rides like the wind. Look under the hair. You'll see the ear-ring.

Most people born today have two strong sides to their nature, the organised and the exotic. In some cases these two sides combine with firework flare at work, when great sums of money can be made. Let them loose on the stockmarket or in any investment and watch the gold coins pile into a gleaming, tumbling mountain.

In private, unlike many people born at this time, they do seek long term relationships and want children. If children don't come along, most January 26 people will do all they can to acquire a family either by use of medical help or by fostering and adoption. But if this doesn't work, then our strong minded air traveller can put the problem out of her mind and live a happy life realising other ambitions.

Always forgive your enemies – nothing annoys them so much.

(Oscar Wilde)

27 January

January 27 is an enchanting child. The trouble is that he goes on being one well into middle age. If he can find a nice steady Taurus, or a leader Leo then it may not matter. Otherwise this once charming characteristic gets burdensome for those around tweety pie. Can somebody help me do up my shoelaces and sort out the nasty taxman? And it's just as irksome in either sex. The women constantly consulting other women about exactly the right shade of hair dye and if they should go to the doctor with their itch.

It's an indulgence that doesn't show at work, nor gets in the way of ambition for career success, money or love. Or of driving too fast, charming the socks off people and getting their Aquarian way. The dummy is subtly waved. Ms and Mr Highpowered Supernova relies on a PA as if she was nanny, to fix lunch dates, buy Christmas presents and hide them from enthusiastic lovers. *In extremis,* Highpowered wants nanny/PA to wear a bleeper or carry a portable telephone everywhere, to lunch, to the loo, so that the big baby in the big office can find them. Otherwise both sexes will scream and scream until they're sick.

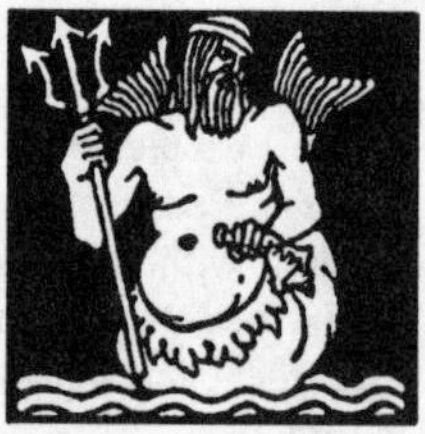

In private January 27 evades responsibility if possible. Many men pretend that the kitchen is their wife's empire into which they DARE NOT TREAD. This exonerates them from having to help. Only over-admiring mates go along with this so January 27 should be careful to pick a life-long partner from the grateful gene pool. The baby character isn't so noticeable in women, who the world still forgives for behaving like ten-year-olds, especially if they're pretty.

But it can give January 27's children the pip, because the adult tries to relate to their own child as if they were another adult. Notice the mother who trillingly laughs that she and her daughter are like sisters. She thinks so. Her daughter doesn't.

Flamingoes and mustard both bite. And the moral of that is – 'Birds of a feather flock together'.

(Lewis Carroll)

Body

Bad circulation is a common Aquarian affliction. Eastern medicine suggests foot massage as a remedy. Pay particular attention to the arches of both feet, related to the heart and kidneys. Then massage the fingers, especially the middle one, related to circulation, and ring fingers, related to the autonomic nervous system. Also turn the ankle to the left and right with one hand, while bending and flexing the toes with the other. Saffron promotes blood circulation and the digestive function. Add it to rice. Pine nuts are also recommended. Add 100g to 750ml of sake. Let it sit until alcohol begins to evaporate, becoming sticky. Drink 20ml a day after meals.

☾

Mind

An old magic spell to zip up sex. Let the full moon shine through the window, put rose essence in a burner, pink satin sheets on the bed and as passion builds murmur, 'Awake, awake, your heart mine, for Moon and love they intertwine.'

Dateshare

Died: **Lilli Palmer**, *movie beauty. Born:* **Wolfgang Amadeus Mozart**, *Austrian master composer, violinist, court musician, child prodigy.* **John Ogden**, *pianist.* **Ingrid Thulin**, *Swedish film actress.* **Ilya Ehrenberg**, *Russian-Jewish dissident author.* **Lewis Carroll**, *aka Charles Dodgson, photographer of children, mathematician, writer,* Alice In Wonderland. **Elmore James**, *blues singer.* **Donna Reed**, *Hollywood film star.*

January 28 lives for love. If there is none, this timid moorhen puts her head under her wing, doing nothing, but longs for something to happen. Fortunately both sexes have fine Aquarian looks, large empathetic eyes, shapely heads and excellent noses and usually something happens eventually. In matters of love the problem is they wait too patiently at all of life's bus stops. If the double decker comes along and the conductor says it's full, 28 would never dream of leaping on board anyway.

If 28 is partnerless for a time, everybody understands that this good-looking individual does hang back rather than coming forward and fortunately they have lots of friends who spend lots of time matchmaking them. Also fortunately, the blind dates and planned outings with possible new partners work.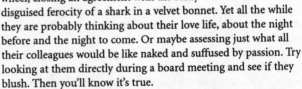

All shyness forgotten during the day, our winter child may be the most brilliant person at meetings. They deftly deal and wheel, closing an agreement with the softly disguised ferocity of a shark in a velvet bonnet. Yet all the while they are probably thinking about their love life, about the night before and the night to come. Or maybe assessing just what all their colleagues would be like naked and suffused by passion. Try looking at them directly during a board meeting and see if they blush. Then you'll know it's true.

Many make money but few spend it generously, more of a savings bank date than dinner for four at the Savoy. Certainly there seems no point in buying a £600 suit when bargains can be spied in the nearby 'Nearly New' shop. (Compliments bring the triumphant response that their dress cost £3.50.) Although January 28 is generous enough with lovers, especially before marriage, and usually with children.

Most have a dreamy, talented side which needs to be encouraged outside work. Involved with a local theatre group or choir they give pleasure to others and to themselves.

The bridegroom's gift to the bride was an antique pendant.

(London *Times report on Lord Redding's marriage to a woman forty years his junior*)

29 JANUARY

January 29 has a massive Hercules Complex. They keep setting themselves impossible tasks and think that they alone are holding up the world. HC people always do too much, get exhausted and complain about it, then make everybody around them feel guilty. Which is a pity because this is a lovely, generous sweetheart who would be completely perfect but for the martyr streak in it psychology.

It's all probably the result of stress – although there's a smidgeonette of vanity here. This date can do a lot more than most, faster, and likes to show off about it. They find it difficult to lie about doing nothing, but this is exactly what benefits January 29 because they are thoughtful creatures with big ideas and they need time to get their minds clear of the everyday round. Most January 29s are surprised when they take their hands down to discover that nothing more important tumbles to the ground than their own exaggerated sense of duty.

Women particularly need to learn time-management and how to let others do things. As do the men, who are given to instructing people half-way through a job they are more than capable of completing by themselves. Stick to the maxim 'Never give advice' and in particular, 'Never tell someone to do what they're already doing'.

Not all members of January 29's family group admire him or her. Most Aquarians ignore uppity relatives, but they do get up January 29's shapely nose. It's best if our star stays steady, resisting

all temptation to send sharp little meteorites in the direction of the indignant sister-in-law who thinks January 29's spoiling his children by allowing them to eat crisps.

Like most Aquarians, this person may expect to live an exceedingly long life and may find romance sweeps them off their feet well into their fifties or sixties. It's the nature of this young at heart psychology. Should this lead to a much younger partner just ignore the quizzical looks.

What contemptible scoundrel stole the cork from my lunch?

(W C Fields)

Sometimes portly January 29 should try the Food Combining Diet, based on the idea that inadequate elimination of waste products occurs when protein and starch are mixed at the same meal. There are five basic rules. 1. Don't mix sugar or starch foods with proteins within one meal. 2. Increase intake of fresh fruit, veg and salads. 3. Always eat fruits in isolation. 4. Don't mix milk with protein or starch within one meal. 5. Avoid processed foods. Typical Day: Breakfast (starch): homemade Muesli. Mid-morning (alkaline): bunch grapes. Lunch (alkaline): veg. crudities with avocado dip. Dinner (protein): grilled lemon sole with green salad.

☾

MIND
A simple good/bad relative test is whether he or she, having used up the loo roll immediately fetches another roll and puts it in place. Even when not planning to return to the house that day.

DATESHARE
Died: Hollywood heart-throb **Alan Ladd**. **Jimmy Durante**, *movie great.* Born: **Oprah Winfrey**, *TV confessional programmes hostess.* **Germaine Greer**, *academic, beauty, wit, writer, revolutionised female thinking,* The Female Eunuch. **Katherine Ross**, *Hollywood film beauty.* **Tom Selleck**, *tough guy, film and TV actor.* **John Forsyth**, *film star, TV actor.* **Frederick Delius**, *British composer.* **Thomas Paine**, *political theorist.* **Anton Chekhov**, *Russian author, playwright,* The Cherry Orchard. **W C Fields**, *early Hollywood film comic, misogynist.* **Ernst Lubitsch**, *film director,* Ninotchka.

They are the golden apples of the sun, the silver apples of the moon. Bite them and everything changes for the better. There's nothing snakey about January 30 and certainly not likely to cause goofy Snow White harm. Because this remarkable person is the mature wise sign of the zodiac, he only wishes good to others. Both sexes have the generosity which goes with complete self-confidence in deeply established talents. When either sex is around things go right for others.

So this is also a magical apple, a little intoxicating for some, a little sophisticated for others. Quite a few January 30s do work extremely successfully in big companies, impervious to politics or bureaucratic irritation, but it's not unlikely that the silliness of some managers finally causes him to go off by himself and be much more successful. Essentially this is an independent operator. Slightly less confident people born today take longer to leave, sometimes sufficiently outstaying their welcome to get sacked or made redundant. Fear not. Given time everything comes right for The Admirable Aquarius. In fact both sexes make the sack or redundancy into a style statement.

It's a psychic day, manifesting itself in both sexes so strongly that they have an inside track on life. Hunches pay off. Many can tell a wrong 'un as he walks in the door, and although they always reserve their judgement, it usually turns out that they were right. Involved in artistic, creative fields, which now of course can include many sciences, there are many new ideas and discoveries, helped by their psychic talent, which means mean that oodles and snoodles of cash comes winging into their magnetic hands.

Rich or poor, January 30 lives peaceably. Both sexes surround themselves with family and friendly affection, welcoming the odd, the beautiful and the talented without any kind of snobbery – anathema to this fair-minded person whose mind soars away from mundane gossip.

There are two ways of meeting difficulties: you alter the difficulties, or you alter yourself meeting them.

(Phyllis Bottome)

31 JANUARY

This is a psychic date. Many Aquarians have some measure of this capacity but it comes out strongly in January 31 and, as always, it's a good idea to talk to professionals and get a measure of what's going on. A lot will find they can see other people's auras for instance – rainbow coloured when healthy, dull if not. And some have healing hands.

People born today are extremely intelligent, with logical minds, and may try to reject their talent, even suspecting that the psychic ability is in their imagination. There will also be many only too willing to discourage them. Like any other gift, it's a tragedy to suppress it. January 31 does no one a service if they absolutely know there is something unpleasant about the house a friend is buying but doesn't say.

In part, this reticence grows from January 31's horror of coincidence conversations. They want to burst into laughter when people get going about how they were standing at a bus stop willing a bus to come and then an utterly amazing thing happened – it did. And how they were just thinking about their neighbour's cat when it walked into the garden! This isn't psychic. It's luck.

If this individual wishes, he or she could make a profession of their talent. Or something allied, such as aromatherapy, where their empathy is valuable. If she's brave enough to go with her hunches, she could make a killing on the horses or the stockmarket, but in this case you do have to be careful – even psychics must retain a sense of humour for when they got the message slightly wrong.

January 31 must also guard against those who want too much help and who could become over-dependent. Unless a deliberate choice is made to openly use the powers, the role of an amateur soothsayer is exhausting and sometimes dangerous. It certainly provokes mockery and gets in the way or normal life.

If a man could pass through Paradise in a dream, and have a flower presented to him as a pledge that his soul had really been there, and if he found that flower in his hand when he awoke – Aye and what then?

(Samuel Taylor Coleridge)

BODY

Health conscious 31 eats lots of fresh fruit and vegetables, the key to a vitamin-rich diet. But you need to preserve their vitamin values. Avoid storing fresh produce for long as their vitamins diminish with age. Chop vegetables just before cooking because exposing cut surfaces to air reduces many nutrients. Vitamins C and the B complex vitamins are lost in boiling water, as are calcium and iron. So eat raw food, or cook without water by stir-frying. About 80 per cent of zinc disappears in flour milling and 50 per cent in rice polishing. The answer is to eat wholewheat flour and brown rice.

MIND

In Tarot the Major Arcana's card for today is The Emperor. In matters of love it indicates that risks should not be taken around your birthday. During this month, women are likely to find or renew an enduring love.

DATESHARE

Died: **Samuel Goldwyn**, film director, producer. Born: **John Lydon**, Johnny Rotten, punk singer, songwriter, Sex Pistols. **Philip Glass**, minimalist composer. **Phil Collins**, singer, songwriter, drummer, Genesis. **Norman Mailer**, novelist, The Naked and The Dead. **Carol Channing**, comedian. **Tallulah Bankhead**, stage, film actress, muse to Noel Coward. **Eddie Cantor**, vaudeville, radio, movie star. **Jean Simmons**, film star. **Franz Schubert**, Austrian composer. **Anna Pavlova**, Russian ballet dancer, emigré to London, Paris, New York. **Mario Lanza**, Italian tenor, film star, musical star.

FEBRUARY I

There's a great deal of zeal about this crusader of the dark skies. February 1 loathes unfairness and snobbery. Neither sex can understand why some people think they are superior and both find unfair privilege, by birth or simple money grabbing,

repulsive. When Aquarius gets going they can be formidable. Their blazing honesty and articulacy is formidable. And although this is a kind date, they won't be if anybody frivolously gets in their way.

They fight their battles in the public forum, blazing down on darker starlets, and turning the opposition to toffee. Let nobody try to bribe February 1, nor persuade them to modify their position for future career reward. It won't work. And this creature doesn't forget perfidy in a hurry.

Madame Aquariana is gentler than the male, more sophisticated but often deadlier because her manner is silken and at first opponents take her lightly. The male of the species is a more aggressive attacker. Naturally these talents are in demand in the political arena and in local authority work. Maybe in medicine or any kind of teaching. In ordinary commerce, this gleaming crusader can be lethal if he gets a notion that something is wrong. For this reason, many fail to win promotion because their potential for trouble frightens bosses.

At home the crusader takes off his red cross, dons a t-shirt and plays the domestic pussycat. Not entirely reliable in love – the men are worse than the women – they are delightful while they stay. And domestically skilled. Most of the men are better cooks than the women, but the crusaderette is better at making the home beautiful. Which she can do for little money.

Neither cares much about cash, and in particular they don't like to spend it. February 1 always has the old age pension in mind, even when they're twenty-five. What they love most is to bargain-hunt, combing car boot sales, street markets and old junk shops for astonishing, enviable bargains.

Oh not at all –
just a straight away pounder.
(Lily Langtry on being asked if the
Prince of Wales was a romantic lover)

BODY

February 1 is romantic, sometimes promiscuous but sometimes unlucky in love. When they want someone, they are rejected; but they are hotly pursued when they don't. Since it's harder to keep than to lose, here's some love binding magic. On the important night, put three drops of neroli in a scent burner at foot of bed. Throw a red cover on the bed and two red candles on either side – to ensure the presence of the Fire element. If the moon is shining full at the window the night will be memorable with more nights to come. If waning, some difficulty. If none, don't get involved. Just have fun.

MIND

This individual should try to remember that conversation is the civilised exchange of ideas, opposing or not. It is not a bull ring, nor an opportunity for shouting others down. It also helps if you can remember other people's names.

DATESHARE

Died: **Buster Keaton**, Hollywood silent movie comedian. Born: **John Ford**, master Hollywood film director, Stagecoach. **Clark Gable**, Hollywood film star, heart-throb, played Rhett Butler in Gone With The Wind *with memorable line 'Frankly my dear, I don't give a damn'.* **Princess Stephanie** of Monaco, survived 120ft car crash over cliff, mother Princess Grace later died. **Hugo von Hofmannsthal**, Austrian poet, playwright. **Don Everly**, singer Everly Brothers. **Boris Yeltsin**, first popularly elected Soviet president.

2 FEBRUARY

A lot of men born today pride themselves on their logic. And drive everybody mad. February 2 is fond of telling people that if they will just view the situation logically, without emotion, then they will come to their senses. This individual is keen on buttoning down emotions and directing others to do so. Maybe it's innate, a gruesome gender symptom. Maybe there's a flicker of the stern side of Uranus coming through. Or perhaps Mr Sensible is a bit of an emotional coward.

It's of course the stuff magnates are sometimes made of and stands February 2 in good stead in his steady climb to the top of the corporate heap. But when life's unexpected upsets come along, as they do, this individual can't empathise. He says about his recently widowed mother 'She's fine', and about his best friend who's got the sack, 'He'll be OK.' But he's not stupid and he knows it's not the case. It's just a way of coping. The women are almost as tough and maybe their saving grace is that they will be the first to offer practical help. If family or friends fall on hard times too, this individual is first to offer financial help – no strings.

February 2 may sometimes give more emotional dates the pip, but there are areas where their determination to make sense of things by not giving in and organising the situation can be helpful. If the church roof needs mending or the local homeless hostel needs cash for a mini bus, they sort it in double-quick time, cutting through bureaucracy and shaming rich meanies into helping. A powerful aggressive streak emerges and you'll find February 2 queue jumping for grants and telling mealy-mouthed official no-people where to get off.

Naturally they drive their children insane. But those same children know how much they are loved and in the end don't want their mum or dad to turn into Madame Butterfly.

In a museum in Havana there are two skulls of Christopher Columbus, one when he was a boy and one when he was a man.

(Mark Twain)

BODY

February 2 often works long hours at a computer and suffers from screen glare. Eyes get dry and blurry after a few hours and sometimes ache. Always consult a doctor. Yawning can help tired, blurred eyes by releasing tension in face muscles and producing flowing tears to bathe and soothe the cornea. Make a loud, animal yawn, jaws wide open and grunt like a hippopotamus. (Do it in private to avoid astonishment.) Yawn until tears flow down your cheeks. Imagine that the toxins within your eyes are flowing away and healthy nutrients are flowing in. After a while you will find your eyes relaxing and vision much clearer.

MIND

To alleviate the spiritual fatigue and despondency which comes to those who behave like a rigid high performance engine, try the Bach Flower remedy Oak, (Quercus robur), especially designed to calm and give strength to just this type of person.

DATESHARE

Died: **Boris Karloff**, horror movie star. **Donald Pleasance**, actor. Born: **Graham Nash**, singer, songwriter, Crosby Stills and Nash. **Nell Gwyn**, actress, woman of pleasure, mistress to King Charles II. **Garth Brooks**, country and western singer. **Valéry Giscard D'Estaing**, French president. **Havelock Ellis**, psychologist, writer on sexual deviation, The Psychology of Sex. **Farrah Fawcett**, TV actress. **James Joyce**, Irish poet, author Ulysses. **Elaine Strich**, Broadway comedian.

BODY

In ancient China the emperor had one wife with whom he copulated once a month and three other consorts, nine wives of second rank, 27 third rankers and 81 concubines. Conserving sperm was the only way he could handle 121 women. Old Chinese sexual guidebooks preach that the more times one has sex without ejaculating, the greater the benefits to health. So once, and vital essences are strengthened; twice – sight and hearing improve; three times – all diseases cured. More result in a sublime experience. By recycling semen they thought the brain would be nourished and longevity assured. Don't believe it? Try and see.

MIND

February 3 can be heedless to others' broken hearts. Very often this individual flirts, then flees with boredom. But such unkind behaviour is irresponsible and unattractive in such a sophisticated star. This tiger should tone it down.

DATESHARE

*Died: **John Cassavetes**, movie star. Born: **Ray Davies**, rock musician, singer, Kinks. **Morgan Fairchild**, actress, film star. Shelley Berman, American comedian, filmstar. **Lillian Armstrong**, jazz pianist, singer, wife to Louis. **James A Michener**, novelist. **Gertrude Stein**, poet, critic, novelist, The Making of Americans. **Norman Rockwell**, graphic artist, illustrator. **Jaques Soustelle**, French anthropologist, right wing political activist.*

FEBRUARY 3

The crackle around this star is electric. Like lightening, they snap across the firmament to strike their latest prey, who absolutely adores every moment of the drama. February 3 has been dangerously attractive since teenage years. The kind who smoulders rather than smiles, who everybody looks at and longs for the look to be returned.

Ruled by the mighty planets Saturn and Uranus, February 3 is a highly-charged bedroom warrior. A skilled lover who may simply walk away from the latest love victim and never look back. When they do love, like sapphires in moonlight they burn with brilliance, casting such a glamorous light that those they love also shimmer. And they have such a powerful sense of humour that nobody they touch ever gets over the addiction.

Naturally 3 has a brilliant career, if he or she chooses. Who can match their charm and persuasive ways? Certainly not the company chairman or any opponent. People who stand in February 3's way just give up, sidle off, maybe go out and buy the same perfume or jacket that 3's wearing in the vague hope that some of this style can be bought. But the speed this tiger brings to any job can't be purchased. Nor can the fascinating sense of danger they generate.

Surprisingly this dominant creature is gentle with the sick, small children, the elderly and animals, although they don't like small

dogs. By their side on winter's evenings find a favourite Alsatian loping across the snowy side of a hill, although they are just as likely to go down to the local animal shelter and rescue an old racing greyhound abandoned by its heartless owner.

It's a two or three career star. The women may run more than one business which they do with ease, often employing less successful friends who they treat like partners and indeed run the whole thing as a fun club as much as a profit-making organisation.

Come, let us take our fill of love until morning, let us solace ourselves with love.

(Proverbs 7)

4 FEBRUARY

Some of the women born today are cleanerholics and some of the men carcleanerholics. February 4, which is a fun-loving, frivolous creature has this one Achilles' heel about spick and span surroundings, odd when it goes with late-night partying, high heels and a penchant for taking off its clothes in public.

They have great bodies so the streakerette streakerette in them is fun for onlookers. Find them in clubs taking off blouses, then pale green silk bras, or tight jeans, then maybe even the red cotton boxer shorts. Of course they do it on beaches, but may try it in restaurants and even at the office Christmas party.

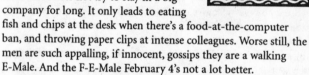

Which brings us to 4's general work behaviour: never completely serious. Complete aces at the computer they earn snoozles of dough, can't be bothered with rules and better not try to stay in a big company for long. It only leads to eating fish and chips at the desk when there's a food-at-the-computer ban, and throwing paper clips at intense colleagues. Worse still, the men are such appalling, if innocent, gossips they are a walking E-Male. And the F-E-Male February 4's not a lot better.

This little toots is better off, like so many Aquarians, running his own business. If either sex do, they have all the fun they like, never impose a no smoking or tidy desk policy and certainly not a pick-up-the-phone-after-three-rings policy. They also work hard and make lots of money. Which they rush out and spend, on beautiful new dining-tables and flash cars. And then, as we've said, vigorously over-clean.

Fame is written in the stars for some born today, which February 4 adores because it gets her the best tables in restaurants and opportunities to sign lots of autographs each time she goes to Tesco's. The flip side of fame for February 4 is sometimes notoriety for some extravagant act, which neither sex mind much either.

I find I always have to write something on a steamed mirror.
(Elaine Dundy)

BODY
If you are going to take your clothes off, you might as well have extra beautiful breasts – if you're a woman. Men don't have so many erogenous zones to show off. Try these essential oil recipes, also invaluable for private display. Bosom Enhancer. Massage breasts once a week with the following blend to tone and enlarge: 2 drops geranium, 2 drops clary sage, 2 drops ylang ylang, 2tsp camellia oil. Petite Bust. To tone and reduce, take 1 drop rose oil, 1tbsp jojoba. Massage this blend into the bosom. Jojoba emulsifies fat tissue, while rose is astringent.

MIND
Dreaming of undressing in public may reflect a rebellious streak, refusing to play roles others cast you in. Also warns where such an attitude may lead. It can also express fears that others may see through you.

DATESHARE
Ida Lupino, early Hollywood movie star. **Betty Friedan**, comedian, talker, broadcaster, feminist, author, The Feminine Mystique. **Alice Cooper**, style addict, rock star, sweet guy. **Dan Quayle**, US vice-president. **François Rabelais**, French humanist, comic satirist, Gargantua. **Charles Lindbergh**, aviator, first successful solo Atlantic crossing. **Isabel Peron**, Argentine president, first South American woman head of state, ousted on corruption charges.

BODY

February 5 should use juniper oil in a burner to strengthen her overburdened psyche when other people's problems weigh too heavily. Otherwise both sexes should take care of their luxuriant Aquarian hair, which may become dull when they are exhausted. The chosen blend of oils mixed in the appropriate oil base will feed hair roots while coating each strand with a fine protective layer. Try 1 drop rosewood, 1 drop lemon, 1 drop rosemary, 3 tsp base oil. To energize the body try the Goddess Bath, with 6 drops myrtle to a full bath. Swirl water with hand to distribute oil through water.

MIND

Plain old itching can be a good or bad traditional folk lore omen. An itch on the right knee means a happy journey, right eyebrow a meeting with old friends, palm of right hand, a legacy, loins, a reconciliation and thighs, a house move.

This is the Concorde of Aquarius, streamlined, fast and desired by the rich and powerful. To travel with February 5 makes the rest of the world feel first class. And the extra long, famous nose gives every other star a deliciously invaded feeling, that somehow this psychic creature knows their every thought. When February 5 came to earth trailing clouds of 24 carat glory, Mercury flew alongside and threw an extra bucket of empathy over the heavenly one.

If ever eyes were windows to the soul, this person has them. Other troubled stars beat a path to his or her door, just to talk for a moment and look for comfort there, and while February 5 is always willing, a kind sort of person, he must be careful not to take on everybody else's problems. Because this magic child has problems of his own.

Neither sex can make up its mind what to be. Talented in arts and sciences, should they choose brain surgery or go for the Odette/Odile role in *Swan Lake*? The latter is best for February 5 because it's an opportunity to play two completely different people, which suits this multi-faceted moodster.

Most pursue several careers, in sequence or simultaneously. They are all-rounders who play football, cricket, the double bass and can fix the electric wiring. Money interests them but they can't stand working out what to do with it, although when forced to concentrate they make excellent investments and property deals. Both sexes thrive in broadcasting because they have the kind of lullaby voice which delights listeners. And this is useful in private where the women sing about the house and at bedtime, endless lullabies to delighted sleepy children.

Many will radically change their way of life in the middle years, either seeking to live in another country, or by sea or amongst mountains. All three help their meditative side, never to be forgotten, whatever the demands of social life or work.

I always keep a supply of stimulant handy in case I see a snake – which I also keep handy.

(W C Fields)

6 FEBRUARY

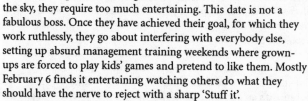

This ripe little banana is just waiting to be peeled, but when the great moment happens it often gets browned off. The trouble with February 6 is that it's always better to travel than to arrive. And that's the case in career, love, travel, moving house. Just about everything. Basically this twinkling star is utterly eclipsed by the thought of boredom.

Lovely they are, delightful to look at and some of the time heaven to know. But for many companions in the great dome of the sky, they require too much entertaining. This date is not a fabulous boss. Once they have achieved their goal, for which they work ruthlessly, they go about interfering with everybody else, setting up absurd management training weekends where grown-ups are forced to play kids' games and pretend to like them. Mostly February 6 finds it entertaining watching others do what they should have the nerve to reject with a sharp 'Stuff it'.

In love there may be trouble ahead. Ms Banana adores the chase, the presents and likes catching impossible-to-get men. And maybe the first night or two of love. But when there's talk of permanence, she flies off shrieking, to wash her hair. She'd rather stay at home and dye her underwear electric blue, her favourite colour, or passionate violet. The men are also bad, terrified of any girl who asks 'Where have you been?'.

They do often marry in the end, and many live happily as long as they can continue with separate interests and friends. Many of the men, who are often good at sport actually need to go off and watch cricket with other men, play golf or in some cases hockey. The women prefer to spend the weekend in Paris with a girlfriend, sitting giggling in cafés. Both sexes adore the Channel Tunnel and any other long trans-European train journey, much preferring the romance of train travel to cars and planes.

Apathy is worse than antipathy.
(*George Bernard Shaw*)

BODY
Maximum vitality is necessary for this energetic creature who like many winter people suffers from fatigue and because of his fast life, tends to eat junk food which exacerbates the problem. Follow these simple guidelines.

Eat less fat, especially the saturated type found in meat, cream and cheese. Less sugar. Less salt – never add it to food at the table. More low-fat foods: low-fat yoghurt, skimmed milk. More complex carbohydrates, more wholegrains, wholewheat pasta and brown rice. More fruit and vegetables – aim to eat five generous portions a day, not including potatoes, which count as starches. Drink more water.

MIND
Think before you show off. Bear in mind the awful example of Vice-President Quayle, who on visiting an American school corrected what he thought was an incorrect spelling in a work display, deftly adding an 'e' on the end of potato.

DATESHARE
Gayle Hunnicut, British beauty, movie star, stage actress. **Bob Marley**, Jamaican reggae singer, songwriter. **Eva Braun**, Hitler's mistress, married moments before mutual suicide. **Patrick MacNee**, film star, TV actor. **Zsa Zsa Gabor**, Hungarian-born beauty, film star. **Manuel Orantes**, Spanish tennis champion. **George Herman 'Babe' Ruth**, American baseball hero. **Ronald Reagan**, US president, film star. **François Truffaut**, French film director, Jules et Jim. **Christopher Marlowe**, Elizabethan playwright, knifed to death in Deptford pub.

AIR

FEBRUARY 7

February 7 seems to be afraid of money, as if it were a mad hippopotamus, lurking boulder-like in the nearby soda lake, waiting to lunge through its sugar-frosting of pink flamingos and crunch poor February 7 just when he thought he'd got by in his boat. Some don't even open bills, especially the women, who just hope everything will go away.

It's not that they don't have money, but they think they won't have if they spend it. This is really a miser date and the miser date's telephone and electricity will get cut off if it doesn't mend its ways. Nor will friends ever buy February 7 a drink again if he or she doesn't return their round. Nor will anybody ever go to a

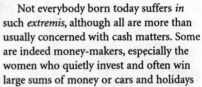

restaurant again with them if they insist on popping to the loo just when the bill comes.

Not everybody born today suffers *in* such *extremis*, although all are more than usually concerned with cash matters. Some are indeed money-makers, especially the women who quietly invest and often win large sums of money or cars and holidays from newspaper competitions and off the back of cornflakes packets. There are even those who spend their lives raising money for charity, some professionally. And there is just a smattering who make it illegally.

Apart from the money complex, this February child is a tender lover, a great inventor of treats and sometimes a wild, adventurous romantic. Sweet 7 can't always take a lover out to tea at the Ritz, but he will take her to swim in pure water high in the Scottish mountains one rare sunny day. While they dry in the sun, February 7 picks a hatfull of blueberries and then kisses his partner and WHAM. This individual is one of the great kissers, which is a talent admired by every woman in the kissing world. She's not such a great kisser, but can do other things.

Why do birds fly south in winter? Because it's too far to walk.

AIR

8 FEBRUARY

This is one of the more contemplative Aquarians. While many February 8 people are forced to live in urban centres because of jobs, their preference is for wide open spaces and green hills. In city centres they try to make their homes an oasis of peace, decorating the walls in soft dove greys, gentle warm blues and on occasion fantastic sky blue and pink combinations which are breathtaking but always harmonious.

Many born today are music lovers, preferring to listen to Classic FM while they paint their homes, rather than a rock station. Find a state of the art sound system in their room and somewhere there's usually a musical instrument, particularly the piano and flute, much loved by the great god Pan, caretaker of woods and fields. Expect also to find poetry on the book shelves.

In any kind of work, February 8 is often extremely successful. They are nice to people, easygoing about rules and regulations, great smoothers-over at the workplace and have something extra to

offer. A snappy way with words may take them into television or advertising, PR or retailing and an easy capacity for organising makes any place they run fun rather than onerous. Naturally they like to be rewarded properly, so don't mistake February 8's compliant ways as a sign of the pushover. Try paying them too little and they'll push you over.

Not necessarily people who need marriage, they may form life-long faithful partnerships, but can live the single life with joy and cope with single parenthood better than many. But what they need and enjoy most is some solitude and life in the country suits them best. With a patch of garden, time to think and be creative, many will take to writing for a living. And some of the women may be exquisite potters, embroiderers or patchwork quilt-makers, enjoying the easy companionship of country neighbours and the sound of church bells pacing the hours.

Nothing makes you more tolerant of a neighbour's noisy party than being there.

(George Santayana)

BODY

February 8 adores summer entertaining chiefly for the pleasure of decorating a table, preferably one out of doors. Scattered leaves and flowers look beautiful on a summery white cotton tablecloth, especially white hydrangea florets, white roses, and daisies mixed with mint sprigs, bay leaves, rosemary and darkly shiny ivy tendrils. For a touch of drama tuck in the occasional pink or dark-red busy lizzie flower and maybe some brilliant nasturtiums. Wind ivy around white linen napkins, winding a length of cord over the stem and tying the ends together on the underside to hold it in place.

MIND

In Tarot, the Major Arcana's card for the eighth day is Strength, which indicates that this creature should try to avoid forcing anything forward in their lives. Relaxing into what happens to you usually makes everything clear.

DATESHARE

James Dean, handsome 50s Hollywood film star, died young in car crash. **Jack Lemmon**, Hollywood film star, stage actor, director, Some Like It Hot. **Mary Steenburgen**, movie star, stage actress. **Nick Nolte**, Hollywood star. **John Williams**, film composer, conductor. **John Ruskin**, poet, art critic, utterly disgusted at the sight of his wife's pubic hair on their wedding night. **Lana Turner**, film star, glamour puss, eight marriages. **King Vidor**, film director, producer, The Crowd. **Jules Verne**, French science fiction novelist, Twenty Thousand Leagues Under The Sea.

Take the Over Stressed Test. Tick where appropriate. 1: Do you sleep poorly, wandering about at night and raiding the fridge? 2: Suffer from intense anxiety, especially if there is a disaster story on the news? 3: Feel nobody appreciates, even notices what you do? 4: Over-eat, golloping down biscuits when distressed? Or even when not apparently distressed? 5: Fly into sudden rages? 6. Spend too much time looking for things? 7: Can't understand new technology, which includes how to work the video? 8: Think you're going to be found out? More than three ticks and you should take a look at your lifestyle.

MIND

Tarot's card in the Major Arcana for February 9 is The Hermit. This indicates a person who enjoys solitude and takes responsibility for themselves. Best policies always include taking time out from too many social activities.

DATESHARE

Holly Johnson, *bass guitarist, singer, Frankie Goes To Hollywood.* **Mia Farrow**, *film star, ex-wife of Frank Sinatra and André Previn, natural and adoptive mother to numerous children.* **Joe Pesci**, *TV and film actor, comedian.* **Carole King**, *singer, songwriter.* **Ronald Coleman**, *British romantic film star, made good in Hollywood.* **Alice Walker**, *novelist, The Colour Purple.* **Brendan Behan**, *Irish writer, playwright, Borstal Boy, alcoholic.* **Mrs Patrick Campbell**, *actress, first Eliza Doolittle in Bernard Shaw's Pygmalion.*

FEBRUARY 9

February 9 needs to avoid stress, because it can literally make this sensitive individual ill. There's a streak of depression here which needs to be watched, and although February 9 can reach the heights of the world if he wants, it may be better for all concerned if he decides not to.

In later life the female of the species may develop such wisdom she becomes a shamanic figure, the one in the family or amongst a group of friends whom others turn to because somehow she can always make sense of a situation. Not to be mistaken for an Earth Mother. This airy creature is not devoted to the home-making skills although she has them. She is more devoted to the basic meaning of things, and has a desire to comfort others in distress.

Because these are fixed air people, money may very easily come their way. Aquarians enjoy money, conserve it and this date doesn't spend frivolously, choosing to buy a painting rather than a new frock – although they adore fancy underwear in fancy colours, particularly electric blue and aquamarine. Because they are so fascinated by the human lot – people orientated – expect also to find in February 9's household porcelain or marble figures which may be part of a collection.

Neither sex is patient with whingers or the extremely weak. They have a horror of them almost amounting to whingerophobia, probably because this most developed sophisticated sign of the year regards whimperers as a lesser species. Most February 9s' philosophy is not so much to congratulate success – although they do very generously- but to regard with admiration those who cope bravely and constructively with adversity. It's how you pick yourself up which appeals to February 9, who understands that life's trials come to us all.

Children born to this person should be grateful. They make marvellous parents, always praising, always planning the next good time, directing like a paternal sheep dog rather than controlling.

Let us permit Nature to have her way; she understands her business better than we do.

(Michel de Montaigne)

10 FEBRUARY

Most February 10s are a little too preoccupied with money and things. Given to rapid resentment they're also a smidgeonette too competitive. There's nothing wrong with their warm heart, but it just doesn't show enough. They spend much energy on house improvement, which makes this exocet of the furnishing department over-fussy and houseproud.

They terrify guests, especially children, by watching them lynx-eyed, in case their bottom squashes a valuable old cushion. In other people's houses they ferret about examining the ornaments as if it was a car boot sale and openly coveting a new way of doing curtains they haven't thought of and suspect is smarter than theirs. Some become instantly angry if they feel their taste hasn't been appreciated enough, suffering festoon blind rage if someone laughs at their general frilliness.

Mr February 10 is usually a fanatical do-it-yourself person and can talk for hours about shelves.

More outgoing people excel in hotel management, catering and any decorative area of retailing where their prissiness is an advantage. But they suffer temper lapses with colleagues who fail to put the correct number of roses on the table. Away from soft-furnishings, this is an amusing date, with brilliant anecdotes full of naughty gossip, which you shouldn't listen to but can't resist. In particular they're noted for irreverence with authority and the rich and famous, and they're wonderfully indiscreet about people they work for.

As lovers they're passionate, going to great lengths to please, always gentle and supportive to partners, although there can be money rows which undermine sex temporarily. The girls love babies if they have them. If they don't it doesn't matter in the end. But this is not someone who is delirious about staying home with the kids. Either sex feels impossibly isolated, suffers from low self image and mild depression if they don't get out into the workplace. Try to, even if it's just a couple of days a week.

Orgasm ~
is like a slight case of apoplexy.
(Democritus)

BODY
What not enough people realise is that the foot is an area vital to our health. Massage can help relax you and put zest into your sex life. Two points on the foot are of major importance. The solar plexus, a point under the sole, in the centre just beneath the ball. And on either side of the heel. In reflexology, the solar plexus is connected to a person's 'will', arouses sexual energy in women when massaged and helps prevent premature ejaculation in men. Massaging the ankle area traditionally helps with infertility, causes pleasing sensations and eases menstrual problems.

MIND
Tarot's 10th card in the Major Arcana is The Wheel of Fortune. For lovers it indicates someone who likes sensuous variety, which sometimes leads to promiscuity. However, switching your sex life from bedroom to the stairs should be change enough.

DATESHARE
Robert Wagner, *film star, TV actor*, Hart to Hart. **Laura Dern**, *film star*, Jurassic Park. **Roberta Flack**, *singer, arranger, pianist.* **Bertolt Brecht**, *German poet, playwright, writer of music theatre with* Kurt Weill, Three Penny Opera. **Boris Pasternak**, *Nobel Prize-winning Russian poet (refused award), author*, Dr Zhivago. **Leontyne Price**, *concert, opera singer.* **Mark Spitz**, *American Olympic swimmer, won eleven gold medals.* **Greg Norman**, *Australian golfer.* **Harold Macmillan**, *British prime minister.* **Jimmy Durante**, *comedian, film actor.*

FEBRUARY 11

U npunctuality is a mania with this dreamy creature, whose idea of 'on time' is half an hour late. February 11 is not a friend of Time and rarely gets a lift on Time's wingèd chariot. They think they have all the time in the world when they have none, and regard other's fury with mild mockery.

Quite often other more reliable stars have to persuade young February 11 to get going and do his stint in the universe's midnight dome. None of this gets in the way of career, sex life or their massive social life, which gives the pip to other more punctilious twinklers. Life's unfair that way.

Clock-watchers despair of February 11 at work. Most just arrive late and apologise without explaining, not out of arrogance, but because they've run out of fresh excuses having used up all the 'car wouldn't start', 'telephone call from great aunt' and 'accident on the underground' variety. Because unpunctuality doesn't go with lack of brilliance, most bosses forgive the heedless one just because they need his originality.

Many February 11s suffer the reverse of unpunctuality. They make a fetish of being on time, harder to bear because of the little itsy-bitsy-witsy self-righteousness you always get with Punctuality Pushers. Males of the species turn the clocks back half an hour to get their partners off to a do on time, then spend fifteen minutes sitting in the car outside their destination because they're too early, while their mate moans because she's got to do her mascara in the

car. Worse still, some turn up so early that the hostess is still in curlers and slippers.

The women are not quite so frenetic, but get worked up about employees who are never there. Never mind, when Ms and Mr Unpunctuality rises up the career ladder he soon joins top executives who make a point of being late to show how important they are.

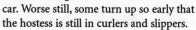

Living is entirely too time-consuming.

(Irene Peter)

12 FEBRUARY

This intensely competitive miss is ultra keen to prove she can do anything better than a man, and by golly Miss Molly she can. February 12 is a mission-minded kid and wherever eleven strong men are gathered for a cricket game, she's in there demanding to play. This is a good sportswoman and can run and throw faster than most men anyway, skills she uses when evading an unwanted male pursuer or to teach him a lesson with the contents of a water jug.

Often technically skilled, but not necessarily, February 12 barges her way through the ranks of light engineering, or the local factory, gets her own department, revolutionises the production department run by a man and before you know it, she's in charge of the shooting match. Since Aquarian's dominant tendency is to be fair-minded, she'll be popular with everybody and sweep out old male fuddy-duddy cobwebs, including the executive loo and dining-room. With February 12 in charge, everybody gets the same facilities.

Both sexes have a strong sense of fairness and neither will brook promotion on the grounds of anything other than talent. Nor can they stand snobs in private life, not on any subject and that includes birth into any family and money. Nobody buys February 12's affection.

Away from work this fierce defender of right is a goddess or god in the kitchen, the wizard cook of the zodiac. They can throw a dinner for ten together in half an hour and their idea of fun is to take a crowd home, feed them, settle them for the night on sofas and camp beds, then cook up a storm of croissants with fried eggs, Tabasco sauce and champagne for the next morning. Those who live in the country can exhaust guests with long walks, tennis matches and charades into the small hours, but their witty, friendly gossip makes it fascinating and worth being slightly hungover and puffed.

A miss is as good as a male.
(Old Greek proverb)

BODY
Being gossiped about is good, a healthy sign that your physical and mental impact is strong enough for others to take notice. Experts have discovered that subjects of gossip are happier, more socially vibrant and possess greater body confidence than those who are not. And their sex lives are better, which goes without saying as this is often the subject of the gossip. If you are considered worthy to be buzzed about on the grapevine, you are 'in'. If you have valuable information you are also 'in'. If you don't fit either group, then you're out of the loop and out to lunch alone.

MIND
Fortunate precious stones for February 12 include garnet, jacinth and jargoon. Dark or golden red garnets bring constancy. The cinnamon coloured jacinth, brings peace of mind and refreshing sleep. And the water coloured jargoon brings good fortune.

AIR

BODY

February 13 likes living so fast they often skip lunch. Medical research says those who do, may feel fatigue, depression and get angry over the most minor things. They also think less clearly, and in many cases experience a loss of sex drive, unusual and unwelcome for 13. Nobody says you have to go out and eat lunch. Busy people who can't be bothered can throw together a glass of extra energy juice which will do the trick.

Juice one parsnip, 6 white cabbage leaves, 2 carrots, seasoning to taste. Have this for lunch and you'll be a lot better tempered.

☾

MIND

Tarot's card for 13 in the Major Arcana is Death, which doesn't mean that. It's the little death or orgasm. For sexpots, this card indicates a person who avoids getting stuck in the missionary position, but continually experiments.

DATESHARE

Aung San, *Burmese National Movement leader, left husband and children in Oxford to help her country, one of the most admirable, bravest women in today's world.* **Kim Novak**, *Hollywood film bombshell.* **Stockard Channing**, *movie star.* **George Segal**, *Hollywood film star, musician.* **Peter Gabriel**, *singer, guitarist, songwriter, rock élite, mega-rich composer.* **Georges Simenon**, *French mystery writer, Maigret police novels.* **William Shockley**, *Nobel Prize-winning physicist, transistor inventor, electronics genius.*

These dancing sparklers are some of the snappiest movers in the zodiac, thriving at night on dance floors in clubs where they quickly draw everybody's gaze. February 13 is also good-looking and wears a snazzy outfit with sufficient flare to make others copy it. Natural style leaders, many followers of February 13 will adopt their mannerisms simply because what 13 does today, the rest of the world cottons on to tomorrow. In any kind of style business they are the dominant stars, making dominant money and if they're particularly flashy examples of the day, travelling all over the world. Catwalk queens are born today, as are designers and people who see to it that films look good.

Many can play musical instruments and could have their own successful band. Some may write, including stage and television scripts which may have people all over the world coining their phrases. When 13 says 'I'll be back' it catches on. When they write 'I did it my way' the world never stops singing and saying it. Shimmying across the world, their dancing stage, always travelling first class with a glass of champagne in their hand, they could be forgiven for forgetting old friends, lovers and Auntie May. But not a bit of it. This tough-minded star always values his or her roots and finds more pleasure in a phone call with their brother than Brad Pitt any day.

Away from the world stage, February 13 is much the same, only quieter, never having wished to stray or make a fortune or create a huge splash with their talents.

They look for endless love in a companion, which is OK because they're the hottest thing in town in bed, often exhausting eager partners. Which doesn't matter either, because nice 13 makes a powerful platonic friend and is just as happy to sit sipping wine and listening to music as to indulge in sweatier activities.

You know how to whistle, Steve –
just put your lips together
and blow.
(*Lauren Bacall,* To Have And Have Not)

14 FEBRUARY

February 14 people are a bunch of mixed aspects of love. All are sex orientated but some achieve less happiness than others. Because they were born on St Valentine's Day, many are expected to be love experts. But some are sourer in the grape department. For these, money plays an important part in their sex life. They may flit from rich flower to flower, scooping up honey and passing on until they accumulate their own wealth. This is definitely an own-yacht person and it's often got by making a series of lucrative marriages and divorces.

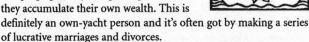

Naturally when either sex makes a career out of love, every chess move this pecuniary poppet makes must be a winning one, but quite often rich partners lose their money, won't divorce or won't die which is where the sour grapes come in. Still, he who lives by the sword dies by the sword.

Fortunately most February 14s use their oodles and boodles of sex appeal less complicatedly. They make their own living in a variety of professions, including transport and manufacturing, and what they want, outside work, is a good time. This less complicated little butterscotch tart knows little of depression and less of manipulation, and only gets into trouble in youth when they run of with too many mate's mates. Unlike sensibler people they also indulge in work affairs, immune to advice that it will all get sticky when they go off the unfortunate quarry. They are amazed later when colleagues tick them off because the rejectee is glumly sitting staring out of the window. And incorrigibly they make a play for the dishy new accountant with saucy eyes.

Goodish in bed, it's more quantity than quality February 14 appreciates. They settle down when somebody makes an honest man or woman of them, raise children and learn to keep their hands to themselves. What's left of their sensuous greed is now devoted to eating and drinking in copious quantities.

Can't Buy Me Love.

(The Beatles)

BODY

Excessive drinking can cause stomach disorders, gastritis, bleeding and ulcers, depression and other psychiatric and emotional disorders, high blood pressure, vitamin deficiency, sexual difficulties, brain damage, muscle disease, problems with the nervous system (especially nerve pains in legs and arms), hepatitis (inflammation of the liver), and cirrhosis, permanent scarring of the liver, cancer of the mouth, throat and gullet and even more problems for people with diabetes. And if that's not enough, it makes you fat. A half-pint of bitter contains 90 calories; 1 pub measure of whisky, 50 calories; an ordinary tonic, 35 calories; a cream sherry, 70 calories and a glass of wine 75 calories.

☾

MIND

Not content with drinking in waking hours, February 14 also dreams of doing it. Sparkling champagne signifies a forthcoming celebration and excitement, warm drinks indicate sexual desire, water is a sign that you are currently seeking spiritual awakening.

DATESHARE

Alan Parker, film director Midnight Express. **Thomas Malthus**, British clergyman, writer, economist, An Essay on the Principle of Population. **James Hoffa**, Robin Hood-style US union leader, aimed for presidency, arrested for crimes, let off, disappeared, suspected murder. **Jack Benny**, comedian, TV personality. **Carl Bernstein**, Watergate journalist, co-author of All The President's Men.

BODY

These fine, imaginative cooks love to serve you something different they have made themselves. And naturally they've grown the ingredients. Try Carnation Petal Cream. Fold petals picked in the early morning into sweetened cream. Stand in cool place for several hours, then remove petals and whip cream. It goes beautifully with pears poached in vanilla syrup or with fresh strawberries or blackberries. Scatter a few petals on top. Borage flowers, traditionally thought to be an anti-depressant, newly opened primroses, slightly bitter marigolds, peppery nasturtiums and young broom flower buds are also excellent added to salads.

MIND

You can tell rain is coming when trees rustle their leaves in calm weather and the scarlet pimpernel, known as 'farmer's weather glass', convolvulus, and clover leaves draw their petals and leaves tightly together.

DATESHARE

Jane Seymour, *long-haired film star, beauty-book writer.* **Cesar Romero**, *movie star, original Joker in* Batman. **Sir John Barrymore**, *stage, film actor.* **Matt Groening**, *cartoonist creator of* The Simpsons. **Galileo**, *Italian astronomer, suggested earth revolved round the sun, forced to recant by Inquisition.* **Jeremy Bentham**, *Utilitarian philosopher whose mummified body was displayed at London University.* **Sir Ernest Shackleton**, *Irish Antarctic explorer, writer,* Heart of the Antarctic.

February 15 is the gardener date, always occupied with the delights of flowers, trees, herbs and vegetables in the garden. To this steady creature growing things, their fresh scent in both the day and night air, is all the occupation he needs and often having to go and earn a living is deeply resented. Many try to make a career of working on the land, in farming, parks, landscape gardening or gamekeeping, just to keep themselves outside four walls.

Both sexes also adore animals and will have three or four dogs roaming about the house if they can, usually with mongrel blood, and always well-trained because practical February 15 thinks a properly behaved dog is a happy dog. It's also true to say they think much the same about the human race. Their courtesy is exceptional, utterly charming, with the old-fashioned habit of warmly thanking a telephone caller for calling even if they weren't really welcome. With February 15, handwritten thank you letters are a must as is polite attention and thoughtfulness paid to older people. They can therefore be sticklers with their children, good as

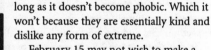

long as it doesn't become phobic. Which it won't because they are essentially kind and dislike any form of extreme.

February 15 may not wish to make a splash in the world, but she makes an impact in her neighbourhood. Drawn into the social and religious life of the church, she becomes a power in the land. When it comes to organising social events, everybody in the county always wants to come if she's involved.

The men and women are extremely superstitious. Garlic is always hung by the garden gate to ward off evil spirits. Black cats are never kept. Large numbers of shooting stars are always noted for the thunder they'll bring, and every fairy ring is jumped inside so as not to break the circle (which could bring bad luck) and so that a silent wish may come true.

A mackerel sky
Twelve hours dry.
(Country rhyme for fine weather)

16 FEBRUARY

Nothing is ever good enough for February 16, whose level of self-doubt plagues this self-critical star all his life. Friends throw themselves into a new craze, job or love affair, but for February 16 nothing promising comes along without the downside highlit. This habit of looking for potential problems actually gives them a useful overview, because we aren't talking hopeless galaxy pessimist here – more Messrs Caution. So when they start their own business, a strong possibility, they examine money flow and the nearest competition with discerning eyes. Thus everything February 16 embarks upon has been well thought through.

Both sexes take longer to complete tasks than their flash and dazzle colleagues at work. But they never present arguments with gaping holes. Nor have apparently good ideas they expect others to pull off, but which are impossibly flawed. Madame Aquarius in particular is good at assessing others' capabilities. She gives tasks to the inexperienced, but chooses those she knows can do it. She doesn't expect miracles and if miracles do happen, she acts cautiously.

In private these good-lookers choose partners with ideas that complement theirs. Marriages may not be made in heaven, but they are heavenly. However, expect lots of pre-marriage colliwobbles, broken engagements and partners left standing at the altar. Because they are such talented all rounders Aquarians often engender great wealth and frequently hit the lucky money jackpot. Their good eye means they spot a rare, fabulously valuable early teddy bear lying among jumble at a car boot sale. Random luck hovers over their golden heads and could bring a National Lottery win. Wealth brings freedom and happiness, but not before they've agonised over the downside – begging letters, requests for loans from friends and relatives.

Expect dissatisfied 16 to keep changing their looks. One day they've dyed their hair red. The next they've had a hair weave. It's a more frivolous side of their search for perfection and it's fun.

> *Many an optimist has become rich simply by buying out the pessimist.*
>
> (Michel de Saint- Pierre)

BODY

Could you try to be more happy-go-lucky? Try the HP Test (Habitual Pessimist) 1: A ravishing creature you desire invites you to a night of love, do you wonder if you're up to it? 2: The company gives you a beautiful red car. Do you think it will get stolen? 3: Exam results are brilliant. You think 'I could have done better'? 4: The genie says, 'You've got three wishes.' You think, 'I know I'll get this wrong.' 5: Stephen Spielberg rings to offer you a part in Jurassic Park II. You think 'Who'll feed the cat?' Any ticks at all and you're an HP.

❧

MIND

Concentrate on the good things. Lucky days for February are 1, 3, 10, 19, 21 and 28 excellent days for working things out, unexpected good fortune, including financial, a marriage proposal, a romantic meeting, possible pregnancies and joy for February 16's kids.

DATESHARE

Geraint Evans, world-famous Welsh baritone. **John McEnroe**, tennis star bad boy, Wimbledon champion. **Sonny Bono**, singer, ex-husband of Cher, massive hit 'I got you Babe', politician. **Anthony Dowell**, British ballet dancer, choreographer, ballet school founder. **John Schlesinger**, film director, Midnight Cowboy, Marathon Man. **Francis Galton**, inspiration for eugenics craze earlier this century, suggested working classes should have their fertility limited. **LeVar Burton**, film star, Kunta Kinte in Roots. **Robert Flaherty**, film director, Nanook of The North.

February 17 is like Tigger from Winnie the Pooh. They bounce about, expect everybody to be their friend and they're always looking for new games to play. Likeable, friendly, energetic Tigger is a favourite star amongst other stars and blessed by the gods.

When Tigger makes mistakes, he's so forlorn the world rushes to help. When lady Tiggers get into hot water because two concurrent boyfriends have found out, people shrug and say 'Silly girl'. The conclusion is that there's not a bad bone in their lovely Aquarius bodies. But they do create problems which often require a lot of sorting out. This is the creature who loses his passport abroad having drunk too much the night before and left it in a café. And the fact is that someone else will have to sort it out.

This is the girl who forgets to take her birth control pills on holiday and drives the wrong way up a one-way street. Lady Tiggers get away with murder because they can look helplessly fetching. When a policeman sternly tells her to park the car, then get out to discuss the one-way situation, she can't get it into the parking space – this isn't a spatially orientated date – but the nice policeman does it for her. And then says he quite understands

about the mistake. His wife is like that too.

They make terrific journalists because people always talk to them. On buses and trains there's always somebody who wants to confide in Tigger. There's also usually somebody who wants to get off with them.

Charm rests on them like a golden cloak. They get the best tables in restaurants and discounts where there are none. Strangers lend them their mobile telephones. People pay them for just being around. Lady Tiggers make good parents but often forget to go to parents' evenings. Husbands forget anniversaries. It never matters.

Knock knock.   *Who's there?*
Euripides.   *Euripides who?*
Euripides and you'll
not get a new pair.

18 FEBRUARY

February 18 longs for spring to come and for summer's warm days. Some may even suffer from mild depression brought on by damp and dingy light outside and at work. Some February 18s find it all so discouraging that they go abroad to a warmer place to live. This problem may dominate February 18's otherwise optimistic psycheology and it's essential that they don't sink into moans every year, but pre-plan instead.

Since many born today have a good eye for colour, and make their living with this clever design vision, the obvious thing is to create a brightly-coloured home. Their houses have touches of bright yellow and blue, uplifting colours. And summery flowers. You find startling shades of orange or carnivorous crimson in hallways and bedrooms.

Many of these individuals take a winter/spring holiday, maybe somewhere hot but also in snow covered mountains where sunlight bounces vigorously off white snow and cheers the most melancholy soul. Since this individual is often sporty and as fast on her feet as a shooting star, there'll be expert swimming and skiing to take others' breath away.

Women born today are extremely conscious of the right price for their work. So they move from job to job until satisfied that they are properly rewarded. Neither sex is at all backwards about coming forwards with what they want and since you do get more if you ask – at the right time – they do get.

In spite of this February 18 puts off to tomorrow what should be finished today. Not so bad at work where pay packages discipline them. But at home procrastination causes the perennial Aquarius problem of unpaid bills, due to reluctance to part with money, and it's not surprising when the electricity gets cut off. Worse, both sexes are so busy putting off decisions they miss the partner of their dreams and let love opportunities drift away. Nor can the women decide when to have a baby.

A little learning is a dangerous thing, but a lot of ignorance is just as bad.

(Bob Edwards)

BODY

If you suffer from winter dumps you should make sure to get out into natural light, preferably amongst green trees, at least once a day for half an hour. Otherwise it may be good to take one of the famous Bach Flower remedies. Olive (Olea europoea) is designed to shoot energy and optimism into the system. It's designed for the 'I'm so exhausted I could cry' person. Formulated by Dr Edward Bach from natural ingredients, it produces a feeling of balance, mental and physical vigour, the return of good humour and an easy ability to cope.

MIND

Syntonics, a branch of optometry, has been demonstrating for the past eighty years how colours can heal eye conditions and generally revitalise the body. Yellow, orange and red are stimulating; green, harmonizing; blue, violet and magenta are relaxing.

DATESHARE

John Travolta, Hollywood megabite. **Yoko Ono**, Japanese wife of John Lennon, author, painter, singer, songwriter. **Cybill Shepherd**, TV actress, Moonlighting. **Helen Gurley Brown**, magazine guru, editor-in-chief of Cosmopolitan, writer, Sex and The Single Girl. **Matt Dillon**, film star. **Jack Palance**, Hollywod star. **Vanna White**, dippy blonde American TV hostess, socialite. **Milos Forman**, Czech film director, Amadeus. **Andres Segovia**, Spanish guitarist. **Alexander Volta**, Italian physicist.

AIR

FEBRUARY 19

February 19 is the sort who thinks there are fairies at the bottom of her garden. And who knows but she's right. Celtic people born on this day are particularly aware of others who people the world just beyond our sight, and in Ireland awareness of the fairy people is part of every day life for many. So February 19 shouldn't heed those who mock. They only do it out of blockheaded embarrassment.

Both sexes will prefer alternative medicines to conventional ones, country life to city dwelling and if they must live in an urban high rise, expect it to be full of mystical wind chimes and wafting essential oils designed to heal and help. Whether they be behind the counter in the high street bank, or on a building site, February 19 holds true to his or her beliefs. And because of them often has a happy, confident life.

Many raise enormous sums of money for environmental benefit. Others sit up trees to stop them being torn down for car parks. Because their theory of life is advanced, they are excellent social workers, listening gently to other people's problems, and trying to instil in their clients the idea of self-help. Basically both sexes dislike being at the mercy of authority, whether it be lawyers or doctors and will avoid these people if they can at all costs.

Sex is a matter of soul as well as body and these people keep lovers happy with real magic as well as ordinary old sex skills of the Ancient Orient. They regard children as a gift of God and treat them as such. They are often vegetarian, so not at the mercy of today's food scares. Many February 19 people's idea of bliss is to live in a group with uncles, aunts, grannies and hangers-on all joining in with child rearing and domestic duties. It's a very long-lived date and no wonder.

Behind every successful man is a woman – with nothing to wear.

(Grant Glickman)

20 FEBRUARY

This dangerous creature doesn't know the power of its impact on others. Someone at birth threw an extra bucket of charm their way as they arrived in the world trailing pink clouds of glory, but forgot to add the extra teaspoonful of self-awareness. Lovely spring children, they are gifted with beauty and eyes that potential lovers want to drown in. Wherever he or she goes, people want them to stay. But sweet February 20 trips away, thinking how kind everybody is for throwing gifts, new cars, best theatre tickets, with no notion that the givers are desperately in love, but don't dare say because February 20 is liable to not only be surprised, but will deem it only kind to never see the poor declarer again.

It's a luscious peach on the tree, but not an easy nibblette and too far to reach for most people. Heads in the stars, they dream of what is to come, a better career, a first book, or decorating their home. Sexy when aroused, it's a cerebral peach, frequently goes without romance for months. Without a partner, February 20

never worries that she might not be kissed again, because a kiss is always just around the corner.

Duplicitous at work, their career rise is often phenomenal. Nobody pins down February 20's intent to deceive because both sexes constantly change the rules and are always surprised that anybody expected them to be consistent. The big ideas are worth waiting for. Nobody else has them quite like this, and nobody else can accomplish them quite like that. Expect astonishing originality and the frequent crackle of pure excitement.

Find February 20 in retail, sales, the media and tourism, where people pleasing is paramount. Although they may not care personally how many people feel, they do care collectively and their strong imagination makes this vision absolutely masterful. In later life they settle down, after one to ten false starts.

Come as you are,

as you were,

as I want you to be.

(Nirvana)

BODY

As they change their mind, so both sexes in youth change their hair colour. Since the desire is for frequent change, why not try something alternative to chemical colourants, which will wash out and leave the way free for another colour experiment?

Try gentle, subtle rinses you make yourself as flower teas. For red lights in fair hair: simmer 75g crushed marigold flowers in 600ml water in non-metal pan for 20 minutes. Remove from heat, strain when cool. Use as an after wash rinse, pouring it over, catching it in a basin and pouring over again. Allow hair to dry naturally in sunshine.

MIND

The older February 20 likes to maintain their youthful charms. To disguise grey hair, steep 3tbsp each of black tea and sage in freshly boiled water. Allow to cool and use as a rinse, pouring repeatedly over your hair. Rinse with tepid water.

DATESHARE

Died: **Robert Bolt**, film producer, director. Born: **Ivana Trump**, ex-wife to Donald 'The Trump', beauty, socially dextrous entrepreneur in own right. **Patty Hearst**, heiress, kidnapped, fell in love with and married kidnapper. **Gloria Vanderbilt**, heiress, designer. **Kurt Cobain**, lead singer, Nirvana, suicide at 27, icon. **Sidney Poitier**, film actor. **Robert Altman**, film director, The Player.

February 21 is like a bowl of cherries. They please everybody. You can do all sorts of things with them. And they don't make you feel sick. Cherry Ripe's stony centre doesn't indicate a hard heart, but a hard head. Versatile creatures, they work well in teams, their verbal skills and often good scientific brains putting them at the cutting edge of new discoveries. At work, they're the ones helping others, turning each project into an exciting party. The young cluster near. Older colleagues are consulted for advice and valuable experience. Nobody is left out. February 21 thinks everybody has something to give.

Outside work this soubrette of the skies is a problem. They're flitters. Rockets firing, they zoom in pursuit of a star, the more difficult to attain, the more zoom. The conjunction in space that follows rocks the heavens, days and nights of star kissed pleasures, love in the grass under the moon's cool smile, declarations beneath the burning rays of the sun. February 21 takes his co-star high into the Welsh mountains, where pearl soft water in rock pools cradles lover's limbs, ice cold and heat for memories.

Suddenly the tricky flitter flees. Boredom is their great fear and by golly, do they get bored fast. Don't ask them if they're happy. Both sexes will think 'no' to everything, including you. Lovers mustn't let themselves be entirely won, because this creature fears being trapped.

They're serial lovers and marryers. High earning, both sexes can afford it. But February 21's child will never be abandoned. Once a parent, they stick like goose grass, stay put out of love for the other partner /parent, with the emphasis on parent. They raise happy kids, inspired by the dreaming imagination of their mother or father. If there aren't children, watch out. You can spot their home anytime. Full of vibrantly coloured walls, flowers, fruit, paintings, shimmering textiles. Done by their own artistic hands.

Should dreams haunt you,

heed them not,

for all, both sweet and horrid

are jokes in dubious taste.

(W H Auden)

22 FEBRUARY

Late February people can let their worries overwhelm them. February 22 is a What-Iffer. What if I go to the country and have a picnic and a wasp stings me, I trail my hand in the river and catch some awful disease, I set foot out of the house and a car knocks me down? Everybody has worries and they're often the same ones, but you have to get on or life gets you down. In extreme cases this creature should seek counselling, which is excellent in this area. Otherwise they should share their worries, but not to burden. Nor should this date give in to constantly seeking reassurance. There was no dark star reigning on this day when Ms and Mr What-If came into the world.

If this person can keep worries in check, he or she will have an excellent time both at work and in their private life. A little worry is useful at work, making them double-check, so February 22 is reliable and accurate. Give them a plan and ask them to tear holes in it and they will find all the weak spots you can't see. Many flourish in scientific and research areas, and in accounting, or anything to do with retail or entertainment, where accurate checking is vital to please the public.

A great lover of natural beauty, this individual loves those who share this enjoyment. Expect to tramp mountain and moor, walk by river and sea. During this time, expect February 22 to collect natural things. Both sexes are passionate about plants, birds and indigenous rocks. Favourite precious stones will be those they can find, such as amethyst, rock crystal, fluorite and haematite. A lump of haematite is as likely to be a present to the dearest as any shop-bought goodie. Partners should learn to see the glittering world through February 22's eyes, or they might be offended by receiving some dusty old pebble.

You remain my power,
my pleasure, my pain.

(Seal)

BODY

Rock crystal is a colourless, transparent variety of quartz and very commonly found on beaches. People in many lands use amulets, worn at night to give them sound and peaceful sleep. It is also said to protect against spells and evil thoughts. Amethyst, commonly found in the north of Scotland, is supposed to counteract hangovers, nervous headaches and ward off ill fortune. It was commonly worn in medieval times by doctors and was often the choice for a prelate's Episcopal ring. It is also a favoured stone for beads of rosaries and one of the chosen stones set into the breastplate of a Jewish high priest.

MIND

Tarot's Major Arcana gives the 22nd card as The Fool. It indicates an unmaterialistic person, a strong sense of empathy and spiritual awareness of the world. It also indicates minor worries overcome and lessons well learned.

WATER

BODY

Late February people often suffer from tired, aching feet and sometimes swollen ankles, especially after a day at work, and especially in a hot summer. Try to get up every so often and move your legs about, or pop out for a quick walk. Try upturning a metal waste paper basket and putting your feet up. Experts suggest avoiding too much tea and coffee. Stick to lemon and water and eat citrus fruit, known to be a natural diuretic. Cut down on salt. It promotes water retention. You may find that you are one of those people whose feet swell up because of an allergy to bread, cakes or biscuits. Cut them out for a few days and eat as much fresh fruit and vegetables as you can.

MIND

Total responsibility for others readily transforms itself into martyrdom, which is the bid for power often chosen by those who have no claim on political and economic power. Hence its popularity amongst househusbands and wives.

February 23 suffers from the Cinderella Complex and they're very entrenched. Although they dream of bright lights and happiness there's a perverse little streakette which urges them to miss opportunities. When the Fairy Godmother says 'You shall go to the ball', Cinderella replies 'I think I'll give it a miss. I've got all this work to finish. I probably won't know anybody, anyway.' She needs hours of morale boosting and by the time the exhausted Godmother has magicked the girl into agreeing that a glittering evening of pleasure could be fun, it's too late. Fortunately for Ms C Complex, there will always be another party with another prince just waiting to admire the glass slippers. Or a princess in the case of Mr Cinderella.

If people born on this day don't stir their stumps, nothing interesting will happen, and they'll feel taken advantage of. At work, they sort out the boss's work, while she is out drinking champagne. Both sexes take on too much. It makes them useful, but who'd choose useful, when exciting's on offer? You are talented. So shine. Many February 23s so afflicted are second sons or daughters in families large enough for them to spend too much time deferring to older siblings and caring for younger ones. But adults don't need to carry the baggage of their childhood. Beware the martyr's streak at home. Dinner parties are a never ending story of self-imposed lack of enjoyment. Partners and family get used to cries of 'Why am I always the one to de-fluff the tumble dryer?' Resolve to do nothing unless it is with pleasure, personally and for others. And never play the martyr again.

Resolution taken, February 23 rediscovers a lovely frivolity and often a quick, amusing wit. It's a rare person who can make others laugh, but also surprise those nearest and dearest with imaginative treats. Expect exotic trips on water. And a fountain installed in the living-room.

I do every possible thing I can for my family. And I never let any of them forget it for a moment.

24 FEBRUARY

They are great believers in fate. Everything always seem to turn out for the best and if it doesn't, it was meant to be that way. February 24 wears a golden mantle of optimism. Both sexes have a habit of being in the right place at the right time. They turn up at the fashion department of *Marie Claire* just as someone has flounced out and Sharon Stone is waiting for help putting on her hat.

Artistically capable with their hands and apparently extremely self-confident this person adjusts it to the right angle and wins the immediate right to angle for the job and land it.

They take a bet on an outsider and the horse comes in first. It's February 24 who is watching telly when a huge finger pokes through the ceiling and a voice says 'It's You.' There won't be any depression about money. They don't suspect others of only liking them for it. They'd just laugh, hire a private jet and take all their friends to Paris for oysters and champagne.

He isn't remotely concerned about being thought vulgar, and nor is she. Big rocks on fingers, small ones in fat wristwatches are their idea of bliss. Grand parties, with thousands of pounds spent on flowers and a flock of doves to let fly at midnight are also their idea of fun, but a barbecue with old mates and masses of good red wine will do just as well.

As lovers they are faithful, reassuring and will never stray. Look for twenty- and thirty-year marriages. Many will have strong beliefs and put their good luck down to the machinations of a kind god, whichever one they choose to follow. But it's worth remembering they have a fatalistic streak, always aware that each fleeting moment is precious because there may not be another.

Birds sing after a storm;
why shouldn't people
feel as free to delight
in whatever remains to them?
(Rose Kennedy)

BODY

February 24 has a racing mind and often finds it goes on racing and prevents sleep. A new, insomnia treatment using small rubber cones, Isocones, is based on acupressure, an ancient Chinese practice to exert pressure at key points to promote sleep. Worn on the inside of the wrist at night, the cones work on a pressure point called Heart 7 (H7) acupoint. The cones are designed to fit comfortably in the dip beneath the wrist and are held in place by aerated plasters. Clinical trials have shown Isocones improve the quality of sleep by up to 79 per cent.

MIND

Memorise these lists.
A: Virtue, history, silence, life, hope, value, mathematics, dissent, idea.
B: church, beggar, carpet, arm, hat, teapot, dragon, cannon, apple.
If your A (abstract and more difficult) was as good as your B (concrete), your memory is excellent.

DATESHARE

Wilhelm Grimm, *German fairytale author with brother Jacob.* **Alain Prost**, *French racing driver, Formula One champion.* **Dennis Waterman**, *star of The Sweeney and Minder, married to actress Rula Lenska.* **Brian Close**, *former England cricket captain.* **Paul James**, *singer with '60s pop band.*

*Are you bored with sex? Here's a
test. Maybe it's just too
predictable. Give yourself a 5
score for each question if you're
very predictable ranging
through 4, 3, 2 to 1 if not at all.
a) The time of day we have sex.
b) The day of the week we have
sex. c) The place we have sex.
d) Who initiates. e) How we get
started. f) What we are wearing.
g) What we do to arouse each
other. h) The order of events.
i) What we say or don't say
during sex. j) What we do after
we finish sex. Over 30? Dear
me. Around 10? Not bored.*

MIND

*A healthy drink for an energetic
mind: Chop carrots into chunky
strips for juicer. Rich in beta-
carotene, folic acid, vitamin C,
small amounts of B1, B2, B3,
B5, B6, and E. Minerals include
calcium, potassium, sodium,
magnesium, small amounts
copper, iron and zinc.*

DATESHARE

Zeppo Marx (Herbert Marx)
member of Marx Brothers
comedy team. **Bobby Riggs,**
amateur champion tennis
player. **Dame Myra Hess,**
pianist. **George Harrison,**
singer, guitarist, songwriter,
Beatle. **Herb Elliott,**
Australian Olympic gold
medalist mile runner. **Sir
David Puttnam**, film director,
Chariots of Fire. **Gert Frobe,**
German film actor,
Goldfinger. **Pierre August
Renoir,** French Impressionist
painter. **George Friederic
Händel,** composer, Water
Music. **Tom Courtenay,**
actor, film star.

FEBRUARY 25

February 25 is kind to all animals, especially spiders in the bath. This arthropodophile is so addicted to the hairy scuttlers that she builds spider ladders up behind the plug so they don't get washed down waving eight sad goodbyes. Most likely both sexes are also vegetarians, particularly pleased with themselves now there's so much concern about meat.

Both sexes are interested in alternative living. Solar power attracts them and many grow their own organic vegetables. Windowsills are crowded with burgeoning cucumber plants and they breakfast off bean sprouts. But take note, scoffers, this person is no pushover. In unexplored depths of science you will find them working brilliantly to discover a giant step forward for mankind. Genetics and neuroscience are a passion. More ordinarily find the girls working as ace car mechanics or computer networking Neptunites (as well as the men). Ms 25 can rewire your house. It's just that she'll take a carrot juice, not a beer break.

Both sexes have great legs, strong thighs, long from knee to fine ankle and big, capable feet, good for dancing and caressing potential partners under the dinner table in unsuitable ways on unsuitable occasions. Many make fine sportsmen and women in youth and continue to play in clubs and local teams well into old age.

It's maybe the good life and maybe the sex life which keeps them springing like arthropods at play into their nineties. Fortune

says this day may have a child or children late in life, in the fifties, sixties, seventies, or even later. Either their own or adopted due to unexpected circumstances. If this is the case, expect February 25 to play great games, tell brilliant stories and with their good voices, sing a great deal of 'Ring a ring of roses' and 'London's Burning'.

February 25 has a lot to say about life and could write a best-selling book about his or her views, or make a film or TV programme.

*All animals are equal,
but some animals are more equal
than others.*

(George Orwell)

26 FEBRUARY

They're made for love. Pisces is a pearl of pure sex appeal. Precious, rare, flattering to all who possess it. The colour of moonshine, it reflects the moon's own alluring light of love but isn't perfectly faithful. Like silky water, they slide through your fingers giving pleasure for a moment, and then it's gone.

What's worse, they get your sympathy vote with tales of woe. They get you to put up shelves, cook pearl attracting dishes, shop for nectarines (they're mad about fresh fruit and veg) and negligees, fix their computer in nanoseconds. They murmur compliments in your ear, get other stars to loan them all their sparkle for a big occasion and then they get bored and shoot off across the dome of the darkened sky with another space biker.

Privately Pisces is afraid of boredom. So much so that he or she can almost sniff it when it's coming and sometimes they can sniff it when it's not there. They thrive on uncertainty. The telephone call that doesn't come keeps them excited and so does something casually dangerous in the air. Let them demand attention, weep for reassurance and they're yours. Give either and they'll be somebody else's.

This child of Neptune simply ebbs away with the night and when you wake, they're gone. The men are always looking at their watches and flipping through their address books. Strangers telephone Pisces in bed with a lover and he pretends it's work. Actually it's the next darling on his list, phoning to say she can't understand why she hasn't received the expensive underwear itemised on his last credit card bill.

If you think he's terminally cheating on you, ask his local grocer to send round their entire stock of cauliflowers to his house. Just one makes a kitchen pong. Multiply that by fifty. Or try the old trick of telephoning him from a box and leaving it off the hook.

Better by far
you should forget and smile
Than that you should remember
and be sad.
(Christina Rossetti)

WATER

Both sexes eat fast-food and have heavy thighs, the women showing a tendency to cellulite. Eliminate all refined and processed foods laden with chemical additives, sugar and white flour products, salty foods such as smoked fish and preserved meat products, coffee, alcohol and to a slightly lesser degree, tea. Try herb teas. The following are particularly good for cellulite sufferers, because they are natural diuretics and are renowned by herbalists as blood purifiers: nettle, golden rod, dandelion and meadowsweet. Try frictioning with a loofah, or brushing with long-handled brush up from ankles and over thighs towards the heart.

☾

MIND

Lucky days in February are 1, 3, 10, 19, 21, 28. These are traditionally thought to be good for business transactions, except speculations. They are also good for field sports achievements and particularly fortunate for all young people.

DATESHARE

Died: **Lillian Gish**, *early Hollywood sex bomb. Born:* **Elizabeth Taylor**, *film actress.* **Ralph Nader**, *consumer advocate.* **Lawrence Durrell**, *novelist,* Alexandria Quartet. **Joanne Woodward**, *film star.* **John Steinbeck**, *Nobel Prize-winning novelist,* The Grapes of Wrath.

FEBRUARY 27

These are some of the nicest people in the year, balancing all the sensuous virtues of Pisces, with Jupiter's kindness and Neptune's brains. There's only the slightest hint of pompous snapping lobster in February 27, when he is pushed very far and loses his temper. Let's take the temper first, get it out of the way.

Our satinette sweetheart's flip side is a steely resolve so tough that if you so much as hint, particularly at work, that you won't be doing what you promised, February 27 will bite your bottom. Both sexes are prepared to work all hours, joined at the fingertips with their computer. And they'll make it fun for companions. Make

them laugh. Buy drinks. Compliment everybody. But they can't stand people who wriggle out of commitment. And the same goes for a domestic promise not kept.

Otherwise, it's good. February 27 likes teams and likes people. He's the ticket sales person at the station who tells you the right platform and looks up when you can return. He's the shopkeeper who carries your bags to the car, the builder who wears his trousers attached to the waist so as not to offend. They don't gossip. They rise high in creative jobs. And they give to charity.

This is a water baby who makes money. Although they worry about losing it – a cash crisis upsets them terribly – February 27 people buy generously for friends and family, and spend a lot of money on themselves. Both sexes are exceedingly fancy dressers, the men favouring dark blue, the traditional colour of truth, sincerity and earnestness. And the women, slightly lighter, brighter shades, indicating the qualities of friendship, frankness, innocence, virtue and steadfastness.

If you want a wrong put right, or if you just need a hand, ask February 27. Both sexes will help out, never breathe a word and never remind you later, or make you feel beholden.

I must govern the clock, not be governed by it.

(Golda Meir)

28 FEBRUARY

They've got the brains and sensibilities of the Great White Whale. February 28 understands so much, and some of it comes from other times and other centuries. They can sense a disaster or a spectacular success miles off, or even years off. Hunches are their signposts. Theirs is a very grown up psychology and any companion will be in awe of their vision and their grandly non-materialistic habits. Maybe irritated by the latter.

In the wrong company they are an endangered species, speaking no evil, seeing and hearing none, but sometimes they are wrong to shut their eyes to reality. It can harm them and those they love. All February 28 people scatter money like falling meteorites. And sometimes more than they've got. Capable of high earning – find them in transport, anything to do with travel, and often in the army or church – they will give everything to a needy, even deceitful, relative or friend. True friends of this fabulous monster worry and query, but February 28 waves them away.

Because they have such an understanding of the human condition, many may develop an interest in mysticism. This is a complicated psychology with a naturally psychic streak. Find them living surrounded by their parents' and grandparents' things, because these inanimate object put them in touch with the friendly beings who owned them.

It's better for February 28 if others watch out for their money. Let this creature dream and sing its mystical songs in the moonglow sea, while others sort the bills. Because apart from giving cash away, this individual has the financial brain of a sea anemone and could make drastic mistakes, drawing down the wrath of authority on its hapless head. It doesn't have much dress sense either and will choose awful bright orange and acid yellows, too-short trousers and shirts whose buttons pop open, just because they are an amazing bargain at the sales.

The present moment is all you ever really know.

BODY
February people can suffer from cold hands and feet and regular massage with essential oils will relieve this. Choose floral or citrus essences, especially lavender, rose, mandarin and bergamot adding one or two drops to a carrier oil such as almond. Work the oil in circles with your thumbs over the whole foot or hand, concentrating on the ankle or wrist joint. Work gently, always massaging towards the heart. To ease stiffness in the fingers and toe joint, gently stretch them to the point of resistance, again causing no pain, and rotate first clockwise then anti-clockwise.

☾

MIND
There was a Young Lady whose chin
Resembled the point of a pin;
So she had it made sharp,
And purchased a harp,
And played several tunes with her chin.
Edward Lear's sensible advice on making the best of yourself.

DATESHARE
Died: **Ruby Keeler**, *Hollywood screen babe. Born:* **Sir John Tenniel**, *cartoonist, illustrator,* Alice In Wonderland. **Sir Stephen Spender**, *British poet.* **Linus Pauling**, *Nobel Prize-winning chemist, vitamin C advocate.* **Vincente Minnelli**, *film director,* An American In Paris, *father of Liza.* **Bugsy Siegal**, *gangster, built Flamingo Hotel and Casino in Las Vegas.* **Tommy Tune**, *Broadway dancer, choreographer.* **Zero Mostel**, *comic film and stage actor.* **Charles Blondin**, *French tightrope walker, crossed Niagara Falls on stilts.*

FEBRUARY 29

BODY

Fast deals mean fatigue and perhaps the best reviver for this unusual creature is Rescue Remedy, first put together by the famous Dr Edward Bach in the 1930s, who roamed our fields and woods for curative plants. Just use a couple of drops in a glass of water. Rescue Remedy contains impatiens (Impatiens glandulifera) for impatience and stress-induced agitation, clematis (Clematis vitalba) for spaciness and fainting, rock rose (Hlianthemum nummularium) for hysteria, cherry plum (Prunus cerasifera) for retaining mental and physical control and star of Bethlehem (Ornithogalum embellatum) for trauma both mental and physical.

MIND

Just an interesting snippet: Julius Caesar created February 29, occurring every four years to solve the few hours extra to 365 days in the solar year. Pope Gregory deemed it overkill, so only one in four century years – 2000, not 1700, 1800 or 1900 – gets February 29.

DATESHARE

James Mitchell, film star. **Anne Lee**, founder of the Shaker movement. **Gioacchino Rossini**, Italian opera composer, William Tell, The Barber of Seville. **Jimmy Dorsey**, jazz saxophonist, bandleader. **Dinah Shore**, film actress, film star, singer.

Naturally this is an unusual day. And there aren't many of them. February 29 seems a restless sort, like a mermaid or merman, unsure of what it is or where it wants to be. Quite a lot of time is therefore spent sitting on a rock combing its long golden hair and gazing in a hand mirror, or actually eyeing the seascape/landscape for any passing boatmen, especially treasure-laden feckless pirates who think they're on to a good thing with Ms Mermaid until she clasps them in her arms and sinks to the bottom.

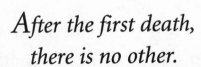

There's a tremendous optimism about this individual, probably the result of having to go without proper birthday parties and put on a brave face. They don't mind privation, and do like living dangerously. Money makers all, and not fussy about how it's done. The ogling pirate will not be clasped until this merperson has been showered with all his booty. And then he's a goner. Deals are made in seconds, and always with a splash. Nobody knows how they do it, but they know they're good. And they go on being good. Find them in any kind of market, money, goods, fruit and veg, antiques. They're the ones with the snazzy suits and fast cars with an account at a pleasing restaurant. He weighs the bank manager up in his scales and then flips the money out of him like an obedient fruit machine.

Many people born today choose one partner and stay put for life. If something parts this creature from his love he pines and won't be comforted for years. Most like to travel with their partner to far away lands. Pisces adores the Middle East, could swim around in Egypt then down the Arabian Gulf forever. Best bet for both sexes is a cruise, where they keep on the move, yet have a secure base. They're lethal and lovely. Lethal to foes. Lovely to the rest.

~

After the first death, there is no other.

(Dylan Thomas)

I MARCH

March 1 is a homemaker. Her rooms are perfumed. The paint effects on her walls, or maybe it's stylish paper or even fabric, is an inspiration. She can put curtains together at lightening speed. The men conjure up a magnificent dolls' house for their daughter. If they can't afford to buy paintings, they take a brush and make one.

With such flair, if either sex chooses they have an obvious and brilliant career. Fortunes can be coined, plus fame and cosseted popularity with rich, eager and socially persuasive customers. Punctuality may be a problem for our sparkling water sign. If they are swimming along, three quarters of an hour away from a meeting scheduled in the next half hour, it's not late until the actual time has passed. Managing as they do with an uncommonly slippery sleight of hand, this time optimism doesn't legislate against success.

Find them also in the media. But better in their own businesses, where their originality inspires clever, extremely marketable ideas. Redundancy brings no fear. Money whizzes into their hands, plus a better social standing and more relaxed life outside the confines of corporate life, where their maverick qualities either bring

exceptional success, or ground them in other's inertia.

March people are usually extremely socially concerned and work hard for charity. Snobbery also lurks in this beautiful head. The pebbles in another stretch of water always glisten more brightly and like salmon, they can take great leaps up the rockiest social waterfall.

They may therefore choose a mate who fits in with the social whirl, always preferring someone who looks after them to a dependent lover. Women in particular resent the househusband because if anyone's going to stay at home and care for the children, they want it to be them. Being financially taken care of is important, and although Mrs March will love and nurture her family and partner, penury is a pain in the pantaloons.

The man who makes no mistakes
does not usually make anything.
(Edward John Phelps)

BODY
A dolls' house is a basic wooden box with divides and a curtain or attached door over the front. A large old drawer may make the basic structure. Paint or paper the rooms with leftover bits of birthday wrapping. Add lighting, magic for a child, using a torch battery with tiny torch bulb set into ceilings with the help of soft solder. (Perfectly safe.) Postage stamps make excellent pictures, framed with tiny strips of coloured Sellotape. Shells, set in glue, make handsome decorations for front doors. Use cotton reels for coffee tables, and three matchboxes glued together for a chest of drawers.

MIND
March 1 has vivid dreams, sometimes recurring. Most have an optimistic meaning. Walking in the dark because the electric light has gone foretells good news from abroad. Dreaming of floods? To the traveller it means calm seas and safe journey.

DATESHARE
Roger Daltry, *lead singer of The Who, film actor.* **David Niven**, *film actor.* **Sandro Botticelli**, *Italian Renaissance Florentine master painter.* **Oskar Kokoschka**, *Austrian-born British Expressionist painter.* **Robert Lowell**, *poet.* **Glenn Miller**, *bandleader.* **Harry Belafonte**, *singer, film actor.*

BODY

Practical March 2 prefers plants in the garden which have two functions: good to eat and attractive, effective hedging and aromatic, alluring to butterflies and easy to cut. Violas, pansies and nasturtiums, whose flowers are all edible can be decorative in the front of a border. As can marjoram's golden leaves and dusty pink flowers, chives, with their edible pink purple flowers, borage – for summer drinks – with its stamened, blue flowers and winter savoury with its mauve blooms and leaves for stews, salads and fish. Not forgetting, of course, solid orange marigold whose petals spice up salads and which conveniently self-sows each year.

MIND

Superstitious March rarely walks under a ladder, but should also beware of other harbingers of ill luck. These include the unlucky giving of gloves to a friend and the fastening of a button into the wrong buttonhole, a bad omen.

March 2 is a great enthusiast. Magazines and newspapers litter this creature's home. There are books on do-it-yourself, cookery, bird spotting, winemaking kits under the stairs and a half made rug tucked beneath the bed. Like water-boatmen, these darling bugs of March skim enthusiastically across the liquid surface of the night in search of new ideas, only to be put off by other more rapacious and frightening stars. The busy waterboatman or woman, (*Notonectidae*) with its ever-flailing, oarlike hindlegs, sometimes feels it's putting in a huge amount of effort for nothing. And it's true. March 2 does tend to go about things the slow way, fixing everything by hand when it could use the machine.

Theirs is an unsullied belief that the woven thread fresh from a sheep's back makes a nicer sweater than any shop bought, chemically dyed wool. Worldlier stars, without March 2's quaint rose-tinted spectacles, understand this is not the case and somehow manage to do everything faster and more prettily. And make March 2 look foolish. At least that's what this sensitive creature thinks.

Faithful to all the old ways, March 2 frequently attaches him or herself to a boss or even admired friend and follows everything they do like a faithful shadow. Even as far as adopting their tastes and mimicking their speech. To some this is flattering, but this creature doesn't understand what a fantastically embarrassing burden it can be for others. Naturally they do brilliantly as aides-de-camp, the man or woman in the shadow behind the great one, but only if the great one has a sense of self-discernment, because March 2 lacks the critical faculty and can't warn when a personal idiosyncrasy has become risible.

What saves them is their quiet and private wit. But they are happiest living a peaceable life, without undue competition, raising a family, or living perfectly serenely alone with time to attend to whichever hobby is taking their fancy that particular year.

Be wise with speed;
a fool at forty is a fool indeed.
(Edward Young)

3 MARCH

This is such a forgetful star that one day he'll be blithering about in outer space and, forgetting the time, become the star that forgot to shine. March 3 leaves his wallet on top of the car as he drives away and sticks the front door keys on the outside of the lock for the rest of the world to turn. They need at least two pairs of glasses and a special place to put the current book they're reading. And both sexes really need a filing cabinet for bills, letters passports and car documents plus all those loseable things like washing machine and iron guarantees.

Baby March 3 has all the psychological indicators for a future of hunting under cushions. They can't find their blazer and the protractor desperately needed for homework. Their best skinny black top goes missing for days and suddenly smiles startlingly from the spin dryer. Best to evolve an attitude. Missing things, like recalcitrant teenagers, usually come out of hiding if you just ignore them.

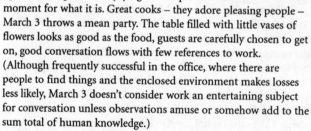

Apart from this anxiety, individuals born on this day are incredibly optimistic, capable of enjoying the simple moment for what it is. Great cooks – they adore pleasing people – March 3 throws a mean party. The table filled with little vases of flowers looks as good as the food, guests are carefully chosen to get on, good conversation flows with few references to work. (Although frequently successful in the office, where there are people to find things and the enclosed environment makes losses less likely, March 3 doesn't consider work an entertaining subject for conversation unless observations amuse or somehow add to the sum total of human knowledge.)

Magical in bed, like most Pisces, bedroom decor is of paramount importance to sensuous well-being. Blue is the best bedroom colour for water people. And shared wine or cocktails from a silver cup, the magic potion which binds your love.

*I'm always fascinated
by the way memory diffuses fact.*
(Diane Sawyer)

BODY

Fresh mussels delight water people. (Must be fresh and properly prepared.) Mussels in Cider. Take 1.2kg mussels, scrubbed, de-bearded, 1 finely chopped leek, 1 onion, finely chopped, chopped parsley, 860ml cider, 45g butter, 30g flour, 570ml milk, salt, pepper, nutmeg. Put leek, celery, onion, parsley, cider in saucepan, bring to boil, turn heat to low, add mussels, cover, cook for 10 minutes. Strain mussels, discard any unopened, reserve broth. Melt butter in saucepan, add flour, mix until smooth, add milk slowly, stirring continuously. Bring to boil, turn heat low, add mussels, salt, pepper, nutmeg. Cook for few minutes. Eat with chunks of bread.

MIND

Women tend to have better memories than men, according to Bristol University psychology Professor Alan Baddeley. And their memories don't decline so early with age. Men's memory starts to go at 65, women's not until at least 70.

DATESHARE

*Died: **Danny Kaye**, actor, singer, great portrayer of fairy stories. Born: **Lee Radziwill**, jetsetter, Jackie Kennedy's sister. **Jackie Joyner-Kersee**, US Olympic (three) gold medal winning heptathlete, long jump champion. **Ronald Searle**, illustrator, cartoonist. **Perry Ellis**, designer. **Jean Harlow**, blonde film actress, died at 27 of uremic poisoning. **William Godwin**, novelist, political philosopher, Mary Shelley's father. **Ion Iliescu**, Romanian president.*

BODY

An alert brain means you can think more quickly, concentrate better and work harder. Fresh juice is better than a cup of coffee for that rapid lift because it provides the body with valuable nutrients. The minerals potassium, calcium, zinc and the B group of vitamins are all vital for healthy brain function. Try juicing 6 red cabbage leaves, ¼ large cucumber and 2 tomatoes. Or 1½ large carrots, 7 large spinach leaves and 2 stalks celery. Or 2 pears and a handful of watercress leaves. Makes one 250ml glass. Adults can drink up to three glasses daily.

MIND

Stop the children getting bored at Christmas. They adore making Sweet Chains to hang on the tree (or anywhere). Simply take sweets in plain, shiny wrappings and wire them, or tie them to a long length of thin ribbon or cord.

DATESHARE

Hans Eysenck, psychologist. **John Garfield**, film actor. **Jim Clark**, Formula One world champion racing driver. **Paula Prentiss**, film actress. **Antonio Vivaldi**, Italian composer. **Don Pedro** of Portugal, great navigator, teacher to explorers, observatory and navigation school builder. **Alan Sillitoe**, playwright, novelist, Loneliness of the Long Distance Runner.

Just a small, smidgeonette of overkill on the sentimental here. There's altogether too much in the world that makes this willow weep and March 4 must understand that the world does not love eyes that are always brimming with tears. A little brimming is fine to get attention or maybe just change the pace. But snivelling – alter the word and look how you change the emphasis – ain't attractive. It also means that companions have to heave themselves out of a chair, or off the telephone, or away from their buttered bun, and do something about you.

Snivelling apart, this is a pretty nice fellow or fellowess. They say a soft heart is never good in business, and maybe not if it's dominant. But in many areas of work it puts this person ahead of the game, seeing dimensions others can't. Because of this sensitivity, they are often superb writers, painters or musicians. Not so hot on journalism where their innate honesty/niceness can disadvantage, nor any kind of politics. But they make great teachers and social workers, fired by imagination and empathy with others.

Fortunately there's also a streak of arrogance and fire in March 4's psychology, which makes them extremely interesting thinkers and capable of the most successful maverick behaviour. Some even become flashy style leaders, can make wearing sequins the only way to dress for wind surfing and feathered curtains de rigeur for shielding eyes from the shimmering night sky.

Not a faithful starfish, however. It longs for the fisher's net to pluck it out of rock pools, but when his back is turned after the catch, March 4 shimmers away into the sand, leaving just a little wet dent where she was only a moment ago. She never leaves children. Both sexes would have six and some will. So watch out for contraceptives which 'don't work', or unconsciously aren't used correctly. March 4's beloved string of 'accident babies' will always come first.

Ever since Eve gave Adam the apple, there has been a misunderstanding between the sexes about gifts.

(Nan Robertson)

5 MARCH

March 5 have great feet. Long, slender, strong, with even toes, an elegant instep and fetching ankles, these are the feet that could launch a thousand ships. Their feet are their fortune. Many are terrific runners, fast on the sprint and steadfast in the decathlon. For some ice skating is their forte, while others could probably earn a fortune in shoe and tights adverts. Many more simply go barefoot all the time and enjoy the

 admiration. So with feet, so with shoes? The answer's no. Shoes are merely what cover the beautiful attribute and are often chosen for comfort and to be kind to their plates of meat rather than to attract.

Apart from drawing other people's attention to their feet, which is natural with such a gift of Jupiter and Neptune, Pisces' ruling planet, March 5 people are an intelligent, spiritually gifted and extremely decent bunch. Many are drawn to the Christian church, where they will be active in all aspects of parish work, both the social and the ecumenical. Both sexes may respond to a religious calling and enter the church, most usually to become a vicar, because theirs is a sociable nature. In this area some rise very high. The beauty of their feet may not be useful in a church setting, but the drive, determination, generosity of spirit and again that old magic worked with empathy, make them popular in parishes. Otherwise, both sexes organise a good fête or theatre in the local hall in aid of church funds. They're also so clever with their hands they paint the scenery and sew the costumes.

March 5 resists his natural temptation to flirt and flit and settles down with a chosen partner. In mid life, both sexes may change their earning style completely and begin a new, much more profitable phase, usually in the country. All their dreams will be realised.

BODY

Teenagers need good food and should be discouraged from adopting fads. It is not unusual for a teenager to grow 10cm in height or add more than five kilos in body weight in a year. These dramatic changes need to be fuelled by the best form of nutrition. Active adolescent boys may need up to 4000 calories a day (twice the normal adult man's recommended intake). Less active boys, who spend more time watching television and playing computer games, will need less, as do teenage girls. But good levels of vitamins and minerals are essential at this important stage in human growth and development.

MIND

Lucky animals include the hedgehog – to meet one brings wealth. Also to encounter a flock of sheep is lucky, especially if the flock is coming towards you. And a squirrel betokens approaching happiness.

It's better to have a rich soul

than to be rich.

(Olga Korbut)

Many Pisces people are fairly psychic, but March 6 has a powerful streak and should take care to listen to its dictates and be aware of the talent lurking there. Psychic promptings often come at the oddest moments and crowded in with all the hurley burley, they can be easy to dismiss. But March 6 has strong images about people which influence his life and it's best to get those psychic flashes as accurate as possible. Nothing is written in stone. Different paths can always be taken. So there is no need to be afraid of your talent. It acts as a signpost, but signposts come at a fork in the way and don't have to be taken. Even so, a great many people with psychic talent know when they are about to meet a future partner, or understand at a glance that this is a partner for life.

They also get a strong feeling about a deal, which is worth listening to. And about lending or borrowing money. And of course, it's a useful talent when buying a house. Some houses are good and others certainly are not, and just because it's a fantastic bargain at £48,000 with five bedrooms, one acre of land and a sea view, doesn't mean you want to take your family to live there, if the temperature drops to freezing in the far corner of the master bedroom. Usually estate agents know about these problems from previous owners, but may not tell you. And 'bargain' houses such as these aren't always easy to sell on.

Good fortune comes to March 6, who has great interest in jewellery. And may even find hidden caches where others failed. If they are lucky they may even find Roman jewels in East Anglian fields or torcs made for a Celtic queen and her daughter from gold, silver and copper alloy just before Jesus Christ was born. Whatever they find, March 6 always prefers antique jewellery.

A legend is a lie which has attained the dignity of age.
(Winston Churchill)

7 MARCH

Many people born today are quite egotistical and extremely self-reliant. Periods of solitude attract them. There is great pleasure in putting up the feet with a book, a long night's read and the occasional pause for a cup of tea and some rice pudding. (They're suckers for the tinned sort, chilled and eaten with honey.) Strawberries and yoghurt are perfect for slimmers, in fact many eat plain yoghurt instead of some meals and exist perfectly happily on fruit and vegetables for days.

Other, less balanced people have nibbling trouble. Like fish idling in the stream, they would dearly like to nibble all day. A little graze here, maybe a packet of chocolate cream biscuits, a little more grazing there, some fresh bread thickly laced with butter, sliced tomatoes, salt, black pepper and maybe a lettuce leaf, seems not to be really eating. They forget what has passed their lips and sit down to large meals, then wonder why their clothes don't fit.

It's particularly hard for working March 7 people, who skip lunch to slave at their desk. Eating makes not going out seem less of a sacrifice and that's when the triple decker sandwiches and doughnuts come in. Nor does this watery sign relish much exercise. Swimming is popular and horse riding; they are exceedingly good. But in a game of tennis they are a menace, lacking the true competitive spirit and skipping about giggling when they miss the ball. Not that they lack competitiveness at work. Theirs is a ferocious intellect, an unequalled capacity for concentration. No shilly-shallying here. If they rise to manager, they can be inspiring to underlings. Also terrifyingly fierce with a cold sting.

Partners must share their interests, which include rambling, collecting and frequently trainspotting. So must children, which leads to arguments in teenage years, because these are not young peoples' interests. March 7 must not push here or the mid-teens become alienated.

The trouble with being in a rat race is that even if you win, you're still a rat.

(Lily Tomlin)

BODY

The most effective way to use essential oils for skin care is to use them as a periodic treatment either once a week or daily for two weeks at a time during one month. This prevents your skin from growing accustomed to the essences and failing to respond. You can doctor an unperfumed face cream with the appropriate essence, two or three drops to 50g of face cream. For dry skin use camomile or lavender. Oily skin: cedarwood, lemon, tea tree. Ageing skin: sandalwood, frankincense. Normal skin: neroli, geranium. Puffy skin: cypress, patchouli. Acne: camomile, juniper, rosemary, tea tree.

MIND

The Tarot gives the 8th card in the Major Arcana as Courage. This gives you moral and physical stamina, plus charisma and determination to succeed. With March 8 there is also a strong likelihood of financial luck.

DATESHARE

Anthony Armstrong Jones (Lord Snowdon), British photographer, married to Princess Margaret. **Aidan Quinn**, Irish actor, film star, Desperately Seeking Susan. **Ivan Lendl**, Czech tennis champion. **Cyd Charisse**, dancer, film star, best legs in the world, born Tulla Ellice Finklea. **Anna Magnani**, Italian film actress. **Sir Edwin Landseer**, English painter, sculptor. **Peter Carey**, Australian novelist, Oscar and Lucinda. **Piet Mondrian**, Dutch painter. **Maurice Ravel**, French innovative composer.

March 8 people are drawn to gossip and although they know they should, they can't stop. A banana for all seasons, this sweet fruit of tropical rain and sun, is welcome everywhere and initially liked by everyone. Everybody wants to take a bite of banana-sweet's pure white flesh. Then our miscreant whisks off to another bowl game and unzips all its newly learned secrets.

Mayhem usually ensues. People slipping about on banana skins everywhere, cursing, explaining themselves, writing letters of apology, making desperate telephone calls and endless trips to the florist for apologetic flowers. Gossipers should understand before their little malicious ways become second nature, that others always discover the source of the gossip and if secrets were told in confidence – and many usually are – this is one banana which will get squashed flat and black.

Why do they do it? One part excitement at knowing something others don't. Four parts an overwhelming desire to let others know it. One part saying anything that comes into their empty heads. And one part is trouble-making. Gossip rage is commoner than road rage. Miscreants are attacked and their own reputation ruined. Once a gossip, it's hard to live it down. Promotion is harder because people fear that company secrets will get out. People avoid March 8 after a drink or two at parties, knowing they may say something indiscreet. Potential partners aren't so potential, because who wants to go to bed with a kiss-and-teller, and find next day that the whole world knows you've got a beauty spot nowhere that shows?

So we're talking a touch of the unpopularity stakes here. Best way to cure it is to be seen to say nothing. At work, when everyone's talking, make no personal comments. In a scandal, pretend you didn't know. Protect a vulnerable person's back. Talk about general interests. Don't be drawn.

His talk was like a stream, which runs with rapid change from rocks to roses.

(Winthrop Mackworth Praed)

9 MARCH

They tend to get involved with much older or younger partners. It's a growing trend. Latest figures comparing the 1990s to the 1970s show a 32 per cent increase in men marrying a woman at least 11 years their senior, and there were twice the number of marriages between women and men older by 16 years. And statistics, as far as they can in a sometimes unrecorded area, show that there are many more such couples living together but not married.

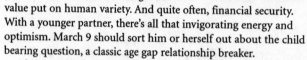

Age gap relationships do work or there wouldn't be so many. March 9 is emotionally flexible, loving and kind and finds benefit in an age gap. From an older person there's wisdom, and a greater value put on human variety. And quite often, financial security. With a younger partner, there's all that invigorating energy and optimism. March 9 should sort him or herself out about the child bearing question, a classic age gap relationship breaker.

It's essentially a jolly sort born on this day, a try anything once person, with buckets of charm and enthusiasm. They make brilliant PRs. At work, nothing's too much trouble. They always return telephone calls and write thank you letters. They're full of ideas, adore travel and never mind its privations and give a whacking good party. Cooking is their strength. Party rooms will be decorated in style but for few pennies. At Christmas they really come into their own.

A Christmas party will look festive, perhaps with a mass of one colour balloons, all blue if this water sign goes for its best colour, all red or silver if she branches out. Trailing ribbons gleam, mistletoe hangs at the right kissing level and all the grown ups get to take away their own balloons at the end of the evening.

Christmas at home is always imaginative. March 9 lies in bed, planning the tree, the flowers – always scented – and the presents, often handmade for love, originality and inextravagance.

What do snowmen dance at?

A snowball.

BODY
March 9 has wonderfully creative, practical skills. Children and aunties adore homemade tiny miniature gardens, with small mirrors as lakes and rivers, bearing a glass swan, tiny pebbled pathways up hills covered in turf (imitation will do), a bridge fashioned from twisted florist's wire, little lavender, curry or rosemary plants as trees and tiny embroidery silk French knot flowers glued onto half a matchstick stalks. Paint the matchbox 'drawer' in bright colours for a boat. Children love to make these too. Use a tin tray as a base for the earth, with a few intermingled stones in the soil to help with watering and keep your garden alive.

MIND
Make the Christmas house both smell good and revive jaded livers and heads with invigorating oils, ravansara, rosemary and myrtle in a burner. Try pine, seasonal fragrance, sandalwood, love, and ylang-ylang, to smooth Christmas tempers.

DATESHARE
Juliette Binoche, French beauty, movie star. **Robin Trower**, guitarist, Procul Harum. **Bobby Fischer**, world chess champion. **Micky Spillane**, author, Kiss Me Deadly. **Andre Courréges**, French fashion designer. **Mickey Dolenz**, drummer with The Monkees. **Yuri Gagarin**, Soviet cosmonaut, first man in space, icon. **Bill Beaumont**, British Lions and England international rugby captain.

March 10 is a solitary star and doesn't want to be part of a galaxy. It avoids the jolly members of the Milky Way, always cackling with laughter and moving with the crowd. It's a shy Pisces star. They are happiest in laboratories, libraries or working at a home computer, their social communication with big business by telephone.

Both sexes like money and find making it easy. Riches shoot across the firmament like rockets homing into the docking station of March 10's hands. Bank managers adore them. This creature has portly pension plans and innovative insurance. There will be stunning stock market kills. Expect large houses, good collections of antiques and baths with jacuzzis. Many become writers, musicians or artists for which the solitary life is best.

March 10 loves to roam the countryside, thinking, watching for rare plants, birds, perhaps the badger's nocturnal appearance and when there are jolly tumbling fox cubs about, both sexes leave titbits. A favourite occupation is a long ride across hills and clifftops with a companionable horse. Many hunt, enjoying the excitement and handsome spectacle of man and horse against the skyline. These people often loathe hunt saboteurs, regarding them as anthropomorphically driven townies, with a Disney concept of animals. But others born on this day very powerfully take the reverse stance, loathe hunting and although they are too shy to join pressure groups, will help finance them.

Discerning family people, they pick a partner for life. Often clumsy in courtship, theirs is a compelling passion and they win surprisingly glamorous, often socially desirable partners, on the basis of their honesty and simplicity of feeling. As parents they are excellent, loving but not coercive, understanding a child's need for its own space.

Time fascinates these people, so expect the collection to be of clocks, homes full of musically chiming longcases, and pretty porcelain and silver pocket watches made to keep our Edwardian ancestors punctual.

Patience is what love is, because how could you love somebody without it?

II MARCH

March 11 is a good leader, pulls a team along behind her with such enthusiasm that work seems more like a privilege. They have something infectious about them. People will work for this person for little money, putting in long hours and sometimes clearing up after March 11 who leaves a trails of paperwork and half-finished ideas behind him. They work for the praise and instant comprehension of their work this creature always shows. And ignore the flashes of contempt and terrifying temper, usually displayed for an excellent reason.

They're also anti-ageist. Captains of industry born on this day delight in using older people, relying on their experience and understanding the wealth of talent which contemporary prejudice ignores. Also find about them the very young and inexperienced, given their first chance to shine brilliantly with support from a boss who may have silently redone their work to help out and to show the correct way.

Great bosses, good colleagues and firm friends, they are not so comfortable with everlasting love, nor will close work relationships necessarily translate to out of office hours, or last after March 11 has gone to pastures new. Some colleagues feel let down by this and never forgive what they see as a slight. But there's a tough side to this water creature. He doesn't really care. You'll rarely find either sex turning up to a reunion. They live for the present, are immediately bored with the immediate past, except for their close circle.

This creature easily travels abroad to work, adapting fast. They take family if they can, but are content to carry on distant relationships if they must, sometimes proving slightly less than faithful to partners. It makes them a natural for businesses with overseas offices, oil mining and the armed forces. Look for a streak of ruthlessness here. If they want to push an idea through at work, at home or in the local community, they won't brook opposition.

BODY
For such clever people, March 11 is awful at finding his way to places, a hopeless map reader. Detailed instructions like take the M94, turn off at junction 16 on to the A663, then left round the second roundabout etc irritate, so they don't listen properly. Women turn the map upside down to accord with the direction they're going in, only half-hear roadside instructions, so have to stop frequently. The men won't ask for directions, so get seriously lost. Car rage ensues, inter couple shouting and frostiness on arrival. In these circumstances a little pre-journey concentration with the great brain is a fruitful thing.

MIND
True quiet means keeping still when the time comes to keep still, and going forward when the time dictates to go forward. Rest and movement are now in agreement with time's demands. Thus there is light in life.

DATESHARE
Harold Wilson, British prime minister. **Douglas Adams**, science fiction writer, A Hitchhiker's Guide To The Galaxy. **Rupert Murdoch**, Australian newspaper and media magnate, The Times, Sunday Times, News of The World, Sun, *Sky television.* **Dorothy Gish**, stage, silent film actress, sister to Lillian.

You will do foolish things, but do them with enthusiasm.

(Colette)

BODY

When planning conception, avoid drinking alcohol and smoking and take additional vitamin and mineral supplements – especially folic acid. This nutrient has been shown to reduce the risk of spina bifida in babies. A well-balanced vitamin and mineral supplement is also good, during pregnancy, although pregnant women should limit their intake of vitamin A (retinol) and avoid eating liver products such as paté. During the last months many vital vitamin and mineral reserves are used up and new mothers do well to take B complex vitamins and zinc. Both have been shown to help combat post-natal depression or common baby blues.

MIND

Pisces is the sign of the fish, a lucky creature. In the east, seeing a fish is a fortunate omen, foretelling wealth and fertility. A large fish swimming by itself promises a life of happiness and prosperity.

DATESHARE

Liza Minnelli, *singer, film star, dancer, daughter of Judy Garland.* **Jack Kerouac**, *beat poet, writer, On The Road.* **James Taylor**, *folk rock singer.* **Paul Kantner**, *singer, songwriter, Jefferson Airplane.* **Giovanni Agnelli**, *Italian industrialist, Fiat chairman.* **Vaslav Nijinsky**, *Russian dancer, suffered from schizophrenia.*

People born on this date have eyes you could drown in. Just one look is all it takes for most March 12ites to turn potential partner's brains to jelly. It's a seductive tiger in the jungle. Luminous stripes make it an awesome hunter in the dark and most victims give in to the pleasurable sensations of being seized and born away. Stealthily sensuous, March 12 is master or mistress to sexual techniques other stars haven't heard of – nothing unpleasant, just languorously imaginative.

When they have time, between romancing, they're also totally unbeatable in the market place. And therefore not only employable, but sought after by employers. Which is good, because this big cat has a habit of disappearing when it falls in love, maybe for days, and, when young, needs a sympathetic and patient boss.

Older tigers settle down into domestic life and in middle age you only see the occasional flash of their claws and those to-die-for eyes, just enough to let you know that the tank in this tiger is still fully fuelled. The girls have a strong maternal drive and once they have offspring, their lives may revolve around the children's needs. It makes them exceedingly happy and contented. The men are not quite so domesticated, but fatherhood means a great deal and they will sit up all night nursing a sick child with just the same energy as the mother.

If there is difficulty in conception, March 12 women are easily tempted to misery, as can be the male. But their balanced brains and thinking help them get a hold on the situation, investigating medical help and adoption. One or the other will succeed if these creatures set their minds to it. Adopted children will have a lovely life with a parent who loves them as much as any natural child. And March 12 will find, if the adoption route is taken, that theirs was wholly the right choice.

So in a voice,
so in a shapeless flame
Angels affect us oft.
(John Donne)

13 MARCH

D eeply dippy. Deeply psychic. Who knows what will happen around March 13, but better get hold of the controls or it may just become irritating. Nothing is certain. These are only signposts. No need to follow a path, especially a bad one. But this creature, although it sets out perfectly well balanced, can get right out of hand. Unless it stops generally floating about with its head in the clouds.

March 13 just leaps on the fadwagon and goes on about it until the next one comes along. This is a space capsule which careers about the sky apparently unmanned. And the trouble is that criticism or even hesitation is paranoidly dismissed. The psychic talent is there and could be useful, but the power is often waylaid into less sensible areas. Both sexes, but in particular the women, may decide to wear nothing but white, a Pisces colour, or blue, a good water personality colour. And so should everybody else, they think, leaping on someone's red trousers and asking very seriously if this is a show of aggression.

They may choose to lie naked at night in their back garden under the light of the full moon, hoping for something to happen. Not what you think and March 13 doesn't think that's funny either. Or maybe the entire garden has to be planted white only, symbolising innocence, the horrid buttercup plucked out for its insinuating yellowness. This person goes to India without injections or pills because of their new faith in a guru's power to create balanced health in followers, and then can't comprehend why he or she has diarrhoea the whole time. At parties they turn up in sandals and kaftans, the men with long beards, influenced by another foreign journey. They buy a Georgian house and make it so authentic, the lighting is from candles and there's no central heating. Fortunately they haven't worked out a legal way yet to recycle the sewage into the vegetable patch.

Though this be madness,
yet there is method in it.
(Hamlet, *Shakespeare*)

BODY
They have good brains and are proud of their memories, which stand them in good stead at work, where if they keep putting in the eight hours a day, some of the loopier fads can be well kept at bay. March 13 astounds everybody with his capacity to remember telephone numbers and number sequences. They use mnemonic systems, such as these ten pegwords, each of which rhymes with a number. One = bun, two = shoe, three = tree, four = door, five = hive, six = sticks, seven = heaven, eight = gate, nine = wine, ten = hen. Once these words are securely in your head, number sequence memory feats aren't particularly difficult.

MIND
Change is the conversion of a yielding line into a firm one. This means progress. Transformation is the conversion of a firm line into a yielding one. This means retrogression. Firm lines represent light, yielding ones, darkness. (I Ching)

DATESHARE
Died: **Busby Berkeley**, great Hollywood director of formation dance musicals. Born: **Neil Sedaka**, singer, songwriter. **Tessie O'Shea**, entertainer, Two-Ton Tessie. **L Ron Hubbard**, Church of Scientology founder, science fiction writer. **Dick Katz**, co-founder Milestone records, jazz pianist.

MARCH 14

BODY

March 14 often suffers from insomnia, perhaps both sexes take other's woes too greatly to heart, disturbing their rest. Aromatherapy will probably help more than any shop-bought remedy. A ten- to fifteen-minute shoulder massage given before bedtime, using sedative oils in a carrier oil, may induce sleep without any other aid. If you wake in the night another five minute massage of the central and upper back area may help you get back to sleep. Good sedative oils include lavender, neroli and marjoram. Lavender drops on the pillow, or on a piece of cotton inside the pillowslip, help sleep.

☾

MIND

'Never imagine yourself not to be otherwise than what it might appear to others that what you were or might have been was not otherwise than what you had been would have appeared to them to be otherwise.' Alice's Adventures In Wonderland

DATESHARE

Albert Einstein, *Nobel Prize-winning physicist, mathematician,* Theory of Relativity. **Paul Ehrlich**, *Nobel Prize-winning immunologist.* **Michael Caine**, *Cockney, good sort, film actor.* **Billy Crystal**, *comedian, entertainer, film star.* **Rita Tushingham**, *film, stage, TV star.* **Tessa Sanderson**, *British Olympic gold medal-winning javelin thrower.* **Georg Telemann**, *German composer.* **Quincy Jones**, *jazz trumpeter, composer, bandleader.*

This nice little stickleback is a good fatherfish and househusband. A catch for any discerning sticklebackess. March 14 wants a house, an attractive partner, children, a car and a television, and to settle down. He is an excellent father and takes care to protect his young, while his frequently flighty mate has carelessly swum away. Other star people shouldn't presume upon his gentle, nurturing nature though. Those who interfere too greatly with either ambition or life, will soon discover those fifteen sharp spines on his back can be lethal.

Both sexes are family people, the ones you want to have, not the ones you don't, at seasonal gatherings. Fun at parties, caring with relatives, they give a lot of time to others. Theirs is also a quiet spirituality, which seeks to smooth over others' ill temper and wrong direction taking. Yet they aren't pushovers and maintain their own powerful convictions.

As nature's nest-builders they are natural designers, architects, plasterers, electricians, plumbers, both the men and the women. And therefore, quite often some of nature's most gifted freelances. In any commercial company, March 14 holds much together, sometimes innovative, but often content to remain quietly expert, and happy to pass this on to younger people. Nor are they afraid of anybody. If something seems very wrong in the workplace, both sexes will firmly point it out, no complicity here with corner cutting or questionable 'fixing'.

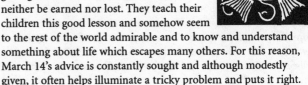

He or she who finds pleasure in a good book, a lovely piece of music or in making a good garden has inner riches which can neither be earned nor lost. They teach their children this good lesson and somehow seem to the rest of the world admirable and to know and understand something about life which escapes many others. For this reason, March 14's advice is constantly sought and although modestly given, it often helps illuminate a tricky problem and puts it right.

There is only one thing in the world worse than being talked about, and that is not being talked about.

(Oscar Wilde)

WATER

15 MARCH

Ill met by E-net, proud Titania. Dating on the computer isn't satisfactory and it won't blossom into a normal way of romance in the year 2000. This is because people who surf the Net have exceedingly similar interests so dating each other could be very like dating yourself. And as computer buffs at this level don't go out much, there's little chance of meeting your contact in the flesh.

But March 15 adores the idea. Those who live by the computer cause others to sigh by the computer. Madame 15 may be a brilliant IT hitwoman, but her preoccupation is so great that her conversation is too dense for other less devoted persons to follow. It was probably Ms or Mr 15 who devised the spellchecks on the damned things. Our Microsoft denies the word 'golly', suggesting you substitute Goole, insists that borate replace borage and cauliflowers is incorrect, the plural being cauliflower's, also prefers pongee to the word pong, and substitutes Chopping for Chopin. 'Golly, it's borage said a delighted Chopin, politely failing to admit he preferred cauliflowers which have less pong,' now reads, 'Goole, it's borate said a delighted Chopping, politely failing to admit he preferred cauliflower's which have less pongee.'

Stick to books Ms and Mr March 15. At least they'll teach you how to speak proper.

That apart, and it's a long way apart, there's a sweet side to both sexes and they do earn enough money to travel widely, where they will learn a lot about the human world and being adventurous, independent creatures, may decide that life at home pongees and they'd be better off in more exotic climes. Being able to spell your own language doesn't matter if you're speaking a foreign one, so that's another advantage. Latterly March 15 grows away from the early computer obsession. Both sexes find flesh and blood friends and lovers and use their expertise as an aid to life and not a prop.

Take care of the sense and the sounds will take care of themselves.

(Lewis Carroll)

BODY

Sweet things cheer March 15 up. Since both sexes can eat pretty well everything, and neither puts on weight, it's OK to indulge. This disgracefully good ice cream dish is excellent at Christmas. And it makes an exotic indulgence for lovers in bed together. Vanilla Ice Cream with Mincemeat: buy the best vanilla ice cream. Take a 400g jar of mincemeat, 50g butter, 60ml Cognac, orange segments.

Mix Cognac, butter and mincemeat in a saucepan, bring to boil stirring continuously until bubbling. Place large portions of vanilla ice cream in two chilled bowls and pour over mincemeat mixture. Garnish with oranges.

☾

MIND

In Tarot, card 15 of the Major Arcana indicates The Devil. There's a strong need for security here, which binds this date unusually close to its work. There's also romance, passion, a capacity for vivid expression and a soaring spirit.

March 16 makes every occasion one for a party and makes everybody at that party have a good time. All the world adores this child of pleasure, admires them as they flash through the water, taking everything in their stroke. They are realists too, and when they see danger coming, like the lobster, they can swim backwards just as fast as they advanced. Christmas and Easter are heaven for this water sprite. And picnics in the summer, boat trips on the river. They were made to play.

Fortunately this creature can turn play to money earning. They're a gift to any catering or tourist industry, to teaching, or anything to do with leading and entertaining a group. In truth, there's not a depressive bone in this person's body. Psychiatrists, to them, are adorable people they invite to their parties who have the further plus of making money – March 16 likes lots of money scattered about, preferably paving his or her apartment with gold.

Fortune indicates plenty of love affairs and quite a few cracks to the heart. But while March 16 may pine for a long time, this steady, sturdy psychology regains its sense of balance in the end and remembers how its mother always said there were plenty more fish in the sea where that one came from. At last, when this individual settles down, it's likely to be with someone very much older or younger, with family money and very likely more than one home – the second being abroad. It's nevertheless the case that March 16 never forgets old friends and never gets too grand for anybody.

Some may suffer from chronic fatigue and should visit their doctor. If nothing comes of the visit, then try alternative medicine, or another doctor. This individual is vulnerable to viruses and thyroid problems, which may affect their weight. And on occasion they encounter irritating allergies, which they are usually clever enough to be able to track themselves.

In the cathedral of my heart a candle will always be lit for you.

(Hardy Kruger)

WATER

17 MARCH

A lover of all beautiful and natural things, March 17 can't get over the gloriousness of the world. They're born to be painters, film makers, designers, flower arrangers, quilt makers, cooks, gardeners, sewers, embroiderers, tapestry enthusiasts. They're not born to drudgery in a factory or shop, bank or even the civil service. And while they will always do their best, unhappiness in the work place is physically bad for this tender person. It can even make them ill, with skin afflictions, palpitations and bad attacks of hayfever and blurry eyes.

March 17 needs fresh air and since air in towns is not now so fresh, this person must try to get to the country regularly, or preferably live there. And preferably by water. Not every star born under Pisces needs to be near water quite so physically as March 17, but this radiant starry creature's brilliance is reflected back when he looks into a watery mirror, reinforcing energy and a sense of well-being. Like Tinkerbell, March 17's belief in himself fades easily and that sense of self-esteem produced by water flowing brightens the sensitive soul.

Find this individual messing about in boats. There's nothing quite like it. Seaside towns are packed with them. The male of the species fishes – just a chance to dream by water. The female needs no such excuse and can sit for hours looking at the light reflected as small fish and frogs busy themselves and the languorous grass

snake makes her way laboriously across the surface. The seashore is a favourite walking place. And the rocks and shells found there are favourite ornaments and furnishings for March 17's home.

Both sexes paint, embroider, write about and compose music for seas and rivers. Some may develop such a skill in swimming that they can achieve international status, because, of course, they are in their element.

Come unto these yellow sands
And then take hands.
(Ariel's song, Shakespeare)

BODY

Use shells everywhere in the house because it will make you feel good. At Christmas large and small shells can be gold sprayed together with pine cones and arranged in a small basket on a swirl of old red, dark blue or any rich-coloured velvet. Tuck in glittering single earrings when you've lost one, a broken string of pearls or a brooch to make the basket look like treasure trove. Spray paint over shells lightly held along a wall border top and bottom for charming effect. Stick them on mirror frames. Stick tiny ones in swirling patterns on wooden boxes.

MIND

In Tarot, card 17 in the Major Arcana, shows The Star. It can mean awareness of sudden renewal and changes in life. Spiritual power indicates that if misfortune arrives as an expected guest, it will not disrupt March 17's equilibrium.

DATESHARE

Died: **Lucino Visconti**, *Italian film maker.* **Mai Zetterling**, *glamorous film star.* **Capucine**, *film actress. Born:* **Rudolf Nureyev**, *Russian dancer, choreographer, icon.* **Nat King Cole**, *singer, jazz pianist, film actor.* **Bobby Jones**, *golfer, Masters Tournament founder, Grand Slam winner.* **Kurt Russell**, *film actor.* **Rob Lowe**, *film star.* **Kate Greenaway**, *children's book illustrator.*

BODY

Eating the right diet for you is often the key to well-being. Jacqueline Kennedy Onassis kept her shape and vigour by eating a favourite meal of one large baked potato, heaped with fresh caviar, and a glass of champagne. Michelangelo preferred a spartan diet of bread and wine, eating a little pasta with fresh fruit in the evening after a day's work. George Bernard Shaw avoided meat, tea and alcohol. For breakfast he had a grapefruit or porridge, for lunch beans and lentils or spaghetti and enjoyed snacking off raw vegetable sandwiches with yoghurt, and glasses of apple juice and milk.

MIND

Exercise feeds oxygen to the brain and keeps the flab away. Calorie counts for activities include dancing, 300 cals per hour; making love, 150 cals per act; playing golf, 133 (no cart); walking slowly, 115 cals; standing at cocktail parties, 20 cals; talking on the telephone to mum, 15 cals.

DATESHARE

Neville Chamberlain, British prime minister. **John Updike**, novelist. **Richard Condon**, writer, The Manchurian Candidate. **Robert Donat**, stage, film actor. **Stephane Mallarme**, French poet, symbolist. **F W de Klerk**, South African president, apartheid reformer, released Nelson Mandela.

In spite of an exceptionally long life spent in rude health, much success and being blessed with good brains and good looks, March 18 is a pain spotter. She has to lie down a lot in a darkened room.

But he is worse. The briefcase rattles with pills. Between high-powered telephone calls he takes out the bottles and reads them, then looks up the drugs in a reference book about prescribed drugs  and their effects which he keeps in his desk. It says possible impotence can result and he panics. Which is worse? A tickle in the nose or no response at all to tickling elsewhere? He opens the *Financial Times*, but tucked inside is the *Daily Mail*'s health section. It's yet another cosmetic surgery story, this time about men in the USA having jutting chin implants to make them seem more assertive in deals. March 18 slips off to the loo to examine his chin and finds the mirror space crowded with male colleagues examining theirs.

Hypochondria is measured by the amount of affliction inflicted on others. The truly inflicted upon absolutely insist you go and lie down – for a long time. When this pathetic individual lurches off to find a hot water bottle, everybody in the family continues to watch *ER*, and shouts as he/she leaves the room 'Can you make a cup of tea?' March 18 comes in from work each evening, slumps into a chair and moans 'I'm utterly exhausted', never asking the children, who have been doing GCSEs and A levels how they've done.

They excel at work because it's crowded with hypochondriacs and there's usually a Big Boss who wants to discuss a pain he's just spotted with a like-minded enthusiast. Out of work, the hypochondriac is not interested in other people's broken legs and probably wouldn't notice if the entire family sat watching *ER* swathed mummy-like in bandages from head to toe.

I have learned one thing:

> *not to look down.*
>
> *(Geoffrey Hill)*

19 MARCH

This creature has sex on the brain and not much else. Whether it's at school, at the theatre, in the local club, at work or in church, what they do is speculate about those around them. In the eyes of their imagination all are naked. It's hard concentrating on most other things because of this.

Both sexes are equally intent. At least the girls remember to ask 'Is he available and single?' Mostly. Much of the time is spent planning accidentally bumping into the latest quarry. Hours drift past at the coffee machine before the discovery is made that the stalkee doesn't drink it. Attention-seeking stunts are pulled. Sheaves of paper are dropped at feet. Telephone calls are

eavesdropped on. So much time is spent by the girls doing their hair that the ozone layer above their office is shot with aerosol hairspray.

At clubs where everybody is eyeing everybody else anyway, this person pleads with friends to intercede, go over and drop the hint that they are expiring for love. March 19 dances embarrassingly alone in

order to attract attention and both sexes wear too much scent. So much effort, however, usually pays off, and surprisingly, once this creature has the desired one in tow, they radiate with happiness. This doesn't stop them assessing everybody else, but people born on this date are usually content to stick where they are thrown.

It's true to say that people with a great deal of sexual energy are usually extremely creative. It all comes from the same source. He or she who makes love a lot, usually makes food a lot and makes plans for fun a lot. March 19, both sexes, are drawn to sexy sporting occasions. Motor racing makes their blood swirl and so does the spectacle of horses racing urged on by skilled, intent riders. Boat racing is full of deft-handed, willing bodies. And any girl might die for a handsome man in cricket whites.

He gave her a look
you could have poured on a waffle.
(Ring Lardner)

BODY
Love in a bed is plain dull for March 19. They prefer something entirely more original. Love on a train rumbling through the night is spectacular, and in Europe, when the train pulls into a platform at three in the morning you can nip out and buy a reviving continental snack from the ever-present trolleys. Love in a river or ice cold pool high in the Scottish mountains is surprising. In a swimming pool a more civilised pleasure, as long as it's empty. Love on a park bandstand is an arresting offence. It's not advisable anywhere in Harrods, especially not in the Food Hall.

MIND
He who will feed for seven days on eggs cooked with myrrh, cinnamon and pepper will find an increased vigour in his erections and in his capacity for coition. This is from the famous Perfumed Garden. Can it be true?

DATESHARE
Glenn Close, film star, singer, Sunset Boulevard. **Bruce Willis**, actor, film star, restaurateur, Planet Hollywood. **Philip Roth**, novelist, Portnoy's Complaint. **Patrick McGoohan**, film and TV actor, The Prisoner. **Ursula Andress**, film actress, James Bond star famous for striding bikini-clad out of the sea. **Adolf Eichmann**, Nazi official, mass murderer. **Albert Speer**, Nazi architect. **David Livingstone**, Scottish explorer, found in jungle by Sir Henry Morton Stanley – 'Dr. Livingstone, I presume.'

WATER

BODY

March 20 people are keen on keeping their beautiful hair, which both sexes like to wash every day as it makes them feel fresher and look glossier. Try natural recipes for delicious hair. Champagne Rinse is a French method of bringing out golden lights in fair hair. Mix half a cup of old champagne with half a cup of hot water. After shampooing and rinsing well, pour the mixture through the hair. Do not rinse. Vinegar Rinse: three tablespoons raspberry vinegar added to your rinse water removes last traces of shampoo and gives hair extra shine and soft, smooth texture. Can be used after every shampoo.

MIND

Correct lighting in your bedroom is a key to love. Place two table lamps on surfaces, one nearer the bed than the other, with 60 or even 40 watt bulbs. Dim, low-angled lights provide flattering, suggestive mysterious shadow.

DATESHARE

Theresa Russell (Theresa Paup), actress, film star. **Holly Hunter**, actress, film star. **Michael Redgrave**, stage and film Shakespearian actor, father of Vanessa and Lyn. **Heinrich Ibsen**, playwright. **Ovid**, the poet of love. **Spike Lee**, film director, actor, Malcolm X. **Benjamino Gigli**, Italian operatic tenor. **Sviatoslav Richter**, Russian pianist. **William Hurt**, film actor.

Come live with me and be my love and we will all the pleasures prove. This is exactly what March 20 has probably said a thousand times to different partners. In youth many have the sexual attention of gnats, bored before they are halfway through. Much of the time they spend hiding from newly ex and heartbroken lovers, sometimes unable to get home because of the furious throng on the pavement.

Egotists at heart, what saves both sexes is ambition, which sobers them up. This spangly individual would give up a love meeting if their boss asked them to nip out and buy everybody in the office fish and chips. They'd rather work extra time than turn up to their own wedding – the first one anyway.

Success comes early because they work so intensively at catching the eye of power as well as completing the job. And with several love affairs under their belt, this individual discovers, late, the difference between lust and love. Having enjoyed a lot of lust, they throw their hat at love and frequently lose the first few times. Accustomed to easy success they have no judgement. This finally learned the hard way, both sexes settle down with a sigh of relief and quite often live happily ever after, once they've got the ambition bug out of their systems and have stopped staying late at the office and working at weekends.

There's a charming naïvety which they retain all their lives. A rush of enthusiasm and pleasure in others which attracts some, but causes envy and destructiveness in others. March 20 can't understand why anyone would want to hurt or destroy him and at first blames himself for making a mistake. Later in life he learns better, and uncoils like a deadly snake, unseen in its accurate attack on any ill-bringer.

Some are too easily impressed, even frightened by authority and should learn a little discernment.

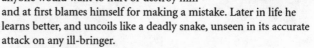

I'm a-weary of my life
If you'll come and be my wife
Quite serene would be my life!
('Yonghy-Bonghy-Bo', Edward Lear)